The Far Right in Europe

The Far Right in Europe

An Encyclopedia

Edited by Peter Davies with Paul Jackson

Greenwood World Publishing
Oxford / Westport, Connecticut
2008

EDITORS

Peter Davies with Paul Jackson

CONTRIBUTORS

Peter Davies
University of Huddersfield, UK

Hans-Georg Betz
York University, Toronto, Canada

Tor Bjørklund
University of Oslo, Norway

Brendan Evans
University of Huddersfield, UK

Matthew Goodwin
University of Bath, UK

Roger Griffin
Oxford Brookes University, UK

Paul Hainsworth
University of Ulster, UK

Paul Jackson
Oxford Brookes University, UK

Rob Light
University of Huddersfield, UK

Stan Markotich
Middlebury College, Vermont, USA

Peter Shearman
University of Melbourne, Australia

TO MY MUM AND DAD.
Peter Davies

First published in 2008 by Greenwood World Publishing

1 2 3 4 5 6 7 8 9 10

Copyright © Greenwood Publishing Group 2008

Greenwood World Publishing
Wilkinson House
Jordan Hill
Oxford OX2 8EJ
An imprint of Greenwood Publishing Group, Inc
www.greenwood.com

Library of Congress Cataloging-in-Publication Data

The far right in Europe : an encyclopedia / edited by Peter Davies with Paul Jackson.
p. cm.

Includes bibliographical references and index.

ISBN 978-1-84645-003-7 (alk. paper)

1. Europe--Politics and government--Encyclopedias. 2. Right-wing extremists--Europe--Encyclopedias. 3. Right and left (Political science)--Encyclopedias. 4. Conservatism--Europe--History--Encyclopedias. I. Davies, Peter, 1966- II. Jackson, Paul, 1978-

JN12.F37   20082008005755

320.5--dc22

ISBN 978-1-84645-003-7 (hardback)

Designed by Fraser Muggeridge studio

Typeset by Softwin

Printed and bound by South China Printing Company

Contents

Acknowledgements

We would like to thank all our excellent contributing authors and Simon Mason and Liane Escorza at Greenwood for all their help and assistance throughout.

Alphabetical List of Entries

Guide to Related Topics

Events

Algerian War (1954–1962)
Alliance for Austria's Future, Foundation
    by Haider (2005)
Bologna Bombing (1980)
British National Party, Acquittal of Members
    (2006)
Communism in Central and Eastern Europe,
    End of (1989)
Danish People's Party, Growth of (2001–2005)
Denazification Laws (1946–1947)
England, Race Riots in the North (2001)
European Union, Treaty of Maastricht (1992)
Flemish Bloc, Disbandment (2004)
France, Student Riots and the French Far Right
    (1968)
France, Success of the National Front
    (1982 to 2002)
Franco, Death of (1975)
Freedom Alliance, Victory in Italian Elections
    (1994)
Freedom Party, Coalition Government
    in Austria (2000)
The Holocaust (1939–1945)
The Identity, Tradition and Sovereignty Group,
    Rise and Fall (2007)
Irving and Holocaust Denial (2006)
Italy, Coalition of Northern League and
    National Alliance (2001)
Kosovo War, Responses (1999)
Latvian Marches (2005)
Milošević, Arrest of (2001)
Norway, Far-Right Gains (2001)
Paris Riots (2005)
Pim Fortuyn, Assassination of (2002)
Romania, Far Right Enters Coalition
    Government (1994)
Russia, Far Right Makes Electoral Gains (1993)
Salazar, Death of (1970)
Switzerland, Far Right Makes Electoral Gains
    (2003)
Waldheim, Austrian President (1986–1992)
'War on Terrorism'

Geographical Essays

Central Europe and the Far Right
Russia and the Far Right
Scandinavia and the Far Right
South-Eastern Europe and the Far Right
Southern Europe and the Far Right
Western Europe and the Far Right

Issues and Ideas

Anti-Semitism
Cold War
Collaboration and Collaborationism
Communism
Cosmopolitanism
Democracy
Economy
Education
Environment
Europe
Family
Freedom
Homosexuality
Immigration
Law and Order
Nation and Nationalism
Patriotism
Protest and the Protest Vote
Regionalism
Religion
Violence
Women
Workers
Youth

Movements and Parties

Attack Coalition (Bulgaria)
Austrian Freedom Party
British National Party
Croatian Democratic Union
Danish People's Party
Empire Europe (Malta)
Flemish Bloc/Flemish Interest
French Algeria
German National Democratic Party
German People's Union
Greater Romania Party
Greek Front
Hungarian Justice and Life Party
Italian Social Movement/National Alliance
Latvian National Front
League of Polish Families
Liberal Democratic Party of Russia
List Pim Fortuyn (The Netherlands)
Memory (Russia)
National Bolshevist Party
National Front (France)
National Front (Great Britain)
National Front (Spain)
Nationalist Action Party (Turkey)
New Democracy (Sweden)

Northern League (Italy)
Norwegian Progress Party
Portuguese Popular Party
Republican Party (Czech Republic)
Republican Party (Germany)
Russian National Unity
Serbian Radical Party
Slovak National Party
Spanish Circle of Friends of Europe
Swiss People's Party
True Finns Party
Ukrainian Conservative Party
United National Workers Party (Lithuania)

People

Blocher, Christoph (Switzerland)
Curska, Istvan (Hungary)
Degrelle, Léon (Belgium)
Fini, Gianfranco (Italy)
Fortuyn, Pim (The Netherlands)
Franco, General Francisco (Spain)
Garda, Aivars (Latvia)
Giertych, Roman (Poland)
Griffin, Nick (Great Britain)
Hagen, Carl (Norway)
Haider, Jörg (Austria)
Kjaersgaard, Pia (Denmark)
Klarström, Anders (Sweden)
Le Pen, Jean-Marie (France)
Lefebvre, Archbishop Marcel (France)
Mégret, Bruno (France)
Milošević, Slobodan (ex-Yugoslavia)
Murza, Mindaugas (Lithuania)
Salazar, Dr António de Oliveira (Portugal)
Schönhuber, Franz (Germany)
Sládek, Miroslav (Czech Republic)
Slota, Jan (Slovakia)
Soini, Timo (Finland)
Stoyanov, Dimitar (Bulgaria)
Tschokin, Georgy (Ukraine)
Tuđman, Dr Franjo (Croatia)
Tudor, Corneliu Vadim (Romania)
Türkeş, Alparslan (Turkey)
Voridis, Makis (Greece)
Waldheim, Kurt (Austria)
Zhirinovsky, Vladimir (Russia)

Places

Algeria
Antwerp (Belgium)
Auschwitz-Birkenau (Poland)
Bernabeu Stadium (Spain)
The Berlin Wall (Germany)
Bradford, Burnley and Oldham
  (Great Britain)
Carinthia (Austria)
Carpentras (France)

Dreux (France)
Kosovo (Serbia)
Meligalas (Greece)
Marignane, Orange, Toulon and Vitrolles
  (France)
Oresund Bridge (Denmark)
Padania (Italy)
Padina (Romania)
Srebrenica (Bosnia and Herzegovina)

Publications

Against the Islamisation of our Culture -
  Dutch Identity as Fundamental Value
  by Pim Fortuyn (The Netherlands)
Aspects of France Journal (France)
Blood and Honour Magazine (Great Britain)
Campaign in Russia: The Waffen SS on the
  Eastern Front by Léon Degrelle (Belgium)
Diorama Letterario Magazine (Italy)
Figaro Magazine (France)
Freedom Newspaper (Great Britain)
The Freedom I Mean by Jörg Haider (Austria)
German Voice Newspaper (Germany)
Gothic Ripples Magazine (Great Britain)
Horrors of War by Franjo Tuđman (Croatia)
I Was There by Franz Schönhuber (Germany)
Ivan Close Your Soul by Vladimir Zhirinovsky
  (Russia)
Mein Kampf by Adolf Hitler (Germany)
National Weekly Newspaper (France)
National-Socialist Battlecry Newspaper
  (USA - Germany)
Netherlands-Europe Journal (Belgium)
Neue Kronen Zeitung Newspaper (Austria)
Protocols of the Elders of Zion Document
  (Russia)
Redwatch Magazine (Great Britain)
SANU Memorandum (Serbia)
Spearhead Magazine (Great Britain)
Switzerland and the Second World War:
  A Clarification by Christoph Blocher
  (Switzerland)
Taking Liberties: A Third Way Special on
  the Attack on Civil Liberties in the UK
  Essays (Great Britain)

Thematic Essays

The Origins of the Far Right
The Ideology of the Far Right
The Development of the Far Right
The Far Right in the Twenty-First Century
Islam and the Far Right

Preface

The encyclopedia is divided into two sections. Section A supplies the reader with a geographical and thematic guide to the phenomenon of the European Far Right. Meanwhile, Section B – the A-Z Glossary – explores far-right politics via the people, movements, issues and ideas, events, places and publications that have, over six decades, served to constitute it.

Section A begins with thematic essays on the Far Right. Roger Griffin explores the origins and philosophical basis of the contemporary Far Right, while at the same time investigating the various strands of far-right political activity. In his chapter on the ideology of the Far Right, Brendan Evans discusses a number of key topics, including: national contexts and their effect on the ideology of individual far-right parties; the merits of studying extremist ideas, however distasteful they may seem; and the relationship between Far Right and more mainstream movements.

Peter Davies builds on this, chronicling and then also explaining the trajectory of the European Far Right in the decades after 1945. Matthew Goodwin offers a broad-ranging survey of the Far Right as it stands today, in the first years of the twenty-first century. He makes reference to an array of electoral data and is interested in both the success and failure of far-right parties across Europe. His prognosis is that, 'the potential for future growth or, at the least, the opportunity to retain a position of influence within their party systems appears relatively healthy'.

Hans-Georg Betz rounds things off by focusing on one vital and highly contemporary issue: the radical right and its attitude to culture, identity and the question of Islam. He interprets hostility to immigration and Muslim immigrants as evidence of a nativist agenda at the heart of far-right political discourse.

The approach then becomes geographical. Peter Davies investigates the legacy of fascist dictatorship. The shadow of Hitler and Nazism is ever-present in Germany and Austria; while in Switzerland Christophe Blocher's SVP has only recently transformed itself into a radical populist party of the Far Right. Peter Shearman moves the spotlight to Russia, where the key theme is the fall of Communism.

Tor Bjorklund focuses on Scandinavia. A key theme in his essay is the contrast between Denmark and Norway (where strong far-right parties have emerged) and Sweden and Finland (where they have not). Stan Markotich, in his essay on South-Eastern Europe, surveys the various forms of nationalism that were unleashed in the years following 1989. In the Balkans as well as in Hungary, Romania and Bulgaria, new demagogues and new political parties emerged. The genie was well and truly out of the bottle.

In Italy, the Far Right has had to distance itself from the memory of Mussolini in order to progress and now actually describes itself as 'post-fascist'. On the Iberian Peninsula, the experience of right-wing dictatorship has also been troublesome. It could be argued that no major parties of the Far Right have emerged in Spain or Portugal and this is often attributed to the fact that Franco and Salazar both tried to muzzle right-wing extremism in their respective eras in an effort to consolidate their political power. These issues are discussed by Peter Davies in his section on Southern Europe.

Paul Hainsworth completes Section A with a tour round Western Europe. He offers a general overview and argues that far-right movements have emerged sporadically here.

Section B is the Glossary. Lives and careers are assessed and important dates chronicled. This section also focuses on political parties and other organisations which have come to be viewed as 'of the Far Right'. The discussion is broadened out to cover major themes and topics which the Far Right has taken a particular interest in, or which have come to be linked with the Far Right.

Entries on key events detail a variety of landmarks and turning-points: from assassinations and bombings to elections and wars. The aim is to narrate the key moments in the history of the Far Right, to understand why and how events have shaped the nature of the phenomenon.

Section B also offers a topographical element. The spotlight falls on villages, towns, cities, regions and countries that have become associated with the Far Right. We also examine the significance of a bridge, a wall, an imaginary state and the site of one of the Nazis' most ghastly concentration camps. Certain publications enable us to survey a cross-section of far-right literary output: from books, memoirs and autobiographies, through journals and newspapers, to pamphlets, memos and one infamous forgery. In summary, the Glossary will add context and insight, and will take a novel and unique slant on the political tradition that is the focus of this volume.

So, the book is a mix of longer and shorter entries and is the product of a variety of contributions. We also need to be clear about its parameters.

If an encyclopedia about the Far Right in Europe had been published two decades ago, it would have been shorter and arguably less interesting. With the countries of Eastern Europe in thrall to Communism, there was little independent political activity there. People were subjected to top-down Communism – or what passed for Communism – and the idea of the Far Right having any constituency in this part of the continent was absurd. But the fall of the Berlin Wall and the collapse of the USSR changed all this; suddenly, ultra-nationalist and neo-fascist movements were emerging almost everywhere. As such, the subject matter for this book – published in 2008– is rich and varied in texture. It deals with the whole of Europe: from Britain in the west to Russia in the east, and from Scandinavia in the north to the Mediterranean in the south.

The chronological parameters are simple. The death of Hitler and Mussolini in 1945 marked the end of classical Fascism. World War II was over and the post-war period had commenced. This volume, therefore, is a survey of the Far Right in the years 1945–2008. There are sixty-three years of political history to explore, analyse and interpret.

The Far Right is a controversial political tradition and there is no black and white about what is or is not 'of the Far Right'. Definitional problems abound, but this is part of the fascination of the subject. In our research, we have made use of academic literature on the subject, media sources and material now available on the internet. Of course there will be overlap in certain places and specific chapters or sections may emphasise particular aspects of far-right politics rather than others. But overall we are confident that coverage of the Far Right in Europe will be comprehensive and – hopefully – the volume as a whole will be useful and informative.

Disclaimer

In this book the phrase 'Far Right' is not employed to abuse or indict movements and politicians; rather, it is a technical term – part of the lexicon of political science and a taxonomic category of political analysis – and it can assist us usefully in our efforts to understand the world around us. Likewise, the implication is not that movements and politicians labeled 'Far Right' are guilty by association for the suffering inflicted on millions of people by the Hitler and Mussolini regimes.

Introduction

Today, no political current is in ruder health than the Far Right. Across the continent of **Europe**, from Britain to the Baltics and from Munich to the Mediterranean, those movements and ideas we choose to classify as of far-right orientation are in pretty good shape. This may not be a particularly healthy thing but, if we can put aside our partisan feelings for a moment and look at the situation from the perspective of a political scientist or modern historian, it turns out that the rise and continued development of far-right politics is both beguiling and worthy of serious study.

The world around us is constantly fascinating and it is the duty of academics to try and make sense of it. Let us be frank: there is something unpleasant and worrying about the rise of the Far Right, but in many countries it is now an integral part of political life, sometimes in government, or sharing power, or racking up impressive electoral performances. And given its topicality there is an onus on us – yes, an onus – to try to understand it, rationalise it and put it into context as dispassionately as possible.

So, the *Encyclopedia of the Far Right in Europe* is necessary. The aim of the volume is to explore the phenomenon and work towards classifying the people, movements, issues and ideas, events, places and publications that constitute the Far Right in Europe. We are never going to be able to execute this task to perfection because, as a contemporary phenomenon, the far right is constantly changing, updating and reinventing itself. It is difficult to pin down and make judgements about something that is so current and modern. Depending on your taste in metaphors, it is like shooting at a moving target, or playing a game of football and realising that the goalposts, at both ends of the pitch, are constantly moving.

There are also challenges implicit in compiling a reference work of this nature. What balance do you strike between incarnations of the Far Right in different parts of the continent, in different eras, which have achieved different levels of success? To illustrate this point, we have had to balance the claims of parties that have no history and no real achievements to their name (like, for example, the confusingly-named **Ukrainian Conservative Party**, established in 2005) with parties that have super-rich histories (like the MSI in Italy or Freedom Party in Austria). There is no easy way to deal with this kind of dilemma. All we can say is that we have done our best and used our academic judgement, as well as our human instincts, to try and produce a book that is as balanced, sensible and useful as possible.

We have also encountered the problem of definition.

What is the Far Right?

One anecdote serves to emphasise the difficulties inherent in defining 'the Far Right'. As I, as editor, recruited fellow academics to write articles for this encyclopedia, nearly every one came back to me with the following line: 'I'd be delighted to help, and prepare the article you suggest, but can I ask you just one preliminary question: how exactly are you *defining* the Far Right in this context?' On each occasion it was a tricky question to answer, but I invariably responded with something like this: 'Well, I'm writing an introductory section on "What is the Far Right?", so I'll send you a copy of that when it's ready'. Now as I come to writing this section, I realise once again what a difficult question I have left myself with to address.

There are no easy answers to the question, 'What is the Far Right?'. The Far Right is an often confusing and bewildering part of the political spectrum, inhabited by a range of strange and controversial political formations. One of the few things we could probably agree upon from the outset is that Far Right usually implies post-war, in the sense that far-right political movements of the pre-1945 era are usually labeled simply as 'fascist'. But still, Far Right could imply late-1940s or early twenty-first century, so we are still dealing with a phenomenon that straddles seven decades.

There are also terminological difficulties: 'far right', 'extreme right', 'hard right', 'neo-fascist', 'post-fascist'. Are these terms all interchangeable or do they each connote something specific and different? This question will form an interesting undercurrent to the ensuing discussion.

Over the years, commentators have exerted much time and energy debating the character and ideological makeup of this thing we have come to refer to as the 'Far Right'. As a starting-point, let us consider the definition of the international Far Right offered by the controversial website, Wikipedia:

> In the modern world, the term Far Right is applied to those who support authoritarianism, usually involving a dominant class ... and/or an established church ... Their favored authoritarian state can be an absolute monarchy, but more often today it is some form of oligarchy or military dictatorship ... The term Far Right also embraces extreme nationalism, and will often evoke the ideal of a 'pure' ideal of the nation, often defined on racial or 'blood' grounds. They may advocate the expansion or restructuring of existing state borders to achieve this ideal nation, often to the point of embracing expansionary war, racialism, jingoism and imperialism ... More generally, the term Far Right has been applied to any stream of political thought that rejects **democracy** in favour of some form of elite rule (including monarchy, plutocracy, and theocracy).[1]

Unintentionally perhaps, this definition highlights the central problem. It is designed to offer students and the general reader an accessible introduction to the topic; yet, if we are being harsh, it offers only an odd mixture of the obvious and some other confused points about authoritarianism, **religion** and monarchy.

For Paul Wilkinson, the emergence of this modern Far Right is a cause for both regret and alarm. The first words in the preface to his book are as follows: 'My aim in writing *The New Fascists* was to alert the general public, and particularly the young generation, to the resurgence of neo-fascist and related movements of the ultra-right, and the implications for the liberal democracies'.[2] In a slightly more detached manner, Hans-Georg Betz portrays the Far Right is an amalgam of radicalism and xenophobic populism.[3] Paul Hainsworth defines it in a similar way. He talks about the 'emergence or resurgence of extreme right-wing or neo-populist politics and parties that, to some extent, have revived fears of a return to the dark past, but which, in other ways, are very much the products of more contemporary developments'.[4]

This last point is significant, for the post-war Far Right is, by its very nature, something distinct from the inter-war fascist right. Of course there are echoes of Mussolini's Fascism and Hitler's Nazism on the contemporary Far Right, but on the whole this post-war phenomenon is the product of new circumstances and influences. This is something Roger Griffin agrees on. He defines neo-fascism as 'offering something new with respect to inter-war phenomena' rather than 'attempting to resuscitate an earlier movement'.[5] Robert Paxton takes the argument a step further.

He explains that far-right leaders, 'have become adept at presenting a moderate face to the general public while privately welcoming outright fascist sympathisers with coded words about accepting one's history, restoring national pride or recognising the valor of combatants on all sides'.[6] And in this context, Roger Eatwell cites the example of the MSI in Italy. He claims that the aim of Gianfranco **Fini**, the leader of the movement, was to turn the MSI 'into a "post-fascist", moderate right-wing party, modeled loosely on the lines of French Gaullism'.[7]

Given the topicality and controversiality of the Far Right, news organisations have also had to grapple with the same issue. In 2000, *The Guardian* in its special online report – 'Europe's Far Right' – identified the following individuals and movements as representative of the phenomenon:

Austria
Austrian Freedom Party (FPÖ)
Key figures: Jörg Haider … Susanne Riess-Passer …

Belgium
Flemish Bloc (VB)
Key figure: Frank Vanhecke (VB's president)

Denmark
Danish People's Party (DPP)
Key figure: Pia **Kjaersgaard** (leader, DPP)

France
National Front (FN)
Key figure: Jean-Marie **Le Pen** (leader and founder, FN)

Germany
Republican Party (REP), **German People's Union** (DVU), National Democratic Party (NPD)
Key figures: No dominant leaders.

Greece
Hellenic Front
Key figure: Makis **Voridis** (leader, Hellenic Front)

Italy
Northern League, **National Alliance**
Key figures: Umberto Bossi (leader, Northern League), Gianfranco Fini (leader, National Alliance)

The Netherlands
Pim Fortuyn's **List** (LPF), Liveable Netherlands
Key figure: Mat Herben (leader, LPF)

Norway
Progress party
Key figure: Carl **Hagen** (leader, Progress party)

Portugal
Popular party
Key figure: Paulo Portas (leader, Popular party)

Switzerland
Swiss People's Party (SVP)
Key figure: Christoph **Blocher** (leader, SVP)

United Kingdom
British National party (BNP)
Key figure: Nick **Griffin** (leader, BNP)[8]

In the same year, the BBC produced another online survey called 'Rise of the Right':

Norway
Political parties: Progress Party
Popular support: 15 percent
Key figures: Hagen

Sweden
Political parties: none
Popular support: none
Key figures: none

Denmark
Political parties: **Danish People's Party**
Popular support: 18 percent
Key figures: Kjaersgaard

Netherlands
Political parties: Livable Netherlands, Pim Fortuyn List
Popular support: 16 percent
Key figures: **Fortuyn** (assassinated 6 May 2002)

Belgium
Political parties: Vlaams Blok
Popular support: 9.9 percent
Key figures: Dewinter

Spain
Popular support: n/a

France
Political parties: NF, MNR
Popular support: 17 percent
Key figures: Le Pen

Italy
Political parties: Northern League, National Alliance
Popular support: 5 percent
Key figures: Bossi, Fini, Alessandra Mussolini

Switzerland
Political parties: Swiss People's Party
Popular support: 22.5 percent
Key figures: Blocher

Germany
Political parties: German People's Union, National Democrats, The Republicans
Popular support: 3 percent

Austria
Political parties: **Freedom Party**
Popular support: 20 percent
Key figures: Haider, Riess-Passer

UK
Political parties: BNP
Popular support: 1–2 percent[9]

The first thing to say is that there is generally quite a lot of agreement about what constitutes the 'European Far Right'. That said, the *Guardian* included two countries that the BBC had ignored (Portugal and Greece) and the same was true vice-versa (Spain, Sweden). It is also interesting that both surveys neglected to mention the far-right movements of Eastern Europe. This would seem to be an error because the majority of ex-communist states in Eastern Europe have witnessed the growth of far-right political activity since 1989. The movements that have emerged have been very different from their equivalents in Western Europe. Invariably, they have been shaped by the pre-1989 communist experience, and have turned out to be loud, aggressive and ultra-nationalist in political persuasion. As Luciano Cheles, Ronnie Ferguson and Michalina Vaughan have written: 'The Far Right is no longer an exclusively Western European phenomenon; its presence in Central and Eastern Europe is by now a fact'.[10]

Furthermore, the issue of influence is a curious one. Does one measure the impact of a far-right movement by its electoral success? Or by its presence 'on the ground'? Or via some other criteria? Here, Sweden is an interesting case. The BBC survey entered the word 'none' next to 'political parties, popular support, key figures', but it goes on to state:

> Sweden has no organised far-right parties, but in recent years the country has seen a wave of neo-Nazi **violence** – including murders and bombings which have targeted immigrants. Many Swedes have found it difficult to come to terms with the existence of racist violence in a country that prides itself on its egalitarian social democracy. Some suspects have been arrested and charged, but there remains an organised underground of white supremacist **youth** who conduct such attacks, as well as posting violent neo-Nazi material on the internet and communicating with similar organisations in the U.S. and Britain. Immigrants account for about 1 million of Sweden's population of nearly 10 million, but the number is growing.[11]

Here we learn that far-right activity isn't always 'official' or 'engaged with the political process'. It *can* be visible, but more often than not it is 'clandestine' or 'underground', as the report on Sweden notes.

All this goes to show that neither political scientists nor commentators or journalists can agree on the defining characteristics of the Far Right – which doesn't bode particularly well for our search for definitions and meanings.

Problems of terminology and definition

We must also take account of how those on the Far Right – those who are happy to be situated there – perceive themselves in terms of their own ideological makeup. Here a suitable starting point is Jean-Marie Le Pen, leader of the *Front National* in France. He is probably the most famous – and notorious – of modern far-right leaders, and also, in his writings, a politician who is totally frank and unambiguous about being 'of the right'. His core values are nation, family, religion and hierarchy. According to Le Pen, these values are permanent and unchanging, and are 'concrete' rather than 'abstract'. As such, the FN is convinced that its doctrine is fully in tune with a sense of 'nature' and 'tradition'. The FN is always proud to proclaim itself as a movement of the right, but at the same time it sees itself as 'transcending the artificial division between left and right'.[12] It has no truck with egalitarian ideas and has put forward various justifications for natural selection and inequality.[13] Furthermore, Le Pen has ridiculed the 'rights of man' and has consistently viewed his values as the antithesis of left-wing principles. In particular, he contrasts his brand of nationalism with the '**cosmopolitanism**' and 'internationalism' of the Socialist and Communist parties in France. If one attitude has underpinned almost every utterance of the FN leader since 1972, it is hostility to the left; he argues that, particularly in the French context, it is obsessed with 'individualism' and the 'rights of man' and that as a result social institutions like the family and the nation are being undermined.

Maybe at this point we can come to an interim conclusion – that, when it comes down to basics, Far Right equates to having some relationship with inter-war Fascism (in terms of leadership, ideology or membership, for example) and/or being of the right to an outlandish or dangerous degree. In France, for example, Le Pen has trivialised the **Holocaust** by portraying it as a 'detail' in the history of World War II. Perhaps it is no coincidence, therefore, that his party and others find themselves sitting on the Far Right – literally – of parliamentary chambers throughout the length and breadth of Europe. Or that in some countries there have been calls for far-right political movements to be outlawed.

In some cases such calls have been successful and parties have been banned. In Belgium in 2004 the *Vlaams Blok* was the subject of a high-court ruling. It was considered to be a racist political movement and was forced to disband. However, it reinvented itself soon after as the *Vlaams Belang*. Episodes like this have led to much debate about strategy in the face of the Far Right. State authorities have invariably argued that the best policy is to deny far-right movements the 'oxygen of publicity' and to legislate them 'out of existence' (as was the case in Belgium). However, it occurs to both friends and foes of the Far Right that this may not be the most astute and intelligent of tactics. The debate was played out in almost text-book fashion in Belgium. One right-wing sympathiser posted this message to an online discussion forum: 'I am a great admirer of the *Vlaams Blok*. While the politically-correct thought police in Belgium have attempted to outlaw the largest party in the country, their censorship will only serve to increase its popularity. The Blok is a group of bright, disciplined, white nationalists who show a real tenacity to protect our wonderful shared European culture from the asinine leftists who would turn Europe into a multicultural cesspool. The leftists have met their match. We will triumph'.[14] From a different perspective, Abou Jahjah – a political campaigner in Belgium – has argued: 'The banning of *Vlaams Blok* only allowed them to start up a new party with more clubbable members ... their persecution has not held them back. Pragmatically, it has helped them'.[15]

Throughout, there are complicating factors that cloud the issue and make the challenge of defining the Far Right even more daunting. First, it is clear that the term 'Far Right', just like its sister term 'fascist', has, over the years, become nothing more than a term of abuse, pinned on anyone or anything that is offensive, particularly to those on the left. Let us examine some archetypal left-wing perspectives. In *The Socialist* in 2006, the former editor of *Marxism Today*, Martin Jacques, commented: 'Not since the 1930s has the threat of racism and fascism been so great in the West'.[16] Likewise, in the same year Christian Bunke of the Socialist Party turned the spotlight on the leader of the BNP:

> Cambridge graduate and rural landlord Nick Griffin ... said that British **workers** had always fought against 'the gaffers'. Today, he claimed, this struggle is against the Muslims. In classic far-right fashion, Griffin takes the vocabulary of class struggle and turns it into its opposite ... Nick Griffin told *Newsnight* that Muslim protests on the Danish newspaper cartoons 'will swell the ranks of the BNP'. The BNP is a parasitic organisation that would support a conflict between Muslim and non-Muslim workers. Such conflict would not be in the working class's interests; the BNP is a right-wing anti-worker organisation. In office on local councils, BNP councillors have failed abysmally to oppose cuts, for example in **Burnley**. Workers cannot rely on these people to fight for their interests. But it would also be foolish to rely on courts to get rid of the BNP.[17]

Left-wing commentators are also liable to exaggerate the internal divisions and disputes evident within far-right parties.[18]

However, commentators with a more balanced approach – some even on the left – are keen to dispel the idea of a 'resurgent fascism'. Lynn Walsh, writing in *Socialism Today,* is representative of this trend:

> The growth of the Far Right certainly poses a threat to the working class. Racism, unless effectively countered, opens up dangerous divisions within the working class. If Le Pen were to come to power in France ... he would launch brutal attacks on the working class, just as Berlusconi is doing in Italy. But a Le Pen government, though a serious setback, would not be a totalitarian fascist regime. It would be a right-wing capitalist government – and would provoke massive resistance from the working class and other strata. Despite the neo-fascist antecedents of many of the leaders of the far-right parties, these formations are not fascist-type parties with their own para-military forces ... Leaders like Le Pen and Haider have past links with neo-Nazi organisations ... But they have grown on an electoral level, presenting a respectable face, distancing themselves from the tiny neo-fascist groups on the fringes of far-right politics.[19]

Similarly, Brendan O'Neill, writing on www.spiked-online.com, asked: 'Is Europe really heading for a new Dark Age, with its Nazi past coming back to haunt it? Are fascistic far-right parties really "on the march again" everywhere from Greece to France, from Italy to Holland? In a word, no. The current obsession with the rise of the Far Right tells us far more about the European elites' crisis of confidence and legitimacy than it does about any Nazi reality'.[20] Perhaps these opinions should be viewed as a necessary corrective to the slightly predictable comments emanating from old-style leftists, who seem to detect the fascist threat almost everywhere.

Second, and without too many exceptions, it seems to be the case that some individuals and movements on the Far Right do not particularly like being characterised as 'being of the Far Right'. That description could be viewed as the ultimate insult or the 'kiss of death', or even a libelous statement, by anyone who is not comfortable with, or proud of, the description. This point particularly relates to movements with serious political aspirations who, for all kinds of reasons (the desire for credibility or access to state funding perhaps), would like to be considered mainstream. The obvious contradiction here is that many movements generally considered to be Far Right are actually proud of this fact, and make great play of the fact that they do not wish to be tainted by being bracketed with the other, traditional parties who are invariably portrayed as 'corrupt' and 'old fashioned'. During the 1980s, Le Pen in France crusaded against 'la Bande des Quatres' – the disparaging nickname he assigned to the 'ruling coalition' of PS, PCF, RPR and UDF. Even though these four parties were totally independent and fundamentally distinct, he came to realise that pigeon-holing them together was a useful tactical device.

Third, what is in and what is out? Do we debate and discuss the public or private utterances of movements we suspect of falling into the Far Right category? And is it significant that, in some cases, there is a divergence between the two? Likewise, are we interested in the discourse of movements or individuals? Or both? Do we content ourselves with analysing the party line as articulated by far-right political parties, or can we also build in analysis of individual activists and thinkers, who could be slightly out of line with the corporate philosophy of their movement? Similarly, is there a sense in which far-right attitudes can permeate a *society* rather than being, merely, the basis of one party's political platform? This spectre has certainly been raised in Germany, where some analysts fear that extreme attitudes are now becoming mainstream. In 2006, *Der Spiegel* announced that:

> Far-right views are not just the domain of skinheads and neo-Nazis but are firmly anchored throughout German society, regardless of social class or age, according to a study of attitudes towards foreigners, Jewish people and the Nazi period. A new survey has found that right-extremist attitudes are firmly anchored in German society. A study based on a survey of 5,000 people found that 9 percent of respondents agreed with the statement that a dictatorship can in certain circumstances be a preferable form of government, and 15.1 percent agreed with this: 'We should have one leader to rule Germany with a strong hand for the good of everyone'. 'The term "right-wing extremism" is misleading because it describes the problem as a peripheral phenomenon. But right-wing extremism is a political problem at the centre of society', says the report commissioned by the Friedrich Ebert Foundation ...[21]

Surf the web and you will invariably find other studies in other European countries saying similar things.

Fourth, it is clear that, in the context of Europe, the Far Right is neither uniform nor homogenous, but configured slightly differently in each individual country. This should come as no surprise to us. Each European country has its own unique history and political culture. It is not just the strength and popularity of the Far Right that differs from country to country, but also – perhaps more significantly – the nature of its political discourse. Different issues matter in different places. For example, in countries where **immigration** is a topical subject, it is maybe easier to detect a far-right party than in countries where it isn't a prominent issue. Different countries and continents have differing political cultures, and what is Far Right in one context may not be, or may be different from, what is Far Right in another context. Likewise, the backdrop can vary: in Germany and Austria memories of the Nazi period are ever-present; in Scandinavia the welfare state is a major bone of contention; while in Eastern Europe, the legacy of the communist period is all-enveloping.

Fifth, and in a related sense, it is apparent that the European Far Right – if it is possible to speak of such a demarcated phenomenon – has changed and evolved over time. By way of illustration, let us consider, for example, three specific eras: the 1880s/1890s, the 1920s/1930s and the 1990s/2000s. In France in the 1880s and 1890s we see the birth of a new type of right-wing politics, variously described as 'new', 'radical' or 'revolutionary'. This was exemplified by the 'right' forged by Maurice Barrès, General Boulanger and the League of Patriots – novel on account of its belief in some kind of republicanism or executive government rather than royalism and aristocracy. This 'right' was 'right' in the sense that it was nationalist, xenophobic and sometimes racist, and thus emphasised the *inequality* of peoples, nations and races. It was also authoritarian and viewed the masses as vulnerable to manipulation and propaganda. Importantly, though, it was a 'right' that had no qualms about campaigning on terrain that was traditionally working class and on integrating archetypal left-wing concerns into its manifesto programme (for example, training, **education** and workers' welfare). Its signature policy was the repatriation of immigrant workers – thereby blending typical right – and left-wing political instincts (in a nutshell: latent xenophobia and concern for native French workers). Not surprisingly, therefore, Barrès labelled his movement in Nancy as 'national-socialist' in political orientation – a key marker for the future.

As in so many other spheres, the Great War also had a significant, catalysing effect on politics and political ideas. By the 1920s and 1930s this 'right' had evolved into a 'right' that was incontestably revolutionary. The variants of fascism that existed in Italy, Germany and France, and also across swathes of Western and Eastern Europe, were viewed by opposition groups as both dangerous and threatening. It was posited that the very essence of western civilisation was in jeopardy. There was still an association and alignment with left-wing or socialist values (Mussolini, for example, was an ex-syndicalist and the former editor of *Avanti*, a socialist newspaper), but the revolutionary right of the inter-war period was interested in more than just winning votes and putting in place new forms of executive government. In Germany, Hitler institutionalised his extreme ideology in the Holocaust and *Lebensraum*, and sought a legacy in the creation of a master race. By the final years of the twentieth century, the extreme right had, to an extent, redefined itself. In fact, it had been forced to re-invent itself. In the post-1945 period, it was untenable to try to maintain any kind of connection with the Hitler era. So, movements like the MSI in Italy and FN in France – and many others across the continent – have attempted to re-configure the political space in which they seek to operate. Of course, they have found it difficult to smother their hard-line, occasionally neo-Nazi, attitudes, but in some cases they have made a decent fist of this.

Here it is also pertinent to consider the way in which far-right movements have interested themselves in 'green' issues. Until relatively recently, ecology and environmentalism were regarded as 'left-wing' issues. Green MPs and councillors habitually aligned themselves with socialist and communist parties in parliaments and other legislatures *ergo* ecology was viewed as an exclusively 'left-wing' concern. However, over the last two decades, far-right activists have tried to claim the issue for themselves. They have utilised the language of 'conservation' and 'protection', and linked the idea of the 'natural world' to the idea of the 'nation'. The FN in France unveiled this new way of thinking in 1990. Other movements have followed suit. The Danish People's Party puts it like this:

> We must take care of the natural world. We will work to ensure that we and future generations are able to live in a clean and healthy **environment**. Denmark must develop in unison with the natural world, exercising caution when it comes to long-term consequences of the way we live. Moreover, we will work both at national and international levels to ensure that the way in which the earth's resources are used bears the stamp of consideration, care and a sense of responsibility, which includes showing care for the natural world and all its living creatures, for which we, as stewards of the earth's riches, are responsible.[22]

It is clear that, in the context of far-right discourse, a link has been made between the environment as an issue and various myths of idealised homelands. In the Nazi era, for example, Walther Darré established himself as one of Hitler's leading 'blood and soil' ideologists. He served as Reich Minister of Food and Agriculture between 1933 and 1942.

Finally, we need to be aware that far-right political movements do not necessarily exist in neat, compartmentalised units. In fact, it is usually taken as read that traditional conservative parties across Europe – like the Tories in Great Britain and the RPR in France – contain their own far-right fringes eg –ie. radical and often eccentric political activists whose ideas and beliefs are slightly out of synch with their leaders'. The most famous example of this phenomenon is Enoch Powell. Powell was a Conservative MP and shadow cabinet minister when, on 20 April 1968, in Birmingham, he produced his 'Rivers of Blood' speech:

> It almost passes belief that at this moment twenty or thirty additional immigrant children are arriving from overseas in Wolverhampton alone every week – and that means fifteen or twenty additional families a decade or two hence. Those whom the gods wish to destroy, they first make mad. We must be mad, literally mad, as a nation to be permitting the annual inflow of some 50,000 dependants, who are for the most part the material of the future growth of the immigrant-descended population. It is like watching a nation busily engaged in heaping up its own funeral pyre. So insane are we that we actually permit unmarried persons to immigrate for the purpose of founding a family with spouses and fiancés whom they have never seen … As I look ahead, I am filled with foreboding; like the Roman, I seem to see 'the River Tiber foaming with much blood'.[23]

In France, in more recent times, Charles Pasqua, a minister in the RPR government during the 1990s has become notorious for his hard-line attitudes and policies towards immigrants. The RPR was an avowedly conservative movement, but it is argued that Pasqua's policies had more in common with the Far Right and actually played into their hands. According to Christian E. O'Connell, 'The Pasqua laws were enacted in 1993 at the instigation of then-Interior Minister Charles Pasqua, whose vigorous endorsement of "zero immigration" set the tone for recent French policy in refugee and asylum matters … the legislation encompassed a broad panoply of severe measures … a toughening of visa requirements, a reduction in the number of visas issued, an expansion of police enforcement powers, an extension of the permitted detention period and a narrowing of the administrative review scheme'.[24]

We could also quote the example of Nicholas Sarkozy who, as Interior Minister in 2005, caused controversy by describing those responsible for the **Paris Riots** as 'troublemakers' and 'a bunch of hoodlums' – a form of words that was taken by many to have distinctly racial overtones.[25] There is no doubt that the Far Right has helped to make immigration a major political issue. Even Labour prime minister Gordon Brown was accused by Conservative leader David Cameron of aping the language of the Far Right during the Queen's Speech debate of November 2007.[26]

Common features

So, having aired our misgivings about the term, and debated its merits and drawbacks, the question now is a simple one. Assuming the term does have some value, what characteristics are most commonly exhibited by, and associated with, the Far Right of the political spectrum? It is possible – and perhaps actually quite desirable – to work towards some kind of consensus based on the judgement of academics and the statements of key political players.

Some preliminary points need making straight away. While it must be acknowledged that the European Far Right has had a significant impact and influence over the last few decades, and that it has proved both newsworthy and controversial, it would also be true to say that it is still only a minority force in political and electoral terms, and also prone to splinter and implode organisationally. Nowhere has it been a majority force in any sense of the term. But, the Far Right probably makes up for its lack of formal success by constantly provoking controversy and media interest. The phrase 'all publicity is good publicity' could have been invented with the parties and politicians of the Far Right in mind. One story goes that Le Pen in France aims to involve himself in a scandal 'every September' – the start of the French political and parliamentary year – so that he can maintain his profile in the media. Not surprisingly, therefore, the FN leader has been embroiled in his fair share of 'colourful' controversies – from fisticuffs with members of the general public to allegations of torture during the **Algerian War**. Furthermore, in an effort to discredit him, his ex-wife posed naked for a pornographic magazine. Across Europe, far-right leaders have displayed a similar ability to make news for the 'wrong' reasons, though without obvious comeback: for example, Jörg Haider and his 'pro-Nazi' views, Zhirinovsky and his demand for a 'new Russian empire', and Richard Barnbrook (leader of the BNP in London), who was subject to allegations that he produced and directed a gay porn film.[27]

It could also be argued that as a political entity the Far Right is associated with what could be termed 'male' values and perhaps even 'machismo'. Far-right movements do not particularly sell themselves as such, but there is no doubting the fact that, on the whole, the 'image' of the Far Right is a 'masculine' one. There are also appeals to aggression and violence – perhaps exemplified best by the 'skinhead' culture that has attached itself to the Far Right. Moreover, most far-right leaders are male. Across Europe, the only real exceptions have been Susanne Riess-Passer of the **Austrian Freedom Party** and Pia Kjaersgaard, leader of the Danish People's Party. (We should also note that Marine Le Pen – daughter of Jean-Marie – is being groomed for the leadership of the Front National in France when her father stands down,[28] and that two other famous 'daughters' have hit the headlines: Alessandra Mussolini and Jennifer Griffin[29]). Note also that the electorate of the Far Right is overwhelmingly male and membership figures reveal a male bias.[30]

In the popular imagination, the Far Right is probably best known for its nationalism and racism. The names employed by contemporary far-right movements are the best indicators of doctrine and ideology: for example, Front National, National Alliance, National Democratic Party, Danish People's Party, Swiss People's Party and Hellenic Front. Beyond the titles, each of these movements is clear that its primary reference point is the nation. The BNP takes a historical perspective on this issue:

> The British National Party exists to secure a future for the indigenous peoples of these islands in the North Atlantic which have been our homeland for millennia. We use the term indigenous to describe the people whose ancestors were the earliest settlers here after the last great Ice Age and which have been complemented by the historic migrations from mainland Europe. The migrations of the Celts, Anglo-Saxons, Danes, Norse and closely related kindred peoples have been, over the past few thousands years, instrumental in defining the character of our family of nations.[31]

Many far-right movements are prone to simplify their message. The FN have used 'The French First' as one of their banner slogans. Likewise, the Sweden Democrats are linked to the 'Keep Sweden Swedish' movement.[32] The corollary of this nation-centredness is a general hostility to foreigners, immigrants and any manifestation at all of 'the other'. The Hellenic Front has talked about 'Islamic infiltration in Greece and Europe' and argues:

> The problem of illegal immigration in Greece is not a question of principles or ideology, but a policy issue, if we assume that there exists a structured national state. If there is a state, then there are borders too. It is known that three are the elements which define the existence of a state: the existence of definite territory, the existence of people living on this territory and the existence of power exercised within the boundaries of the territory and for the benefit of the people. And if there exists a state, then the legal distinction between a native and an alien is absolutely legitimate and founded on our Constitution … Say YES to the immediate DEPORTATION of ALL ILLEGAL IMMIGRANTS … Say NO to ILLEGAL IMMIGRATION.[33]

Likewise, the Danish People's Party has stated:

> The country is founded on the Danish cultural heritage and therefore, Danish culture must be preserved and strengthened. This culture consists of the sum of the Danish people's history, experience, beliefs, language and customs. Preservation and further development of this culture is crucial to the country's survival as a free and enlightened society. Therefore, we wish to see action on a broad front to strengthen the Danish national heritage everywhere. Outside Denmark's borders we would like to give financial, political and moral support to Danish minorities. Denmark is not an immigrant-country and has never been so. Therefore, we will not accept a transformation to a multiethnic society. Denmark belongs to the Danes and its citizens must be able to live in a secure community founded on the rule of law, developing only along the lines of Danish culture.[34]

And according to BBC reports, the People's Party was able to make immigration the primary issue in the 2005 national elections.[35]

These passages are highly illuminating. They are critiques of the state in different parts of Europe, and point to its reluctance, if not outright failure, to place control of national identity at its core. From this stems other points. In the language of the Far Right if the state is failing in its duties, then nationalist parties have a legitimate right to organise the defence of their respective nations. And it is then a short step to policies of 'national preference' and manifestoes and doctrines that are deemed by ordinary people and mainstream political parties to be xenophobic and racist.

One step on from xenophobia and racism is **anti-Semitism**. Even though the 'immigrant question' has become more topical in recent decades, far-right movements still exhibit, and can't let go of, a very pointed and unpleasant anti-Semitism. This is less a doctrine or ideology than an instinct and impulse that manifests itself in certain situations and contexts, sometimes simply in 'wordplay' or off-the-cuff comments.[36] Also, aside from its racist aspect, anti-Semitism still works on the level of a conspiracy theory, as in the inter-war era. On occasions, too, anti-Semitism breeds revisionism – a criminal activity whereby the reality of the Holocaust is called into question. We have already cited Le Pen's infamous statement in 1987. In more recent times, there have been other instances of revisionism in action. In January 2005 the following report appeared in the media:

Far-Right German Party Belittles Holocaust

A week before Europe hosts a series of memorial services in honour of the freeing of Auschwitz, a group of far-right German politicians caused a stir by walking out on a state ceremony for Nazi victims … In Germany, the historic moment when Soviet forces freed the infamous **Auschwitz-Birkenau** camp in Poland in 1945 will be remembered throughout the country. On Friday, a week before the anniversary, the state parliament in Saxony paid tribute to the victims of the Nazis – some 6 million Jews – with a moment of silence. Instead of being a solemn moment of reflection, the tribute turned into a political bashing as twelve regional lawmakers for the far-right National Democratic Party (NPD) refused to participate and stormed out of the chamber.[37]

In this general context, nostalgia has played a key role. Just like the 'new radical right' activists of the 1880s and 1890s and the Fascists of the 1920s and 1930s, the far-right militants of the post-war era have long memories. Whereas Boulanger and Barrès, under the Third Republic in France, reminisced about a strong and patriotic France, and Mussolini and Hitler looked back to 'golden age' periods in the history of their respective countries, the far-right agitators of today have a variety of historical reference points. For Le Pen in France it is the glory of *Algérie française* (the period prior to independence being granted to France's Algerian colony in 1962), while for Zhirinovsky in Russia a world in which Russia's borders took in the Baltic states and others. Thus, the notion of empire, and lost empire, is important for the Far Right. And in Austria Haider's views on the Nazi era have caused great controversy. One of his most infamous utterances came in December 1995 when he declared: 'The Waffen SS was a part of the Wehrmacht (German military) and hence it deserves all the honour and respect of the army in public life'.[38] When Haider entered government, the EU was forced to act. As a mark of **protest**, they inaugurated a period of sanctions. In time, the FPÖ was pressured into disassociating itself from Haider's remarks. Thus, in 2000, a joint manifesto was issued by the FPÖ and their partners in government, the centre-right Austrian People's Party:

The federal government affirms its unshakeable commitment to the spiritual and moral values which are the shared heritage of the peoples of Europe and which underlie the personal **freedom**, political freedom and the rule of law upon which all true democracy is based. The government will work for an Austria in which xenophobia, anti-Semitism and racism have no place. It espouses its own particular responsibility for respectful dealings with ethnic and religious minorities ... Austria embraces its responsibility arising from the disastrous history of the twentieth century and the monstrous crimes of the National Socialist regime. Our country shoulders as its responsibility the light and dark aspects of its past and the deeds of all Austrians, good and evil ... The uniqueness and incomparability of the crime of the Holocaust are a warning to be eternally vigilant concerning all forms of dictatorship and totalitarianism.[39]

Likewise, in Germany the contemporary Far Right is linked to the Nazi period. The former leader of the Republikaner Party, Franz **Schönhuber**, was a Waffen-SS sergeant, while the NPD still likes to associate itself with the colours of the German Empire: black, white and red.

For political movements on the fascist right during the inter-war years, leadership was always an important issue. Leaders, whether they were in government or opposition, had a vital role to play: to inspire, rally and organise. Hence, the 'cult of personality' that developed around leaders such as Hitler in Germany, Mussolini in Italy and Franco in Spain. It was also interesting the way in which fascist leaders in other countries tried to copy and ape the Central European dictators. In France, for example, Jacques Doriot called himself the 'French Führer' and started to dress like Hitler and also pose and gesticulate like him. In the post-war years, far-right movements have placed a similar emphasis on charisma. Le Pen in France has led his party since 1972 – over thirty-five years – mainly because potential rivals cannot compete with him as an orator or *médiatique* personality.

Parties on the extreme right have also emphasised their lack of faith in established parliamentary and governmental institutions. The BNP is representative: 'The struggle to secure our future is being waged on many fronts. The need for political power is crucial to bring about our goals. Without effective political representation the majority of Britons, who are deeply concerned about the future, have no voice in the chambers where decisions are made. Increasingly numbers of voters are expressing apathy and discontent with the endless incompetence, lies, false promises and sleaze coming from the three parties that make up the Old Gang. The BNP will contest and win elections at council, parliamentary, Assembly or European level in order to achieve political power to bring about the changes needed'.[40] So, as with other far-right parties around Europe the avowed aim is to work within 'the system' in order to change it. At some junctures far-right parties have also been happy to endorse and encourage extra-parliamentary activity, whether through riots or demonstrations. Occasionally, these events have spiralled into violence. In France in March 2006, the FN was implicated in a wave of political riots. In the previous year, Le Pen had claimed that direct-action tactics had the potential to be advantageous and beneficial for his movement: 'We are receiving thousands of new members, tens of thousands of e-mails. All of our offices are submerged, we don't know how to respond because we don't have the staff to reply to the wave of people who, 95 percent of them, salute and approve our positions'.[41]

It is also clear that far-right movements thrive on, and put great store by, propaganda. Of course, in today's world all political groupings want to spread their message effectively, 'spin' stories to their advantage and produce converts. But it would be fair to say that the Far Right puts a special emphasis on this, perhaps because they exclude themselves (or feel excluded) from mainstream political processes or because, historically, fascist, extreme-right and far-right parties have resorted to propaganda quite instinctively and successfully.

In recent years, far-right political propaganda has taken various forms. On one level it is quite traditional: hard-hitting posters with a powerful political message, aimed especially at the young.[42] On another, it is about the different types of media that can be employed to influence people. Take, for example, the FN in France. They have created a cottage industry out of merchandising their political message and making it accessible to ordinary people through such things as CDs, videos, books, badges, stationery and even key rings.[43] There is general agreement, too, on the fact that the FN was the first French political party to upload an effective and stylish website.[44] Far-right movements across Europe have followed suit – and some have even provided an English-language version.[45] Today, YouTube even hosts BNP songs.[46] Propaganda is also about the nature of the political message being conveyed. The names that far-right movements choose for themselves are particularly interesting. In Austria: the Freedom Party. In Russia: the Liberal Democratic Party. Do these monikers accurately reflect the nature and character of the movements concerned, or are they are a form of propaganda in themselves?

The attitude of the Far Right toward the mainstream right is also an interesting issue. The relationship is normally characterised by mistrust and mutual dislike. However, on some occasions, far-right movements have been courted by the mainstream. It has been argued that in Denmark in 2002 the liberal premier Anders Fogh Rasmussen moved his party rightwards as part of a strategy. His rhetoric changed and became much more alarmist about the 'threat' posed by immigrants. The strategy was so successful, it is claimed, that the far-right Danish People's Party claimed 12 percent of the national vote and thereafter Rasmussen was able to use the DPP as a 'parliamentary safety net'.[47] It is also clear that, almost without knowing it, the Far Right has the ability to stir, galvanise and sometimes unite 'the opposition'. In October 2000, for instance, the BBC reported that in Belgium, 'Opposition parties have vowed to co-operate to prevent the far-right Flemish Bloc from gaining power in Belgian town and city halls. The Bloc increased its share of the poll in **Antwerp**, Ghent, Mechelen and other northern Dutch-speaking towns during weekend elections. But politicians from across the political spectrum said they would boycott the Bloc and form local coalitions to keep the party out of local government'.[48]

Opponents of the Far Right can try to 'stereotype' it or 'exterminate' it.[49] The academic response is to try and understand it. Attempting to define the 'Far Right' is a troublesome business. We can focus on perceptions and self-perceptions, and then try to identify the main characteristics of the majority of far-right movements. But it isn't easy. There is something quite nebulous and elusive about the Far Right. What is 'far'? What is 'right'? And how do we gauge the nature of political extremities?

Academics across the world are divided on the nature of the post-war Far Right. They cannot assume that everyone is following a single definition that simply does not exist. Indeed, the onus is really on students of the phenomenon to develop their own version of the 'story', their own timeline and lexicon. That said – and we have got to try and move towards some kind of conclusion – it is clear that across Europe far-right parties do harbour some common political impulses and instincts.

To recap, almost all movements of the Far Right are united by a powerful and vehement anti-**Communism**, although the irony is that many of the most vociferous ultra-nationalists (especially in Eastern Europe and the Balkans) are former communists and were actually brought into being, politically and ideologically, by the fall of the **Berlin Wall** and the collapse of the USSR.

There is also an interesting and important relationship with the individuals who embodied 'classic fascism' between the wars. At first, the instinct on the post-war Far Right was to ape and mimic, and even to aim for the reconstitution of, the fascist movements of the 1920s and 1930s. But there was a gradual realisation that this would be counter-productive, and so many movements now style themselves as 'post-Fascist' and admit to only a passing, adjacent, contiguous relationship with inter-war fascism, if that. The truth, of course, is that parties have had to adapt and configure themselves adroitly to the exigencies of post-war milieus. And this has had unpredictable outcomes, with fuzzy relationships developing between far-right parties and extremist factions in more mainstream parties, and some boundaries being blurred.

Fundamentally, though, the Far Right has almost taken ownership of such issues as national identity, racism and anti-Semitism, and forms of praxis such as strong leadership, direct action and propaganda.

Peter Davies

Notes

1. Wikipedia, 'Far right', http://en.wikipedia.org/wiki/Far_right (cited 1 January 2008).
2. Paul Wilkinson, *The New Fascists* (London: Pan, 1983), vii.
3. See 'Politics of resentment: right-wing radicalism in West Germany', *Comparative Politics*, 23:1 (October, 1990), 45–60, and also 'The new politics of resentment: radical right-wing populist parties in Western Europe, *Comparative Politics*, 25:4 (July 1993), 413–427.
4. Paul Hainsworth (ed.), *The Politics of the Extreme Right: From the Margins to the Mainstream* (London: Pinter, 2000), 1.
5. Roger Griffin, *The Nature of Fascism* (London: Routledge, 1994), 166.
6. Robert O. Paxton, *The Anatomy of Fascism* (London: Penguin, 2005), 174.
7. Roger Eatwell, *Fascism: A History* (London: Vintage, 1996), 213.
8. See http://www.guardian.co.uk/gall/0,,711990,00.html (cited 1 January 2008).
9. Nones deleted except Sweden which is all none.
10. Luciano Cheles, Ronnie Ferguson & Michalina Vaughan, *Neo-Fascism in Europe* (London: Longman, 1991), xi.
11. BBC News, 'Far right', http://news.bbc.co.uk/hi/english/static/in_depth/europe/2000/far_right/sweden.stm (cited 1 January 2008).
12. P. Hainsworth, 'The extreme right in post-war France: the emergence and success of the Front National' in Paul Hainsworth (ed.), *The Extreme Right in Europe and the USA* (London: Pinter, 1994).
13. Michalina Vaughan, 'The extreme right in France: "Lepenisme" or the politics of fear' in Luciano Cheles, Ronnie Ferguson and Michalina Vaughan (eds.), *Neo-Fascism in Europe* (London: Longman, 1991), 222.
14. Posted at http://www.amren.com/mtnews/archives/2004/11/blok_changes_na.php (cited 1 January 2008).
15. Equality and Human Rights Commission, http://www.cre.gov.uk/Default.aspx.LocID-0hgnew0d4.RefLocID-0hg01b001006009.Lang-EN.htm. On Germany, see, for example, 'Living with the extremist plague', http://www.spiegel.de/international/spiegel/0,1518,451838,00.html (both cited 26 November 2007).
16. Guardian Unlimited, 'The new barbarism', www.guardian.co.uk/comment/story/0,3604,712136,00.html (cited 26 November 2007).
17. Socialist Party, 'Fighting the far-right BNP', http://www.socialistparty.org.uk/2006/426/index.html?id=np3a.htm (cited 26 November 2007).
18. World Socialist Web Site, 'Austria's right-wing Freedom Party riven by disputes', http://www.wsws.org/articles/2001/may2001/haid-m30.shtml (cited 26 November 2007).

19. Socialism Today, 'The character of the far-right threat', http://www.socialismtoday.org/66/farRight.html (cited 26 November 2007).

20. Spiked, 'The myth of the far right', http://www.spiked-online.com/Articles/00000006D931.htm (cited 26 November 2007).

21. Der Spiegel, 'Far-right views established across German society', http://www.spiegel.de/international/0,1518,447255,00.html (cited 26 November 2007).

22. DPP, 'Manifesto', http://www.danskfolkeparti.dk/sw/frontend/show.asp?parent=3293 (cited 6 July 2007).

23. Daily Telegraph, Enoch Powell's 'Rivers of Blood' speech. www.telegraph.co.uk/opinion/main.jhtml?xml=/opinion/2007/11/06/nosplit/do0607.xml (cited 6 July 2007).

24. The Human Rights Brief, 'Plight of France's *sans-papiers* gives a face to struggle. Over immigration reform', http://www.wcl.american.edu/hrbrief/v4i1/pasqua41.htm (cited 30 December 2007).

25. BBC News, 'French riots spread beyond Paris', http://news.bbc.co.uk/1/hi/world/europe/4405620.stm (cited 30 December 2007).

26. This is London, 'Cameron accuses Brown of using language of BNP as PM forces immigrants to learn English', http://www.thisislondon.co.uk/news/article-23419786-details/Cameron+accuses+Brown+of+using+language+of+BNP+as+PM+forces+immigrants+to+learn+English/article.do (cited 30 December 2007).

27. Guardian Unlimited, '"Gay porn" movie raises ripples on far right', http://politics.guardian.co.uk/farright/story/0,,1772052,00.html (cited 30 December 2007).

28. Guardian Unlimited, 'Le Pen dynasty's bid to renew appeal of far right', http://observer.guardian.co.uk/world/story/0,,1973768,00.html (cited 30 December 2007).

29. Guardian Unlimited, 'Jennifer's journey to the front of the BNP', http://www.guardian.co.uk/farright/story/0,11981,1218008,00.html (cited 30 December 2007).

30. Le Monde Diplomatique, 'Women are saying no', http://mondediplo.com/1998/05/06lavau (cited 16 August 2007).

31. BNP, 'Mission statement', http://www.bnp.org.uk/mission.htm (cited 16 August 2007).

32. The Economist, 'Far-right parties up north', http://www.economist.com/PrinterFriendly.cfm?story_id=8418058 (cited 30 December 2007).

33. Hellenic Front, 'Immigration', http://www.e-grammes.gr/index_en.html (cited 14 April 2007).

34. Danish People's Party, 'Programme', http://www.danskfolkeparti.dk/sw/frontend/show.asp?parent=3293 (cited 14 April 2007).

35. BBC News, 'Denmark's immigration issue', http://news.bbc.co.uk/1/hi/world/europe/4276963.stm (cited 30 December 2007).

36. See, for example, P. Jouve & A. Magoudi, *Les Dits et les Non-Dits de Jean-Marie Le Pen* (Paris: Editions La Découverte, 1988).

37. Deutsche Welle, 'Far-Right German Party Belittles Holocaust', www.dw-world.de/dw/article/0,1564,1466245,00.html

38. BBC News, 'Joerg Haider: Key quotes', http://news.bbc.co.uk/1/hi/world/europe/628282.stm (cited 30 December 2007).

39. BBC News, 'Coalition pledge over Nazi past', http://news.bbc.co.uk/1/hi/world/monitoring/media_reports/630901.stm (cited 30 December 2007).

40. BNP, 'Political battle', http://www.bnp.org.uk/?p=227 (cited 30 December 2007).

41. Breitbart News, 'Far-right leader: riots only the start', http://www.breitbart.com/news/2005/11/09/D8DP4IE02.html (cited 26 July 2007).

42. Hellenic Front, 'Posters', http://www.e-grammes.gr/posters/index_en.htm plus (cited 7 August 2006).

43. FN, 'Boutique', http://www.frontnational.com/pdf/boutique.pdf (cited 30 December 2007).

44. See http://www.frontnational.com.

45. See Hellenic Front/Hellenic Lines, http://www.e-grammes.gr/index_en.html (cited 30 December 2007).

46. YouTube, 'BNP Nothing bloody works', http://youtube.com/watch?v=CmmjrLG0ScU&mode=related&search (cited 30 December 2007).

47. CounterPunch, 'The new Danish government and the extreme right', http://www.counterpunch.org/sohn0430.html; The Economist, 'Far-right parties up north', http://www.economist.com/PrinterFriendly.cfm?story_id=8418058 (both cited 16 June 2007).

48. CNN, 'Far-right unites Belgian parties', http://edition.cnn.com/2000/WORLD/europe/10/09/belgium.elections (cited 21 July 2007).

49. Guardian Unlimited, 'Way wrong on the far right', http://commentisfree.guardian.co.uk/ian_cobain/2006/12/post_843.html (cited 16 May 2007).

The Far Right in Europe:
Introductory Essays

The Origins of the Far Right

When the *philosophes* of the Enlightenment first conceived the project of writing an 'Encyclopedia' they assumed that the systematic application of human reason to research into all aspects of reality would eventually lead to a compendium of human knowledge about the world of universal validity. At the end of the nineteenth century, Lord Acton could still fondly imagine that the series of Cambridge histories could be written in such a way that it would be impossible to know where one historian took over from another in the reconstruction of the past. Both the writers and readers of this encyclopedia live in more 'enlightened' and less optimistic times, where the naivety of such assumptions is self-evident. The arbitrary, incomplete, strictly *heuristic* nature of a panoramic account of a topic as extensive and multifaceted as 'the Far Right' can now be openly confronted without it being taken as a sign of weakness. Methodologically speaking, all academics have been 'outed' by postmodernism as falling short of the utopian ideals of scholarly omniscience and objectivity.

This chapter thus cannot be looked at for a seamless, authoritative history of the origins of the Far Right. It is a continually evolving topic that embraces a wide range of political phenomena both generic and particular beyond the ken of any one researcher, even when the scope of the inquiry is artificially restricted to **Europe** – in itself a treacherously simple geographical unit, especially when it is not limited by a specific period of history. Political extremism is also a topic that in any geographical area or period raises definitional and explanatory issues which are intensely contested, both by experts and by the individuals – ranging from a handful to millions according to the variant of Far Right and period of modern history in question – whose political convictions and activities actually constitute or construct it.

Indeed, the first fallacy to be exposed is that the Far Right constitutes an 'it' at all, since the term subsumes several discrete – and in some cases bitterly opposed – currents of ideology and praxis which have coalesced in the minds of upholders of liberal **democracy** and of the (equally mythically homogeneous) Far Left into a single threat to their values and institutions. It is worth stressing at this point that academics whose mindset is shaped by far-left assumptions would write a very different version of this chapter. They would probably argue that it is the need to preserve the hegemony of oppressive feudal or capitalist socio-economic and political structures that provides the mainspring of a Far Right. From a socialist perspective, this explains why in practice it is continually leaking into and entering collusion with the mainstream politics of both authoritarian conservatism and actually existing liberalism despite official or rhetorical attempts to repress it.

The solution to such methodological dilemmas adopted here is first to offer brief notes on the problems of definition and demarcation intrinsic to the subject, providing working solutions to them without which it would be impossible for it to be written at all. It will then offer some necessarily brief reflections on how the specific constituents of the loose conceptual hold-all known as the Far Right came about. The aim is to provide a 'rough guide' to lead those exploring this topic for the first time to investigate it further in secondary and primary sources. In this way, they might produce their own story of how the particular variant of politics that concerns them came into being, thereby deepening their own understanding of the factors determining its current strength or weakness. It will necessarily be a story attuned to their own experience of 'the Right', their own ideological principles and their own vision of contemporary political reality. It should also be informed by more detailed, 'in-depth' studies of Far Right phenomena (some of them contained in this encyclopedia) than can be attempted in this highly condensed synoptic essay. Such complementary sources are essential to provide empirical colour and texture to the schematic account offered here.[1]

'Far'

The 'Far Right' is a binomial expression both of whose elements are problematic. The adjective 'far' evokes the comforting illusion that the writer is somehow located at the 'centre' of normal, moderate, healthy, rational, human values, and is dealing with something safely removed and remote from his or her universe. By definition, no-one on the Far Right would use the phrase to define themselves. For them it is the status quo that is 'extreme' in its decadence and failure to safeguard essential values. Clarifying what it means is not made any easier by the fact that this political use of the adjective is peculiar to the English language, and has to be translated in most European languages into the equivalent of 'extreme' or 'radical'. The first of these connotes both geographical remoteness and intensity ('extreme heat'), while the second implies 'going to the roots', seeking fundamental as opposed to superficial change, and hence bent on wholesale and often immediate rather than piecemeal and gradualistic transformation of political society.

Whereas in English 'extreme' and 'radical' are frequently used interchangeably – as the titles of several books cited in the endnotes to this chapter illustrate – in German *'radikal'* is a legal term for forms of politics still operating within the bounds of democratic legitimacy. By contrast, *'extrem'* is beyond the pale, and is considered to pose a threat to liberal society and values. As a consequence 'radical' parties receive state funding, while those officially deemed 'extreme', and hence illegal, face prosecution and a ban on their activities. The Office for the Protection of the Constitution (*Verfassungsschutzamt*) in Federal Germany has drawn up a set of criteria on the basis of which organisations are officially tolerated or not. Obviously such a bureaucracy constantly faces teasing legalistic issues of definition and evaluation with respect to specific cases, but at least a German political theorist would have the advantage of writing a chapter on a more manageable, less elusive subject than the untranslatable 'Far Right', and would have to decide clearly at the outset whether to consider the extreme right, the radical right, or both. The present chapter, written for an Anglophone readership, thus works with considerably more fuzzy boundaries.[2]

'Right'

The vagueness inherent in the epithet 'far' is compounded by the difficulties intrinsic to the term 'right'. Twentieth-century history, which proliferated hybrids such as Christian Socialism, National Bolshevism, National Syndicalism, National Socialism and Soviet Nationalism, considerably compromised – if it did not destroy altogether – the heuristic value of the left-right spectrum as a conceptual tool for analysing politics. How are politologists to classify Pol Pot's regime, based as it was on a lethal fusion of the fundamentalist Maoism of China's Cultural Revolution with extreme racist nationalism, a hybrid signalled in the name 'Khmer Rouge'? No less confusingly for those bent on neatly pigeon-holing such products of ideological syncretism is the profound kinship existing in practice between 'actually existing' communist systems and fascist regimes in the way they blend totalitarian transformation with ultra-nationalism, even if they are theoretically and historically sworn enemies.[3] Equally problematic for taxonomic purists is the fact that some factions within the highly nationalistic and thus apparently 'right-wing' separatist movements, such as the Irish Republican Movement (IRA), had hosted factions that pursued a staunchly Marxist vision of the New Ireland. This 'touching of extremes' was a feature of classic Fascism itself. There is more than rhetoric in the phrase 'National Socialism', or in the title that Zeev Sternhell chose for his groundbreaking study of French Fascism, *Neither Right nor Left*.

The contemporary Far Right perpetuates this 'coincidence of opposites'. By the end of the century, following the collapse of the Soviet Empire, intellectuals of the European (not neo-liberal, or 'Thatcherite') New Right were announcing they had transcended the outdated distinction between Left and Right altogether. It was a claim apparently vindicated by the publication of some of their articles in the American journal *Telos* which formerly could boast impeccable left-wing credentials. It is symptomatic of the same phenomenon that a Third Positionist *groupuscule* such as Luc Michel's National-European Communitarian Movement blends communist with fascist critiques of EU Europe and globalising capitalism in a way that defies traditional categories.

To abandon the concept of 'the Right' altogether, however, would cause not just this chapter but the whole encyclopedia to disappear – like God does at one point in Douglas Adam's *Hitchhiker's Guide to the Galaxy* – in a 'puff of logic'. The less drastic, more pragmatic solution adopted here is to combine a historical perspective on individual phenomena widely associated with the 'Right' in common usage, with the recognition that the term, as in the case of all generic concepts in the human sciences, is an ideal type rather than an objective, definitively definable entity.[4] This approach can air-lift us from the quicksands of definitional conundrums and self-deconstructing methodological musings into an engagement with specific empirical realities.

The Far Right

Any concept of the Far Right implies the existence of a moderate, liberal, non-extreme Right with which it is being contrasted. For the purposes of this chapter, this 'democratic Right' is approached as a modern descendent of a tradition of liberal politics symbolically inaugurated with the French Revolution, which, in order to guarantee the social stability and *order* of a state based on representative government and individual human rights, upholds the values of rootedness, history and traditional hierarchies such as monarchy and bourgeois property relations. By contrast, the democratic Left focuses on the possibility of achieving greater *social justice* by replacing historically forged communities with new ones, and by adopting more radical policies designed to transform existing power hierarchies and distribute power and wealth more equitably. The paradigmatic party-political manifestations of these contrasting positions in the context of Anglophone democracy are – despite significant differences – the British Conservative Party (and its equivalents in Canada and Australia) and the US Republicans for the Right, and the various Commonwealth Labour Parties and the US Democrats for the Left. Every European parliamentary system will have its uniquely constituted tradition of Left and Right.

The 'far right' and 'far left' represent versions of these positions that go *beyond* – though not necessarily *far* beyond – the sphere of legitimate liberal politics (a sphere whose boundaries are being constantly renegotiated), by rejecting several cornerstones of democracy, notably the principle of open debate, **freedom** of speech, free elections, the separation of powers, the commitment to non-violence and individual human rights and the tolerance of cultural, religious and ethnic pluralism. The modern European far left, now apparently reduced to a 'Paper Tiger' in comparison with earlier decades, retains an ideological kinship with the – sometimes warring – factions that fought against Franco's fascist forces in the Spanish Civil War, and embodies various strands of revolutionary socialism and anarchism bent on transcending or destroying the bourgeois state and the global forces of capitalism and militarism that underpin it. The militant European students, who four decades ago felt inspired by the Red Guards of China's Cultural Revolution and the Red Brigades, some of whom turned their ideals into terrorist praxis in Europe, both defined themselves in terms that corresponded to the 'Far Left' in this sense.

In contrast, the Far Right rejects liberal democracy, pluralism, individualism and often free-market capitalism as well, not in the name of a system of universal social justice for all, but in the name of a society in which a sense of national, ethnic or religious identity and belonging has been restored and the alleged forces of decadence and dissolution have been overcome. In inter-war Europe a host of far-right movements and regimes arose which were dedicated to combating both the spread of Bolshevism and to replacing or fending off the advent of a liberal democracy, sometimes in its infancy. They did so because the parliamentary system and liberal values – especially after the horrors of World War I and the ensuing socio-economic chaos – were equated in their eyes, not with progress, but with national weakness, the atomisation of society and a modern civilisation in terminal decline.

For the inter-war Far Right, the basic unit of humanity whose health and strength were to be preserved or intensified was usually the nation-state, so that both (reactionary) conservatives and (revolutionary) fascists upheld militant forms of ultra-nationalism. However, the ultra-nationalism of the Third Reich already created a hybrid between the political cult[5] of 'Germany' as a historically formed nation-state, and of 'the Germans' as a discrete and potentially pure *ethnie* embodying the mythic qualities of a presumed Aryan root-race. This hybrid has exerted a profound influence on some currents within the contemporary Far Right, several of which have abandoned the primacy of the nation-state as a unit of social organisation altogether. Nevertheless, 'by definition' no form of Far Right can survive without a heightened sense of belonging to some – essentially mythical – historical, natural or ethnic reality as the cornerstone of spiritual values, civilisation and ultimate purpose of existence. The cohesion and mobilising potential of any form of Far Right depends ultimately on its ability to satisfy human needs for 'belonging' which express themselves differently in different phases of history, and whose origins arguably lie within primordial features of the human relationship to time itself.[6]

Superseded Forms of the Post-War Far Right

Before considering in general terms the origins of contemporary, still active variants of the Far Right, it is helpful to gain a broader sense of its developments since the dramatic symbolic end of the 'fascist epoch' in April 1945 when the corpse of the *Duce* was strung up from a petrol station gantry in Milan's Piazza San Loretto, and the Führer's body was burnt beyond recognition in his Berlin bunker. The Third Reich's defeat, the revelation of the extent of the horrendous crimes against humanity it had committed under the cover of war, and the discrediting of imperialist and racist ultra-nationalism as the basis of state power form the backcloth of the way the Far Right presents itself today and the abject failure of it to break through politically whenever it openly celebrates its kinship with its inter-war forebears. The three forms of the Far Right that dominated the period 1918–1945 but that have comprehensively disappeared from contemporary history, are authoritarian nationalist regimes, fascist regimes and fascist mass movements.

The Authoritarian State

Inter-war Europe was an era marked by the inability of the liberal state in its nineteenth-century incarnation to provide a peace settlement that enabled viable and stable nations to emerge after the collapse of the Austro-Hungarian Empire, to establish the League of Nations as an effective international body for the peaceful settlement of international crises, to create an effective economic system to maintain stability and growth, or to accommodate the rise of the masses as socio-political actors. Instead of mutating smoothly into liberal or social democracy, political liberalism thus became widely identified with the impotence to resolve acute domestic and international problems, and more generally with the structural crisis of modern civilisation which had become manifest in the Great War. Almost every European nation hosted tensions, sometimes acute, between different factions within liberal society and between liberalism, the Far Left – which itself was split between Bolsheviks and other forms of revolutionary politics – and the Far Right, which in countries without a well-embedded democratic tradition consisted of a wide array of radical conservatives and revolutionary nationalists. It was a situation that led to a number of authoritarian regimes being installed in Southern and Eastern Europe, and provided the preconditions for the fascist 'conquest of the state' in Italy and the Nazi 'seizure of power' in Germany.

By contrast, the first decades of post-war Europe proved to be an era of growing economic and political stability in the democratic (capitalist) West, and saw the creation of the Russian Empire in the East which imposed communist states on nations that would otherwise have completed the transition to liberal democracy. This made the perpetuation of the right-wing authoritarianism of **Salazar** in Portugal and **Franco** in Spain increasingly anomalous relics of a bygone age, rather than the embodiments of political modernity they could still claim to be in the late 1930s. Though they lingered on until 1970 and 1975 respectively, there was no question of them continuing after the death of their increasingly geriatric leaders. Instead, both countries quickly made the transition to democracy, and are currently enthusiastic member-states of the European Union with minimal popular nostalgia for the fascist or even imperialist era.

The general sense of material progress of liberal capitalist society, the urge to put an end to an age of crisis, war and extermination camps, dominated the whole of Western Europe after 1945. Thus, when a military regime was created in Greece lasting from 1967 until 1974 it was entirely out of step with the ethos of modern Europe, and its inevitable demise had a democratic outcome that would have been far less likely in inter-war Europe, Latin America between the 1920s and 1980s, or contemporary Africa. Meanwhile the imposition of nationalist communist dictatorships in Eastern Europe was successful in mostly disseminating not **Communism** but an almost universal longing to be part of the liberal capitalist West. As a result there was little danger that the vacuum created when Soviet Russia collapsed would be filled by openly authoritarian right-wing regimes, whatever the imperfections of the parliamentary systems that did emerge. Notable among these imperfections in the period of transition to a civil society was the rise of populist racism towards Jews, gypsies and other ethnic minorities fomented by the chaotic conditions that prevailed before stability and prosperity started returning to former Soviet satellites – a racism that created an ideal habitat for the rapid re-emergence of the Far Right.

An extreme instance of this process manifested itself in Yugoslavia, which, in the wake of the Soviet Empire's dissolution, saw the resurfacing of powerful currents of racism and ultra-nationalism,[7] as well as the emergence of a new genus of Far Right with no precedent in inter-war Europe. Both Croatia and Serbia elected governments in 1991 – under Franjo **Tuđman** and Slobodan **Milošević** respectively – which blended the formal apparatus of democratic institutions with charismatic leadership, authoritarianism and the militarisation of society. These served to realise domestic and foreign policies based on extreme nationalism, xenophobia, religious hatred and anti-Islamic sentiments. It was a development that soon resulted in bitter internecine wars throughout much of the area, culminating in horrendous episodes of ethnic cleansing, war crimes and genocidal purges carried out with ferocious **violence** and sadism by the armies and militias of democratically elected governments. A possible neologism for the ideology underpinning the unique form of regime created by Milošević and Tuđman is 'ethnocratic liberalism', since its most fanatical supporters see no contradiction in creating an 'ethnocratic state' where civil rights are enjoyed, as under the Third Reich, strictly on the basis of racial and nationalist criteria, but without abolishing the formal apparatus of pluralist democracy. Another evocative term might be 'democratic fascism' to the extent that the bloodshed and atrocities were justified by evoking the vision of a new Croatia and new Serbia.[8] The regimes of Milošević and Tuđman exhibited some points of analogy with the Republic of South Africa in the years of apartheid, another variant of 'ethnocratic liberalism'. However, within the extended family of the European Far Right both were largely *sui generis*, originating in a fatal coincidence of post-communist democratisation with the resurfacing of age-old ethnic tensions whose roots lie deep in irreconcilable and intensely mythicised nationalist histories of the Balkans. More immediately they arose from the legacy of the First and Second Balkan Wars (1912–1913), and from the ferocious ethnic conflicts between Serbs and Croats that took place during World War II. All these involved blood-chilling atrocities committed against the demonised enemy which have been officially commemorated only by the nation of the victims, while remaining in hermetic denial about its own genocidal past. The Third Balkan War (1991–2001) – which subsumed at least nine discrete conflicts – was brought to an end only under sustained diplomatic and military pressure from the international community.

With the prospect of the EU being eventually enlarged to include all former communist states, Europe now seems to have eliminated for the foreseeable future the possibility that authoritarian regimes might re-emerge in either their familiar authoritarian or new democratic forms. Integrated economies, the age of rampant individualism, globalised media and consumerism and the watchful presence of NATO and the United Nations condemn any would-be Salazar, Franco, Tuđman, or Milošević to living in a world of wishful thinking.

The Fascist Totalitarian Party/Regime and 'Mimetic' Fascism

World War II and the various genocides that accompanied it left such deep scars on the collective European memory that 'fascism' is still widely used as a synonym for the Far Right. Moreover, there is a natural tendency for ghosts of the Third Reich to be summoned forth whenever a party identified with it, such as Jean-Marie **Le Pen**'s Front National or Jörg **Haider**'s **Austrian Freedom Party**, has given the impression that it might be manoeuvring its way towards state power. Yet someone of the generation born after the **Cold War** and the collapse of the Soviet Empire – unless steeped in the history of the twentieth century – would find it impossible to infer from the paltry residues of Fascism detectable today that by 1941, the Berlin-Rome Axis, a shot-gun marriage between two highly different variants of fascist regime, credibly threatened not just to occupy practically the whole of Europe, but to determine the long-term fate of European civilisation.

A minute stream now trickles where a highly destructive mountain torrent once surged. There are no more mass movements of national rebirth led by charismatic (or would-be charismatic) leaders, no political parties backed by powerful squads of uniformed militias holding mass-rallies in public squares and sports arenas announcing the dawning of a new age and a new man. For practical purposes the 'fascist epoch' is dead. The hostile conditions created by post-war developments for right-wing extremism did not, however, prevent initiatives in every part of Europe where communist dictatorship was not enforced from above to emulate 'classical fascism'. Many hundreds of revolutionary fascist groupings have formed since 1945 in Europe, nearly all of which have remained of negligible size or have quickly withered on the vine, despite the utopian fantasies of their founders that they were the vanguard of a 'national revolution'.

As for the origins of this superseded form of Far Right, it is stating the obvious that every would-be mass-party movement which invokes the symbolism or ethos of inter-war Fascism has its origins in the era that produced the regimes of Mussolini and Hitler – whose genesis, of course, has its own convoluted history[9] – and will present an alternative history in which any national variant of Fascism that developed in that era is presented in a positive light. Less self-evident is the role played by another factor, namely the way the events of the inter-war period have lent themselves to Romanticisation by new generations who have never been exposed to the horrors caused by Fascism and who are thus able to turn them into a mythic narrative through which to express their own, very different, struggle for social order and racial homogeneity, even though the conditions that made mass movements of revolutionary nationalism no longer prevail. Thus it was not surprising if the attempt of the UK's **National Front** to adapt the Fascism of Oswald Mosley and Adolf Hitler to the conditions of post-war Britain won some temporary popular support in areas of high **immigration** and social deprivation in the 1960s and 1970s, even if the idea that it could ever begin to emulate the success of the NSDAP was sheer fantasy on the part of militant members and opponents alike. Similarly, it was predictable that within months of the overthrow of Nicolae Ceaucescu's dictatorship in Romania in 1989 attempts were under way to reestablish the Iron Guard, an extremely virulent home-grown variant of Fascism led by Corneliu Codreanu in the 1920s and 1930s. Equally inevitably this experiment in 'nostalgic' or 'mimetic' Fascism had a negligible impact on the progress of the new state towards democracy, and failed to channel the powerful currents of racism and xenophobia that resurfaced from an earlier age like its legendary ancestor. A synoptic chapter on the origins of the European Far Right thus requires us to focus on the new, more viable forms it has assumed since 1945.

The Origins of the Far Right

Active Forms of the Contemporary Far Right

Groupuscular Neo-Fascism

Given the horrors of the World War II, it is legitimate to wonder how Fascism could resurface in any form at all after 1945. However, it should be remembered that millions of Europeans found Far Right attitudes to the nation and race in their fascist permutation 'normal' by 1942, a normalisation of extremism fed by the apparent collapse of liberal democracy as a historical force, as well as intense – and far from imaginary – fears of anarchy and Communism after the Wall Street Crash further destabilised a Europe still reeling from the impact of World War I. It would thus be mysterious if fascist attitudes had evaporated entirely after the Allied victory, especially in countries with powerful home-grown fascist movements or experiences of **collaboration** with the Third Reich, notably Italy, Germany, France and Belgium. Instead, small pockets of nostalgic Fascism survived in countries which created their own self-perpetuating subculture. Surveys into racist and anti-democratic attitudes carried out by sociologists and the EU provide another causal factor at work in the resurgence of Fascism after 1945. They have indicated that even in stable modern societies, a small percentage of any given population has a latent predisposition towards xenophobia and ultra-nationalism as a matter of temperament or personality. This provides the basis for the existence of a permanent constituency of far-right activists scattered throughout Europe, one which can swell locally to provide marginal support for racist groups and parties if socio-economic conditions are 'right'. This is true even in countries famous for the strength of their democracies such as Sweden and Switzerland. The permanent presence of a racist Far Right, however small, in every European state, despite the atrocities committed under Nazism between 1939 and 1945, should thus not come as any surprise, especially since collective historical memories are such malleable and largely mythicised entities.

The immediate context for the perpetuation of Fascism under new guises in post-war Europe was a constellation of new factors that threatened national identity, such as decolonisation, the EU, globalisation, Americanisation, the rise of the multi-ethnic and multi-cultural society and, more recently, insecurities following the collapse of the Soviet Empire. To these can now be added the growing threat posed by the possibility of acts of terrorism committed against European targets by Islamist extremists. It is possible to speculate that had the astonishing rise of the media culture not provided an increasingly atomised society with the technical possibility for every individual to inhabit his or her private mental room decorated and furnished with a personalised choice of music, communication and entertainment – a phenomenon epitomised in the proliferation of cell-phones, MP3 players and PCs connected by broadband to the Web – modern Europe would be awash with currents of far-right extremism. Indeed, were all technological means of accessing private space to offset *anomie* suddenly to be turned off, fascistic forms of politicised racism might find a powerful popular resonance and no longer be the preserve of minute groups of fanatics or isolated loners. After all, had Adolf Hitler been forced to contend in his struggle not just with Communism but with Sky TV, his charisma might have been stillborn.

Perhaps sociologists and political scientists would do well to devote more time to explaining the general *lack* of populist momentum gathered by the fascist Far Right since the war rather than treating its continued presence as an anomaly to be explained. Certainly it would have been an aberration if the mass immigration that took place in the 1950s and 1960s into countries such as West Germany, France,

Holland, Belgium and Britain had not led to a resurgence of populist racist sentiments in the areas of society most directly affected. However, xenophobia is not to be confused with fascism, despite the widespread colloquial use of the term which perpetuates such confusion. What is significant in the context of this encyclopedia is that a genuinely fascist Far Right has, against all the odds, continued to survive in its most extreme or pure form, one which has stayed true to its uncompromising and, in its own terms, *revolutionary* struggle against liberal democracy. Precluded from operating as a party-movement, it is now made up of myriad minute, and mostly ephemeral and individually insignificant, *groupuscules* scattered across Europe which collectively enable far-right extremism to survive in a hostile environment.[10] Its attempts to usher in a new post-liberal era can take one of several forms. Each form has its roots in inter-war Fascism but, at the same time, has been shaped by the disappearance in Western Europe of popular sympathy for classic fascist visions of a new national order achieved through violence, and hence the impossibility for any fascist formation to gather the momentum needed to become a fascist *movement* in a meaningful sense of the term.

In this sense all fascistic variants of the Far Right have dual origins and can be called 'neo-fascism' to mark their novelty with respect to the 'classic' forms of Fascism whose epoch-making power – if not their specific contents – they would so much like to emulate. It should be noted, however, that some experts maintain that the gulf separating inter-war Fascism from the post-war racist right is so profound that it is more appropriate to use a term such as 'the new radical right' instead (or rather, in line with German usage, 'the new extreme right').[11] Whatever term is used, it is important to apply a bi-focal approach, which highlights *both* the novelty of revolutionary variants of the Far Right *and* their continuity with inter-war Fascism.

Neo-Nazism

At least in its extra-parliamentary forms, Neo-Nazism makes no attempt to disguise its debt to the regime that was responsible for the military and industrialised slaughter of millions of human beings between 1939 and 1945. As a politicised form of racism it is, in Darwinian terms, the most successful post-war form of neo-fascism, with *groupuscules* and individual acolytes in every Europeanised nation in the world celebrating in public or private mythicised versions of the goals and achievements of the Third Reich – though in Germany any *public* display of pro-Nazi sympathies is, of course, illegal. However, it would be simplistic to trace the origins of neo-Nazism simply to Hitler's movement. When Swedish, English, or Russian youths sport Nazi insignia and greet each other with the Hitler salute they are no longer celebrating Germany's rebirth. Instead they are openly defying liberal norms of tolerance by parading the alleged supremacy of the White race in a way that both dramatises and politicises their hatred of local racial enemies, whether immigrants, ethnic minorities, Blacks, Jews, Roma or any social group categorised as 'foreign' or 'scum'. In doing so, the historically-specific national goals and racial hatreds of Hitler's original followers have been universalised into an international racist creed adapted to the local social and historical conditions outside Germany, with only a small minority of neo-Nazis at all interested in probing beyond the theatrical element of Führer-worship and its ritualisation of racial hatred and violence.

It is the radical-ness with which the Nazis pursued their policies of destroying Bolshevism, of making the world 'Jew-free', and of asserting their supremacy over 'racial inferiors' that continues to exert its fascination on an extremely marginalised, politically impotent section of disaffected racists intent on taking a stand against contemporary decadence and the Americanisation (or, for American Nazis, the domination by 'Zionism') of their nation – an entity they conceive in terms of racial purity rather than shared citizenship. The origins of neo-Nazism thus lie as much in the post-war rise of xenophobia, the rejection of mass immigration and multiculturalism and the erosion of a clearly conceived national identity, as in the historical Third Reich, and fully reflects the social and historical ethos of contemporary society – especially its **youth** culture and technological advances – rather than the 1930s.

A symptom of the dual origins of neo-Nazism is the attempt by activists to infiltrate the 'hooligan' sections of football support in order to politicise their violence and racial hatred and bring them into the Nazi fold. Another is the development of a (for its organisers, highly lucrative) 'White Noise' music scene that uses a travestied form of punk rock performed on semi-clandestine CDs and illegal concerts to incite its far-flung audience to live out their repressed resentments and to engage in racial warfare.[12] Both these developments would have been unthinkable under the 'original' Nazis. Equally innovative is the use of the Internet to create an 'imagined community' of Nazis as a potent player in global politics. This offsets the reality of extreme marginalisation and fragmentation that has led to Nazism's *groupuscularisation* and almost total social invisibility as a political force, certainly in contrast to 1930s Germany. The proliferation of 'virtual fascism', the growth of international linkages between minute Nazi groups, most of them identified by their own name, logo and website and the alliance that some form with kindred racist groups, such as the US Ku Klux Klan or Christian Identity, are symptoms, not of strength, but of a fundamental impotence to change the status quo.

The unique conditions in which Nazism thrived in the 1930s are gone forever, and neo-Nazis have no prospect of changing the course of history beyond the sporadic execution of racially motivated crimes, such as the murder of three Turks in Mölln in November 1992 by German neo-Nazis. Warnings that the upsurge of neo-Nazi violence in Germany after unification announced the dawning of a new Reich thus turned out to be hysterical over-reactions which misread the changed conditions of post-war Europe for incubating fascism, even if they corresponded to the utopian fantasies of the extreme right itself.[13] Against this, some might argue that such crimes create a climate of fear in which democratic governments are more likely to take illiberal measures against 'foreigners', but this still falls far short of the neo-Nazis' own visions of a 'new order'.

Black Terrorism and the 'International Third Position'

Neo-Nazism has a direct bearing on another aspect of the contemporary European Far Right; one which has its own complex origins. David Copeland's 'lone-wolf' nail-bombing campaign against black, Asian and gay communities in London in April 1999 was precipitated partly by his membership in a minute English neo-Nazi *groupuscule*, the National Socialist Movement. It consisted of an elite with a handful of followers, and was essentially a form of 'virtual fascism' until Copeland took it upon himself to turn the rhetoric of utopianism and hatred, as promulgated on its website, into the self-appointed mission to carry out terrorist attacks against ethnic minorities and homosexuals in London in order to trigger a race war. Again, the blend of inter-war and contemporary causal factors is striking: Copeland downloaded bomb-making instructions and the hate literature of various US far-right religious groups from the Internet.[14] It is worth underlining the fact that his private 'mission impossible' would have been unthinkable at the height of the 'fascist epoch' when paramilitary movements such as the Nazi SA or fascist Militia would have accommodated his fanatical hostility to liberal society. His personal crusade reflects the anomic ethos of modern urban and suburban life explored in Martin Scorsese's *Taxi Driver* rather than that of Weimar Germany.

However devastating the impact was on the lives of the victims and their relatives of the 3 dead and 129 injured, some maimed for life, Copeland's three-bomb campaign still represents a considerable dwindling of 'black terrorism' in Europe since the high point it reached with the **Bologna Bombing** of 2 August 1980, which killed 85 and injured over 200.[15] This was the most lethal outrage of a series of attacks on the civilian population during the period of the 'Strategy of Tension', when the Far Right set out to destabilise Italy with a series of terrorist attacks in the utopian hope of bringing about a right-wing military coup backed by Fascists. Again, this was no straightforward re-enactment of inter-war Fascism. Though historical memories of Fascism and Nazism played a role, the upsurge of neo-fascist violence in the 1970s was bound up with the polarisation between left-wing and right-wing youth in the years of the 'hippy' and student counter-cultural rejection of mainstream Western values. An essential role was also played by the chronic instability and corruption of Italy's governments at the time, as well as by romanticised memories of Italy's 'rebirth' as a strong, proud nation under Mussolini.

One of the main inspirations behind Italian black terrorism was the prolific philosopher and cultural critic Julius Evola.[16] Though a major theorist of fascist racial doctrine under Nazism and an admirer of the Third Reich, his main influence on post-war far-right ideologues lay in two ideas: his analysis of how Fascists should behave in an age when fascist parties were impotent to develop mass support, and his vision of a Europe freed of US and American domination. The adoption of Evola, rather than Hitler, as guru was symptomatic of the emergence of the internationalist form of Far Right known as 'Third Position', alluded to above, at the core of which lay the vision of a new breed of 'Political Soldier' dedicated to bringing about the new post-capitalist and post-communist world. It is a vision whose roots lie both in inter-war Europe and in the reactions of hardcore revolutionary fascists to the crushing defeat of the Axis Powers and the need to resort to guerrilla tactics to perpetuate their cause. This led to the Europeanisation of fascism as a clandestine, potentially terroristic counter-culture, the main theorists of which were high-profile figures such as Oswald Mosley, but also far more shadowy ones such as Francis Yockey,[17] Francois Thiriart and Christian Bouchet, and more recently, Luc Michel. The fact that some former members of the UK's neo-Nazi National Front also became Third Positionists in the 1980s, when it had become a spent political force, was a sign of the times.[18]

Despite producing voluminous, sometimes ingenious, political writings in several languages, as well as scores of factions and *groupuscules*, especially in France and Belgium,[19] Third Positionism has remained an utterly marginalised, practically invisible, force at the level of mainstream politics. Its main interest to political scientists lies in the degree to which some Fascists were prepared to adapt a nationalist ideology born of the revolutionary conditions of inter-war Europe to the anti-revolutionary ethos of the post-war world, even to the point of promulgating Colonel Qadafhi's *Green Book* and rhetorically pledging support for the 'Third World' as a way of transcending both capitalism and Communism. Such developments emphasise how

The Origins of the Far Right

Fascism has in some instances changed ideologically and organisationally almost beyond recognition by those who still identify it narrowly with the Nazi party under Hitler.[20]

The European New Right

One of the most important manifestations of the European Far Right's adaptation to the overwhelming impotence of post-war Fascism is the rise to prominence of the *Nouvelle Droite* (New Right) during the 1970s. The immediate background to this development was France's loss of the **Algerian War**, a cause which had rallied the support of the Far Right to stop the process of decolonisation, as well as the 'years of contestation' with the far left which culminated in the events of May 1968. The New Right was pioneered by the formidably prolific intellectual Alain de Benoist[21] with the support of growing ranks of other intellectuals, academics and cultural commentators, not to mention think tanks, study groups, journalists, publishers, seminar organisers and a section of the 'quality press'.

The New Right has always maintained the position of being above conventional politics and hence resolutely 'metapolitical'. Yet forensic study of the New Right's origins[22] reveals that it was born of the painful recognition by sophisticated ideologues within French neo-fascist circles of the bankruptcy of their creed in the transformed conditions of European history in the 1960s compared with the 1930s, and of the urgent need to combat the intellectual domination of the left-wing intelligentsia by creating a sophisticated 'right-wing culture'. The solution they adopted was the deliberate creation of a new discourse which perpetuated core elements of the fascist world view while radically dissociating them from the horrors of World War II. This was to be achieved by cutting all formal links to political activism, whether party-political or terroristic, and abandoning the narrow nationalism and biological racism of inter-war fascism for a purely ideological campaign for a French renaissance as an integral part of the cultural rebirth of Europe. Under de Benoist's tireless intellectual leadership, the New Right soon established itself as the most ideological cohesive and innovative product of the combined processes of 'metapoliticisation', 'Europeanisation', and *groupuscularisation* that had been forced on Fascism by the destruction of its inter-war habitat after 1945.[23]

The main feature of the *Nouvelle Droite* as a form of far-right ideology is a sustained, multi-front attack on several core principles of democracy. This it carries out in a discourse that presents contemporary society as utterly decadent when contrasted with a fundamentally ahistorical vision of a future Europe in which an end has been put to the process of homogenisation and levelling down inflicted by liberalism and the forces of *mondialisation*. The goal inferable from its vast outpouring of intellectually demanding cultural analysis is a post-democratic continent made up of homogeneous national *ethnies*. These will draw their vitality from a primordial root culture whose spiritual, heroic vision of the world – already debilitated by Judeo-Christianity – is currently threatened with extinction by the impact of such forces as consumerist materialism, multiculturalism, Americanisation, globalisation and abstract theories of universal human rights and equality. The theoretical underpinnings of this ideology are derived from the writings of the inter-war Conservative Revolution associated with thinkers such as Friedrich Nietzsche, Ernst Jünger and Martin Heidegger combined with the neo-Gramscian tactic of achieving cultural hegemony as a precondition to political power. This leads its thinkers to adopt a deliberate strategy of drawing on all critiques of modern liberal society, Left or Right, which can be used to argue against the alleged loss of spiritual values and the erosion of identity, difference and spirit.

The resulting 'vision of the world' carefully dissociates itself from the traumatic events of inter-war Europe, and in particular, sheds neo-fascism of the intolerably heavy baggage associated with Nazism, notably World War II, the German occupation of France and the **Holocaust**. Instead, core far-right principles are relocated in a 'clean', 'new', apparently 'apolitical' context which is presented as upholding cultural diversity, pluralism and identity, and opposed to (historical) Fascism, Communism and the creeping 'totalitarianism' of liberal democracy. Its most insidiously powerful ideological product is 'differentialist' racism. This attacks multiculturalism not in the name of biologically conceived racial supremacy but of culturally conceived 'difference', the ethnic and ethnological equivalent of 'biodiversity'. Such sophistry, combined with the claim to have transcended the distinction between Left and Right, has created considerable confusion for commentators, some of whom have been reluctant to associate it with Fascism or the Far Right at all. Yet it demonstrably grew out of French neo-fascism and its reverence for the Conservative Revolution is deeply indebted to theories of the post-war thinkers and self-confessed Fascists such as Armin Mohler and Julius Evola. Moreover, it has in the past openly used the term 'right' in descriptions of itself: a canonic text of ND thought is de Benoist's *Vu de Droite* ('Seen from the Right'),[24] while one of its seminal essays was entitled 'For a right-wing Gramscism'.[25]

The most telling reason for locating the New Right within the Far Right, however, despite its eagerness to cover its tracks, lies in its rejection of democracy not in the name of universal social justice, but of core right-wing values of identity and rootedness that even turns anaemic Europe into a mythic, organic homeland for 'true' Europeans. If its metapolitics were ever adopted as the basis of policy by the European Union they would lead to the 'Balkanisation' of the whole continent. Apart from the economic chaos this would unleash, this would mean devastating the lives of millions in implementing programmes of ethnic and cultural cleansing designed to realise myths of homogeneous, differentiated *ethnies* and of higher values based on anthropological fantasies of a rooted European race and culture.

It is precisely the utter utopianism of such a vision that presumably explains why, in a post-war Europe where extremist activism is so impotent to bring about structural change, the New Right has become the most powerful ideological manifestation of the Far Right throughout Europe. Disaffected intellectuals who in the 1930s might have been swept into the arms of Fascism and directly complicit in its actions have instead devoted themselves to emulating Alain de Benoist in their own society. This they do by dubbing French New Right cultural discourse into an ideology of cultural revolution appropriate to their own national history and context.[26] The result has been the development of significant New Right political cultures in Belgium, Italy, Germany and especially in post-Soviet Russia, where the 'Eurasianist' variant of the New Right promoted by Aleksandr Dugin's Arctogaia has influenced mainstream politics.[27]

There is even an outpost of the European New Right in the UK, where it is currently attracting the attention of some ideologues formerly associated with Third Positionism. Despite its efforts to remain invisible on the radar screens of conventional political analysis, the New Right is to be taken seriously as a major component of the contemporary Far Right. Like the 'dark matter' that constitutes so much of the universe, its presence as a counter-cultural force in several major democracies as a 'meta-political' – but still extremist and implicitly revolutionary – political discourse, enables it to influence the political **education** of activists, some of whom go on to play a role in politics of a more conventional and visible kind, in both its extreme and radical forms.

Neo-Populism

One form of politics which has absorbed the influence of the European New Right is neo-populism,[28] otherwise known as 'radical right populism',[29] or 'the post-industrial right'.[30] It first started attracting the attention of academics as a European phenomenon in the mid-1990s,[31] and continues to be the most actively monitored and analysed aspect of extremism in contemporary Europe.[32] In fact, several books claiming to cover the extreme-right focus almost exclusively on this one form of it.[33] This is a useless simplification, especially since in German terms, it is clear that neo-populism represents an outstanding form of radical politics operating strictly *within* the system of parliamentary democracy as far as official policies are concerned. (This does not preclude *extremist* attitudes being held by some of its supporters or activists). Meanwhile, the far left has few scruples in regularly calling neo-populism a form of fascism – an attribute it also uses, with somewhat more justification, about the European New Right.[34]

Neo-populism is the generic term for the type of politics displayed by a number of electoral parties dispersed throughout Europe, notably in France (the **National Front**, or FN), Austria (Austrian Freedom Party), Italy (**Northern League** and National Alliance), Belgium (**Flemish Bloc**), Holland (**List Pim Fortuyn**), Germany (Republicans), Denmark and Norway (Progress Party), Sweden (**New Democracy**),[35] Switzerland (**Swiss People's Party**) and Russia (Russian Liberal Democratic Party). Their broad, ill-defined common denominator, alongside numerous idiosyncrasies that make them highly heterogeneous, is that they all articulate anxieties about the erosion of national or regional identity under the impact of multiculturalism, the atomisation of society and mass immigration. Such concerns are often combined with attacks on the breakdown of law, order and morality, the representativeness of traditional parties, state corruption, the high level of taxes and the inefficiency of central government.

Neo-populism represents a hybridisation of xenophobia or national or regional chauvinism – which can assume extreme-right levels of intensity among some politicians and supporters – with classic elements of conservative politics. Though it rejects inter-war Fascism's totalitarian and revolutionary vision of a new order, in one respect it can be regarded as an extremist (illiberal) form of right party masquerading as a radical (liberal) right one. Certainly, if the policies of all the most openly racist neo-populist parties were implemented – notably those of France, Belgium, Italy (the Northern League) and Russia – they would destroy the basic principles of liberal democracy, turning it into a form of ethnocratic, and hence fundamentally anti-democratic, liberalism. Given the affinity of neo-populism with the extreme right despite its radical guise, it is no coincidence that New Right differentialism – an overtly anti-liberal ideology[36] – has had a direct impact on the policies and discourse of France's FN, the German Republicans and Russian Liberal Democrats.

Against this background Gianfranco **Fini**, the leader of Italy's neo-fascist **Italian Social Movement** (*Movimento Sociale Italiano*), decided to take advantage of the crisis of Italy's corrupt post-war political system known as *'tangentopoli'* in the early

1990s to turn his party into a neo-populist party, the **National Alliance**. Revealingly, his rationale for doing so was that the end of the Soviet Empire had signalled the dawning of a 'post-fascist' age. The MSI's roots lay in the Nazi-Fascist Republic of Salò, but once cleansed of its extremist image and liberated from the political ghetto in which it had languished for over four decades, it rapidly established itself as Europe's most successful neo-populist party, becoming a cornerstone of Silvio Berlusconi's two coalition governments. Nick **Griffin** was thus following a trend and, once elected leader of the **British National Party**, he set about converting its neo-Nazi image to that of a 'user-friendly' neo-populist party modelled on the FN ostensibly concerned primarily with preserving a beleaguered but essentially mythic British identity.[37]

The origins of neo-populism lie in the further erosion of the political habitat for extremism in Europe which occurred after the end of the **Cold War**. Whereas Fascism would once have been the natural outlet for populist resentment about the inability of mainstream democratic parties to address issues of identity, deep-seated fears of being swamped by immigrants and their alien culture and a general sense of the instability of the modern world, they now have to be articulated not 'extra-systemically' but 'democratically'. Historical or classical Fascism thus plays a minimal role in neo-populism's dynamics, except for a minority of hardcore racists who may tactically assume the strategy of parliamentary reform rather than revolution to pursue a racist agenda, or hope to use neo-populism to build up mass support for a crypto-fascist vision of society. The tensions between the ethno-regionalism of the Northern League and the muted ultra-nationalism of the National Alliance in the same country illustrate how difficult it is to generalise about neo-populist policies.

Postscript and Prognosis

There are three main common denominators to the various forms of Far Right we have surveyed in this chapter. The first is that they are all symptoms of the way the crisis conditions of inter-war Europe, which incubated a host of different extremist assaults on liberalism, gave way in 1945 to a generalised sense of stability and progress in Western, and then the whole of Europe, making democracy the norm. As a result, centrifugal forces replaced centripetal ones, and the critical mass needed for a charismatic mass movement could not be generated. The three discrete components of political extremism that had coalesced within Fascism and Nazism – a revolutionary nationalist ideology, a paramilitary movement, and a political party with a wide base of public support – thus separated out like curds from whey, each element taking on a life and evolution of its own. Even in Italy and Germany (where fascist regimes enjoyed the support of the consensus of millions of citizens at their peak), attempts by unrepentant Fascists to relaunch their cause as a party-based movement with watered down, euphemised extremist agendas, utterly failed to make headway: both the neo-Nazi Nationaldemokratische Partei Deutschlands and the neo-fascist MSI remained pariahs within the post-war parliamentary system.

The second feature that stands out is the way all residual forms of Far Right have adapted ideologically and organisationally to the new age of mass democracy, mass consumerism and technological advance (in post-Christian Europe 'European' Turkey is undergoing its own democratisation). Signs of this evolutionary process at work are the general abandonment of narrow forms of chauvinism, imperialism and the public display of militarism, the extensive use of the Internet as a form of communication enabling networking between far-right *groupuscules*,[38] and the importance to far-right programmes of such new issues as identity, security, the EU, globalisation, the growing ecological crisis and the threat posed by mass immigration.

A third trait which they all share is that they assert the primacy of communal belonging and the defence of spiritual values over individualism and materialism as the precondition of a healthy socio-political existence. This makes them the modern descendent of the radical right tradition that formed in the nineteenth century and assumed such virulent forms in inter-war Europe. It also makes them expressions of a fundamentally *modernist* response to the impact of modernity in generating mass *anomie*. As such, their attempts to supply a new sense of community and purpose in a modern age of perceived dissolution acquires a *futural* rather than reactionary dynamic.[39] (Obviously this interpretation of the Far Right as revolutionary would be hotly disputed by academics and ideologues of the Far Left.)

The fact that resistance to the alleged forces of cultural and social dissolution is still capable of manifesting itself in Europe, with some of its inter-war intensity in the Third Millennium, was vividly demonstrated by the attacks on London's transport system in July 2005 and the advanced plot to blow up ten airliners simultaneously *en route* from the UK to the US in August 2006. The planning and execution of both operations were not the responsibility of imported fanaticism and know-how, but of British citizens committed to an internecine 'war against the West' carried out with extra-European support. Both were chilling expressions of religious militancy, not only the latest and potentially most devastating form of Far Right to be encountered in Europe in the last six decades, but seemingly set to become an authentically European, home-made form of extremism. Religious militancy is no new phenomenon. In its Christian form it has long been a factor of the Far Right in the US where it has exerted a profound influence on mainstream government policies,[40] while politicised Hinduism, Hindutva, has long exerted an impact on Indian politics.[41]

In both UK incidents, the specific form of religious militancy involved was Islamist extremism (NOT synonyms) and terrorism (again NOT synonymous) operating semi-autonomously and 'rhizomically' in collaboration with an international network of terrorist *groupuscules*.[42] Though the shifting epicentre of this network is currently in Eastern Afghanistan and Western Pakistan, it has clearly begun recruiting 'martyr bombers' from second or third-generation Muslim Britons. In other words, a new form of Far Right has now appeared involving European citizens who may only speak the language of their host nation, but have developed a personal sense of mission to defend the integrity of their faith and culture in the most extreme way possible.[43] There is every likelihood that young Muslims are joining the cause in other European countries, and that European variants of Islamist extremism may come to have a major impact on the course of contemporary history in the terrorist acts it causes, the repressive measures used to combat it and the general atmosphere of insecurity and psychosis it generates.

The origins of European Islamism – often referred to by the media simplistically but misleadingly as 'Islamic fundamentalism' – are intimately bound up with the complex causes of the politicised Islam of such groups as Hamas and Hezbollah and the rise of Al Qaeda.[44] Its Europeanisation reflects the emergence of a generation of European Muslims deeply disaffected with the society to which their parents or grandparents migrated to secure a better future for their families, and outraged at US, British and, to a lesser extent, EU foreign policy towards the Islamic world, especially in respect to Israel's intransigence on the issue of the Palestinians' right to statehood.[45] It stems, too, from an arch-*conservative* bid to stem the secularising tide of materialism, secularisation and Americanisation that in the long term threatens to wipe out Islam as a living faith. However, this conservatism is imbued with the powerful *futural* dynamic of all radical modernist politics, since the fanatics of Islamism know full well that the idealised past of their culture cannot be simply restored. Militant Islamism thus represents a radical break with traditional Islamic society and **religion**. Paradoxically, it has no scruples in deploying in its war against globalisation the full potential destructiveness of modern terrorism provided by globalised communications and technology.[46] It thus has the potential to unleash more political violence and instability in Europe than all the other post-war forms of Far Right put together. To complicate matters further, for political scientists the anti-Zionist, anti-American, anti-globalisation positions hosted by both the revolutionary fascistic Far Right and Islamist extremists has brought about curious instances of synergy between the two, as when Muslim 'Jihadist' bookshops sell Hitler's ***Mein Kampf***.[47]

This chapter has attempted to produce a coherent overview of the Far Right while stressing the heuristic nature of its 'ideal-typical' definitions and taxonomy, and the incompleteness of the causal explanations it can offer of its origins. It is necessarily open-ended, inviting readers to refine their understanding of the aspects of the Far Right of most interest to them, and to stay on the constant lookout, whether as academics or upholders of civic values, for new hybrids and permutations which reject liberalism and universal human values in the name of nebulous organic communities, mythic roots, or holy causes. What André Taguieff says of fascism and racism in an essay on the French New Right thus holds equally well for the European Far Right in general:

> Neither 'fascism' nor 'racism' will do us the favour of returning in such a way that we can recognise them easily. If vigilance were only a game of recognising something already well-known, then it would only be a question of remembering. Vigilance would be reduced to a social game using reminiscence and identification by recognition, a consoling illusion of an immobile history peopled with events which accord to our expectations or our fears.[48]

There is nothing 'cut-and-dried' about the Far Right. This chapter is not a comforting retrospective of a largely superseded and understood form of politics. Instead, it stresses the need for students of the Far Right to be concerned with the general and the unique, the historical and the contemporary, the old and the new, as befits a phenomenon which is living, evolving and multifaceted. It appeals for vigilance as new events unfold and new fears are awakened by seismic shifts in the social, economic, political and ecological foundations of our world, summoning forth in new forms, primordial and essentially utopian dreams of cultural or racial homogeneity, purity and strength. For all committed liberals the next decades promise to be what the Chinese sage called 'interesting times'.

Roger Griffin

Notes
1. For some useful country-by-country analyses of the constellation of far-right forces in particular European nations see Paul Hainsworth (ed), *The Politics of the Extreme Right* (London: Pinter, 2000); Piero Ignazi, *Extreme Right Parties in Western Europe* (New York: Oxford University Press, 2003).
2. For a discussion of the complexities of defining the contemporary Far Right see Piero Ignazi, *Extreme Right Parties in Western Europe* (New York: Oxford University Press, 2003), 4–19. For an overview of the inter-war Far Right and its contrast with the post-war Far Right see Peter Davies & Derek Lynch, *The Routledge Companion to Fascism and the Far Right* (London: Routledge, 2002), Part II, 87–166.

3. See James Gregor, *The Faces of Janus: Marxism and Fascism in the Twentieth Century* (New Haven, Conn.: Yale University Press, 2000). It is also worth noting that some 'liberal causes', such as anti-globalisation and animal rights, have been fought for by militants prepared to use 'right-wing' forms of violence. For an illuminating case study, see 'Political protestors and Amsterdam's South Africa Institute, 1984' in Rebecca Knuth, *Burning Books and Leveling Libraries* (Westport, CT: Praeger, 2006), 43–70.

4. For more on this, see Rolf E. Rogers, *Max Weber's Ideal Type Theory* (New York: Philosophical Library, 1969).

5. On the primary role played by cultic politics within both civil and totalitarian societies, see Emilio Gentile, *Politics as Religion* (Princeton: Princeton University Press, 2006).

6. See Roger Griffin, *Modernism and Fascism. The Sense of a Beginning under Mussolini and Hitler* (London: Palgrave, 2007), chs.2–3.

7. Sabrina Ramet (ed.), *The Radical Right in Central and Eastern Europe* (University Park, PA: Penn State Press, 1999).

8. The 'palingenetic' vision of a 'new order' purged of anarchy and decadence (and hence racial chaos) is central to most definitions of Fascism, eg. in Roger Griffin, *The Nature of Fascism* (London and New York: Routledge, 1993) and Michael Mann, *Fascists* (Cambridge: Cambridge University Press, 2005).

9. The definition and origins of fascism is a highly contested area, the most authoritative account of which remains Stanley Payne's magisterial *A History of Fascism 1914–1945* (London: UCL Press Limited, 1995). This presents fascism as largely the product of the crisis conditions that affected Europe at the turn of the century and which were brought to a head by the First World War. For a contrasting theory that makes *fin-de-siècle* France the birthplace of fascism see Zeev Sternhell, *The Birth of Fascist Ideology* (Princeton NJ: Princeton University Press, 1994).

10. See the July 2002 edition of *Patterns of Prejudice* (36.3) devoted to the 'groupuscular right'.

11. For an article that develops this point while offering a detailed picture of the state of development of the Far Right and of academic engagement with it in the early 1990s see Diethelm Prowe, '"Classic fascism" and the new radical right in Western Europe: comparisons and contrasts', *Contemporary European History*, 3.3 (1994), 289–314.

12. N. Lowles & Steve Silver, eds., 1998, *White Noise* (London: Searchlight).

13. M. Schmidt, *The New Reich* (London: Hutchinson, 1986).

14. See R. Eatwell, 'The internet: extremist strategies and the problem of control', *Patterns of Prejudice*, 30:1 (1996), 61–71. Graeme McLagan & Nick Lowles, *Mr Evil. The Secret Life of the Racist Bomber and Killer David Copeland* (London: John Blake, 2000).

15. Franco Ferraresi, *Threats to Democracy* (Princeton: Princeton University Press, 1996).

16. See Richard Drake, 'The children of the sun' in *The Revolutionary Mystique and Terrorism in Contemporary Italy* (Bloomington: Indiana University Press, 1989), 114–134. On the esoteric ('traditional') Far Right embodied in Evola see Mark Sedgwick, *Against the Modern World* (Oxford: Oxford University Press, 2004).

17. K. Coogan, *Dreamer of the Day* (New York: Automedia, 1999) - an essential book for understanding the ideological and organisational transformations of fascim and the rise of the 'International Third Position' after the defeat of the Axis powers.

18. See R. Eatwell, 'The esoteric ideology of the National Front in the 1980s' in M. Cronin (ed.), *The Failure of British Fascism* (London: Macmillan, 1996).

19. For an insight into the highly syncretic ideology of the Third Positionist Far Right see its main English website at http://www.rosenoire.org/essays/itp.php (cited 7 September 2006).

20. For a case study in this development see J. Bale, 'National Revolutionary' groupuscules and the resurgence of 'left-wing' fascism: the case of France's Nouvelle Résistance', *Patterns of Prejudice*, 36:3 (2002).

21. See the entry on de Benoist in Philip Rees, *Biographical Dictionary of the Extreme Right* (New York: Simon & Schuster, 1990).

22. The most authoritative work here is Pierre-André Taguieff, *Sur la Nouvelle Droite* (Paris: Descartes & Cie, 1994). For a brief Anglophone introduction, see Roger Griffin, http://youtube.com/watch?v=CmmjrLG0ScU&mode=related&search 'Plus ça change! The fascist pedigree of the Nouvelle Droite' in Edward Arnold (ed.), *The Development of the Radical Right in France 1890–1995* (London: Routledge, 2000), 217–252. For two sympathetic accounts of the European New Right see: Tomislav Sunic, *Against Democracy and Equality* (Noontide Press, 2004 1st edition 1990); and the more scholarly Michael O'Meare,. *New Culture, New Right. Anti-Liberalism in Postmodern Europe* (Bloomington: 1st Books, 2004).

23. On the Far Right's 'metapoliticisation' and 'Europeanisation' see Roger Griffin, 'Interregnum or endgame? Radical right thought in the "post-fascist" era' in Michael Freeden (ed.), *Reassessing Political Ideologies* (London: Routledge, 2001), 116–131. On 'groupuscularisation', see Roger Griffin, 'From slime mould to rhizome: an introduction to the groupuscular right', *Patterns of Prejudice*, 37:1 (March 2003), 27–50.

24. De Benoist, Alain, *Vu de Droite* (Paris: Copernic, 1977).

25. De Herte, Robert (pseudonym of Alain de Benoist), 'Pour un "gramscisme de droite"', *Éléments*, 20 (February 1977).

26. For a synoptic account of the New Right as a European phenomenon, see Tamir Bar-On, *Where Have All the Fascists Gone?: The European New Right (ENR) and the Emergence of a 'Post-Fascist' Synthesis* (Aldershot: Peter Lang, 2007).

27. See Markus Mathyl, 'The National-Bolshevik party and Arctogaia: two neo-fascist groupuscules in the post-Soviet political space', *Patterns of Prejudice*, 36:3 (July 2002), 62–76.

28. See Yves Mény (ed.), *Neopopulism in Western Europe* (London: Macmillan, 2002).

29. Hans-Georg Betz, *Radical Right-wing Populism in Western Europe* (New York: St. Martin's Press, 1994).

30. See Piero Ignazi, *Extreme Right Parties in Western Europe* (New York: Oxford University Press, 2003), 200–204.

31. Herbert Kitschelt, *The Radical Right in Western Europe: A Comparative Analysis* (University of Michigan Press, 1995). For the US context see Chip Berlet & Matthew Lyons, *Right-wing Populism in America: Too Close for Comfort* (New York: Guilford Press, 2000).

32. Yves Mény & Yves Surel (eds.), *Democracies and the Populist Challenge* (Basingstoke: Palgrave, 2002).

33. Cas Mudde, *The Ideology of the Extreme Right* (Manchester: Manchester University Press, 2000); Piero Ignazi, *Extreme Right Parties in Western Europe* (New York: Oxford University Press, 2003); Roger Eatwell & Cas Mudde (eds.), *Western Democracies and the New Extreme Right Challenge* (London and New York: Routledge, 2004).

34. E.g. the article on the Austrian Freedom Party (no author cited), 'Sinister fascist Haider behind rightist government in Austria', *The Internationalist*, 8 (June 2000), 20–40. Contributors to the UK socialist periodical *Searchlight* dedicated to anti-fascim regularly refer to Jean-Marie Le Pen's National Front and Gianfranco Fini's Alleanza Nazionale as 'fascist'.

35. Paul Taggart, *The New Populism and the New Politics: New Protest Parties in Sweden in a Comparative Perspective* (London: Macmillan, 1996).

36. On 'differentialism' as a euphemised form of racism see Pierre-André Taguieff, 'The new right's view of European identity', *Telos*, 98–99 (Winter 1993–Fall 1994), 99–125.

37. On the BNP's attempts to pass itself off as a neo-populist party see Nigel Copsey, *Contemporary British Fascism. The British National Party and the Quest for Legitimacy* (Basingstoke: Palgrave, 2004).

38. See the chapter, 'The use of the internet by far right extremists' in Douglas Thomas & Brian Loader, *Cybercrime: Law Enforcement, Security and Surveillance in the Information Age* (London: Routledge, 2000).

39. See Roger Griffin, *Modernism and Fascism. The Sense of a Beginning under Mussolini and Hitler* (London: Palgrave, 2007), ch.12.

40. See Martin Durham, *The Christian Right, the Far Right, and the Boundaries of Conservative Politics* (Manchester: Manchester University Press, 2000); Jeffrey Kaplan, *Radical Religion in America. Millenarian Movements from the Far Right to the Children of Noah* (Syracuse, NY: Syracuse University Press, 1997); Michael Barkun, *Religion and the Racist Right: The Origins of Christian Identity Movement* (Chapel Hill, NC: University of North Carolina Press, 1997).

41. See Robert Frykenberg, 'Hindutva as a political religion: a historical perspective' in Robert Mallet, John Tortorice & Roger Griffin (eds.), *The Sacred in Politics* (Madison, WI: University of Wisconsin Press, 2007).

42. On the concept of the 'rhizome' as a metaphor with which to conceptualise the way the Far Right operates outside the sphere of formal 'arborial' organisations such as the NSDAP, see Roger Griffin, 'From slime mould to rhizome: An Introduction to the Groupuscular Right'.

43. See Roger Griffin, '"Shattering crystals": the role of "dream time" in extreme right-wing political violence', *Terrorism and Political Violence*, 15:1 (Spring 2003), 57–96.

44. For the international rather than European background to 'Islamist extremism' - which requires completely different sets of historiographical, cultural, sociological, and linguistic skills to

understand than the 'fascis' Far Right -- see Jason Burke, *Al-Qaeda: Casting A Shadow of Terror* (London: I.B.Tauris, 2003), 7–22; Jeffrey M. Bale, 'Islamism' in Richard F. Pilch, & Raymond A. Zilinskas (eds.), *Encyclopedia of Bioterrorism Defense* (New York: Wiley & Sons, 2004); Mary Habeck, *Knowing the Enemy: Jihadist Ideology and the War on Terror* (New Haven, CT: Yale University, 2006).

45. John K Cooley, *Unholy Wars: Afghanistan, America and International Terrorism* (London: New Ed. Pluto Press, 2000).

46. Cf. Benjamin Barber, *Jihad vs. McWorld* (New York: Times Books, 1995). The historical and ideological complexity of the phenomenon of Islamist extremism makes talk of 'Islamo-fascism' not just politically unhelpful, but highly misleading from a historical point of view, sowing yet more conceptual confusion about a topic that demands intelligent understanding rather than demonisation.

47. See George Michael, *The Enemy of My Enemy: The Alarming Convergence of Militant Islam with the Extreme Right* (Lawrence, KS: University of Kansas Press, 2006). The association of Islamism and Nazism has its origins in inter-war Europe. For a journalistic study of their collusion under the Third Reich see the self-published book by US newspaper columnist Chuck Morse, *The Nazi Connection to Islamic Terrorism: Adolf Hitler and Haj Amin Al-Husseini* (Publisher not known, 2003). This postulates Nazism's direct contribution to making 'Islamo-fascism and Jihad terrorism' what he describes (misleadingly) as the dominant political philosophy of the Arab world.

48. Pierre-André Taguieff, 'Discussion or inquisition: the case of Alain de Benoist', *Telos* 98–99 (Winter 1993–Spring 1994), 54.

The Ideology of the Far Right

In the immediate post-war decades the extreme right in European politics 'began a metamorphosis into something far more than a throwback to Fascism and Nazism', and it 'exploited the backlash against the left'.[1] Yet, with the collapse of **Communism** in the east of **Europe** in the 1980s and 1990s, the extreme right has now reverted to emphasising the old keynote fascist ideas of **nation** and race.[2]

Extreme right-wing political parties are always perceived by both mainstream parties and political commentators as a potential menace to social and political stability. Normally, the parties that are associated with the farther shores of right-wing politics have failed to secure an electoral foothold sufficient to warrant consideration as an immediate threat. Yet, in all European countries, there has emerged an array of parties which are customarily classified as belonging to the extremes of right-wing politics. Periodically, one party may secure a high level of support, as with **Le Pen**'s **National Front** (*Front National*, FN) in the French presidential election of 2002, when he garnered 19.9 percent of the poll on the second ballot, having beaten the Socialist candidate into third place in the first ballot, and the **Austrian Freedom Party** (*Freiheitliche Partei Österreichs*, FPÖ), which secured 26.9 percent in elections to the national parliament in 1999, and for a short period secured a role in the **coalition government**.[3] There have been other recent examples of significant support, such as the Flemish Blok (*Vlaams Blok*, VB) and the Danish and Norwegian Progress parties. If in other European countries such as Britain, Sweden and Spain the performance of such parties has been less impressive electorally, far right-wing politics has become a sufficiently significant political phenomenon in Europe in general for it to be important to understand it, what causes it, what its main tenets are and to consider the extent to which there is a European-wide extreme right movement, or a 'Black International'.

It is necessary as a starting point to offer a definition of the terms 'ideology', 'extremism' and 'the far-right' if this analysis is to be meaningful.

The Concept of Ideology

Ideology is one of the most elusive concepts in the study of history and politics.[4] It is often associated with disgraced political movements, such as Communism and Nazism, rather than with the beliefs of mainstream political parties. This association is the product of a restrictive and pejorative version of the concept which enables some commentators to refer to the ideology of the extreme right while they would refrain from describing liberalism, **democracy** and conservatism as ideologies.[5] There are other negative associations with ideology since it has been viewed frequently as serving the purposes of domination, the concealment of social contradictions in the interests of ruling elites, the antithesis of science and truth, emotional verbiage, a product of social crisis, a device to manipulate the masses, a rigid dogma confined to the political extremes and a rejection of openness to evidence. There is also a tradition of regarding ideology more neutrally, but still restrictively, as an internally consistent set of political ideas. It is also argued that ideology is a flexible form of discourse, one that unites social groups even where the ideas themselves are nebulous.

The difficulty of producing a definitive conception of ideology is apparent. One survey of the extensive literature on the subject assembled a list of twenty-seven elements which, variously defined, constitute the repertoire of definitions of ideology in the social sciences.[6] For the purposes of this introduction, a working definition is required. Eschewing the labyrinthine and inconclusive debates on the subject, it is argued that ideology can operate at any one of four levels, and can also be the result of both individual and group allegiances. At its lowest level, ideology can be discerned by an individual expressing support for a single belief or value, such as an enthusiasm for capital punishment; at the next level, ideology can exist for both individuals and groups as a form of ideology by proxy through adherence to a political party without necessarily subscribing to all of the specific doctrines and policies of that party. At the third level, ideology represents a set of ideas that may not be recognisable as one of the 'isms' in the contemporary world, but rather as an idiosyncratic construct for groups or individuals that lack what the political cognoscenti might consider to be intellectual, or governing, coherence. Finally, at the highest or purest level, it forms an adherence and commitment to a specific, coherent and recognised global ideology, such as socialism or fascism.[7]

There are evident merits in applying this ultra-inclusive definition of ideology. It is a non-elitist and judgemental conception of ideology through its avoidance of the pitfall of confining the ability to be ideological to the approximately 2.5 percent of the population which opinion surveys have found capable of allocating to themselves an ideology, and being able to describe its tenets accurately.[8] To confine ideological support for extreme right-wing parties only to those voters able to recite all the main items in the manifesto of a far right-wing party, and then to understand the relationship between the policies contained within it is, therefore, to set up so demanding a definition of ideology as to be of no practical value in interpreting the real world of electoral politics.

At the lowest level of ideological awareness, many of those who vote for extreme right parties, whether on a long or short-term basis, may be motivated solely by one concern, for example, the repatriation of immigrants. This is not to deny that such support can be perceived as behaving ideologically when casting such a vote. In any event, probing below the surface of such a voter's world-view is likely to yield some unarticulated link between dislike of immigrants and, for example, views about the dangers of multiculturalism or on the relationship between **immigration** and criminality. At the next level of ideological commitment, voters who merely support an extreme-right party without an understanding of its manifesto are also acting ideologically, if only by proxy, as their support tends to be interpreted either as contributing to the quantity of extreme right-wing beliefs or, at least, as a general and calculated **protest** against the values of the political establishment in their country. Naturally, those supporters of an extreme right-wing party who fully subscribe to the entire ideology of that party must count as fully-fledged ideologues. Classifying voters for extreme-right parties, or people who display a visceral dislike of immigrants, as ideologues denies them the pretext of arguing that they are virtuously immune from ideological infection while permitting them to accuse the advocates of multicultural diversity as being trapped in a harmful ideology allegedly threatening the health and wellbeing of the nation.

In summary, 'political ideology' is a term to describe political ideas, whether of the right, left or centre of the political spectrum, and without regard to their orientation towards the status quo. Therefore, whether the conception of ideology is defined inclusively, or in a highly restrictive-pejorative manner, extreme right-wing parties must be considered as unquestionably ideological in character. If the term ideology were to be abandoned owing to its elusive nature, it would simply be necessary to invent another word to describe the political functions that it performs.[9]

If ideology is sometimes used as an abusive term in political discourse to discredit opponents, then the same applies to 'extremism'. Extremism is patently a pejorative term exploited to demonise those political ideologies seen as irrational and illegitimate in a civil society, and as a technique to further some rival political cause. Governments wishing to defend their own position frequently invoke the term extremism, for example attacks on the 'extremism' within the Muslim community in Britain and across the world. Some academics have also been charged with seeking to apply the label 'extreme' only to the Far Right, but to avoid applying it to the far left. The traits that are often identified as characterising political extremism include 'name calling, sweeping generalisation, inadequate proof for assertions, viewing opponents as evil, possessing a Manichean world view, identifying opponents as dangerous enemies, resorting to intimidatory methods of argument, doomsday thinking and justifying taking "bad" actions to further a "good" cause'.[10] It must be recognised that, in practice, it is often the mainstream political parties in a country who determine which of their opponents are to be stigmatised as extreme.

Right-Wing Political Parties in Europe

It is profoundly difficult to construct a typology of political parties which classifies parties as belonging to the extreme right of the spectrum, and more difficult still to portray those parties as a clearly identifiable and trans-national group. Some of the parties considered in this volume would object to the extremist label being applied to them. There is an evident problem of where precisely ideological boundaries are to be drawn. Where is the line to be drawn between parties understood as belonging to the extreme right, on the one hand, and conservative parties on the other? Even if agreement is possible on that issue, should no distinctions be made about degrees of extremism within the extreme right? Is the French FN really similar to the Danish Progress Party (*Fremskridtspartiet*)? The FN is not an advocate of extensive state welfare, for example, whereas the Danish party, which shares an animus towards immigrants and foreigners with the FN, is also as enthusiastic as the Danish Social Democrats for the provision of state social welfare.[11] The Scandinavian Progress parties could be excluded from the category of extreme-right parties. For example, the Danish leader Pia **Kjaersgaard**, now with the **Danish People's Party** (*Dansk Folkeparti*, DPP), is sometimes cited as being too 'soft' in her allegiance to be a true leader of the extreme right-wing, yet she has talked of immigrants 'multiplying like rabbits', and urges that there should be a barrier built on the **Oresund Bridge** between Denmark and Sweden because she alleges that the Swedish state has not been vigorous enough in keeping out Muslims, who she regards as unwelcome intruders in Danish culture.[12] Similarly, some would question categorising the **Northern League** (*Lega Nord*, LN) in the Lombardy province of northern **Italy** as a far-right party since it has been considered a regional and sub-national party concerned with economic autonomy from the rest of Italy, rather than as a member of the 'extreme right' **family**. Yet its stigmatisation of southern Italians for belonging to a lower race and its leader's description of North African immigrants as 'bingo-bongos' reinforce ideas of ethnic superiority.[13] Both the Scandinavian Progress parties and the LN should be included within the extreme right-wing 'family', then, as both are in competition with mainstream conservative and Christian Democratic parties and both express an exclusionist stance against others with whom they do not desire to share nationhood.

The Ideology of the Far Right

There are also variations in the national contexts that generate ideological differences between parties of the extreme right. For example, in Britain, immigrants can acquire national citizenship whereas in Germany, Switzerland and Spain, the acquisition of citizenship is very tightly controlled and is normally confined to people born within the boundaries of the country.

It might also be difficult to determine whether the definition of far-right parties should be confined to those organisations which display some nostalgia for pre-war Fascism and Nazism, and those which deny such links and exclusively purport to address contemporary issues. These definitional dilemmas are not to be swept under the carpet. Analytical progress can be made, however, by differentiating extreme far-right parties from mainstream, and long established, conservative parties such as the British Conservative Party, the Swedish Moderate Party and the German Christian Democrats. The more extreme label can be applied to those parties which visibly display nostalgia for the symbols and rhetoric of Fascism, such as the **Italian Social Movement** (*Movimento Sociale Italiano*, MSI) and parts of the FN, and those that condone interwar Fascism and Nazism, such as the **German People's Union** (*Deutsche Volksunion*, DVU).[14]

A further sign of those parties which have a retrospective character is their endorsement of the phenomenon known as **Holocaust Denial**. The suggestion that the **Holocaust** is an invention must be regarded as a device designed to boost extreme right-wing parties, for example, by enabling them to overcome stigmas from the past and lifting the burden of guilt from the minds of voters. Since the publication of Richard E. Harwood's *Did Six Million Really Die?* in 1977, the phenomenon has developed apace and so the concept of a Jewish and Zionist conspiracy remains a strong theme for some groups on the Far Right of the political spectrum.[15] It is also argued that the **British National Party** (BNP) contains pseudo-Nazi elements and, as a consequence, that it has not so much abandoned ideas of a Jewish conspiracy but absorbed Muslims into a contemporary version of this narrative. According to this interpretation, the BNP loathes liberalism, has a revolutionary ethos and subscribes to the 'palingenetic myth' or the idea of 'rebirth' and 'renewal', to offer the United Kingdom a new start after decades of decline and decadence.[16] While the BNP and some other parties who maintain continuities with Fascism and Nazism might play down such associations for public consumption, their backstage propaganda sometimes reveals such tendencies.

The ideological differences between individual parties of the extreme right must be recognised, and these distinctions will be demonstrated in the chapters that follow. However, there is enough in common between them, particularly in their focus on the threat to national identity from ethnic diversity, to provide a common ideological 'inner core', even if some of the other ingredients in the programmes advanced by these parties are different. The problem of analysing the ideology of these parties is intensified by the fluidity, factionalism and ephemeral organisational identity which occurs on the Far Right. Some parties change their agendas, divide into rival factions and even alter their names. In the Netherlands, for example, four significant extreme-right parties have been involved in the last thirty years: the Netherlands People's Union (*Nederlandse Volksunie*, NV), the Centre Democrats (*Centrumdemocraten*, CD), the Centre Party (*Centrum Partij*, CP '86) and the **List Pim Fortuyn** (*Lijst Pim Fortuyn*, LPF).[17] Other parties change their ideological identity over time, such as the FPÖ, which altered its nature with the accession to the leadership of Jörg **Haider** following a putsch in 1986. He turned the party from an essentially anti-corporatist and anti-social democratic party into a 'highly authoritarian-populist party attacking foreigners, welfare spongers and criminals'.[18]

After due allowance is made for the methodological problems of national party distinctiveness, and for internal party change, it remains the case that analysing political parties on the basis of a shared ideology has both theoretical and practical merit. Klaus von Beyme suggests nine discrete party 'families' based on ideology. One of his categories is that of 'right-wing extremist'. It does not follow that there are official links between the parties in the far-right 'family' although there are some personality-based associations.[19] Supporting von Beyme's classification is the fact that there is a far-right grouping in the European Parliament. Most ultra-right parties are not represented there simply because they fail to secure any seats. The case for accepting the idea of a 'family' of extreme right–wing parties is ultimately justified since 'to ignore professed policies altogether when looking for similarities between parties would clearly be to stick our heads in the sand'.[20] While the policies of extreme right-wing parties in each European country are nationally centred, the advantage in testing for a common ideological link between all of their party programmes is that it leads to an appreciation of the normative fundamentals which unites them all.

The unique permutations of the policies of extreme right-wing movements in particular countries are apparent. Undoubtedly, immigration is a central issue for them all, and especially since 1994 the control of immigration, asylum and the integration of migrant minorities has been at the centre of electoral campaigns across Europe.[21] However, many illustrations of significant policy variations between them can be cited: the Swiss Democrats (*Schweizer Demokraten*, SD) stress environmental protection;[22] the Italian MSI argues for action against pollution and for more support for pensioners;[23] the **Norwegian Progress Party** (*Framstegspartiet*, FrP) combines a classical extreme-right populist stance on immigration and **law and order** with a right-wing firmness on the threat of terrorism, a centre-right agenda in favour of competition and private enterprise, a left-wing position on welfare and public services and neutrality on membership of the European Union;[24] the German far-right Republicans (*Republikaner*, RES) and the DVU focus on reuniting Germans in a state extending further east than the current boundaries up to the Oder-Neise line in order to restore congruence between the cultural nation and the state.[25] These German parties also display **anti-Semitism**, with the DVU not only obsessively concerned about the iniquities of Israel but also expressing anxiety about an international conspiracy to create a single world government – a preoccupation that they share with CP 86.[26] As with its German counterparts, the Belgian VB also desires to re-unite the Flemish nation with those that it considers its compatriots in the Netherlands. In France, the FN proposes drastic cuts in income tax and also advocates that **women** should work in the home as housewives and mothers.[27] Finally, in Britain the BNP combines traditional xenophobia with nostalgia for the British countryside, the superiority of small local communities and the encouragement of traditional arts and crafts and folk culture. Its leader, Nick **Griffin**, advocates Mummer's Plays, Padstow Obby Osses, Green Men, Abbots Bromley Horn Dancers, vegetable and cookery competitions, celidhs, folk music and many other manifestations of 'long buried English identity'.[28]

The plethora of such country-specific, and frequently idiosyncratic, policies challenges the argument that there is a family of extreme-right parties because, transcending similarities, there are 'country-level specificities that derive from different political and historical circumstances'.[29] In some respects, the debate about the existence of a coherent 'family' of far-right parties reflects the methodological differences between historians and social scientists. The historical approach can be summed up with the claim that 'the definitions, typologies and taxonomies beloved of social scientists tend to fit uncomfortably the intractable realities which are the raw material of the historian … Lines stubbornly refuse to be drawn … exceptions disprove more rules than they prove'.[30] The alternative view is that there are sufficient commonalities and patterns in the extreme right-wing European parties for the idea of a 'family' to possess heuristic value. In this volume, the preferences of students of history and the social sciences are both satisfied. There are evident dangers if the historical approach is neglected, as differences are as significant as recurring patterns. Simply to emphasise shared characteristics of parties of the Far Right and to neglect national diversities is both lazy and misleading. However, there is also good reason to maintain the generic approach preferred by social scientists because it allows some account to be taken of the generic normative values that underpin the ideology of most of the extreme right-wing parties in Europe. It also enables an appreciation of the Europe-wide outrage at the inclusion of extreme right-wing parties in coalition governments which will be referred to later in this chapter.

Applying the generic analysis of the idea of a 'family' of parties of the extreme right may lead to a reductive analysis of the ideology of these parties and to the assertion that they are all purely focused on immigration and the 'solution' of repatriation. However, there are nuances even in this policy area. While many parties reject the immigration of all foreigners, and others the immigration of non-European migrants, there is a growing convergence among many of the parties of the extreme right which argues that the real threat is now specifically posed by Muslim immigrants. The BNP has shifted substantially towards this interpretation, although its concern about laws banning racist comments may also have encouraged them to re-focus their hostility towards **religion** in order to avoid prosecution. This theme capitalises on the anxieties felt in some parts of Britain about Muslims, for example arguing that 'the Clash of Civilisations can only be ended by the total separation of civilisations; the free nations of the west can only be free of Islamic terrorism when they are free of **Islam**. They've got to go home'.[31] The changing focus towards the condemnation of Muslims is well illustrated in the case of the Flemish VB which, increasingly since the mid-1980s, has viewed Islam as a national and international danger. It asserts that Muslims are a fifth column in Belgium, are reluctant to integrate and that they practise a 'backward' religion.[32] Material produced for a local election campaign has asserted that Flemish cities and municipalities 'must remain cities and municipalities of towers and cathedrals and must not become North African ghettos with mosques'.[33] Similarly, the upsurge in support for the charismatic Pim **Fortuyn**'s LPF in 2002 had an anti-Muslim focus. This is evident from the groups which he specifically targeted – 'the guest labourers from Turkey and Morocco as well as from the former colonies of Surinam and Indonesia' – and his demands for integration. This was fertile territory for his party because the events of 9/11 led to half the Dutch population believing that the members of the Dutch Muslim community had 'failed to distance themselves from these events'.[34]

While none of the parties defined as belonging to the extreme right-wing family would reject the related policy goals of ending immigration and championing national cultural identity, a reductive view that claims to explain the ideology of extreme right-wing parties solely on that basis is too simplistic. This is because the parties are not single-issue based and the immigration issue itself is inextricably linked to other questions, such as law and order and the need for strong leadership. Their enthusiasm for strong leadership and their often palingenetic, revolutionary tendencies makes them unsuitable partners for alliances. It is also to be noted that, despite the phenomenon of *ideological pluralism*, in which specific ideological tenets are shared between ideologies, and in which mainstream parties might share a particular idea with the extreme right, it is unusual for far-right parties to be invited to join in coalition governments.[35] This is because, despite the sharing of certain political goals with other parties and ideologies, it is in the particular 'mix' of ideas, and the specific combination of ideological ingredients, that a 'family' of discrete extreme right-wing ideologies can be discerned. It is the intensity of their racist focus on repatriation, combined with the anti-democratic proclivities, that the capacity of parties of the Far Right to engage in coalition politics with mainstream conservative parties becomes strained. Indeed, parties of the Far Right are anti-democratic in their hostility towards existing political structures and elites, and in their advocacy of strong leadership. This explains why, when Haider's FPÖ first joined just such a governing coalition in 1999, there were European-wide sanctions taken against Austria. Such a reaction suggests the existence of a set of common European values which extreme-right parties violate. As the Belgian Foreign Minister put it at the time, 'my home is Belgium of course, but I also have another home, Europe. European politics is domestic politics'.[36]

Therefore, the ideology underpinning the extreme right consists of a set of related values which have internal coherence and which claim to solve contemporary dilemmas. The current and recent parties of the extreme right present an ideology which is a mix of racism, xenophobia, **nationalism**, strong law and order and a strong state: a mixture of ingredients which have anti-democratic implications.

Factors Conducive to the Growth

It is difficult to separate the principles of far right-wing parties from the social conditions and the political environment in which they develop. Extreme right-wing parties are reactive in character, and the political climate has to be conducive to their growth if they are to succeed. In the **twenty-first century**, there are certain Europe-wide issues, whether real or perceived, which promote the growth of far-right parties. They include the need to address the protection of national identities against the perceived threats of migration, the power of the European Union, boundary incongruence between ethnic and national boundaries, globalisation of the world **economy**, law and order, and American hegemony over international affairs and cultural life.

Historically, when particular societies have been under severe stress they begin developing far right-wing movements as part of a general drift towards political extremism.[37] This occurs when mainstream political parties appear unable to resolve the tensions generated by such stresses. This explains historical Fascism and Nazism. Following World War II, conditions in postwar Western European countries has not warranted entire populations from feeling beleaguered by a sense of national crisis. However, these same countries have suffered the impact of demographic changes, shifts that have been detrimental to particular groups in different ways. Immigration has appeared to threaten specific groups, and some sections of certain societies have felt more vulnerable to the rise of crime, lawlessness and moral decay, and others have attributed these problems to immigrants and consequentially to cultural diversity.

The Ideology of the Far Right

It is often assumed that high unemployment generates support for parties of the Far Right and that the vote for these parties reflects a **protest vote** rather than an ideological endorsement. Recent research casts doubt on these assumptions. It is correct that it tends to be in the particular localities in European countries, where social problems and unemployment are most evident, that the extremism of the right-wing flourishes. But the conclusions of recent research suggest that it is the combination of ideological and social factors which generate high concentrations of electoral support for the extreme right. This section of the chapter examines the impact of economic conditions, and particularly unemployment, on the growth of the Far Right. It argues that the strength of the vote in particular places is to be explained by ideology, and is only partly related to economic and social circumstances.

High unemployment does not appear to be a significant variable impacting on levels of support for the Far Right. In fact, high unemployment actually tends to lead voters back to the mainstream parties to solve the problem.[38] Intuitively, it is convincing to assume that existing populations in a similar socio-economic position to immigrants are likely to be attracted to the exclusionary and xenophobic policies of the extreme right-wing in order to protect their social stratum from economic competition. A major cross-European survey in which 49,081 people were interviewed suggests that, while support from sections of the working class for the Far Right is likely to be higher where there is competition from immigrants, unemployment is not the key. Apparently, it is the working classes, and sometimes the lower-middle classes, whose economic situation is strong, but who are insecure about the prospects of losing that prosperity, who are attracted to the Far Right.[39] This interpretation is supported by observing areas of far-right electoral strength, such as Austria, Norway and Flanders, as well as in richer regions within countries such as northern Italy. Even those people surveyed who were unemployed placed more emphasis upon their cultural objections to immigrants. Another survey suggests that, among the unemployed themselves, concern about asylum seekers was slightly more troubling to them than the impact of unemployment in their own lives.[40]

There is powerful evidence that the combination of local insecurities resulting from objectively poor social conditions, combined with the ideological traditions which are themselves an independent variable, nurtures support for extreme right-wing parties. This is apparent in Britain. For example, it was only in certain areas where inadequate housing was a problem that pro-**National Front** (NF) ideologies were evident in the 1980s. It was locally based traditions that explained hostility towards black people. These particular areas displayed a working class 'conformity effect and a predilection for racial exclusiveness'.[41] Social conditions contributed to the success of the BNP in parts of East London such as Barking, Dagenham and Epping in the local elections of May 2006, but here also it appears that immigration 'acted as a symbol for a host of other dissatisfactions, such as poor housing and **education**'. In East London, the largest single group of voters for the BNP were older, white and working class.[42]

Certain northern towns, such as **Oldham** and Halifax, have also experienced BNP electoral breakthroughs since 2003. The core vote was different here than in London. It was not disgruntled and elderly voters rebelling against change, but young people, mainly male, aged between 18 and 25 who were angry about local quality-of-life issues, such as anti-social behaviour, low-level crime and the need for a cleaner **environment**, and only 3 percent considered that asylum and immigration was the most important single issue. Yet a common local issue was the misperception that immigrants were favoured by the allocation of resources, so the 3 percent figure is probably an underestimate. In areas of BNP strength, false stories about grants to enable immigrants to buy houses intensified the white hostility toward ethnic minorities. The BNP is also able to exploit racial incidents, in particular localities, such as instances where a gang fight or inter-racial attack has led to the death or injury of a white person. It is evident that the BNP intervenes in those areas to exploit the situation; but it also appears that there are localities where ideology is already in play, possibly because of a previous history of anti-alienism. Issues of race and ethnicity are both the essential element in the ideological appeal of extreme right-wing parties, but also serve to trigger discontent with a wider range of issues.[43]

Ideological causes loom large in explaining the rising vote for far-right parties, so the complacent assumption by mainstream politicians that these votes are necessarily ephemeral protest votes must be challenged. Survey evidence again supports the view that parties of the Far Right attract support because of their specific prescriptions for contemporary problems and that the ideology of the parties matters. They are not mere receptacles for voters temporarily alienated from mainstream politics. Some votes may be explained as emanating from mere protest because there appears to be a distinction in some countries between 'first' and 'second' order elections. Voters in the Netherlands provide evidence for the view that while some might utilise right-wing parties for purposes of protesting, they do so mainly in 'second order elections'; for example, in local, provincial or European elections rather than in elections where national political power is at stake.[44] Similar patterns have appeared in Germany and in European elections in Britain; contests where strongly Euro-sceptic parties performed well only to disintegrate in the succeeding General Election. Some of these transient voters would appear to be less intensely committed ideologically, although in their Euro-scepticism and chauvinism they are exercising more than merely protest voters.[45]

Voting can be classified into one of four types; pragmatic, idealistic, protest and clientilist. These categories can overlap and a protest vote is not incompatible with an ideological vote depending upon the exact nature of the protest. For example, if the protest is a complaint about immigration, that is itself also an ideological statement. Rejections are as much a feature of ideology as are prescriptions.[46] Non-voting is more likely to be the form that a pure protest takes rather than casting a vote for a party with a clear programme. In 1994, anti-immigrant parties performed well in Italy, Belgium, Austria and Denmark and performed much less well in France, Germany and Holland. The themes advanced by extreme right-wing parties shift over time and, by 1999, extended to include economic and environmental issues. Studies of the programmes of parties of the Far Right reveal a common factor of anti-immigrant sentiment, and while the vehemence on the issue varies across European far-right parties, it always plays a central role. The same research suggests that, while the less educated generally are more prone to the ideological appeals of the extreme right than the more highly educated, large sections of European electorates do not regard these parties as evil. Therefore, far from dismissing the significance of extreme right-wing parties as mere receptacles for protest votes, their political strategies are compatible with post-modernist conceptions of partisan de-alignment and the decline of the established ideological narratives. Their focus on a core issue gives them a more contemporary ethos. It certainly enables them to consolidate support among lower-class, male voters with limited education and cultural capital who vote against their economic class interest.

The Ideology of the Far Right

Political Opportunity Structures

While the ideological and issue-based appeal of extreme right-wing parties must be recognised, so must the structures for political opportunity within which these parties operate. These opportunity structures include the ideological positions adopted by other political parties within the party system. These exogenous factors are crucial in determining the extent to which parties of the Far Right can be electorally successful. Opportunity structures are a combination of institutional and short-term factors. The institutional elements comprise such structures as the electoral systems and the question of whether the state is unitary or federal in organisation. Agency factors are also relevant, however, in influencing the electoral performance of far-right parties. For example, we should ask whether the issues which these parties seek to exploit at any given time partly reflect short-term factors such as: the state of the economy, the levels of immigration, whether there really is an influx of allegedly 'bogus' asylum seekers, as well as evidence for racial disturbances. Whether these issues are 'hot button' issues is affected by the choices of the mainstream parties about which issues they wish to emphasise. Also, whether the main parties choose to emphasise or ignore these contentious matters affects the voting strength of the Far Right. The location of the rival parties on the far right of the ideological spectrum, particularly mainstream conservative and Christian Democratic parties, is vital in affecting the appeal of extreme-right parties to the electorate.

Electoral systems are only one of a number of factors which influence the electoral appeal of parties of the extreme right. The classic political study of political parties by Maurice Duverger asserts the conventional wisdom that proportional systems allow all points on the political spectrum to form an electorally significant party.[47] Conversely, simple majority, or 'first past the post' systems, act as a brake on the emergence of fringe or minority parties. This would offer a simple explanation for the weakness of the BNP in British national elections. Yet, even if majoritarian electoral arrangements act as a brake on the emergence of minority parties, a powerful social force, or the ideological identity between a far-right party and a substantial portion of the electorate, means that the constraints imposed by the electoral arrangements are overcome. For example, in contrast to Britain, the FN in France, despite a simple majority electoral arrangement, has scored a mean vote of 11 percent during the period from 1979 to 2002 while the comparable figure for the UK's BNP and NF hardly registers. Equally, some extreme-right parties have performed badly even when competing under proportional formulas over the same period. In Germany, for example, at the national level, the mean figure is under 2 percent.[48] These statistics underline the importance of ideology. They suggest that, for voters of the extreme right, their awareness of the impact of electoral systems on the access of their favoured party to political office is overshadowed by more expressive concerns. Equally, there is no correlation between the appeal of the extreme right and whether or not a state has a federal constitutional structure.

A vital element in the political opportunity structures for parties of the Far Right is the ideological character of their party competitors, particularly on the right wing, and the cultural status of the voters who might veer between support for conservatism and the hard right.[49] It is commonly asserted, for example, that the strongly nationalist appeal of Margaret Thatcher on immigration was to the detriment of the Far Right, particularly after she expressed the concern that British people felt 'swamped' by immigrants in 1978, stressed her Euroscepticism from 1979 and adopted an aggressively militarist stance after her government defended the Falkland Islands in 1982. This would suggest that if the mainstream far-right party generates a harder right-wing appeal, the vote for the parties of the extreme right in that party system is diluted. This view is reinforced by the widespread attribution of the success of the Far Right in local elections in 2002 to the virtual disappearance of the Conservative Party in urban England at the time. The phenomenon of the rise of extreme right-wing voting in 2002 in some northern English towns could also be attributed to the convergence of the two major parties. This was caused by New Labour deserting its traditional supporters in relatively deprived areas in order to appeal to 'middle England' with centrist policies. This interpretation gains further support by examining other countries. There is research evidence which suggests that in Bavaria the ultra right-wing vote was diminished by the Christian Social Union (*Christlich-Soziale Union in Bayern*, CSU) whose policies are distinctly more right-wing than those of its Christian Democratic coalition partner in northern Germany.[50] Similarly, the countries in which there is a crowded centre of the political spectrum provide the opportunity for the Far Right to develop, and where there is a centrist coalition government the opportunity is the greatest of all.[51] There is scant evidence to support the view that the advocacy of far-right policies by mainstream right-wing parties strengthens the Far Right by making those issues respectable, although it has been suggested that when the debate takes on a hysterical tone, as has sometimes happened recently over the issue of political asylum, this can lead both the mainstream and the official parties of the right to take up the issue.[52] The increasingly volatile nature of social life and the growing volatility of party systems in recent decades ensure that this question will need frequent re-researching.[53]

The electoral fate of extreme-right parties is not an entirely dependent variable, however, as they can utilise the resources at their disposal with varying degrees of skill. If the relevance of the ideology of far-right parties to the perceived social issues in a country is a crucial variable in determining their appeal, the other salient factor is based on agency: that of the character of the parties themselves. Well-organised parties are more likely to be able to gain support. The VB performs better than many of its counterparts because it is better at mobilising support through a network of Flemish nationalist clubs. Leadership is also important, regardless of whether it is defined by charisma or media skills. Le Pen and Haider magnified the appeal of their parties by presenting themselves as heroic figures.[54] Good leadership supported by an effective cadre and a strong organisation, preferably with some roots in civil society, are decisive in helping parties to propagate their programmes effectively. These factors are important in explaining the success of the VB, the FN, the LN, the two far-right expressions of the FPÖ and the Scandinavian Progress parties.

Responding to the Extreme Right

The Far Right is often seen as evidence that European countries cannot eradicate the impact of Europe's 'dark past'.[55] Certainly, on a European-wide basis there is conflict between whites and non-whites. Even the Scandinavian social democracies have the same concerns, with the Danish and Norwegian Progress parties acquiring support through the 'rising tide of racism' and 'political disillusionment'; while in Sweden, half of the population surveyed blame immigrants for crime.[56] The evidence suggests that retreating from proportional electoral systems would have little effect. The debate is centrally about the best strategy for dealing with the threat displayed by the Far Right.

The Ideology of the Far Right

Is it more effective to 'kill it with kindness', to steal, but modify its policies, or to erect a *cordon sanitaire* and campaign energetically against it by offering alternative policies? The debate is about which strategies by other parties are most effective in negotiating, diffusing and isolating the impulses of the radical right.

There is evidence to support the view that the extreme right needs to be taken seriously and that to excoriate it is an inappropriate response. The argument for a counter campaign strategy is that mainstream parties should preach the merits of diversity with the result that the threat of the extreme right will evaporate, and antipathy to immigrants and fears of 'Muslim hordes' will be overcome, as happened with Catholics in the past.[57] The counter view is that popular nativist sentiments must be acknowledged in mainstream party political dialogue. It has already been argued that the strong leadership and anti-immigrant sentiments of the Thatcher Conservative Party was a factor in weakening the NF in the 1970s, although the party had been addressing the issue since the 1960s, when it introduced immigration restrictions.[58] The Conservative Party can capitalise on the issue more effectively than their rivals on the Far Right because it can play the race card with a more solid hand. This is because of its electability and its developed programme across the entire field of policy.[59] The case of the Bavarian CSU has also been cited as an example of the mainstream right weakening the Far Right by focusing on race and immigration issues. Mainstream party leaders in Belgium also argue that the *cordon sanitaire* does not achieve the desired results as it promotes the image of the VB as 'an anti-establishment party and strengthens its power base in cities such as **Antwerp**'.[60] More contentiously, the liberal and conservative ruling party in the Netherlands proposed banning the burkha for Muslim women in order to reduce the appeal of the Far Right in the November 2006 elections. This may be simply symbolic, however, and contribute towards an alienation of Muslims which is more problematical than allowing far right-wing parties to garner more votes.[61]

In contrast to these efforts, the gradual transformation of Scandinavian conservative parties into moderate parties and their acceptance of the main elements of social democracy have actually assisted the growth of the Progress parties which have been developing over decades, while erstwhile conservative parties were punished by their former voters.[62] A variant of the tactic of competing with the Far Right is to dilute its effect by taking it into a coalition. The Austrian FPÖ was actually weakened by its entry into a coalition after 1999. The imposition of sanctions on Austria proved counter-productive and boosted support for Jörg Haider's party. What emasculated the FPÖ was the skilful manipulation by Prime Minister Schussel, who 'attended to some of the more reasonable of the **Freedom Party**'s causes, rather than immigration policy' which weakened the appeal of Haider.[63] The approach in Denmark is to ally with the DPP but to allow it to hold no government positions.[64] It is likely that a complicated embrace of the extreme right can be more detrimental to their cause than attempting to erect a *cordon sanitaire*, as such a calculated response recognises that its vote is not simply one of transient protest. Extreme right-wing parties tap into the deeply embedded sentiments of nations. The realisation that the ideology of **nationalism** is 'the simplest, the clearest and the least theoretically sophisticated (ideology), but also the most widespread, and the one with the strongest grip on popular feeling' explains why the specific emphasis placed by far-right parties upon it gives them electoral appeal.[65] This is further supported by the recognition that nationalism, as a 'thin' ideology, is hosted by such other 'thick' ideologies, such as conservatism and liberalism.

Nationalism appeals, even in the more extreme forms advocated by the extreme right, because it 'institutionalises and legitimates emotion as a motive force of political, not just private, life'.[66]

The European Union and Globalisation

The European Union (EU) and a vague alienation from the process and consequences of globalisation also affect the sensitivities of particular groups in Europe. While the potential decline of national identities, and certainly the loss of substantial sovereignty, alarms many who toy with the idea of supporting extreme-right parties, the concrete evidence that it translates into votes for the extreme right is thin. It is necessary to distinguish between 'soft' and 'hard' Euro-scepticism. The softer version is signalled in Britain and Sweden by the rejection of membership of the Euro, and it brings together strange bedfellows on left and right. The costs for mainstream parties of adopting a harder version of Euro-scepticism is such that it is normally left to the peripheral parties of left and right to advocate opting out of the European Union entirely. These parties can bolster their appeal, however, in a cost-free manner.[67] Nevertheless, it tends to be a second order issue, although there are specific factors at play in Switzerland, which heightens the salience of the issue there. In Switzerland, the German-speaking Swiss are the dominant section within the society, and while in countries lacking such internal cleavages there is less concern about a measure of integration into the EU, in a divided country the German speakers have a dominant, or 'niche', position which would be undermined by incorporation into a larger entity. Further, in Switzerland, the German speakers do not identify themselves with other Germans, as the Swiss German language is different from High German. This phenomenon serves both to separate them from Germany and to keep them together.[68] As a group they wish to retain their identity against the Romands, as they term the French and Italian speakers in Switzerland. The **Swiss People's Party** (*Schweizerische Volkspartei*, SVP), which is formally their mainstream centre-right party, has acquired considerable strength in recent years on the basis of an anti-EU and an anti-foreigner appeal.[69]

If immigration is the issue *par excellence* for extreme right-wing parties in Europe, it is rooted in a sense of ethnocentrism and a strong sense of nationhood drawing upon language, religion, culture and history. Concerns about Jews, Communism, crime and general anti-establishment sentiments among the alienated in society are all potent, but immigration and its consequences are central. There is a clear difference with the United States, where the historical legacy of slavery and racist fears fuelled support for the Ku Klux Klan and various other bodies such as the White Aryan Resistance.[70] There is some differentiation also in Eastern Europe, where the legacy of Communism, coupled with economic traumas linked to the move to a free market economy, has played a part. This is also exemplified in the case of East Germany.

It is apparent that in Germany it is the perceived sense of relative economic disadvantage felt by those in the former German Democratic Republic (GDR) which fuels support for the National Democratic Party (*Nationaldemokratische Partei Deutschlands*, NPD). The historical connections between the Nazi era are in evidence, here through the use of insignia such as the swastika.[71] It is mainly comprised of disaffected young people who, by rejecting the eastern-bloc Communism of the past, have found in neo-Nazism a means of 'fighting back' against the wrongs caused by Communism, yet they remain economically socialist in their views. These ideas, combined with an aversion to the Slavic countries, to foreigners from **Russia** and to the former western part of the country, have given rise to a violent type of neo-Nazi behaviour. In the German case, the issue of aligning the cultural and linguistic group with a set of national boundaries has always been problematic. Before the reunification of East and West Germany, this was a particular preoccupation. Even though reunification has now been achieved, however, it still leaves the issue of re-uniting all Germans up to the Oder-Neise line. The legacy of Nazism also has resonance with some groups in Germany, and there is the disturbing phenomenon of neo-Nazi behaviour among the **youth**. The tensions involved in the failed efforts to integrate foreign-born Germans, as well as other foreigners, and the arrival of over 1.6 million immigrants from the former Soviet Union alone between 1993 and 2004, has intensified conflict. Many new immigrants choose to barricade themselves into miniature societies, complete with their own laws. **Violence** has erupted between young foreigners and young neo-Nazis, who have their own skinhead style and dress code.[72] This upsurge is linked to the rise in support for the NPD, which secured 9.1 percent of the vote in the parliamentary elections for Saxony in 2004, and 7.3 percent of the vote in the 2006 parliamentary elections in Mecklenburg-Western Pomerania. Yet, while the ideological support given to extreme right-wing parties should not be underestimated, in most European countries most voters for such parties should not be associated with pre-war Nazism. The parties appeal to an intense **nationalism**, but appeals to weaker forms of nationalism are evident in parties across the political spectrum.

It is important to study extreme right-wing parties and movements as the threat that they pose to established party systems, particularly those committed to a policy of erecting a *cordon sanitaire* around the hard right, is real. The parties of the extreme right express issues which concern substantial numbers of European citizens. The parties of the Far Right have a sufficient amount in common ideologically to be studied as a single group, but the need to study parties in the context of their individual countries is also apparent. No European country is free from the challenges posed by hard right-wing political parties, but the strength that they demonstrate is a product of specific national histories and cultures. The salience of particular concerns varies between countries as with the issue of Euroscepticism. However, there is general evidence to suggest that the social groups who fear that the position they've acquired within their societies might be under threat are those who respond to the appeals of the extreme right and not merely the most underprivileged. Divided societies, or those whose citizens fear the possibility of internal divisions, tend to generate the anxieties which far right-wing ideologies seek to assuage. Such factors often override more common explanations such as unemployment.

While many will find it distasteful when mainstream parties adopt highly diluted versions of the ideology of far right-wing parties on issues such as immigration, there is evidence that such a stance tends to weaken hard right parties, as evidenced in the Netherlands General Election of November 2006. There are also many other factors at work specific to particular countries. In the British case, for example, the reasons for the limited electoral appeal of the hard right include the lack of a severe national economic depression, the transformation in people's lives through the National Health Service, a stable party system and a sense of British grandeur linked to the World War II. Correspondingly, the extreme right-wing has Germanic connections, especially to Nazism, and much of British national identity can be traced back to the impact of that war on society. The decline of electoral socialism has permitted extreme right-wing parties to play down the socialist threat, but immigration has filled the vacuum. Political opportunity structures also determine the electoral prospects of the Far Right. There is a myth that the electoral system is an independent variable, but the effectiveness of the organisation and leadership of extreme-right parties themselves matters more, as does the avoidance of too moralising a tone by political elites on the issues that far-right parties seek to exploit.

Psychological explanations for the allegiance of individuals to the extreme right may have some purchase, as nationalistic and ethnocentric appeals carry emotional resonance for many, but economic and social causes are more potent. In the years ahead, it appears to be the ideology of Islamophobia associated with the **'war on terror'** which extreme right-wing parties will emphasise. The behaviour of both European governments and Muslim leaders, together with the personal attitudes of millions of non-Muslim Europeans and Muslims alike in everyday interactions, will determine whether tensions increase or diminish. This is because extreme-right parties are capable of developing appealing ideologies to address the prejudices and concerns of certain social groups. If the issues on which they concentrate are not handled with skill, the parties of the hard right will remain ready to pounce.

Brendan Evans

Notes

1. Peter Davies & Derek Lynch (eds.), *The Routledge Companion to the Far Right* (London: Routledge, 2002), 100.
2. Ibid., p.100.
3. Paul Hainsworth, 'The extreme right in France: the rise and rise of Jean-Marie Le Pen's Front National', *Representation*, 40:7 (2004), 101; and *The Guardian,* 29 September 2006.
4. J. Larrain, *The Concept of Ideology* (London: Hutchinson, 1979).
5. Martin Seliger, *Ideology and Politics* (London: Allen and Unwin, 1976). The central argument is that ideology should be regarded as a technical and not a neutral term, and that political ideologies are located across the entire political spectrum. They can advocate conservatism, reformism, radicalism and revolutionary politics alike.
6. M.B.Hamilton, 'The elements of the concept of ideology', *Political Studies*, 35:1 (1987), 18.
7. Evans, Brendan, 'Political ideology and its role in recent British Politics' in L. Robins (ed.), *Updating British Politics* (London: The Politics Association, 1984), 125–142.
8. Angus Campbell, *The American Voter* (New York: Wiley, 1960), 229.
9. A. Vincent, 'The ambiguity of ideology', *Politics*, 16:1 (1998), 47–52; and R. Christenson & H. Waltzer, *Ideologies and Modern Politics* (London: Nelson, 1972), 5–8.
10. L. Wilcox, 'Traits of extremism', http://www.lairdwilcox.com/news/hoaxerproject.html (cited 10 September 2006); see also http://en.wikipedia.org/wiki/extremism (cited 10 September 2006).
11. P. Hainsworth (ed.), *The Extreme Right in Europe and the USA* (London: Pinter, 1992), 197.
12. G. Mulgan, BBC Radio 4, 25 October 2006; and C. Mudde, *The Ideology of the Extreme Right* (Manchester: Manchester University Press, 2000), 8.
13. Wikipedia, 'Northern League', http://en.wikipedia.org/wiki/Northernleague-Italy (cited 14 November 2006).
14. C. Mudde, *The Ideology of the Extreme Right* (Manchester: Manchester University Press, 2000), 175.
15. M. Billig, 'The extreme right: continuities in anti-Semitic conspiracies in post-war Europe' in R. Eatwell & N. O'Sullivan (eds.), *The Nature of the Right: American and European Politics and Political Thought Since 1789* (Twain Publishers, 1989), 153–156.
16. N. Copsey, 'The BNP and fascist politics', *Politics,* 14:3 (1994), 102.
17. H. Dornsen, 'Pym Fortuyn and the new far right in the Netherlands', *Representation*, 40:2 (2004), 131.
18. D. Morrow, 'The Austrian parliamentary election of 1995', *Politics*, 17:1 (1987), 39.
19. K. Von Beyme, *Political Parties in Western Democracies* (Aldershot, UK: Gower, 1985). Von Beyme proposes nine types of party families. They are liberal and radical, conservative, socialist and social democratic, Christian democratic, communist, agrarian, regional and ethnic, right-wing extremism and ecology.

20. Michael Gallagher, Michael Laver & Peter Mair, *Representative Government in Modern Europe* (New York: McGraw Hill, 1995), 181.

21. C. Lahav & V. Guiradon, '"Actors and venues in immigration control": closing the gap between political demands and policy outcomes', *West European Politics*, 29:2 (2006), 201.

22. Michael Gallagher, Michael Laver & Peter Mair, *Representative Government in Modern Europe* (New York: McGraw Hill, 1995), 200.

23. R. Chiarini, 'The Moviemento Sociale Italiano': a historical profile' in Luciano Cheles, Ronnie Ferguson and Michalina Vaughan, *Neo-Fascism in Europe* (London: Longman, 1991), 38.

24. N. Fitter, 'Norway's Storting election of 2005: back to the left', *West European Politics*, 29:3 (2006), 578.

25. C. Mudde, *The Ideology of the Extreme Right* (Manchester: Manchester University Press, 2000), 169.

26. Ibid., p.172.

27. *Le Monde Diplomatique* at http://mondediplo.com/1998/64/leader (cited 31 August 2006).

28. http://chairmanscolumn.blogspot.com, 10, 19, 29 and 34 (cited 31 August 2006).

29. C.T.Husbands, 'Flemishness on the march' in P. Hainsworth (ed.), *The Extreme Right in Europe and the USA* (London: Pinter, 1992), 126.

30. M. Blinkhorn, 'Introduction: allies, rivals or antagonists? Fascists and conservatives in modern Europe' in M. Blinkhorn (ed.), *Fascists and Conservatives* (London: Unwin Hyman, 1990), 1–2.

31. http://chairmancolumn.blogspot.com/p.3 (cited 2 September 2006).

32. C. Mudde, *The Ideology of the Extreme Right* (Manchester: Manchester University Press, 2000), 173.

33. C.T.Husbands, 'Flemishness on the march' in P. Hainsworth (ed.), *The Extreme Right in Europe and the USA* (London: Pinter, 1992), 138.

34. H. Horussen, 'Pym Fortuyn and the new far right in the Netherlands', *Representation*, 40:2 (2004), 136–142.

35. Martin Seliger, *Ideology and Politics* (London: Allen and Unwin, 1976). For example, the idea of a strong state can be linked to non-fascist ideologies and individualism to liberalism and anarchism.

36. M. Van de Steeg, 'Does a public sphere exist in the European Union? An analysis of the content of the debate on the Haider case', *European Journal of Political Research*, 45:4, 269.

37. E. Shils, 'The concept of ideology', D.L.Sills (ed.), *International Encyclopedia of the Social Sciences* (New York: Macmillan and the Free Press, 1968), 69.

38. K. Arzheimer & E. Carter, *European Journal of Political Research*, 45:3, 434.

39. M Lubbers, M. Gizsbents & R. Scheeps, 'Extreme right-wing voting in Western Europe', *European Journal of Political Research*, 41:3, 371.

40. Ibid.

41. C.T.Husbands, *Racial Exclusionism and the City: The Urban Support of the National Front* (London: Allen & Unwin, 1983), 142.

42. http://www.irr.org.uk/2005/october/ak00035.html (cited 7 September 2006).

43. One survey suggested that people with middle school diplomas are most heavily represented rather than those experiencing higher or lower level education. Ibid., Arzheimer & Carter, *European Journal of Political Research*, p.42.

44. C. Mudde & J.J.M. Van Holsteyn, 'Over the top: Dutch right-wing extremist parties in the European Elections of 1994', *Politics*, 14:3 (1994), 127–134.

45. P. Pulzer, 'Germany votes for deadlock? The Federal Election of 2005', *West European Politics*, 29:3 (2006), 569; Thomas Quinn, 'The British General Election of 2005', *West European* Politics, 29:1 (2005), 176. In Britain the United Kingdom Independence Party (UKIP) is on the margin between the conservative and far-right positions and secures votes in such 'second order' elections as to the European Parliament. In addition to hostility towards the EU, its rhetoric is about strong law and order, firm leadership and blaming the politicians not the immigrants for immigration and asylum problems. These views were expressed by Nigel Farage MEP on BBC TV on 15 October 2006.

46. Martin Seliger, *Ideology and Politics* (London: Allen and Unwin, 1976), 64.

47. M. Duverger, *Political Parties* (London: Methuen, 1954).

48. Elizabeth Carter, 'Does PR promote political extremism? Evidence from West European parties of the extreme right', *Representation*, 40:2 (2004), 89.

49. P. Achtenberg & N. Houtman, 'Why do so many people vote unnaturally? A cultural explanation of voting behaviour', *European Journal of Political Research*, 45:1, 75.

50. W. Van Der Bring & F. Fennema, 'Protest or mainstream? How the European anti-immigrant parties developed into two separate groups by 1999', *European Journal of Political Research,* 42 (2003), 55–76.

51. A. Abedi, 'Challenges to the established political parties: the effects of party systems features on the electoral fortunes of anti-establishment political parties', *European Journal of Political Research*, 41:4 (2002), 551.

52. M. Lubbers, M. Gizsbents & R. Scheeps, 'Extreme right-wing voting in Western Europe', *European Journal of Political Research*, 41:3, 349.

53. Andrew J Drummond, 'Electoral volatility and party decline in Western democracies', *Political Studies*, 54:3 (2006), 628–647.

54. M. Lubbers, M. Gizsbents & R. Scheeps, 'Extreme right-wing voting in Western Europe', *European Journal of Political Research*, 41:3, 351–352.

55. M. Van de Steeg, 'Does a public sphere exist in the European Union? An analysis of the content of the debate on the Haider case', *European Journal of Political Research*, 45:4, 610.

56. Ignazi & Yemal (eds.), 'The silent counter revolution: hypotheses on the emergence of extreme right parties in Europe', *European Journal of Political Research*, 27:1.

57. G. Mulgan, BBC Radio 4, 25 October 2006.

58. M. Schain, 'The extreme right and immigration policy-making: measuring direct and indirect effects', *West European Politics*, 29:2 (2006), 286–287.

59. S. Saggar, *Race and Representation: Electoral Politics and Ethnic Pluralism* (Manchester: Manchester University Press, 2000), 185.

60. http://www.Economist.com/displayStory.cfm.story-id=1800764 (cited 10 October 2006).

61. *Guardian*, 19 November 2006.

62. N. Sitter, 'Norway's Storting election of September 2005: back to the left', *West European Politics,* 29:23, 580.

63. http://www.economist.com/display/Story.cfm?story-id=1459609 (cited 20 November 2002).

64. *Guardian*, 10 October 2006.

65. I. Adams, *Political Ideology Today* (Manchester: Manchester University Press, 1987), 82.

66. Michael Freeden, 'Is nationalism a distinct ideology?' *Political Studies*, 46:4 (1988), 754.

67. P. Taggart & A. Szczerbiak, 'Contemporary Euroscepticism in the party systems of the European Union: candidate states of central and eastern Europe', *European Journal of Political Research*, 43:1 (2004), 4.

68. T. Theiler, 'The origins of Euroscepticism in German-speaking Switzerland', *European Journal of Political Research*, 43:4 (2004), 639–650.

69. BBC News, 16 September 2003 and 24 October 1999.

70. P. Hainsworth (ed.), *The Extreme Right in Europe and the USA* (London: Pinter, 1992), chapter 13. See also W. Craig, *The Fiery Cross: The Ku Klux Klan in America* (New York: Simon and Schuster, 1987).

71. http://en.wikipedia.org/wiki/Neo-Nazism (cited 2 October 2006).

72. http://www.spiegel.de/international/spiegel (cited 2 October 2006).

The Development of the Far Right

Over the past 50 years, the Far Right has evolved from an insignificant presence
to a major force on the European political stage. This ascent from the margins to
the mainstream has been both impressive and undeniable. Firstly, this chapter will
present a narrative of this evolution, explaining when and where movements of the
Far Right have made their mark, whether in electoral or broader political terms. It
will also be interested in the way that such groupings have entered and exited the
political stage and the factors inherent in both. It is a feature of far-right politics that
organisations – however successful or unsuccessful – have had (and continue to have)
a limited shelf life, and this will emerge as a major underlying theme in this section.
Secondly, by necessity, the chapter will consider the different ways in which far-right
movements have operated: in power and opposition, and from parliamentary to extra-
parliamentary strategies. In doing so, we will dwell on some of the most significant
parties and leaders to emerge in the period.

1945 to the Present Day

The year in which World War II ended – 1945 – was a black year for those who had
positioned themselves on the Far Right. The German Nazi Party collapsed, Hitler
killed himself, Mussolini was murdered by Partisans at Dongo, and Germany
surrendered. In the same year, the Norwegian leader Vidkun Quisling – the arch-
disciple of **collaboration** as a policy of state – was shot as a traitor. The Nuremberg
Trials also commenced. Thereafter it was going to be almost impossible for those with
far-right sympathies to organise and position themselves again with any kind
of credibility.[1]

Analysing the story of the Far Right in the late 1940s and early 1950s, there are two
key strands that we should be aware of. On the one hand, individuals and movements
of the Far Right continue to be targeted by the post-war authorities; on the other,
small, splinter movements are founded in the hope that the ideas of the Far Right can
emerge again. Thus, in 1946 two notorious fascist leaders from Eastern Europe are
executed: Antonescu in Romania and Szálasi in Hungary. In 1947 Maurice Bardèche
is imprisoned in France, while in Italy in the same year, the authorities outlaw any
attempts to reconstitute Mussolini's Fascist Party. The new regime in Germany was
particularly sensitive to the idea of a resurgent Far Right, so in 1952, the courts banned
the SRP and in 1953 – as if pre-empting a resurgence in extremist ideas – a new law
stated that parties must pass a 5 percent threshold before they could gain parliamentary
representation. By 1955, the Dutch authorities had also banned the NESB.

During the same period, however, small far-right movements were being
founded around **Europe**. In Belgium, the Flemish *Vlaamse Concentratie* (1949),
the *Mouvement Social Belge* (1950) and the Flemish *Volksunie* (1954). In France,
the *Mouvement Socialiste d'Unité* (1947), the Union of National and Independent
Republicans (1951) and the *Parti Patriotique Révolutionnaire* (1954). In Britain, the
Union Movement (1947) and the League of Empire Loyalists (1954). In West Germany
the Fellowship of Independent Germany (1949) and the *Sozialistische Reichspartei*
(1950). In the Netherlands, the Dutch National European Socialist Movement
(1953). In specific countries, far-right activists would also have been encouraged by
early election showings. Shares of the vote were tiny, but at least parties on the Far

Right were registering with the electorate when some experts were predicting a total wipe-out. Thus, in Italy in 1947, the MSI claimed 1.9 percent and five parliamentary deputies in national elections (and later cemented an alliance with the Italian monarchist movement), while in Greece in 1950, the National Alignment of the Working People scored 2 percent in a nationwide contest. Far-right activists were also beginning to organise themselves across the continent. In 1950 we see Nation Europa being established and in 1951 the Malmö International and the European Social Movement.

The **Algerian War** – fought out between Paris and the combined forces of Algerian nationalism – gave the Far Right a new lease of life, at least in France. The conflict lasted for eight years (1954–1962) and by its very nature was of enormous significance for those on the French nationalist right. The idea that France might 'sell off' one of her prized possessions in North Africa – which is how **Algeria** was viewed – was a sacrilegious idea for nationalists, and so the campaign to keep Algeria French became a crusade for those who positioned themselves on the nationalist right. In May 1958 the French army and the French settlers in the colony (the *pieds noirs*) revolted against the administration in Paris. When de Gaulle came to power in the aftermath of this revolt, and set about establishing a new regime (what became the Fifth Republic), those on the Far Right assumed that, as a 'man of the right', he would make defence of *Algérie française* a guiding principle for his regime.

However, de Gaulle soon outlined his plans for Algerian independence. In so doing, he alienated the forces of the nationalist right. 'Barricades Week' (January 1960) and the 'Generals' Putsch' against the Fourth Republic (April 1961) were important symbols of the right's annoyance and frustration. For the (highly politicised) army in Algeria, the *colons* (the French settlers in Algeria) and the newly established parties and movements of the Far Right, de Gaulle had no right to 'sacrifice' Algeria. The integrity of the French nation was 'sacred'. It could be argued that divisions over Algeria had created a situation of near-civil war. In February 1961, the *Organisation de l'Armée Secrète* was formed to spearhead the campaign to keep Algeria French. In December of the same year, an 'Anti-OAS Day' was staged in Paris. This sequence of events seemed to symbolise the sense of division in France.

In a strange way, the Algerian War was a godsend for the extreme right. On one level it was a catastrophe: it threatened everything they cared about and stood for. But on another level it was an issue that helped to crystallise and catalyse activity and agitation. If ever there was a *cause celèbre* for those on the Far Right – one that could foster unity and militantism – this was the one. Almost in parallel, there were other developments on the **French Far Right**. In 1956 the political wing of the Poujadist movement, *Unité et Fraternité Française*, claimed fifty-two seats in parliamentary elections. The issue they cared about most was the **economy** and, in particular, prospects for small-business owners or, as they liked to put it, the 'little man'. The roots of Poujadism lie in the economic situation France found herself in following World War II. Shopkeepers were being forced out of business by the spread of supermarkets and hypermarkets, and Poujade proclaimed himself the saviour of the 'little man'. And of course, as a movement of the nationalist right the Poujadists were pro-*Algérie française* – it was almost a badge of honour – but in no way were they dominated by it.

For students of far-right history, France during the 1950s and 1960s was a fascinating case study. There was *Algérie française*, Poujadism and also myriad other groups. In 1960 two movements, *Europe-Action* and the *Societé des Amis de Robert*

Brasillach, were founded. The former was a neo-fascist formation that stressed the integrity and profundity of Europe as a geo-political entity, while the latter was a political club that looked back nostalgically at the life and work of Brasillach – a Fascist in the inter-war period and a pro-Nazi collaborator during World War II. Other movements were founded too: Occident in 1964 and Ordre Nouveau in 1969. It is also interesting to note the electoral performance of Jean-Louis Tixier-Vignancour in the presidential elections of 1965. He took 5 percent of the vote for the extreme right – hardly an earth-shattering performance but it did demonstrate that the Far Right could be an electoral force, albeit a minor one, and that the shadow of World War II had slightly lessened. The 1950s and 1960s was also an era when the French state became more vigilant in its dealings with shady movements on the Far Right. So, in 1958, *Jeune Nation* was banned and in 1968, *Occident* was outlawed. The authorities indicated that they would always have the final say on which movements were legal and which were not.

Across Europe this period witnessed the birth of many movements that would come to be classified as 'of the Far Right'. Most would remain small and splintered: for example, in 1956 *Ordine Nuovo* was founded in Italy; in 1958, the National Labour Party and the White Defence League came into existence in Britain, while in the Netherlands, the Dutch *Boerenpartij* was founded. In 1960, another grouping was born in Britain – the **British National Party**. In the same year, *Mouvement d'Action Civique* came into being in Belgium and *Avanguardia Nazionale* in Italy. More groups were born as the 1960s progressed: *Were Di Verbond van Nederlandse Werk-Gemeenschappen* (Belgium, 1962), National Socialist Movement (Britain, 1962), National Democratic Party (West Germany, 1964), National Revolutionary Front (Portugal, 1966) and **National Front** (Britain, 1967). The same period also witnessed the birth of far-right movements with a trans-national focus: the **Northern League** (1958), World Union of National Socialists (1962), *Fédération Ouest-Européene* (1963) and **Spanish Circle of Friends of Europe** (1965). We should also note two landmarks in the history of the Far Right. In 1956 the **Freedom Party** of Austria (FPÖ) was founded and in 1967 the 'Colonels' coup' put the army into power in Greece.

The student-driven revolutions of 1968 were a major fillip for the left. They incorporated a root-and-branch critique of 'bourgeois society' and no country in Europe was left unaffected by them. In general the period that followed was anything but fertile for those who positioned themselves diametrically opposite the left and far left on the political spectrum. By way of example, we should note that in 1968 – the year of rebellion – **Salazar**'s authoritarian right-wing rule in Portugal came to an end and in East Germany the new constitution contained a specific article that warned of the dangers of 'fascism'.

Of course, there was no let-up in the ambition of far-right activists and many new movements came into being across Europe in the aftermath of 1968:

1969 – Neo-Nazi Friendship Circle for Independent Intelligence in West Germany
1971 – West German Deutsche Volks Union
1972 – Front National in France
1973 – Flemish Vlaams-Nationale Raad, Faire Front in France and Wehrsportgruppe Hoffman in Germany
1974 – Parti des Forces Nouvelles in France
1975 – Parti des Forces Nouvelles in Belgium

1976 - Nationalist Student Confederation and Voorpost in Belgium, Fuerza Nueva in Spain
1977 - Vlaame-Nationale Partij and Vlaamse Volkspartij in Flemish Belgium, neo-Nazi movement ANS in West Germany, National Alignment in Greece, Movimento Independente para a Reconstrucão Nacional in Portugal
1978 – Vlaams Bloc and Union Démocratique pour le Respect du Travail in Belgium, Légitime Défense in France
1979 – Securité et Liberté in France, United Nationalist Movement in Greece
1980 – New Order in Portugal
1982 – Belgian Nationalist Young Students Association and British National Party

In the same period, key names began to emerge on the Far Right. Giorgio Almirante emerged as leader of the Italian MSI in 1969 and thereafter became a pillar of the movement. Eight years later, in 1977, **Fini** was appointed head of the MSI's **youth** movement – the first step in what would turn into a spectacular political career. He would later become deputy prime minister and foreign minister of Italy. In France, Alain de Benoist claimed the *Académie Française* prize. An innovative new-right thinker, he would become a key reference point for political activists who wished to dress up some of their more unpleasant ideas in the cloak of respectability. The late-1970s were also important to **Le Pen**. He had yet to make his electoral breakthrough, but he equates the period to his 'wilderness years' – the time when he formulated a political doctrine and awaited his opportunity. We should also note the election of Blas Piñar Lopez to the Spanish parliament in 1979. He was to become the mainstay of the Spanish Far Right for years to come.

The post-1968 era was not a great one for the Far Right in terms of electoral advances. Notable achievements were few. The NPD scored 4.3 percent in the West German elections of 1969, the MSI registered 8.7 percent in the Italian national elections of 1972 (its best ever result), and in 1973 the Danish Progress Party claimed a 16 percent share of the vote in 1973. Results continued to be poor. In 1979 *Unión Nacional* won 2 percent of the vote in Spanish elections and in March 1980 National Democratic Party candidate Norbert Burger scored 3.2 percent in the Austrian presidential elections. Theories abound as to why the Far Right achieved so little success during the 1960s and 1970s. In the main, though, they boil down to two: the post-war European democracies were becoming stronger and more confident and economies across the continent were maturing and any sign of crisis seemed to be a long way off.[2]

Other events in this period also help to illuminate the nature of the developing Far Right. In 1969 elements on the Italian extreme right were implicated in the Piazza Fontana bombing in Milan and in December of the following year the Italian Republic had to withstand an attempted coup led by neo-fascist militant Junio Valerio Borghese – 'The Black Prince'. In 1980 the **Bologna bombing** rocked the Italian body politic, and the suspicion was that neo-fascist activists were responsible. In the same year neo-Nazis were blamed for the Octoberfest bombing in Germany.

There were other indicators of how the Far Right was beginning to configure itself. In 1978 François Duprat, a hardline French nationalist, was assassinated. A.K.Chesterton resigned from the British National Front in 1971 and Enoch Powell left the Conservative Party in 1974. The Portuguese dictatorship collapsed in 1974 and **Franco**, Spain's nationalist dictator, died in 1975. In Germany the *Wehrsportgruppe Hoffman* was banned in 1980 and the Strasserite German Popular

Socialist Movement of Germany/Labour Party was outlawed in 1982. In the same era we also encounter the first stirrings of 'historical revisionism' – the campaign to deny the existence of the **Holocaust**. In 1978 the Institute for Historical Review (IHR) was founded and an array of highly controversial studies accompanied this development. In 1977 David **Irving** published *Hitler's War* and in 1978 and 1979 French professor Robert Faurisson argued in *Le Monde* that the gas chambers used by the Nazis to exterminate the Jews did not exist. The phenomenon of **Holocaust denial** demonstrated that elements on the Far Right – individuals who were sympathetic to the Third Reich – had the ability to reinvent themselves and engage in new, novel and provocative posturing.

The electoral breakthrough of Jean-Marie Le Pen's *Front National* (FN) in 1983 is a significant moment in the history of the Far Right. Up until this point, the FN had been a fringe grouping that hadn't been taken seriously by the French political classes. But the party's by-election victory in **Dreux**, to the west of Paris, was a landmark. The poll result had national ramifications and reverberations, and the FN consolidated its breakthrough in the 1984 European elections (polling 10 percent of the vote) and the 1986 legislative elections (winning 35 seats).

Dreux, 1983, was no 'flash-in-the-pan' result for the FN. It heralded a period of national political influence for Le Pen and the FN that has still not abated. The factors that explain the Dreux result – voters' disillusionment with unemployment, crime, levels of **immigration** and the impotence of the established political parties – were not purely France-specific. The continent was in the midst of economic depression and the attitude of a growing minority of voters was clear: if the traditional parties can't supply the answers, maybe the newer, fringe movements are worth a try.

So, in the mid- and late-1980s we witness the birth of many new movements that are instantly pigeon-holed on the Far Right: in Spain the *Junta Coordinadora de Fuerzas Nacionales* (1985) and *Frente Nacional* (1986), in the Netherlands the Dutch *Centrum Democraten* (1984) and *Centrum Partij* '86 (1986), in Belgium the *Front National-Nationaal Front* (FN-NF) and in West Germany the *Republikaner Party* (1983). Also, in 1986 Austria became a focal-point for far-right-watchers, for this was the year of Kurt **Waldheim**'s controversial campaign for the presidency. Throughout, he was dogged by allegations that he was more embroiled in the Nazi era than he had admitted. Significantly, in the same year, Jörg **Haider** took over the leadership of the **Austrian Freedom Party**. But in a sign of things to come, his party was subjected to a special investigation by the Liberal International (LI), 'the world federation of liberal and progressive democratic political parties'. Ominously, this organisation said that it wanted to 'find out more' about the politics of the FPÖ. By 1993 Haider's party had withdrawn from the LI as expulsion became more and more likely.

During the last years of the twentieth century there were key themes at play on the Far Right. Firstly, there was a wave of impressive electoral performances. In 1989 Le Pen's party won a parliamentary seat at Dreux – where the big breakthrough had come in 1983. In the same year the Republikaner Party had taken 7.5 percent of the poll (and eleven seats) in West Berlin, and then a 7.1 percent share of the German vote in the 1989 European elections.

The movement lost its Berlin seats the year after, with **Schönhuber** resigning, and then being re-elected, as party leader. But in 1992 it returned to win 11 percent of the vote in Baden-Württemberg. Schönhuber didn't last long, though – he was sacked again in 1994. In Austria the FPÖ was also on the electoral march:

1990 – 15 percent (federal elections)
1991 – 23 percent (Vienna)
1994 – 22 percent (parliamentary)
1996 – 28 percent (European)
1999 – 43 percent (**Carinthia**), 23 percent nationally and 5 seats in European elections

Across Europe there were other landmark poll results. In 1993 the Latvian Independence Party scored 13 percent in national elections, and in Britain the BNP won 34 percent of the vote in a local election on the Isle of Dogs, thereby gaining its first elected councillor. In 1994 the Alleanza Nazionale won 13.5 percent of the vote in Italian elections, and two years later increased this figure to 15.7 percent in a parliamentary poll. In Scandinavia parties pigeon-holed on the Far Right of the political spectrum also came of age. The **Norwegian Progress Party** claimed 15 percent of the national vote in 1997, while the **Danish People's Party** scored 7.4 percent in a 1998 poll. That said, the European elections of 1999 were, on the whole, a disappointment for the Far Right. The Alleanza Nazionale won 10.3 percent of the vote in Italy, but in Germany the Republikaner Party scored 1.7 percent and the NPD won a paltry 0.4 percent, while in France, the FN totalled only 5.7 percent (the breakaway FN-MN didn't help their cause, polling 3.5 percent). However, the FN became a 'serious' political player when in local elections it gained control of four southern municipalities: **Marignane, Orange** and **Toulon** in 1995 and **Vitrolles** in 1997.

By this time, immigration and asylum had become major election issues throughout Europe. Far-right parties devoted massive chunks of their manifestoes to these topics. They also thrived on 'racist incidents' that made it into the European media. In the newly-reunified Germany there was a series of episodes: in 1991 in Hoyerswerda, in 1992 in Rostock and in 1993 in Solingen. As far as far-right parties were concerned, these incidents were 'fuel to the fire'. A decade later, Britain was affected. In 2001, tension between 'indigenous' and 'Asian' communities in **Bradford, Burnley and Oldham**, spiralled into weeks of urban **violence**. And as could be expected, the BNP weren't slow to exploit these 'race riots' for potential political gain.

The other defining feature of this period was the political explosion in Eastern Europe. The fall of the **Berlin Wall** in 1989 and the collapse of the USSR had enormous political reverberations, one of which was the outpouring of powerful nationalist feelings that, up until this point, had been forcibly discouraged by the communist authorities.

The end of **Communism** was a watershed. For existing far-right politicians and new, aspiring ultra-nationalists - often these individuals were former communists – the fall of the Berlin Wall and the collapse of the USSR were interpreted as landmark events with a powerful political message.

Veteran far-right leaders like Le Pen and Franz Schönhuber believed they had been vindicated. Throughout their careers they had railed against the dehumanising 'communist system' and communist parties (in their own countries and elsewhere) which had faithfully toed the Moscow line, glorified the memory of Lenin and Stalin, and 'brainwashed' voters into opting for far-left parties in domestic elections. As such, a loathing of communist ideology and a hostility to everything the USSR stood for became the touchstones of nationalist, far-right ideology.

In Eastern Europe, the situation was different. By necessity, far-right parties only really emerged in the period *after* the fall of the Berlin Wall. Prior to 1989 the communist authorities held an iron grip on the political process. Nothing could happen, and certainly no political organisations could emerge, without being sanctioned by them. Dissent and opposition did not exist, at least in theory.

But, as communist regimes were toppled in 1989 and after, so the political landscape of Eastern Europe started to change. Ideas, attitudes and emotions that had for so long been suffocated by the authorities, and deemed 'not to exist' in official terms, were given some kind of house room. There was a new political framework based around **freedom** and **democracy**, and there would be a very new unpredictability about the kind of activity and the kind of political parties that would now emerge.

1. Several hundred skinheads march through central Prague, 21 August 1999, in commemoration of the death of Rudolf Hess.

As stark evidence of this, ultra-nationalist movements sprang up like mushrooms after a storm and a 'new Far Right' began to configure itself.[3] Dozens of new parties were founded, including:

Baltic states: **Latvian National Front** (2001), **United National Workers Party** (2005)
Bulgaria: **Attack Coalition** (2005)
Czech Republic: **Republican Party** (1990), Patriotic Republican Party (2000)
Hungary: **Hungarian Justice and Life Party** (1993)
Poland: **League of Polish Families** (2001)
Romania: **Greater Romania Party** (1991), Movement for Romania (1991), Party of the National Right (1992), Romanian Cradle (1990)
Russia: Derzhava (1995), **Liberal Democratic Party of Russia** (1990), **National Bolshevist Party** (1993), **Russian National Unity** (1990)
Slovakia: **Slovak National Party** (1989), Real Slovak National Party (2002)

The new political mix was even more interesting, and potent, in the Balkans. Here it was not simply a case of new nationalist movements emerging. Rather, the 1990s turned out to be a decade of inter-ethnic conflict in the area, with the various wars actually predicated – in Serbia and Croatia, in particular – on the exigencies of far-right-style nationalism.[4]

The Development of the Far Right

Here, the key individuals involved were Slobodan **Milošević**, president of Serbia, and Franjo **Tuđman**, the Croatian leader. Both men were dyed-in-the-wool Communists who had, almost overnight, grafted a dangerous brand of bellicose ultra-nationalism onto their respective ideologies. Subconsciously, and sometimes very consciously, both also harked back to the Nazi occupation of the Balkans for their inspiration. While Milošević made policy like a latter-day Chetnik, Tuđman did very little to dampen down the impression that the Ustaše had been re-born half a century on from World War II.

New movements that emerged in the former Yugoslavia, and that were immediately classified as Far Right, included:

Croatia: **Croatian Democratic Union** (1989), Croatian Party of Rights (1990)
Serbia: Socialist Party of Serbia (1990), **Serbian Radical Party** (1991)

Furthermore, the phenomenon of 'ethnic cleansing', as a strategy for realising an ethically pure nation, re-entered the psyche of European countries and peoples. It is no exaggeration to say that the ghastly goings-on in the Balkans could be legitimately equated to the horrors of the Third Reich. Milošević and Tuđman both used murder and terror as instruments of state, and tried to justify this through recourse to fanatical ultra-nationalist ideologies. Paxton captured the mood of the times when he wrote in 2004: 'No place on earth has harboured a more virulent collection of radical Right movements in recent years than post-Soviet Eastern Europe and the Balkans'.[5]

The Emergence of the Far Right

The question begged by these details is how and why. How has the Far Right – across the continent and in individual countries – become such a key player? And why: what factors have played a part in this transformation? Since 1945, all far-right movements have had to work out a strategy. If the ultimate end is power and influence, what should be the means? Here there have been many different approaches.

Most movements on the Far Right have been determined to engage with democracy, to fight elections and to try and gain influence that way. In the aftermath of World War II and the victory of democracy over the Hitler dictatorship, there was absolutely no other way to go. So, the vast majority of parties have made the pledge, even though the sincerity of some must be questioned.

In the manner that it advertises its democratic credentials, the Progress Party in Norway is representative of this strain in far-right politics: '[We are] Norway's second largest political party and [are] represented by 38 out of 169 members in the Storting, Norway's Parliament. The largest party is Arbeiderpartiet (Labour), with 61 representatives. The Progress Party holds several important positions within Parliament, including chairmanship of the Health and Social Affairs Committee, the Committee on Scrutiny and the Constitution and the Transport and Communications Committee. Carl I. **Hagen**, the Party's former chairman is also Vice-President of the Storting'. The movement obviously sees itself as part of the democratic infrastructure and, significantly perhaps, the passage cited above is the first thing that people will read when they visit the party's English-language web page.[6]

The National Front in Britain takes things a step further and actually flaunts its democratic structure as a party:

[We are] a party of genuine democracy which belongs to its members and whose policy is determined by its members. [Our] governing body is the National Directorate which is an elected body and which elects from within its ranks a Chairman, Deputy Chairman and other national party officers. The policies of the party are determined by the members at Annual Conferences and, unlike some other parties, such decisions are binding upon the party. The same democratic principles govern the operation of all local party organisations. The NF seeks to promote in Britain a genuinely democratic political system and advocates a fairer electoral system which includes an aspect of proportional representation. In government the NF would like to see an increase in the powers of the House of Commons Select Committees.[7]

On paper, this is a not unimpressive statement. But unfortunately, on occasions the practice has not matched up to the theory, and the NF has been involved in a number of unsavoury episodes.[8]

Other movements – or, occasionally, some individuals within these movements – have been intent on following another path: attempting to seize power illegally or actually trying to bomb their way into power. Here we might cite the examples of the National Bolshevist Party in Russia and the Baltic states (leaders Limonov and Aksyonov have both been imprisoned for possessing arms), the *Nuclei Armati Rivoluzionari* (the Italian neo-fascist terrorist organisation implicated in the Bologna bombing of 1980), and a variety of neo-Nazi groups in West Germany/Germany (many of whom have actually been proscribed).[9]

A 'third track' was to seek influence on a metaphysical level, to work on people's minds, ways of thinking and attitudes. This strategy had been employed by Charles Maurras and the monarchist-fascist *Action Française* in the first half of the twentieth century. Their aim – much ridiculed at the time – was to create a 'state of mind' in France that would favour the restoration of the monarchy. After 1945 others took the same tack, including Alain de Benoist, doyen of the French *Nouvelle Droite*, and the Italian Julius Evola, whose interest in 'Third Positionism' meant that he saw himself as being 'above' conventional politics.

So, there have been a variety of approaches. With hindsight, it is clear that parties of the Far Right have not achieved all their aims, far from it in fact. But, on the other hand, they have not been unmitigated failures either. Whatever barometer we use – votes or seats gained, political impact or some other measure – it is demonstrably the case that far-right parties have achievements to their name.

As has been noted elsewhere in this work, the 1940s and early 1950s were pretty barren periods for the Far Right in Europe. Activists and militants found it almost impossible to throw off the stigma of Hitler and Nazism. But gradually, and in certain countries rather than across the continent in one fell swoop, those who defined themselves as being 'of the Far Right' were able to come out of hiding and fight for their beliefs again.

It could be argued that the coming together of extreme-right parties in the European Parliament was, and is, a symbol of the development and growing credibility of the Far Right. In the 1980s and 1990s, the FN in France and other like-minded parties at the Strasbourg parliament formed the 'Group of the European Right'. The name of this new coalition implied moderation and conservatism, but it was misleading because leading members of the coalition were Jean-Marie Le Pen (elected to Strasbourg in 1984, but unseated in 2000 after assaulting a rival politician in 1998) and Franz Schönhuber (who took up his seat in the parliament in 1989).

Up until only recently, it was the **Identity, Tradition and Sovereignty Group** that, almost out of view, flew the flag for the Far Right in Strasbourg. It boasted members from France (**National Front**), Romania (Greater Romania Party), Belgium (**Flemish Interest**), Bulgaria (Attack), Italy (Social Alternative and Tricolour Flame) and Austria (Freedom Party) and the UK (an Independent). However, in 2007, the group ceased to exist after an internal dispute, prompting British Green MP Jean Lambert to say: 'This collection of unsavoury European politicians were united only by hatred – be it of other races, nationalities, sexualities or, ironically, the EU'.[10]

In recent years we have also witnessed amazing electoral advances by far-right parties and the appearance of far-right movements in government.

The emergence of Vladimir **Zhirinovsky** and the Liberal Democrats in Russia, and Le Pen and the FN in France, has convinced many commentators that the Far Right is a serious pan-European phenomenon. Zhirinovsky's popularity soared through the 1990s. His LDP emerged as a key player in Russian politics following a period on the margins. During the 1990s, the party's electoral scores were:

1991 – 7.8 percent (presidential)
1993 – 22.8 percent (parliamentary)
1995 – 11.2 percent (parliamentary)
1996 – 5.7 percent (presidential)
1999 – 6 percent (parliamentary)

What is more, in 1993 the LDP was the top party in 64 out of 87 regions. In 1997, Darrell Slider tried to explain the rise of the Russian Far Right:

The 1993 elections represented an important new phase in Russian politics in the post-Soviet era ... [The] polls, along with almost all Russian-sponsored surveys, underestimated the amount of support that would be given to Zhirinovsky's party in the 1993 balloting. As confirmed by other studies, the poll data show that supporters of Zhirinovsky tended to live in small towns and rural areas (helping to explain the poor accuracy of the surveys, since these areas are relatively poorly represented in Soviet and post-Soviet polling). One interesting result of this study is the finding that party identification was aided by the campaign, and that 'as the campaign progressed parties increasingly came to represent distinct sections of Russian society'.[11]

Between the early 1970s and the late 1990s, the rise of Le Pen's FN was equally as impressive:

1974 – 0.7 percent (presidential)
1981 – 0.3 percent (parliamentary)
1984 – 11 percent (European)
1986 – 10 percent (parliamentary)
1988 – 10 percent (parliamentary)
1988 – 14.4 percent (presidential)
1995 – 15 percent (presidential)
2002 – 16.86 percent/17.79 percent (presidential)

In other countries too, far-right political parties have grown significantly in popularity – for example, Austria, Denmark, Italy and Norway.

Here we should not overlook two other areas of impact. The media focuses on the headline news – the national elections, whether presidential or parliamentary – but far-right parties have a long history of success at local level. This might take the form of creditable electoral performances and/or actually moving into the realms of decision-making. As case studies of this phenomenon in action, we might alight on the *Vlaams Blok* (VB) and **Antwerp** (Marc Swyngedouw has explored the VB's strength in municipal elections between 1982 and 1994)[12] and the FN and its four southern mayoralties (**Marignane, Orange, Toulon and Vitrolles**).[13]

We should also take account of movements' ability to affect the national political debate, engineer kudos-enhancing alliances and gain significant, and perhaps even favourable, media exposure. These aspects of the Far Right's activity are often overlooked, but they should not be. Why have immigration and asylum gravitated towards the top of most countries' political agenda? External factors, of course, have played their part, but in many parts of Europe it is only the Far Right who have dared to talk about nationality-related issues, and they are now reaping the reward in terms of being associated with, and also being able to exploit, such topics.

Some far-right parties have actually achieved power at a national level. This has been a major achievement. In 1945 would any political commentators have predicted that, within a couple of generations, parties representing far-right attitudes and values would have entered government? 'Pariahs' in the corridors of power? Almost certainly not.

A key landmark for the MSI was 2004 when Fini was named as Italy's foreign minister. Under the words, 'Gianfranco Fini has shaken off his party's neo-fascist roots', the BBC reported that, 'Italy's Deputy Prime Minister Gianfranco Fini, the leader of the **National Alliance** (AN), has been appointed foreign minister. He replaces Franco Frattini, who is moving to Brussels as Italy's new European Commissioner. Analysts say Mr Fini's promotion crowns a remarkable transformation for the head of a party that emerged from the neo-fascist **Italian Social Movement** …The National Alliance is the second-biggest partner in Prime Minister's Silvio Berlusconi's centre-right coalition'. Arguably, this moment was Fini's crowning glory. He had been elected to parliament in 1983, had taken on the leadership of the MSI in 1987, and been appointed deputy prime minister in 2001.

In 2000, the Austrian Freedom Party gained a place in government after strong poll showings throughout the 1980s and 1990s. This created storms of **protest** across the world. In Washington the authorities decided to act and recalled its ambassador to Vienna. Secretary of State Madeleine Albright said: 'We have decided to limit our contacts with the new government and we will see whether further actions are necessary to advance our support for democratic values. [There should be no place in a European government for a political party that] doesn't distance itself clearly from the atrocities of the Nazi era and the politics of hate'.[14] Even on the other side of the globe governments were taking note. Australian foreign minister Alexander Downer chose to make an official statement on 6 February 2000:

> The Australian Government understands and shares the concern expressed by Austria's EU partners and other governments about the entry of Joerg Haider's Freedom Party into the Austrian Government. Mr Haider has in the past made statements expressing sympathy for the Nazi era. He has since recanted these views but other recent statements by the Freedom Party have also brought into question the party's democratic orientation and commitment to human rights. It is for the Austrian people to decide their own government. However, I am concerned that Austrian democracy could be put at risk if extremist views expressed in the past were ever put into practice. Australia is a country which took a strong stand against the Nazis, fought alongside our anti-Nazi allies in World War II and is home to many victims of the Holocaust.[15]

The Development of the Far Right

And in neighbouring Switzerland, the SVP of Christophe **Blocher** gained a second seat in the Federal Council in 2003 to add to the one it had traditionally held. This was hugely significant because during the 1990s the party had remodelled itself as a radical and populist movement that articulated a powerful anti-immigrant, anti-Islamic message.

In a very different context, ultra-nationalist movements came to dominate the imploding former Yugoslavia. The Croatian Democratic Union (HDZ) ruled war-torn Croatia between 1990 and 2000 and, in coalition, after 2003. Likewise, in Serbia the Socialist Party of Serbia (SPS) was in government, and supported by the Serbian Radical Party (SRS) in the late-1990s. In reality, the HDZ and SPS became inseparable from the leaders who came to dominate them: in the case of the former, Franjo Tuđman, and the latter, Slobodan Milošević. They were merely vehicles for the aggressive and expansive nationalisms of two modern dictators.

Elsewhere in Europe, far-right parties have either supported or propped up mainstream governing coalitions: the DPP in Denmark, the Northern League in Italy, **List Pim Fortuyn** in the Netherlands, the Progress Party in Norway, the Popular Party in Portugal and the Slovak National Party in Slovakia.

Looking back on the post-war years, how have these achievements been made possible? Here we must alight on a number of key explanatory reasons. The first factor is time. At the end of World War II the Far Right was in disarray and tainted horribly by Hitler and Nazism. There was no future for any politicians or movements proclaiming themselves as 'of the Far Right' or connected in any way to inter-war fascist groups. So, the late 1940s and early 1950s were a difficult period for those on the Far Right.[16]

It was only in the late 1950s and 1960s that movements on the Far Right – small and generally insignificant - were able to emerge. By the 1970s and 1980s, two generations on from Hitler and World War II, the conditions were altogether more favourable. It wasn't as if people had 'forgotten' about the evils and atrocities of Nazism. Rather, that there had been a passage of time: across Europe, new cohorts of activists had few inhibitions about establishing political parties and making their voice heard. Some of these movements played on the Hitler legacy, while others ignored it. Both sets of people benefited from the fact that things had 'moved on' since 1945.

Second, far-right groupings in post-war Europe have benefited from having strong leadership. On the whole, their leaders have been forceful, charismatic and effective. Given the emphasis within Fascism on the 'cult of the leader', this should come as no surprise. Whether it is the old-fashioned strongmen like Schönhuber or Le Pen, sharp-suited frontmen like Fini or Haider, or mavericks like Zhirinovsky, parties on the Far Right have not noticeably been short of persuasive, or controversial, bosses.

What is more, the political acumen of individuals such as these is easily overlooked. For a group of 'thugs', 'irrendentists' and 'fascists', they have done remarkably well in steering their own parties into the limelight and, in doing so, confounding the critics. Fini, for instance, is a fine example of an astute political strategist. Eatwell acknowledges his qualities, arguing that he 'cleverly adapted the AN-MSI's appeal to help it break out of its largely ghettoised southern roots'.[17]

Third, it could be argued that far-right parties across the continent have also had good fortune. For example, commentators are forever pointing to the weakness, ineffectiveness and incompetence of liberal, left-wing and centre-right parties across the continent. Frequently, in the last few decades, they have buried their heads in the sand when difficult issues have made themselves known. Paxton puts it vividly: 'Governments and mainstream parties coped badly with the new problems faced by Western Europe after the 1970s. They could not solve unemployment ... The state ... was losing part of its authority ... Welfare programmes now came under serious strain ... An interlocking set of new enemies was emerging: globalisation, foreigners, multiculturalism, environmental regulation, high taxes and the incompetent politicians who could not cope with these challenges. A widening public disaffection for the political Establishment opened the way for an "antipolitics" that the extreme Right could satisfy better than the far Left after 1989'.[18]

Indeed, it would be fair to say that the left has a case to answer. It not only lost credibility after the fall of the Berlin Wall, but was genuinely perplexed about how to deal with the Far Right, this new and uninvited political guest. Ban it? Ignore it? Be indifferent to it? Talk to it? Or actually do business with it? It was a horribly new and frightening dilemma and the best that one can say is that the left was often devoid of a convincing strategy. At times, in Machiavellian fashion, the left might even have encouraged the growth of the Far Right to cause maximum electoral problems for the mainstream right – in effect, a policy of 'divide and rule'. This was certainly the suspicion in France when Mitterrand introduced PR – so helping smaller parties like the FN – prior to the 1986 parliamentary elections.

Moreover, the major issues of the day have seemed to play into the hands of right-wing extremists. This has been slightly fortuitous. It is not as if far-right parties could have planned this in any way. Rather, they have been 'lucky' in the sense that their main concerns and interests have dovetailed neatly with issues which have hit the headlines in recent years – such as immigration, crime, unemployment, globalisation, asylum and the war on terror. That said, parties of the extreme right have also become increasingly savvy regarding ways to exploit populist issues and present liberal politicians as incompetent.[19]

In the 1950s and early 1960s the Algerian War gave ultra-nationalists in France the chance to parade their patriotic credentials, while also rehearsing a virulent anti-Arab message. Organisations like the OAS and individuals such as Jean-Marie Le Pen and Pierre Poujade gained a reputation for their virulent nationalistic discourse that bordered on outright racism. As such, the 1954–1962 conflict was a staging post and a training ground for future far-right activists. Myriad groups emerged on the extreme right in France during the 1970s, and by 1972 Le Pen himself had founded the Front National (FN), which in time would become one of the most high-profile of modern far-right movements. What is significant is that for all post-1962 movements on the **French Far Right**, the issue of Algeria was of central importance. And far-right militants were still 'fighting' the war long after the peace accords had been signed. Of course, those on the Far Right would not say they have been 'lucky'. They would argue that they have had the foresight and presence of mind to focus on the issues that matter – and thus it is no coincidence, or surprise, that in recent years their concerns have juxtaposed with those of ordinary voters to such a degree.

Fourth, we must acknowledge that some far-right parties have evolved into highly professional organisations. In terms of internal structure, public relations and the art of media manipulation, or 'spin', one or two movements on the Far Right could teach some mainstream parties a lesson. This has been a major factor in the growth and evolution of the Far Right. It is also noticeable how in recent times far-right groupings have broadened out their policy platforms. At one point in time, most parties on the extreme right were branded 'single-issue movements' on account of their over-zealous attitude to immigration and their inability, or unwillingness, to move beyond attitudes of xenophobia and racism. This has now changed, and the topic of the **environment** is a good example of a policy area that some far-right parties have almost made their own.

So, the Far Right has made great strides. In Austria, Switzerland and Italy – 'moderate' democratic states – it has held genuine political power, albeit causing controversy and consternation at the same time. In objective terms, this has been a major achievement. In Croatia and Serbia, forces of the ultra-nationalist right have had a major say in the direction of government, and have also been responsible for some of the worst outrages committed on European soil since 1945.

In some countries (for example, France, Romania) representatives of the Far Right have come close to success in presidential polls, and in others (for example, Belgium, Denmark, the Netherlands, Norway, Russia, Switzerland) political parties standing for xenophobic and racist ideas have scored impressively in legislative elections. These scenarios would have seemed almost unthinkable in the late 1940s and early 1950s when neo-fascist movements were finding it hard to break through the 1 percent barrier or were being legally prohibited.

Far-right movements have also gained influence in another way. Even where such groupings are a million miles away from political power, they have helped to set the agenda. They have influenced mainstream parties in terms of doctrine and policy. Sometimes this has happened in very indirect fashion, but on occasions specific parties have been able to bask in the limelight of having had direct strategic dealings with other political groupings (mainly on the conservative right – in Austria and Italy, for example). This has added immensely to their kudos and credibility as organisations. In this sense, across Europe, the Far Right has carved out a significant role as a 'pressure group' in European politics, both on a national level and on the level of the European Parliament.

It should also be emphasised that the Far Right has come a long way since 1945. Of course, there have been, and still are, plenty of 'nutters' prepared to engage in terrorism, anti-democratic tactics and Holocaust-denial activities, and most have ended up serving time in prisons across the continent. But, at the same time, it has to be said that the majority of far-right groupings have become more populist and sophisticated in their approach.

It is not just the sharp suits worn by leaders such as Haider and Fini or the impressive PR techniques employed by many a party which have steered the media towards a new batch of issues and controversies. Rather, it is the political strategies employed by movements the length and breadth of Europe which has enhanced the Far Right's respectability.

In Scandinavia, for example, parties have blended progressive notions of welfarism with anti-immigrant and anti-Islamic attitudes. In Italy, Fini and his colleagues have re-invented themselves as 'post-fascists' and tied themselves to Berlusconi rather than Mussolini. And in France, the FN has tried, not altogether successfully, to (re)claim the issue of ecology for the nationalist right.

The Far Right is now a truly pan-European phenomenon. Whatever their opponents might say, from the UK to the former USSR, and from Scandinavia to the Mediterranean, parties of the Far Right are playing a significant role in the political process. This may well be a worrying development, but it is one that cannot be overlooked.

Peter Davies

Notes

1. Roger Eatwell, *Fascism: A History* (London: Vintage, 1996), 279–280.

2. See Paul Wilkinson, *The New Fascists* (London: Pan, 1983), 8–9 and Roger Eatwell, *Fascism: A History* (London: Vintage, 1996), 280–281.

3. Hence the appearance of a second edition of the book edited by Cheles *et al.*, and with a new title: Luciano Cheles, Ronnie Ferguson & Michalina Vaughan, *The Far Right in Western and Eastern Europe* (London: Longman, 1995).

4. R. Paxton, *The Anatomy of Fascism* (London: Penguin, 2005), 189–191.

5. Ibid., p.188.

6. See http://www.frp.no/Innhold/FrP/Temasider/Flere_sprak/English/ home page (cited 18 December 2007).

7. National Front, 'The National Front: the real alternative', http://www.natfront.com/nfsop.html (cited 18 December 2007).

8. For example: BBC, 'Violent clashes at NF march', http://news.bbc.co.uk/onthisday/hi/dates/stories/august/13/newsid_2534000/2534035.stm (cited 18 December 2007).

9. See Paul Wilkinson, *The New Fascists* (London: Pan, 1983), ch.4.

10. BBC News, 'European far-right bloc collapses', http://news.bbc.co.uk/2/hi/europe/7094861.stm (cited 18 December 2007).

11. JSTOR, 'Review', www.links.jstor.org/sici?sici=0966-8136(199701)49percent3A1percent3C173percent3AEAPOIRpercent3E2.0.COpercent3B2-Y (cited 16 July 2007).

12. Marc Swyngedouw, 'Belgium: explaining the relationship between Vlaams Blok and the city of Antwerp' in Paul Hainsworth (ed.), *The Politics of the Extreme Right: From the Margins to the Mainstream* (London: Pinter, 2000), Ch.6.

13. Peter Davies, *The National Front in France: Ideology, Discourse and Power* (London: Routledge, 1999), ch.4.

14. BBC News, 'US acts over Austrian far-right', http://news.bbc.co.uk/1/hi/world/europe/631376.stm (cited 18 December 2007).

15. Australian Government, 'New Austrian government', www.foreignminister.gov.au/releases/2000/fa008_2000.html (cited 18 December 2007).

16. See Paul Wilkinson, *The New Fascists* (London: Pan, 1983), ch.3.

17. Roger Eatwell, *Fascism: A History* (London: Vintage, 1996), 287.

18. R. Paxton, *The Anatomy of Fascism* (London: Penguin, 2005), 181.

19. Legend has it that when Le Pen was setting up the FN he commissioned an opinion poll to find out the ten issues that French people cared about most; he then made these ten issues the focal-point of his party's first manifesto.

The Far Right in the Twenty-First Century

Far-right parties are political organisations that campaign predominantly on issues of **immigration** and **law and order**, and that exhibit anti-democratic and anti-system features. They have become a significant political force in a number of party systems in Western Europe, as well as beyond. In the contemporary political arena the majority of these parties have increasingly downplayed their 'fascist' credentials and extremist discourse in an attempt to promote an image of political legitimacy and electoral credibility.

From the late 1970s onward, far-right parties have exerted a growing impact upon a number of political systems in Western Europe. Unlike previous instances of far-right success, for example the Democratic Party of Germany (*Nationaldemokratische Partei Deutschlands*, NPD) in the 1960s or the French Poujadist movement in the 1950s, the contemporary Far Right has achieved a relatively sustained presence in a number of electoral arenas. This success is often accompanied with worldwide media attention, for instance Jean-Marie **Le Pen**'s performance in the 2002 French presidential elections. In some instances, for example the **Austrian Freedom Party** (*Freiheitliche Partei Österreichs*, FPÖ) in Austria and the **National Alliance** (*Alleanza Nazionale*, AN) in Italy, parties commonly considered 'far-right' have entered governing coalitions at national level. Elsewhere, for example in Britain and Germany, parties such as the **British National Party** (BNP) and **German People's Union** (*Deutsche Volksunion*, DVU) have achieved notable success in local and regional polls. The contemporary Far Right has also appeared able to influence the 'mainstream' political agenda, particularly on issues such as immigration and law and order. Centre-right parties are often accused by political commentators of replicating far-right appeals by 'talking tough' on immigration or law and order. Nor has the emergence of the Far Right remained confined to Western Europe. Political parties commonly considered to be 'far-right' have achieved significant election gains in countries throughout Central and Eastern Europe, for instance the **Hungarian Justice and Life Party** (*Magyar Igazság és Élet Pártja*, MIEP) in Hungary, as well as beyond the borders of **Europe**, for example Pauline Hanson's One Nation party in Australia or the Indian's People's Party (*Bharatiya Janata Party*, BJP) in India. In a number of cases, there is little doubt regarding the ability of the Far Right to move 'from the margins to the mainstream'.[1]

For some academics, such parties constitute a distinct far-right **family**. For others, these parties owe more to specific national political characteristics. However, what remains unquestionable is the ability of the Far Right to emerge as an important political force in contemporary politics. This chapter proceeds as follows. First, some definitional issues will be explained. In the popular and academic literature, a plethora of terms have been used when defining these parties, including: neo-fascist, extreme right, radical right-wing populist, national-populist and neo-nationalist. What differentiates these terms and which most aptly describes these parties? Second, the general performance of this party type will be noted. Third, different interpretations of this success will be considered. For example, does the breakthrough of the Far Right owe more to 'single issues' (i.e. immigration), or to broader trends, such as the transition toward a post-industrial society? Finally, the prospects for future growth will be discussed.

The Far Right in the Twenty-First Century

The War of Words

Attempting to define the 'far-right' is far from a straightforward task. For instance, debates typically focus upon whether the French **National Front** (*Front National*, FN) is 'neo-fascist', 'radical right-wing populist', or 'national conservative'. Likewise, there is disagreement over the extent to which it is accurate to consider parties that are rooted in regional concerns, for instance the Italian **Northern League** (*Lega Nord*, LN), as fully-fledged members of the 'far-right' family. To what extent is it appropriate to group these parties together underneath the common label of 'Far Right'? Often, such parties differ markedly in their outlook and general characteristics. Parties in Britain, Germany, or Eastern Europe, for instance, have traditionally been associated with the more 'extreme' side of far-right politics; they espouse overt racism, **anti-Semitism** and their ideological and organisational development is clearly influenced by interwar variants of 'fascism', such as Nazism. Yet parties in Scandinavia have appeared generally more moderate and have eschewed association with extremism, at certain times appearing primarily as anti-tax populist movements, rather than 'genuine' far-right organisations. It is also important to take note of the post-1945 transformation of several parties once considered unequivocally 'neo-fascist'. For instance, recent years have witnessed the **Italian Social Movement** (*Movimento Sociale Italiano*, MSI), now the AN, undertake a comprehensive modernisation process, and it has attempted to transform itself into a more 'respectable' member of the mainstream right-wing scene. Parties such as the MSI have sought to shed their 'fascist' credentials by marginalising their 'hard-line' members, downplaying blatant racism, and attempting to present themselves as legitimate mainstream parties. Such developments are often accompanied by highly symbolic acts, for instance the visit to **Auschwitz** by the leader of the AN, Gianfranco **Fini**, in 1999. In a similar fashion, parties such as the French FN and British BNP have selected black and Jewish party candidates as a means to distance themselves from accusations of racism and anti-Semitism. In this sense, the Far Right has increasingly experimented with 'political marketing', altering its appeal and programmatic mix as a means to improve its political legitimacy and escape the electoral 'ghetto'. However, such attempts have not been taken by each and every party. Thus, the participation in national governing coalitions by the AN stands in stark contrast to the complete marginalisation of the British **National Front** (NF). Yet, despite the uneven process of modernisation, the majority of commentators continue to view the Far Right first and foremost as a distinct political family in its own right. While these parties typically share common ideological and/or organisational features, at the same time there exist important 'sub-types' within the broader party family.[2]

In the literature on the Far Right, numerous features have been identified in an attempt to label this distinct group of parties. Characteristic of such attempts is the tendency to place an emphasis upon what extreme-right parties are *against*, as opposed to what they are *for* – e.g., their attitudes of anti-democracy, anti-parliamentarianism, anti-immigration, anti-Semitism, anti-cosmopolitanism, anti-equality, anti-materialism, anti-globalisation and anti-Americanism. Alongside these features, we might note more general characteristics common to most far-right organisations: ethnic nationalism, racism, authoritarianism, populist appeals, and, in some cases, conspiracy theories. In addition, these parties are often led by strong and charismatic leaders who favour a highly centralised organisation, displaying little enthusiasm for intra-party **democracy**. Figures such as Fini and Le Pen are often viewed as leaders in complete control of their party apparatus, determining party direction and ideological development, and requiring complete dedication from party members and activists.

However, drawing together these various features into a unified and relatively concise definition is not without its problems. Surveying the literature, one academic examined twenty-eight existing studies and identified fifty-eight possible different features of 'right-wing extremism'.[3] The task remains similarly complex today, with much discussion centring upon the preferred label: should parties be considered 'far-right' or 'radical right', 'populist' or 'national populist', 'neo-fascist' or 'anti-establishment'?

Though commonly appearing in typically alarmist media accounts, the term 'neo-fascist' is rejected by the majority of writers on the contemporary Far Right. Most obviously, this is due to the way in which the Far Right today has made a concerted attempt to distance itself from historical Fascism. Importantly, this is not to deny that 'neo-fascist' or 'neo-Nazi' groups and parties do not exist and that, at certain times, these groupings have constituted significant threats to liberal democracies. The activities of groups such as Combat 18 (C18) in Britain and neo-fascist *'groupuscules'*,[4] should not be downplayed. Yet in terms of the broader 'far-right' category, neo-fascist parties are significantly less prominent in the contemporary political environment than they previously were.[5]

American writers have traditionally favoured the term 'radical right', though in recent years, European scholars have also adopted the term. Thus, Herbert Kitschel refers to the European 'radical right',[6] while others refer to right-wing radicalism, or radical right-wing populism. However, a problem with this usage is that the term 'radical right' has been applied to a range of movements not commonly associated with right-wing extremism, for instance American-based movements such as the John Birch Society and McCarthyism.[7] These latter movements often differ significantly from their 'far-right' counterparts in regard to their ideology, goals, support and overall nature. By utilising 'radical right' we therefore become susceptible to including movements, or parties, which, while radical in their general outlook, may not necessarily hold much affinity with far-right politics.

A more concerted challenge arrives from the use of 'populism', whether in the form of 'neo-populist', 'radical right-wing populist', or 'national populist'.[8] For authors such as Betz,[9] the term 'extreme right' is ultimately flawed in that it implies a fundamental rejection of liberal democracy, as well as support for **violence**, which not all parties of the populist right exhibit: 'what we propose is that what unites these parties and movements is programmatic radicalism and populist appeal'. These writers typically stress the ability of parties to appeal directly to the 'common man', and to launch effective attacks against the political establishment. For the far-right, contemporary society may be divided into two realms: the ordinary hard-working members of the public (i.e. 'us') versus the corrupt, inefficient and increasingly detached political elite (i.e. 'them'). Indeed, Betz was one of the earliest writers to utilise this definition, placing his emphasis upon these parties' 'unscrupulous use and instrumentalisation of diffuse public sentiments of anxiety and disenchantment, and their appeal to the common man and his allegedly superior common sense'.[10] From this perspective, a principal defining feature of far-right parties is their ability to launch scathing attacks against the allegedly corrupt establishment, and the way in which they present themselves as the guardians of 'real' democracy. Thus, many far-right parties call for the increased use of referenda, and initiatives designed to promote 'direct' democracy. The BNP, for instance, like others, claims to speak on behalf of Britain's 'silent majority'.

While populist appeals and style unquestionably appear frequently in the discourse and publications of the Far Right, in terms of aptly describing the party family, there are a number of problems. First, it can be argued that by devoting greater attention to the populist credentials of these parties, analysts are led away from focusing upon the underlying 'extreme' nature of these movements. A second weakness concerns that mentioned above, namely that populism is in fact a political *style* as opposed to an ideology. Populism has been linked to numerous political figures, from Hugo Chávez in Venezuela to Tony Blair in the UK. As Carter explains,[11] the result is that many parties which are markedly different from one another are nevertheless grouped together under the same heading. In addition, there is a specific problem when attempting to link the term to parties such as the French FN: 'just as not all populist parties are of the extreme right (or even of the right), not all parties of the extreme right have adopted a political style that may be described as populist'.

It is the label 'extreme right' which appears to be used most often and which is most apt in terms of describing the contemporary Far Right. One leading advocate of this term is Piero Ignazi, who presents a useful classificatory system, identifying two sub-types within the broader 'extreme right' party family.[12] The first – the traditional, *old* extreme-right party – may be linked directly to the fascist legacy, and can be viewed as a direct heir to movements such as the German NSDAP through ideological linkages. These 'old' neo-fascist parties include small, and typically unsuccessful, movements, such as the BNP and the German DVU. The transition of established nation states toward post-industrialism, however, brought with it accompanying value changes. Consequentially, a *new*, post-industrial 'type' of extreme-right party emerged. Although no longer viewed as a direct heir to the fascist tradition, this 'new' party-type remains both critical and opposed to the central tenets of liberal democracy, for instance tolerance of pluralism, liberty and human rights. No longer viewed as directly linked to 'historical' Fascism and fascist movements, the contemporary 'new' Far Right nevertheless exhibits clear anti-establishment credentials. Examples of this sub-type can be seen in the French FN, the Austrian FPÖ and the German Republicans (*Die Republikaner*, REP). Likewise, others have stressed the difference of contemporary manifestations from Fascism, albeit in different ways. For instance, Kitschelt argues that the Far Right today draws upon markedly different constituencies than previous movements of a similar ilk, and has launched altogether different appeals.[13] For the majority of scholars, it is the term 'extreme right' which is generally considered the 'appropriate generic term' for this respective political family.[14] Not only does 'extreme right' overcome the problems associated with those competing terms discussed above, but it's also concerned foremost with party ideology, not political style. Thus, for Carter, the usefulness of the term arrives from the way in which it directs attention toward the anti-democratic and anti-system features, both of which 'lie at the very heart of the concept of right-wing extremism'.[15]

Scholars also differ in terms of their specific approach toward the **ideology of the Far Right**. While some provide a comprehensive 'checklist' of ideological features, others seek to provide a more concise definition. Hainsworth, for instance, stresses a number of issues and themes: immigration, nation, security, moral questions and identity.[16] In contrast, Carter is more specific, arguing that, in terms of ideology, there exist five distinct far-right party sub-types: first, 'neo-Nazi' parties which are radically xenophobic, promote biological racism and reject existing democratic arrangements; second, 'neo-fascist' parties which are neither xenophobic nor racist but which still reject the democratic system; third, 'authoritarian xenophobic' parties which are radically xenophobic, embrace 'cultural' racism and demand reform of the existing system with a greater role for the state; fourth, 'neo-liberal xenophobic parties' which are radically xenophobic, culturally racist, demand reform of the existing system, but which want less state intervention and greater 'democracy'; finally, 'neo-liberal populist' parties which are neither xenophobic nor racist, but demand reform of the system with greater democracy and less state.[17] As explained below, it is specifically when the Far Right distances itself from blatant xenophobia and a radical critique of the political system that it is able to achieve higher levels of success.

Towards the Mainstream

As stated at the outset, from the late 1970s onward, the Far Right has increasingly scored significant advances in elections at a variety of levels in several party systems. As Ignazi highlights,[18] the number of far-right parties entering national parliaments in Western Europe, or the European Parliament, has increased from six, at the beginning of the 1980s, to ten by the end of the 1980s, and then rising to fifteen in the mid-1990s. Furthermore, in the same period, the share of votes awarded to these parties more than doubled, from 4.75 percent (1980–1989) to 9.73 percent (1990–1999).

For most students of far-right politics, this trend can be traced back to the performance of the French FN in 1984. Having first scored electoral success at the municipal level, in the town of **Dreux**, the FN went on to receive over 11 percent in the 1984 European elections. Receiving similarly high scores in the European elections of 1989 (11.7 percent), in the same year the party subsequently achieved important results in by-elections in Dreux (43.5 percent) and Marseilles (33 percent), credited by some as the beginning of a new electoral trend in favour of the French extreme right.[19] Receiving just 0.2 percent in the 1981 legislative elections, by 1997 the FN's support had jumped to almost 15 percent. Furthermore, the FN leader – Jean-Marie Le Pen – received 15 percent of the electorate's support in the first round of the 1995 French presidential elections and, in 2002, received worldwide attention when he defeated left-wing candidates in the first round, receiving over 16 percent, to face the centre-right Jacques Chirac in the second ballot, receiving almost 18 percent.

The performance of the French FN is important for several reasons, not least because some interpret the FN's success from the 1980s onward as important in both publicising and making available a new 'winning formula', which far-right parties throughout Western Europe (and potentially beyond) could adopt and apply to their respective political environments.[20] What is certain is that from the early 1980s onward, far-right parties experienced significant increases in support. In Italy, the transformed AN received 15 percent in the 1994 elections, entering into a governing coalition alongside Silvio Berlusconi's Forward Italy (*Forza Italia*, FI) and the LN. This electoral pact was resumed in 2001, and in the 2006 national election the AN received a respectable 12.3 percent. Also on the ballot was the party of Benito Mussolini's granddaughter, Social Alternative (*Alternativa Sociale con Alessandra Mussolini*, SA), which received just under 1 percent. Likewise in Austria, under the leadership of the charismatic Jörg **Haider**, the FPÖ scored consistent increases in its support at national level, from 9.7 percent in 1986, to 22.5 percent in 1994, peaking with

27 percent in 1999 and a place in a governing coalition with the Austrian People's Party. In the Netherlands in 2002, a party under the flamboyant leadership of Pim **Fortuyn, List Pim Fortuyn** (*Lijst Pim Fortuyn*. LPF) came out of nowhere to take 17 percent of votes cast and 26 seats in the Dutch House of Representatives. Meanwhile in Belgium, the Flemish Blok (*Vlaams Blok*, VB), now **Flemish Interest** (*Vlaams Belang*, VB) has likewise experienced consistent and dramatic growth in electoral terms. Achieving only 1.6 percent in 1981, by 1995 the party's support had risen to almost 12 percent, continuing to rise to nearly 17 percent in 2003.

Importantly, the Far Right has often proven able to mobilise significant support at local and regional level. For instance, the Belgian VB has achieved notable levels of success in the city of **Antwerp**. Similarly, the FPÖ has scored consistently well in the southern province of **Carinthia**. German parties have recently received significant support in eastern states such as Saxony, while in Britain the BNP's support is particularly significant in the north-west and the outer ring of London. At the other end of the spectrum, via elections to the European Parliament, the Far Right has seen the opportunity to acquire additional funds, representation and political legitimacy. Indeed, the importance of 'secondary' elections to the Far Right's political development should not be underplayed.

However, despite noticeable gains in recent years, the Far Right has found it increasingly difficult to sustain this momentum. Heavily prone to factionalism, parties such as the French FN and Austrian FPÖ have, at various times, been seriously weakened by internal divisions. In 1998–1999, the FN suffered a serious internal split with its support temporarily dropping to 10 percent. In Austria, infighting within the FPÖ precipitated a national election in 2002 in which the party received just 10 percent of votes cast and 18 seats in the Austrian Nationalrat (National Council). More recently, Haider abandoned the FPÖ altogether to establish a new movement, the **Alliance for Austria's Future** (*Bündnis Zukunft Österreich*, BZÖ) which managed to receive only 4.1 percent in the 2006 federal elections.

It is also important not to overstate the success of the Far Right in general. Though prominent in north European states, for instance the Danish Progress Party (*Fremskridtsparti*), in Britain far-right parties have consistently failed to secure representation beyond local level. Though in recent years the BNP has become the first far-right party in British electoral history to have more than a couple of candidates elected at local level – for example, in May 2006, the party doubled its number of local council seats to over forty-five and, in Barking and Dagenham, became the second largest party, winning eleven of the thirteen seats that it contested – it has failed to win seats in elections to either the national or European parliaments. Indeed, throughout British history, both in the interwar and post-1945 periods, the Far Right has consistently failed to secure parliamentary representation. Similarly, elsewhere parties such as the Spanish New Force (*Fuerza Nueva*) failed to capitalise upon early gains, while the Dutch Centre Party (*Centrumpartij*, CP) and Centre Democrats (*Centrum Democraten*, CD) likewise never became serious challengers for political power. Meanwhile, in countries such as Finland, Greece and Ireland, political systems have, seemingly, remained relatively immune from far-right party politics. Therefore, while we should be careful to avoid blanket descriptions of far-right 'success' we can nevertheless summarise that, at least in national electoral terms, these parties 'have made an uneven, but appreciable impact, stretching from the margins to the mainstream of power'.[21]

Success of the Far Right

Numerous hypotheses have been advanced in an attempt to explain the 'third wave' of far-right parties.[22] For some, the success of the Far Right owes much to the way in which these parties mobilise support on single issues, such as immigration and law and order. For others, success should be linked more closely to the impact of socio-economic factors such as levels of immigration and unemployment. Numerous additional explanations have been advocated, from the impact of charismatic leaders to the capacity of national and local media to set an agenda favourable to far-right party growth. For Eatwell,[23] it is helpful to divide the plethora of approaches into a neat dichotomy between 'demand' and 'supply' theories. While the former focuses attention upon the impact of socio-economic developments external to the party, the latter places greater emphasis upon the 'supply' of appeals to the electorate, and therefore examines factors such as leadership, programmatic appeals and the media. In terms of understanding the abundance of explanations, it is perhaps useful to briefly outline this framework.

In terms of 'demand', Eatwell identifies five relatively distinct theoretical approaches. First, the 'single issue' thesis focuses upon the role of individual issues such as welfare, law and order, or immigration. From this perspective parties such as the French FN and Flemish VB are foremost anti-immigrant movements, with their support a response to specific unidimensional campaigns such as '*Les Français d'abord*' (French people first) or '*Eigen volk eerst!*' (Our people first!) Second, the **protest** thesis emphasises the ability of the Far Right to profit from 'anti-establishment' sentiment among the populace – i.e. distrust of mainstream parties and politicians. The British BNP, for instance, frequently launches attacks against the 'Old Gang' mainstream parties, while the Austrian FPÖ have placed a heavy emphasis on criticising Austria's historic 'social partnership' and co-operation between the Social Democrat and Christian People's parties. From this angle, there is a direct correlation between rising anti-establishment attitudes throughout established democracies and rising support for the Far Right. Third, the 'social breakdown' thesis devotes more attention to feelings of alienation and marginalisation among voters as leading them toward parties which promote "'traditional' values. Rising levels of **education**, and the growth of information sources, has contributed to the increasing fragmentation of society amid an increasingly globalised world. As traditional associations and linkages, such as party identification and class-based loyalties, erode, an increasing number of modernisation 'losers' are left susceptible to far-right campaigns. Fourth, the reverse 'post-material' thesis stresses the rising salience of material concerns, such as job insecurity, for some voters who express little sympathy for the 'new' cultural issues stressing matters of 'lifestyle' (e.g. ecologism, feminism, etc). From this approach, the emergence of the Far Right is viewed as a response to deeper undercurrents in contemporary society linked to the transition towards a post-material society.[24] Fifth, the 'economic interest' thesis follows on from the rise of 'rational choice' theorising in political science to examine the link between voters' material interests and their support for the Far Right. From the perspective of this last approach, support for the Far Right occurs when individuals face competition over typically scarce resources such as housing or local regeneration funds. Often, far-right supporters perceive ethnic minorities to be a 'threat' to their own political, cultural and socio-economic interests, and thus respond favourably toward parties seen to be defending these resources.

However, a key problem with placing exclusive emphasis upon 'demand-side' explanations is that they typically interpret far-right support as grievance-based. A vote for the Far Right is viewed as a protest against current political arrangements, as a response to feelings of alienation, or as a revolt against broad societal changes. In other words, studies often neglect the possibility that rather than voting *against* mainstream parties and current political arrangements, voters might actually vote *for* the Far Right. Support may not be strictly reactive in nature, but rather it may owe more to the appeals launched by the parties themselves.

Therefore, it becomes equally important to address the 'supply-side' of the equation, and Eatwell also identifies five relatively distinct approaches. First, the 'political opportunity' thesis examines the way in which the behaviour of mainstream parties might facilitate or constrain far-right development. For instance, in the late 1970s, a right-wing Conservative Party in Britain sought to undercut far-right support as Margaret Thatcher proclaimed that immigrants were 'swamping Britain'. Conversely, should mainstream parties move toward the centre-ground, then the degree of 'political space' available for extremist movements on either the left or right will increase.[25] Similarly, in those instances where mainstream parties ignore issues linked to immigration and race-relations generally, they provide significant opportunities for far-right movements to mobilise support. Second, some stress the role of the media and agenda-setting in contributing to a political climate which is receptive to appeals rooted in racism and exclusionary attitudes. The coverage of the asylum-seeker issue in Britain in 2001, for instance, arguably facilitated the BNP's anti-asylum campaigns. Third, the 'national traditions' thesis examines the specific impact of national history in providing a political culture which far-right entrepreneurs are able to exploit. The national histories of Germany and Italy are the prime examples in terms of providing a clear fascist 'legacy' on which more recent parties can draw. Fourth, advocates of the 'programmatic thesis' argue that, rather than representing a vehicle capable of mobilising only anti-establishment sentiment, the Far Right in some instances presents a comprehensive ideological 'package' in its own right. As argued by Hainsworth, 'it would be incorrect to see the extreme right as a single-issue movement or to draw simple correlations between levels of extreme right support and immigrant presence. The reality is more complex ...'[26] Not confined to the single issue of immigration, parties such as the French FN have, in stark contrast, launched a broader offensive, providing a range of detailed policies and innovative appeals. These parties also exhibit significant programmatic flexibility, and are able to respond to issues quickly. Finally, the 'charismatic leader' thesis, as the name suggests, examines the role of strong and 'colourful' leaders in an increasingly media-dominated political arena. For instance, the personalities of Jean-Marie Le Pen in France or Gianfranco Fini in Italy are widely regarded as figures capable of attracting significant support by themselves. Conversely, those parties without strong and charismatic leaders, for instance in Britain, have not enjoyed similar levels of success. In addition to these theories, for others greater importance should be placed upon the specific institutional arrangements in national states. Peculiarities of the electoral system are also significant. For example, proportional representation may well provide more fertile soil for insurgent parties than a 'first-past-the-post' system which raises significant barriers to small challenger parties. Similarly, the way in which systems differ in terms of state subsidies or media access provided to parties may also play a pivotal role. However, the evidence appears far from clear.[27] For instance, why has the Far Right proven able to engineer significant success in Flanders, but remained less successful in Wallonia, despite the fact that both regions use the same electoral rules?

Individually, no single theoretical approach is able to adequately explain the recent development and success of the Far Right. Rather, what is required is a combination of both demand and supply factors. While levels of unemployment and immigration are important, also central are the strategies of the far-right parties themselves. Indeed, recently scholars have turned to examine 'party-centric' factors in greater depth, emphasising, for instance, the centrality of party organisation, ideology and leadership to any comprehensive account of far-right success. Much of this work can be traced back to Kitschelt's study, a leading argument of which was that the contemporary Far Right is not merely affected by the behaviour of its mainstream competitors, 'but also by the capabilities and choices of the incipient rightist entrepreneurs and parties themselves'.[28] More recently, attempting to explain cross-national variation in far-right support, Carter's conclusions likewise point heavily toward this direction:

> Organisation and leadership are by far the strongest supply-side predictors of extreme right party success, and given that a pool of disenchanted voters, susceptible to varying degrees of extreme-right sympathy, exists in all Western democracies, much depends on contingent factors such as the availability of skilful political leaders who are capable of exploiting this potential.[29]

From this perspective, parties which are well led, well organised and which disassociate themselves from historical Fascism and extremist discourse, generally enjoy greater success than those which do not. Likewise, recently, Pippa Norris has similarly argued for a broader approach: 'What is needed is a more comprehensive understanding of this phenomenon which provides insights into the interaction of the distribution of public opinion ('electoral demand') with how parties respect in their ideological location ('party supply')'.[30] Reflective of the growing interest in supply-side factors, Rydgren places particular importance upon the ability of the contemporary Far Right to construct a new 'master frame' (i.e. ideological formula) which places specific emphasis upon anti-establishment populist appeals and 'ethno-pluralist' xenophobia.[31] This latter element refers to the rise of a 'new' racism which downplays 'traditional' hierarchical and biological conceptions of race in favour of cultural, or 'differentialist', racism. Emerging predominantly from the French New Right (*Nouvelle Droite*) intellectual circles, this 'new' racism instead stresses the need to preserve the unique national features of different peoples. Rather than stress racial supremacy, the contemporary Far Right advocates the separation of ethnic groups based upon the need to retain cultural diversity. For Rydgren, the importance of this new discourse arrives from the way in which it enables far-right spokesmen to avoid being stigmatised as 'racists', while anti-establishment populism similarly allows these parties to refute claims that they are 'anti-democrats'.[32] The central point is clear: the more the contemporary Far Right distances itself from strategies and ideas associated with the inter-war and immediate post-1945 environment, the greater the opportunity for political success.

Furthermore, as argued by Eatwell, interpretations which examine only the international and national (*macro*) level at the expense of the local and group (*meso*) and individual (*micro*) levels may well ignore important additional dynamics.[33] For instance, the breakthrough of the BNP in East London in 2006 owed much to specifically local issues, such as rapid demographic changes in the area and strains upon the local housing market. Similarly, the ability of the German NPD to capture seats in Saxony in 2004 can be explained likewise, in part by reference to the peculiarities of eastern Germany's post-unification transition, and also in part by the strength of the local party branch. Therefore, any understanding of far-right breakthrough must not only address the demand/supply distinction, but must also adopt a multi-level focus. Combining all of these attributes, Eatwell outlines his own formula to explain far-right success: growing perceptions of far-right *legitimacy* + rising personal *efficacy* + declining political *trust*.

Prospects for Future Growth

Though in some states far-right parties have experienced notable setbacks in terms of their electoral support, as well as intense factionalism, the potential for future growth or, at the least, the opportunity to retain a position of influence within their party systems appears relatively healthy. Voter disillusionment with political parties and national political institutions remains high. Similarly, high levels of electoral volatility in contemporary European states, the general uncertainty and insecurities that have accompanied the post-9/11 environment and the rise to prominence of the debate on Islam have all contributed to a fertile soil on which voters can be mobilised through racist and exclusionistic discourse. Urban 'disorders' on Parisian estates and in the northwest of **England** are reflective of a growing unease over the utility of current integration policies and the apparent disillusionment of predominantly second and third generation Muslim youths. In addition, questions over how best to respond to the rise of far-right parties are yet to be solved. For Belgium, the answer lay in imposing a restrictive '*cordon sanitaire*' around the Far Right and, by ruling the VB to be a 'racist' organisation, the party was effectively shut down. The effectiveness of such strategies, however, is highly questionable as arguably initiatives like these merely serve to reinforce the 'outsider' nature of the Far Right. In contrast, experience in Austria has suggested that, by co-operating with the Far Right, and handing these parties governmental responsibility, they are forced into moderating their message and, consequentially, internal schism and disintegration as factions dispute party direction.

Matthew Goodwin

Notes

1. Paul Hainsworth, 'Introduction: the extreme right' in Paul Hainsworth (ed.), *The Politics of the Extreme Right: From the Margins to the Mainstream* (London: Pinter, 2000).
2. Ibid., pp.4–5.
3. Cas Mudde, 'The war of words: defining the extreme right party family', *West European Politics*, 19:2, 225–248.
4. Roger Griffin, 'From slime mould to rhizome: an introduction to the groupuscular right', *Patterns of Prejudice*, 37:1, 27–50.
5. P. Ignazi, *Extreme Right Parties in Western Europe* (New York: Oxford University Press, 2003).
6. H. Kitschelt in collaboration with A.J.McGann, *The Radical Right in Western Europe: A Comparative Analysis* (University of Michigan Press, 1995).
7. P. Ignazi, *Extreme Right Parties in Western Europe* (New York: Oxford University Press, 2003), 28.
8. For example, see: H.G.Betz & S. Immerfall (eds.), *The New Politics of the Right: Neo-Populist Parties and Movements in Established Democracies* (London: Macmillan, 1998), 1–10.
9. Ibid., p.3.
10. Hans-Georg Betz, *Radical Right-wing Populism in Western Europe* (London: Macmillan, 1994), 4.
11. E. Carter, *The Extreme Right in Western Europe: Success or Failure?* (Manchester: Manchester University Press, 2005), 23.

12. P. Ignazi, *Extreme Right Parties in Western Europe* (New York: Oxford University Press, 2003).

13. H. Kitschelt, *The Radical Right in Western Europe* (University of Michigan Press, 1995).

14. P. Hainsworth, 'Introduction: the extreme right' in Paul Hainsworth (ed.), *The Politics of the Extreme Right: From the Margins to the Mainstream* (London: Pinter, 2000), 6.

15. E. Carter, *The Extreme Right in Western Europe* (Manchester: Manchester University Press, 2005), 23.

16. P. Hainsworth, 'Introduction: the extreme right' in Paul Hainsworth (ed.), *The Politics of the Extreme Right: From the Margins to the Mainstream* (London: Pinter, 2000), 14.

17. E. Carter, *The Extreme Right in Western Europe* (Manchester: Manchester University Press, 2005).

18. P. Ignazi, *Extreme Right Parties in Western Europe* (New York: Oxford University Press, 2003), 1.

19. For example, see: P. Bréchon & S.K.Mitra, 'The National Front in France: the emergence of an extreme right protest movement', *Comparative Politics*, 25:1 (1992), 63–82.

20. For example, see: H. Kitschelt, *The Radical Right in Western Europe* (University of Michigan Press, 1995); and J. Rydgren, 'Is extreme right-wing populism contagious? Explaining the emergence of a new party family', *European Journal of Political Research*, 44:3, 413–438.

21. P. Hainsworth, 'Introduction: the extreme right' in Paul Hainsworth (ed.), *The Politics of the Extreme Right: From the Margins to the Mainstream* (London: Pinter, 2000), 14.

22. K. Von Beyme, 'Right-wing extremism in post-war Europe', *West European Politics*, 11:2, 1–18.

23. Roger Eatwell, 'Ten theories of the extreme right' in P. Merkl & L. Weinberg (eds.), *Right-Wing Extremism in the Twenty-First Century* (London: Frank Cass, 2003).

24. P. Ignazi, 'The silent counter-revolution: hypotheses on the emergence of extreme right-wing parties in Europe', *European Journal of Political Science*, 22:1 (1992), 3–34.

25. H. Kitschelt, *The Radical Right in Western Europe* (University of Michigan Press, 1995).

26. P. Hainsworth, 'Introduction: the extreme right' in Paul Hainsworth (ed.), *The Politics of the Extreme Right: From the Margins to the Mainstream* (London: Pinter, 2000), 11.

27. E. Ivarsflaten, 'reputational shields: why most anti-immigrant parties failed in Western Europe, 1980–2005', paper presented to the 2006 Annual Meeting of the American Political Science Association, Philadelphia, 2006.

28. H. Kitschelt, *The Radical Right in Western Europe* (University of Michigan Press, 1995), 3.

29. E. Carter, *The Extreme Right in Western Europe* (Manchester: Manchester University Press, 2005), 213–214.

30. P. Norris, *Radical Right: Voters and Parties in the Electoral Market* (Cambridge: Cambridge University Press, 2005), 16.

31. Ibid., J. Rydgren, 'Is extreme right-wing populism contagious? Explaining the emergence of a new party family', *European Journal of Political Research*.

32. Ibid.

33. Roger Eatwell, 'Ten theories of the extreme right' in P. Merkl & L. Weinberg (eds.), *Right-Wing Extremism in the Twenty-First Century* (London: Frank Cass, 2003).

Islam and the Far Right

In March 2003, a few months before the parliamentary election, Filip Dewinter, the leader of the *Vlaams Blok* (today's *Vlaams Belang*), accorded an interview to one of Belgium's small newspapers. This was hardly exceptional. After all, Dewinter had established himself as one of Belgium's most prominent and notorious politicians, known well beyond Belgium's borders. What made the interview noticeable – given the *Vlaams Blok*'s past association with negationism (the party's founders included Nazi collaborators), racism and right-wing extremism in general – was the fact that it was published in *Hamishpacha*, an orthodox Jewish newspaper. In the interview, Dewinter not only presented himself as a great admirer of Jewish culture and traditions, but declared that the Jewish cultural heritage represented an essential part of European culture and identity. Therefore, the *Vlaams Blok* had no problems with the Jewish community in Belgium. In fact, Dewinter urged the Jewish community to accept the *Vlaams Blok* as an ally against a common enemy – Islam. For, as Dewinter put it, there was no way European culture could adapt itself to the Muslim customs. Neither could the two sides live in harmony with each other since the way each side looked at the world was 'completely different'. In his attempt to appeal to Jewish voters, Dewinter went so far as to project himself as an enthusiastic supporter of Israel, 'a piece of Europe in the Middle East', equating Israel's fight against Palestinian terrorism with his party's fight against Islam in **Europe**.[1]

Dewinter's attempt to court Belgium's Jewish community was part of a strategy to gain political respectability for a party which, despite its growing popularity at the polls, had remained a pariah on the margins of Belgian politics. In 2004, the party was even forced to disband after the Belgian Supreme Court charged the *Vlaams Blok* with inciting racial hatred. This, however, did not prevent the party from returning to the political scene under a new name (*Vlaams Belang*), but with the old programme. What remained too was Dewinter's vociferous championing of the Jewish cause at home and abroad, designed above all to deliver a fatal blow to the *'cordon sanitaire'* imposed on the *Vlaams Belang* by all the other political parties. Gaining respectability was particularly urgent in view of the upcoming 2006 municipal elections, where Dewinter hoped to play a decisive role in **Antwerp**, Belgium's most prosperous city. In the short run, however, Dewinter's 'philosemitism' gained him new venues for espousing his views. Thus in August 2005, *Haaretz* published a substantial article on the *Vlaams Belang* leader, which cited lengthy passages of an interview with Dewinter. Among other things, Dewinter was given the opportunity to distance himself publicly from 'individuals and groups with anti-Semitic tendencies and from **Holocaust** deniers' while reiterating his support for the state of Israel 'in its struggle to survive'. Most important of all, Dewinter was accorded space to propagate his party's views on Islam, which had increasingly come to dominate the *Vlaams Belang*'s programmatic agenda. In Dewinter's words, 'Islam is now the number one enemy, not only of Europe, but of the entire free world'. However, Europe was completely unprepared to face the fundamental threat posed by Islam: in Dewinter's view, in 'its current situation, Europe is like the Roman Empire – indulged, decadent, flooded with immigrants and unprepared to fight for its culture'.[2] In this situation, as Dewinter put it a few days before the 2006 municipal elections to *Haaretz*, his party and the Jews were 'brothers-in-arms' in the struggle against extremist Islam.[3]

Islam and the Far Right

As it turned out, Dewinter's strategy yielded mixed results. To be sure, the *Vlaams Belang* fell far short of the ambitious goals its leader had set for it before the election. On the other hand, however, the party proved that it was well entrenched in Antwerp and elsewhere in Flanders, where it managed to almost double its seats in local councils.[4] At the same time, the Flemish radical right's gains at the polls during the past several years demonstrated, in a particularly impressive way the persuasive power of a political project founded almost exclusively on cultural grounds, and centered around questions of values and identity. In recent years, this political project has been adopted by virtually all relevant radical right-wing populist parties as a new ideological justification for their policies of selective exclusion, which no longer immediately evokes the spectre of racism. We will now move on to the idea of nativism.

European-Style Nativism

The emergence of identitarian politics on the radical right is not, as is sometimes proposed, a revival of Fascism or neo-Fascism in post-modern guise. Rather, it represents a revival of an older strand of exclusionary nationalism – nativism. Historically, nativism emerged first in settler societies, such as Australia, Canada and particularly the United States, where it gave rise to strong political movements which, albeit only for a short period of time, gained considerable influence on both the state and national level. Nativism was a defensive response on the part of the original settlers to newcomers perceived as posing a threat to the culture, values and institutions of the community. Ideologically, nativist tendencies in the United States (what Rogers M. Smith has called 'ethnocultural Americanism') have a long pedigree, going all the way back to the founding moments of the country.[5] However, it was not until the early nineteenth century that nativism turned into a significant political force. The first nativist movements targeted Roman Catholic immigrants from Ireland and Germany entering the country in the early nineteenth century.[6] In the nativists' eyes, Catholic **immigration** was part of a 'Papal plot' to undermine American **freedom** and liberty and, ultimately, seize political control of the United States. The newly arriving immigrants were suspected of holding values that were fundamentally incompatible with American democratic traditions and institutions, a direct threat to 'the ideological backdrop of America's consensual faith'.[7] To the nativists, Catholicism, with its hierarchical structure, posed a 'clear challenge to America's civil liberties and republican institutions'. Catholicism and **democracy**, as one prominent nativist warned, 'are diametrically opposed; one must and will exterminate the other'. Immigration represented nothing less than a 'foreign conspiracy' against the United States and its liberties fostered by an institution (the Catholic Church) that was not only fundamentally undemocratic, but supposedly sought 'world domination'.[8]

In the American context, nativism represents a form of defensive nationalism, based on the notion that 'some influence originating abroad' poses a fundamental threat to 'the very life of the nation from within'.[9] The result is a 'suspicion of disloyalty' directed against minorities deemed unable or unwilling to conform to the rules and way of life of the nation. In the nativists' eyes, new immigrants entered the country with 'the set purpose to form and maintain distinct communities within the community, not only unable but unwilling to be assimilated politically or socially, intellectually or morally'.[10]

In the final analysis, nativism is thus all about defending and maintaining the foundations of existing ethno-cultural and ethno-national dominance, which are taken as given and therefore above and beyond questioning. Samuel P. Huntington, in one of his recent contributions to the revived debate on American identity, has summed up what this means with regard to the foundations of America's national culture. In his view, American society owes its success and stability, to a large extent, to its 'distinct Anglo-Protestant culture' inherited from the country's 'founding settlers. Key elements of that culture include the English language; Christianity; religious commitment; English concepts of the rule of law, including responsibility of rulers and the rights of individuals; and dissenting Protestant values of individualism, the work ethic and the belief that humans have the ability and the duty to try to create a heaven on earth, a 'city on a hill.'[11] Newcomers had better accept these values lest they run the risk of both threatening national cohesion and provoking a nativist backlash on the part of the majority intent on defending the basis of their culture.[12]

Nativism should not be confounded with racism *tout court*, nor is it merely another word for xenophobia. Traditional racism maintains that humanity is divided into 'hierarchical types' whose relative ranking depends on their level of civilisation. Xenophobia refers to an indiscriminate fear of all that is foreign and strange. By contrast, underlying nativism is a strong belief that different societies and cultures espouse entirely different values, which are neither inferior nor superior, but essentially incommensurable and incompatible with each other.[13] Thus Nativism generally accepts and tolerates difference, as long as it does not transcend cultural boundaries. In its most radical form, nativism goes so far as to postulate that 'cultural differences and distinctions must be preserved among an enduring plurality of groups' and in this way provides 'a discriminatory rationale for practices of inclusion and exclusion'.[14] In either case, nativism fundamentally rejects the notion that there exist universal standards, values and rights, and has nothing but contempt for the cosmopolitan, denationalised elites, which espouse and propagate this chimera. Instead, nativism champions what Pierre-André Taguieff has called the 'defence of cultural identities' based on the 'privileging of difference'.[15] At the same time, it vehemently opposes multiculturalism, which it considers, in the words of the late Samuel Francis, one of America's most outspoken contemporary nativists, a 'deliberate device by which the power-hungry can subvert a culture, whose moral codes deny them power, and build an alternative culture whose different moral codes yield power for themselves and none for their rivals'.[16]

With nativism, racism reinvented itself, exchanging culture for race. However, as Walter Benn Michaels has most forcefully argued, the adoption of culture is 'not a critique of racism; it is a form of racism'. In fact, as 'skepticism of the biology of race' increased, the new focus on culture became 'the dominant form of racism'.[17] Emphasising cultural pluralism, nativism 'transforms the substitution of culture for race into the preservation of race'. For, as Michaels argues, 'the commitment to pluralism requires, in fact, that the question of who we are continues to be understood as prior to questions about what we do'.[18] In other words, cultural identities are fixed, which makes it impossible to assimilate those who do not share in the common cultural heritage. They remain 'strangers in the land', as an American Supreme Court justice put it in 1889 in defence of the *Chinese Exclusion Act*, which denied citizenship to labour immigrants. Adhering 'to the customs and usages of their own country' these immigrants were not only deemed incapable by the Court to 'assimilate with our people' but given their numbers, which approached 'the character of an Oriental invasion' were seen as constituting a 'menace to our civilisation'. By couching the question of Chinese labourers in terms of a 'narrative of race-as-culture', the Court presented 'Chinese otherness', not only in terms of 'an inassimilable subject', but also as an 'inassimilable, and therefore constant, threat'.[19] This is the essence of nativism.

Contemporary radical right ideology represents a fusion of nativism and populism. This is hardly surprising. What the two have in common is a shared hostility to elites – political, academic, intellectual and business – who, in the words of a notorious contemporary American nativist, are either unwilling 'to preserve the land they grew up in for their children' or are 'indifferent to its disappearance, or long for its death'.[20] The nativist right claims for itself to represent and express the 'defensive instinct' of ordinary people against the nefarious multicultural fantasies and experiments of deracinated, cosmopolitan elites.[21] In the United States, populist nativism has largely remained confined to the margins of politics; by contrast, in Western Europe, it has played an increasingly important political role, largely as a result of the success of radical right-wing populist parties to turn questions of culture and identity into important political issues. Dewinter maintained as early as 2000 that in the future, the conflict between identity and multiculturalism would constitute the main political cleavage separating right and left.[22] In the years that followed, the fight for the 'survival of the nation' as a culturally distinct entity and against multiculturalism has become pivotal for the ideological development of radical right-wing populist discourse, from the most radical parties such as the *Front National* and the *Vlaams Belang*, to the more moderate ones such as the *Schweizer Volkspartei* and the *Lega Nord*.

The 'nativist turn' has had important repercussions on the radical right's programmatic strategy. Whereas in the past, radical right-wing populist parties distinguished themselves primarily by their extreme anti-immigration stance, with the nativist turn, the focus increasingly shifted toward questions of integration, ie. how to deal with those foreign populations already in the country. Yet, while a growing number of radical right-wing populist parties started to acknowledge that the majority of foreign residents were here to stay, they vehemently rejected the notion that integration would only be successful within a multicultural context, which, based on the recognition of ethnic and cultural diversity, allows immigrants to maintain their distinctive identities in the context of the laws and regulations of the respective country.[23] As the *Front National* put it in 2000, the party's fight was not for 'the sovereignty of a France that is multicultural and multi-religious, but for a France that is French'.[24] In fact, as the party stated one year later, the 'rejection of the multicultural society in the name of the identity of France' represented the 'fundamental battle of the *Front National*'. This meant, above all, putting an end to the political experiments, which not only accorded immigrants the right to preserve their identity but actively advanced programmes designed to promote cultural awareness and understanding. Instead immigrants should be given a choice – either to integrate themselves or go back to their country of origin. For the radical right, integration presupposes both willingness and the ability to fully and completely adopt the host country's culture, values and way of life. In other words, as the *Vlaams Blok* stated in its 2002 party programme, if immigrants planned on staying they had better 'unequivocally opt for assimilation'.[25]

Here we come to the pivotal argument informing the radical right's nativist position. For the radical right, successful integration depends first of all on the foreigner's willingness to assimilate, and assimilation, in turn, depends first of all on the compatibility of an immigrant's cultural predispositions with the host society's values and way of life. The *Front National* was the first radical right-wing populist party to develop this argument in a coherent fashion and spell out the consequences.[26] According to a pamphlet from the early 1990s laying out the party's position on immigration, France's experience during the past two hundred years had demonstrated that integration posed few problems as long as immigrants were of European origins and predominantly Catholic (eg. Italians, Spaniards and Portuguese). By contrast, the more recent experience had amply shown that it was impossible to integrate immigrants from North Africa, Turkey and elsewhere in the Third World. In fact, if European and world history taught anything, it was that 'enduring, peaceful coexistence between peoples of different ethnic and religious origins sharing the same territory' was virtually impossible. From this it followed, as the *Front National* stated at the beginning of the new century, that uncontrolled immigration, if allowed to continue unchecked, posed an elementary challenge to the cultural survival of the indigenous population threatened with 'being replaced on their own soil by other populations, which neither want nor can assimilate'.[27] It was hardly a secret that if the party referred to immigrant 'populations' it essentially meant to say Muslims. For the *Front National*, like other radical right-wing populist parties, it was an illusion to believe that Muslims would be able to integrate themselves into European societies, given the fundamental differences in cultural heritage. As Bruno **Mégret** – until his 'betrayal' in 1999, Jean-Marie **Le Pen**'s right-hand man – has recently put it in an article on Turkey's integration into the European Union, 'Islam is the carrier of a civilisation that is incompatible with the European civilisation. This is not meant to be injurious or aggressive; it is a simple statement of a reality, which nobody can deny'.[28]

This was hardly a new position. As early as 1992, the *Vlaams Blok* had stated in its '70–point programme to solve the problem of immigration' that Islam was an 'intolerant religion', fundamentally incompatible and 'irreconcilable' with Western values. For a **religion** that preached, among other things, holy war, the oppression of **women** and the extermination of infidels was, by its very nature, fundamentalist and therefore dangerous.[29] A few years later, Filip Dewinter, in a speech celebrating his party's victory in local elections, reaffirmed the party's position on Islam. In his view, Islam represented an 'anti-Western religion, which has no business being here'. Anyone, he warned, who claimed to take his inspiration from Islam had 'bought his return ticket to his country of origin'.[30] The threat of expulsion, however, was hardly a credible weapon to meet the challenge posed by an increasingly assertive Muslim immigrant population. In the long run, Europe would only be able to hold its own in what the radical right increasingly characterised as a collision of two fundamentally different cultures if it asserted its cultural identity. Among the first to make this point was Pim **Fortuyn** in his 1997 anti-multiculturalism pamphlet entitled ***Against the Islamisation of our culture – Dutch identity as a foundation***. The central argument here was that Islamic culture, values and norms were diametrically opposed to those predominant in modern Western societies: values such as democracy, gender equality, religious tolerance, freedom of opinion, individual responsibility and respect for minorities in general. Like others on the radical right, Fortuyn believed both that the main line of conflict informing current world affairs was one between the Islamic world and that contemporary Europe was experiencing precipitous cultural decline, comparable to the last years of the Roman Empire. In this situation, Europe could only be saved if it reasserted the foundations of its cultural identity, grounded in Judeo-Christianity and the Enlightenment.[31]

Islam and the Far Right

Fortuyn's writings, although inspired by libertarian beliefs, were exemplary of the line of nativist argumentation adopted by the radical right starting in the late 1990s in their attempt to mobilise anti-Islamic fears and *ressentiments*. As we have seen in the American case, the ideological core of nativism consists of two related propositions. One asserts that the nation's inherited culture, values and ideals are crucial for the survival of the nation. The other claims that there are cultures, values and ideals that are the very antithesis to the ones informing the nation, and therefore represent, as the *Front National* would put it in 2001, a 'deadly threat' to the continuity of the collective identity. Once the radical populist right started focusing on questions of integration and citizenship, rather than immigration more broadly, it quickly adopted the central tenets of nativism.

Contemporary radical right nativism subscribes to the notion that what we are witnessing today is a 'clash of civilisations', a notion first introduced by the renowned historian of Islam and the Middle East, Bernard Lewis, and then popularised by Samuel P. Huntington.[32] Like Lewis, the European nativist right assumes that the resolution of the East-West conflict, instead of bringing about the end of history, marked the beginning of a new – and in many ways significantly more dangerous – conflict, pitting Western civilisation against the Muslim world.[33] In this conflict, the nativist right asserts, Europe has become the main battleground of a revolutionary religious and cultural war, waged by what Jean-Yves Le Gallou and others on the French Islamophobic right have characterized as *'l'Islam conquérant'*.[34] Unlike in the past, however, the Muslim world, given its technological backwardness, is no longer in a position to threaten Europe with military conquest. Today, Islam's strategy of conquest relies primarily on inundating Europe with immigrants intent on subverting and ultimately subjugating Europe. As Morton Messerschmidt, a leading member of the *Dansk Folkeparti*, put it in an interview with the far-right American online magazine, *FrontPage*, if nothing is done against immigration from Muslim countries, in a few decades, Muslims will constitute a majority of the population of Europe. That would mean 'the end of our culture and the end of European civilisation'. [35] In Austria, where the FPÖ had made the question of Islam the central issue in its 2006 election campaign (the main campaign slogan was 'Daham statt Islam' – at home, instead of Islam), the party leader Heinz-Christian Strache announced in spring 2007 the foundation of a *'Kulturschutzverein'* (Association for the Protection of Culture) with the telling name *'SOS-Abendland'* (SOS-Occident). The project was designed to contribute to the protection of the country's history, culture and identity, particularly against the growing threat of an increasingly radicalised Islam seeking to bring about 'the destruction of Western society'.[36] As Strache put it at the New Year meeting of his party in 2007, there was only one place in Austria for the crescent, and that was 'in the evening sky'.[37]

The Nativist Case against Islam

The FPÖ was hardly the first radical right-wing populist party to make the question of Islam the central issue of a national election campaign. A prominent example is the *Dansk Folkeparti*, whose hard-line position on immigration from Muslim countries had been a decisive factor in the party's success in the 2001 national election. A few months before the election, the party issued a book-length pamphlet entitled *Danmarks fremtid: dit land – dit valg* (Denmark's future: this country – this choice) whose cover provided a clear indication of its content.[38] It showed two Muslim militants, one brandishing a pistol, surrounded by a group of young Muslim demonstrators taken during an anti-Israeli demonstration in Copenhagen a year earlier. In a series of images, interspersed throughout the text, the party sought to illustrate the choice Danish voters had in the election: on the one hand idyllic landscapes with serene lakes and flowery fields, blond women and children; on the other hand, scenes from Berlin Kreuzberg (a district with a large concentration of Turkish immigrants) dominated by women wearing headscarves, if not a chador. The message was clear: Muslim immigrants represent a fundamental threat to Danish values and the Danish way of life.

Mogens Camre, the party's lone member of the European Parliament, had set the tone as early as 2000. In his view, it was naïve to believe that it would be possible to integrate Muslims into Danish society, if only because the vast majority of Muslim immigrants were not interested in integration, seeking instead to transform Danish society into a Muslim society. Most people mistakenly regarded Islam merely as a religion. In reality, Islam was above all a 'fascist ideology mixed with the fanaticism of the Middle Ages, an insult to human rights and any other condition necessary to create a developed society'. There was nothing the West could do to prevent Muslims from 'ruining their own societies'. But at least, 'we should protect our own society' against people intent on 'waging a holy war'[39] A year later, several prominent party members reiterated the *Dansk Folkeparti*'s intransigent position on Islam. Charging that wherever Islam is in the majority, 'there is a dictatorship because Islam is also a political system', Søren Espersen, the party's press secretary, warned that his party would continue to 'fight Islam in the same way we fight **Communism**'. Søren Krarup, a leading representative of the party's ultra-Christian wing, stressed a second point that had assumed increasing importance in the fight against Islam – the country's Christian heritage. For this reason alone, Krarup noted, it 'is and remains impossible' to integrate Muslims into Danish society.[40] For, as the 2001 election pamphlet had noted, 'Christianity and Islam are irreconcilable'.[41] The party's hostility towards Islam was perhaps best expressed by Michael Rex, a town councilor from Næstved, who during the party's annual meeting in September 2001, characterised Islam as a 'terror organisation' intent on gaining 'world domination' by violent means.

The *Dansk Folkeparti*'s successful mobilisation of anti-Muslim sentiments did not go unnoticed. Following the events of September 11, Islamophobia assumed an increasingly central role in the radical populist right's anti-immigrant rhetoric. Characterising Islam as a fundamental threat to the West, the radical right largely adopted Fortuyn's line of argumentation and thus managed to promote itself as a staunch defender not only of secularism and Enlightenment values, but also of democracy and even Christianity. A prime example is the Dutch politician Geert Wilders, whose newly-formed *Partij voor de Vrijheid* gained nine seats in the 2006 national election on a largely nativist platform designed to stop 'the tsunami of Islamisation'. Like Pim Fortuyn before him, Wilders is convinced that 'Islam and democracy are totally incompatible and will always be incompatible', not least because Islam is a 'violent religion', which preaches 'a fascist body of thought, which threatens to destroy our democracy'. Like Fortuyn, Wilders considers Islam a 'backward religion' deeply steeped in pre-modern, medieval practices, which unlike Christianity never went through a process of reformation leading to the separation of church and state. The result is a 'retarded' political culture, hostile to genuine democracy and the rule of law. Under the circumstances, it makes no sense 'to invest in a moderate Islam'.

It is therefore absolutely essential that Muslim immigrants intent on making the Netherlands their permanent home must put the Dutch constitution above the Koran. In fact, given the 'horrible things' contained in it, Wilders suggest that they tear out half of the Koran and throw it away – together with it at least half of their beliefs.[42]

The charge that Islam represents a backward culture, medieval if not worse, proved highly effective if only because it allowed the radical right to evade accusations of racism. By invoking the values of the Enlightenment, even ideologically extremist parties such as the *Vlaams Belang* could denigrate one of the main world religions with impunity. In 2002, for instance, Filip Dewinter held a programmatic speech in Antwerp, in which he characterised Islam as the 'green totalitarianism' threatening Europe with 'colonisation'. So far, Dewinter warned, Europe had failed to understand Islam's true nature – a religion of conquest, which disdained and rejected everything the West stood for. However, Dewinter continued, 'democracy and freedom of opinion, the separation between church and state, equality between men and women, in short, our complete way of life, are too valuable to us to allow them to be replaced by the green totalitarianism of Islam'.[43] A few years later, after having repeatedly asserted his commitment to the foundations of Western culture and civilisation, Dewinter would state that compared to 'Muslim culture (…) our culture is superior. Our values, our way of life are superior and we have to say so. I don't think the way of life of Muslims is compatible with our way of life'.[44]

The only way to fight against 'the Islamisation' of Europe and reverse the Muslim invasion, Dewinter charged in his 2002 speech, was 'to drive Islam back to where it belongs – namely the other side of the Mediterranean Sea'. This was also the goal of the *Lega Nord*, which in October 2002, organised a mass rally to commemorate the four hundred and thirty-first anniversary of the 'Christian victory' over the Turks at Lepanto in 1571. Initially founded to bring about the 'liberation' of the prosperous northern provinces of Italy from the rest of the country – and particularly Rome - the *Lega Nord* increasingly adopted questions of identity and immigration as central issues. In this context, the party tried to promote itself not only as the defender of Western values but also of Christianity, in an effort to appeal to practising Catholic voters, particularly in the north-eastern part of the country. The tone was set by the *Lega Nord* daily newspaper, *La Padania*, which in June 2002 published an open letter by the noted priest Gianni Baget Bozzo calling on Bossi to turn the *Lega* into a 'bulwark against the Islamic invasion'. A few months later, the party voiced its strong support for a law designed to make it obligatory to display a crucifix in all public offices, including schools and universities. For the *Lega*, the law was meant not only to strengthen Italy's Judeo-Christian cultural heritage and identity, but also to counter the 'arrogance and intolerance' of Muslim organisations, which had denigrated and attacked the crucifix (demanding that the cross be removed from schools).[45] The *Lega*'s hostility toward Islam found its most vocal representative in Roberto Calderoli, senator and Reforms Minister under Berlusconi. Calderoli made no secret of his belief that if nothing was done to stop the Muslim invasion, Islam would one day 'dominate all of Europe'. Like his counterparts in Denmark, Belgium and the Netherlands, Calderoli considered the confrontation between Islam and the West as a clash between 'a civilisation and a non-civilisation'. If Muslims believed theirs was a great civilisation, they should prove it. Otherwise 'let them return to the desert and talk with the camels, or to the jungle and talk with the apes'.[46] Shortly after making these statements, Calderoli was forced to resign. In the wake of the Danish cartoon affair, Calderoli wore in public a t-shirt emblazoned with one of the offending cartoons. Calderoli's resignation, however, had little impact on the *Lega*'s anti-Muslim campaign. On the contrary. The party continued to promote itself as the defender of 'Europe's Christian roots' against the Islamic invasion.[47]

Under no circumstances, the *Lega* maintained, would Muslim immigrants be allowed, in the name of the 'Islamically correct', to undermine Italy's system of values, its Judeo-Christian heritage and its way of life. As an article in *La Padania* put it, 'Milan must remain Milan, not Milanistan! Turin must remain Turin, not Turinistan. Treviso must remain Treviso, not Trevisistan. Florence must remain Florence, not Florencistan!'[48] Immigrants seeking to settle permanently in Italy had better respect the cultural identity of the country, its Catholic traditions and Western values. As Andrea Gibelli, the president of the *Lega Nord*'s parliamentary delegation put it in a programmatic speech on Islam in Europe, there exists a 'culture of reference', and 'those who come here either refer to this culture or they don't come'.[49] Mario Borghezio, the leader of the *Lega Nord*'s representatives in the European Parliament, reaffirmed his party's position in an interview with the French far-right magazine *Le Choc du Mois*, a few months after the centre-right's narrow defeat in the 2006 parliamentary elections. Although denying that the *Lega Nord* as a movement was tied to any religious confession, he maintained that, nevertheless, his party had 'a strong commitment to the defense of the Catholic identity, particularly in view of the unimpeded Islamisation of our territory and of Europe', which had to be fought with all means, including 'the defence of our own religious identity'. This meant that the *Lega Nord* was above all a 'resistance organisation against the Muslim invasion', its members and activists 'political soldiers in the European tradition, defenders of our natural cultural identity'.[50]

Politically this was reflected in a number of anti-Islamic initiatives. Among other things, the *Lega Nord* introduced various motions to ban the burqa, at least in public. Not only did the burqa represent a 'form of oppressive integralism', it also made it difficult, if not impossible to recognise a person, which according to Italian law is illegal.[51] At the same time, the *Lega* continued its campaign against the construction of mosques and Muslim cultural centres, arguing that mosques, rather than being houses of prayer, more often than not were places 'where they make politics, where they ghettoize themselves, and where they think they can live according to their own rules (…) creating a state inside the state'.[52]

This was also the position of the **Swiss People's Party**, which in the course of its dramatic electoral gains in the late 1990s had established itself as a leading voice of nativism in Western Europe. In the process, the party increasingly focused on the question of Islam, warning, among other things, of the 'creeping introduction of the sharia' as well as the danger that if there was not a significant reversal in the country's naturalisation policy, Muslims would 'soon' constitute a majority in the country.[53] In early 2007, a few months before the national elections, leading representatives of the party launched a signature drive in support of a popular initiative designed to forbid the construction of minarets in the country. Characterising Islam as a 'declaration of war against the Christian world' and minarets as a symbol of Islam's 'imperialist' ambitions and the 'Islamisation of the country', the SVP adopted the nativist notion that Islam was not a religion, but an ideology fundamentally incompatible with the country's constitution, an ideology which, in the words of one SVP politician, sought 'to conquer the world'.[54] With this initiative the SVP meant to make clear, once and for all, that Switzerland was 'part of the Christian-occidental cultural community' whose values stood in sharp contrast to those propagated 'in the name of Allah'. At the same time it was meant to reaffirm the party's position – formulated by the leading SVP politician Hans Fehr a year earlier – that Switzerland would only be able to preserve its liberal values and its cultural heritage if 'people belonging to other cultural communities and religions remained a small minority in our country'.[55]

The Deviant Case of the Front National

A survey of radical right-wing nativism would be incomplete without a brief discussion of the paradoxical case of the *Front National*. The *Front National* was the first significant radical right-wing populist party to make the question of identity central to its political project.[56] It was also one of the first parties on the radical right to conjure up the spectre of Islam characterised as a religion incompatible with Europe's cultural traditions.[57] In early 2007, Bruno Gollnisch, in his capacity as chair of the newly created far-right group – **Identity, Tradition and Sovereignty** – in the European Parliament reiterated his party's position that it was of central importance to 'properly defend Christian values, the **family** and European civilisation'.[58] Unlike most other radical right-wing populist parties, however, during the most recent years, the *Front National* has guarded its tongue with respect to the question of Islam. To be sure, in the party's 2001 programme, *300 Mesures pour la Renaissance de la France*, the *Front National* devoted several paragraphs of the chapter on 'Freedom of Culture' to the potential threat emanating from the Muslim immigrant community residing in France. Among other things, the party asserted that Muslims by the very nature of their religion belonged to a 'community of believers' which considered itself superior to the rest of the world. As a result, Islam constituted a 'threat to our national sovereignty' by creating a 'system of double allegiance'. Under the circumstances, the only way to protect France against 'Islamisation' and its consequences was to severely curb immigration.[59]

Six years later, Islam had virtually disappeared from the FN's programme for Jean-Marie Le Pen's campaign for the presidential election. Le Pen himself, in an interview with the Catholic newspaper *La Croix*, repeated the party's traditional position that Islam only represented a threat when it became 'dominant'. The question of Islam was thus a 'demographic' problem, which could only be solved by preventing the further growth of the Muslim immigrant community in France. At the same time, however, Le Pen affirmed his support for the neutrality of the state *vis-à-vis* all religions, including Islam, even with respect to the question of the head scarf – a central issue for the nativist radical right. If Muslim women chose to wear it in public, it was their right, as long as they did not violate public rules.[60]

There are a number of reasons that explain the *Front National*'s comparatively moderate position on Islam. For one, Le Pen has been far less hostile toward Islam than radical right-wing populist leaders in Belgium, the Netherlands, Denmark and elsewhere in Western Europe. For the *Front National*, the main issue has remained immigration, not Islam. If Le Pen has maintained that in the Muslim world, Islam is generally 'totalitarian', he also seems to believe that it is possible to contain these tendencies in the West – as long as Muslims represent a relatively small minority of the population.[61] A second reason for the transformation of the *Front National*'s position on Islam is closely linked to organisational developments. Until the late 1990s, the party's discourse on Islam was largely shaped by two intra-party circles, Catholic traditionalists led by Bernard Antony and *nouvelle droite*-inspired 'racialists' led by Bruno Mégret. Many of its leading figures left the party in late 1998, joining Mégret's newly-founded *Mouvement National Républicain* (MNR), which quickly began to distinguish itself by its pronounced hostility toward Islam.[62] At the same time, some of the younger leaders in the *Front National* launched various initiatives to modernise the party's image and make it more presentable in an attempt to broaden the party's appeal. Thus, during the campaign for the presidential election in 2007, the *Front National* made a conscious effort to appeal to naturalised immigrants, including Muslims.[63] A few weeks before the election, it was no longer excluded that Le Pen might make inroads among North African voters (*les beurs*).[64] Sensitivity to France's North African community, many of whom were forced to flee **Algeria** at the end of France's colonial adventure in North Africa, is a final reason for the *Front National*'s ambiguous position on Islam. As the party's 2001 *300 Mesures pour la Renaissance de la France* put it, the *Front National* had 'always respected the religious practice of the former French Muslim fighters and of those who genuinely chose France, often risking their lives'. This also explains why the *Front National* has counted among its elected officials a small number of Maghrebi, such as Sid Ahmed Yahiaoui, son of a French-Muslim senator from Algeria assassinated by the FLN in 1962. One of them (Farid Smahi) was even elected to the party's *Bureau Politique* (provoking the resignation of several pro-Mégret members).

Identity Politics, Nativism and the Quest for Political Recognition

Contemporary radical right-wing populist parties have often been dismissed as cynical opportunists without vision and political project. This image is clearly false. As the analysis presented here suggests, during the past several years, the radical populist right has developed a coherent ideology, largely centered around the notion of identity. The result has been what Anniken Hagelund has called an increasing 'problematisation of culture', which has become central to the radical populist right's identitarian project throughout Western Europe.[65] Identitarian politics, by definition, always involves establishing opposites and constructing 'others' whose actuality, as Edward Said has pointed out, 'is always subject to the continuous interpretation and reinterpretation of the differences from us'.[66] Under the circumstances, it is hardly surprising that the radical right has made the question of Islam – both in terms of the presence of a substantial number of Muslim immigrants in Western Europe and of the challenge posed by Islam to Western Europe's highly secularised societies – its leading cause.

For the radical right, Islam is not only an alien religion; it is also an all-encompassing – and in this sense 'totalitarian' – ideology, which is not only fundamentally inimical to liberal democracy, Western Europe's secular values and its way of life, but which is inherently prone to use violent means to pursue its objectives. In other words, Islam is an extremist ideology. Søren Krarup of the *Dansk Folkeparti* expressed these sentiments most provocatively when, in April 2007, he characterised the head scarf worn by Muslim women as a 'totalitarian symbol' comparable to the symbols associated with Communism and Nazism, such as the swastika.[67] The message is clear: Muslim women wearing the head scarf in public demonstrate their cultural identification with a transnational Muslim identity (the *ummah*), which means a rejection of Western values, the unwillingness to assimilate and a disloyalty to the host country. For the radical right, it is particularly this transnational identity which makes

Islam and the Far Right

Muslims the enemy within, for, as the prominent SVP politician Christoph Mörgeli has put it, 'a religious Muslim is always also a political Muslim'. Those who follow the religious laws must invariably come into conflict with 'the Western rule of law, which places itself above the commandments of the Koran'.[68]

The parallels in rhetoric between contemporary right-wing populist Islamophobia and nineteenth-century American nativism are striking. American nativists opposed Catholicism not only because it was, at least in their view, fundamentally different from other religious denominations, but also because they believed that Catholic allegiance rested ultimately with Rome rather than the Constitution. Samuel Morse expressed it most poignantly in one of his anti-Catholic tracts when he wrote that the truth was that, 'Popery is a political as well as a religious system', which, in this respect, differed 'totally from all other sects, from all other forms of religion in the country'.[69] For the American nativists, as for the contemporary radical populist right, the practical political consequences were obvious. As the Know-Nothing Party put it in 1855: 'America for the Americans! (…) The politico-religious foe is fully discovered – he must be squarely met and put down. We want in this free land none of his political dictation'.[70]

If the contemporary radical right has managed to turn Islamophobia into a major political asset, it is largely because of the mistakes committed by the established parties in dealing with the question of Islam. For too long they adhered to the notion that 'liberal pluralism meant respecting the rights of communities rather than individuals' while at the same time, in the name of multiculturalism, leaving Western Europe's growing Muslim communities 'in isolated ghettos, which then became fertile grounds for the growth of a highly intolerant version of Islam'.[71] Under the circumstances, it was easy for the radical right to promote itself as the only force that dared to violate the conventions of political correctness and say out loud what the majority of the population thought.

Surveys, as far as they exist, suggest that, at least with regard to the question of Islam, the radical right has public opinion to a large extent on its side. Thus, in 2001, 40 percent of respondents in Denmark thought that Islam represented a serious threat to the country's culture. In 2003 in France, more than 60 percent of respondents agreed with the statement that Islamic values were incompatible with those of the French Republic. One year later in Germany, more than two-thirds of those surveyed thought that Islam was incompatible with the 'Western world'. Two-thirds associated Islam with 'backwardness'. And more than 60 percent agreed with the notion that there was a 'clash of cultures' between Islam and the Christian world. In the same year in Sweden, two-thirds of respondents felt that Islamic values were incompatible with the basic values of Swedish society; more than half objected to the statement that 'Swedish Muslims were just like other Swedes'. (A noteworthy exception was Switzerland. In 2004, more than 75 percent of those surveyed rejected the notion that Muslims living in Switzerland represented a threat to the country).[72] The results of British surveys suggest that there has been a worsening of sentiments toward Islam in recent years. In late 2001, a few weeks after September 11, only a third of British respondents agreed with the statement that 'Islam (as distinct from Islamic fundamentalist groups) poses a threat to Western liberal democracy'. Five years later, more than half of those surveyed agreed with the statement.[73]

Given the extent of anti-Islamic sentiments prevalent among a significant part of Western Europe's public opinion (and increasingly also in the media, Christian traditionalist circles, and among some intellectuals), the radical right's embrace of nativism in recent years represents a rational strategy not only to mobilise the 'silent majority', but also to gain political legitimacy as defenders of Western values, liberal democracy and cultural identity in general. At the same time, it also represents a political project that aims at the reaffirmation of European history, culture and values as equal, if not superior, to other cultures and values;[74] a project that is in direct opposition to the 'internationalist-global view', the multicultural 'experiments' and political correctness campaigns associated with the political establishment and the cultural elite. Islamophobia thus fits perfectly into the radical right's larger populist agenda, whose main objective has always been the restoration of ethno-national and ethno-cultural dominance.[75]

Hans-Georg Betz

Notes

1. 'Antwerpse joden achter Vlaams Blok,' *Hamishpacha*, 12 March 2003.
2. Haaretz, 'Between Haider and a hard place', 28 August 2005, http://www.haaretz.com/hasen/pages/ShArt.jhtml?itemNo=617761 (cited 27 February 2007).
3. Haaretz, 'Belgian far-rightist calls on Jews to join battle against Muslims', 8 October 2006, http://www.haaretz.com/hasen/objects/pages/PrintArticleEn.jhtml?itemNo=771558 (cited 27 February 2007).
4. Wildman, Sarah, 'Guess who's coming to seder. Dewinter's tale', The New Republic Online, posted 17 January 2007, http://www.tnr.com/doc.mhtml?i=20070122&s=wildman012207 (cited 27 February 2007).
5. Rogers M. Smith, 'The "American Creed" and American identity: the limits of liberal citizenship in the United States', *The Western Political Quarterly*, 41:2 (June 1988), 225–251.
6. Thomas J. Curran, 'Assimilation and nativism', *International Migration Digest*, 3:1 (1966), 15–25.
7. Michael W. Hughey, 'Americanism and its discontents: protestantism, nativism, and political heresy in America', *International Journal of Politics, Culture and Society*, 5:4 (1992), 42.
8. Robert William Gall, 'The past should not shackle the present: the revival of a legacy of religious bigotry by opponents of school choice', *New York University Annual Survey of American Law*, 59 (2003), 415–416. See also Ray Allen Billington, *The Protestant Crusade 1800–1860* (Chicago: Quadrangle Paperback, 1964).
9. John Higham, *Strangers in the Land: Patterns of American Nativism, 1860–1925* (New Brunswick, N.J: Rutgers University Press, 1955), 4.
10. The historian Hermann Eduard Von Holst, himself an immigrant from Germany, cited in Edward N Saveth, *American Historians and European Immigrants, 1875–1925* (New York: Columbia University Press, 1948), 156.
11. Samuel P. Huntington, 'The Hispanic Challenge', *Foreign Policy*, March/April 2004, available online at http://www.foreignpolicy.com/story/cms.php?story_id=2495&popup_delayed=1 (cited 1 March 2007). The opposite case is late-nineteenth-century French anti-Protestantism. At the time, protestants were characterised by their detractors as a fifth column in the services of Germany and Great Britain accused of plotting to 'conquer France' by subverting and destroying French identity. Protestantism, born of defiance and revolution, was deemed to undermine authority and destroy the established order and France's time-honoured (Catholic) traditions. See Steven C. Hause, 'Anti-protestant rhetoric in the early Third Republic', *French Historical Studies*, 16:1 (Spring 1989), 183–201; Jean Baubérot & Valentine Zuber, *Une Haine Oubliée. L'Antiprotestantisme avant le 'Pacte Laïque' (1870–1905)* (Paris: Albin Michel, 2000).
12. See Paul Starr, 'The return of the native', a review of Huntington's book *Who Are We? The Challenges to American Identity* in *The New Republic* (21 June 2004).
13. Thus Jean-Marie Le Pen, in response to charges that he was a racist, said during a speech in 1996 that in his view, races were 'neither equal nor unequal, but simply different' (speech at La Fête des Bleu-Blanc-Rouge, 29 September 1996. This position was reaffirmed by Pierre Vial, at the time the party's leading exponent of its most extremist 'identitarian' wing (he left the FN in 1999), in an interview with an American White Identity publication: 'We are often called "racist", but for the word to have any meaning, it must imply a hierarchy of races, or the domination of one race over another. That is not at all the position of the Front National. But we do recognise differences.

This does not mean hierarchy; only that each group has the right to pursue those differences.' 'The view From Lyon', *American Renaissance*, November 1998, available online at http://www.amren.com/9811issue/9811issue.html. A similar statement was made by Vlaams Blok spokesman Filip Dewinter during an interview with BBC: 'The Vlaams Blok isn't racist. We want to preserve our identity and our culture. After all, racism means a belief that on the basis of racial features a group of people is superior or inferior to another. This isn't what we believe; everyone is equal but not the same.' *Our Nationality*, 13 May 2000, transcript, available online at http://news.bbc.co.uk/hi/english/static/audio_video/programmes/correspondent/transcripts/746195.txt

14. Douglas R. Holmes, *Integral Europe: Fast-Capitalism, Multiculturalism, Neofascism* (Princeton: Princeton University Press, 2000), 7. Holmes refers here to Isaiah Berlin's analysis of the core ideas espoused by the German romantic philosopher Herder. But his remarks are equally valid for nativism. For a similar argument see Robert Antonio, 'After postmodernism: reactionary tribalism', *American Journal of Sociology*, 106:2 (2000), esp. 57–64.

15. Pierre-André Taguieff, 'The new cultural racism in France', *Telos*, 83 (Spring 1990). See also Alberto Spektorowski, 'The French New Right: differentialism and the idea of ethnophilian exclusionism', *Polity*, 33:2 (Winter 2000), 283–303.

16. Samuel Francis, 'The other face of multiculturalism', *Chronicles* (April 1998), available online at http://www.lrainc.com/swtaboo/taboos/sf_multc.html.

17. Walter Benn Michaels, *Our America: Nativism, Modernism and Pluralism* (Durham, N.C.: Duke University Press, 1995), 129.

18. Ibid., pp.14–15.

19. Hoang Gia Phan, '"A race so different": Chinese exclusion, the slaughterhouse cases, and Plessy v. Ferguson', *Labor History*, 45:2 (2004), 155.

20. Pat Buchanan, 'America in 2050: another country', 24 March 2004, available online at http://buchanan.org/blog/?p=588.

21. See Alan Wolfe's review of Huntington, 'Native son: Samuel Huntington defends the homeland', *Foreign Affairs* (May/June 2004), available online at http://www.foreignaffairs.org/20040501fareviewessay83311/alan-wolfe/native-son-samuel-huntington-defends-the-homeland.html (cited 3 April 2007).

22. F. Dewinter, *Baas in Eigen Land* (Brussel: Egmont, 2000), 14.

23. A prime example is Sweden's integration policy, guided by the notion of 'diversity'. This means that integration is 'no longer regarded as a unilateral process of incorporating immigrants into mainstream society but a process of mutual adjustment and adaptation of migrant minorities and mainstream ethnic Swedes' - Charles Westin, 'Sweden: restrictive immigration policy and multiculturalism', Migration Policy Institute, June 2006, available online at http://www.migrationinformation.org/Profiles/print.cfm?ID=406 (cited 3 April 2007).

24. Front National, *Les argumentaires: l'identité*, February 2000, available online at http://www.frontnational.com/argumentaires/identite.php (cited 3 April 2007).

25. Blok Vlaams, *Een Toekomst Voor Vlaanderen: Programma en Standpunten van het Vlaams Blok* (Brussel: Vlaams Blok, 2002), 19.

26. On the Front National's 'selective xenophobia', see Pierre-André Taguieff, *L'Illusion Populiste* (Paris: Berg, 2002), 143–144.

27. Front National, *Les argumentaires: l'identité*, February 2000, available online at http://www.frontnational.com/argumentaires/identite.php (cited 3 April 2007).

28. Bruno Megret, 'Contre la chimère de l'élargissement asiatique de l'Union', *Dossiers* (20 January 2005), available online at http://www.m-n-r.net/news408.htm (cited 3 April 2007).

29. Blok Vlaams, no.6, 1993, cited in Cas Mudde, *The Ideology of the Extreme Right* (Manchester: Manchester University Press, 2000), 103.

30. Dewinter quoted in Rink van den Brink, *L'Internationale de la Haine* (Paris: Luc Pire, 1996), 120.

31. See Tjitske Akkerman, 'Anti-immigrant parties and the defence of liberal values: the exceptional case of the List Pim Fortuyn', *Journal of Political Ideologies*, 10:2 (October 2005), 347.

32. Bernard Lewis, 'The roots of Muslim rage: why so many Muslims deeply resent the West, and why their bitterness will not be easily mollified', *The Atlantic* (September 1990), 47–60.

33. See Guillaume Faye, *La Colonization de l'Europe: Discours Vrai sur l'Immigration et l'Islam* (Paris: L'Æncre, 2000).

34. Le Jean-Yves Gallou, 'Le retour de l'histoire', speech, 8 December 2001, Paris; see also Philippe de Villiers, *Les Mosques de Roissy* (Paris : Albin Michel, 2006).

35. Jamie Glazov, 'Europe's Suicide?', FrontPageMagazine.com, April 2006 (cited 3 April 2007).

36. 'SOS Abendland: Strache warnt vor Werteverfall und Verlust der Freiheit', www.hcstrache.at (cited 3 April 2007); http://www.hcstrache.at/index.php?style=9&ID=373&PHPSESSID=53073eaf5d d2751104d281fbcf2f84d2 (cited 3 April 2007).

37. Freiheitlicher Parlamentsklub, Press release, 14 January 2007, available online at http://www. ots.at/presseaussendung.php?schluessel=OTS_20070114_OTS0017 (cited 3 April 2007).

38. Dansk Folkeparti. 2001. *Danmarks Fremtid: Dit Land – Dit Valg*. Dansk Folkeparti.

39. Mogens Camre, 'Islam kan ikke integreres', 20 December 2000, available online at http://www. df-dragoer.dk/sw/frontend/detail.asp?parent=6645&typeid=13&id=879&menu_parent=&layout=0 (cited 3 April 2007).

40. Søren Espersen quoted in Sasha Polakow-Suransky & Giuliana Chamedes, 'Europe's new crusade', American Prospect Online, 25 August 2002, http://www.prospect.org/web/page.ww?section =root&name=ViewPrint&articleId=6436 (cited 3 April 2007); Søren Krarup, speech in Sønderborg, 13 November 2001, cited in René Karpantschof, *Er Dansk Folkeparti Racistisk?*

41. *Danmarks Fremtid*, p.40.

42. See 'Islam verderflijk gedachtegoed', *De Volkskrant*, 31 October 2001; Groep Wilders, 'Onafhangkelijksheidsverklaring', 13 March 2005, p.12; 'Het heeft geen zin te investeren in een gematigde islam', NU.nl, 13 November 2006; Bruno Waterfield, 'Islam is taking over, says Dutch politician', *Daily Telegraph*, 2 March 2007; 'Geert Wilders: "Ik heb goede bedoelingen"', *De Pers*, 13 February 2007; Ari Paul, 'Mr. Backlash', *The American Prospect*, 26 March 2007.

43. F. Dewinter, 'Het groene totalitarisme: de kolonisatie van Europa!', Antwerp, 20 November 2002.

44. Angus Roxburgh, 'Blow to Belgium's far right', BBC News, 9 November 2004.

45. See Gianluca Savoini, 'Lega baluardo contro l'invasione islamica', *La Padania*, 26 June 2002; 'Crocifissi control l'Islam: la Lega li vuole dovunque', *La Repubblica*, 18 September 2002.

46. Roberto Calderoli, 'Ho detto basta alle strumentalizzazioni', *La Padania*, 19 February 2006; Emanuela Fontana, 'In Arabia paragonano i leghisti ai terroristi', *Il Giornale*, 22 September 2005.

47. Renzo Guolo, 'L'uso politico dell'odio', *La Repubblica*, 21 February 2006.

48. 'Siamo vittime dell'islamically correct', *La Padania*, 19 February 2006.

49. Andrea Gibelli, 'Islam, terrorismo e sicurezza', Scuola Politica Federale, Bellaria Igea Marina, 5–6 November 2005. For the Lega, the main pillars of this 'reference culture' are, Gibelli explained, the separation between the secular and the religious realms, democracy, and human rights.

50. 'Entretien avec Mario Borghezio', *Le Choc du Mois* (November 2006), 20–21; see also Edouard Ballaman, *Piccola Guida alla Cultura Islamica* (Lega Nord Federazione Padana, 2005); and also Maurizio Parma, Mauro Manfredini & Roberto Corradi, *Islam e Immigrazione: I Numeri di un'Invasione* (Bologna: Gruppo Consiliare Lega Nord Padania Emilia e Romagna, 2006).

51. Lega Nord, 'Commune di Drezzo (Co): ordinanza generale in material di pubblica sicurezza', Milan, Secretaria Politica Federale, 17 July 2004.

52. Andrea Gibelli, 'Islam, terrorismo e sicurezza', Scuola Politica Federale, Bellaria Igea Marina, 2005, 4.

53. Christoph Mörgeli, 'Auswüchse einer falschen Einwanderungspolitik', SVP Pressedienst, no.49, 6 December 2004, available online at http://www.svp.ch/index.html?page_id=1359&l=2 (cited 3 April 2007). On the question of Islamophobia in Switzerland see Damir Skenderovic, 'Feindbild Muslime – Islamophobie in der radikalen rechten' in Urs Altermatt, Mariano Delgado & Guido Vergauwen (eds.), *Islam in Europa. Zwischen Weltpolitik und Alltag* (Stuttgart: Verlag W. Kohlhammer, 2006), 79–95.

54. Sylvie Arsever, 'L'islam dans le collimateur', *Le Temps*, 4 May 2007; Jürg Sohm & Patrick Feuz, 'Im wahljahr gegen minarette', and interview with Jasmin Hutter, St. Galler Tagblatt, 4 May 2007.

55. 'Das ringen der parteien um "Muslim-Papiere"', 27 February 2006, available online at http://www.svp.ch/index.html?page_id=2205&l=2 (cited 3 April 2007).

56. See Jens Rydgren, *The Populist Challenge: Political Protest and Ethno-Nationalist Mobilization in France* (New York: Berghahn, 2004), 131–156; Pierre-André Taguieff, 'Biopolitique de l'identité', *Raison Présente* (July 1998), 37–63. The party states in its 2001 programme: 'Le refus de la société multiculturelle, au nom de l'identité de la France, est le combat fondamental du Front National'.

57. See 'Islam: "Une religion incompatible avec nos traditions culturelles"' in Pierre-André Taguieff (ed.), *Face au Racisme, Vol. 1: Les Moyens d'Agir* (Paris: Editions La Decouverte, 1991), 189–214.

58. Gollnisch quoted in Bruno Waterfield, 'New far-right group launches its mission to defend European identity', www.telegraph.co.uk, 17 January 2007 (cited 20 January 2007).

59. Front National, *300 mesures pour la renaissance de la France*, available online at http://www. frontnational.com/doc_liberte_culture.php (cited 20 January 2007).

60. 'Jean-Marie Le Pen, candidat du Front national: "L'État n'a pas à encourager ni à combattre les religions"', *La Croix*, 2 February 2007.

61. See 'Entretien avec Chiheb Nasser', *Le Choc de Mois* (March 2007), 21.

62. See the discussion on 'islam' in Erwan Lecœur (ed.), *Dictionaire de l'Extrême Droite* (Paris: Larousse, 2007), 183–186.

63. See Jean-Marie Le Pen's famous speech delivered at Valmy on 20 September 2006, during which he invited all French people, including those 'French of foreign origins', to join him in his quest for the presidency.

64. Akram Belkaïd, 'Ces beurs qui vont voter Le Pen', *Le Quotidien d'Oran*, 12 April 2007; François Bousquet, 'Moi, Maghrébin, électeur de Le Pen', *Le Choc du Mois* (Mars 2007), 19–20.

65. Anniken Hagelund, 'The Progress Party and the problem of culture: immigration politics and right wing populism in Norway' in Jens Rydgren (ed.), *Movements of Exclusion* (New York: Nova Science Publishers, 2005), 153.

66. Edward Said, *Orientalism* (New York: Vintage, 1979), 332.

67. Morten Henriksen, 'Pia K. enig i hagekors-udtalelser', *Berlingske Tidende*, 17 April 2007.

68. Christoph Mörgeli, 'Auswüchse einer falschen Einbürgerungspolitik', *SVP Pressedienst*, 49 (6 December 2004), 4–5.

69. Cited in Terry Golway, 'Return of the know-nothings', *America*, 29 March 2004, available online at https://www.americamagazine.org/gettext.cfm?articleTypeID=7&textID=3508&issueID=479 (cited 20 January 2007).

70. Cited in Richard C. Sinopoli & Teena Gabrielson, 'Mirroring modernity: America's conflicting identities', *Polity*, 32:1 (Autumn 1999).

71. Francis Fukuyama, 'Europe vs. Radical Islam', slate.com, posted 27 February 2006.

72. Mette Tobiasen, 'Danskernes verden var den same efter 11. September: terror, islam og global solidaritet' in Jørgen Goul Andersen & Ole Borre (eds.), *Politisk Forandering* (Aarhus: Systime, 2003), 351; Ipsos-LCI-Le Point survey, cited in *Le Point*, 16 May 2003, p.39; Wilhelm Heitmeyer, 'Die gespaltene Gesellschaft', *Die Zeit*, 2 December 2004; Elisabeth Noelle, 'Der kampf der kulturen', *Frankfurter Allgemeine Zeitung*, 15 September 2004; Göran Larsson, '"Muslims" in Swedish media and academia', *Isim Review* (Autumn 2006), 36; Iso Public survey, November 2004, results published in Blick Online, 28 November 2004.

73. *The Observer*/YouGov poll, November 2006, results published in *The Observer*, 4 November 2001; Johnston, Philip, 'Islam poses a threat to the West, say 53pc in poll', *Daily Telegraph*, 25 August 2006.

74. As Geert Wilders has put it, 'Why aren't we allowed to say that Muslims should conform to us given the fact that our norms and values are on a higher, better, and more humane level? No integration. Assimilation!' Cited in 'VVD'er Wilders halt uit naar college-Kamerleden', *De Telegraaf*, 4 February 2004.

75. See Hans-Georg Betz & Carol Johnson, 'Against the current – stemming the tide: the nostalgic ideology of the contemporary radical populist right', *Journal of Political Ideologies*, 9:3 (2004), 320–324.

Central Europe and the Far Right

On 20 October 2003, under the headline 'Swiss right in political avalanche', the BBC reported: 'The far-right **Swiss People's Party** (SVP) has won the biggest share of the vote in parliamentary elections, throwing a decades-old system of consensus government into turmoil. The party won 11 extra seats in the lower house of parliament, taking its total in the 200-member parliament to 55. It took nearly 27 percent of the vote. The party, once the smallest of four governing parties in the Swiss coalition, is now the largest. Flamboyant party figurehead leader Christoph **Blocher** has been put forward to take a second seat for the party on the seven-member cabinet'.[1] This is an unusual but pertinent point on which to begin this survey of the Far Right in Central Europe.

Austria and Germany might seem more obvious starting-points. The **Freedom Party** has gained significant electoral success in Austria in recent decades and is now a key player on the political stage. Between 1990 and 1999 its share of the vote ranged from 16.6 percent to 26.9 percent, and in 2000 and 2003 the Freedom Party joined Austria's governing coalition. Since then, however, decline seems to have set in. Poll ratings have been less impressive and the movement's flamboyant former leader, Jörg **Haider**, has moved on and founded another political party, the **Alliance for Austria's Future**.[2] Likewise, since 1945 Germany has had a strong tradition of far-right movements, many of whom have tried to ape and mimic Hitler's Nazi party. In recent times, the DVU and the *Republikaner Party* have become prominent. This section will consider the nature of the Far Right in the three countries. It will also offer some general observations about the configuration of the Far Right in Central Europe.

Switzerland: The Rise of the SVP

On the face of things, Switzerland is hardly fertile territory for the Far Right. In the inter-war period, its tradition of 'neutrality' seemed to immunise it from the growth of Fascism – impressive given the geographical proximity of both Italy and Germany. This is the theme of Stephen P. Halbrook's book, *The Swiss & The Nazis: How the Alpine Republic Survived in the Shadow of the Third Reich*. Halbrook tells the story of all those Swiss who helped to defend the integrity of the country against the threat of German domination and totalitarianism. Other themes also emerge: the help that Switzerland gave to wartime refugees; the Americans' reliance on Swiss intelligence; and also the hostility of many Swiss to representatives of the Hitler regime (hence the phrase 'Nazi Pigs').[3]

Between 1945 and 2003 Switzerland managed to escape extremism in all its forms, including right-wing extremism. Two authoritative country-by-country surveys of the European Far Right, broadcast in 1992 and 2000, simply ignored the country.[4] If the country had been tainted by Fascism it was in a totally different way. In the 1990s, stories started to emerge about the country's 'hidden' Nazi links. On 21 August 1998, the BBC reported:

SWISS BANKS DODGE SANCTIONS IN HOLOCAUST DEAL
JEWISH GOLD: STOLEN BY THE NAZIS, STASHED IN SWISS BANK VAULTS

Swiss banks have agreed to compensate Jewish victims of the Nazi Holocaust – narrowly avoiding sanctions from some US states. Three of the country's leading banks struck a deal with representatives of **Holocaust** survivors whose stolen money and assets ended up in Switzerland's vaults during World War II. The deal with the World Jewish Congress will lead to a major programme of compensation as the banks finally hand over secret records of war-time accounts. The agreement came as some US states prepared to bring sanctions against the Union Bank of Switzerland, the Swiss Bank Corporation and Credit Swisse in an effort to force them to pay up.[5]

At the same time, new books were being published such as *Nazi Gold* by Tom Bower.[6] This volume was subtitled: 'The Full Story of the Fifty-Year Swiss-Nazi Conspiracy to Steal Billions from Europe's Jews and Holocaust Survivors'.

But then came Blocher. The emergence of the SVP as an authentic and electorally successful far-right movement in 2003 was an enormous surprise – and shock – for ordinary Swiss people. It was not that they were smug or blasé about the country's political future, but rather that they felt Switzerland had an excellent track record when it came to combating, or at least minimising, any sign of right-wing extremism. The key to this success was the 'magic formula', whereby, in the post-war years, the four main political groupings shared out the seven seats on the Federal Council – the cabinet-style ruling committee chosen by parliament. The parties in question were the left-wing Social Democrats, the social-conservative Christian Democrats, the middle-class Radicals and the People's Party.

The People's Party underwent a major transformation during the 1990s. It had been founded in 1971 as a result of the amalgamation of the Farmers, Artisans and Citizens' Party and the Democratic Party. During the 1970s and 1980s it spoke for the country's farming community and espoused an inoffensive brand of centrism; at election time it regularly claimed between 10 percent and 15 percent of the national vote. In the 1990s the movement changed course. It began to champion a radical manifesto based around national-populism and neo-liberalism, and articulated its opposition to **immigration** and the EU. In the 2003 poll the People's Party not only claimed two cabinet seats rather than the usual one, but also grasped the opportunity to put forward its new extremist agenda. In 2007 it tightened its grip on power, winning 29 percent of the popular vote, gaining 6 extra seats of parliamentary representation and maintaining its influence at cabinet level.[7]

Explaining the political earthquake that struck Switzerland in 2003 is no easy task. Blocher is a charismatic political operator and has been likened to other far-right leaders, such as Haider in Austria and **Le Pen** in France. As *The Guardian* put it: 'Although it does attract extreme right support, the SVP is best described as hard right. The party takes a strongly anti-immigrant line, but its populist leader, Christoph Blocher, insists he is not racist'.[8] The SVP was also well known and had a respectable history. Blocher himself was a former industrialist and veteran political campaigner who had always been interested in Swiss history and his country's place in the world. In 2003 – the 'breakthrough' year – the key factor appears to have been immigration and race. The Swissinfo news service stated that 'international observers' were taking a keen interest in 'Blocher's stance on the issue of race and his repeated attacks on those immigrants and asylum seekers who "abuse" the system'.[9]

In recent times, the SVP has made a great play of its opposition to mosques. Here the key individual has been Ulrich Schlüer MP. He has been quoted as saying: 'Unlike other religions, Islam is not only a **religion**. It's an ideology aiming to create a different legal system. That's sharia. That's a big problem and in a proper **democracy** it has to be tackled. If the politicians don't, the people will. We've got nothing against prayer rooms or mosques for the Muslims. But a minaret is different. It's got nothing to do with religion. It's a symbol of political power'.[10] The call has been for a referendum on the issue, with Schlüer and his colleagues arguing that ordinary people have a right to decide on such matters.

In 2007 the party caused further controversy by proposing a 'Federal Popular Initiative for the Deportation of Criminal Foreigners'. The advert it used to publicise the policy featured a cartoon of three white sheep grazing against the backdrop of a red and white Swiss flag, with a lone black sheep being ejected from the area reserved for the white ones. The accompanying text read, 'Bringing safety'. The ad seemed to cross the line of decency, and Blocher and his movement stood accused of promoting a policy that had more in common with Nazi Germany than anything else. In 2003 the BBC had also given prominence to the 'race' angle, reporting that, 'The party ran an anti-foreigner campaign, in which asylum seekers were portrayed as criminals and drug dealers. But the campaign seems to have found favour with more voters than it offended'.[11]

Commentators could not ignore the issues of asylum and immigration, but there were other themes, too, like the SVP's aversion to the EU and the economic backdrop to the party's advances. Jack Ewing in *Business Week* put the spotlight on financial matters: 'To the outside world, Switzerland may look as cosy and prosperous as ever, with just 3.8% employment and some of the lowest taxes of any industrialised nation. But morale has been dented by the collapse of national icons such as flag carrier Swissair, which went bankrupt in 2001, and massive layoffs in the all-important banking industry'.[12] Meanwhile, Elizabeth Olson in the *International Herald Tribune* focused on political culture in Central Europe:

> Outwardly, Switzerland's embrace of fervent nationalism in last weekend's elections was about refugees and the country's place in Europe, but it was also very much about Swiss identity shaped by the recent furore over its less-than-glorious role in World War II and its uncertainty over what path to take in the future. After four decades of national consensus, the gains made by Switzerland's most rightist party in the parliamentary elections have dramatically upset governing traditions and thrown the political landscape into chaos. Its tilt to the right placed the Alpine republic firmly in the conservative camp established by neighbouring Austria, which recently gave its far-right party a resounding electoral victory.[13]

Mention of Austria muddied the waters somewhat. There were no doubt some general European and Central European patterns at play, but also some country-specific factors. Blocher and the SVP emerged unexpectedly in 2003 but the country's past wasn't as untainted as some might have assumed.

Austria: Haider and the Freedom Party

Austria has a far stronger tradition of far-right politics. Hitler was born in Braunau, Upper Austria, and it was natural for him to want to unite Germany with Austria in the *Anschluss* of 1938. After World War II, the Austrian authorities, like their German counterparts, did everything in their power to discourage the growth of far-right movements. But as in Switzerland it was a 'moderate' right-wing party that eventually flowered into an 'extremist' one.

Before the rise to influence of Jörg Haider and the Freedom Party (FPÖ), Austria was home to a constellation of small extreme-right movements. One official document published in 1979 detailed around 50 far-right movements active in the country.[14]

By then, though, some parties had come and gone. The League of Independents (VdU) emerged in the late 1940s and claimed 12 percent of the votes, and 16 seats, in the National Council elections of 1949. It was founded and led by Dr Herbert Kraus and Dr Viktor Reimann and lasted until 1955. During its short life it became a 'gathering of the discontented around particular local figures'.[15] It recruited particularly well among ex-Nazi officials who – in the light of legislation passed in 1948 – were now free to become involved in politics again.[16] Commentators are generally agreed that the VdU became the natural repository of the 'German nationalist vote'. The rise of the party was also quite useful for the Austrian left as it had the effect of 'splitting' the right. Strangely perhaps, the emergence of Kraus – the dominant personality at the top of the party – was quietly welcomed by American diplomats in Vienna. According to Max Riedlsperger: 'This perception of a split was fundamentally accurate and anticipated the subsequent history of the VdU. Clearly, Kraus was the kind of leader the American Legation wanted to promote, describing him as ... one of the most interesting and important personalities in the province and in all of Austria today. Undoubtedly, his popular following consists to a large extent of former Nazis, but it would be wrong for that reason to accuse Kraus of sympathizing with Nazism'.[17]

But prior to the Haider-FPÖ breakthrough, another party of the extreme right – in fact an 'explicitly neo-Nazi'[18] one – made its presence felt. The *Nationaldemokratische Partei* (NDP) was formed in 1966 by Norbert Burger and a group of fellow ex-members of the infant FPÖ. Although Burger scored a respectable 3.2 percent in the 1980 presidential elections, he and his party were generally viewed as being beyond the pale. Earlier in his life he had been found guilty by an Italian court of terrorist offences in South Tyrol; and in 1988 his NDP movement was prohibited on account of its openly neo-Nazi standpoint.

It has to be said, though, that the 1960s through to the 1980s was not the most fertile or conducive period for those on the Austrian Far Right. The authorities were still suspicious of extreme-right activity (even though some of the key pieces of anti-Nazi legislation had been repealed), the left was in the ascendant, and 'effective enlightenment programmes (... on Austrian identity, democratic traditions) [were being] carried out in secondary schools and universities'.[19] Another movement in the same boat as the NDP was the *Ring Freiheitlicher Studenten* (RFS), a student organisation. It came to national prominence in 1953 when it won a 33.4 percent share of the vote in the Austrian Students' Union elections. But, 'at the beginning of the 1980s neo-Nazi student groups never attained more than 1 percent of the student vote and went through a period of stagnation and defeat'. By 1987 the RFS was scoring only 2 percent of the student vote, and in 1995 it was 4 percent.[20]

The plot, however, is thickened by the story of Kurt **Waldheim**, Austrian diplomat and politician. Waldheim served as secretary-general of the United Nations between 1972 and 1981, and then as president of Austria between 1986 and 1992. He attracted worldwide controversy in 1985 – while he was running for the presidency – by purposefully underplaying his role as a Wehrmacht intelligence officer during World War II.

Waldheim was an individual with skeletons in his cupboard. This was very different from belonging to an organised party or movement, but still it hinted at a national political culture that was connected implicitly to the Nazis and the Nazi era. The same could also be said of Haider and the FPÖ.

The history of far-right politics in Austria is complicated, but at the same time brought into sharper focus, by the story of the Freedom Party. This movement was founded in 1956. In general terms it would be true to say that there have been three main phases in its history. In its early days it saw itself as the successor movement to the VdU: it was fundamentally nationalist – albeit with liberal strains – and its membership comprised many ex-Nazis. In 1980 the profile of the party changed and under Norbert Steger's leadership it began to stress its essential liberalism. As if to emphasise its new 'moderate' image, the FPÖ entered a coalition government in 1983 with the Social Democrats. This 'liberal interlude' didn't last long. By 1986 Jörg Haider had taken over the leadership of the party and in 1993 two significant events occurred: the movement split from the Liberal International and the few remaining *bona fide* liberals in the party resigned to form a new political grouping, the Liberal Forum. Thereafter, the FPÖ reverted to type and, in and out of government, exhibited classic far-right tendencies in terms of its anti-immigrant and anti-Semitic discourse.

Probably the defining feature of the FPÖ is its experience of coalition government at a national level. As Morrow puts it: 'By 1966, it was clear that the larger parties were interested in the FPÖ only in as far as it was useful in winning advantage over their main opponents'.[21] In 1970 and 1971 it agreed to support Bruno Kreisky's minority government and in 1983 the FPÖ joined with the social-democratic SPÖ under Fred Sinowatz. This liaison lasted for three years and was ultimately undone by the FPÖ's lurch to the right in 1986. But for all serious far-right-watchers, 2000 was the landmark date – when, after scoring 27 percent in parliamentary elections, Haider's party was invited into coalition government with Wolfgang Schüssel's ÖVP. The FPÖ was only a junior partner, but even so its emergence in government provoked a storm of outrage, both within Austria and across the world. For a brief period, the EU decided to boycott the Austrian government – this meant purposefully not shaking hands with government ministers, minimising communication and cooperation, and also instituting minor sanctions in the sphere of diplomacy.[22] In February 2000 Haider resigned as leader of the Freedom Party, mainly, it would seem, to try and quell the torrent of international criticism. Leadership of the party passed to Susanne Reiss-Passer – widely regarded as the 'acceptable face' of the movement'[23] – but it was assumed that Haider was still the 'power behind the throne' and, as if to emphasise this, he retained the governorship of **Carinthia**, his political powerbase. After more elections, the coalition government of the People's Party and the Freedom Party was renewed in February 2003.

This overview of the development of the Austrian Far Right raises a number of questions. First, a neutral observer would surely ask: How could a country so aware of its Nazi past elect Waldheim as president and then, decades on, embrace a political current with so many links to that dark period? After a period of making friendly and positive noises about the Nazi era – he described Hitler's employment policies as sound and used the phrase 'penal camp' to describe a concentration camp[24] – Haider has reined in slightly. But this does not alter the fact that, half a century on from the Nazi era, **Europe** witnessed the spectacle of a charming, popular politician exalting the Hitler regime. We also know that the first two leaders of the FPÖ were former SS officers. How could this be so? According to Morrow, the answer is simple: 'Since its foundation in 1955, the FPÖ has always served as a political vehicle for integrating former Nazis. Technically, this was meant to allow those with unsavoury past connections to enter into mainstream post-war politics, avoiding the creation of a permanent and large anti-democratic opposition'.[25] There seemed to be an assumption that the country's 'Nazi past' would not simply disappear. It was a 'constant' and an intrinsic component of modern Austrian political culture. It would actually need managing and controlling and, seemingly, the FPÖ made itself available as the natural repository. Against this backdrop, it is slightly easier perhaps to understand how an individual with some pro-Nazi views (Haider) and a political party with anti-immigrant and anti-Semitic instincts (the FPÖ) has been able to effect influence. Of course, Austria is a modern, democratic and wealthy country, and of course in an ideal world it should be able to immunise itself from the Far Right, but this perhaps is to underestimate the power of the Nazi legacy. But there are positive indicators. In 2006 a court in Vienna found British historian David **Irving** guilty of denying the Holocaust and sentenced him to three years in prison. Maybe this verdict should be viewed by the outside world as a statement of intent.

Second: What explains the liberal/illiberal dichotomy at the heart of the party? The issue of the FPÖ is complicated by the fact that sitting side by side with the authoritarian, pro-Nazi, far-rightist discourse is a discernible liberal strand. As we have already noted, the FPÖ has had its 'liberal' phases. In the early days and into the 1980s, the party advanced what was, in part at least, a traditional liberal agenda. Then, opposition to immigrants and other minorities took over and the policy platform started to look distinctly illiberal. But Haider is no old-fashioned bully boy. He is actually the incarnation of the 'yuppie fascist' – suave, smooth-talking and thoroughly modern in outlook.[26] But still, ever since the FPÖ exited the Liberal International and the *bona fide* liberals haemorrhaged from the movement it has become increasingly obvious that the Freedom Party is ironically named. Morrow's feeling is that, even back in the 1980s, the 'liberal presentation of the party programme ... looked like a veneer which hid an authoritarian core'.[27]

Finally, and perhaps most importantly: How do we explain the rise of the FPÖ into government? As we noted, the party claimed 27 percent of the vote in the parliamentary elections of 2000 and this was enough to catapult it into the governing coalition. Recriminations – and sanctions – followed, but for academic and media commentators the question was how and why. Many theories have been advanced to explain the FPÖ's rise to power: Haider's authoritarian, pro-Nazi rhetoric has touched a significant nerve in the Austrian body politic; the legacy of Kurt Waldheim's candidacy in the 1986 presidential election (which opened up the debate about Austria's wartime past); the increasingly multi-cultural nature of Austrian society; Haider as a man – he has come across as a charming and savvy modern-day politician; and the mixture of responses which greeted his initial breakthrough – from complacency to panic.

Just like Le Pen in France, Haider has portrayed his political career as a crusade. He is fighting for 'ordinary Austrians' and trying to improve their 'everyday life'. Hence his interest in the immigration issue. As *The Guardian* put it: 'Haider loves the political show and is a master of political effect. Haider and his Freedom party waxed as the main parties waned. He drew his support both from those who felt excluded by the old system, and those who did benefit, but felt those benefits threatened. Increasingly he got the young, who were impatient at waiting in the queue for advancement, particularly as the queue seemed to be breaking down'.[28] He is helped by his own character and personality: 'Haider also is (in purely descriptive terms) a rhetorically brilliant politician and exceptionally effective with the media. Austrian journalists, who have been sparring with Haider in the media ring for the past ten years, have taken considerably more punches than they have landed'.[29]

In 2005 Haider split from the FPÖ and founded a new political movement, the Alliance for the Future of Austria (BZÖ). The BZÖ described itself as 'unideological'; in reality, it stayed loyal to core FPÖ ideas such as opposition to immigration and the EU but also upped the ante on issues such as ecology, economic liberalism and direct democracy. In the nationwide elections of 2006 the rump FPÖ took 11 percent of the vote and the BZÖ, 4 percent.

Germany: The Legacy of Hitler

It is arguably no surprise that Germany has a strong and powerful far-right tradition. The rise of Hitler and the Nazi regime was an inspiration to many on the Far Right after 1945. Somehow these activists had to promote their ideas and methods in the new West Germany, while at the same time avoiding the glare of hastily erected – and stringent – anti-fascist legislation. Fast forward to today and it seems that the Far Right is visible and fragmented, legal and illegal. And needless to say, it has been buoyed by the fall of the **Berlin Wall** and the instabilities that have afflicted Europe since 1989. In 2000, the BBC identified a new wave of political activity in Germany:

> The election of the controversial right-wing former judge Ronald Schill as Hamburg's interior minister has prompted fears that a new generation of far-right politicians with strong views on crime and immigration may be poised to emerge. Germany's Christian Democrat party has also recently flirted with far-right policies. It sparked controversy with an anti-immigration advertising campaign which urged people to put *'kinder statt Inder'* (children before Indians) … Germany has strict laws against any rehabilitation of its Nazi past, and many Germans feel a heavy moral responsibility not to allow nationalist politics to return.[30]

And according to *The Guardian*, the post-war German Far Right has become intertwined with **youth** culture, 'with plenty of unpleasant rallies by disaffected and racist youths from both the east and west of the country. However, none of Germany's three minor far-right parties has made headway at national level. In the 1998 parliamentary elections, the REP and DVU mustered just 1.8% and 1.2% respectively – way off the 5% hurdle over which votes can translate into seats under Germany's dual PR/first past the post electoral system'.[31]

The consensus among academic commentators is that there have been three waves of far-right activity in Germany since 1945. The first, covering the late 1940s and early 1950s, involved neo-Nazi parties such as the German Reichs Party (DRP) and Socialist Reichs Party (SRP). The second, in the 1960s and 1970s, revolved mainly around the National Democratic Party (NPD), which was fiercely anti-immigrant and advocated a revolutionary brand of 'Third Way' politics. And the third, from the 1980s onwards, has centred on the **Republican Party** and the DVU. It is argued that these two parties are crypto-fascist in nature – on the surface they have committed themselves to the democratic process, but they have also inspired street-level **violence**.[32]

This kaleidoscope of far-right activity is both easy and difficult to explain. As with the Austrian case, but probably to an even greater degree, Germany cannot deny its Nazi heritage. The end of Hitler did not mean that national-socialist ideas and instincts were eradicated or simply became invisible. They lived on and re-emerged swiftly in the late 1940s and after. Whatever his notoriety and infamy, Hitler also became an idol for some Germans. After 1945 it became a *cause célèbre* to reclaim his legacy and emphasise his 'noble' and 'legitimate' objectives while in power. Groups and individuals on the Far Right saw it as a challenge to defy the post-war legislation that aimed at full-scale denazification. In fact, after 1945 both the Allies and the Americans predicted 'substantial right-wing opposition' in the country.[33]

Later, in the 1990s the newly reunified Germany metamorphosed into a modern, multi-cultural and cosmopolitan country. It welcomed hundreds of thousands of immigrants and asylum-seekers, mainly from Turkey, Africa and Asia.[34] In this new environment it was easy for far-right political movements to turn on 'foreigners' and blame them for whatever social, economic and political woes Germany was suffering from at the time. So, of course, the increase in far-right political activity was easy to explain and rationalise. But in another sense, it was extremely difficult to fathom how and why pro-Nazi ideas could gain a foothold in a country that had suffered so horrendously under Hitler. Had Germany not learned anything from the rise and fall of the Third Reich? And why was the post-war anti-Nazi legislation so weak and ineffectual?

Surveying more than sixty years of post-war German history, there are key points to make about far-right activity. First, it is clear that there has never been *one* Far Right. There has been a multitude of short-lived organisations, each with their own leader and constituency. Two statistics will suffice to emphasise the point. In 1984 the *Bundesamt für Verfassungsschutz* (BfV) – the state body charged with monitoring political extremism – calculated that there were thirty-four 'militant neo-Nazi groups' active in Germany.[35] Obviously, this figure would rise even further if far-right movements of all persuasions were counted. We are also told that in 1988 there were seventy-three different far-right publications on the market.[36] Again this may underestimate reality. Nevertheless, these are significant statistics that point to a Far Right that is both eclectic and fragmented. At the same time we also witness intra-party disputes. Franz **Schönhuber**, leader of the *Republikaner party,* was deposed as party leader in 1990, reinstated, and then sacked again in 1994. The first time around it was relations with the neo-Nazi NPD that seemed to be the key issue; the second time, a possible coalition with the anti-immigrant DVU. It appears also that German neo-Nazism has split into Strasserite and non-Strasserite factions eg. one faction that believes in the masses and a revolutionary brand of Fascism (in effect, followers of Nazis Gregor and Otto Strasser) and one that does not.[37]

Second, 'Far Right' should only be used as a shorthand term. Likewise, 'right extremism', the term preferred by Eva Kolinsky.[38] Both phrases can be used to describe the constellation of groups that have emerged since 1945, but they conceal a slightly more complex reality. No two academics classify these groups in exactly the same manner, but if we were to summarise it could be said that three types of movement have existed since 1945:

> Ultra-right-wing – these started to emerge immediately after the war; movements such as the German Reichs Party and the Socialist Reichs Party.
> Militant neo-Nazi – preponderant from the late 1970s onwards; between 1977 and 1988 there were, on average, twenty-three such groups existing at any one time.[39]

> Populist/**protest** – as incarnated by the *Republikaner party* from the mid-1980s.[40]

And needless to say, different experts on the Far Right would draw different boundaries between the different sub-families.

Third, a distinction should be made between political parties and other groups. Many far-right movements have joined the democratic fray but other groupings have been content to operate outside electoral politics. Statistics used by Childs reveal that in 1987 there were a total of 1,447 infringements of the law (from arson attacks to daubing graffiti) by right-wing extremists. We are also told that 143 charges were made in the same year.[41]

An individual who embodied this illegal brand of political activity was Michael Kühnen. A militant neo-Nazi activist, he was involved in a variety of post-war German groups including *Aktionsfront Nationale Sozialisten* (founded by Kühnen in 1977 and banned two years later), ANS/NA and 'The Movement'. Throughout his political career he displayed intense admiration for Hitler and always dreamed of formally reconstituting the Nazi Party. His ideology was consistently hardline: elitist, anti-Semitic, anti-communist and anti-capitalist. He was heavily influenced by Nietzsche and said that he was committed to political violence – hence his regular prison sentences.

Kühnen died from AIDS in 1991, but the cause he stood for was taken on by others. Throughout the last few decades, German neo-Nazis have been constantly in the news, engaging in violent tactics and making provocative public gestures. In August 2000, the BBC reported that Germany was clamping down on the Far Right after a series of attacks: 'A recent bomb attack in the city of Duesseldorf wounded ten immigrants, most of them Jewish. At the weekend, police arrested more than 100 far-right extremists, and the government has vowed to do more. German politicians, though, are divided on how to prevent the growth of the right wing, especially in eastern Germany, which has become a hotbed for neo-Nazi attacks'.[42] Six years later a report with a similar tone appeared:

> The Israeli ambassador to Germany has said he is concerned for Jews in Germany, against the background of what he says is rising **anti-Semitism** there. In a newspaper interview, Shimon Stein said the number of neo-Nazis in Germany had also increased. The interview appeared as neo-Nazi sympathisers gathered outside Berlin's Tegel Prison to demand the release of a singer jailed for three years. A court ruled that Michael Regener's band was spreading racial hatred. Mr Stein told the *Neue Osnabruecker Zeitung* he believed there was a greater willingness on behalf of neo-Nazis to use violence. 'I have the feeling that Jews in Germany do not feel safe. They are not always able to practise their religion freely,' he said. He said tightened security had been put in place around synagogues and other institutions.[43]

Both reports hint at the major problem that has faced, and is still facing, the authorities, namely what to do, politically and legislatively, in the face of a growing and violent Far Right. As recently as 2006 Germany's parliament was debating whether to proscribe the far-right NPD. As if to help the discussion along, *Spiegel* magazine declared: 'But such a step [banning the movement] may prove to be neither feasible nor advisable. In fact proponents of democracy in Germany would be better off focusing on their strengths and trying to make the NPD irrelevant'.[44] The same debate has ensued in other European countries (for example, France), with some observers airing the view that banning unpleasant parties may force them underground and, in the long run, actually make them stronger. The *Spiegel* line has also been reiterated: better exert energy engaging with the relevant issues than on banning a movement that obviously has a constituency.

Fourth, it is interesting to note the development of far-right politics in what was East Germany. In 2006 the BBC stated: 'The NPD's support is partly explained by its hard anti-immigrant stance in Mecklenburg-Western Pomerania, where unemployment runs at more than 18% – the highest in the country. Manufacturing has collapsed across the former East German state following reunification in 1990, forcing many of its residents to go west in search of work. Two states in former Communist East Germany already have far-right MPs. The NPD has lawmakers in the state of Saxony, following regional elections in 2004. Another far-right party – the **German People's Union** (DVU) – entered parliament in the state of Brandenburg'.[45] Eight years before, reports were equally pessimistic after the DVU polled 12.9 percent in the eastern state of Saxony-Anhalt and so become the first far-right movement to enter an East German statehouse: 'The surge by the far-right party coincides with an increase in rightist violence and growing anti-immigrant sentiment throughout East Germany … A study by the Berlin-based Center for German Culture found that one in three East German youths expressed some form of rightist leanings … Unemployment in Saxony-Anhalt is the highest in Germany … 'Social disintegration' and the erosion of **family** structures leave Eastern youth without bearings in society, [said a BfV spokesman]'.[46] For Kolinsky the fact that far-right and neo-Nazi ideas have taken root in the geographical area covered by the former East Germany is one of the 'shock discoveries' of recent items.[47]

Finally, decades on from the end of the war, the German authorities are still 'on watch'. The BfV is charged with 'monitoring both left and right-wing extremism'.[48] It is doubtful whether any country in the world has such a methodical and rigorous way of surveying and categorising far-right movements. In 1981, for example, the BfV identified five types of far-right organisation:

(a) those associated with groups that were explicitly terrorist, violent and/or militaristic;
(b) those associated with organisations and parties that the BfV explicitly labelled 'neo-Nazi';
(c) the NPD and its spin-off affiliates;
(d) the so-called 'national liberal right', a category apparently used solely to accommodate [Gerhard] Frey's numerous initiatives, particularly the DVU; and
(e) a residual category for other extreme right-wing groups, especially various youth groups, nationalist cultural groups and an organisation for former soldiers in the Waffen-SS.[49]

Today, the scale and thoroughness of the organisation's website is testament to the seriousness with which the German authorities treat any manifestation of right-wing extremism.[50] The BfV states: 'Right-wing extremist ideology has its roots in nationalism and racism. It is governed by the idea that ethnic affiliation to a nation or race is of the utmost importance for an individual. All other interests and values, including civil and human rights, are subordinate to it. Right-wing extremists propagate a political system in which the state and the people amalgamate – as an alleged natural order – to form a unity ("ideology of the ethnic community")'.[51] It goes on:

Actually, this results in an anti-pluralistic system, leaving no room for democratic decision-making procedures. Right-wing extremism in Germany is not homogeneous in terms of ideology, but all right-wing extremists have in common that ethnic affiliation and xenophobia directed against the principle of equality are overestimated. As concerns its image, right-wing extremism is no homogeneous, self-contained phenomenon, either. It occurs in various forms, in particular in a juvenile sub-culture of violence-prone, right-wing extremist skinheads, neo-Nazi groupings propagating a totalitarian state, parties striving to gain political influence by running in elections, literature of right-wing extremist authors and publishing houses, agitating intellectually or propagandistically. The ideology which is hostile to the constitution and mostly contemptuous of human life vents itself in right-wing extremist and in particular xenophobic acts of violence directed against minorities only because of their ethnic origin.[52]

As if to illustrate the efficiency of the organisation, we are also told that since 1992 twenty-four right-wing extremist organisations have been banned by the German authorities.[53]

What this essay has demonstrated is that Central Europe is fertile territory for the Far Right. Today, in Switzerland, Austria and Germany there is a natural constituency for political parties, and other movements, that trade primarily in hard line nationalism and xenophobia. In Switzerland and Austria, far-right parties are currently coalition partners in government. Could we have even contemplated making such a statement thirty or forty years ago? In Germany, such a scenario is less likely because of the fragmented nature of the Far Right and also because of the strict monitoring of far-right political activity that takes place. That said, it is curious to say the least that the Far Right has blossomed in a part of the world which is dominated by – perhaps almost paranoid about – the legacy of the Nazi era. To put it bluntly: How could Germany and Austria fall prey, *again*, to such a pernicious ideology?

There are no easy answers to this question. Obviously, social and economic change has created an environment in which far-right leaders have been able to talk about 'problems', 'blame' and 'scapegoats'. And obviously, it has been natural to point the finger at large and extremely visible immigrant communities. But maybe we also need to examine German and Austrian political culture. The reflexes and the instincts: is there still a hangover from the Nazi period? At times, the continuities are too blatant to ignore. There are the Haider speeches that have lauded various aspects of the Hitler regime. There are also developments elsewhere. The Jewish Telegraph Agency has highlighted one disturbing trend: 'In 1997, when Switzerland was confronting charges that it profited from wartime dealings with the Nazis, Blocher launched a campaign to prevent public funds from being used to support victims of the Holocaust. That same year, Blocher, a millionaire businessman, told a rally that Switzerland had no reason to apologise for doing business with Nazi Germany. Now, Jewish leaders are warily watching the ascent of Blocher and his party'.[54]

Peter Davies

Notes
1. BBC News, 'Swiss right in political avalanche', http://news.bbc.co.uk/1/hi/world/europe/3204412. stm (cited 31 December 2007).
2. BBC News, 'Haider founds new Austrian party', http://news.bbc.co.uk/1/hi/world/europe/4409953. stm (cited 31 December 2007).
3. See http://www.stephenhalbrook.com/swiss&nazis.html (cited 10 May 2007).
4. See Paul Hainsworth (ed.), *The Politics of the Extreme Right: From the Margins to the Mainstream* (London: Pinter, 2000) and Paul Hainsworth (ed.), *The Extreme Right in Europe and the USA* (London: Pinter, 1994).
5. BBC News, 'Swiss banks dodge sanctions in Holocaust deal', http://news.bbc.co.uk/1/hi/world/europe/70515.stm (cited 31 December 2007).
6. Tom Bower, *Nazi Gold* (New York: HarperCollins, 1997). See also http://www.amazon.com/Nazi-Gold-Fifty-Year-Swiss-Nazi-Conspiracy/dp/0060175354 (cited 10 May 2007).
7. Guardian Unlimited, 'Rightwing SVP tightens grip in Swiss election', http://www.guardian.co.uk/farright/story/0,,2196563,00.html (cited 31 December 2007).

8. Guardian Unlimited, 'Special report: Europe's far right', http://www.guardian.co.uk/gall/0,,711990,00.html (cited 31 December 2007).

9. SwissInfo, 'Blocher', http://www2.swissinfo.org/sen/swissinfo.html?siteSect=2051&sid=4360268&cKey=1066717182000 (cited 28 October 2003).

10. Guardian Unlimited, 'The rise of mosques becomes catalyst for conflict across Europe', www.guardian.co.uk/farright/story/0,,2188275,00.html (cited 31 December 2007).

11. BBC News, 'Swiss right in political avalanche', http://news.bbc.co.uk/1/hi/world/europe/3204412.stm (cited 31 December 2007).

12. Business Week, 'Switzerland: A hard-right kick in the pants', http://www.businessweek.com/magazine/content/03_47/b3859082_mz054.htm (cited 31 December 2007).

13. International Herald Tribune, 'Shift to the right undermines Swiss "magic" formula', http://www.iht.com/articles/1999/10/26/swiss.2.t_0.php (cited 31 December 2007).

14. Documentation Centre of Austrian Resistance, 'Right-wing extremism: history, organisations, ideology', http://www.xn--dw-fka.at/english/right/englre.html (cited 31 December 2007).

15. Duncan Morrow, 'Jörg Haider and the new FPÖ: beyond the democratic pale?' in Paul Hainsworth, *The Politics of the Extreme Right: From the Margins to the Mainstream* (London: Pinter, 2000), 41–42.

16. In fact, around 480,000 of the 520,000 former Austrian Nazi Party were allowed to vote again.

17. Refer to http://cla.calpoly.edu/~mriedlsp/Publications/GSA98.htmlrfs (cited 10 May 2007).

18. Duncan Morrow, 'Jörg Haider and the new FPÖ: beyond the democratic pale?' in Paul Hainsworth (ed.), *The Politics of the Extreme Right: From the Margins to the Mainstream* (London: Pinter, 2000), 40.

19. Brigitte Bailer-Galanda & Wolfgang Neugebauer, 'Right-wing extremism: history, organisations, ideology', http://www.xn--dw-fka.at/english/right/englre.html (cited 31 December 2007).

20. Ibid.

21. Duncan Morrow, 'Jörg Haider and the new FPÖ: beyond the democratic pale?' in Paul Hainsworth (ed.), *The Politics of the Extreme Right: From the Margins to the Mainstream* (London: Pinter, 2000), 43.

22. New York Times, 'A Threat by Austria on sanctions', http://query.nytimes.com/gst/fullpage.html?res=9801E5DC1339F937A35754C0A9669C8B63 (cited 28 October 2003).

23. BBC News, 'Far-right row topples Austrian coalition', http://news.bbc.co.uk/2/hi/europe/2246734.stm (cited 1 January 2008).

24. BBC News, 'Haider: Nazi admirer or moderate?', http://news.bbc.co.uk/1/hi/programmes/from_our_own_correspondent/468127.stm (cited 31 December 2007).

25. Duncan Morrow, 'Jörg Haider and the new FPÖ: beyond the democratic pale?' in Paul Hainsworth (ed.), *The Politics of the Extreme Right: From the Margins to the Mainstream* (London: Pinter, 2000), 33.

26. New Statesman, 'Haider: stand by and watch him self-destruct', http://www.newstatesman.com/200002070010 (cited 31 December 2007).

27. Duncan Morrow, 'Jörg Haider and the New FPÖ: Beyond the democratic pale?' in Paul Hainsworth (ed.), *The Politics of the Extreme Right: From the Margins to the Mainstream* (London: Pinter, 2000), 49.

28. Guardian Unlimited, 'Jörg Haider's rise will soon enough be followed by a fall', http://www.guardian.co.uk/comment/story/0,,239273,00.html (cited 31 December 2007).

29. Central European Review, 'Austria's new ÖVP-FPÖ government and Jörg Haider', http://www.ce-review.org/00/7/johnson7.html (cited 31 December 2007).

30. BBC News, 'Far right', http://news.bbc.co.uk/hi/english/static/in_depth/europe/2000/far_right/germany.stm (cited 13 April 2007).

31. Guardian Unlimited, 'Europe's far right', www.guardian.co.uk/gall/0,,711990,00.html (cited 31 December 2007).

32. Eva Kolinsky, 'A future for right extremism in Germany?' in Paul Hainsworth, *The Extreme Right in Europe and the USA* (London: Pinter, 1992), 61; see also Susann Backer, 'Right-wing extremism in unified Germany' in Paul Hainsworth, *The Politics of the Extreme Right: From the Margins to the Mainstream* (London: Pinter, 2000), 89.

33. David Childs, 'The far right in Germany since 1945' in Luciano Cheles, Ronnie Ferguson & Michalina Vaughan, *Neo-Fascism in Europe* (London: Longman, 1991), 67–68.

34. For some interesting statistics, see Susann Backer, 'Right-wing extremism in unified Germany' in Paul Hainsworth (ed.), *The Politics of the Extreme Right: From the Margins to the Mainstream* (London: Pinter, 2000), 108.

35. Christopher Husbands, 'Militant neo-Nazism in the Federal Republic of Germany in the 1980s' in Luciano Cheles, Ronnie Ferguson & Michalina Vaughan, *Neo-Fascism in Europe* (London: Longman, 1991), 87 & 91.

36. Eva Kolinsky, 'A future for right extremism in Germany?' in Paul Hainsworth, *The Extreme Right in Europe and the USA* (London: Pinter, 1992), 65.

37. Christopher Husbands, 'Militant neo-Nazism in the Federal Republic of Germany in the 1980s' in Luciano Cheles, Ronnie Ferguson & Michalina Vaughan, *Neo-Fascism in Europe* (London: Longman, 1991), 86–119.

38. Eva Kolinsky, 'A future for right extremism in Germany?' in Paul Hainsworth, *The Extreme Right in Europe and the USA* (London: Pinter, 1992), 61 & Liane.Escorza@pearson.com92.

39. Christopher Husbands, 'Militant neo-Nazism in the Federal Republic of Germany in the 1980s' in Luciano Cheles, Ronnie Ferguson & Michalina Vaughan, *Neo-Fascism in Europe* (London: Longman, 1991), 91.

40. Susann Backer, 'Right-wing extremism in unified Germany' in Paul Hainsworth (ed.), *The Politics of the Extreme Right: From the Margins to the Mainstream* (London: Pinter, 2000), 93.

41. David Childs, 'The far right in Germany since 1945' in Luciano Cheles, Ronnie Ferguson & Michalina Vaughan, *Neo-Fascism in Europe* (London: Longman, 1991), 82.

42. BBC News, 'Germany agonises over neo-Nazis', http://news.bbc.co.uk/1/hi/world/europe/870086.stm (cited 31 December 2007).

43. BBC News, 'Envoy: 'German Jews feel unsafe', http://news.bbc.co.uk/1/hi/world/europe/6072034.stm (cited 31 December 2007).

44. Spiegel Online, 'Living with the extremist plague', http://www.spiegel.de/international/spiegel/0,1518,451838,00.html (cited 31 December 2007).

45. BBC News, 'Poll boost for German far right', http://news.bbc.co.uk/1/hi/world/europe/5349696.stm (cited 31 December 2007).

46. International Herald Tribune, 'Business association warns of damage to nation's image: surge of far right shocks Germany', http://www.iht.com/articles/1998/04/28/germany.t_4.php (cited 31 December 2007).

47. Eva Kolinsky, 'A future for right extremism in Germany?' in Paul Hainsworth, *The Extreme Right in Europe and the USA* (London: Pinter, 1992), 72.

48. Christopher Husbands, 'Militant neo-Nazism in the Federal Republic of Germany in the 1980s' in Luciano Cheles, Ronnie Ferguson & Michalina Vaughan, *Neo-Fascism in Europe* (London: Longman, 1991), 87.

49. Ibid.

50. See http://www.verfassungsschutz.de/en/index_en.html (cited 12 October 2007).

51. Federal Office for Protection of the Constitution, 'Right-wing extremism' http://www.verfassungsschutz.de/en/en_fields_of_work/rightwing_extremism/?color=0 (cited 31 December 2007).

52. Ibid.

53. Ibid.

54. Jewish News Weekly of Northern California, 'Far right makes new gains - this time in Switzerland', http://www.jewishsf.com/content/2-0-/module/displaystory/story_id/12356/edition_id/238/format/html/displaystory.html (cited 31 December 2007).

Russia and the Far Right

When the Union of Soviet Socialist Republics (USSR) collapsed, so suddenly and unexpectedly in December 1991, there was widespread expectation in the West that the fifteen newly independent states that comprised the USSR, and most significantly the Russian Federation itself, were embarking upon a transition to **democracy**. This was seen as almost inevitable as the communist experiment had so manifestly failed to deliver its promise of a new, classless and non-capitalist post-nationalist society. The most influential articulation of this idea – of a triumph for democracy and the capitalist market – was made by Francis Fukuyama in his 'end of history' thesis.[1] Immediately, a new academic genre of 'transitology' emerged as comparative politics specialists and those scholars who had specialised in the USSR and communist systems sought to track, explain and predict the processes involved as the former communist states transited to democracy and the capitalist market.[2] It was widely considered that liberal democracy had finally won out in a competition of ideas, having defeated both Fascism and **Communism** as the two most powerful alternatives in the twentieth century.

Yet if we stop for a moment to reflect on what the experts were saying before the USSR collapsed, then perhaps we should always have been wary of assumptions being made by the same group of scholars concerning the future trajectory of Russia and the former titular republics of the USSR. For it is the case that not one single expert predicted that the USSR was about to collapse; indeed most were expressing confidence in the Soviet system's durability just as it was about to expire.[3] As I have sought to demonstrate elsewhere, this was largely because those specialising in the USSR failed to appreciate the powerful underlying forces of nationalism within the communist bloc.[4] And those scholars who specialised in nationalism tended to ignore or discount the power of the politics of national identity in the communist states. Yet in the end, we can only understand the demise of the communist system with reference to the powerful forces of nationalism. It was not a strong desire to transit to democracy that was the key to understanding the collapse of these systems (although that was part of the story); it was the desire of the subject peoples of what was essentially the last remaining great European/Eurasian empire for their independence. Old communist elites and new emerging post-communist elites were all very quick to engage in a new nationalist discourse. This of course was for their instrumental interests, as the most potent mobilising force to garner mass support was a national identity dynamic. Slobodan **Milošević**, the former communist official turned far-right nationalist in Serbia, was not the only politician in the bloc to turn overnight from communist to nationalist ideology. It is the case that what happened as a consequence in the former Yugoslavia (the various bloody wars of succession) did not occur in the USSR. However, it is important to recognise that far-right nationalist forces were, and are still, very strong in the Russian Federation and there are therefore lessons to learn from comparing the different trajectories these forces took in the two post-communist countries. The important point to make here, though, is that nationalist forces brought down the communist systems, rather than any overwhelming desire on the part of the elites or masses to transit to liberal democracy (although, again, this may have been an additional strong pull for some). Further evidence of the power of the national idea was the split, after the demise of Communism, of Czechoslovakia into two independent states (Slovakia and the Czech Republic) and the numerous ethnic conflicts that emerged, for example, in various parts of the Caucasus (most notably Chechnya), in Moldova, and between Armenians and Azeris over Nagorno Karabakh

What the fall of Communism clearly demonstrated was that nationalism, including nationalist forces on the Far Right of the political spectrum, was an irresistibly powerful force. This again should have come as little surprise given what scholars already knew about the causes of extreme nationalist sentiments. The experiences of Italy and Germany in the decades leading up to World War II demonstrated that a mix of factors existing simultaneously in any one country can easily lead to extreme nationalism in the form of Fascism or National-Socialism (Nazism). What have generally been considered prerequisites (social and economic) for the successful fostering of democracy simply did not pertain in the Russian Federation after the collapse of Communism. Central to any definition of democracy is the notion of free and fair elections, providing citizens with the opportunity to select their preferred representatives when forming a government. In a functioning democracy, mediating institutions allow civil society to participate in the political process through a plurality of autonomous groups separate from the state. The changing of representative government through a periodic electoral process – contested by a number of competing political parties – is the key component of democracy. However, elections organised to establish representative government do not necessarily result in a stable, liberal, democratic order. Indeed, the electoral process has been used as a vehicle for gaining political power by far-right nationalist forces. In the first half of the twentieth century Hitler gained power through the ballot box. So too, did Milošević at the end of the century. At the beginning of the twenty-first century we have witnessed how democratic elections can produce something other than democracy – as in the case of the Palestinian Authority and in Iraq following the U.S.-led invasion in 2003. Planning for democracy, as with planning in an **economy**, does not work. Democracy cannot be imposed from without or established by indigenous social engineers, if the socio-economic perquisites for democratic development are not in place. The working of an economy and a polity are also determined by social and cultural practices, and these facets cannot simply be restructured by administrative fiat.

In the early 1990s the prerequisites for democratic development were not in place in the Russian Federation. It is, however, the case that Russia was a radically different country in the 1990s than it was under Stalin in the 1930s. Soviet Russia in this earlier period was relatively backward, but by the end of the twentieth century it had been transformed into an urban, highly educated and technologically advanced country with a strong military and it was forging ahead in space exploration. Yet Russia could not keep pace with the capitalist West, and a systemic crisis, linked to the growing manifestation of nationalism among the minor nations of the Union, led to the collapse in 1991. It was now expected that a modernising imperative would lead Russia to become integrated into the global capitalist economy with a modern pluralist, democratic political system. Yet, after centuries of authoritarian forms of government, Russians did not have the experience, or what some have referred to as the appropriate 'political culture', to foster democracy. Old habits die hard, and without the experience of democratic forms of government, Russians, it is argued, are more prone to respect strong leadership within an authoritarian system. Traditional Russian political culture was more conducive to far-right nationalism replacing Communism as a cementing ideology for the new post-imperial Russian state. And if one assesses Russia in terms of Robert Dahl's definition of modern democracy, in which high levels of sustained economic development, high income per capita, decreasing infant mortality rates and increasing life expectancy are all considered necessary for the successful implementation of democracy, then one can readily see that after the demise of Communism, Russia did not fit this picture.[5]

The concern soon became that in the Russian case pluralism, rather than creating democracy, would lead to a new form of authoritarianism based on the logic of far-right nationalism. The fear by the mid-1990s was that Russia was embarking upon a Weimar scenario, or would follow a similar path to that of Yugoslavia, and break up into warring ethnic groups. Central to both scenarios was an assumption of far-right nationalism as the guiding force. By the time Putin had completed his two terms as president, neither of these predictions had proved to be correct. Although it has been a strong force, and Putin has sought to harness it to his cause, the Russian Far Right has not gained power, and far-right nationalist groups have fostered neither empire-building nor a militant expansionist foreign policy, neither have they created conditions leading to intra-state ethnic wars (notwithstanding the problems in the Northern Caucuses). Below we will examine the contemporary **Far Right in Russia**, assessing its current influence in the political process along with its future potential. Some important historical background will also be included where it is considered helpful.

Manifestations of Far-Right Extremism

It is very difficult to keep track of the rise and fall of far-right groups in Russia since the collapse of the Soviet Union, as so many individuals and groups have either come and gone during this period, or have been disbanded to re-emerge in a different guise. Many parties began as independent vehicles for the political ambitions of individuals, and as with many far-right nationalist groups in other countries, their successes have been closely linked to the fortunes of their respective leader.

Vladimir Zhirinvosky, for example, was clearly dominant in the immediate post-Soviet period with the establishment of what, in effect, became the official and acceptable face of the Far Right, in the form of the misnamed **Liberal Democratic Party of Russia** (LDPR). Support for far-right groups in Russia during this period can be gleaned from both attitudinal and opinion surveys and political behaviour, including voting in elections and participation in far-right groups. On the surface support for the **Far Right in Russia** appears to have waned, as evidenced by the much smaller (although still significant) level of support for the LDPR since the early 1990s. Also, the economic and social conditions that are conducive to the Far Right have been ameliorated since Putin came to power. However, as will be shown below, the forces of the Far Right are still influential and pose a danger to Russia's future development towards democracy, and Putin himself has flirted with nationalist forces to embed his own position and increase his popular legitimacy. Perhaps the best way of assessing the forces of the Far Right in Russia is to look at parties with far-right nationalist programmes and their electoral strengths, surveys of Russian attitudes, levels of **violence** perpetrated in the name of nationalism, and official state policies towards far-right and nationalist groups.

Parties, Elections and Polls

Competitive elections for political office are a recent phenomenon in Russia. The only other elections with a universal franchise before those of recent years were for the Constituent Assembly in 1917, an institution which was quickly disbanded by the

Bolsheviks following the October Revolution. In those elections competing parties ranged from pro-monarchist through liberal democrat to various forms of socialism. There was no single strong party representing what would be considered far-right nationalist forces. Before the Revolution the Far Right in Russia was represented by many groups and parties, some with their own periodicals, some linked to the Russian monarchy and the Orthodox Church. Some of the principal parties that formed around the turn of the twentieth century, and were influential at the time following the Revolution in Russia of 1905, were the Russian Monarchist Party, the Union of Russian Men, the Russian Assembly and the Union of the Russian People.[6] These rightist groups were appalled at the prospect of liberalism, especially western forms of liberalism, undermining what they considered to be traditional Russian, or Slav, mores and customs. This reflected the divide at the time between the Slavophiles and the Westernisers, a divide which would reappear following the fall of Communism a hundred years later, as Russians searched for a new identity.

During the civil war rightist forces fought a losing battle against the Communists and were soon forced into exile or became obsolete in the face of total Bolshevik Communist control in what quickly became a one-party state. Other parties were soon outlawed. With only one party offering a career path for aspiring politicians, the Communist Party of the Soviet Union, in effect, became a catch-all party: anyone with ambition had little option but to join. More than this, however, is the fact that the CPSU, from the outset, appealed not just to those ideologically committed to communist revolution. The party was seen by many as a saviour for Russia, offering a programme to make Russia great again following defeat and humiliation in war and the devastation of the civil war, in which foreign powers intervened on the side of the Whites. The party also offered a disciplined instrument with which to catch up with the Western powers rather than being constantly left behind. There was always a small but significant element within the party that reflected a Eurasianist trend, or a Great Russian tendency. It is also worth remembering that Stalin invoked Russian nationalist ideals and Russian military heroes from the Tsarist era in order to mobilise the population when waging war against Hitler's Germany.

When the Soviet Union disintegrated into its separate titular national elements (again the logic of national identity was the rationale for the territorial boundaries of the fifteen new states that succeeded the Union) the Communist part of the Russian Federation (CPRF) carried on the mantle of the CPSU. However, in these radically changed circumstances it was necessary to compete for mass support in elections. The leftist ideology of the CPSU was very quickly transformed into what in essence was a new rightist and nationalist one. The CPRF leader, Gennady Zyuganov, as a member of the CPSU, had opposed the reforms of Mikhail Gorbachev, seeing them as undermining not only Communism, but also Russia's position *vis-à-vis* the West. He considered the reforms of the 1980s as moving against Russia's own national interests and weakening the power of the state.

During the attempted coup against Gorbachev in the summer of 1991 the instigators produced a document setting out their aims and objectives, and it is instructive to note that, despite all being senior members of the Communist Party apparatus, there was no word of Lenin or Marxism or Communism: the rationale was all about the nation and strengthening the state. Zyuganov had in July that year combined with a group of leading far-right nationalists in writing *Message to the People*, warning about the potential for civil war if the Soviet state was to collapse and calling for a coalition of patriotic forces to prevent the slide into chaos.[7]After the USSR expired in December 1991, Zyuganov used the CPRF as an instrument in a struggle against Boris Yeltsin for political power. Yeltsin had won election to the Russian presidency the previous year. Zyuganov not only formed a coalition with nationalist forces, but in formulating the new CPRF policies it was clear that Zyuganov and the Communist Party were taking on more of a far-right nationalist colouring. Yegor Gaidar, one of the leading liberal reformers under Yeltsin, referred to this successor party as reflecting 'National Socialism' rather than anything related to Karl Marx.[8] During this early post-Soviet period, Communists and nationalists were forming a 'Red-Brown' alliance in order to challenge the power of the liberal, westernising reformers around Yeltsin. This alliance was creating a potentially dangerous brew that was becoming openly anti-democratic and hostile to the West. Promotion of economic reform in the form of shock therapy, involving a radical and immediate leap into privatisation and the market, supported by the United States and the West (pace the Washington Consensus), had devastating economic and social consequences for the vast majority of Russian citizens. This further reinforced mass support for both Communists and nationalists, two forces viewed as being strong proponents of Russia's national interest in a time of uncertainty and crisis.

As part of the political reforms under Gorbachev, Russia instituted its first ever presidential election in June 1991; he himself, then riding a wave of popular Russian nationalism, won easily in the first ballot with over 45 million votes. A former Soviet prime minister, Nikolai Ryzhkov, came second with some 13 million votes. The surprise third place went to Vladimir **Zhirinovsky**, head of the LDPR. The LDPR was the official voice of extreme nationalism in the early transition period following the disintegration of the USSR. It was established in March 1990 as a counter to the power of the CPSU at a time of evolving political pluralism under Gorbachev. It was the first organisation to gain official registration as a political party in the Soviet Union since the ban on political parties in the 1920s, hence undermining the CPSU's monopoly of the political landscape.

Zhirinovsky dominated the party practically from the outset, developing his own cult of personality, and even branding and marketing his own Zhirinovsky vodka label. Zhirinvosky was noted for making some bizarre policy proposals, such as reclaiming and then extending the Russian empire further into Asia. But he spoke to the new disposed and poor in Russia, offering salvation in the form of a welfare cushion provided by the state for those most in need. Zhirinovsky articulated four basic goals: to reconstitute the Russian Empire; to secure the position of ethnic Russians living in former republics of the Union; to develop strong state power with an authoritarian structure; and to limit privatisation and restrict foreign ownership in the Russian economy.[9] Zhirinvosky played on the image of poor Russians being abused and taken advantage of by groups including the International Monetary Fund, non-Russian peoples of the former Soviet Union, and Muslims and the Islamic faith in general. The LDRP at this time offered the most potent challenge to the emerging liberal order in the form of a far-right nationalist ideology.

Although Yeltsin was a clear and easy winner with 59.7 percent of the valid vote, the 8.1 percent gained by Zhirinvosky was indicative of the strong potential force of the Far Right, and perhaps a wake-up call to the Communists at that time as regards the force of nationalism in mobilising the vote. However, the national idea was already apparent in the presidential candidacy of Albert Makashov. Openly anti-Semitic, Makashov represented the Communist Party and the military industrial complex, coming a poor fifth with less than 3 million votes, behind Aman-Geldy Tuleev, a miner and minor Soviet official from the regions.

In 1996 Yeltsin faced strong competition from the communist leader, Zyuganov, who looked set to win the election. Yeltsin only managed to hold onto power following a concerted political campaign funded by the new wealthy oligarchs. In addition, most of the media, for the most part in the hands of the same oligarchs, were clearly biased in support of Yeltsin, and were highly critical of Zyuganov. In the first round Yeltsin gained 35 percent of the vote; Zyuganov came a close second with 32 percent, leaving these as the only candidates to contest the second round of voting. Yeltsin went on to win 53.8 percent to Zyuyganov's 40.3 percent, thereby retaining the presidency. Zhirinvosky also participated and was knocked out in the first round of voting in 1996 with 5.7 percent (Gorbachev also ran and got a measly 0.5 percent of the vote). The election indicated that nationalism was still a force to be reckoned with, although now the main Communist Party was competing more effectively against the LDPR for the nationalist vote.

In the 2000 presidential election Yeltsin's hand-picked successor, Vladimir Putin, had only one serious challenger: Zyuganov, but his popularity had lessened since the last election in 1996. Putin won on the first ballot with 52.9 percent against Zyuganov's 29.2 percent (Zhirinovsky received 2.7 percent). Although Putin refused to publish a manifesto or join up as a member of a political party, putting himself somewhat above the political fray, it was clear what he stood for: taking a tough stance against Chechen terrorists, making Russia strong again as an actor in world politics, and putting the economy back on track. Putin was stealing some of the thunder from the CPRF and the LDPR by articulating a clear 'Russia first' policy that portrayed him as the saviour of the Russian nation, whether fighting Chechens at home, or challenging the West abroad in defence of Russian national interests. His was not a far-right message; but it was taking some of the force away from the Red-Brown parties and nationalist groupings by his strong and confident patriotic stance. By the time Putin's term ended in 2008 all contenders for the highest political office in the Federation were strong supporters of maintaining Russia's status as a world power, but within the context of global interdependence in the capitalist market.

The big shock for many in the first post-Soviet elections to the new Russian parliament was the very strong showing for the LDPR. As noted, in the presidential election of 1991 Zhirinovsky was the surprise recipient of 8 percent of the vote. But even more significant, and at the time surprising to all observers, was the very high vote the LDPR received in the elections to the State Duman in 1993, the first post-Soviet democratic elections to the Russian parliament. In the party-list portion of the votes (the one where voters are forced to choose between competing parties) the LDPR won the highest share, some 22.9 percent against 15.51 percent for Russia's Choice, then the 'party of power' (i.e. the party linked to the president, although Yeltsin was not an official member of any party). The CPRF came in third in the party-list system with 12.4 percent of the vote. These parliamentary elections demonstrated clearly the powerful forces of nationalism.

In subsequent elections the Far Right lost its appeal to Russian voters and also the dominant parties of the Far Right moderated their positions to become more mainstream, if not outright supporters of Putin and the status quo. In the 1995 elections to the Duma the LDPR received only 11.2 percent of the party-list vote, although the CPRF increased its party-list vote to 22.3 percent (from 12.4 percent in 1993), and gaining 25.8 percent of the single-member constituency votes also, giving the Communists 34.9 percent of the seats in the new Duma (compared to 11.3 percent for the Liberal Democrats; Our Home is Russia gained 12.2 percent). This still left the Communists as the main opposition to the Kremlin. Apart from the liberal Yabloko party (which gained 6.9 percent of the party-list vote), no other party among the dozens that competed got over the 5 percent hurdle needed to gain representation in parliament (although some minor parties did get a very small number of individual seats in the constituencies).

In the Duma elections of 1999 the CPRF once more retained its position as the dominant party in the parliament and as the major opposition to Putin, gaining 25.1 percent of the total seats. Unity, the new party of power, supporting Putin and the Kremlin leadership, gained 16.2 percent of seats. Zhirinovsky's LDPR now held only 3.8 percent of the seats, having barely crossed the five percent threshold (6 percent) to gain representation on the party-list part of the vote. The LDPR failed to get a single member elected in the constituency portion of the vote. Other groups that did well in 1999 included the Fatherland-All Russia Bloc (15.1 percent of total seats), and the Union of Right Forces (6.4 percent). Fatherland represented a patriotic bloc, and a fairly tame one that did not offer real opposition to the Kremlin; and the Union of Right Forces was right in an economic sense, calling for further liberalisation, marketisation and democratisation. By this time too, the CPRF had become more pliable and was often itself supportive, if not compliant, in relation to policies emanating from the Kremlin.

In the 2003 elections to the Duma, United Russia won fully 49.3 percent of the total seats (winning 37.6 percent in the party-list ballot). The CPRF received the second largest share of seats (fifty-two seats, or 11.6 percent of the total), and the LDPR received 36 seats (8 percent of the total) all of which came from the party-list ballot (where the party gained 11.5 percent of the total vote).

It should also be noted that there were more extremist groups contesting elections, both for the Russian presidency and to the Duma. And these parties and individuals gained a very small percentage of the vote indeed, hence marginalising the main far-right nationalist groups. People voted for the CPRF and the LDPR, for Zyuganov and Zhirinvosky, not out of any sympathy for far-right nationalist causes, but because they were considered the best among the alternatives to improve the economic and social situation of the average Russian citizen.

One of the most influential far-right organisations in the transition period from Communism was *Pamyat*, meaning '**memory**' in Russian. *Pamyat* was established by a group of leading artists and writers, including the famous 'village writer' Valentin Rasputin, who was later one of the signatories of the 1991 *Message to the People*, also signed by Zyuganov. The organisation was designed, according to its stated objectives, to preserve Russia's cultural monuments, its name deriving from the title of a book by Chivilikhin. In *Pamyat*, written in the 1970s, Chivilikhin covered the Aryan origins of the Russian people.[10] *Pamyat*'s origins precede the reformism of the 1980s by a decade, having been established in the 1970s out of a concern for the deteriorating condition of Russia's churches, monuments, and traditional buildings of historical significance. But Gorbachev's moves towards pluralism gave what was originally a disparate coalition of patriotic groups concerned with cultural questions the momentum to engage more directly in the political sphere. *Pamyat* evolved into an aggressive and hyper-nationalist exponent of Russian ethnic interests. In 1987 the group published what in effect was its manifesto, entitled *Appeal to the Russian People*, which was riddled with hostile anti-Jewish sentiments. One regional grouping of *Pamyat* in Novosibirsk claimed that Jews organising a plot to deliberately pollute Lake Baikal.[11]

Eduard Limonov, head of the banned National Bolshevik Party, has as his party's flag a mixture of fascist and communist symbolism: a black hammer and sickle on a red background. Once on the extreme right and associated with skinheads and mob violence, Limonov had served two years in prison for plotting to split off part of Kazakhstan dominated by ethnic Russians. By 2007 he was calling for a coalition of nationalist oppositionists to challenge the dominance of Putin and the power elite.

In 2007 a number of other far-right organisations were active in the Russian Federation, including the Movement against Illegal Immigration, the Russian All-National Union (RONS), the National Imperial Party of Russia (NDPR), the Slavic Union, and Russian Order. The leader of RONS, Igor Artyumov, led and coordinated the demonstrations in Moscow against the first gay pride march in May 2007. Another new group, the National Bolshevik Front, formed a coalition with Alexander Dugin's Eurasian Youth Movement. The National Bolshevik Front is a split-off from Limonov's original National Bolshevik Party. Keeping track of these shifting groups and parties and individuals is very difficult, but suffice to say by the end of 2007 they had not penetrated deeply into the electoral landscape, or even made a significant impact on political debates. The official Kremlin position was that Limonov's NBP, an increasingly left-wing and openly oppositional party, was 'fascist' in orientation, whereas the actual right-wing forces of the BNF and ESM can now claim some government support - because they have abandoned their opposition to Putin.

In a poll carried out by the widely respected Yuri Levada Centre in Moscow, fully 54 percent of Russian **youth** said they had a positive attitude to Stalin, considering his legacy to be more positive than negative. Not only did the poll show that the majority of Russia's youth admired Stalin, it also demonstrated that they wanted to expel migrants from the country (62 percent agreed with the statement that the 'Russian government should evict most immigrants'. The majority also saw the collapse of the Soviet Union in 1991 as a 'tragedy').[12]

Survey results, however, have not revealed any widespread anti-Semitic tendencies, even though individual party leaders including Zhirinovksy and Zhuganov have publicly made anti-Jewish comments. Despite the fact that political leaders have sought to mobilise anti-Jewish sentiments, it appears, according to this kind of evidence, that the vast majority of Russians are not anti-Semitic.

Violence, Vandalism and Anti-Semitism

Violence and vandalism aimed at symbols of ethnic, national or religious identities are clear manifestations of xenophobic and far-right extremism. Russia in recent years has become unsafe for some foreigners, especially those easily identifiable by the colour of their skin. Students from African countries and those from the Caucuses, for example, have been physically assaulted and even killed by neo-Nazi groups. In 2006, some seventy separate incidents of vandalism were reported in Russia in which religious hatred was the key motive, with Jewish organisations being the predominant targets. Hatred, discrimination and violence against Jews have, in fact, been a recurrent issue in Russia since prior to the Russian Revolution in 1917.

It was in the late period of the Russian Empire that *The **Protocols of The Elders of Zion*** was published – the word *pogrom* came from the original Russian – and it was

Russia that witnessed the emergence of the Black Hundreds groups and also gave birth to the term 'beyond the pale'. In the aftermath of Tsar Alexander ll's assassination in 1882, a new state law forced Jews out of urban areas and the rural *shtetls* of Western Russia and into the newly created 'Pale of Jewish Settlement'. In fact, '[t]here was no other state on the European continent which officially pursued such repressive anti-Jewish policies in the nineteenth century as the Russian Tsarist Empire'.[13] Due to subsequent *progroms* in the early 1900s, large numbers of Russian Jews, estimated at some 2 million, emigrated to the United States. Despite their clearly bogus and fictional character, *The Protocols* were accepted by a wide section of influential Russians as evidence of a global Jewish conspiracy aimed at world domination. During the civil war rightist organisations, such as the Union of Russian National Communities and the Russian Assembly, operated under the slogan 'Beat the Jews, Save Russia'.[14] The Assembly also adopted the catchphrase 'Russia for the Russians' and opposed Jews having equal civil rights, for this would enable them to enjoy even more power over the dominant Russian population.[15]

During the Soviet period Jews in the USSR suffered discrimination in gaining access to the highest levels of political power in the Communist Party apparatus. It was only Stalin's death in 1953 that prevented him from unleashing a new purge, this time against Jewish medical practitioners in what was termed the 'Doctors' Plot'.[16] A recent study has documented how Russian history is 'replete with instances of scapegoating and persecution of Jews'.[17]

Anti-Jewish sentiments in the post-Soviet period have become more openly articulated in Russia. The leaders of the two main opposition parties have both pandered to these sentiments. Zyuganov, for example, has written for anti-Semitic newspapers and Zhirinovsky has exploited **anti-Semitism** when it has served his political objectives. Albert Makashov, a leading communist and presidential candidate in 1991, openly blamed the problems besetting Russia on its Jewish population.[18]

In the late 1990s there was a series of bomb attacks on synagogues in the Russian capital and the director of Moscow's Jewish arts centre was stabbed by a far-right sympathiser. As Engel put it at that time: 'The sight of swaggering Jew-hating skinheads has been one of the most startling images of the post-Soviet era'.[19]

In the first decade of the twenty-first century violent attacks against immigrants and people from the Caucuses have increased. Attacks on Georgians, farmers from Central Asia or the Caucuses selling their produce in Russian markets, foreign students on the streets of St. Petersburg, and other hate crimes have become increasingly common. A young student from Armenia was killed on the Moscow Metro in 2006 by a gang of skinheads in the middle of the day. An explosion in the Cherkizovo market in Moscow in August 2006 killed thirteen innocent traders. An annual report on radical nationalism published in Moscow in 2006 refers to what it calls some 'formerly unthinkable' alliances between members of the State Duma and regional legislative bodies openly collaborating with skinheads.[20] The report documents 539 victims of violent hate crimes in 2006, of whom 54 were killed. This marked a 17 percent increase in such crimes compared to 2005. In January 2006 a neo-Nazi stabbed eight people in a Moscow synagogue.

Anti-extremism laws originally introduced in 2007, devised to counter growing hate crimes, racism, ultra-nationalism and terrorism, were strengthened in 2007 after a large increase in extremist crimes. However, these laws are widely criticised as being an instrument that the state wields to target any group that opposes Putin, enabling authorities to categorise almost any opposition as 'extremist'.

The State and the Far Right

As noted, the Russian Tsarist authorities had used a nationalist discourse and anti-Jewish policies in the nineteenth century. This partly explains the relatively large number of Jews in leading positions among the Russian Marxist revolutionaries in the early part of the twentieth century (in both the Bolshevik and, in particular, the Menshevik factions after the split in 1902). Fast forward to today and according to Russia's Prosecutor General, citing figures from the Interior Ministry, in August 2007 there were 150 extremist organisations in Russia with approximately 10,000 members, mostly between the ages of 16 and 25 years.[21]

One increasingly influential youth group, *Nashi*, is considered by many to be a front for the Kremlin leadership. It was established in 2005, reportedly with help from Vladislav Surkov, Putin's deputy chief of staff. The extent to which *Nashi* is a vehicle established and funded by the state under Putin to support the president's policies is a question that requires careful analysis. It is the case that *Nashi* does tend to act as a cheerleader for Putin, and often holds rallies in which the president's basic policies are supported. *Nashi* itself has claimed that it represents the Putin generation (most members are aged between fourteen and twenty-five years), and critics refer to it as 'Putin's Youth League'. Although *Nashi* spells out the Russian word for 'ours', it is in fact an acronym for Young Democratic Anti-Fascist League. Its title would imply that its chief objective is to oppose any form of extremist far-right nationalism, and so the idea that it represents a kind of nationalist front is wide of the mark.

During a period when Russia was flexing its muscles in relation to energy prices and in other areas of foreign affairs, Paul Kennedy suggested that these moves of a resurgent great power should not be of primary concern; instead he saw something else, 'more purposeful, and potentially quite sinister'.[22] Kennedy was referring to *Nashi*, seeing this as an example of Putin deliberately developing a 'cadre' of 'ultra-Russianists' to 'buttress [his] regime against domestic critics'. While it is true that members of *Nashi* have harassed foreigners, including the British ambassador to the Russian Federation after he attended a meeting of Russian NGOs, it is an exaggeration to see, as is implied here, *Nashi* as a kind of Hitler Youth-style movement.

It should be noted that since the demise of the Soviet Union there have been no organised state-run pogroms against Russian Jews, nor any discrimination or legal restrictions against Jews in the political and economic spheres. Yet many predicted a Weimar scenario for the post-Soviet Russian state. The sale of Soviet economic and trading infrastructures under Yeltsin was accompanied by the rapid impoverishment of the bulk of the Russian people and the sudden catapulting into great wealth of a small number of oligarchs, many of whom, if not most, are Jewish. The Russian tendency to scapegoat did not result in any state-sponsored anti-Semitism. Right-wing groups and even the main opposition parties such as the CPRF and LDPR have sought to make political capital by noting that many of the new rich are Jewish, but the public has clearly not taken the bait. As one evaluation of anti-Semitism in Russia has concluded: '… if Russian public opinion has not turned against Jews, it is certainly not owing to the absence of efforts by prominent political leaders to stir up anti-Jewish sentiment'.[23] One can reasonably conclude on the evidence of opinion surveys, voting behaviour and the level of support for far-right groups that anti-Semitism in contemporary Russia is not a strong enough factor to gain widespread electoral support. Indeed, if one group has been used by the state authorities as a scapegoat it is the Chechens, and maybe even immigrants.

It is also the case that, through the central electoral commission, the state authorities can manipulate the electoral system for their own benefit. For example, it is claimed by the head of the Russian think-tank *Panorama* that the Kremlin, through the electoral commission, prevented nationalist parties from being able to register for the December 2007 elections to the Duma. Pribylovsky argued that the Kremlin had done its arithmetic and 'it doesn't need independent ultra-nationalists', concluding that groups such as Great Russia posed too big a potential challenge and hence needed to be outlawed.[24]

Great Russia was set up by Dmitry Rogozin, an influential political personality and former head of Rodina. The Kremlin preferred to have more tame opponents, like the LDPR, rather than ones that could gain electoral support and be more independent of the Kremlin line. Other extreme nationalist groups that have been banned include Eduard Limonov's National Bolshevik Party. Limonov's political fate is perhaps symbolic of that of the extreme right in Russia more generally. He has served time in prison and was once a leading member of the LDPR before splitting with Zhirinovsky to form the National Bolshevik Party, a left-fascist organisation. It was always a remote prospect that the NBP could ever gain power in its own right through the ballot box, although it was always warning of the potentially dangerous avenues that Russia could have journeyed down if economic and social circumstances had deteriorated further.[25] In more recent times, Limonov has moved away from association with skinheads and leading up to the 2007 Duma elections he was calling for a coalition of liberals and nationalists in opposition to Putin.

To conclude, one can state clearly that liberalism and the idea of democracy is weak in the Russian Federation, largely a consequence of the Yeltsin era which associated democracy and liberalism with greed, poverty, corruption and humiliation at what were viewed as Western-imposed reforms. And where liberalism is weak, national sentiments are fairly strong, and these have been harnessed by Putin to both give his regime legitimacy and to create the conditions necessary to rebuild a strong Russian state. However, this is neither a fascist state, nor the installation of a national-socialist system, nor a return to Soviet Communism. Putin can be seen to have harnessed (some would say hijacked) Russian nationalism for his own cause.

We should also recall that far-right nationalism has been a constant feature of, and an influential force in, Russian politics and society for centuries. With the victory of the radical 'left' in October 1917 right-wing nationalist forces were either defeated or forced into exile. However, small numbers of far-right figures found sanctuary in the CPSU itself; although never jettisoning Marxism-Leninism, they developed a form of (what we might term) National Bolshevism, a type of national-socialism.

Stalin's 'Socialism in One Country', as opposed to Trotsky's conception of permanent revolution, harnessed Great Russian nationalist sentiments as part of his quest for legitimacy and fight against German Fascism. The collapse of Communism can only be fully explained with reference to nationalist sentiment as the empire struck back at the end of the twentieth century. This left Russia with a crisis of national identity.

Russians went to bed one night and woke up the next to discover, with no warning, that their country had disappeared while they slept. Russia had lost an empire, its superpower status and its belief system. Initially she was to 'join the West', to integrate as a wealthy, confident and major democratic player in the global capitalist economy. But during the Yeltsin years, Russia saw the most radical decline in living standards ever experienced by a state in peacetime. As a consequence, many predicted a move towards ultra-nationalism and violence as Russia turned against the West and sought to reestablish its lost empire. This would seem to have at least partially occurred.

Peter Shearman

Notes

1. Francis Fukuyama, *The End of History and the Last Man* (New York: The Free Press, 1992).
2. For a critical review of this literature, see Valerie Bunce, 'Should transitologists be grounded?', *Slavic Review*, 54:1 (1995), 15–24.
3. See for a trenchant critique of the failure of Soviet Studies see the special issue of *The National Interest*, 1993, on 'The strange death of Soviet Communism'.
4. M. Cox, & P. Shearman, 'After the fall: nationalist extremism in post-communist Russia' in Paul Hainsworth (ed.), *The Politics of the Extreme Right: From the Margins to the Mainstream* (London: Pinter, 2000).
5. R. Dahl, *Democracy and its Critics* (New Haven, Conn.: Yale University Press, 1991).
6. Donald C. Rawson, *Russian Rightists and the Revolution of 1905* (Cambridge: Cambridge University Press, 1995).
7. M. Cox & P. Shearman, 'After the fall: nationalist extremism in post-communist Russia' in Paul Hainsworth (ed.), *The Politics of the Extreme Right: From the Margins to the Mainstream* (London: Pinter, 2000), 235.
8. B. Clark, 'Nationalist ideas move from the margins', World Today, 52:5 (1996), 119–121. See also M. Cox & P. Shearman, 'After the fall: nationalist extremism in post-communist Russia' in Paul Hainsworth (ed.), *The Politics of the Extreme Right: From the Margins to the Mainstream* (London: Pinter, 2000).
9. M. Cox & P. Shearman, 'After the fall: nationalist extremism in post-communist Russia' in Paul Hainsworth (ed.), *The Politics of the Extreme Right: From the Margins to the Mainstream* (London: Pinter, 2000).
10. W. Laquer, *Black Hundreds. The Rise Of The Extreme Right In Russia* (New York: Harper Collins, 1993), 114.
11. J. Devlin, *The Rise Of The Russian Democrats: The Causes And Consequences Of The Elite Revolution,* (Aldershot: Edward Elgar, 1995), 76
12. JRL (Johnson's Russia List), 27, July 2007, www.cdi.org/russia/johnson.
13. Robert Wistrich,. *Anti-Semitism: The Longest Hatred* (London: Mandarin, 1992), 171.
14. S.K.Carter, *Russian Nationalism: Yesterday, Today, Tomorrow* (New York: St. Martin's Press, 1990), 39.
15. Donald C. Rawson, *Russian Rightists and the Revolution of 1905* (Cambridge: Cambridge University Press, 1995), 52.
16. J. Brent & V.P.Naumov, *Stalin's Last Crime: The Plot Against the Jewish Doctors, 1948–1953* (New York: HarperCollins, 2003).
17. J.L.Gibson & M.M.Howard, 'Russian anti-semitism and the scapegoating of jews', *British Journal Of Political Science*, 37 (2007), 193–223.
18. M. Cox & P. Shearman, 'After the fall: nationalist extremism in post-communt Russia' in Paul Hainsworth (ed.), *The Politics of the Extreme Right: From the Margins to the Mainstream* (London: Pinter, 2000).
19. M. Engel, 'A History Of Hate', *Guardian*, 16 August 1999.
20. Annual Report on Radical Nationalism, 2007.
21. Izvestia, 8 August 2007.
22. P. Kennedy, 'Worried about Putin's Russia?', *International Herald Tribune*, 20 August 2007.
23. J.L.Gibson & M.M.Howard, 'Russian anti-semitism and the scapegoating of jews', *British Journal Of Political Science*, 37 (2007), 193–223.
24. *Moscow Times*, 25 July 2007.
25. Stephen Shenfield, *Russian Fascism: Traditions, Tendencies and Movements* (New York: M.E.Sharpe, 2000).

Scandinavia and the Far Right

As of 2006, the main parties on the Far Right in Scandinavia are: the Danish People's Party (*Dansk Folkeparti*, DPP) in Denmark, and the Progress Party (*Fremskrittspartiet*, FrP) in Norway. Both are well-established parties with a long record. The DPP – founded in 1995, but the successor of the Progress Party which was represented in the Danish Parliament from 1973 – gained 13.3 percent in the 2005 election, up from 12.0 percent in 2001. Since 2001, it has been the key coalition partner of the Liberal-Conservative minority government. The FrP, has also been represented in Parliament since 1973. Though it has had less direct influence on government, the FrP has been even more successful in electoral terms as it won 22.1 percent in the 2005 election, up from 14.6 percent in 2001.

In Sweden and Finland, there are no true equivalents. The True Finns (*Perussuomalaiset*, TF), which in 1995 succeeded the populist Finnish Rural Party, bears some resemblance to the Danish and Norwegian parties in its resistance to **immigration**, but is otherwise quite dissimilar. It gained 1.6 percent and 3 seats in the 2003 parliamentary election, up from 1.0 percent in 1999, and its chairman, Timo **Soini**, received 3.4 percent in the 2006 presidential election. In Sweden, the populist New Democrats (*Ny Demokrati*, NyD) came out of nowhere shortly before the 1991 election and won 6.7 percent of the votes, only to disappear almost as rapidly as it emerged after the next election. By 2006, the closest relative was the Sweden Democrats (*Sverigedemokraterna*, SD) which, historically, has roots in the extreme right. It gained 2.9 percent in the 2006 election, up from 1.4 percent in 2002. However, this result was not sufficient for it to pass the 4 percent threshold for representation. Local elections were held at the same time as the parliamentary election, and here the SD were represented by at least 200 members in the municipal councils, with a stronghold in south-western Sweden (Scania). Even if the result was an all-time high, it was still far below the election results for the Norwegian and Danish parties.

For this reason, this chapter focuses on the Danish and Norwegian parties. Below, we take our point of departure as Klaus von Beyme's identification of three waves of mobilisation of the Far Right in postwar **Europe**. The following section will describe the mobilisation of anti-immigration policies and the transformation of the parties. Then the chapter will analyse the movement from anti-tax policies to a broadly pro-welfare position, and relate this change of party position to the changing cleavage structure in western European societies. The final section will then briefly discuss why the Far Right has been so successful in Denmark and Norway and equally unsuccessful in Sweden and Finland.

Three Waves of the Far Right

To describe the development of the Far Right in Scandinavia, we can begin with the identification of three waves of post-war mobilisation of the extreme right in Europe, as postulated by Klaus von Beyme.[1] He distinguishes between a first wave of neo-fascist, or neo-Nazi, parties that emerged shortly after the war; a second wave of tax revolt parties that began with Pierre Poujade's party in France in the second half of the 1950s, and finally a third wave of xenophobic parties which have emerged from the mid-1980s onwards.

Scandinavia and the Far Right

First Wave: Neo-Fascism

The first wave was virtually non-existent in Scandinavia. Like elsewhere, Nazi parties had been established in Scandinavia in the 1930s, but they obtained very little electoral support. In both Denmark and Norway, the parties had a peak support of just over 2 percent, and the Swedish parties remained even smaller. After the war, all organisations with a past as collaborators and supporters of Nazism were silenced in Denmark and Norway. For Swedish Nazis, old networks were slightly easier to sustain, but the number of sympathisers was small. One of the oldest organisations, the national-socialist Nordic Reich Party (*Nordiska Rikspartiet*, NRP), founded in 1956, occasionally put up candidates in national elections, but the number of votes it received is estimated to be in the low hundreds.[2] However, the first chairman of the SD, Anders **Klarström**, had a history as an NRP activist.

In Denmark, a small Independent Party ran for elections between 1953 and 1968 and typically obtained between 2 and 3 percent of the vote. In 1973 after putting a few candidates on the party list of the Progress Party, one representative was elected. However, even though the Independent Party was far to the right, it was not a 'far-right' party. It was founded by a former Liberal prime minister as a reaction to the abolition of the two-chamber system in 1953, and simply advocated more orthodox liberal and non-socialist policies.

In Norway, there were no parties on the Far Right at that time. However, Anders Lange, who became the founder of the FrP in 1973, had unsuccessfully tried to launch a far-right party in the 1950s. Lange was a strange political propagandist operating on the fringe of the established right wing. Before the war, he had been affiliated with a right-wing organisation sympathetic to Fascism, but he later became definitely anti-Fascist and actively opposed the German occupation.

To conclude, the first wave of far-right mobilisation was virtually absent in Scandinavia. Even though there are a few links to the past, especially in the Swedish case, a balanced assessment suggests that modern far-right parties in Scandinavia are not rooted in any historical tradition of right-wing extremism. Further, it is debatable whether the term 'extremist', in this context, is an appropriate one.

Second Wave: Tax Protest

The parties of the second wave – the Progress parties in Denmark and Norway and, two decades later, the NyD in Sweden – were populist tax **protest** parties. Nevertheless, these parties were quite different from the party of Pierre Poujade a couple of decades earlier. First and foremost, they had a less *petite bourgeois* outlook. In particular, there were no traces of petite bourgeois anti-capitalism or nostalgia for the past. Unlike Poujade's party, the second-wave parties in Scandinavia were *parties of the mature welfare state*, to some extent forerunners of the neo-liberal retrenchment. However, the Danish and Norwegian parties succeeded in transforming themselves from second-wave parties to very successful representatives of the third wave. The Swedish variant, on the other hand, turned out to be a flash-in-the-pan party similar to Poujadism in 1950s France.

The Danish Progress Party (*Fremskridtspartiet*) was launched by the tax lawyer Mogens Glistrup in 1972, and immediately experienced an explosive growth in opinion polls. In the election of December 1973, it obtained 15.6 percent of the votes, and in the subsequent elections of 1975, 1977 and 1979 its support remained above 10 percent. Inspired by Glistrup's success, Anders Lange established a similar party in Norway in 1973. The founders of both parties argued strongly for tax cuts and against the 'lavishness' of the welfare state. Nevertheless, they were distinguishable from conventional right-wing parties not only on account of their anti-elitist, populist style and by their radicalism, but also by demanding more money for health care and old-age pensions – especially in the Danish case.

As has already been mentioned, these parties were, to some extent, forerunners of the neo-liberalism of the 1980s, which started when Margaret Thatcher became the prime minister of Britain in 1979, and Ronald Reagan became President of the US in 1980. The subsequent wave of neo-liberalism reached Norway in 1981, when Kåre Willoch of the Conservative Party was appointed prime minister. The following year the Danish Conservative Party leader, Poul Schlüter, became prime minister of a centre-right government that introduced tough measures to stop the Danish economy's 'course towards the abyss'. With such government measures, the Progress parties were rendered superfluous as proponents of neo-liberalism. Further, taxes were no longer a salient issue among voters.

Accordingly, support for the parties fell to below 4 percent in elections, and even lower in opinion polls in the early 1980s. Moreover, the founder of the Danish party was sentenced to prison for tax fraud, and spent about eighteen months in jail between 1984 and 1985. The situation was critical, and new initiatives were needed. The opportunity for a new platform came when the number of asylum-seekers, who were typically of non-western origin, exploded in the mid-1980s.

The latter issue was also, to some extent, exploited by the Swedish NyD, which was launched shortly before the 1991 election. However, the NyD must be classified primarily as a second-wave party. In Sweden, welfare state retrenchment was largely postponed until the 1990s, thereby creating the political space for criticism of the welfare state as too lavish. After the extremely severe economic crisis in Sweden, and the unprecedented retrenchment that followed after 1991, this part of the party's agenda soon became unusable. At that time, however, the party had already destroyed itself through political and personal disagreement, and what little remained of the party erroneously radicalised the neo-liberal aspects of the party's programme, while dropping the xenophobic tenor. It does not come as any surprise, then, that the party went bankrupt a few years later.

Third Phase: Xenophobia
This brings us to the third phase which, according to von Beyme, began across Europe from the mid-1980s, and was characterised by a xenophobia that was, in part, linked to unresolved social problems. The new parties of this third phase have variously been dubbed 'anti-immigration parties', 'New Populist/Neo-populist Parties', 'Radical Right-wing Populist Parties', 'New Radical Right Parties' and 'Extreme Right Parties'. The term 'new right' is preferable, but this chapter will continue to use the term 'far-right' during the course of its discussion.

Unlike the 'old extreme right parties' from the first phase, typically the third-wave parties have no ideological relationship to Fascism or neo-Fascism. Most of these parties undisputedly defend **democracy**, and they are also clearly against classical ideas of racism based on biological arguments and the idea of hierarchies of races. Rather, they argue that immigration is costly; that ethnic groups are culturally different; and that multiculturalism should be avoided because it undermines cohesion and generates conflict. This 'ethno-pluralist xenophobia' is often surrounded by a broader perception that the nation-state is undermined and threatened by Europeanisation and globalisation and, consequently, needs to be defended.[3]

In Denmark and Norway, immigration arrived on the political agenda when the number of asylum-seekers exploded in the mid-1980s. In Norway, the figures increased from 200 in 1983 to 8,613 in 1987. In Denmark, the corresponding figures were 800 in 1983 and 9,300 in 1986. Thus there was a possibility of revitalising the Progress parties. In Denmark, Mogens Glistrup had already started to fraternise with racist groups in 1979, but that only resulted in internal unrest and electoral losses, in particular among better-educated voters. But, in 1985, the time was ripe. Immediately upon his release from prison, Mogens Glistrup made some very provocative statements that went far beyond the bounds of acceptability, but attracted attention in the media. Subsequently, the statements were 'translated' into a more socially acceptable language by the new *de facto* party leader, Pia **Kjaersgaard**. In the parliamentary elections of 1987 and 1988, the Progress Party was revived, with 4.8 percent and 9.0 percent of the vote respectively (even though part of the increase from 1987 to 1988 must be ascribed to increasing political distrust). In Norway too, the issue of immigration resulted in a second breakthrough for the FrP, which elevated itself from 3.7 percent in the 1985 parliamentary election to 12.3 percent in the 1987 local elections. The party presented itself as the only movement that opposed immigration, arguing that money spent on asylum-seekers should be better spent on taking care of the elderly and sick people of an ethnic Norwegian background. Subsequently, this form of welfare chauvinism has been an important part of the political message of the far-right parties in both countries, while in Denmark the old tax issue has gradually been relegated. This process was catalysed in Denmark when former party leader, Pia Kjaersgaard, broke with the Progress Party in 1995 to launch her new DPP, which abandoned tax protest altogether in favour of a position as a pro-welfare, anti-immigration party.

In Sweden, the Far Right did not benefit much from the issue. After the disastrous 1994 election, the remaining elements of the NyD took the opposite course to Pia Kjaersgaard and largely dropped the immigration issue in favour of classical neo-liberalism. The party went bankrupt a few years later. Only the SD, formed in 1988, took up the issue. The party gained only a negligible number of votes in the general elections of 1988 and 1991; by 1994 it received 14,000 votes; in 1998, it received almost 20,000; and in 2002 it received 76,300 votes, corresponding to 1.4 percent of the electorate. In the September 2006 election, the party's support increased further, but still not enough to a high level to pass the 4 percent threshold.

However, as will be pointed out in the description of party transformations below, the three parties are in many ways dissimilar, and they have had differing levels of success in disassociating themselves clearly from more extremely racist and nationalist parties.

The Politicisation of Immigration

Until the Mid-1980s: No Political Divisions

As will be pointed out, the issue of immigration has triggered strong political divisions that cut across traditional left/right affiliations, and it has generated a new, two-dimensional political cleavage structure in Danish and Norwegian politics. As late as 1985, attitudes towards immigration among Norwegian voters did not vary much according to party preference, and FrP voters did not deviate from the population at large in this respect. But, from 1988 onwards, regarding attitudes to immigration, all surveys locate FrP voters at one extreme and left-socialist voters at the other, with the Social Democrats in an uneasy and divided position around the centre.

Likewise, a Danish opinion poll question from 1979 concerning guest **workers** revealed no difference at all between Progress Party voters and the adherents of other parties, except for a slightly more liberal attitude among left-socialist voters. This indicates that the issue was not politicised in Denmark either. The flow of migrant workers from circa 1970 had not made immigration an issue: their numbers were modest, they were not expected to stay, and there was nearly full employment. Few people objected to a situation where guest workers accepted the low-status jobs that the indigenous population left vacant. Nor was it a political issue when the decision was made in the early 1970s to stop immigration of guest workers. This was supported even by the left. But, with the massive arrival of refugees from the mid-1980s, the issue was redefined and became salient among voters. This started the third phase of the Far Right's development in Scandinavia.

The Mobilisation of the Immigration Issue

Even though their figures remain modest, the number of 'non-western' immigrants has increased rapidly in the Nordic countries. By 2006, 'non-western' immigrants and descendants constituted about 6 percent of the population in Denmark, and about 5 percent in Norway. However, immigrants are not evenly spread geographically, especially in Norway where there is a large concentration in the capital, Oslo. Further, the age profile of migrants is such that the proportion of immigrant schoolchildren is about twice as high as in the population at large. As labour market integration of non-western immigrants remains very low in the Nordic countries, problems are visible. Not least, there has been increasing public attention on social problems like ghettoisation, schooling, juvenile delinquency, language issues, unemployment and welfare dependency – as well as growing awareness of prejudices and discrimination.

Further, because the Scandinavian countries – with the exception of the Sami people in the far north – traditionally have been very homogeneous in religious and ethnic terms, and also not especially religious, learning to live with cultural diversity has also proved quite difficult. This issue is particularly problematic because, at the same time, **religion** has become an important source of identity-formation among immigrants themselves. In recent times, Islam has become the second largest religious denomination next to state Lutheranism. In Denmark, the number can be estimated to be around 200,000 - 225,000,[4] and in Norway just below 100,000, or, in relative terms, approximately four and two percent of the respective populations.

Election studies show that the issue is higher up in terms of voters' interest in Denmark than in Norway. This is indicated by analysing questions put to the public about what formed the most important criteria when supporting a party (Norway), or about the most important issues that politicians should address (Denmark). In the last three Norwegian parliamentary elections – 1997, 2001 and 2005 – only around 5 percent of answers have been about immigration. In Denmark, the level has been much higher, especially in the 2001 parliamentary election, when one half of voters, 20 percent of all answers, spontaneously referred to immigration as a central issue.

In addition, the issue of immigration is more polarising in Denmark. In Norway, the prominence of immigration almost always involves negative attitudes: the vast majority among those who mention immigration as the most important issue for party choice also voted for the FrP. Contrastingly, in Denmark the pro-immigration camp have also mobilised on the issue. By 2005, people who were sympathetic to immigrants were about as likely to point to immigration as the most important issue as those who were negative. In particular, the centre party, the Radical Liberals, have benefited from this issue.

From an Economic Issue to a Cultural Issue
In Norway as well as in Denmark, the arguments against immigration have also shifted from the economic to the cultural. In the manifestos of the Progress parties from the 1980s, immigration was discussed almost purely in economic terms. The FrP argued for supporting **education** in Norwegian, against subsidising housing and against all sorts of affirmative action policies that were seen as favouring immigrants and as discriminating against Norwegians. Thus, the party presented itself as the only one that did not discriminate according to ethnicity, religion and culture. This theme was also echoed in the manifesto of the Danish party in the early 1990s.

However, gradually the manifesto of the FrP revealed a shift from economic to cultural arguments, and was based on a critique of multiculturalism. It was argued that a multicultural society generates conflicts, whereas an ethnically homogeneous society was seen as a precondition for peace and harmony in society. This was because different ethnic groups would always find it hard to co-exist peacefully. Following on from this view, by 2006 the FrP recommended a very restrictive policy towards new immigration, allowing only a quota of 1,000 'non-western' immigrants per year, including people seeking asylum and attempting to reunify families.

In particular, both the Norwegian and Danish parties have argued against liberal rules of citizenship (which were granted almost automatically after seven years in both countries until the rules were tightened in Denmark from 2002), and against the right of foreign citizens with three years of legal residence to vote in local elections. Further, they have demanded that the criteria for **family** reunion should be tightened, and that immigrants who commit crime should be expelled from the country. In the Danish case, these demands have to a large extent been satisfied since 2001.

Internal Conflict over Immigration
The reorientation towards immigration as the key rallying issue has not only increased electoral support for the far-right parties, in Norway it also resulted in a party split. A group of die-hard neo-liberals, who stuck to ideological doctrines such as the free movement of the workforce, had put their mark on the party's manifesto in the 1980s. According to the manifesto, in principle the party would favour free immigration, provided that migrants could manage without public support. Similar formulations also found their way into the manifesto of the Danish Progress Party, which stated that foreigners were welcome if they did not impose extra social expenditure on Danish citizens or commit any crimes. Neo-liberals were still allowed to put forward their views in parts of the party programme, but in its public statements the party increasingly emphasised welfare alongside immigration, with the issue of tax more or less dropped.

The notion of free immigration disappeared from the Norwegian party's manifestos when the anti-immigration faction won over the hardcore liberalists in 1994. Four out of ten MPs left the party, along with the **youth** organisation, which was itself a neo-liberal stronghold. In spite of this dramatic split, the party subsequently won a convincing victory in the 1995 local elections where immigration once again emerged as a central issue. In the 1995 election survey, one-half of those who voted for the FrP mentioned immigration as the most important issue for their party choice. During the 1995 election, to many voters the FrP appeared as a single-issue party. About 90 percent of those who regarded the immigrant question as the most important issue voted for the FrP.

In the Danish case, a more thorough break with the past took place when the DPP became the successor party of the Progress Party. In the first half of the 1990s, the Progress Party almost disintegrated. At first, Mogens Glistrup became more and more extreme and frustrated over not being in control of 'his' party. In 1990, he tried unsuccessfully to run for office on his own list, and was subsequently excluded from the party. However, this did not bring an end to the unrest. After a prolonged period of internal strife over the control of the Progress Party, in 1995 the former party leader Pia Kjaersgaard decided to leave the party and form a new party of her own: the Danish People's Party. This gave rise to the opportunity to get rid of most of the party's older neo-liberal legacy.

The manifesto of the DPP is built more strictly around the notion of nationalism. Rather than low taxes, this nationalism explicitly involves a social obligation to take care of the weak within society. The party has adopted a positive attitude towards welfare, and has deliberately tried to steal the welfare agenda from the Social Democrats, for example by successfully demanding more money for poor pensioners and the disabled, by opposing retrenchment in early retirement programmes and the like. The party has served as a loyal and reliable coalition partner for the Liberal-Conservative government since 2001, but it has deliberately sought to present itself as the guarantor of welfare schemes. In this respect, it has moved much further than the Norwegian party, which, to a greater extent, is in competition with other bourgeois parties, whereas the Danish party is in competition more directly with the Social Democrats.

As far as immigration is concerned, both the Danish and the Norwegian parties have been keen to maintain a 'socially respectable' image, and they have explicitly dissociated themselves from racism, as well as from radical right movements like **Le Pen**'s **National Front** (*Front National*, FN). Here, the art is to go as far as possible without overstepping the invisible line of public decency. On quite a few occasions, the leadership of the DPP has gone too far. But the main task has been to maintain strict control over its members and representatives in order to ensure that they do not destroy the party's image as a non-racist and respectable party. The DPP is extremely centralised, and exclusions have often taken place. In the summer of 2006, an undercover journalist from a Danish newspaper phoned some of the DPP's local chairmen and asked whether he could become a member of the party even though he had previously been more or less affiliated with the racist movement Danish Front. Immediately after the appearance of this story in the press, those who, according to the newspaper, had answered positively, were excluded without any inquiry or interrogation whatsoever. This approach may cause some frustration within the party organisation, but it is of the utmost importance in the effort to keep the party's image 'clean'. By and large the party has succeeded in this effort.

The Switch to Pro-Welfare Parties

Alongside the increasing emphasis on immigration, the DPP and the FrP have increasingly marketed themselves as pro-welfare parties, or even as parties that carry the legacy of classical social democracy. In particular, this is the case with the Danish party. As stated by Pia Kjaersgaard at the party's annual meeting in 2006: 'A true Social Democrat votes for the Danish People's Party'.[5]

Over the years, the Norwegian party has also become more and more friendly towards the welfare state. However, in Norway, there was greater continuity between the second and the third wave: i.e. no change of party and no change of party leadership. This also means that the party's critical attitude towards taxes has been maintained, and the party still embraces a number of policy positions from its liberal past. This includes a number of proposals for reforming the public sector, such as outsourcing, partial privatisation of hospitals and budgeting according to the 'taxameter principle', that is, allocating money in proportion to production in schools, universities, hospitals etc. Increasingly, such principles have been implemented in both countries, but the DPP has not pressed for changes in this direction. Further, as a pure opposition party, the FrP also seeks to use discontent in a somewhat more opportunistic way than the DPP, which is essentially loyal to the government.

The Norwegian party still argues for tax cuts, but not as vigorously as during the first years of existence, and for a long time the party has demanded that more money should be appropriated to welfare programmes, especially for the elderly. Indeed, the FrP has successfully built an image of a party that promotes care for the elderly. In the 2001 elections, no other party received a higher score among voters regarding which party they believed forwarded the best policy in terms of caring for the elderly. In the 2005 elections, the party's reputation in this respect was somewhat weakened, but it still scored well, coming in second only to the Social Democrats. Also in Denmark, a study of party images in 2006 showed that, when people were asked which party protected the interests of elderly people, an absolute majority of voters pointed at the DPP.

The pro-welfare stance of the DPP has implied that the party has completely abandoned any demands for lower taxes. Since 2001, it has supported the government's 'tax stop' policy which forbids any increase in any tax rates, but it has tried to modify the government's proposals for tax relief even when it was not accompanied by any savings. For example, in 2003, the party successfully demanded that the amount of tax relief should be reduced in favour of more welfare benefits to pensioners.

The FrP is able to argue for increasing welfare benefits and decreasing taxation at the same time. Because of the enormous oil revenues received by the country, this is not quite as contradictory as it might seem. Indeed, an important new conflict has developed in Norwegian politics concerning the issue of whether to save or spend more oil money. In the 1997 election campaign, one of the party's slogans was: 'Use the oil revenues for the people's welfare'. Nearly all the other parties followed the advice of economists which said that such a policy would be irresponsible and would cause the **economy** to over-heat. As the economy was already working close to its capacity limit, such a policy could lead to serious problems regarding inflation.

At any rate, both parties have moved towards the political centre. The FrP has even proposed that the government should act as an investor in the market, and argued for the establishment of large government funds in order to ensure that Norwegian businesses are kept in Norwegian hands, thus preventing acquisitions by foreign investors. But first and foremost, both parties have sought to position themselves as pro-welfare parties close to the Social Democrats. This reflects a rational exploitation of the new political opportunities provided by a changing cleavage structure that has thoroughly altered Danish and Norwegian politics, including the notions of 'left' and 'right'.

The Contemporary Far Right

One might say that contemporary far-right parties in Denmark and Norway are strong *because of* the weak historical traditions of the Far Right. This has not only helped them avoid the image problems associated with interwar extremism, but has also allowed the parties to be more flexible and to adapt their policies to reflect changing socio-political situations. These situations have altered substantially in both countries, due to the emergence of a new, two-dimensional political cleavage structure. In Denmark, the DPP and the Liberals have jointly been able to attract former core Social Democrat voters, and have built a new majority situated to the right, one that would have been unthinkable until the late 1990s.

However, the meaning of 'left' and 'right' has changed. In a way, this is nothing new. Basically, these concepts have changed their meaning ever since they were introduced during the French Revolution. At that time, the left-right dimension centred on a liberal fight for political rights, democracy and representative government. This fight ended long ago, but in Denmark it is still visible in the names of the two parties usually considered to be to the right of the centre line on the *economic* left/right dimension.

In Denmark and partly Norway, the left/right economic axis has been dominant from the early twentieth century until the 1990s. In Norway, the centre-periphery cleavage has in short periods been a challenger. The economic left/right axis has its origin in the emergence of industrial society, and arose from the conflict between labour and capital. This conflict crystallised into two blocs of political parties, which for many years were called the socialist and bourgeois parties. The divisive issues were questions regarding economic distribution, taxes and welfare, and state control versus free markets. Such economic conflicts will always remain relevant, even though some issues relating to state ownership or state control have become obsolete. In addition, broad support for the welfare state has softened the left/right economic dispute in Scandinavia. Nevertheless, this political cleavage structure remained dominant in Denmark until it was challenged by new value-based politics. Due to a simple political cleavage structure between bourgeois and proletarian politics, Denmark and Sweden used to be the class-polarised polities *par excellence*, even though class conflicts were peaceful and moderate.

With the emergence of post-industrial society and globalisation, new issues such as environmentalism, gender equality and immigration have come to the forefront. Even though conflicts over such issues are conceptually different, increasingly they can be seen to converge empirically into a new value politics with its own left/right dimension. We use the terms 'left' and 'right' to describe the new value dimension of politics as this reflects how positions are perceived and political identities are formed among the general population. The new value dimension to politics comes close to what has been dubbed 'materialism-postmaterialism' by Ronald Inglehart. His book, *The Silent Revolution*, was written with reference to the youth and student rebellion of the late 1960s. Even though the explanations in terms of affluence and socialisation may be open to question, Inglehart's theory, with an emphasis on environmentalism and public influence on governance, at least provided an account of the emergence of the 'new left'.

However, the emergence of the 'new right' at the opposite pole is difficult to explain in terms of Inglehart's theory. As suggested by Ignazi, the new right might be conceived as a 'silent counterrevolution' i.e. as a reaction to the new left.[6] But this is also too narrow a viewpoint. Rather, the new right is related to an authoritarian/liberal polarisation that was triggered by immigration. Lipset had already talked about 'working-class authoritarianism' in *Political Man*, but at that time this phenomenon was unimportant for electoral behaviour, which was determined mainly by economic and class interests. Further, as working-class parties were anti-authoritarian, the practical implications in western democracies were small. With the increasing significance of immigration, and with more 'rational' voting behaviour leading to people voting increasingly in accordance with their political attitudes, the situation has fundamentally changed.

Empirically, the 'materialist versus post-materialist' and 'authoritarian versus liberal' value dimensions increasingly tend to converge in Scandinavia. Attitudes towards Europeanisation and globalisation are sometimes linked to either one of these dimensions but, at least up until the point of writing, attitudes towards the European Union stand out as a separate conflict line in Scandinavian politics. The crucial point here is that values reflecting levels of education have become at least as important as distributional attitudes or economic left/right positions, which reflect class structures, as determinants of party choice and the construction of political identities that are seen to operate on 'the left' or 'the right'.

Electoral researchers in Denmark have demonstrated that an individual's position on the economic/distributional dimension, and their position on the value dimension – both measured by issue positions – are approximately of equal importance in determining self-placement on a scale ranging from 0, representing the 'left', to 10, representing the 'right'. The latter is a subjective scale where voters themselves decide the meaning of 'left' and 'right'. Also, in Norway, this value-dimension has increased our ability to determine voters' position on the left/right dimension. However, the economic/distributional dimension is still the most important factor.

When voters are asked to place the different parties on the 0–10 left/right scale, the values of the FrP and the DPP are usually equated to the 'most right' positions of all parties, even among the parties' own followers. However, when it comes to the position of the parties' supporters on the distributional left/right scale, these are much closer to the centre, and this also holds for voters' evaluations of the parties' position on distributional issues. On the values dimension, both the followers themselves and voters' assessment of party positions unambiguously locate new right parties on the Far Right.

The economic and value-based left/right axes have different social compositions. The economic left/right dimension reveals a well-known pattern. At the left pole we find lower-class people, people with minor educational attainments and people with low incomes, whereas the rich and well educated are located to the right. Support for politics of redistribution reflects social class. Education can be interpreted both as a class variable and as a socialisation variable. Higher education offers a better position in the class structure, but also breeds humanistic values that pull individuals to the left on the value dimension.

On the value dimension, the left pole attracts people with high education and income, whereas the lower-educated tend to be attracted to the right. Consequently, manual workers are typically positioned towards the right pole on the value dimension, but to the left on the economic left/right dimension. This contradiction, strengthened by increasing significance of the value dimension of politics, has alienated workers from what might be viewed as their traditional parties.

This has opened great opportunities for far-right movements. Because they are closer to the average worker than socialist parties on the value dimension of politics, they are able to attract substantial numbers of working-class voters, provided that the parties' positions on the economic left/right axis are not too far to the right. Therefore, it is rational for these parties to adapt their policy image on distributional and welfare policies. And this is exactly what we find. Workers are increasingly over-represented among far-right supporters, and the DPP and the FrP today have higher proportions of manual workers among their supporters than the social democratic parties. Among 'new left' parties, we find the very opposite trend in social composition of supporters.

However, there remains a difference between the Danish and Norwegian parties, as the DPP has increasingly moved towards a centrist or even centre-left position on issues of welfare, taxation and economic inequality. By pursuing this strategy, the DPP has consolidated its victory over the Social Democrats, which has decisively tipped the balance between the parties and weakened the centre-left alternative. To some extent, this may be seen as a reflection of the changes in the strategy of bourgeois parties, in particular the Liberals, who have also adopted a much more pro-welfare and anti-immigration stance than was previously the case. It seems likely that part of what is mobilised by the Liberals in the Danish case would be mobilised in Norway by the FrP. It is also worth noting that, in spite of the close similarities between the Danish and the Norwegian parties, there is virtually no contact between them. The FrP has even openly declared that it does not want any contact with the DPP.

Sometimes, workers' attraction to far-right parties is interpreted in terms of threats of marginalisation rather than in terms of values. In the labour market, globalisation and the transition from an industrial to a post-industrial society generates winners and losers: as a consequence of automation and outsourcing, routine jobs in manufacturing tend to disappear, and in this process of de-industrialisation manual workers can easily end up as losers. Thus, according to this theory – which resembles classical explanations of Fascism as expression of 'panic of the middle class' – the radical right has a special appeal to the losers in modernisation or globalisation, or at least to those groups of voters who do not benefit from socio-economic change.

However, the Scandinavian experience does not fit easily within this theory. In the first place, the success of far-right movements in the first decade of the new century coincides with economic prosperity and record-low unemployment. Furthermore, skill differences in unemployment are unusually low in Scandinavia – there are few potential 'modernisation losers'. These are also the countries where sentiments regarding globalisation in the general population are the most optimistic. Paul Taggart has stressed that 'new protest parties', including far-right parties, have optimum conditions in which to operate when there is long-term economic success and there are strong welfare states.[7] To some extent, this is a plausible perspective. At least the absence of other problems, such as economic crisis and unemployment, leaves more space for issues, including welfare, immigration and even the **environment**, to develop on the political agenda.

However, the surge of the Far Right must be related to structural changes and new political cleavage structures. First and foremost, the Far Right is structurally related to globalisation and concomitant immigration. How globalisation affects nation-states economically, politically and culturally, is somewhat different from one state to another. In Scandinavia, with prosperous economic conditions, value-based conflicts that reflect the emergence of a new social-cultural cleavage are the 'natural' outcome. Politics is about conflict, and even though immigrants remain a relatively small minority, a large number of new issues which mobilise strong conflicts of values have entered the political agenda. To take the extreme cases, the tragic killings of Muslim girls by their own fathers, however infrequent such cases are, have shocked the Scandinavian public. So have instances of genital mutilation. To take a more general issue, clashes between cultural traditions and individual rights, such as forced and arranged marriages, serve to generate tensions. A clash has also emerged between feminism and multiculturalism. Feminism has argued for universal rights irrespective of culture, whereas multiculturalism celebrates cultural diversity. And the increasing visibility of religion – sometimes fundamentalist religion – in some of the world's most secular and unreligious societies also serves to generate negative attention and tensions, in particular in societies where other social problems are relatively few.

These considerations suggest that we are dealing with more general phenomena which are not peculiar to specific nations. Rather, it is the absence of similar conflicts in other Scandinavian countries that needs to be explained. In particular, why is it the case that the Far Right has, until now, been unsuccessful in Sweden and Finland? This chapter does not offer a fully-fledged explanation of this, but will present some considerations that are worth mentioning.

The Failure of the Far Right in Sweden and Finland

Differences in attitudes

Of course, the first possible explanation is simply that there is not a similar demand for far-right movements in the Swedish and Finnish populations. This explanation is not entirely without credibility. All international comparisons describe the Swedes as the most tolerant people in Europe,[8] even though immigrants constitute a larger part of the Swedish population than in most other countries. However, this argument does not really apply to Finland,[9] and in comparative terms, all the Nordic populations appear as relatively tolerant,[10] with negative attitudes towards Islam forming an exception. Interestingly, Islamophobia in Denmark is stronger among those who have fewer affiliations with Christianity (with the exception of the most orthodox Christians). In other words, Islamophobia is nourished by negative attitudes towards religion.

Differences in attitudes of tolerance may contribute to an explanation of why far-right parties have less appeal in Sweden. However, it cannot explain the *absence* of significant far-right parties. Besides, one may ask why Swedes are more tolerant than the people of the other Nordic countries. Further, what matters the most is not minor differences in attitudes to immigration. Rather, it is the prominence of the issue which is consistently lower in Sweden and Finland than in Denmark. However, even explanations in terms of the saliency of immigration are inadequate because there are also large differences between Denmark and Norway in this respect. At this point, it is probably the *institutionalisation* or *'freezing'* of new political cleavages that are significant in the Danish and Norwegian contexts. And at any rate, we need an explanation of this difference in the prominence of immigration. In Finland, this might be explained by the fact that immigration is a more novel phenomenon, and that the composition of immigrants is quite different. The latter explanation even has some relevance to Sweden, but on the other hand, Sweden hosts by far the largest proportion of immigrants, and its problems with labour market integration and cultural tensions are very much similar to the other countries.

The Supply of Parties

One may argue quite convincingly that the Norwegian and Danish parties are better equipped to mobilise significant groups of voters due to their positions on key issues with appeal to the working class, and due to their image as relatively moderate parties. The SD carries a legacy of past excesses and an image of extremism that is regarded as far more outspoken. At the same time, the party suffers from a programmatic weakness on other issues, and from obsolete ideas, such as very traditional ideas about the family. This is also the case with the True Finns (*Perussuomalaiset*, TF). Indeed, it is questionable whether the TF belongs to this party family at all, in spite of the strong anti-immigration stance of some of its spokesmen. However, such issue positions may also, to some extent, be considered a dependent variable: with a strong and professional party organisation, parties are better equipped to design vote-maximising policies.

Institutional and Media Barriers

In Sweden, there is a 4 percent threshold for representation in parliament, as has also been the case in Norway since the 1989 election. If Denmark and Norway had also enforced such a threshold before 1989, the Progress parties would have been out of parliament in the early 1980s, and it is questionable whether they would have been given a second chance to develop as a political force. However, it is also worth noting that Finland does not have such barriers to parliamentary representation.

Access to the media is important. In the 1973 election campaign, the Danish Progress Party and Anders Lange's party participated in television and radio programmes on the same terms as the established political parties. In contrast, during the 2006 election, the SD were expelled from all the important mass media outlets. They even experienced problems when trying to buy advertising space. Some of the most influential newspapers had an advertising ban on the SD.

The success of the Danish and Norwegian parties, in contrast to the failure of NyD, illustrates another characteristic, namely that new parties are very vulnerable during their first years of existence, and that it is very difficult to establish new political movements.

Preconditions for the Formation of New Parties

In 1971 Sten Berglund and Ulf Lindstrøm published a book entitled *The Scandinavian Party System(s)*, which described the party systems as relatively similar, dominated by five party types: Conservatives, Liberals, Agrarians, Social Democrats and Communist/ Left Socialist Parties. As these countries are relatively similar in terms of culture and social and political structures, this similarity was not very surprising. However, in Sweden no tax revolt parties emerged during the 1970s and the 1980s. This is puzzling. The formation of new parties is difficult, and there are at least two important hurdles. It takes extraordinary circumstances to launch a new party, and it is very difficult to consolidate a new movement. High thresholds of representation of course serve to augment such problems.

In all countries, the end of the 1960s and the beginning of the 1970s was the most expansive period for the welfare state, with unprecedented tax increases. However, in both Denmark and Norway the incumbent parties were coalitions of non-socialist parties, which followed on from a long period in which the Social Democrats were in office. This aroused frustration and distrust among non-socialist voters, who had hoped for a change of regime, but only saw taxes escalating even faster than before. In Sweden, however, the Social Democrats remained in office during the period of the most expansive growth of the welfare state. Accordingly, bourgeois voters in Sweden did experience a similar disappointment, and distrust did not really escalate until 1976 when a bourgeois coalition took over.

Another difference is that Denmark and Norway both had referendums regarding membership of the European Community (EC) in 1972, one year before the 1973 breakthrough for the far-right parties. The referendum campaign generated considerable polarisation between voters and party elites, especially in Norway, and contributed to an atmosphere of political distrust. The bonds of loyalty between voters and their parties deteriorated, facilitating the breakthrough of new parties.

The 1973 polls in Denmark and Norway have been called 'earthquake' elections. In Denmark, the number of parties represented in parliament doubled from five to ten. Due to the referendum and bourgeois disappointment, the political establishments had lost some of their defence mechanisms, which normally precluded the emergence of new parties. In 1991, after a referendum about nuclear power, Sweden experienced a similar 'earthquake'. A new far-right party, NyD, gained 6.4 percent of the vote, and in the same election Christian Democrats succeeded in gaining representation for the first time. By 1991, Swedish voters had also learned that the differences between a social democratic and a non-socialist government were small.

Even though the new issue of immigration was on the political agenda and was reflected in the party programme of NyD, it was basically a second-wave party. Further, it turned out to be a short-lived movement. The party disintegrated after only one parliamentary term. This was a reminder that the conditions conducive for the breakthrough of a new party are dissimilar to the conditions favourable for consolidation.

Conditions of Consolidation: Leadership and Organisation

The survival of a party leadership is an extremely important factor, yet rivalry and internal conflicts tend to be the rule. After a short period of time, a serious split occurred between the two founders of NyD, Bert Carlsson and Ian Wachtmeister. They were unable to cooperate, and neither of them wanted to remain in charge of the party. NyD was exceptional in the fact that both leaders retired. Indeed, its survival would actually have been a miracle.

In short, leadership is a decisive factor in the initial phase of the life of a political party, when it is most vulnerable. This applies to all parties, but even more so to populist parties where charismatic leaders often become synonymous with the parties themselves. However, different skills are required to launch and to consolidate a new party. This is perhaps an explanation as to why populist parties tend to be 'flash-in-the-pan' parties. However, in both Norway and Denmark, the Progress parties were, so to speak, rescued from their founders, Anders Lange and Mogens Glistrup. Both leaders soon experienced problems with running the party on a daily basis.

The competence of Anders Lange's leadership was questioned immediately after the parliamentary group was established. Lange argued against ordinary party organisation while another faction led by the later chairman, Carl I. **Hagen**, argued for the same style of organisation that was found in other parties. After one year in parliament, Lange suddenly died, and the party was expected to collapse. However, Lange's replacement as MP, Carl I. Hagen, who had actually temporarily left the party at this point, rejoined and managed to reorganise the party.

Like Carl I. Hagen, Pia Kjærsgaard was a replacement MP for the Danish Progress Party's founder, Mogens Glistrup, who was imprisoned for tax evasion in 1984. She managed to capture *de facto* leadership of the party at a time when Glistrup had become increasingly extreme, unpredictable and isolated within the party. Upon his return from prison, Glistrup was re-elected MP in 1987, but found himself without much influence. He finally defected in 1990, when he tried to launch a new party, The Party of Wellbeing. Eventually he was invited to rejoin and lead the party in 2000, but only managed to kill the party, even though the events of 11 September 2001 offered him a platform for his extremely xenophobic viewpoints. The Progress Party only managed to obtain 0.4 percent and no seats in the 2001 elections. Ironically, Mogens Glistrup, who formed the Danish Progress Party in 1972, became the same person who led the party to its downfall thirty years later.

Later in the 1990s, personal conflicts accumulated within the Progress Party's parliamentary group as the majority worked to prevent a concentration of power in the hands of Pia Kjaersgaard. It ended in the birth of a new party. Kjaersgaard became a strong and firm leader of the DPP. In this way, a parallel can be drawn with Carl I. Hagen. From 1978 to 2006, Hagen was the chairman and undisputed leader of the FrP. He has even been described as the owner of the party. This has not prevented quarrels and controversies; for example, several vice-chairmen and aspiring leaders have dropped out in protest, though none of them have seriously tried to launch new parties. Hagen and the FrP have been regarded as synonymous. He began a gradual retirement from the party after the 2005 elections, as a new and younger generation emerged. After his victory in the 2005 election, it was seen as a personal triumph for Hagen that he passed over the position as leader of the parliamentary group to the aspiring new chairman Siv Jensen. She was elected the new chairman of the party during the 2006 party conference. With twenty-eight years as chairman, Hagen had been party leader longer than any other political leader in Norwegian political history.

Hagen and Kjærsgaard have put emphasis on cooperation and respectability. They have practised firm leadership based on a strong, hierarchical and centralised party organisation. Strong party discipline has been combined with exclusions and lay-offs. According to the statutes of the FrP, party members who publicly harm the party can be excluded. Consequently, both parties can easily rid themselves of disobedient members. Members who have fraternised with right-wing extremism have been excluded. In Norway, MPs have been forced to leave the FrP's parliamentary group when they have crossed the boundaries of political acceptability, especially in reference to the immigration debate. Carl I. Hagen's long-term plan was to redefine the party in order to prepare himself for a position in government. In order to succeed, the party must, in Hagen's words, be 'responsible and predictable'. This strategy implies that the free-speaking elements within the party, especially on the immigration question, are silenced or expelled. Exactly the same strategy has secured great influence for the DPP in government since 2001.

Party Competition and Prominence

As mentioned, an important factor in understanding the collapse of NyD was probably the extremely severe economic crisis which occurred soon after the 1991 election. Accelerating unemployment, exploding state debt and the bankruptcy of the major banks created an atmosphere of uncertainty among voters where issues like taxation, and even immigration, appeared completely irrelevant.

However, another major variable is whether the issue of immigration enters the field of party competition. In Sweden and Finland, the absence of a major anti-immigration party and consensus among the major parties not to compete over this issue serve to make the issue less salient to voters. Just prior to the 2006 election, the immigration issue was not even mentioned during the final Swedish party leaders' debate.

In Denmark, the situation is different. The issue of immigration has even entered party competition between the 'established' parties. The gains of the DPP, and to some extent the Liberals, on this issue have not only seriously eroded support for the Social Democrats, but also, for a decade, left the party in a state of confusion and internal strife. Such intra-party conflicts, in turn, are the kind of stories that are most attractive to journalists, and contribute to secure permanent media coverage of the subject.

Thus, it comes as no surprise that the new political cleavage structure is strongly institutionalised in Denmark – indeed it would be correct to describe this new cleavage line as more or less 'frozen', as supporters of the Danish People's Party reveal no sign of returning to the parties they came from, in particular the Social Democrats.

If the diagnoses above are true, we should not look for factors that explain why there are relatively large far-right parties in Denmark and Norway, but not in Sweden and Finland. It is likely that the latter countries may witness the emergence of significant far-right parties in the years to come, even though a number of factors, such as the opinion climate and the threshold of representation, are somewhat less conducive in Sweden. However, it does seem to be the case that the current small parties are not too well equipped to represent broad, critical voter segments, like the Danish and Norwegian parties. And it must be underlined that the breakthrough and consolidation of new parties is a very difficult process, one that depends on a large number of factors, including leadership and the weakening of voter ties to the existing parties. As far as the latter precondition is concerned, both Sweden and Finland have revealed a long-term decline in political trust, party identification and electoral participation – all of which signal a relatively fertile ground for the formation of new parties.

Perhaps the most important fact about the Danish and Norwegian parties is that they show how such parties can survive and prosper: not only by exploiting dissatisfaction with existing parties among lower-educated voters, but also by consolidating this support through an image as pro-welfare and 'moderate' parties.

Tor Bjørklund

Notes
1. Klaus von Beyme, 'Right-Wing extremism in post-war Europe', *West European Politics* 11 (1988) 1–18.
2. Heléne Lööw, *Nazismen i Sverige 1980–1997: Den Rasistiska Underground-Rörelsen: Musiken, Myterna, Riterna* (Stockholm: Ordfront Förlag, 1998).
3. Jens Rydgren, *From Tax Populism to Ethnic Nationalism: Radical Right-Wing Populism in Sweden* (New York and Oxford: Berghahn Books, 2006).
4. Statistics Denmark. 2006: 41.
5. *Politiken*, 17 September 2006.

6. Piero Ignazi, 'The silent counter-revolution. Hypotheses on the emergence of extreme right-wing parties in Europe', *European Journal of Political Research,* 22 (1992) 3–34.

7. Paul. A. Taggart, *The New Populism and the New Politics: New Protest Parties in Sweden in a Comparative Perspective* (London: Macmillan, 1996).

8. Hans Jørgen Nielsen, *Er Danskerne Fremmedfjendske?* (Rockwool Foundation Research Unit/ Aarhus University Press, 2004).

9. Elina Kestilä, 'Is there a demand for radical right populism in the Finnish electorate?', *Scandinavian Political Studies* 29:3 (2006), 169–191.

10. Jørgen Goul Andersen, *Immigration and the Legitimacy of the Scandinavian Welfare State,* AMID Working Paper, 53 (2006).

Also used as references:

Jørgen Goul Andersen & Tor Bjørklund, 'Radical right-wing populism in Scandinavia: from tax revolt to neo-liberalism and xenophobia' in Paul Hainsworth (ed.), *The Politics of the Extreme Right. From the Margins to the Mainstream* (London: Pinter, 2000).

Jørgen Goul Andersen & Tor Bjørklund, 'Anti-immigration parties in Denmark and Norway: the progress parties and the Danish People's Party' in Martin Schain, Aristide Zolberg & Patrick Hossay (eds.), *Shadows over Europe: The Development and Impact of the Extreme Right in Western Europe* (New York: Palgrave Macmillan, 2002).

South-Eastern Europe and the Far Right

After being front-page news throughout the 1990s, the Balkans are now relegated to obscurity. It was in 1991 that socialist Yugoslavia began disintegrating, unleashing a wave of ultra-nationalism and war that threatened to destabilise the entire region. Some feared a wide conflict, threatening to pull in every country from Hungary to Turkey. But with the incarceration and death of Serbian president Slobodan **Milošević** and the passing of his Croatian counterpart, Franjo **Tuđman**, all worries have faded. The international community is now preoccupied with other crises, such as the Middle East, Iran, Pakistan, Afghanistan and North Korea.

For the attention it receives in the media now, the Balkans might be thought of as an island of stability. This, however, is far from the truth. In recent years, radical right movements and parties across the region have shown signs of reawakening, while for the most part outsiders, particularly in the West, remain fixated on regional investment opportunities.[1] In Serbia and Croatia, extreme nationalism has never really fallen out of favour. In other countries, such as Bulgaria, it was slow to find support at first, but now seems to be gathering a following. In Romania, where ultra-nationalists once admired communist leaders, recent developments show that such practices are giving way, and a move towards embracing the country's fascist past is filling the void. A country like Slovenia, where extremist politicians are losing ground, may prove to be the exception.

What will happen to the region in the longer term is a subject that may prove to serve up ammunition for lively futurologists' debates. But what may be said with a high degree of certainty is that while the radical right is gaining momentum, for the foreseeable future it is not likely to produce consequences that might destabilise the area all over again.[2] While some analysts may see the sudden collapse of **Communism** as having created a void that reactionaries may fill, the reality is, simply, that in many cases they have either failed to do so, or while they may be said to be working on such an objective, are moving at a painfully slow pace.[3] Moreover, in some places, such as the former Yugoslavia, radical nationalists have had their day, and while broad-based and seemingly unqualified public support continues to exist, it may be withering. The reality is that in many cases any void provided by the fall of left-wing extremism has not been convincingly filled by the Far Right.

In Yugoslavia, a country that will be taken up as a separate series of case studies, it was ultimately the leadership of Slobodan Milošević, manipulating political and diplomatic variables, which turned the Western Balkans into a dark geopolitical and diplomatic nightmare for the international community. There is no one like Milošević anywhere in the region who is ready to seize power. Perhaps ultra-nationalist parties will come to influence a government, or even find themselves in office, but it is unlikely they will be able to reignite the broad regional instability of the 1990s. Perhaps some states will implode, decay, or merely falter under radical right regimes, becoming difficult, if not impossible, to govern, but their ability to export social instability will not be at a premium.

This chapter considers each country separately, beginning in the north with Hungary, and moving south. The states of the former socialist Yugoslavia will be analysed in detail in a separate section. Again, it is important to keep in mind that, in many of the cases taken up, one must note that the radical right remains very much in development, evolving into perhaps viable political movements, and now, more and more assuredly, turning to pre-socialist history for inspiration, guidance and symbols. While the collapse of Communism provided an opening for alternatives, there were few fully formed ultra-nationalist organisations waiting to seize power.

From Hungary South

Hungary

While Hungary's government is nowhere near falling prey to any radical movements, it must also be acknowledged that ultra-nationalist politicians have scored some notable successes. In the 1998 elections, the tactical concordat between the governing Alliance for Free Democrats (*Szabad Demokraták Szövetsége*, SZDSZ) and the Hungarian Socialist Party (*Magyar Szocialista Párt*, MSZP) gave way, opening the door of opportunity for Istvan **Csurka** and his **Hungarian Justice and Life Party** (*Magyar Igazság és Élet Pártja*, MIÉP), founded in 1993, to win 14 of 386 seats and 5.5 percent of the popular vote.[4] This marked the first time since World War II that an extreme right, openly anti-Semitic party would win representation in the Budapest parliament. Since 1997, Csurka had crafted his aggressive populist push for the country's middle and lower-middle classes, who felt abandoned or victimised by economic and political reforms. And his accomplishments the following year seemed to hint at an even brighter future.

But ultimately this move was a failure. Csurka's harsh rhetoric, a hallmark of his debating style, gradually served to alienate even many who had at first flocked to his constituency, and when elections again came in April 2002, the party fell back to 4.4 percent of the popular vote, taking no seats. What followed were attempts to build bridges with like-minded, yet almost invariably hostile, rival leaders. In recent years, the party had formed and later abandoned an alliance with David Kovacs' Movement for a Better Hungary (*Jobbik Magyarországért Mozgalom*), originally forged out of a clique of college friends at Eötvös Loránd (ELTE) University in 1999, and surfacing publicly as a political organisation in 2002 with support from campuses across the country. Prior to the *anschluss*, there was a period of intense rivalry, muddled intrigue, name-calling and jockeying for power between Csurka and Kovacs who, at one time, had been a MIÉP member. The truce emerged in 2005 and the two parties managed to iron out a common strategy, finally reconstituting themselves under the united banner of MIÉP–Jobbik Third Way Alliance of Parties (*MIÉP–Jobbik a Harmadik Út pártszövetség*) under Csurka's tutelage.[5] Now allied and aiming to contest for seats in the 2006 nationalist elections, the new body, keenly aware of the limitations of its harsh anti-Semitic rhetoric, repackaged itself as a benign promoter of nationalism with a domestic law-and-order agenda. Again, there was no victory, and the new approach yielded only 2.2 percent of the popular vote, translating into no seats.

Since parting ways with Csurka, Kovacs' followers have been linked with the very public formation of armed paramilitary units, perhaps attracting the support of fewer than 1,000 followers. Nevertheless, the development was viewed with alarm by those who regard the evolving situation as having negative consequences and implications not only for the country, but the wider region.[6] It's possible that these new paramilitaries will manage to ratchet up **violence** in neighbouring countries, or undermine civil society in Hungary, although such a possibility remains extremely remote for the foreseeable future.

Yet just as the organised extreme right seemed poised to slide off the political stage for good, events in late 2006 suggest a rebound must not be ruled out. On 17 September 2006 an audio recording surfaced in which Prime Minister Ferenc Gyurcsány makes several contentious and explosive remarks, including the observation that 'we have obviously been lying for the past one and a half–two years.' Gyurcsány, who admits making the comment,[7] found himself the target of mass demonstrations. At first, protesters numbered around several thousand. But within days ranks swelled to perhaps 40,000 – 60,000 in Budapest, with sympathy rallies, also demanding resignations, springing up country-wide. Some have gone on record insisting such political actions may have destabilised the Hungarian government, and that Csurka and MIÉP were key in the planning and staging of the protests.[8]

In order to understand the roots of contemporary extremism, one must delve further back in time, and examine developments that did not, at least at first, directly include disaffected members of the dying totalitarian regime or conservative intellectuals with residences in university debating societies. Lower-class **youth** subculture holds the key, and it may well be the case that in Hungary the socio-economic origins spawning such developments might mean these movements and organisations will have greater staying power and deeper roots in Hungarian society than fleeting rightist political parties. The Hungarian radical right's renaissance can be traced back to its roots in youth movements in the late 1970s and early 1980s.

Youth gangs, many either forming out of, or affiliating with, skinhead groups, dedicated themselves to the destruction of the state and communist authorities. Never a major social force, the skinheads and satellite groups suffered their first major setback with the collapse of socialism across Eastern Europe in the late 1980s, leaving followers and organisers in disarray and without any sense of mission. If nothing else, Hungarian skinheads proved resilient, reconstituting themselves rapidly, redefining their new purpose as one of defence of the fatherland, with many enthusiastically dusting off the ignominious symbols of Hungary's World War II fascist past. In this context, groups deemed antithetical to the national interest, invariably defined in terms of the survival of an ethnic Hungarian state, became quick and convenient targets. Ethnic non-Hungarians came to be viewed as little more than potential objects of violence, with arguably the country's Roma and Jews being singled out for particularly harsh rhetoric and assaults.[9] Other favourite targets have been and remain non-Caucasian foreign exchange students. Visitors to the country have also been victimised, and Hungarian public opinion in the nation's capital was shocked in 2006 when a group of skinhead youths attacked young French tourists for cheering a rival team during the last football World Cup.

The first serious organisational steps undertaken by skinheads took place in the early 1990s, with many groups, although not all, devoting themselves to reconstituting the heritage and legacy of the Arrow Cross (*Nyilaskeresztes Part-Hungarista Mozgalom*), Hungary's Nazi Party led by Ferenc Szálasi, which had taken power briefly from October 1944 to January 1945.[10] Szálasi, regarded as a national hero and near-deity by many skinheads, was himself executed on war crimes charges. Back in the 1990s, the leader of the most well-known of the skinhead units, the Szálasi Guards, conferred his personal respects on Germany's notorious death camp doctor by becoming known and identified only as 'Mengele'. In addition to paying homage to the Arrow Cross's Szálasi, the swastika had a revival, as did other key symbols from Hungary's Nazi past, including styles of dress, flags and social clubs and rituals.

Perhaps the most important year for the extremist movement remains 1990, when in the town of Eger, leaders from various groups met at the first political congress, setting in motion a series of events that prompted Hungarian skinheads to seek out an international role and solidarity with like-minded groups across Europe, notably in Austria, Germany, and the Czech Republic.[11] Additional support was sought, and relations were forged, with groups across the Western world, including in Australia, Canada and the United States.[12] Rumours persist that Hungarian radicals continue to receive financial support from these sources abroad, and while such allegations are difficult if not impossible to prove, it is certain they have received encouragement. Among the first accomplishments of the Hungarian movement was the successful launching of several propaganda forums, including journals such as *Kitartas,* financed and published by Germany's Far Right. Outsiders from as far away as the other side of the world have played a key role in fostering Hungarian extremists' literary efforts, with such benefactors as American neo-Nazi Gary Lauk serving up backing for the journal *Uj Rend* from his far-away Nebraska base.

Alongside efforts to organise skinhead gangs, there came attempts to influence or become active within many splinter far-right political parties, with the radicalised youth readily supporting the objectives and ideologies of extreme nationalists.[13] Since the mid-1990s, and up until today, symbiotic relationships have evolved between youth gangs and ultra-right parties. While the details of party platforms varied, they found common ground in any ideology that emphasised four key points: staunch opposition to Communism or left-wing politics of any ilk; unquestioning and uncritical support for an ethnically and culturally pure Hungarian homeland, which includes dealing with social elements deemed undesirable through expulsion, deportation and violence (with the most extreme continuing to advocate violence as the only solution); denouncing all efforts at association with Western institutions; and, calling for the restoration of national greatness, principally through a reconstructing of an enlarged state, a 'Greater Hungary', by laying claim to territories from neighbours, such as Transylvania from Romania.

Mainstream Hungarian political leaders have acted to safeguard and promote civil society. Usage of Nazi symbols has been legislated against, and violence has been deplored each time it has occurred. Moreover, some groups once thought to have been part of the far-right fabric have denounced the extreme aspects of their ideology and redefined themselves, in order to fit into the mainstream. Perhaps the most notable in this respect is József Torgyán's Independent Smallholders, Agrarian Workers and Civic Party (*Független Kisgazda, Földmunkás és Polgári Párt*), which in 1997, quietly stepped back from its harsh **anti-Semitism**, resurfacing as a conservative party.[14] Other groups opt to defy laws by going underground, and periodically resurfacing under new names, all the while remaining loyal to their ideological convictions. The staunchly pro-Nazi Hungarian Welfare Association (*Magyar Népjóléti Szövetség*) – a name adopted in the 1990s by the largest grouping within the Arrow Cross movement – remains well out of the political mainstream, publishing a journal reaching only an estimated 5,000 readers.

Romania

At first, the Far Right's evolution was halting in Romania. Could those recently deposed by the communist regime possibly have a role to play in new radical extremist parties? Would communist strong-man Nicolae Ceauşescu remain a hero and an inspiration even after his death and disgrace? Early on, it seemed the reward would go to those political leaders who were wise enough to recognise that a complete break with the communist dictatorship was unnecessary. More recently, that heritage finds itself being thrown off, and the legacy of the fascist period gaining prominence.

Undoubtedly, Romania's most successful extremist politician has been, and remains, Corneliu Vadim **Tudor**, known simply as Vadim, head of the **Greater Romania Party** (*Partidul România Mare*, PRM).[15] In 1990 he and his mentor, the author Eugen Barbu, a former Ceauşescu advisor, founded the journal *Romania Mare* (*Greater Romania*) and the next year established their party. In the early days, Tudor was known for his anti-Semitic, anti-Hungarian, anti-Roma, and homophobic rants. In equal measure, there was defence of a 'Greater Romania'. By 1996, the PRM began attempts to place a distance between the party and the communist legacy, with an even stronger Romanian nationalism filling the ideological vacuum. Then towards the late 1990s there were even attempts to move into the mainstream. In 2000 these efforts were reflected in the presidential campaign, which showed that Tudor had substantial public backing.[16] He won roughly 28 percent of the popular vote, coming in second, and losing in run-offs.

In the years since the 2000 elections, Tudor worked on reforming his image, at various times claiming that his ideology and beliefs, while conservative, were also mainstream. He went on record as saying that he was wrong to have been anti-Jewish, recognising his **Holocaust denials** had been unfounded. But none of this produced political advantage. He managed to win only 11 percent of the vote in the 2004 presidential race, placing a distant third. And over the past several years, after briefly flirting with alliances with other parties, Tudor has returned to head a reinvigorated the PRM, very much following the form of the party in the early 1990s. Despite Tudor's claims of having moved into the political mainstream, evidence suggests otherwise.[17]

Openly posing a challenge to Tudor as the champion of ultra-nationalist causes is George Becali, leader of the New Generation–Christian Democratic Party (*Partidul Noua Generaţie - Creştin Democrat*, PNG-CD) since 2004. Becali rejected categorically the notion that there can be a place for, or any ties with, left-wing authoritarianism, and claims his **family** was harassed by the former Marxist authorities for their inter-war involvement with Codreanu and membership of the Iron Guard. For Becali, inspiration and guidance is to be drawn from inter-war Romania's fascist movement, and he argues that this past shall serve as an inspiration for a Romanian 'Cultural Revolution'. Like Tudor, Becali is known for racist, homophobic rants.[18] Yet relations between the two leaders are strained, with both men often engaging in insulting, inflammatory and sometimes public exchanges.[19] So far, Becali's following has proved small; in 2004 presidential elections he won only 1.77 percent of vote.

Nevertheless, Becali may be the personification of the future, embodying a new and dominating trend in extremist Romanian politics. In particular, his rejection of the legacy of the communist authorities has placed him at odds with some. Also, the fact that he may ultimately enjoy some public favour was demonstrated in early 2007, when at least one poll suggested that, if elections were held at the end of March, he would have the support of 18 percent of voters.[20]

When it surfaced in the late 1980s, Romanian extremism, unlike any vision served up by Becali, was marked by a deep schizophrenia. On the one hand, leaders of the country's fringe radical right appealed to constituents by calling for the restoration of Romania's greatness, accomplished by working towards a 'Greater Romania' which is to include land from neighbouring states and all of Moldova. At other times, rather than appealing to a sense of public confidence, leaders opted to exploit fear, angst and a sense of cultural weakness, arguing that Romania is besieged by hostile powers intent at aggrandising themselves by gorging on Romanian territories. Usually singled out during such campaigns was Hungary, which, it is alleged, will never be appeased until it forcibly swallows up all of Transylvania, home to a large and potentially destabilising Hungarian minority.

Unlike extremist movements in some other Balkan states, the Romanian schizophrenia has produced a series of radicalised parties that can, and have, venerated strong political leadership irrespective of its ideological origin. Ultra-nationalists have embraced former communist dictator Nicolae Ceauşescu, using him to appeal to those who advocate a strong Romanian foreign policy and who are nostalgic for the social and political stability of the socialist era. Alternatively, and occupying equal status in the pantheon of ultra-nationalist heroes, is Corneliu Zelea Codreanu, Romania's fascist leader in the inter-war period, who was murdered in 1938, probably on orders from the monarchy.[21] Veneration for both the Far Left and Far Right has led one insightful author to observe that Romania's extremists are 'pioneers' in establishing and promoting 'red-brown' alliances, or cooperation between parties of the Far Right and Far Left. The only prerequisites for membership appear to be advocacy of strong national leadership and willingness to denounce Western-style reforms. Subsequently, 'following the parliamentary elections of the autumn of 1992, the minority government of the Democratic National Salvation Front (later renamed the Party of Social Democracy in Romania–PSDR), headed by Prime Minister Nicolae Văcăroiu, was supported in parliament by the party of Romanian National Unity (PRNU), the Greater Romania Party (GRP) and the Socialist Labour Party (SLP). There are red elements in all four components of the alliance.'[22] The question for the coming years is whether or not Becali, or others like him, may succeed in putting to rest once and for all the Marxist legacy.

Bulgaria

What are the boundaries or limits to Bulgarian extremism? What happens to the far-right **Attack Coalition** (*Natsionalen Săyuz Ataka*, or *Ataka*) in the coming months or years may serve to answer this question. Further, what is perhaps the most remarkable or noteworthy aspect of extremism in Bulgaria was its slowness to launch. When socialism toppled, there was first an immediate reversion to that country's tradition and legacy of ethnic and political toleration.

Perhaps the most surprising aspect of Bulgaria's collapse of socialism has been the Far Right's reticence to revert to racism and specifically anti-Semitism. At least, this has been the case until very recently. Centuries of occupation by the Ottoman Empire has, however, seemingly left parts of the national psyche scarred, and when the argument is made about the dangers of lingering threats posed by the country's remaining Turkish minority, some segments of the population have been receptive. Perhaps this sentiment combines with fears of possible retaliation by Bulgaria's Turks over the negative consequences and subsequent failure of the over half-decade policies that culminated in 'Bulgarisation'.

Certainly between 1984 and 1989, ethnic Turks were turned officially into second-class citizens. In 1985, cultural chauvinism found policy expression in the 'Bulgarisation' campaign, an effort to assimilate the roughly 10 percent of the

Turkish population by first forcing them to exchange personal names for names more appropriately 'Bulgarian'.[23] It was also from this late-Zhivkov period that some of the ultra-nationalists, who still attract some public support, assumed a measure of prominence. However, it must be understood that they and their parties were a marginal political phenomenon.

Some tiny parties used both Bulgarisation and most especially its collapse, along with the fall of the totalitarian regime, to whip up fear and develop a constituency. And at least one extremist organisation, the Committee for the Defence of National

2. A cyclist passes posters of the ultra-nationalist candidate Volen Siderov in Sofia, Bulgaria, 28 October 2006.

Interests, had its direct roots with activists and social protests that sprouted up in 1990 in reaction to the failure of 'Bulgarisation'. Not by accident, ethnic Bulgars living near or alongside thriving Turkish communities, offered CDNI the greatest support. There were others, and among those in the early 1990s veering towards anti-Turkish policies were the Fatherland Party of Labour and the Liberal Democratic Party.

It is with the rise of *Ataka* that it may be possible to argue that intolerance is slowly finding a way to survive, if not thrive, and that it may come to inform political discourse and ideology in ways heretofore unseen. Before *Ataka* is examined, what must be understood clearly is that while Bulgaria does have 'a history of repressive anti-minority policies', for the time being organised racist extremism is weak. Since the Bulgarian political discourse is not strongly ideologised, racism and xenophobia have failed to develop into an ideology, or, even, into a political issue.'[24] Even the Bulgarian Far Right can lay some, perhaps feeble, claims to the traditions of tolerance. True, in the post-Zhivkov, post-'Bulgarisation' era many far-right parties adopted more chauvinistic, and in rare cases racist, rhetoric and policies, but rarely has this extended to denying equal treatment to most national minorities, including the tiny Greek, Romanian, Russian and Ukrainian populations. It has almost invariably been the ethnic Turkish, subsequently lumped alongside the country's roughly 3.5 percent Roma population, who have been the intended victims of demands for repression.

Perhaps the most notorious exception to the rule of Bulgarian tolerance remains Father Georgi Gelemenov, leader of the Revival Movement, Bulgaria's neo-Nazi party. In the early 1990s, Gelemenov gained a reputation for his inflammatory, racist rhetoric, most of which was directed against the Roma and Turkish populations.[25] Gelemenov, who was among the pioneers in seeking supporters from within the country's tiny skinhead movement, has appealed to followers to commit criminal acts of violence against individuals and groups, and has taken pride in having recruited fighters who served in the former Yugoslavia alongside 'brother' Serbs. Yet Gelemenov, in style, substance and approach, stands out even among parties of the Far Right.

The most curious aspect of many of the tiny early radical right-wing groups was the fact that, by some standards, they seemed to actively fight efforts at being categorised as extremist. First, none was absolute in its opposition to Western-style reforms. In some instances political organisations that might have sought to resurrect traditions of a 'Greater Bulgaria', by identifying with names and symbols of a past that made irredentist claims against neighbours, developed platforms and advocated policies that expressly rejected territorial expansion. The Bulgarian National Legions, in the early 1990s, was among the first of the nationalist splinter groups to disavow territorial claims. Moreover, the leader of the Internal Macedonian Revolutionary Organisation–United Macedonian Associations, (IMRO-UMA), Krasimir Karakachanov, used at least one occasion to tell the media that demanding real estate from another country was simply out of the question.[26]

It has only been very recently that a far-right political party has emerged, seemingly surging from nowhere, to chisel out a base of mass public support. In the 25 June 2005 elections, *Ataka* managed to win 21 of 240 seats, also claiming about 8.15 percent of the popular vote. Headed by the charismatic media personality Volen Siderov, *Ataka* was formed when three minor parties, the National Bulgarian Patriotic Party, the National Movement for the Salvation of the Fatherland, and the Union of Patriotic Forces and Militaries of the Reserve Defence, agreed to an alliance. What was striking about *Ataka*'s accomplishment was that the coalition wasn't created until about 60 days prior to the election, and its leader had previously experienced disastrous failure when attempting to carve out a career in public life. As recently as 2003, Siderov campaigned to become mayor of Sofia in local elections, but his efforts netted less than 0.5 percent of the popular vote and his campaign – which included promises to 'purge the city of beggars, Roma and drug addicts'[27] – and its result went almost unreported.

Siderov's opponents allege he is an extreme racist, preaching anti-Semitism, homophobia, and hate against Turks and Roma.[28] Every mainstream party rejects the idea of entering into any kind of alliance or coalition with *Ataka*. For his part, however, Siderov claims his politics are not at all extremist, merely patriotic, and that his views come neither from the far left nor far right, but from an understanding of the Bulgarian national interest that happens to be shared by the average person. Mention is made of the fact that, while *Ataka* opposes NATO membership and seeks greater ties with Russia, there is no great problem working with the EU, except for the fact that agreements may need periodic amending to reflect Bulgarian concerns. He also notes that *Ataka* support, which allegedly continues to grow, stems from the failure and decay of the establishment parties, especially the Bulgarian Socialist Party.

Nevertheless, groups aware of Siderov's history continue to assert that his support of radical-right causes can be well documented. In 2002, evangelical leaders observed 'a wave of anti-Semitism spreading in the country', suggesting an obvious linkage with work published by Siderov, dubbing it nothing more than 'Holocaust-denying literature […] nothing but a collection of anti-Semitic stereotypes', also taking aim at 'Roma and other minorities.'[29] Whether or not Siderov's popularity has peaked does at this point remain very much an open question. On 30 October 2006, he lost in a presidential run-off to incumbent Georgi Parvanov; however, he did receive 27 percent of the popular vote.

Greece

Traditional and conservative politics are alive and well in Greece, and while appearances of ultra-nationalist or extremist parties are known, they tend to be rare and infrequent. What is very likely the case is that the far-right segment of the population is well accommodated by the country's catch-all, stable right-wing parties, and extremist public opinion is therefore muted by the political process. Greek scholars, however, give a variety of reasons for why extremism does not thrive in their political culture, though invariably they return to the point that the radical right is incompatible with traditional Greek values. As Vassilis Lambropolous urges:

> Look at the fascinating exception of Greece, where the extreme right does not even have a party [… There] is the total absence of support for extreme right-wing positions among artists, writers, intellectuals, scholars and academics. Greek intelligentsia has not lacked fanatics of several persuasions (Communist, Trotskyite, anarchist, Christian, Byzantine, classical, etc.), but not the Far Right. Over the last two centuries, among the lines of philosophers, authors, journalists, teachers, directors or musicians, there has been no-one, not a single figure of distinction, who advocated consistently far-right positions — no Gentile, Pound, Benn, Lewis or Brasillach. This is an astonishing record by any standard. In fact, Greeks have considered a thoroughly right-wing position incompatible with cultural engagement, artistic creativity and free inquiry.[30]

While it is true that extremism outside the framework of mainstream parties has little support in Greece, it is myth to suggest that it does not now, or ever, existed. One of the most high-profile proponents of the radical right today is Georgios Karatzaferis. A former media producer and journalist, he turned to political life only to find himself expelled from the New Democracy Party in 2000. His response came in founding the Popular Orthodox Rally (LA.O.S) that same year, an organisation that pulled the remnants of various far-right and far-left political organisations and parties into its ranks. While never a major political force, LA.O.S did provide the means for Karatzaferis to take up his party's lone seat in the European Parliament, after it won 4.12 percent of the vote in 2004 European parliamentary elections. According to some analysts, there is no, or very little, difference between LA.O.S and other neo-Nazi parties, and Karatzaferis may be linked to anti-Semitism. For example, a report by the Stephen Roth Institute observes that 'right-wing extremist parliamentarian George Karatzaferis claimed there were no Jews among the victims of the World Trade Centre attacks, for which he implied Israel was responsible.'[31]

Greece's vocal neo-Nazi Party Golden Dawn (*Chrysi Avyi*, CA), was disbanded at the end of 2005. Violence against the group, allegedly perpetrated mostly by anarchists and leftists, was cited as the cause for the action, while members were instructed to resume their political activities discreetly and through other political organisations. Undoubtedly, the attention and opposition it received made daily operations difficult. Party chief Nikolaos Michaloliakos styled his leadership after the main figures of Germany's Third Reich, and also advocated an ideology borrowed directly from Hitler. The party's main publication, launched by Michaloliakos in December 1980, was also called *Chrysi Avyi*. It laid out an ideology that could be summarised as anti-Semitic, anti-immigrant, anti-capitalist, anti-Marxist and pro-'Greater Greece'. Michaloliakos pirated Nazi symbols liberally, advocated a *fuhrer princip,* and when in doubt about any course of action drew inspiration from ***Mein Kampf***. The party charter says, 'the leader is unassailable and inviolate and is the supreme leader of the party. He stands above electoral procedures.' Upon coming into, or leaving party offices, 'a national socialist salute […] is mandatory.' The party's main 'belief is Nation-Race. Above everything for us is Greek blood and the National Legacy.'[32] And while the party claimed to be the victim of violence, it was reportedly involved in numerous attacks against minorities,[33] with Cypriot chapters implicated in aggression against ethnic Turks.

Even Michaloliakos claims the party had limited appeal prior to the early 1990s. However, he insists that in 1991–1992, following the disintegration of socialist Yugoslavia, he made inroads in mainstream public opinion. According to his boasts, the prospect of an independent Macedonia, a territory claimed as an integral part of a 'Greater Greece', turned party fortunes, as such a potential regional development could not be supported or even tolerated by any Greek. While it has never been proven that actual membership exceeded a few hundred, and sympathisers numbered several to perhaps five thousand, the early 1990s saw the party garnering a higher public profile. During the Yugoslav wars, CA members and recruits travelled to fight alongside their Orthodox Serb brethren. At least a handful of CA loyalists fell in with Drina Corps, involved in the Serb campaign at **Srebrenica** (Bosnia and Herzegovina), and raised a Greek flag in the ruins of an Orthodox church following the fall of the city. Any possible CA involvement in war crimes remains a subject of hot debate.

After 1 December 2005, and following the disbanding of CA, most supporters shifted loyalties to the Patriotic Alliance. Critics say the Patriotic Alliance is little more than a neo-Nazi front and CA under a new name. The party was co-founded in 2004 by Dimitrios Zaphiropoulos, a former member of CA and close friend of Michaloliakos. This new vehicle has almost no popular support. In 2004 it participated in the European parliamentary elections, taking a paltry 0.17 percent of votes.

Turkey

Turkey is perhaps the most unique country in the study. There is little that can be defined as a radical party, movement or organisation in the sense in which those terms apply to other entities in countries across the region. Rather, secular Turkey is home to at least two types of parties that would seek to undermine and destroy the existing authority and state structure. First, there is the ethnic-national Kurdish-based Kurdistan Workers Party (*Partiya Karkerên Kurdistan*, PKK), which seeks independence and a separate state hived out of Turkey and neighbouring countries.[34] While primarily Turkey-based, the PKK operations are, strictly speaking, not confined to South East Europe, as irredentist claims are made on lands well outside the region.

Second, there is the religious and pro-radical Islamic movement in Turkish politics, today represented best by the most mainstream of the religious organisations, the

Welfare Party. Founded in 1983 from the National Order Party and the National Salvation Party, the Welfare Party was banned in 1998, and its support and base remain difficult to gauge. Many tiny radical Islamist groups remain mostly out of sight, with Turkish authorities regarding them to be no, or only a minor, threat to state stability. Very broadly speaking, the objective of the Islamist parties is to overthrow, or quicken the demise of, a secular authority in favour of a **religion**-based governance. The holy Koran would be taken as the foundation for the state system. At times over past decades, Ankara has suspected neighbouring states, or interests in them, of promoting and backing, and sometimes financing, Islamic groups in Turkey. This has periodically seen a strain in relations with neighbouring countries, principally Iran.[35]

Today, a very real issue is emerging with the PKK. Again, the party's ideology is not what can be dubbed rightist, or even remotely extremist in the way the term may be applied to other regional far-right parties. Certainly, PKK ideology has a strong nationalist component, but the inspiration for that lies in a legacy of Marxist-Leninist radicalism, formulated by the Communist International beginning back in the 1920s. Very briefly, the PKK has simply adopted the position that Kurds, as any avowed Leninist might argue, are a repressed national minority. As such, theirs is a struggle made just, as, in their opinion, the shackles of imperialism are meant to be overthrown violently. National self-determination is the aim, and guerrilla tactics serve the agenda. While Turkey has been, at least until the time of the invasion of Iraq, the main base of operations, the PKK recognises that ethnic Kurds are oppressed in Iran, Iraq and certainly Syria, and there can be no true conclusion to agitation while those populations remain oppressed.[36]

In fact, the PKK has demonstrated that it is truly a global organisation, with ties to organised crime and the drug trade that span the world.[37] Contacts have been identified in the Far East and even Ireland. While the PKK may want to project the image of **freedom** fighters, its activities allegedly include extortion, kidnapping, murder and bribery. There is no question that it is well organised and capable of emerging as the backbone of a governing structure. The problem, insofar as the PKK may be concerned, is that the organisation is on Western terror lists, and has been deemed a terrorist organisation by numerous multilateral bodies, including the European Union and NATO. Under such circumstances, there would be no international community tolerance for a PKK-backed government.

Right from its founding in October 1978, Abdullah Öcalan has been the party's guiding light. Under his leadership, the PKK, by 1984, began a transformation that would effectively turn the organisation into a paramilitary force. Since the mid-1980s, relations with Turkey can be said to have resembled low-intensity warfare, with perhaps as many as 37,000 people dying in the hostilities and cross-fire.[38] For his part, Öcalan has led an unstable existence, at least depicted in the press, channelling the *joie de vivre* of any Ian Fleming main villain. For years, he evaded spies and police authorities, remaining on the run, seeking refuge in Russia, Greece and various other locations. Finally in early 1999, he was captured in Kenya, and eventually tried and sentenced to solitary confinement in a Turkish prison.

Until about 2004–2005, Turkey responded to the PKK primarily by relying on its armed forces, as well as by enlisting the aid of various ultra-conservative and paramilitary organisations staunchly loyal to the secular Kemalist state and ideology. Such loyal groups at times train members to infiltrate the PKK, where the aim was to identify suspects or key leaders, with the goal of bringing them to street justice.

By 2004, Öcalan himself appealed for calm and an end to hostilities, at times seeming to come close to being critical of the violence meted out by the paramilitary forces of the PKK. In fact, such moves may have been self-serving and calculated to soften the image of the Kurdistan Workers' Party, perhaps in an attempt to reclaim some legitimacy or to stake out some political role. But the reality is that certainly in recent times, PKK-Turkish relations have been degraded to a new low, with a condition of seemingly full-blown warfare in the making, and Turkey's strategy being to confront the PKK in a neighbouring country.[39] Over the past few years, it may be the case that the PKK has shifted its attention and priorities to forming some sort of shadow state authority in the Northern Kurdish territories of Iraq, an opportunity presented as a consequence of the invasion of Iraq. In any case, Ankara alleges the PKK has consolidated a base in northern Iraq, and that it is using the territory as a launching pad against Turkey, which has resulted recently in cross-border raids and the deaths of perhaps several dozen Turkish troops. Ankara's response has been to prepare for more war. In the latest ongoing and rapidly escalating conflict, according to Bloomberg news:

> Turkish jets bombed eight sites in northern Iraq today in the latest in a series of cross-border attacks on the outlawed Kurdistan Workers Party, or PKK, that have killed more than 150 rebels [...] Turkish soldiers also clashed with the PKK inside Turkey, killing 11 rebels in an area close to the Iraqi border in two days of fighting, the military said on its Web site. Today's bombing raid was at least the third air operation in Iraq this month.[40]

Albania

No discussion of radicalism can avoid analysis of the concept of 'Greater Albania'. Yet what must be noted about the ideology is that, throughout most of the past few decades, the concept played a much bigger role within neighbouring states, cited by cultural and political leaders there as a threat to regional order. Having said that, however, it also must be noted that adherence to, or advocacy of, a 'Greater' state is what unites the various Albanian populations across the region, and produces arguably the strongest basis for a broad intra-ethnic public consensus, making the issue a hallmark of the mainstream, and not merely the domain of some fringe rightist elements. After 1945, Albania plunged into a bloody civil war that lasted until 1951, and the resulting social, political and even religious differences were merely papered over by the Stalinist regime of Enver Hoxha. As long as Albania was in isolation and governed by the hard-line Communists, there was no chance Greater Albania would find a meaningful voice. However, geopolitical realities have now shifted. Today, when socio-economic and political cleavages grow too intense, it is becoming increasingly clear that disparate ethnic Albanian populations can be diverted by the call of a Greater Albania, or at the very least, by calls for greater ties between Albanians in the country and those residing in neighbouring states.

Indeed, about as many ethnic Albanians live in states bordering Albania (especially **Kosovo** and Macedonia, but also parts of Greece and Montenegro), enabling radical Serb leaders, for example, to argue that Kosovars, along with their kindred across the region and in Albania, continue to work for the creation of a 'Greater Albania' at the expense of Serbian statehood. As such, much of the discussion of a 'Greater Albania' is to be taken up in the context of the former Yugoslavia. But what must be absolutely understood is that in order for non-Albanian politicians to promote the threat of a Greater Albania, they must do so by insisting the whole of the ethnic Albanian population region-wide is equally energised, politicised and committed to effecting that reality. In truth, that is not the case. While most Albanians may not disapprove of a Greater state, for many it remains a cultural goal, and for some in Albania, it stands as an objective, given current political and diplomatic constraints, realisable in the distant future only, if at all.

Within Albania itself there has, since the collapse of Communism, been almost no threat posed by any radical-right parties. When far-right parties did emerge, their efforts to drum up any public support seemed doomed to defeat from the start, their entire strategy revolving around devising platforms defined by, and confined to, their advocacy of a 'Greater Albania'. It was, therefore, within the context of foreign policy that extremist Albanian political organisations laboured to innovate and differentiate themselves from government.[41] In 1993, Abdi Baleta and Petrit Kalakula were dropped by the ruling Democratic Party, and went on to found the Democratic Party of the Right. During at least the first year of its existence, Kalakula and Baleta were hampered by the inability to generate any following. Ultimately, they were supported by splinter groups that included the Republican Party and the National Front (*Balli Kombetar*, BK). During World War II, the BK was Albania's Nazi party; however, in the early 1990s, the reconstituted entity went without support in Albania, though it did develop some popularity with the diaspora in the West. Nevertheless, the Republican Party and the BK supported the 'Greater Albania' ideal.

In recent years, the entire Far Right can be justly characterised as having died and withered away on the vine, the cause of 'Greater Albania' taken away from it by the country's mainstream politicians. Arguably, Greater Albania's most high-profile advocate is current prime minister and former president Sali Berisha. Since the 1999 NATO bombing of Serbia, the prospects for Kosovan independence have increased dramatically, and an independent Kosovo appears set to become reality in early 2008, when Western powers are slated to extend recognition. In today's climate, an Albanian Far Right has no *raison d'être*, as mainstream politicians are now leading the ideological charge with claims that a 'Greater Albania' might even provide a basis for regional stability; not instability: 'Tirana is increasing pressure on the international community to act fast and impose independence on Kosovo, if it seeks to improve long-term relations between Albanians and Serbs in the Balkans [...] Sali Berisha says independence for the majority-Albanian region offers the only route to normal relations between the two estranged nations.'[42]

The lands of the former Yugoslavia

What happened in and to Yugoslavia between 1990 and 1995 helps to explain continuing interest in the fate and workings of extremists across the region. While Belgrade was mostly accountable for the events of the first half of that decade, the potential threat of any mass violence in Serbia reigniting a regional conflict remains inconceivable, at least for the near term. This is not to argue that political conditions in Serbia cannot deteriorate, and the country may flirt with becoming a failed state. However, any resulting violence is likely to be manageable, without plunging the Balkans back into war.

When discussing the countries of the former Yugoslavia, there are two generalisations which must be kept in mind. First, since the early 1990s, and in fact, prior to the collapse of the socialist country, most of what can be described as 'extremist' was contained within, or represented by, mainstream political parties. In a very fundamental sense, at least insofar as Croatia, Bosnia and Herzegovina and Serbia are concerned, extremist or radical right-wing influences were, and remain, very much part of the political establishment. Of all the independent states of the country, only Slovenia must be held up as the exception: with no prior history of independence or radicalism to draw on, the transition to a civil society, albeit with its problems, has been relatively smooth, and radical conservative movements and ultra-nationalist voices are a fairly recent phenomenon. The case of Slovenia shall be taken up in closing. Second, in many cases, while finding expression through political parties and the political process, there are organisations and institutions throughout the lands of the former Yugoslavia that function outside the law or formal political establishment but are linked to the main parties. For instance, there are paramilitary groups and organisations within Serbia, armed and militant groups in Kosovo and Macedonia.

Croatia

Here, most ultra-nationalists trace their pedigree back to the ideology of Croatian nation-statehood which began to find expression through the writings of Ljudevit Gaj in the 1840s. His work on language and literature laid the foundation for a Croatian cultural, social identity.[43] But it was later, with Ante Starčević, that Croatian political identity would be codified and linked to the political cause of establishing a highly centralised and ethnically-based national state. In 1861, Starčević, an attorney, joined with Eugen Kvaternik to co-found the Croatian Party of Rights (*Hrvatska stranka prava*, HSP).[44]

In reality, the immediate and far more controversial inspiration for contemporary extremism in Croatia is the pro-fascist World War II government of Ante Pavelić. In contemporary Croatia, attitudes towards this controversial figure and opinions about his Ustaše (Insurgency) government serve to define one's position on the political spectrum. In his time, Pavelić was among the most militant leaders, and his government is described as the bringing together of 'the worst of German Nazism and Croatian Fascism. Although the "Independent State of Croatia" was the fulfilment of Croatian dreams of a single, unified Croatian homeland, its population of 6.3 million included about 2 million Serbs, 30,000 Jews, and 750,000 Bosnian Muslims. The Ustashe set out with ruthless determination to eliminate Jews, Gypsies and Serbs.'[45]

One of the very few efforts to organise an anti-establishment far-right party came in February 1990. Dobroslav Paraga attempted a resurrection of the Croatian Party of Rights, boasting that he, in fact, had succeeded in breathing new life into the dream and ideals of Starčević and Kvaternik with the launch of the new organisation. But in very short order, the party's most potent symbol became Ante Pavelić, with many members coming mostly from the underground neo-Nazi and skinhead communities, opting for black attire decked out in images of Pavelić. The intense appeals to Croatian youth translated into some solid support from the arts community, but even at his peak, Paraga never made serious political inroads, stalling out with around 5 percent public support.

Paraga and others like him were relegated to the political sidelines simply because their ideology and pedigree were quickly usurped by elements that came to define the status quo. Franjo Tuđman, president of Croatia from May 1990 until his death on 10 December 1999, and his governing party the Croatian Democratic Community (*Hrvatska demokratska zajednica*, HDZ), account for why others of the Far Right were simply shoved off the political stage. Tuđman was a career Communist who fought on the partisan side, but by the 1960s began his public questioning of orthodoxy, venturing out on a career as a dissident which included time in prison. Eventually, he came to the conclusion that Croatia was mistreated within the federation and that certain assumptions promoted by the communist authorities were destructive. In 1971, Tuđman was questioning Serbian claims that at least 700,000 ethnic Serbs were killed at Pavelić's death camp in Jasenovac. By the late 1980s, Tuđman emerged as a leader within the burgeoning national movement. By the time he ascended to power, his credentials for leading a national revival were impeccable. He had expressed sympathy for the most extreme demands of Croatian nationalism, which included building a 'Greater Croatia', to accommodate Muslim populations from Bosnia and Herzegovina.[46] In office, Tuđman also worked to sanitise and restore the Ustaša legacy, observing that its members deserved recognition as national heroes, and at times, honouring their memories through public campaigns that included renaming place names after Ustaša war dead. Such actions enraged Croatia's minorities, notably its ethnic Serbian communities, but helped Tuđman cement his image as the father of the newly independent Croatia.

Among Tuđman's most significant ties to the Ustaša past was relations with the ultra-nationalist Croatian community from Herzegovina, the ethnic Croats from neighbouring Bosnia and Herzegovina advocating most forcefully for a strong, ethnically-based Croatian state that would include Bosnia. In addition to their support, Tuđman drew financial backing and expertise from the most militant pro-Ustaša diaspora community. Here Gojko Šušak, a Toronto-based entrepreneur, was to play a key role in Tuđman's work as defence minister.

In fact, throughout his career Tuđman's practice was to appear sympathetic to the most extreme demands from his constituents, while balancing these factors against the demands of realpolitik. A vital function of the regime came to be controlling and mitigating the demands of the ultra-nationalist Far Right. But with Tuđman's death, the HDZ fell out of public favour, and efforts to reform the party were undertaken. In recent years, it has made a remarkable comeback, and in the parliamentary elections of 2003 won just under 34 percent of the popular vote and took 66 of 151 seats, enough to form a government with the backing of several other parties. But in 2002, current leader Ivo Sanader had a showdown with the ultra-nationalist Ivić Pašalić, the figure in Croatian politics most closely tied to the ultra-nationalism of the Tuđman era. In challenging Sanader for party control, Pašalić alleged his rival was taking the HDZ down a course that would betray Tuđman's legacy. Ultimately, Sanader's successful campaign meant he could argue that extremist radicalism had been dispelled, and that the HDZ had, at last, resurfaced as a centrist, moderate party. Sanader has since committed himself to European Union reforms, a move that has included a pledge to work with The Hague war crimes tribunal. This is where both Sanader and the HDZ may be tested. According to unconfirmed reports, growing in both frequency and number since late 2005, Sanader's promises to The Hague, most especially over the indictment and case of General Ante Gotovina, have led to growing disapproval and opposition, most notably within HDZ ranks.

Undoubtedly, much of the opposition to the current state of the HDZ, both from within and outside the party, will come from the ranks of the military and veterans associations. Individuals tied to the army, or those retired from the military, have over the years become the most active in organising fundraising campaigns for the defence

of those indicted at the Hague, mass rallies against reforms, and marches in support
of a return to what they regard as the golden era of the Tuđman years. Among the most
vocal, and by far the most prominent, of these ultra-nationalist groups is the Croatian
Handicapped War Veterans Association or HVIDRA. In 2005, retired Colonel Bozo
Drmic made it very public and very clear just how involved in conservative politics and
opposed to a reformed HDZ, HVIDRA planned to be:

> Nacional has learned that, due to the current politicized leadership of Hvidra,
> the Croatian Handicapped War Veterans Society, led by HDZ MP Josip Djakić,
> a movement has begun to destroy this organisation and to establish a new Hvidra.
> Retired Colonel Bozo Drmić, a handicapped war veteran and former member of the
> 2nd Guard Brigade Thunder, one of the founders of the special police in Lučko, is
> leading this initiative to establish a new umbrella association for all the Croatian
> handicapped veterans, as he considers the current organisation to be an extended
> arm of Ivo Sanader and HDZ, which does nothing to protect the veterans and the
> dignity of the Patriotic War. Furthermore, the new Hvidra will demand a review of
> all the handicapped and war veterans of the Patriotic War. [47]

Bosnia and Herzegovina

Bosnia, torn apart by war from 1992–1995, was reconstituted by the 1995 Dayton
Accord. According to the terms of that defining document, Bosnia and Herzegovina
is divided into two entities, a Federation of Bosnia and Herzegovina, home of the
constituent Muslims and Croats of the country, a *Republika Srpska*, and the self-
governing *Brcko* District. Each of the entities has its own constitution, and there are
provisions for a national political life at the level of a federal government. There are
three constituent peoples: Croats, Muslims and Serbs. Efforts throughout the 1990s to
take the word 'Bosniak' to mean any citizen of the country were rejected by Croats and
Serbs, usually amid claims that the term could be linked to Bosnian Muslim political
aims.

When it comes to understanding radicalism, it is best noted that Bosnian politics
are in stasis, and may remain so for some time. While acts of inter-ethnic violence are
common in press reports, for the most part social, political and economic differences
are finding resolution through the political process. Yet having noted this point, it is
also worth noting that all of the mainstream political parties that have been implicated
in the atrocities conducted during the war have either remained active or in office
throughout the 1990s to today. Most radical nationalists in the country have all, at
one time or another, either cooperated with or had membership in the 'mainstream'
parties that represent most ultra-nationalist causes. They remain: the Croatian
Democratic Community in Bosnia-Hercegovina (*Hrvatska demokratska zajednica
Bosne i Hercegovine*, HDZBiH), the Party of Democratic Action (*Stranka Demokratske
Akcije*, SDA) and the Serbian Democratic Party (*Srpska Demokratska Stranka*, SDS).[48]
Some of the most notorious accused war criminals have the status of party founders.
Perhaps the most well-known is the fugitive Radovan Karadžić, indicted by the Hague
on genocide and a host of other charges. In 1989, he was co-founder of the SDS and its
leader from 1989–1996.

Most recently, especially since the attacks against the United States on 11
September 2001, some press reports have speculated that Balkan Muslim populations
have served to provide recruits for radical Islamist movements. At times, Bulgaria,

Albania, Bosnia and Herzegovina have been cited in this context, with some accounts alleging that Al-Qaeda has made profound inroads in Muslim communities in those countries. Many serious analysts dispute such charges. While, for example, Mujahedeen fighters did come to Bosnia during the war, it is believed that their numbers were, and remain, so small as to be insignificant, and their impact on extremist politics non-existent. For the most part, observers continue to point out that most Bosnian Muslims consider themselves European, and the activities of radical Islamists remain anathema.

In Albania's case as well, there is little to support claims that al-Qaeda is having serious influence, since the Albanian national movement is predicated on eradicating differences among Albanian communities based on religion. Yet, it may be the case that through organised crime, Al-Qaeda may find some, albeit very limited, role. As one source, worth quoting at length, notes:

> Central and Eastern Europe has not been reported to be as important a haven for Al-Qaeda and other terrorist groups... However, concerns have been raised about several countries in Southeastern Europe with large Muslim populations e.g. Bosnia-Herzegovina. One legacy of the 1992–1995 war in Bosnia is the presence of Islamist fighters from other countries who stayed behind and became Bosnian citizens. Some Islamic charities that proliferated during and after the war reportedly served as Al-Qaeda money-laundering fronts. Terrorist groups have also operated from Albania. At the same time, opposition to terrorism among indigenous Muslims in the Balkans has been strong...The region's weak governing institutions and problems with organised crime and corruption may make it vulnerable to infiltration by terrorist groups.[49]

Serbia, now independent Montenegro, and Kosovo

As in Croatia, extremism in Serbia has found expression through mainstream political parties. What may be understood as extremist political organisations were in fact ruling parties or major opposition organisations throughout the 1990s and right up until today. As with Croatia, such political parties draw support from extra-parliamentary institutions. In Serbia's case, paramilitaries have been the main base of support, with some political parties being little more than extensions of paramilitary organisations. Some political parties amounted to little more than legal, public expressions for the interests of their paramilitary leadership, or of only one individual. Perhaps the best-known case was the Party of Serbian Unity (*Stranka Srpskog Jedinstva* SSJ), founded by Željko Ražnatović, alias Arkan, long-time leader of the Tigers and linked to organised crime. Arkan's SSJ also clearly illustrates what tends to happen with many of the political parties that have grown up within the paramilitary culture; namely, with the disappearance of its leadership, the party disintegrates. Throughout the 1990s and just after Arkan's assassination in January 2000, support and public sympathy grew. By 2003, the SSJ faded into obscurity, attempting alliances with other like-minded parties, but failing to win any seats or much public support.

What enabled the various paramilitaries to emerge from their nearly five decades of underground hibernation during the socialist period was the politics of Serbian leader Slobodan Milošević, himself in charge of the Socialist Party of Serbia (*Socijalistička partija Srbije*) and the collapsing of Yugoslavia until he was forced from office in 2000. In 1989, on the 600th anniversary of Kosovo Polje, Milošević used the occasion to resurrect a wave of Serbian national sentiment. Ultra-nationalist Serbian public opinion, over the course of the years, served as a main component of Milošević's base, and was energised by two sources. First, Milošević's promoting of ultra-nationalist parties and paramilitaries, who at various times supported his regime while engaging in the conflicts in neighbouring Croatia and Bosnia and Herzegovina.[50] Second, there was a reliance on the mass media to whip up fear of Serbia's neighbours, with, at times, all ethnic Croats, Albanians and Muslims being depicted as striving to destabilise Serbian territories while in pursuit of aims that included 'Greater Croatia' and 'Greater Albania'.

Arguably, it was in the period between 1990 and 1993 that the paramilitaries were most active, and not only because of the regional wars. It was precisely during those years that Milošević sought to establish his image as defender of Serbian nationalism, and thus not only tolerated, but publicly lauded, the paramilitaries. While many groups grew up or surfaced in this period, many with only a handful of members, several of the lesser known – which distinguish themselves as among the most vicious in the conflicts in neighbouring states – deserve mention. Two such groups were Dragoslav Bokan's White Eagles (*Beli Orlovi*) and Mirko Jovic's *Vitezovi*, reputed as being among the most vicious fighters during the time of the Yugoslav wars, allegedly committing numerous atrocities and usually targeting civilian populations.[51] Within Serbia, these groups have been blamed for introducing a widespread culture of violence which thrives to this day.[52] In some cases, the result has even included the assassination of the highest-ranking political officials. On 12 March 2003, Prime Minister Zoran Đinđić was gunned down by police official Zvezdan Jovanović. Jovanović, or 'Snake' (*Zmija*) as he is known, was also a former fighter who participated with Arkan's Tigers during the Bosnian campaigns and had allegedly said that Đinđić had to be removed for being a traitor to the Serbian nation.[53]

While the fortunes of most paramilitary groups and parties have waned over the past decade, including Milošević's own Socialist Party of Serbia, one group must be singled out for special attention. Vojislav Šešelj's **Serbian Radical Party** (*Srpska radikalna stranka*, SRS) was formed in 1991 when the People's Radical Party, a fringe party, merged with the paramilitary Chetnik movement which surfaced in 1990. The ultra-nationalist party was always, and remains, hard-line on Serbian nationalism.[54] Its main plank is the uniting of all Serbian-populated lands into one highly centralised Greater Serbian state; the SRS has never wavered in its support of Serbian hardliners, such as Radovan Karadžić. While never directly condoning the actions of any paramilitary group, Milošević did, during the early 1990s, offer encouragement in the hope of winning their support in the political arena. Until 1993, Milošević described Šešelj as his 'favourite opposition leader'. During that same time, Šešelj did nothing to conceal the fact that the extra-parliamentary Chetniks were the backbone of his support. And also during that period, Chetniks, as well as SRS party functionaries, were involved in ethnic cleansing campaigns, not only in areas where war fighting was taking place, but in Vojvodina province, a multi-ethnic region, where ethnic Croat and Hungarian communities became the main victims.

But in 1993, Milošević attempted to sanitise his image, a move that prompted him to sever ties with some of the most unsavoury ultra-nationalists and paramilitaries.[55] Seselj subsequently became a target of the SPS regime which ordered the Chetniks underground, where they could remain active in politics, but do so discreetly. The aim of Milošević's anti-SRS campaigns in 1993 was, simply, to neutralise the SRS as a political force. In the election campaign at the end of the year, the state-backed media ran stories linking Šešelj and the SRS to ethnic cleansing campaigns in Bosnia, and allegations were made about Šešelj and war crimes. At one point, a major daily newspaper, in the form of a premature political obituary, observed that the time had come for the SRS to slink 'back into the darkness from which it came.'[56] Despite backing from the mass media, Milošević could not destroy the SRS. It has survived both Milošević and over a half-decade of attempts at political reforms in Serbia. Back in December 1993, the party secured 13 percent of the vote and 39 of 250 seats in Serbia's legislature. That may have been the party's low point.[57]

The SRS has consistently won representation, gaining ground since 1993. From 1998–2000, it was involved with the SPS in forming a coalition government. In February 2003, leader Vojislav Seselj voluntarily gave himself up to the Hague authorities and awaits trial, where evidence allegedly suggests his activities in Bosnia brought him and his Chetniks into alliances with various paramilitaries, including the White Eagles. But it was also in the elections of 2003 that the SRS, now headed by Tomislav Nikolić in Šešelj's absence, won just under 28 percent of the vote and a plurality of seats. In the following year, Nikolić won just over 45 percent of the vote in the second round of presidential balloting. And most recently, in the January 2007 parliamentary elections, preliminary returns say the SRS will have under 29 percent of the popular vote and 81 seats, making it the single largest party in the legislature, though not in a position to be part of government.[58]

The SRS continues to expand. On 3 June 2006, Montenegro declared independence, following a 21 May 2006 referendum on the issue. The SRS has attempted to organise in the new country, basing its actions firmly in the belief that Montenegrins are ethnic Serbs and amenable to a political solution defined by a 'Greater Serbia'. Within Montenegro, Muslim and Albanian communities comprise an estimated 8 percent of the population, and in recent years fears have grown that ties may exist with extremist elements in neighbouring states, notably Kosovo.

Within Kosovo, the greatest surge towards extremism has taken place in the past years. Until recently, non-violence played the key role in Kosovo's resistance to Belgrade's rule. The Democratic League of Kosovo (*Lidhja Demokratike e Kosovës*, LDK) was founded in the 1990s and its leader, Ibrahim Rugova, remained the main proponent of non-violent resistance until his death in 2006. During Rugova's leadership, principally throughout the 1990s, ethnic Albanians across Kosovo, who made up roughly 90 percent of the province's population, were encouraged to boycott Yugoslav institutions, while at the same time backing efforts to build up parallel institutions and social structures.[59] The NATO war against Yugoslavia in 1999 brought fundamental change which resulted in the UN Security Council Resolution 1244, placing Kosovo under temporary UN administration. But more importantly, Belgrade was to no longer have power governing the province, and Serbian institutions and laws were no longer valid. While final status for Kosovo is likely less than a year away, the province is functioning as *de facto* independent, and since 1999, members and those affiliated with the Kosovo Liberation Army (*Ushtria Çlirimtare e Kosovës*, KLA) have been linked to surging ethnic Albanian violence, not only in Kosovo but also the Presevo Valley.[60]

Throughout the 1990s, ethnic Albanians were the targets of extreme violence, often perpetrated by members of Serbian paramilitary groups or Belgrade's security forces. Since 1999, international media have recorded scores of reports of violence against the province's ethnic minorities, notably Serbs and Roma, who have been victims of mob intimidation, beatings, and have had property and cultural landmarks destroyed. There are constant allegations that those perpetrating the violence have KLA connections.[61] For its part, the KLA gave up its identity, demilitarised following the 1999 conflict, and re-emerged as the Kosovo Protection Corps (*Trupat e Mbrojtjes së Kosovës*, KPC). Moderate Kosovar politicians regard the KPC as vital to the national interests of Kosovo, many of whom regard it as only a matter of time until Kosovo is granted independence and will need the services of an independent army. Yet the allegations of KLA links to the underworld persist, as do charges that its ultimate aim is independence for Kosovo, only as a first step to eventual union with Albania and other ethnic Albanian territories in a Greater Albania.

Ramush Haradinaj, leader of the Alliance for the Future of Kosovo (*Aleanca për Ardhmërinë e Kosovës*, AAK), became prime minister of Kosovo following elections in October 2004, but served barely a hundred days before being indicted by the Hague. As soon as the indictment became public in March 2005, Haradinaj resigned his post and gave himself up to the authorities.[62] Among the charges against him are accusations that in 1998, while affiliated with the KLA, he planned atrocities against civilians. These and related charges are denied.

Macedonia

Possibly fuelling extremism is the country's very constitutional framework. Ethnic Slavs, who make up roughly 65 percent of the population, are legally the state's only constituent people. Invariably, the roughly 25 percent ethnic Albanian population complains that non-Macedonian groups are, at best, relegated to second-class status. There have been instances over the past decade when inter-ethnic violence has flared.[63] Also, it may be argued that that which defines extremism is itself, very much part of the Macedonian socio-political fabric.

Early observers argued that of all the states of Former Yugoslavia, Macedonia was the likeliest candidate for implosion. Conventional wisdom posits that the fact that Macedonia continues to thrive is nothing short of a minor miracle.[64] Perhaps sustaining the miracle is the reality that, for the most part, the country's two largest communities have opted to live in isolation of one another.[65] While relations have been best with Serbia, they have not been problem-free. In fact, while outside challenges to statehood seem to run rampant, it has been only on few occasions, most notably in February of 2001 when Kosovar Albanian rebels exchanged rounds with Macedonian border guards, that outside threats materialised.[66]

Back in the early 1990s, mainstream Macedonian parties, especially the Internal Macedonian Revolutionary Organisation–Democratic Party for Macedonian National Unity (*Vnatrešno-Makedonska Revoluciona Organizacija-Demokratska Partija za Makedonsko Nacionalno Edinstvo*, IMRO-DPMNU), won public support by campaigning on fear, insisting the country's ethnic Albanian minority plotted to dismember the country for the benefit of a 'Greater Albania' agenda. Very quickly, some IMRO-DPMU members concluded their party's policies were too moderate, and concrete reaction came in 1992 when Vladimir Golubovski broke away, founding the IMRO-Democratic Party, which appealed to the most hard-core xenophobic, anti-Albanian segments of the population.

Aiding and abetting Macedonian nationalism, fanning fears and nurturing extremism, has been the activity of some in the minority communities. Enraging even moderate Macedonian public opinion back in late 1993, for example, were events linked to plots to destroy statehood. In November of that year, reports surfaced purporting a shadowy group calling itself the All-Albanian Army (AAA) intended to launch a revolution with the aim to end repression, win retribution and overthrow the government by brute force. The principal charge was that the AAA was well-regimented and rehearsed, having enough discipline, hardware and access to financial backing to enable suffcient numbers of volunteers to be called up with almost no notice and muster a small army that might easily topple the authorities. For their part, ethnic Albanian leaders deemed the charges absurd, arguing they were made solely to incite fear and whip up anti-Albanian sentiment.

Over the years, simmering inter-ethnic tensions remained a constant.[67] Most recently, a policy of the Albanian Party for Democratic Prosperity (PDP) reignited concerns about plans to create a 'Greater Albania'. In 2006, leader Abdulhadi Vejseli campaigned on a platform of seeking to build the 'Almakos' Project, or what was described as a Benelux-type union of Albania, Macedonia, and, upon independence, Kosovo.[68] For his part, Vejseli stressed that the idea was only to find common ground on questions of trade and economics, and that no political unions ought to be inferred. Yet suspicions were raised, and even though a coalition that involved the PDP, the Democratic Union for Integration and the Democratic League of Bosniaks won the most votes in the Albanian community, the coalition was not represented in government. Instead, Prime Minister Nikola Gruevski asked for and received backing from the Democratic Party of Albanians, a move that prompted widespread demonstrations by Macedonia's Albanians.

And no comment on extremism in Macedonia would be complete without reference to the country's Serbian community and Serbia's Vojislav Šešelj. Though ethnic Serbs make up under 2 percent of the population, they have produced loyalists and followers of the Serbian Radical Party. In the early 1990s, the chief spokesman for the ultra-nationalist voice within the Serbian community was Dragisa Miletich, leader of the minuscule Democratic Party of Serbs in Macedonia (*Partija na Srbite vo Makedonija*, DPSM).[69] Officially, the party sought goals such as the constitutional status for Serbs as an equal, constituent people within Macedonia. Yet, it was little more than a vehicle for the SRS and a means of influence for Šešelj, who, by 1991, was well on record as saying Macedonia was part of a 'Greater Serbia' by virtue of being ancient Serb territory. He also continues to insist that labels such as 'Macedonian', 'Montenegrin', 'Bosnian Muslim' and 'Muslim Slav' are merely fictions, and that all people who describe themselves as such are really nothing more than delusional Serbs. In 2006, the SRS took a final step, opening a branch of the party under the 'Radical' banner. Recently, too, the Radical Party of Serbs in Macedonia (RSSM) was formed and subsequently registered.

Slovenia

On 25 June 1991 this republic declared independence and has since become a regional leader in terms of liberal-democratic reform.[70] There exists no history or tradition of Slovenian independent statehood prior to June 1991, and this explains why the country failed to revert to any radical ideologies. Yet with the wars across former Yugoslavia, there was a tendency among observers to speculate that extremism would manifest itself across the whole of former Yugoslavia, Slovenia not excepted. At times, even the flimsiest evidence was dredged up to argue Slovenes would succumb to the radical right.

South-Eastern Europe and the Far Right

As far back as the 1980s, some signs seemed to suggest that a cultural revolution could sweep reactionaries to prominence, if not power. Back then, the music scene birthed *Laibach*, a punk rock group that took its identity from the German name for the Slovenian capital Ljubljana. When it made its public debut on television in 1982, its members did so decked out in swastikas and fascist attire. They clamoured for the violent destruction of the state, effectively jolting a lethargic Slovenian body politic. Reaction came swiftly and immediately, especially from World War II veterans' groups, who lined up to denounce *Laibach*, arguing that the band was little more than a skinhead front and recruiting tool promoting Fascism. Time, however, proved that *Laibach* used sensationalism only to advance its art; and, when Yugoslavia's disintegration turned bloody, the group resurfaced with messages of tolerance, peace, love and coexistence.[71]

Some events did seem far more serious, and for a time appeared to foreshadow political turmoil. The most infamous of these took place on 4 September 1993. On that day local police in Ljubljana reported a Jewish cemetery had been defiled, with several markers being spray-painted with swastikas and hate slogans.[72] The immediate public reaction was one of shock and revulsion, as this was the first such event witnessed in the city. Immediately there was speculation that the incident may have been the work of a resurgent Nazi splinter group, but investigations could never rule out the possibility that what took place was the deed of one individual or a small group of vandals with no ideological motives.

The closest to an organised extremist right-wing threat over the past few decades has materialised in the form of two political leaders who have led parties that have been consigned to the fringes, at least for much of the time. And at least in one of the cases, any suspicion based on early political activity has proved unfounded. First, mention must be made of Janez Janša, current prime minister of Slovenia, elected by parliament on 9 November 2004. Janša, a dissident during the period of socialist Yugoslavia, has led the Slovenian Democratic Party since 1995. Prior to that, he was affiliated with a number of smaller political groupings and parties that won some public support and enabled him to participate in various parliaments and governments. Very early on, he won the reputation for being a rebel and dissident in socialist Yugoslavia, and in 1988, along with a group of journalists, was arrested by the Yugoslav military on charges of passing secrets. Perhaps the arrest and subsequent in-camera trial cemented Janša's reputation as a heroic leader within the nascent Slovenian nationalist movement.

Indeed, Janša's early involvement with nationalism following Slovenia's assertion of independence, prompted some to portray him as a charismatic ultra-nationalist threat to state security. On 28 March 1994, he lost his post as Minister of Defence amid accusations that he was involved in arms trafficking,[73] a charge ultimately that made more sense about possible involvement with organised crime than extremist politics. Potentially more damaging were accusations by then members of government that he had urged his connections in the military to subvert the civilian judiciary; however, those allegations were subsequently dropped following investigations. Over the past decade Janša has proved himself a moderate, and one who continues to function within Slovenia's political culture of consensus-building.

Arguably the closest and most genuine connection to an extremist right-wing nationalist threat comes in the persona of Zmago Jelinčič Plemeniti, leader of the Slovenian National Party (*Slovenska Nacionalna Stranka*, SNS), founded on 17 March

1991. Insofar as he has a political programme, it is to rail against 'foreigners', who are regarded as a threat to the state, and to act coy whenever the issue of 'Greater Slovenia' surfaces. Jelinčič does not seem to have the sense that any one particular ethnic group is an eternal problem for Slovenian sovereignty. His bogies are drawn from current events and contemporary headlines.

Jelinčič has many times throughout his career gone on record saying that he has nothing against foreigners, refugees and those who are not ethnic Slovenes living in his country. But during the time of the Yugoslav conflicts, he insisted non-Slovenes, and most notably ethnic Serbs, had evolved into the greatest threat to Slovenia's survival. When talking about non-Slovenes back then, he rarely made any distinction between immigrants, refugees and members of ethnic communities born in Slovenia. His vitriolic rhetoric was sharpest in the first half of the 1990s, when he singled out fellow South-Eastern European groups for the harshest criticisms, at times claiming that independent Slovenia had mistakenly welcomed under 200,000 ethnic minorities who were guaranteed to dilute the body politic, if not threaten independence outright. He questioned the loyalties of all other groups from the former Yugoslavia who had found a home in Slovenia, at one stage observing his proud country had become 'a centre for the Serbian, Albanian and Montenegrin Mafias.'[74] These days, it is not necessarily any resident who can trace his lineage to the Western Balkans that is most threatening. Rather, he now takes issue with Muslims all over the world. He has condemned and protested plans for the building of mosques in Slovenia, linking Muslim residents with alleged international terrorist plots and speaks out about **Europe**'s 'Muslim problems'.[75]

Jelinčič and his SNS also endorse policies that would produce Slovenia's isolation, and membership of organisations such as the EU and NATO continues to be strictly opposed. There is no official advocacy of the aim of a 'Greater Slovenia', or the ideology of creating a *Velika Slovenija*, which would aim to bring all ethnic Slovene territories outside the country under Ljubljana's direct control. However, Jelinčič has gone on record hinting he endorses the idea of a *Velika Slovenija*,[76] by saying, for instance, that Istria was never really Croatian territory, a claim substantiated by observing that the region was always incorporated with Slovenia during Hapsburg administrations. In its most extreme form, the *Velika Slovenija* ideology would see lands claimed from Croatia, Italy, Austria and from as far away as Eastern Hungary.

The SNS also derives its constituency and support from those segments of the population who are former communists who remain nostalgic about the order and stability brought about by Tito's authoritarianism. Unconfirmed reports arise periodically claiming that the SNS continues to work with, and recruit within, the skinhead communities. To some of his critics, Jelinčič is little more than a clownish, pathetic figure who serves the needs of a fringe constituency feeling adrift in a post-Tito, post-socialist world. Others, however, regard him as a potent danger in the form of an unrepentant racist whose policies threaten to undermine civil society and whose aim it is to create an ethnically pure state while antagonising neighbouring countries.[77] In reality, support for the SNS has been dwindling steadily. In the national elections of 1992, the SNS took twelve of ninety seats, winning roughly 10 percent of the vote. In 2004, the party captured only six seats and just over 6 percent of the popular vote.

Four Points about the Far Right

Some may be tempted to argue that seismic socio-political events, such as the collapse of Communism, created voids that radical parties might fill, and that such events explain much of what is going on in the Balkans. However, an analysis of happenings over the past decade or so suggests realities across the region are far more complex.[78]

First, some countries, for example Greece and Slovenia, have histories that may inoculate the body politic against movements of the radical right. Greece has no communist legacy. Slovenia's heritage and development is rooted in the multi-ethnic Hapsburg political culture of tolerance and compromise. Greece, on the other hand, has well-established conservative traditions and parties so that voters have little need to turn to any radical movements. Even on those few occasions when Greek extremist parties have found issues, such as the status of Macedonia or the war in Bosnia, where they claim they have broadened their popular support, they have been unable to exploit them in such a way as to make lasting or even significant inroads on public opinion.

Second, there are those states where circumstances led to the revival of extremist organisations well before the final collapse of socialism, most notably, in Croatia and Serbia. The presence of extremist parties in mainstream politics for well over a decade in both of these states demonstrates how controlling political office has limited their appeal and perhaps halted growth potential. In Croatia, a reform impulse within the HDZ has produced intra-party opposition as lively as any afforded by any arguably democratic alternatives. In Serbia, radical fortunes have been tied not only to longevity on the political spectrum, but to the presence of strong leadership. As long as Milošević lived, the Socialist Party could expect to play a political role. With his passing, the party is all but gone. In some cases Serbian paramilitaries establish relations with political parties, but when their charismatic leaders disappear, there is found to be no or little bureaucratic and institutional underpinning, and their parties and organisations wither away, with members either fading back into private life or moving on in search of other affiliations. Such was the case with what the notorious paramilitary leader Arkan built up. And in Serbia today, the Serbian Radical Party appears to be working on consolidating its hold over rightist politics, not only in the homeland, but in newly organized cells and branches across neighbouring states, in Macedonia and Montenegro. But the real question remains: just how lasting can such organisation and activity be? Will Šešelj's time at the Hague eventually cause supporters back home to drift away from the SRS?

Third, there are those states that demonstrate that the collapse of socialism served up no well-defined socio-economic or political vacuum, merely circumstances that even to this day provide opportunities, and not just for extremists, but potentially anyone or any organisation claiming to be able to satisfy a yearning for political order and stability. When Communism collapsed in Hungary, for example, politicised skinheads, demanding the death of Communism, found themselves without a plan. Very quickly, though, the movement found purpose in resurrecting a Nazi past, and affiliating with nationalist parties calling for the restoration of a Greater Hungary. Even more recently, Hungarian paramilitaries have begun organizing, but so far the membership of a few hundred or several thousand individuals does not suggest the stability of the Hungarian state is imperilled. In Bulgaria, there is a similar story, in that the forming of a nativist, nationalist, racist movement took time to develop, much more than was the case in Hungary, but now has a home in *Ataka*. That *Ataka* draws much of its support from voters and especially disillusioned members of mainstream parties, most especially the Bulgarian Socialist Party, may suggest there is more of an appetite for **law and order** and stable strong-man politics than any lasting support or pining for a nostalgic return of some ultra-conservatism. Romania, again, is similar, in that evidence from the early days of the collapse of socialism suggests that any public support was drawn from those segments of the population that craved strong-handed leadership and social stability, and so early radical rightists did not necessarily steer away from venerating the defunct Marxist dictatorship. Only more recently has the extreme right in that country evolved away from such practices, with more and more, almost exclusive, devotion being accorded the Iron Guard and a fascist past.

Fourth and finally, there are those examples that suggest broader geo-political exigencies, rather than simply or exclusively internal crises brought about by the collapse of totalitarianism, might explain some of ultra-nationalism's successes.[79]

Such developments often prompt ultranationalist leaders to convince themselves that the goal of 'Greater' state creation just might be realisable. There is a compelling case to be made that the international community's eventual intervention in the Balkan wars in the 1990s, at the very least, prolonged Milošević's hold on power, providing him with diplomatic opportunities while allowing him to ally with and pander to Serbia's ultranationalist movements, all the while shoring up public opinion with a steady stream of propaganda aimed to suggest to the ordinary Serb that conspiratorial global forces stood united in anti-Serb campaigns. Today, Kosovo and the PKK are in a very real position to be either the beneficiaries or targets of wider political developments. In the case of Kosovo, the province is slated, in 2008, to win independence and recognition, a move fraught with potential political and diplomatic pitfalls. Should ultranationalists in the province continue to view sovereignty as but a step in the eventual union with Albania, they may come to regard independence as tacit international approval for an amalgamation with Tirana.[80] It is not inconceivable that Western powers would have to react in such a case. Meanwhile, the PKK has seized opportunities from the chaos triggered by the Iraq invasion, moving into and setting up base in Kurdistan, where now, as a result, possibly a full-scale war is only just unfolding with Ankara. Will the PKK be able to leverage political and diplomatic circumstances from what is only now taking place? 2008 promises to be an eventful year for politics in Kosovo, Kurdistan and Turkey.[81]

Stan Markotich

Notes
See for example Zoe Dare Hall, 'Property Overseas: Where's Hot, Where's Not, Where's Next?' *Telegraph*, 22 December 2007.
2. BBC News, Dramatic 2008 Beckons for Balkans', 26 December 2007, http://news.bbc.co.uk/1/hi/world/europe/7155439.stm (last accessed 04/01/2008).
3. For discussion of the impact of the collapse of communism on radical right movements, see: Michael Petrou, 'Neo-neo-Nazis: New Fascist Movements Find Fertile Ground in the Turmoil of Eastern Europe', *Macleans*, 24 February 2006.
4. For background on the playwright Csurka, on Hungary's most famous radical leader, and his beliefs see: Edith Oltay, 'Hungary: Csurka Launches "National Movement",' *RFE/RL Research Report*, no.13, 26 March 1993.
5. 'The Nationalist Right Gets Together: "Third Way" Platform,' posted at http://hvg.hu/english/2005 1017nationalistright.aspx (last accessed 04/01/2008).
6. See, for example, Markus Salzmann, 'Hungarian Extreme Right Set up Paramilitary "Guard",' World Socialist Web Site [WSWS], 24 September 2007. Story posted at http://www.wsws.org/articles/2007/sep2007/hung-s24.shtml (last accessed 04/01/2008). Salzmann writes: 'The end of August witnessed the foundation in Hungary of an extreme-right-wing paramilitary [...] Around 1,000 sympathisers and supporters gathered in front of the Budapest Castle, directly before the offices of the Hungarian president, Laszlo Solyom, to swear in the first 56 members of the guard (a number chosen to commemorate the 1956 uprising against Stalinism)'.
7. See http://www.hirtv.hu/?tPath=/belfold/&article_hid=115874 (last accessed 04/01/2008).

South-Eastern Europe and the Far Right

8. See, for example, Roger Boyes, 'Far Right tries to take control of the revolt,' *The Times*, 23 September 2006, http://www.timesonline.co.uk/article/0,,13509-2371248.html (last accessed 04/01/2008).

9. For historical background on the origins of Hungarian radical nationalism, and analysis of the role religion contributed to its development and to impacting anti-Semitism, see: Paul A. Hanebrink, *In Defense of Christian Hungary: Religion, Nationalism, and Anti-Semitism, 1890–1944* (Ithaca: Cornell University Press, 2006), 1–9, 108–191.

10. For background on the Arrow Cross see Stanley G. Payne, *A History of Fascism, 1914–1945* (Milton Park, Abingdon: Routledge, 1996), 415–416.

11. Part of the political development for the skinheads included unleashing a first of several well-orchestrated attacks against the Roma communities in and around Eger. While violence has, on occasion, intensified since, both public response and reaction from mainstream politicians has been characterized by revulsion.

12. The diaspora proved to be an important source of political leadership. For example, Albert Szabo returned home from Australia to found the tiny neo-Nazi World National Popular Rule Party (WNPRP) in October 1993.

13. See, for example, Thomas S. Szayna, 'The Extreme-Right Political Movements in Post-Communist Central Europe,' in Peter H. Merkel and Leonard Weinberg (eds.), *The Revival of Right-Wing Extremism in the Nineties* (London: Frank Cass, 1997), 141.

14. For background on Torgyan and accounts of his early political career see Judith Pataki, 'Hungary's Smallholders Fail to Unite before National Elections,' *RFE/RL Research Report*, no. 10, 11 March 1994.

15. Duncan Light and David Phinnemore, *Post-Communist Romania: Coming to Terms with Transition* (New York: Palgrave, 2001), 49.

16. Tom Gallagher, *Modern Romania: The End of Communism, the Failure of Democratic Reform, and the Theft of a Nation* (New York: New York University Press, 2005), 267–268.

17. Elizabeth Pond, *Endgame in the Balkans: Regime Change, European Style* (Washington DC: The Brookings Institution, 2006), 82.

18. *Evenimentul Zilei*, 24 September 2007.

19. See *Evenimentul Zilei*, 3 September 2004.

20. Polling data published by *Hotnews*, 29 March 2007. Story available at www.hotnews.ro.

21. Codreanu's party was called the Iron Guard. In 2000 a new group surfaced publicly, calling itself the New Right, or Noua Dreapta. For the most part, it has kept a relatively low profile, but is increasingly being linked to vicious attacks against ethnic minorities and homosexuals. The New Right appears to have swallowed up wholesale the ideology, symbols and rituals of the old Iron Guard. Codreanu is almost deified by the rank and file. So far, the organisation has refused to engage in the open political process, opting only to follow the established Iron Guard custom of identifying itself as a 'legion', and members as 'legionnaires'. Its main goals seem to be working for a Greater Romania, and forging a nation grounded in the principle genetic purity. With most activities remaining underground or accessible only to members, it is not possible to say without doubt how much support the legionnaires have. If recent recruiting efforts can provide any insight, it is likely the New Right remains a tiny group well outside the mainstream, perhaps having only or no more than 1,000 followers. After the collapse of communism a tiny Neo-Nazi group calling itself Garda de Fier, or Iron Guard, had resurfaced, but claimed almost no following. Best estimates suggest the organisation may never have had more than a few dozen members, and it is believed that many who were active are somehow affiliated with or have been absorbed by Noua Dreapta.

22. Cited in Michael Shafir, 'Romania,' *RFE/RL Research Report*, no. 16, 22 April 1994.

23. John T. Ishiyama and Marijke Breuning, *Ethnopolitics in the New Europe* (Boulder: Lynne Rienner, 1998), 23–24.

24. Christo Ivanov and Margarita Ilieva, 'Bulgaria,' in Cas Mudde (ed.), *Racist Extremism in Central and Eastern Europe* (New York: Routledge, 2005), 2.

25. For a brief but excellent review of Gelemenov's politics and public reaction to his policies and pronouncements, see Janusz Bugajski, 'Nationalist Majority Parties: The Anatomy of Ethnic Domination in Central and Eastern Europe,' in Jonathan P. Stein (ed.), *The Politics of National Minority Participation in Post-communist Europe: State-Building, Democracy, and Ethnic Mobilization* (New York: East West Institute, 2000), 81.

26. Karakachanov's statement is reproduced in an interview carried by, *24 Chasa*, 2 March 1994.

27. 'Controversial Journalist to Run for Sofia Mayor,' *RFE/RL Newsline*, 23 September 2003.

28. In an August 2005 profile of Siderov, one Standart piece explained the leader exhibited such

190

qualities that many observers would readily 'lump him as a Nazi' and even many nationalist political leaders would view his organisation as being 'even very extreme for them'. See *Standart*, 17 August 2005.

29. Cited in 'Leaders of Evangelical Churches in Bulgaria Warn Against Anti-Semitism in Bulgaria,' *RFE/RL Newsline*, 22 February 2002.

30. Vassilis Lambropoulos, 'Why is there no Extreme Right in Greece?' *The Journal of the International Institute*, 10:1 (Fall 2002). Article posted at http://www.umich.edu/~iinet/journal/ vol10no1/lambropoulos.htm (last accessed 04/01/2008).

31. 'Greece,' The Stephen Roth Institute Report for 2001, http://www.tau.ac.il/Anti-Semitism/ asw2001-2/greece.htm (last accessed 04/01/2008).

32. Cited in http://www.reference.com/browse/wiki/Hrisi_Avgi (last accessed 04/01/2008).

33. Maria Vidali, 'Anti-Jewish Attacks,' *Central Europe Review*, 2:22 (5 June 2000). Posted at http:// www.ce-review.org/00/22/greecenews22.html (last accessed 04/01/2008).

34. Brendan O'Leary and Khaled Salih, 'The Denial, Resurrection, and Affirmation of Kurdistan,' in Brendan O' Leary et al. (eds.), *The Future of Kurdistan in Iraq* (Philadelphia: University of Pennsylvania Press, 2005), 3–46.

35. For a contemporary history and background on radical Islamic activity in Turkey see Ely Karmon, 'Radical Islamic Political Groups in Turkey,' *Middle East Review of International Affairs*, 1:4 (December 1997).

36. Ali Kemal Ozcan, *Turkey's Kurds: A Theoretical Analysis of the PKK and Abdullah Ocalan* (New York: Routledge, 2006), 84–137.

37. 'The PKK's Role in International Drug Trafficking,' posted at http://www.fas.org/irp/world/para/ docs/studies5.htm (last accessed 04/01/2008).

38. See estimates published in 'Kurdish Rebels Kill Turkey Troops,' BBC News, 8 April 2007. Story posted at http://news.bbc.co.uk/2/hi/europe/6537751.stm (last accessed 04/01/2008).

39. 'Bush to Discuss PKK with Turkey's Gul on January 8,' *Reuters*, 28 December 2007.

40. Cited in Ayla Jean Yackley's 'Turkish Army Hits Iraqi Sites, Kills Rebels in Turkey,' *Bloomberg News*, 26 December 2007. Story posted at http://www.bloomberg.com/apps/news?pid=20601102&sid =ajpzbOrblU44&refer=uk (last accessed 04/01/2008).

41. And it is in foreign policy, in relations with Albania's neighbours, that Greater Albania will have its most significant impact. See, for example, Victor Roudometof, *Collective Memory, National Identity, and Ethnic Conflict: Greece, Bulgaria, and the Macedonian Question* (Westport, CT: Praeger, 2002), 154.

42. Cited in Frida Malaj, 'Albania: Support for Kosovo Crosses Left-Right Divide,' *Institute for War and Peace Reporting (IWPR)*, 11 February 2006. Story posted at http://www.reliefweb.int/rw/RWB. NSF/db900SID/TKAE-6VB493?OpenDocument (last accessed 04/01/2008).

43. Alex J. Bellamy, *The Formation of Croatian National Identity: A Centuries-old Dream?* (Manchester: Manchester University Press, 2003), 44–45.

44. Charles Jelavich, 'The Croatian Problem,' *Austrian History Yearbook*, 3 (1967), 83–115.

45. Robert J. Donia and John V.A. Fine, Jr., *Bosnia and Hercegovina: A Tradition Betrayed* (London: Hurst and Company, 1994), 139.

46. In doctrinal terms, stemming back to the nineteenth century. Bosnia and Herzegovina's Muslims were regarded merely as ethnic Croats who had been seduced by Islam. In its most benign form, the Croat nationalism espoused by Tuđman saw as realistic option that these populations could eventually be won back to the true faith, Catholicism. This attitude translated into realpolitik during the wars in Bosnia when, with only a few exceptions, Tuđman and his government opted for cooperation with Muslim authorities in neighbouring Bosnia.

47. Eduard Šoštarić, 'A New HVIDRA to be Established,' *Nacional*, 1 March 2005. Story posted at http://www.nacional.hr/en/articles/view/18479 (last accessed 04/01/2008).

48. *Oslobodjenje*, 7 November 1990.

49. Kristin Archick et al., *CRS Report for Congress: Islamist Extremism in Europe*. Text of full report posted at http://64.233.167.104/search?q=cache:iTEYlen0LE4J:www.fas.org/sgp/crs/terror/RS22211. pdf+bosnia+extremism&hl=en&gl=ca&ct=clnk&cd=8 (last accessed 04/01/2008).

50. Julian Borger, 'The President's Secret Henchmen,' *Guardian*, 3 February 1997.

51. '"Beli Orlovi"–15 godina poslije,' *Vijesti* (Zagreb), 17 August 2006.

52. See Colette Rausch (ed.), *Combating Serious Crimes in Postconflict Societies: A Handbook for Policymakers and Practitioners* (Washington: US Institute of Peace Press, 2006), 59.

53. Miloš Vasić, '"Zmija" u nedrima vlasti,' *Vreme*, no. 638, 27 March 2003.

54. 'Profile: Vojislav Seselj,' BBC News, 7 November 2007. Story posted at http://news.bbc.co.uk/2/hi/europe/2317765.stm (last accessed 04/01/2008).

55. Ogjen Pribicevic, 'Changing Fortunes of the Serbian Radical Right,' in Sabrina Ramet (ed.), *The Radical Right in Central and Eastern Europe* (University Park: Pennsylvania State University Press, 1999), 192–211.

56. *Politika*, 10 November 1993.

57. See Šešelj's remarks concerning the potential for SRS electoral growth in NIN, 18 December 1997.

58. *Beta*, 22 January 2007.

59. See Lenard J. Cohen, *Serpent in the Bosom* (Boulder: Westview Press, 2001), 187–190.

60. 'Eyewitness: A New Balkan Flashpoint?' *BBC News*, 14 March 2000.

61. Carlotta Gall, 'Kosovo Rebels Said to Allow Violence Against the Serbs,' *New York Times*, 3 August 1999.

62. Bekim Greicevci, 'War Crimes Indictee Haradinaj Urges Stability in Kosovo,' *Southeast European Times*, 26 February 2007.

63. For a detailed discussion of Macedonia's ethnic make-up and the possible implications for state security see Peter Jordan, 'Ethnische Gruppen in Makedonien,' in Walter Lukan and Peter Jordan (eds.), *Makedonien* (Vienna: Peter Lang, 1999), 65–114.

64. See Ferid Muhic, 'Macedonia–an Island on the Balkan Mainland,' in David A. Dyker and Ivan Vejvoda (eds.), *Yugoslavia and After* (London and New York: Longman, 1996), 232–247.

65. On the other hand, some have made the argument, now done with less frequency, that Macedonia's stability is largely explainable because its multi-cultural, multi-ethnic character in facts holds all the elements necessary for a thriving liberal democracy. See, for example, Peter H. Liotta, 'The "Future" Republic of Macedonia: The Last Best Hope,' *European Security*, 9:1 (Spring 2000), 68–97.

66. Tensions and hostilities both within the country and between groups in Macedonia and Kosovo escalated to the point where, by 28 February 2001, Macedonian security troops and some ground forces clashed with an organisation calling itself the National Liberation Army. What threatened for over a month to erupt into major fighting calmed.

67. *Frankfurter Allgemeine Zeitung*, 7 May 2001.

68. *SRNA*, 4 May 2006.

69. 'Prv kongres na Demokratskata Partija na Srbite', *Macedonian Information Centre (MIC)*, 11 March 1996.

70. *Report of the Human Rights Committee*, vol. 1, General Assembly Official Records Sixtieth Session, Supplement no. 40 (A/60/40), United Nations Publications (Human Rights Committee), 2005, 74–77.

71. For a detailed analysis and commentary of Laibach's early impact on Slovenian society see Mark Thompson, *A Paper House: The Ending of Yugoslavia* (New York: Pantheon Books, 1992), 43–44.

72. *AFP*, 4 September 1993.

73. *Delo*, 28 March 2004.

74. *Globus*, 14 December 1992.

75. *Mladina*, 26 January 2004.

76. Gerald Henry Blake, Dusko Topalovic *et al.*, *The Maritime Boundaries of the Adriatic* (Durham: International Boundaries Research Unit [IBRU] at Durham University, 1996), 25.

77. *Financial Times*, 5 December 1992. See also, John K. Cox, *Slovenia: Evolving Loyalties* (Milton Park, Abingdon and New York: Routledge, 2005), 119.

78. Just what would it take for most of a population to turn its back on civil society and democratic reform? While it may be tempting to fall back on arguments which say singular events may act as catalysts, forcing social reactions that may be chronicled as conditioned stimulus-response behaviours, some analysts insist a great deal of pain and suffering might be endured, and critical thresholds are invariably reached before any tipping points are triggered. For but one insightful analysis, see Daniel N. Nelson, "Civil Society Endangered," *Social Research* 63:2 (Summer 1996), 345–368.

79. *Le Figaro*, 28 June 2004.

80. 'Ceku: Partition Raises Issue of Greater Albania,' *B92 News*, 26 December 2007. Story posted at http://www.b92.net/eng/news/politics-article.php?yyyy=2007&mm=12&dd=26&nav_id=46491 (last accessed 04/01/2008).

81. For some signs of how the Western powers may address developments within Kosovo and across the Kurdish Middle East see Lokman I. Meho, *The Kurdish Question in U.S. Foreign Policy: A Documentary Sourcebook* (Westport, CT: Greenwood Press, 2004), 11–12.

Southern Europe and the Far Right

Southern Europe – Italy and the Iberian Peninsula – has a history of right-wing dictatorships. In Italy Mussolini held power between 1922 and 1943, in Spain **Franco** ruled between 1936 and 1975, while in Portugal **Salazar** was head of an authoritarian regime between 1932 and 1968. Curiously, though, it has only been in Italy that the Far Right, in contemporary times, has been able to exert any significant influence. In fact, in recent decades, what has distinguished the political landscapes of both Spain and Portugal has been the dearth of meaningful far-right activity. This chapter will consider the nature of the contemporary Far Right in Italy and its links to Mussolini's Fascism in the inter-war period. It will also analyse the legacy of the Franco and Salazar eras in Spain and Portugal and seek to explain the lack of substantive far-right movements in these two countries today.

Italy: From Mussolini to the Alleanza Nazionale

It could be argued that, of all European countries, Italy has the strongest tradition of far-right politics. This incorporates not just the Mussolini regime, but also the MSI, one of the earliest and most influential post-war parties, and the **National Alliance**, which has shared in various Italian governments. Add to this the regionalist and xenophobic **Northern League**, and you have an impressive list of far-right political movements active in post-war Italy. Given that 'Fascism' is, at its root, an Italian word, and given also that Mussolini's was the first fascist regime to gain power in **Europe**, it is no surprise that far-right ideas are embedded in the political culture of Italy in a way that they aren't necessarily in other countries.

That said, for obvious reasons the immediate post-war years were not particularly favourable to the growth of the Far Right. The Axis powers had been defeated and Mussolini hanged. As Chiarini puts it: 'The allied victory against Nazism and Fascism was, above all, an ideological one'.[1] It was the same across Europe. Anyone wishing to resurrect the ideas and ideology of fallen right-wing dictatorships was going to find it hard to attain any level of credibility. The social and economic context had also changed. Italian citizens now had rights and freedoms 'guaranteed by the State'.[2] In fact, it could be said that, 'The Republic came into being as a system explicitly hostile to, and hence incompatible with, any survival of Fascism'.[3]

In the post-Mussolini era, the Italian Far Right has taken on many guises. In 1946, a movement that would evolve into one of the most durable and successful of European far-right movements was established: the MSI. As Gallagher argues: 'Fascism had sunk sufficiently deep roots in Italian society for there to be a successor movement ready to promote the nationalist and corporatist values of the Mussolini era, even in the hostile environment of a fledgling Italian **democracy**'.[4] The founding father of the MSI was Giorgio Almirante, a junior Fascist official who was involved in the formation of the Italian Social Republic in 1944. For almost half a century, the MSI stood as the flag-bearer of Italian neo-Fascism. It exhibited nostalgia for the Mussolini regime, but at the same time, it also sought to adapt to a changed political climate. As such, it dissolved itself in January 1995. Almost immediately, another movement of the Far Right was formed: the *Alleanza Nazionale* (AN). This new movement also took in ex-conservatives, but in terms of membership and manifesto, it was heir to the MSI.

The establishment of the *Alleanza Nazionale* was about re-inventing the Far Right. Commentators argued that the logo of the new movement was reminiscent of one that had been used previously by the left, and also that the name of the new movement had echoes of the left-wing Democratic Alliance. In addition, **Fini**, the first leader of the AN, made a conscious effort to distance himself and his movement from the ideas and imagery of the Mussolini regime. For example, in March 1998 he said he wanted to relaunch the AN as a 'modern, open, right-wing party',[5] and in November 2003, while visiting Israel in his capacity as deputy prime minister, he described the fascist racial laws as 'infamous' (this was viewed as a terrible insult by many AN members).[6] This is why the AN is often labelled 'post-Fascist'. In terms of ideology and policy, it is trying to 'move on' from the Mussolini regime and its legacy.

3. Italian Foreign Minister Gianfranco Fini during a press conference at Rome's Foreign Press Association, 6 April 2006.

For neo-Fascists in Italy, there was a central dilemma: legal or illegal means? While the MSI was contesting elections and attempting to 'play by the rules', another group of far-right militants were committing themselves to a 'strategy of tension' based on **violence**, propaganda and psychological warfare.[7] In 1969, Ordine Nuovo (ON), an MSI splinter group, was implicated in the Piazza Fontana bombing and this was followed by an attempted coup in 1970. In 1974, right-wing extremists were connected to the massacre of Piazza della Loggia. In 1980, Mario Amato, a judge conducting a high-level investigation into right-wing terrorism, was assassinated. In the same year, ON and other far-right factions were linked to the **Bologna bombing**. Fifteen years later, in 1995, the Italian authorities confirmed sentences of life imprisonment on Valerio Fioravanti and Francesca Mambro – members of the neo-fascist Nuclei Armati Rivoluzionari (NAR) – for executing the 1980 attack. Another NAR member, Stefano Delle Chiaie, was also implicated in the event. One estimate – albeit from a communist academic – says that there were 4,384 acts of political violence committed in Italy between 1969 and 1975, 83 percent of them by the Far Right.[8]

Post-war Italy also witnessed the birth of a regionalist movement of the Far Right. The Northern League was formed in 1991 as a merger between various regional 'leagues' including the Lombard League and the Liga Veneta. Under the leadership of Umberto Bossi, the Northern League rose to prominence in the early 1990s. It has made the most of the various corruption scandals that have afflicted Italy in recent years, and especially the way that in the 1980s and early 1990s, corruption became endemic and almost semi-institutionalised in what became known as *Tangentopoli* (Bribeville). In 2001, Bossi's movement entered government, even though it had scored only 4 percent at the polls. It was awarded three cabinet posts by Prime Minister Silvio Berlusconi.

And that, of course, is not to forget those who have thrived on their familial connections with Benito Mussolini, such as his granddaughter, Alessandra. She began her political career in the MSI and AN, but after a falling out with Fini – who called the fascist ideology of her grandfather 'absolute evil'[9] – she founded her own far-right party, *Liberta d'Azione*. Via this new movement, she claimed a seat in the European Parliament in 2004. She was disenchanted with Fini's 'post-fascist' makeover and wanted to speak up for her grandfather, for **women** and against **immigration**. 'The National Alliance is no longer to the right, it is in the centre,' she said. 'There is a huge space in the society of the right for me to occupy. For the first time a woman is the leader of a political party [in Italy]'. The view is that she now personifies 'hard-right politics' in Italy.[10]

How should we interpret the Far Right in Italy? One interesting aspect of neo-Fascism in Italy is its relationship to the left. At bottom, of course, movements such as the MSI have displayed a glaring hostility to the left. This, in fact, has been a unifying feature of the Far Right across Europe for more than 60 years. In Italy, where traditionally there has been a strong communist party, it has been particularly pronounced. Those on the left were still feeling this hatred in the first years of the twenty-first century. The feeling was that the Berlusconi-led coalition – that included the AN – was 'chomping at the bit to extend and deepen the attacks on the working class' and that through 'a series of bills, public statements and interviews given to the media, the ... government has outlined a range of attacks on pensions, the right to strike and the 40-hour work week, immigrants, welfare and public **education**'.[11] Bizarrely, though, commentators were queuing up to argue that, over the decades, the Far Right had actually aped the far left in the way that it had formulated a political strategy. As Sidoti puts it: 'In the 1970s and in the 1980s, terrorism constituted a major element of dispute and ideological self-questioning in leftist culture, posing basic questions about Marxism, democracy, violence, revolution and legality. The debate involved the press, political parties, trade unions, academic circles and militant pundits. Something similar happened within rightist culture through various intricate paths'.[12]

The Far Right has also revealed itself to be fragmented and divided. At any one time during the post-war period there have been scores of different parties, movements and groupings. Even the MSI split in two in the early 1970s.[13] Efforts at creating some kind of unity always failed.[14] But, curiously, this fragmentation and division has not proved fatal. Also, more than in many other European countries, the Far Right has played its part in electoral coalitions; for example, with the Monarchist Party (1972). During the 1960s, it helped keep various coalition governments and presidents in power and in more recent times it has been an integral component part of Berlusconi's Forza Italia administration, with Fini at various times holding the prestigious posts of deputy prime minister and foreign minister.

Underlying everything has been a fundamental dilemma for movements of the Far Right. This has had several strands, but at root it has been about ideology and strategy.

Southern Europe and the Far Right

Should the legacy of Mussolini be embraced or not? Should the Far Right stand for tradition or modernity? For moderation or hard-line attitudes and policies? Different groupings and different factions have supplied different answers to these questions, but in general, and very gradually, the Far Right – or at least key elements on the Far Right – has acknowledged the need for credibility and respectability. The best example of this process in action has come with the AN. In 1998, *Le Monde Diplomatique* said that this movement was 'now considered part of Italy's anti-fascist "constitutional arc"'. It went on: 'Gianfranco Fini has succeeded in turning his National Alliance into an avowedly post-fascist party, which has won a legitimate and increasingly successful place among today's political parties. Much of this new-found legitimacy comes from a new liberal orientation and a refusal to ally itself with the more extreme neo-fascist right.[15] Five years later, in 2003, another news organisation noted a key policy change. 'In recent weeks, Italy's far-right *Alleanza Nazionale* has called for immigrants to be given the vote. The call is seen as a major U-turn from a party striving to break clear from its fascist roots to become a moderate mainstream party. But the Muslim vote still faces stiff opposition from parts of Prime Minister Silvio Berlusconi's coalition government'.[16]

The journey towards respectability has been a long and difficult one, but it seems that key players on the Far Right realised that a line had to be drawn in the sand. They realised that their parties and movements had to be seen to be more moderate, reasonable and electable. For the most part, this about-turn has been executed skilfully. But not everyone has been convinced. For Gallagher: 'Fini's claims to have made a genuine conversion to post-fascism, while genuflecting to Mussolini's memory, have cast doubt on how complete the rethink has been'.[17]

Spain: The Shadow of Franco

Today, Spain is devoid of an influential party of the Far Right, or as the BBC put it recently: 'The Far Right is not currently a significant force in Spanish politics'.[18] But that is not to say this has always been the case. Over the last three decades small, fringe movements have come and gone. Probably the most famous was the *Frente Nacional* (Front National - FNl), founded in 1986 and led by veteran politician Blas Piñar López. It tried to update and tone down Falangist-Francoist ideology. It boasted its own 'trade union' body – the *Frente Sindicalista Nacional* – but did not win any seats in either the 1987 or 1989 elections. The FNl was direct successor to the movement that Piñar led between 1976 and 1982 – *Fuerza Nueva* (New Force - FNa). It had a dedicated **youth** movement (*Fuerza Joven*) and, like the FNl, had an affiliate trade union – *Fuerza Nueva del Trabajo* (FNT).

Piñar has been the nearest the modern Spanish Far Right has had to a unifying leader, but even he has fallen short.[19] His electoral results have been disappointing: 0.4 percent (1977), 2.1 percent (1979), 0.5 percent (1982), 0.63 percent (1987) and 0.38 percent (1989).[20] According to Ellwood, in 1984, Spain was home to 'as many as 400 groups' on the extreme right.[21] The history of far-right movements is certainly rich and varied. In the 1970s, we encounter *Falange Española* (auténtica), the *Junta Coordinadora Nacional Sindicalista*, the Warriors of Christ the King, the *Alianza Nacional '18 de julio'*, *Círculos Doctrinales and Unión Nacional*. Also in existence in the 1970s, was the *Frente Nacional Español* (Spanish **National Front** – FNE) – a nostalgic pro-Falange group that evolved into the FE de la JONS in 1976 – and many other parties and movements.

The absence of significant far-right movements today is obvious, but this does not necessarily connote lack of far-right activity in a more general sense. Far from it, in fact. As one news organisation put it: 'Although Spain lacks a national far-right political party like the French *Front National* or the Italian *Forza Italia*, it does host a bewildering array of smaller extremist groups. Their numbers appear to be expanding as old-style Fascists and Franco supporters are joined by young neo-Nazis, skinheads and the "ultras", or politically extremist hooligans, who congregate at soccer games. Most of these groups espouse racist, anti-Semitic and xenophobic ideas; many promote "white pride". All embrace violence'.[22] Other trends are also apparent: the coming together of far-right parties at election time, the central role played by veterans associations, and the emergence of 'neighbourhood and other neo-Nazi groups' who have a strong presence on the internet and generally coordinate their activities from outside Spain.[23] Another media source put it like this:

> [In Spain] 10,000 people are estimated to belong to far-right groups. The U.S. group Volksfront has become one of Spain's most important neo-Nazi organisations, sidelining a group called Blood and Honour, according to the daily *El Pais*. Police have arrested more than 100 people in 2005 and 2006 on charges such as beating up immigrants or painting threatening graffiti. Spain's Movement Against Intolerance estimates that ultra-right groups attack nearly 4,000 people annually. Skinheads 'go hunting' ... not only for immigrants, but also for leftists, homosexuals, beggars or prostitutes ... So far, the ... far-right groups have been unable to unite under single leaders. But even if that does not happen, their presence could influence the political scene by making conservative parties adopt a tougher discourse on subjects such as immigration, analysts said.[24]

Although the modern Spanish Far Right has evolved and changed, it is clear that nostalgia for the Franco regime is a kind of 'glue' that still unites activists. Ellwood comments: 'For some, the central figure is Franco; for others it is the founder of the *Falange*, José Antonio Primo de Rivera, or one of the other pre-war Falangist leaders. For all the external paraphernalia, the lexicon, the iconography and the ideological content are culled from the 1930s, regardless of the fact that the Falangist yoke and arrows painted on walls, the protests against "reds" and "masons", the blue shirts and roman saluting seem anachronistic in post-Francoist Spain. Indeed, the impression these groups give is that the Spanish extreme right is ahistorical'.[25]

This nostalgia has been in evidence recently. In 2005, hundreds of far-right activists (doing fascist salutes) gathered together to protest at the actions of the Socialist government, which had just ordered the last statue of Franco to be removed from Madrid.[26] Also, one contemporary far-right movement, the Brotherhood of the Old Guard, is an offshoot of the *Falange* and looks back on the Franco era with affection. We are told that members of this organisation meet together 'regularly in what was once Primo de Rivera's Madrid office to uphold the ideals of the *Falange*. At a meeting on March 30, Brotherhood member José Luis Jerez Riesco lambasted homosexuals, "Moors", Freemasons and "Judaizers", as well as the Socialist government. He told the 40 or so mostly elderly men and women gathered there that "bullets are worth more than words." The audience greeted Jerez's words with enthusiastic applause'.[27]

Naturally, the anniversary of the former leader's death is exploited by far-right activists. In 2005: 'Hundreds of right-wing demonstrators made stiff-armed fascist salutes and shouted insults against gays, Muslims and immigrants at a Sunday rally marking the 30th anniversary of the death of former Spanish dictator Gen. Francisco Franco. Waving red-and-yellow Spanish flags with the insignia of the Franco regime's *Falange* Party, the crowd gathered at the Plaza de Oriente beside the royal palace in Madrid's old quarter, where Franco used to address crowds every year ...'[28] But, whatever far-right activists may have us believe, or whatever they would like to imagine, the Franco regime was never a fascist regime in the same sense that Mussolini's and Hitler's were. Gilmour says that the date 18 July 1936, 'the day of the Nationalist uprising against the legally constituted Republican government, occupies pride of place in the mythology of the Spanish extreme right'.[29] But, the general view is that Franco stood for an old fashioned type of conservatism and authoritarianism. Of course there were aspects of his regime that were reminiscent of Italy under *Il Duce* and Germany under the *Führer*, but Spain is often ignored in academic surveys of inter-war European Fascism.[30]

So, parties and movements have come and gone on the Far Right, with many still exhibiting affection for, and loyalty to, the Franco regime. In recent years, there have also been a number of 'incidents' where 'far-right activists' have been blamed for stirring up trouble. The BBC focused on one such episode in early 2000: '[A]n outbreak of racial violence in the southern town of El Ejido...was seen by some as a warning sign. El Ejido's mayor blamed extreme right-wingers for inciting violence which erupted after the funeral of a woman killed while being robbed by a Moroccan immigrant. Huge numbers of Moroccan immigrants work in Spain mainly as low-paid agricultural labourers ... there are fears that the Far Right could find increasing support in communities with large immigrant populations'.[31] And in January 2007 a far-right leader was accused of attacks on immigrants:

> Jose Luis Roberto, head of the España 2000 party, allegedly committed the offences at a demonstration in March 2002. A court in Valencia heard the local leader of an Ecuadorian immigrant group who claimed there was a 'permanent attitude of aggression against the African and Latin American foreigners' in and around Valencia. Hernán Cortés, leader of the Rumiñahui association, said Roberto was involved in a series of protests at different places in eastern Spain 'at which immigrants were attacked'. The entire situation occurred, the Rumiñahui head said, 'with the consent' of the Valencia regional government. Cortes recalled that during the 2002 demonstration, Valencia's Ruzafa neighborhood 'was the object of a brutal and exaggerated virulence,' where the España 2000 followers 'did not come to demonstrate, but to attack vulnerable groups who are working and contributing to the richness of this country'.[32]

These episodes would seem to demonstrate that the ideas of the Far Right have a constituency, even if this doesn't necessarily translate into electoral support.

Why, though, in general terms, is the Far Right on the road to 'obscurity and ineffectuality'?[33] And why are there no influential far-right parties in Spain today? Many theories have been advanced. The conservatism of the Franco dictatorship did little to encourage the growth of radical political groups; the transition to democracy, post-Franco, was so successful that 'anti-democratic' far-right parties had little future; the Far Right has always been fragmented and lacking in unity and leadership; and by its nature, Spain is rural and under-developed rather than urban and industrialised (the ideal conditions for the growth of the Far Right). Or maybe we should relate a joke that was doing the rounds when Mr Aznar was Spanish premier: 'There are no far-right parties in Spain because all their potential members feel very comfortable with the government of the Partido Popular'. Even in 1996 Spaniards were wondering whether the election of Aznar's party to government might herald a return to the authoritarian right-wing politics of the past.

Portugal: The Rise of the Popular Party

The situation is slightly different in Portugal where a party of the Far Right has, in recent times, become prominent. The Popular Party, led by journalist Paulo Portas (founder of the *O Independente* newspaper), won 9 percent of the vote and fourteen seats in the parliamentary elections of March 2002 and thus became the 'third force' in Portuguese politics. It also became a junior partner in the country's centre-right government with Portas becoming defence minister.

In terms of ideology, Portas' movement is strong on trying to combat immigration and multiculturalism. Its practical policies include: special integration programmes for 'violent' second-generation immigrants from Portugal's former empire and asking children to sing the national anthem every day at school. In 2001, it was reported that Portas considered 'the surveillance of Muslim communities a priority'.[34] Soon after the 2002 election, *Agence France Presse* noted: 'In an interview with the newspaper *Publico*, the right-wing defence minister, Paulo Portas, called for a cut in immigration on the grounds that "a country has obvious limits" and that "Portugal does not have, especially at a time of rising unemployment, conditions to accept many more immigrants."'[35] And in 2004, Portas spoke out against the arrival of a 'Dutch abortion ship' in Portuguese waters: 'If Portugal allowed the ship into its waters, it would not have authority against illegal fishing, drug trafficking or clandestine immigration … We cannot allow what is illegal on land to be legal in our waters'.[36] Also, in the area of social policy, the party wishes to tighten abortion laws and reduce the age at which young people can be sent to prison.

The party is hostile to the growing power of the EU and also fearful of Spain. In 2002, *The Independent* reported on the attitudes of the new governing coalition. Under the headline, Portuguese Far Right Revives Old Rivalries With Spain, it declared:

> A fierce nationalism has sprung up in Portugal since the far-right Popular Party joined a conservative government elected in March, stirring up old hostilities towards the country's historic rival, Spain … [S]ince Jose Manuel Durao Barroso became prime minister and brought the PP into coalition with his conservative Social Democratic Party (PSD), commentators and entrepreneurs have warned of the threat of a Spanish takeover, calling upon a spirit of resistance symbolised by the bloody battle of Aljubarrota in 1385 … And the Spanish prime minister, Jose Maria Aznar, was infuriated by Portugal's refusal to extradite a suspected member of the Basque separatist group Eta. Jose Luis Telletxea, accused of involvement in terrorism, fled to Lisbon without identity papers in 1994 … However, the leader of Portugal's Far Right, Paulo Portas, said Mr Aznar had no business giving Portugal lessons on how to rule. Mr Portas is now Defence minister and his views are gaining ground.[37]

Also on the Portuguese Far Right we encounter the National Front, led by Mario Machado, which specialises in direct-action tactics against immigrants and leftist groups. Machado has claimed that party membership has increased by 400 percent since November 2004. There is also the Portuguese National Renewal Party (PNR) – a small movement that was extremely nostalgic for the Salazar years – and New

Order, a neo-Nazi group that existed on the fringes of politics between 1980 and 1982. We must also note the existence, during the 1970s and 1980s, of the PDC and the MIRN-PDP. But these movements were tiny. Standing on its own, the PDC could muster only 0.5 percent of the national vote in 1976, and then 1.1 percent in 1979, 0.6 percent in 1983 and 0.69 percent in 1985. When it joined up with the MIRN-PDP in 1980, it actually registered an even lower electoral score: 0.3 percent.[38]

Thus, since 1974 and the end of the Salazar-Caetano regime, the Far Right has not been a prominent force in Portugal. As Pinto puts it: 'The neo-fascist manifestations which have recurred periodically in European countries since 1945 have had no Portuguese equivalent as yet'.[39] This might strike the unknowing observer as perverse, but the fact is that, in the long term, the authoritarian nature of the Salazar regime actually did little to encourage the growth of independent movements on the Far Right. According to Tom Gallagher: 'It is possible to argue that at the outset of his marathon premiership, Salazar took steps which fatally weakened the prospects of a vigorous movement emerging to defend the principles of the regime, and to keep alive its appeal, either in the absence of its founder or following its own dissolution. Thus, the gravedigger of the populist neo-Fascism of the kind able to engineer electoral breakthroughs in France or West Germany was the architect of the authoritarian era no less, rather than the forces of democracy or of the revolution which had briefly triumphed in 1974–1975'.[40] Add to this the reality of the post-1974 situation. The new authorities made a point of clamping down on all manifestations of the right. They also stood up to an attempted coup by far-right forces in March 1975. Against this background it is no real surprise to discover that the Far Right has been almost non-existent in Portugal over the last three decades.

This last statement, though, should be qualified. Of course, in electoral and political terms, the Far Right has been a negligible force. But in other arenas it has had more of a profile. Pinto talks about a 'cultural and ideological effort [with] various centres of growth'. By this, he means that the Far Right was operating, and seeking influence, outside the traditional milieu: in private universities, in the new emerging press, and within youth movements and other foundations.[41] As in other European countries (the best example being France), the Far Right was shifting the battleground onto a cultural plane.

In Portugal, there were many specific instances of this strategy in action. Far-right activists started to organise on university campuses and new groups started to emerge: for example, *Movimento Jovem Portugal* (Young Portugal Movement), *Frente de Estudantes Nacionalistas* (Front of Nationalistic Students) and *Frente Nacional Revolucionária* (National Revolutionary Front). In 1959, a group of young neo-Fascists founded the review *Tempo Presente*. This publication 'embraced modern aesthetic values' and 'sought to deprive opposition intellectuals of their overwhelming monopoly in the intellectual field'.[42] There were other forays into publishing. In 1976, *A Rua* (The Street) was launched. Its editor was Manuel Maria Múrias, who had his own **family** link to the Salazar era (his father had edited the regime's main paper). The same year saw the first appearance of *O Diabo* (The Devil), a satirical and passionately anti-communist journal.[43] More far-right journals also hit the streets – for instance, *Agora*, *Política* and *Resistência*.[44] Another tactic has been to infiltrate 'mainstream' political parties. As has been argued: 'Rather than establishing new right-wing parties, conservatives and supporters of the old regime were most likely to be active politically through the PSD [Social Democratic Party] or the CDS [Centre Democrats]'. [45]

The relationship between the Salazar dictatorship and the Far Right in Portugal is an odd one. In the words of Gallagher: 'First appearances suggest that the capacity of the ultra-right to mobilise in Portugal ought to be higher than it actually is … Outwardly, neo-Fascists stood to gain from the extent to which two generations of Portuguese were indoctrinated in the schoolroom, from the pulpit, and through the media by conservative propaganda which stressed the values of 'God, Nation and Authority … However, one has to look hard for signs of neo-fascist strength in democratic Portugal, and Salazar is a curiously understated figure in current ultra-right propaganda'.[46] Dr António de Oliveira Salazar was Portuguese dictator between 1932 and 1968. In power, he put heavy emphasis on ideas of hierarchy, economic stability and social harmony. He also took on extra roles: he acted as foreign minister between 1936 and 1947, and war minister during the period 1936–1944. He supported the Nationalists in the Spanish Civil War, but purposefully did not get close to Hitler or Mussolini. Historians tend to view Salazar's regime as para-fascist. Essentially, he wished to give off the impression that his government was populist, dynamic and fascist-like, while at the same time resisting any genuine moves in a radical direction.

Salazar's regime was based around the *Estado Novo* (New State) and *União Nacional* (UN), the 'artificial' movement set up to give the new regime an aura of legitimacy. The *Estado Novo* was a corporate structure established in 1934. Its title suggested radicalism, but in reality it was the opposite: conservative, backward and devoid of modern ambition. Influenced by Charles Maurras and the *Action Française*, it was neither Fascist nor hospitable to Fascism, and ultimately tried to destroy the authentically-fascist NS Blueshirts. During the Salazar era those on the Far Right could belong to the *União Nacional*, created in 1930. It tried to pose as a mass movement, but failed visibly, and simply became part of the state structure. In time it was outflanked by the NS Blueshirts and was on its last legs by the early-1940s.

So, to what extent was Salazar and his regime linked to the Far Right? It was certainly *politique* for him to play at being 'Fascist'. It could draw people into his regime and neutralise them.[47] It was a tactic and strategy. The reality, though, was that the genuine 'Fascists' were distrustful of, and disappointed by, the dictatorship and thus carved out a home for themselves elsewhere, either in the NS Blueshirts or in other movements, such as the *Frente Académica Patriotica* (Patriotic Academic Front - FAP) which operated during the 1940s and was pro-Salazar in orientation. During the 1960s, there also emerged the *Frente de Estudantes Nacionalistas* (FEN), a neo-fascist movement based in the student sector which published a newspaper of the same name. Another neo-fascist grouping was founded in 1966: the *Frente Nacional Revolucionária* (National Revolutionary Front - FNR).

So, why is the contemporary Far Right in Portugal not as strong as one might predict? In one sense, the conditions are ripe. The country is home to more than 700,000 immigrants, mainly from ex-colonies such as Brazil, and there is also a strong tradition of right-wing politics, albeit of the Salazar variety. But the reality is different. Salazar never overtly encouraged the growth of an independent Far Right, and many right-wingers were forced into exile at the end of his regime, with all far-right movements being declared illegal. This meant that only gradually were those on the Far Right able to come out of hiding and re-invent themselves within the new 'democratic' politics. The Salazar experience may well have 'stymied' the growth of the Far Right in Portugal, but today Portas and others appear to be fighting back.

Southern Europe and the Far Right

The three countries covered in this section have one significant thing in common. Each endured its own authoritarian regime during the twentieth century. Mussolini, Franco, Salazar – three dictators whose legacy was both a help and a hindrance to far-right activists after 1945. It has been argued that in Italy, Fascism was so engrained that, after the war, pro-Mussolini activists had little trouble in re-igniting the flame of far-right politics. But within a few decades, a new generation of militants had emerged who had no links with Fascism or Mussolini. Then came Fini and the AN, and the era of 'post-Fascism'.

In Spain and Portugal, the Far Right has been less visible. The Franco and Salazar eras – conservative, traditional and authoritarian rather than fascist *per se* – seemed, actually, to smother the growth of indigenous far-right movements. Genuine Fascist or neo-fascist activity was not encouraged. The end result of the Franco and Salazar regimes was inertia. Looking back, it is clear that neither Spain nor Portugal has ever boasted a strong and significant party along the lines of the MSI in Italy. A multitude of tiny movements have had a temporary presence, but none have actually become permanent. Of course, this does not deny the fact that in these two countries – and elsewhere – the Far Right has regularly operated underground and on the fringes of legality. But this is a *different* Far Right – one that, in truth, has yet to acquire, or even realise the need for, 'respectability' in the same way that the MSI in Italy has done.

That said, in all three countries the Far Right's future prospects are anything but unhealthy. The AN has only recently been in government as part of Berlusconi's Forza Italia coalition. Since the early 1990s, its share of the national vote has remained remarkably steady at around 12 – 15 percent. Meanwhile, activists on the Spanish Far Right continue to idolise Franco. Depending on their attitudes and mentality, they might also be encouraged by the rise of the Partido Popular and the growth in neo-Nazi violence. In Portugal – a country that didn't even warrant a mention in the BBC's survey of the European Far Right in 2000 - things are also on the move with Portas' Popular Party now a key player on the national political stage and also playing a junior role in government.

In Southern Europe, as in other regions, the Far Right has a rich and varied heritage. But it is not a uniform, homogenous *bloc*. Far from it, in fact. At one extreme, elements on the Far Right have engaged in armed combat and violence. At the other, they have entered the corridors of government. And this, in a sense, is the fascination.

Peter Davies

Notes

1. Roberto Chiarini, 'The "Movimento Sociale Italiano": a historical profile' in Luciano Cheles, Ronnie Ferguson & Michalina Vaughan, *Neo-Fascism in Europe* (London: Longman, 1991), 20.
2. Ibid., p.21.
3. Ibid., p.22.
4. Tom Gallagher, 'Exit from the ghetto: the Italian far right in the 1990s' in Paul Hainsworth (ed.), *The Politics of the Extreme Right: From the Margins to the Mainstream* (London: Pinter, 2000), 67.
5. Ibid., p.82.
6. Stephen Roth Institute, 'Italy 2003–4', www.tau.ac.il/Anti-Semitism/asw2003-4/italy.htm (cited 6 April 2007).
7. Francesco Sidoti, 'The extreme right in Italy: ideological orphans and countermobilization' in Paul Hainsworth (ed.), *The Extreme Right in Europe and the USA* (London: Pinter, 1994), 160.
8. Ibid., p.158.
9. BBC News, 'Italy's post-fascists to regroup', http://news.bbc.co.uk/2/hi/europe/3382151.stm (cited 6 April 2007).

10. Independent on Sunday, 'Mussolini in stilettos', http://findarticles.com/p/articles/mi_qn4159/is_20040208/ai_n12751423/pg_2 (cited 1 January 2008).

11. World Socialist Web Site, 'Italy's right-wing government unveils new attacks on workers', http://www.wsws.org/articles/2001/sep2001/ital-s22.shtml (cited 30 December 2007).

12. Francesco Sidoti, 'The extreme right in Italy: ideological orphans and countermobilization' in Paul Hainsworth (ed.), *The Extreme Right in Europe and the USA* (London: Pinter, 1994), 152–153.

13. Ibid., p.158.

14. Roberto Chiarini, 'The "Movimento Sociale Italiano": a historical profile' in Luciano Cheles, Ronnie Ferguson & Michalina Vaughan, *Neo-Fascism in Europe* (London: Longman, 1991), 23.

15. Le Monde diplomatique, 'Italy's post-Fascists bid for respectability', http://mondediplo.com/1998/05/09raff (cited 30 December 2007).

16. Christian Science Monitor, 'A rising tide of Muslims in Italy puts pressure on Catholic culture', http://www.csmonitor.com/2003/1110/p07s01-woeu.html (cited 30 December 2007).

17. Tom Gallagher, 'Exit from the ghetto: the Italian far right in the 1990s' in Paul Hainsworth (ed.), *The Politics of the Extreme Right: From the Margins to the Mainstream* (London: Pinter, 2000), 83.

18. BBC News, 'Far right', http://news.bbc.co.uk/hi/english/static/in_depth/europe/2000/far_right/spain.stm (cited 6 April 2007).

19. Sheelagh Ellwood, 'The extreme right in Spain: a dying species' in Luciano Cheles, Ronnie Ferguson & Michalina Vaughan, *Neo-Fascism in Europe* (London: Longman, 1991), 154–155.

20. Ibid., p.154.

21. Ibid., p.153.

22. John Gilmour, 'The extreme right in Spain: Blas Piñar and the spirit of the nationalist uprising' in Paul Hainsworth (ed.), *The Extreme Right in Europe and the USA* (London: Pinter, 1994), 213.

23. Sheelagh Ellwood, 'The extreme right in Spain: a dying species' in Luciano Cheles, Ronnie Ferguson & Michalina Vaughan, *Neo-Fascism in Europe* (London: Longman, 1991), 153.

24. Internet Centre Anti Racism Europe, 'Far right on the rise on the Iberian Peninsula', http://www.icare.to/news.php?en/2006-11(cited 30 December 2007).

25. Sheelagh Ellwood, 'The extreme right in Spain: a dying species' in Luciano Cheles, Ronnie Ferguson & Michalina Vaughan, *Neo-Fascism in Europe* (London: Longman, 1991), 153.

26. Christian Science Monitor, 'In Spain, signs that far right is on the rise', http://www.csmonitor.com/2005/0411/p05s01-woeu.html (cited 2 January 2008).

27. Ibid.

28. The Scotsman, 'Spanish fascists mark 30th anniversary of Franco's death', http://news.scotsman.com/ViewArticle.aspx?articleid=2680107 (cited 2 January 2008).

29. John Gilmour, 'The extreme right in Spain: Blas Piñar and the spirit of the nationalist uprising' in Paul Hainsworth (ed.), *The Extreme Right in Europe and the USA* (London: Pinter, 1994), 207.

30. See Ernst Nolte, *Three faces of fascism* (London: Weidenfeld & Nicolson: 1965).

31. BBC News, 'Rise of the right', http://news.bbc.co.uk/hi/english/static/in_depth/europe/2000/far_right/spain.stm (cited 30 December 2007).

32. Internet Centre Anti Racism Europe, 'Far right leader accused of attacks on immigrants', http://www.icare.to/news.php?en/2007-01 (cited 30 December 2007).

33. John Gilmour, 'The extreme right in Spain: Blas Piñar and the spirit of the nationalist uprising' in Paul Hainsworth (ed.), *The Extreme Right in Europe and the USA* (London: Pinter, 1994), 227.

34. European Monitoring Centre on Racism and Xenophobia, 'Portugal', http://eumc.europa.eu/eumc/material/pub/anti-islam/collection/Portugal.pdf (cited 2 January 2008).

35. Institute of Race Relations, 'Portugal', https://www.irr.org.uk/cgi-bin/news/open.pl?id=5424 (cited 30 December 2007).

36. Abortion Rights, 'Portuguese ban on abortion ship creates furore over women's rights', www.abortionrights.org.uk/content/view/30/105 (cited 30 December 2007).

37. The Independent, 'Portuguese far right revives old rivalries with Spain', http://www.findarticles.com/p/articles/mi_qn4158/is_20020603/ai_n12625805 (cited 30 December 2007).

38. António Costa Pinto, 'The radical right in contemporary Portugal' in Luciano Cheles, Ronnie Ferguson & Michalina Vaughan, *Neo-Fascism in Europe* (London: Longman, 1991), 184.

39. Tom Gallagher, 'Portugal: the marginalisation of the extreme right' in Paul Hainsworth (ed.), *The Extreme Right in Europe and the USA* (London: Pinter, 1994), 233.

40. António Costa Pinto, 'The radical right in contemporary Portugal' in Luciano Cheles, Ronnie Ferguson & Michalina Vaughan, *Neo-Fascism in Europe* (London: Longman, 1991), 183.

41. Ibid., p.171.

42. Ibid., p.171.
43. Tom Gallagher, 'Portugal: the marginalisation of the extreme right' in Paul Hainsworth (ed.), *The Extreme Right in Europe and the USA* (London: Pinter, 1994), 238.
44. António Costa Pinto, 'The radical right in contemporary Portugal' in Luciano Cheles, Ronnie Ferguson & Michalina Vaughan, *Neo-Fascism in Europe* (London: Longman, 1991), 173–175.
45. Country Studies, 'Political parties', http://www.country-studies.com/portugal/political-parties.html (cited 30 December 2007).
46. Tom Gallagher, 'Portugal: the marginalisation of the extreme right' in Paul Hainsworth (ed.), *The Extreme Right in Europe and the USA* (London: Pinter, 1994), 232–233.
47. Ibid., p.234.

Western Europe and the Far Right

This contribution to the encyclopedia focuses upon extreme right political parties and movements in Western Europe. The emphasis is upon the post-war and contemporary context, and parties on the Far Right of the political spectrum, which contest direct elections in their respective countries. In recent years, there has been much attention in the media, academic writing, reports, research projects, monitoring institutions and so on, devoted to Western Europe in this context. Extreme right-wing parties surfaced intermittently after 1945 in certain circumstances, and their emergence and varied success can be linked to some broad societal developments and changes. At the same time, the extent of their success depends upon their own subjective qualities and capacities. In this respect, the projection of policies that appeal to the electorate is important – and the contribution below examines these aspects, as well as illustrating the sociological profile of extreme right voters. Since the success of extreme right parties cannot simply be measured by the size of their vote though, the contribution assesses also their power and potential to influence policy-making and the consequences of extreme right engagement with certain mainstream political parties.

Context

The inter- and war-time period in twentieth century Western Europe witnessed the emergence, consolidation and defeat of movements and regimes that were seen widely as extremist. National Socialism in Germany and Italian Fascism were the most prominent examples here. But they were not the only ones of note. Thereafter, the post-war era ushered in an understandable reaction and revulsion against the excesses and extremes of the previous period. In this context, liberal **democracy**, free market capitalism and anti-Fascism became the bywords of post-war policy and practice in the nation-states of Western Europe and beyond. As the **Cold War** set in, anti-**Communism**, too, became an important part of Western European policy perspectives.

Because of what had happened in the 1930s and 1940s – notably the **Holocaust**, mass killings, widespread human rights violations, death and destruction – state and society remained vigilant in post-war Western Europe. 'Never again' became the widely held sentiment across much of the continent. As a result, various governments and mainstream political parties in Western Europe brought in legislation, practices and other measures to guard against any recurrence of the above phenomena. However, the post-war world *has* experienced the emergence of various Far Right, extreme or radical right-wing populist parties. Indeed, there is a lively debate among observers about how to define and classify the modern and contemporary phenomena. Here is not the place to rehearse this debate, except to add that, at times, the labels are used interchangeably and, at times, more rigidly.[1] What is not in question, though, is the prevalence of the phenomena of far-right parties. Thus, across Western Europe in recent decades, most countries have experienced the resurgence of far, or extreme right, or radical right-wing populist forms. To be sure, in some countries, the presence and success of such forces has been markedly more significant than in others. Unsurprisingly, then, there has been an uneven and changing picture of extreme right success and failure in post-war and contemporary Western Europe.

The picture is also complicated by the diverse nature of the various parties and movements that can be said to make up this tableau. For instance, unsurprisingly, some are more extreme than are others. Again, some have been more linked to, and are nostalgic about, pre-war and wartime ideas and manifestations on the Far Right. Furthermore, in certain countries, the phenomena in question have emerged at a relatively early stage in the post-war cycle, whereas most of the successful extreme right parties have gathered momentum only since the 1980s. By and large, moreover, the most successful extreme right parties have won support by marking their distance from Fascism and Nazism and engaging with contemporary issues such as **immigration**, security, globalisation, identity and European integration. In this respect, it is important to stress that contemporary extreme right parties are products of their times and need to be understood as such. They are the by-products of socio-political developments and changes that have taken place, and are still taking place, in the contemporary world. The context for extreme right success, therefore, is very important.

Some political commentators have argued that the context for extreme right growth in recent decades has been the emergence of a so-called post-materialist and changing world, in which key issues (such as immigration, **Europe**, identity and the **environment**) have assumed greater importance and political allegiances, and party systems have undergone a process of change. Moreover, in general, voters have identified less and less with a given party, as old alliances based on class and **religion** have receded. The nation (or nation-state), too, is challenged by accelerating trends towards globalisation and Europeanisation, which impinge upon national sovereignty and decision-making – and leave individuals believing that things are beyond the control or care of their traditional political leaders. Other customary forms of belonging and solidarity have also been weakened, such as community, village, Church, trade union and extended **family**, leaving individuals more atomised and potentially more receptive to the populist styles and discourses of extreme right politicians and parties. As would-be saviours, the forces on the extreme right have appealed to voters, offering individuals a sense of place (the nation, the national community) and an easy solution to their various problems such as unemployment. This appeal from political outsiders is enhanced when traditional mainstream political parties have monopolised political power for long periods of time and are identified with failed politics and policies. At the same time, the incidences of coalition governments, of power sharing and of various agreements within and across the political mainstream and establishment have fuelled the extreme right's argument that all the *other* political parties are the same. In this scenario then, the parties of the extreme right purport to offer a different, alternative agenda and priority list, as opposed to offering the mere alternation of political parties and the circulation of traditional elites.

However, in order to take advantage of the political opportunities which come their way, the parties on the extreme right need to be in good shape internally and to be able to offer something appealing to the voters. Thus, strong and charismatic leadership qualities are important attributes, as demonstrated by individuals such as Jean-Marie **Le Pen** of the Front National (*Front National*, FN) in France, Jörg **Haider** of the **Austrian Freedom Party** (*Freiheitliche Partei Österreichs*, FPÖ) and later, in 2005, the Alliance for the Future of Austria (*Bündnis Zukunft Österreich*, BZÖ) and Gianfranco **Fini** of the **Italian Social Movement** (*Movimento Sociale Italiano*, MSI) and later the **National Alliance** (*Alleanza Nazionale*, AN). Effective and centralised party machines, financial soundness, activist supporters and appealing party programmes are all part of the picture here. According to one viewpoint: 'The closer a group gets to sophisticated party organisation, the more likely their prospects for effective policy impact will be'.[2] In this context, the growth of the Internet has provided extreme right parties with a useful tool, enabling them to propagate their message, reach wider audiences and communicate with (potential) supporters. To sum up, therefore, extreme right success can be attributed to the unfolding and confluence of broad societal developments external to the parties in question, and also to the capacity of these organisations to take advantage of circumstances and opportunities.

Parties and movements

It perhaps goes without saying that each country is different, with its own political culture, institutions and traditions, and each extreme right party is also unique within its respective setting. Nonetheless, there is enough in common on the far or extreme right to justify the parties therein being referred to as a 'political family', in much the same way that Green parties or social or Christian democratic parties might be categorised as such. Thus, it is the ideas, the priorities and the style of the extreme right parties that enable them to be examined under the same roof.

In examining the extreme right in a post-war and contemporary setting, a plausible starting point is to ask 'where to begin?' Initially, all roads lead to Rome. The Italian MSI is often put forward as the first post-war extreme right party of significance in Western Europe. Born in 1946 and inspired by Mussolini and late war-time Fascism, it won seats in the Italian National Assembly and in local government and the organisation had thousands of members in the post-war decades. It became a significant, albeit relatively minor, actor in Italian politics. Further afield too, it served as a model for other sister political parties such as the Front National in France. Ignazi makes the point that the MSI paid homage to the fascist tradition and supported a third way between capitalism and Communism.[3] However, the MSI undertook a metamorphosis in later decades – and has reaped the rewards. In the mid-1990s, as the Italian party political system was rocked under the weight of corruption, the MSI was superseded by the National Alliance. The latter party basically replaced the former, albeit leaving in the process a splinter, dissident movement, the Social Movement-Tricoloured Flame (*Movimento Sociale Fiamma Tricolore*, MS-FT). Under the leadership of Gianfranco Fini, the AN performed well at the ballot box – with, for instance, over 100 parliamentary seats and returns of 13.5 to 15.7 percent in the 1990s. Moreover, the party entered into coalition government (in 1994–1996 and 2001–2006) with Italian prime minister and media magnate Silvio Berlusconi's Let's Go Italy (*Forza Italia*, FI) and the **Northern League** (*Lega Nord*, LN) – the latter being another far-right regionalist (and sometimes separatist) movement based in the north of Italy. The National Alliance is projected by its leader as a post-fascist party that has turned its back on the past in order to embrace the present and future. However, there are some doubts prevalent about the completeness of the AN/MSI's transformation into a more mainstream type of right-wing party. These doubts have been fuelled by the findings of questionnaire surveys that have revealed high levels of fascist nostalgia within the party, notwithstanding its metamorphosis into the AN and its two spells of coalition government in recent years.[4]

Ignazi put the MSI forward as an old-style, traditional type of extreme right party, alongside sister organisations such as the **British National Party** (BNP) and the **German People's Union** (*Deutsche Volksunion*, DVU). Simultaneously, Ignazi placed parties such as the Austrian FPÖ and the French FN in the category

of the new post-industrial extreme right, i.e. organisations that were less explicitly
linked to the fascist tradition. These two particular parties have won considerable
success at elections in the last quarter of a century and, in turn, they have served
as role models for other extreme right parties in Western Europe and beyond. At
times, these two parties have had some difficulty in establishing their credentials as
valid participants in the democratic process. In this respect, for instance, utterances
from their respective leaders on matters such as the Holocaust (Le Pen) and Nazism
(Haider) have provoked much criticism and backlash since they served to place these
individuals and their parties in the anti-democratic fold.[5] Nevertheless, alongside the
Flemish Bloc (*Vlaams Bloc*, VB), the FN and the FPÖ have been in the vanguard
of extreme-right success at the ballot box. These parties had difficulty establishing a
presence and winning electoral support in their early years. But, from about the mid-
1980s onwards, they began to assert themselves more, campaigning strongly on issues
that appealed to many in the electorate (see below). The FN, for example, at virtually
every major election (presidential, parliamentary, European) since 1984, has won
double-figure support, with Le Pen peaking at 16.9 percent, and 4.8 million votes, in
the 2002 presidential election (first ballot), when sensationally he was runner-up to
the mainstream right-wing Gaullist French president, Jacques Chirac. The FPÖ, too,
steadily increased its share of the vote in the 1980s-1990s, peaking at 26.9 percent
in 1999, when it became the largest party on the Austrian right. The successful
campaigning of these parties on issues such as immigration, **law and order**, national
identity and Europe has influenced greatly the discourse of other sister parties.
Notably, the Flemish nationalist party, VB added these issues to its initial prime focus
on the national question – i.e. Flemish nationalism counter-posed to incorporation in a
Belgium state. Indeed, VB has been one of the most successful extreme right parties in
Western Europe, especially in its bastion of **Antwerp** where the party has won up to
a third of the vote in recent years and also emerged as the largest party in the regional
Flemish Parliament.

Elsewhere too, notably in Switzerland and Scandinavia, far-right parties have
adopted similar themes and policy emphases belatedly into their policy agendas.
Thus, parties such as the Danish Progress Party (*Fremskridtspartiet*), the **Swiss
People's Party** (*Schweizerische Volkspartei*, SVP), the **Norwegian Progress Party**
(*Framstegspartiet*, FrP), the **Danish People's Party** (*Dansk Folkeparti*, DPP) and
Sweden's **New Democracy** (*Ny Demokrati*, ND) fit less easily under the label 'extreme
right' and are often depicted as radical right-wing populist movements. Whatever the
definition, these parties have sharpened and hardened their discourse on issues such
as immigration and asylum seekers, ceasing to become primarily anti-tax or anti-
bureaucracy movements. For some of these parties in particular, electoral success has
been very impressive. Thus, the SVP made significant breakthroughs in the 1999 and
2003 Swiss federal parliamentary elections. In 1999, the party won 23 percent and
44 seats (out of 200) and in 2003, became the largest party in Switzerland with 26.7
percent and 55 seats. In the most recent election in 2007, the SVP continued to make
further progress with 29 percent and 62 seats, although the party leader, Christoph
Blocher, found it difficult to sustain comfortable relations with coalition government
partners.

Similarly, the last decade has seen the Norwegian Progress Party achieve an
upwardly mobile trajectory. The real breakthrough came in the 1997 parliamentary
election when the party won 15.3 percent and 22 seats. Although the party slipped back

a little in 2001 (to 14.6 percent), by 2005 it had become Norway's second largest party (and the largest on the right) with 22 percent and 38 seats. In neighbouring Denmark, the Danish Progress Party was perhaps the first of the right-wing populist parties to make a significant breakthrough (15.3 percent in 1973). In recent years, though, the party has been overtaken at home by the Danish People's Party, which gathered momentum steadily over the past decade – to reach 13.3 percent and 24 (out of 179) seats in 2005 – and achieved a role in official policy-making (see below).

To some extent, the **List Pim Fortuyn** (*Lijst Pim Fortuyn*, LPF) – named after its leader – fits ideologically into the above cluster of parties. However, unlike its Scandinavian counterparts, the LPF's success was very fleeting i.e. largely confined to the 2002 parliamentary election, when the party won 17 percent and 26 (out of 150) seats, making it the Netherlands' second largest party. But the LPF leader was assassinated during the 2002 election campaign and, deprived of his leadership role and media-friendly personality, the party soon declined. With the collapse of the LPF (to 5.7 percent and 8 seats in 2003 – and with all the seats then lost in 2006), the vacuum has been filled by Geert Wilders's populist and anti-immigrant Party for Freedom (*Partij voor de Vrijheid*, PVV) (5.9 percent and 9 seats in 2006), which has campaigned on similar issues to its predecessor.

In other parts of Western Europe, the results for the extreme right have been less impressive. In the United Kingdom and Germany, for instance, none of the extreme right parties have won seats in the national parliaments – in part due to the respective electoral systems and parliamentary rules in these countries. The legacy of Fascism in Germany, or the threat of it to the UK, has also served to restrict extreme right breakthrough. As a result, electoral success has been limited to local and regional elections, with parties such as the BNP and the National Democratic Party of Germany (*Nationaldemokratische Partei Deutschlands*, NPD) making some significant, but limited, gains in the twenty-first century. In the Mediterranean countries of Greece, Portugal and Spain, post-war authoritarian regimes and one-party states have featured at varying times. However, once these countries moved towards more liberal democratic, multi-party regimes, the electorates therein showed little appetite for returning extreme right parties to the parliamentary mainstream. The legacy of past authoritarianism, the popular desire to embrace a more pluralist style of politics, the opting to join the European Union and the incorporation of nationalist-minded themes within the agendas of mainstream parties, all served to reduce the space for far-right parties to operate and succeed.

Overall, then, the above picture suggests an uneven tapestry of support and success for extreme right political movements and parties in Western Europe. This is not surprising. Each country and party is different; each political culture, party system.and context is also different.

Policies and perspectives

Extreme right political parties are noteworthy both for the issues that they campaign on and the priority that they give to them. The following section focuses on four key aspects of the extreme right's policy agenda – immigration, nation, Europe and economics. Whilst it is too simplistic to call the parties in question 'single issue parties', there is no doubt that immigration control has emerged as a key policy issue for the extreme right. As such, many other policies (security, economics, **education**, culture, etc) are bound up with it in one way or another. Immigration has featured as an important issue for extreme right parties for many years now. To some extent, they have followed the example of mainstream political parties and politicised the issue of immigration. Though usually, this is done in a more populist and robust manner. As a result, the movements, especially the successful ones, on the extreme right have appropriated the issue and, in effect, often set the standard by which immigration is discussed and approached. However, not every party from the extreme right political family has given the issue such prominence in party discourse from the beginning. For instance, Scandinavian political parties such as the Danish Progress Party and the Norwegian Progress Party tended to focus more so on taxation and bureaucracy as primary issues, only belatedly jumping on the anti-immigration bandwagon when it became apparent how well the issue played for extreme right parties in other countries. Territorially focused movements, such as the LN in Italy and the VB in Belgium, became known initially for their attitudes towards the 'national question', but later prioritised the issue of immigration for similar reasons.

Extreme right parties portray immigration as the root cause of many problems within society. Notably, it is argued that it causes unemployment, strips the public exchequer of scarce financial resources, leads to insecurity and dilutes the culture of the host nation. The solution for extreme right parties initially was to halt post-war immigration in Western Europe and to pursue a draconian policy of population return. Zero immigration remains the goal of extreme right policy makers, but recent emphasis has been placed on the practice of assisted return. Extreme right parties approach the issue of immigration with concepts such as 'national preference' and practices that are tantamount to welfare chauvinism. National preference means giving priority to indigenous citizens/nationals in matters such as employment, housing and state benefits. As regards welfare chauvinism, Kitschelt and McGann have defined it as thus: 'The welfare state is presented as a system of social protection for those who belong to the ethnically defined community who have contributed to it'.[6]

As intimated by the above quotation, the parties on the extreme right tend to see the nation, *their* nation, as an ethnically defined, exclusive entity. The myth of a homogenous nation, a more or less fixed and organic entity, is at the core of extreme right values. Accordingly, the parties of the extreme right are not in favour of multicultural, foreign, external influences that might dilute the ethno-national community and its integrity. Therefore, catchy populist slogans such as 'France for the French' or 'Germany for the Germans' are utilised to express the sentiments of the extreme right. In this context, outside influences, such as immigrants, asylum-seekers and refugees, as well as non-Christian religious and cultural doctrines, such as Islam, are largely seen (by extreme right parties) as unwelcome in Western Europe. Again, other socio-economic or political supranational or global developments are seen as threats to the sovereignty and potency of the nation-state. Thus, post-war European integration, new world order American cultural hegemony and increasing globalisation fit into this scenario.

As regards European integration, extreme right parties have benefited from the second order character of European elections and thereby won seats in the European Parliament (EP) on a regular basis. Indeed, notwithstanding their strong sense of nationalism, extreme right movements have formed trans-national party groups in the EP to promote their Euro-scepticism. The latest of these groupings was the **Identity, Tradition and Sovereignty** (ITS) grouping, created in 2007 following the June 2004 European elections and – also following the May 2004 enlargement of the

European Union – bringing together West European and Central and East European parties. However, at the time of writing, the ITS grouping has been derailed by internal divisions among the parties, notably in Italy and Romania.

Extreme right parties have not always been so Euro-sceptic and, indeed, not all fit into this category. Nonetheless, given their strong sense of nationalism and the generally pro-European consensus among mainstream political parties in Western Europe, the issue is an ideal one upon which populist, anti-elitist, plain speaking extreme right parties have campaigned. Institutions such as the European Commission are particularly targeted as non-elected, remote, bureaucratic and encroaching threats to the nation-state. Similarly, major developments in European integration, such as the 1991 (Maastricht) Treaty on **European Union** (TEU) and the 2005 Draft Constitutional Treaty on European Union have been attacked as steps too far and perceived as the building blocks in the creation of a European super-state. In recent years, moreover, extreme right parties have been in the vanguard of opposition to Turkey's membership of the EU, seeing the country as having its own non-European, non-Christian cultural values. Some extreme right parties, such as the French FN and the BNP, have even gone as far as to call for their country's withdrawal from the European Union. In both these cases (France and Britain), though, the above parties are faced with similar-minded rivals on the issue of withdrawal from the EU. Nonetheless, on the issue of European integration, extreme right parties have been able to exhibit their **protest** character and their patriotic colours. Since the process of European integration is often seen to lack transparency and also is not widely understood by the citizens of Europe, extreme right parties can function as the tribune of the people, critical of the European Union and against the establishment and elites supporting it.

At the same time, European integration and globalisation are associated with free trade and enhancing the market, whereas extreme right parties – whilst largely supporting the principle of capitalism – also favour protectionist economic policies that benefit the **workers** and (small) businesses of the nation-state. Indeed, in terms of economic policy, extreme right parties have evolved towards embracing a hybrid or composite perspective in which market and nation are combined in a not always consistent or coherent synthesis. The latter reflects the eclectic make-up of the extreme right's electorate. For, what is evident is the capacity of extreme right parties, in recent decades, to capture more working-class voters to add to the traditional supporters from the cohorts of the lower middle-classes, white-collar employees, small businesses, artisans, shopkeepers and the like. Satisfying the demands and policy perspectives of all these sectors (and more) is not always that easy. Thus, in order to retain support, extreme right spokespersons have needed to juggle their policy appeal and audiences accordingly. Extreme right economic policy has generally been critical of excessive charges and bureaucracy levelled on businesses, as well as excessive public/state expenditure. Indeed, as already intimated, some far-right parties (notably in Scandinavia and Switzerland) have emerged primarily as anti-tax movements, only to take up welfare chauvinism and economic protectionism in later years. Notably, the Norwegian Progress Party called for welfare expenditure cuts in the 1970s, but for greater welfare expenditure in the 1990s, to be financed out of the country's considerable oil industry profits. In Belgium too, initially the VB became identified with a policy perspective of tax cuts, privatisation and neo-liberalism, only later developing sentiments supportive of a social market **economy**, economic protectionism and welfare chauvinism.

Western Europe and the Far Right

Who votes for the extreme right?

As illustrated above, the vote for extreme right political parties fluctuates from country to country, from election to election. In some instances, the most prominent parties here have won millions of votes. Elsewhere, the picture is less impressive. But what is clear is that the parties on the extreme right have won votes from a range of individuals and groups, making it unwise to stereotype or pigeon hole the 'ideal' party voter. Nevertheless, notwithstanding this proviso, certain trends and patterns are apparent and worth noting.

For instance, the sociological profile of electorates suggests that more males than females tend to support extreme right parties. Within the higher echelons of extreme right parties, notably among the leaderships and the ranks of elected representatives, there are fewer **women** too. Indeed, this latter situation (though not necessarily specific to the extreme right parties) most probably is a factor in reducing the proportion of females voting for the extreme right. Another factor too, is the tendency of extreme right parties comparatively to have more traditional perspectives on the role of women in society and to be less in tune with feminist and equality discourses. In particular, extreme right parties perform less well among young, highly educated, middle class females. This suggests that, when coupled with gender, other factors are important too – such as class and education. As regards the latter, there is much evidence to show that extreme right organisations draw comparatively less from voters with formal educational qualifications. The higher the level of education, the less likely is the support for the extreme right. As argued elsewhere, those electors in contemporary society who lack the skills and security that a higher education can provide have a greater propensity to vote for the extreme right.[7] When unemployment (and to some extent, the fear of unemployment) serves as an additional factor here, the potential to vote for the extreme right increases. Regional gains for the NPD in twenty-first century eastern Germany fit into this scenario. The small extreme right party has been able to exploit unemployment and discontent in a reunified post-communist Germany in transition.

Class too is a significant indicator of extreme right voting. One of the most striking characteristics of the sociological profile of extreme right electorates is the presence of sizeable cohorts of working-class voters. Indeed, extreme right parties have been referred to sometimes as the 'workers' parties' of contemporary times – a description traditionally applied to communist and socialist parties of old. Successful extreme right parties, such as the FN in France and the FPÖ, have performed better than mainstream parties on the right, and even on the left among working-class voters. This situation reflects the difficulty that mainstream right-wing parties have in competing with the extreme right on issues such as immigration, law and order/security, economic protectionism, welfare chauvinism and Europe. It also reflects the evolution of mainstream left-wing class-based organisations towards becoming more consciously centrist, catch-all parties – in the process marking their distance from traditional appeals such as class solidarity and struggle. As well as drawing significant support from working-class voters, the extreme right traditionally has enjoyed the support of lower middle class and white collar workers. These layers have felt squeezed between the organised working class on the one hand, and higher paid middle class, managerial, big business and professional layers on the other. They are receptive to extreme right discourse on taxation, bureaucracy and state interference, as well as the emphases on immigration, nation, security and cultural dilution that are popular with working-class voters.

As regards age, extreme right political parties have had success in appealing to younger and first-time voters, as well as to abstainers. The chances of young people voting for the extreme right increases when other factors come into play here – such as, being male, less formally educated, working-class and/or unemployed. Significant parties such as the French FN and the Austrian FPÖ have won disproportionate support from younger cohorts of voters in their upwardly mobile progress in the 1980s and 1990s. Lesser supported parties, such as the BNP in Britain and the NPD in Germany, have performed well in these categories too. Again, the profile of these parties' electorates may vary from election to election and over time. For instance, in the historic 2002 French presidential election, Jean-Marie Le Pen did best amongst older voters (50–64 years old) and less impressively among young voters.[8] Yet, overall, younger voters have been attracted significantly enough to extreme right parties. Sometimes, the vote for extreme right parties from younger voters (and more generally) might be construed as a **protest vote** – a protest against the establishment, the powers that be and other political parties. There is certainly an element of protest voting in this respect, as recent gains for the NPD in Germany suggest. But all in all this interpretation is not the full picture, and rational choice and identification with policies, personalities and party need to be taken into account too.

Coming to terms with extreme-right influence

The standing of the Far Right in Europe today cannot be measured simply by examining the level of its vote from country to country, even though this is a useful and tangible indicator of the strength of its support. In addition, the extreme right has been seen to influence the agenda of other parties, pressurising them to pick up on and address its vote-winning themes. Moreover, mainstream political parties – unable to form governments on their own or with others – have gone into coalition government with extreme right parties, notably in Austria, Italy, the Netherlands and Switzerland. Elsewhere too, such as in Denmark and Norway, the extreme right has remained outside coalitions, but nonetheless, entered into policy making and supportive arrangements that serve to enhance its agenda and influence. In other instances, such as in France, extreme right parties have been able to exercise pressure and influence via bargaining and ad hoc deals done at a regional level. A few concrete examples will serve to illustrate the influential roles of extreme right-wing parties on issues of importance to them. Thus, in Austria in 2005, the coalition government between the FPÖ and the mainstream Austrian People's Party (ÖVP) brought in legislation that made it more difficult for immigrants to accede to citizenship. Again, in Denmark in recent years, the dependence of mainstream parties on parliamentary support from the DPP contributed towards tougher policies on immigration and asylum, with less residence permits forthcoming for persons from these categories. In coalition in Italy in recent years too, the extreme right LN has had some influence on the provision of tougher immigration and asylum-seeker policy. Furthermore, Schain highlights developments in France, where success at a local level by the French *Front National* encouraged mayors from the mainstream right to reduce expenditure on housing and welfare programmes for immigrants.[9] These types of examples are by no means exhaustive and, according to one view, 'centre-right politicians have begun to inhabit the same discursive universe as their far-right counterparts'.[10] Curran, too, has pointed to a sharing of ideas and even political styles across the extreme and mainstream rights – a process she defines as the mainstreaming of populist discourse.[11]

Western Europe and the Far Right

Prior to the mid-1990s, extreme right parties were seen very much as 'outsiders'. Indeed, this was their strength and appeal – they were not part of the establishment and system. As Abedi explains, they functioned as anti-political establishment parties (APEs).[12] However, over the past decade or so, some far-right parties have entered the mainstream and become players on the inside track. Others aspire to do so. To some extent, this situation has involved the parties losing their APE status. Yet, it would be fair to say that the parties in question cannot be viewed simply as parties like the others, despite their new found insider status. They have different agendas, priorities and styles of doing politics. Mainstream parties, notably on the right, sometimes have to make the choice between ignoring extreme right parties and seeing political office escape them or joining forces with the extreme right in order to enter government. Thus, mainstream political parties are faced with the choice of dealing with extreme right parties as partners, or enemies, or as a mix of both categories. There are risks and problems either way for a mainstream right-wing party. Moreover, in order to counter the influence of the extreme right, mainstream parties have had to examine their 'tool-kit' and come up with appropriate strategies, tactics and measures.

4. France's veteran anti-immigration campaigner and National Front leader Jean-Marie Le Pen (L) and BNP (British National Party) chairman Nick Griffin shake hands after a news conference in Manchester, 25 April 2004.

Therefore, in this context, a range of approaches have been adopted by mainstream parties. For example, these measures have included ostracising extreme right parties and refusing to see them as natural partners (as is the norm in Belgium and France), or stealing their policies to varying degrees. Policy emulation is dual-edged (see below): on the one hand, it may persuade voters to support a mainstream party rather than an extreme one. These voters can support their usual political party, believing it to have adopted certain policies and priorities to their satisfaction. In this respect, the 2007 French presidential campaign of the right-wing, mainstream (Gaullist) candidate Nicolas Sarkozy has been seen as a prominent example of successful appropriation of the rival FN ground. Sarkozy flagged up issues such as national identity, immigration and law and order in his campaign – all of which had tended to play well for the FN hitherto. The first ballot share of the vote in 2007 for the FN candidate, veteran leader Jean-Marie Le Pen, dropped from (admittedly an unusually high) 16.9 percent to 10.44 percent and was appreciably below his previous performances (15.3 percent in 1995 and 14.4 percent in 1988). Meanwhile, Sarkozy (at 31 percent) improved on the score of his predecessor (19.88 percent for Jacques Chirac in 2002).

On the other hand, however, policy emulation may enable extreme right parties to claim that their approach had been the correct one, and also that a greater measure of legitimacy and credibility is given to their agenda. Legitimacy is also provided when mainstream parties engage in coalition arrangements with extreme right parties. The latter organisations experience a dilution of their pariah status. They become more integrated into the political system. But, such developments and alliances entail a calculated risk for extreme right parties, who are more used to playing the role of critical outsider than that of a policy maker. There is evidence to suggest that an ascendant FPÖ, in the late twentieth/early twenty-first century, lost much ground within the electorate as it became a government partner. The FPÖ's share of the parliamentary vote dropped from 26 percent (1999) to 12 percent (2002) over a relatively short period of time. The party was subject to considerable divisions and schism and, as a result, its share of the vote plummeted subsequently. In short, it suffered from serious problems of role adjustment and internal management as it exchanged an outsider for an insider status. Likewise, the LPF's brief sojourn in office in 2002–2003 proved to be disastrous for the party, unaccustomed as it was to playing a parliamentary and governmental role. Political inexperience, leadership problems and divisions characterised the party, although undoubtedly a big factor in the rapid collapse of the LPF was the sudden loss of its assassinated leader.

Proscription or banning represents another tool that can and has been used by the political mainstream to contain extreme right parties. Notably, in 1952 in West Germany, the neo-Nazi Socialist Reich Party of Germany (*Sozialistische Reichspartei Deutschlands*, SRP) was proscribed as an anti-constitutional movement. In view of past history, Germany had adopted postwar legislation specifically to arrest the growth of anti-constitutional extremism. Those parties, not only on the Far Right, that were seen to be in contravention of the constitution were liable to proscription. Again, in 2004, the Flemish nationalist party, the Flemish Bloc, was banned for contravening anti-racist legislation and for depicting foreigners as criminals. Such provisions and decisions serve as a warning to extremist parties not to cross certain red lines and thresholds. However, the banning of parties has its problems as an effective mechanism for contending with extreme right rivals. For one thing, other like-minded parties may simply take the place of proscribed organisations. Indeed, in Belgium, the Flemish Bloc was succeeded promptly by **Flemish Interest**, albeit replete with a promise not to reproduce a discourse that might get it into trouble again. In Germany too, proscription of the SRP did not prevent the subsequent emergence of a myriad of extreme right parties and movements, including notably the DVU, the Republicans (*Republikaner*, REP) and the NPD. Also, proscription tends to give the extreme right an oxygen balloon of publicity and, to some extent, even ensures for it the status of victim. Again, proscription may be an unwieldy and heavy-handed process. It is noteworthy that the mechanism has been used sparsely in countries where it exists. Significantly too, in 2003, procedural complications led to the NPD surviving an attempted ban in Germany and then going on to win ground in regional elections thereafter.

Proscription represents simply one of several mechanisms available to the state and mainstream forces in order to constrain extremist parties. Other measures include such devices (e.g. in Germany, Greece and Sweden) as the stipulation of minimum electoral quotas that parties must achieve in order to gain seats in representative assemblies and also the imposition (and deterrent) of non-returnable election deposits (e.g. in the United Kingdom) for parties failing to reach a certain, specified vote ceiling. Again, in France, failure to secure the signatures of 500 elected *notables* can deprive a candidate from contesting a presidential election – as happened to Jean-Marie Le Pen in 1981.[13] In addition to these formal mechanisms and restrictive practices, there are other informal means available to counter the prevalence of extreme right parties and which sometimes come under the label of 'militant democracy' or 'defensive democracy'.[14] The notion here is that the building of initiatives and structures within civil society may well provide a more effective means, than state institutional provision and action, to counter the emergence and ideas of the extreme right. Thus, for example, anti-racist movements, socio-political demonstrations, solidarity networks, cultural initiatives, street politics, publications/newsletters and non-governmental organisations are all part of the picture here.

Extreme right parties in post-war and contemporary Western Europe have become familiar actors in politics and society, not least where they have polled well at elections and possibly entered government office as a result. By offering the electorate something different, something unlike and against the mainstream political parties, they have created a niche of sorts within their respective party systems. They have benefited from popular reaction against the established parties and consensus, and caused the latter bodies to reflect seriously on how to approach and contend with the challenge that the parties on the extreme right present. For the extreme right too, the acquisition of government status represents a momentous step. But it also brings with it problems of identity and character for parties more used to functioning as outsiders. In the future, parties and movements on the extreme, as well as mainstream wings of politics, will continue to weigh up the 'pros' and 'cons' of engaging with one another in such arrangements.

Paul Hainsworth

Notes

1. Paul Hainsworth, *The Extreme Right in Western Europe* (London: Routledge, 2008); Cas Mudde, *Populist Radical Right Parties in Europe* (Cambridge: Cambridge University Press, 2007).
2. M.H.Williams, *The Impact of Radical Right-Wing Parties in Western Europe* (London: Palgrave Macmillan, 2006), 37.
3. Piero Ignazi, *Extreme Right Parties in Western Europe* (New York: Oxford University Press, 2003).
4. Michael Gallagher, 'Exit from the ghetto: the Italian far right in the 1990s' in Paul Hainsworth (ed.), *The Politics of the Extreme Right: From the Margins to the Mainstream* (London: Pinter, 2000); M. Tarchi, 'The far right Italian style' in Xavier Casals (ed.), *Political Survival on the Extreme Right: European Movements between the Inherited Past and the Need to Adapt to the Future* (Barcelona: Institut de Ciences Politiques i Socials, 2005); Piero Ignazi, *Extreme Right Parties in Western Europe* (New York: Oxford University Press, 2003).
5. Paul Hainsworth, *The Extreme Right in Western Europe* (London: Routledge, 2008).
6. Herbert Kitschelt, *The Radical Right in Western Europe* (Ann Arbor, MI: University of Michigan Press, 1995), 22.
7. Paul Hainsworth, *The Extreme Right in Western Europe* (London: Routledge, 2008).
8. David S. Bell & Byron Criddle, 'Presidentialism restored: the French elections of April-May and June 2002', *Parliamentary Affairs*, 55 (2002), 643–663.
9. Martin Schain, Aristide Zolberg & Patrick Hossay (eds.), *Shadows over Europe: The Development and Impact of the Extreme Right in Western Europe* (New York: Palgrave Macmillan, 2002).

10. Tim Bale, 'Cinderella and her ugly sisters: the mainstream and extreme right in Europe's bipolarising party systems', *West European Politics*, 26:3 (July 2003), 67–90.

11. G. Curran, 'Mainstreaming populist discourse: the race-conscious legacy of neo-populist parties in Australia and Italy', *Patterns of Prejudice*, 38:1 (March 2004), 37–55.

12. Amir Abedi, *Anti-Political Establishment Parties* (London: Routledge, 2004).

13. Pippa Norris, *Radical Right: Voters and Parties in the Electoral Market* (Cambridge: Cambridge University Press, 2005).

14. Roger Eatwell, 'Introduction: The new extreme right challenge' in Roger Eatwell & Cas Mudde (eds.), *Western Democracies and the New Extreme Right Challenge* (London and New York: Routledge, 2004); Michael Minkenberg, 'Repression and reaction: militant democracy and the radical right in Germany and France', *Patterns of Prejudice* 40:1 (February 2006), 25–44; Cas Mudde, 'The populist zeitgeist', *Government and Opposition* 39:4 (Autumn 2004), 541–563; A. Pedazhur & A. Brichta, 'The institutionalization of extreme right-wing charismatic parties: a paradox?', *Party Politics* 8:1 (2002), 31–49.

The Far Right in Europe:
A-Z Articles

A

Against the Islamisation of our Culture - Dutch Identity as Fundamental Value by Pim Fortuyn (The Netherlands)

In 1997, the maverick Dutch right-winger Pim **Fortuyn** published *Against the Islamisation of our Culture - Dutch Identity as Fundamental Value*. It was the book that made his name and forged his reputation as a controversial public figure. Soon he had left his academic life behind and was embarking on a new career in politics. In 2001, he was elected onto the Livable Netherlands' party list and by 2002 he had set up his own party, **List Pim Fortuyn**. But nine days before the 2002 parliamentary elections he was assassinated.

The book became notorious because in it, Fortuyn articulated his view of Islam as a 'backward culture'. As he later said: 'In my book I demonstrate that **Islam** ... basically, when it concerns our norms and core values, is hostile towards modernity: i.e. hostile towards the culture of the free and economically developed West. The separation of church and state is not accepted by them. They only accept one state – a theocracy. Consequently those with a minority opinion in the general public domain would have to submit themselves to Islamic law'. And on the back of this kind of thinking, he began to cultivate a public and political life.

As an openly gay man, Fortuyn also confronted the issue of **homosexuality**. This was another issue on which he offered a critique of Islam. Writing in 2001, he said: 'In a so-called liberal Islamic country such as Egypt, fifty-two homosexuals have recently been imprisoned without any trial ... on the charge that they are members of a state-undermining group. These men were caught on a party ship that had already been sailing for years every weekend: as it happens, organising a comfortable meeting for homosexuals and giving them the opportunity to meet. In our country something like that would be unthinkable, in Egypt no-one cares'.

Fortuyn's thesis was condemned by those on the left, with a former Social Democrat minister labeling him 'an inferior human being'. But the former sociology professor was undaunted and was ready to defend himself. As he explained: 'Xenophobia is completely alien to me and Islam is a **religion** and culture which is not bound to any race. There are white Muslims, brown, yellow and black Muslims. Something of everyone, I would say. Moreover, the same could be said for Christians, Roman Catholics and Jews. It's got nothing to do with race. Rather, it's all about culture and religion'. One view is that Fortuyn's book was a landmark in the re-emergence of far-right ideas in the Netherlands; it helped to popularise certain ideas and encourage the author to move into organised politics.

See also Fortuyn, Pim (The Netherlands); List Pim Fortuyn (The Netherlands) *and* Pim Fortuyn, Assassination of (2002).

Further Reading

Fortuyn, Pim. 1990. *Ordening Door Ontvlechting: Een Advies Over de Adviesstructuur in de Volksgezondheid*. Rijswijk/Den Haag, DOP: Ministerie van Welzijn, Volksgezondheid en Cultuur.
Mudde, Cas. 2000. *The Ideology of the Extreme Right*. Manchester: Manchester University Press.
Sniderman, P.M. & Hagendoorn, L. 2007. *When Ways of Life Collide: Multiculturalism and Its Discontents in the Netherlands*. Princeton, NJ: Princeton University Press.

Mudde, Cas & Holsteyn, Joop Van. 2000. 'The Netherlands: explaining the limited success of the extreme right'. In *The Politics of the Extreme Right: From the Margins to the Mainstream*. Edited by Paul Hainsworth. London: Pinter.

Husbands, Christopher T. 1994. 'The Netherlands: irritants on the body politic'. In *The Extreme Right in Europe and the USA*. Edited by Paul Hainsworth. London: Pinter.

Algeria

Between 1830 and 1962 Algeria was a French colony. The fact that the two territories were separated only by the Mediterranean Sea meant that the colonial relationship was a particularly close and emotive one. After a bloody, eight-year civil war, Algeria gained independence in 1962, and relations between the two countries were set to enter a new phase. This was characterised by powerful tensions and recriminations, which were exploited by the French Far Right. One example of this was the Far Right presenting itself as the true defenders of France's right to possess an empire by maintaining vehemently that the, then, French president, Charles de Gaulle, should not have allowed Algeria to become an independent state. The **Algerian War** even spawned far-right, terrorist groups in France. For example, in 1961 the extremist Organisation of the Secret Army (*Organisation de l'armée secrète*, OAS) was formed in response to de Gaulle's policy of Algerian independence. The OAS not only staged an unsuccessful revolt in Algiers, but also waged a terror campaign in mainland France.

After Algerian independence, the far-right figure Jean-Louis Tixier-Vignancour, who had previously represented OAS defendants, ran for president in 1965 – again bolstering right-wing interest in the Algeria issue. Further, this presidential campaign was managed by Jean-Marie **Le Pen**, the future leader of the **National Front** (*Front National*, FN). In the decades that followed, and right up until today, the question of Algeria has remained a bone of contention among the French Far Right. Indeed, Le Pen, who himself fought in the **Algerian War**, still maintains that many of France's modern-day problems stem from the fact that the imperial relationship between Paris and Algiers was terminated. In particular, he is horrified by the scale of Algerian **immigration** into France, and, more generally, he articulates concerns over North African migration. It is little wonder, then, that the biggest, most prolonged cheers at FN rallies always seem to accompany references to *Algérie française* (the notion of an Algeria connected to 'Mother France' through the presence of Algerian Deputies in the French National Assembly, and for Algeria to be subject to French national law). Unsurprisingly, when responding to the riots of late 2005 in Paris and other French cities, Le Pen blamed this unrest on unregulated, third-world immigration. This concern with Algerian immigration, however, sits uncomfortably with his criticism of the end of direct French links with Algeria. Further, in the 2007 presidential elections, Le Pen made play of unrest in Algeria to assert that France's security was undermined by its links with Algerian extremists.

See also Algerian War (1954–1962); Le Pen, Jean-Marie (France) *and* Western Europe and the Far Right.

Further Reading
Davies, Peter. 1999. *The National Front in France: Ideology, Discourse and Power*. New York: Routledge.

Horne, Alistair. 1977. *A Savage War of Peace: Algeria 1954–1962*. London: Macmillan.

Algerian War (1954–1962)

Between 1954 and 1962, France fought a sapping and ultimately unsuccessful war against **Algeria**, one of her most prized colonial possessions. Thousands of soldiers and civilians died in a war that became notorious for the mass torture and systematic murder exerted by the French forces. Both then and now, the French Far Right has used the war as a key reference point. While the war was being prosecuted in the late-1950s and early-1960s, far-right politicians in mainland France often voiced their support for the conflict, essentially arguing that maintaining France's status in Algeria was fundamental to protecting France's empire and, thus, her international prestige. The Poujadist and Young Nation (*Jeune Nation*) movements, for example, were hard-line in their support for *Algérie française*. Even the army was highly politicised in this regard. In 1960, after the 'betrayal' of new French president Charles de Gaulle, army units in Algiers were responsible for an insurrection that came to be known as Barricades Week. A year later, four French generals including Raoul Salan were involved in the Algiers Putsch – a failed attempt to destabilise and overthrow the de Gaulle-led government in Paris. Soon after the putsch, Salan and other disenchanted army officers founded the Organisation of the Secret Army (*Organisation de l'armée secrète*, OAS), a clandestine and short-lived movement that used terrorist methods to block Algerian independence.

In the decades following the war, and the subsequent independence of Algeria, support and nostalgia for the ideals of *Algérie française* has almost become a badge of honour for the Far Right. The **National Front** (*Front National*, FN), which has been a significant player on the French political stage since the early 1980s, contains many *Algérie française* veterans within its ranks. Further, special reverence is reserved for party activists who, almost half a century on, still refer to the notion of *Algérie française* in their speeches and political literature. In fact, at FN rallies and demonstrations the biggest cheers are heard when activists utter the seemingly magic words: '*Vive l'Algérie française!*' The FN's leader, Jean-Marie **Le Pen**, is himself a veteran of the Algerian War – a fact that he takes great pleasure in mentioning at every opportunity, as if to amplify his nationalist credentials.

However, the Algerian issue also raises a key problem for the FN's discourse on race. On one hand, the party wishes to glorify the movement that sought to keep Algeria 'French', yet on the other hand it displays a deep-seated hostility towards the community of Algerian immigrants now living and working in France. This grey area between accepting the idea of an Algeria intimately tied to the French national political structure, and the presence of Algerian immigrants in French cities, highlights the confusion between myth and the reality within the political imagination of the French Far Right. However hard it has tried, the FN has never been able to square this circle in its political rhetoric.

See also Algeria; Le Pen, Jean-Marie (France) *and* Western Europe and the Far Right.

Further Reading
Davies, Peter. 1999. *The National Front in France: Ideology, Discourse and Power*. New York: Routledge.
Horne, Alistair. 1977. *A Savage War of Peace: Algeria 1954–1962*. London: Macmillan.

Alliance for Austria's Future, Founding by Haider (2005)

After breaking away from the **Austrian Freedom Party** (*Freiheitliche Partei Österreichs*, FPÖ), Jörg **Haider** officially founded the Alliance for Austria's Future (*Bündnis Zukunft Österreich*, BZÖ) on 3 April 2005. He did so in association with his sister, Ursula Haubner, and other former members of the FPÖ. They styled themselves as the 'moderate' wing of the FPÖ and, in a radical departure from typical attitudes regarding a new party, the BZÖ had a presence in government from the first day of its existence. Having elected Haider as its leader, the BZÖ remained in office alongside the conservative majority.

Many news outlets responded to the news that, following a split within the FPÖ, Haider had formed a new party. Media speculation attributed the split to the decreasing levels of support for the FPÖ following its rise to notoriety in the 1999 elections. The BBC reported on opinion poll ratings for the FPÖ, which gave the rump party a mere 3 percent support, whereas the BZÖ scored 5 percent. It also reported that 9 FPÖ party members had defected to the new party, with seven of the remaining nine members choosing to stick with the FPÖ, while two remained undecided. Meanwhile, *The Economist* reported on how the new party had adopted the colour orange in order to echo the recent 'Orange Revolution' in the Ukraine and that Haider was ditching his previous praise for Nazism for a macho, charismatic style that he believed was 'young, handsome and cool'.

In a speech that launched the new party, Haider wove pro-European and anti-globalisation themes into his characterisation of the BZÖ. In the 2006 legislative elections, the FPÖ increased its share of the vote from 10 percent to 11 percent, while the BZÖ claimed seven seats after just scraping past the 4 percent electoral barrier.

See also Austrian Freedom Party; Central Europe and the Far Right *and* Haider, Jörg (Austria).

Further Reading

The Economist, 'Jörg Haider's new Alliance for Austria's future', http://www.economist.com/world/europe/displaystory.cfm?story_id=E1_PRJPSTV (cited 31 December 2007).
Müller, Wolfgang C. Forthcoming. 'The surprising election in Austria, October 2006', *Electoral Studies*.

Anti-Semitism

At its most basic, anti-Semitism can be defined as hatred of Jews and Jewishness. It is a prejudice as old as the Jewish community itself – hence the title of Robert Wistrich's book on the subject: *The Longest Hatred*. However, when discussing this issue, it is important to recognise that there is a distinction to be drawn between the older prejudice of anti-Judaism, which has been around for many centuries, and the more modern phenomenon of anti-Semitism. The former prejudice is founded on religious principles, and at least offers a pathway to redemption, namely conversion to Christianity. Modern anti-Semitism, on the other hand, is based on specious theories of racial hierarchy and regards the Jews as an inferior racial stock. Inferiority, then, is literally in the Jewish blood according to modern anti-Semites.

The writings of many nineteenth-century theorists saw the development of modern anti-Semitic ideology. In France, Arthur de Gobineau's *The Inequality of Human Races* was one such text, while in Germany Houston Stewart Chamberlain's *The Foundations of the Nineteenth Century* became another highly-influential tract in this literature. Meanwhile, the issue was crystallised by the Dreyfus Affair of the 1890s. Indeed, the latter helped to create the link between the nationalist right and anti-Semitism. By the 1930s, Jews were used as a scapegoat figure by all kinds of far-right groups – who presented them variously as: plutocratic capitalists, parasites on the nation's wealth, decadent, diseased immigrants, and revolutionaries, to name but a few of the negative stereotypes. In Germany, notoriously the Nazi regime turned biological anti-Semitism into state policy, leading to the extermination of an estimated six million Jews during the **Holocaust**. Like many anti-Semites before him, Hitler blamed the Jews for all the various failings of society, and targeted them in uncompromising terms.

Given the anti-Semitic heritage associate with far-right politics from the first half of the twentieth century, it was predictable that most post-war groupings within the Far Right would seek to replicate this hostility towards the Jews. Indeed, this prejudice has been a natural and instinctive attitude for many post-war parties of the Far Right. Meanwhile, after 1945 new social issues have emerged, changing the way the Far Right has viewed the issue of race. Most importantly, additional targets for the Far Right to represent as the 'other' have developed. Although the Far Right has always regarded non-whites as inferior, the post-war trend of mass migration from Asia, Africa and the Caribbean to **Europe** was a significant change within European society. These new waves of migration have seen Jewish stereotypes increasingly superseded as the main target of far-right scapegoating, and so the rhetoric of prejudice has moved on. Nevertheless, it would also be accurate to say that anti-Jewish and anti-Semitic impulses and attitudes are omnipresent within the Far Right. They will never disappear.

The language used by far-right leaders and groups regarding Jews has been significant. It is difficult to generalise across a number of countries, but there are some key themes and patterns. The word 'Aryan' has remained a key part of extreme-right vocabulary. In the era of interwar Fascism, Hitler used the term to refer to Caucasians, thereby excluding the Jews from the Nazis' 'pure' race. Particularly in the early post-war period, when the European Far Right was unreconstructed, the word was also used regularly and basically meant white, and it is still used by some far-right groups that exist on the fringes of legality. But on the whole, the parties that have gained a good measure of electoral success – like the **National Front** (*Front National*, FN) in France and the **Austrian Freedom Party** (*Freiheitliche Partei Österreichs*, FPÖ) – would rarely, if ever, use such a loaded term now. They have realised that such anti-Semitic language is now dated; their cultural sensitivities to racism have become more refined. So, in order to make themselves appear electable, the populist Far Right now realises that it has to drop such language because of the negative image it projects.

That said, even 'modern' parties like the FN and the FPÖ have not been averse to alluding to the Jewish issue. For example, both **Le Pen** and **Haider** have questioned the scale of the Holocaust. Le Pen has also engaged in his own brand of wordplay – using terms like 'oven' and 'genocide' in a way that he claims is innocuous, but which, in reality, demonstrates his near-obsession with the Holocaust and the Jews. Not surprisingly, Le Pen has lost friends and colleagues as a result of such tasteless rhetoric. Elsewhere, Nick **Griffin** of the **British National Party** (BNP) has referred to the Holocaust as the 'Holohoax', and allegedly criticises the convicted Holocaust denier David Irving for his partial admission to the deaths of Jews at the hands of the Nazis. Such examples of Holocaust denial should be regarded as further examples of modern, far-right anti-Semitism. Another example is Roland Raes of the **Flemish Bloc** (*Vlaams Blok*, VB). In 2002, he gave a TV interview in which he questioned how many Jews were killed by the Nazis, and how many gas chambers were used in the Holocaust. In the end, he was forced to resign from his high-level role within the party.

Looking eastward, Vladimir **Zhirinovsky**, the leader of the Russian Liberal Democratic Party (*Liberal'no-Demokraticheskaya Partiya Rossii*, LDPR), has also singled out the Jews. He has wildly accused them of: holding all the power in modern-day **Russia**; treating **women** and children badly; and even of causing the Holocaust themselves. Zhirinovsky has also argued that Jewish people have attempted to destroy Russia by claiming that, although in other parts of the world Jews may be pleasant people, in Russia they are cruel and aggressive, and detest Russian values. It is also worth noting that he has demonstrated his admiration for American politician Pat Buchanan, who once characterised the US Congress as 'Israeli-occupied territory'. Referring to this suggestion, Zhirinovsky said that, like the US, Russia was also under Jewish 'occupation', and added that both the US and Russia needed to create special zones on their territories to house what he dubbed a 'small but troublesome tribe'. Another layer of confusion regarding Zhirinovsky's anti-Semitism emerged in 2001, when he admitted in a book that he too was of Jewish blood. Despite characterising his father, Volf Isaakovich Eidelshtein, as a 'Polish Jew', he again asserted his love of Russia over his Jewish roots, asking: 'Why should I reject Russian blood, Russian culture, Russian land, and fall in love with the Jewish people only because of that single drop of blood that my father left in my mother's body?' These comments were viewed as particularly hypocritical given that he has snubbed Holocaust commemoration events in the past, and has also encouraged many Jews to emigrate from Russia through his anti-Semitic comments.

Despite its propensity towards anti-Semitic views, it is difficult to make too many sweeping generalisations across the far-right spectrum regarding this issue. At one extreme, the Romanian far-right politician Corneliu Vadim **Tudor** has deployed an anti-Semitic political message, as have other, far-right politicians in the country. Meanwhile, at the other extreme, Filip Dewinter has offered to protect Belgian Jews from the influx and alleged dangers of Muslim **immigration**. Anti-Semitism, then, remains a key issue within far-right politics. However, in an era of increased racial complexity, the relatively simple discourse of anti-Semitism of the interwar era has been replaced by a more multifaceted set of prejudices and racist viewpoints.

See also The Holocaust; The Ideology of the Far Right *and Mein Kampf* by Adolf Hitler (Germany).

Further Reading
Lacquer, Walter. 1996. *Fascism: Past, Present and Future*. New York: Oxford University Press.
Lee, Martin A. 1998. *The Beast Reawakens*. London: Warner Books.
Wistrich, Robert Solomon. 1991. *Anti-Semitism: The Longest Hatred*. London: Thames Methuen.

Antwerp (Belgium)

Part of the Flemish-speaking area of Belgium, Antwerp is both a province and a city port. In recent years, Antwerp has also gained notoriety as the capital of far-right politics in Belgium. In a recent example of this far-right dominance of the city, in the municipal elections of 1999 the **Flemish Bloc** (*Vlaams Blok,* VB) claimed 33 percent of the vote. Indeed, if it were not for the impressive anti-fascist unity and solidarity of the other parties, one of the movement's leading lights, Filip Dewinter, would have been elected Antwerp's mayor. This would have left Flanders – the northern half of Belgium, which incorporates Antwerp – even more vulnerable to VB's autonomist message. More recently, in the regional elections of 2004, VB took a 24 percent share of the vote in Flanders; while in the 2006 municipal election, the reformed version of VB, **Flemish Interest** (*Vlaams Belang*, VB), increased its share of the vote in Antwerp, gaining 33.5 percent of the vote. However, it is also worth noting that the Socialists gained 35.5 percent in these polls, and so ultimately the 2006 election was a setback for the VB in its Antwerp homeland.

Meanwhile, in May 2006, Antwerp was also the scene of a double murder, a story that soon encapsulated VB. The fact that the perpetrator of the crime, Hans Van Themsche, had **family** links to VB (he was the son of one of its founders, and the nephew of one of its MPs), and that one of the victims was African, the other Turkish, merely added to the city's far-right notoriety. Significantly, a silent protest march was staged in Antwerp soon after this controversy. This demonstration highlighted the fact that the majority of local people did not want to be associated with the crime or with far-right politics in general.

Interestingly, Antwerp is also home to 15,000 Jews. One might have assumed that this fact would encourage VB in its racist discourse, but actually the party has worked hard to attract Jewish voters. This strategy has borne some fruit, mainly because there is a tense relationship between the city's Muslim and Jewish communities, and so Jews have seen in a vote for VB a means of demonstrating their hostility to North African and Arab **immigration**.

Not many Belgian cities have been the focus of special *Time Magazine* features in recent years, but in 2005, Antwerp reversed this trend. Under the heading 'Life on the Front Lines', Vivienne Walt reported on the growing social tensions in Antwerp, alongside the role of Dewinter in this trend. Her article highlighted how Dewinter had worked hard to prevent the creation of the first official mosque in Antwerp North. Indeed, a few minarets and a boarded up shell are all that currently exists of this site following Dewinter's 'stop-the-mosque' campaign, which was founded on alleged fire regulation irregularities. Both non-Muslim residents and anti-immigration lawyers fought against this development, symbolic both of the attempts by the Muslim community to develop its presence in Antwerp, and the way this subject has acted as a flashpoint issue. Far-right, anti-immigration politics, then, have been able to make much play of the negative emotions that Muslim immigration and architecture can generate. In particular, Walt's article also demonstrated Dewinter's belief that such buildings undermined a sense of Christian identity: 'It's just a few doors from the church,' he lamented. Dewinter also decried the way Antwerp North has become a significant site for immigration, with locals moving away from the area and into the city's suburbs. The new multicultural milieu that has emerged, comprised of ethnic food stores and the like, leaves him cold. Walt's report stresses the fact that, when walking through Antwerp, Dewinter is clearly a recognisable figure. Unsurprisingly, then, Dewinter is an unpopular personality among the city's new population, as both Muslim and African immigrants shout 'Racist!' as he tours the area. Meanwhile, one VB supporter shouts out from her window: 'You're doing great things, Dewinter. Keep it up!'

See also Flemish Bloc, Disbandment (2004) *and* Flemish Bloc/Flemish Interest.

Further Reading
Erik, Jan. 2005. 'From Vlaams Blok to Vlaams Belang: the Belgian far-right renames itself'. *West European Politics* 28.3.
Ignazi, Piero. 2003. *Extreme Right Parties in Western Europe*. New York: Oxford University Press.
Walt, Vivienne. 2005. 'Life on the Front lines', Time, http://www.time.com/time/magazine/article/0,9171,1029799,00.html (cited 31 December 2007).

Aspects of France Journal (France)

Aspects de la France is the journal of the Action Française – a far-right and monarchist movement in France. The AF's heyday was in the early twentieth century and inter-war period when it became an influential voice on the Far Right. It wasn't a political party in a traditional sense; rather, it saw itself as an elitist and intellectual talking shop that was above the cut and thrust of normal party politics. Its leader, Charles Maurras, was branded a Fascist – an accusation that seemed to gain ground after 1940 when Marshal Pétain, leader of the pro-Nazi French government at Vichy, announced that Maurras was his ideological inspiration. *Aspects de la France* was launched in 1947 after the Liberation authorities had banned the AF's erstwhile journal, *Action Française*, in 1944. It was launched by Georges Calzant and Maurice Pujo as a weekly paper and was initially known as *Aspects de la France et du Monde*. After the death of Maurras in 1952, *Aspects de la France* fought it out with the movement's other paper, Pierre Boutang's *La Nation Française*, for influence until the latter ceased publication in 1967. *Aspects de la France* still exists today and continues to advocate the reestablishment of the French monarchy – even though there is little possibility of this occurring.

See also Western Europe and the Far Right.

Further Reading
Shields, J. 2007. *The Extreme Right in France: From Pétain to Le Pen*. London and New York: Routledge.
Davies, Peter. 2002. *The Extreme Right in France, 1789 to the Present: From De Maistre to Le Pen*. London and New York: Routledge.
Hainsworth, Paul. 1992. 'The extreme right in post-war France: the emergence and success of the Front National'. In *The Extreme Right in Europe and the USA*. Edited by Paul Hainsworth. London: Pinter.

Attack Coalition (Bulgaria)

The Attack Coalition (*Ataka*) is a nationalist movement in Bulgaria formed out of three organisations: the National Movement for the Salvation of the Fatherland, the Bulgarian National Patriotic Party and the Union of Patriotic Forces and Militaries of the Reserve Defence. It is led by TV personality Volen Siderov and has included many key military people in its ranks.

In terms of ideology and its '20 Principles', Attack blends nationalism and **anti-Semitism** with suspicion of other political parties in Bulgaria, NATO and the US. Its nationalism is hard-line and can be summed up in the phrase: 'Neither left, nor right, but Bulgarian'. Because of its broad appeal, Attack has taken a significant portion of support away from the Bulgarian Socialist Party. But, at the same time, all political parties in the country have stated unambiguously that they will never make an electoral pact with *Ataka* because of its xenophobic platform.

The movement does not believe in any kind of diversity; hence its attacks on ethnic minorities, including gypsies, and its championing of the Bulgarian Orthodox Church as a national institution. It would also like to introduce a new crime of 'national betrayal' so as to bring to account all those individuals – mainly politicians – who, in its opinion, have let the country down, whether in word or deed. This, in fact, is part of Siderov's appeal. He is willing to stand up and be counted and talk about things that other politicians would rather ignore.

A major theme in Attack discourse is hostility to Turkey. Within Attack ranks there is a perception that Bulgaria – formerly under the rule of the Ottoman Empire – is still dominated by the Turks. As Siderov has argued: 'Bulgaria is not yet free. Bulgaria is still under Turkish rule'. Consequently, the party has engaged in the ritual burning of fezzes (these felt hats are seen as a symbol of Turkishness). It also attaches great importance to 3 March every year. This date marks the liberation of Bulgaria from Ottoman rule, and so today, Attack uses this anniversary for the purpose of anti-Turk propaganda. It has organised demonstrations and rallies, but these have proved extremely controversial – with the party forced to ask for official permission each time it wishes to stage an event.

In the 2005 legislative elections, Attack claimed a 9 percent share of the vote, which gave it 21 out of 240 seats. And by 2006 – if opinion polls are to be believed – it had become the second force in Bulgarian politics after the Bulgarian Socialist Party. In the same year, Siderov finished second in the first round of polling in presidential elections.

The party also has one deputy in the European Parliament, who joined up with the Identity Tradition and Sovereignty group. *Ataka* representative Dimitar **Stoyanov** said: 'When I first went to the European Parliament as an observer, I was greeted very warmly by the other nationalist parties. They weren't especially against Romania and Bulgaria, they were against what enlargement would bring. That's why we decided to shake hands and cooperate'.

See also South-Eastern Europe and the Far Right *and* Stoyanov, Dimitar (Bulgaria).

Further Reading
http://www.ataka.bg (party website).
http://www.europarl.europa.eu (European Parliament).
Ganev, V.I. 2007. *Preying on the State: The Transformation of Bulgaria After 1989.* Ithaca, New York: Cornell University Press.
Giatzidis, E. 2002. *An Introduction to Postcommunist Bulgaria: Political, Economic and Social Transformation.* Manchester: Manchester University Press.
Crampton, R.J. 2005. *A Concise History of Bulgaria.* Cambridge Concise Histories.

Auschwitz-Birkenau (Poland)

Located near Krakow in Poland, Auschwitz-Birkenau was one of the largest of the Nazi concentration camps. Indeed, it lays claim to the grizzly notoriety of being the site of the largest-known mass-murder in history. Nazis killed an estimated 1,100,000 people at the camp complex following its creation in May 1940. Since the end of World War II,

Auschwitz-Birkenau

Auschwitz-Birkenau has become symbolic of the Nazi's wartime atrocities, leading Donald Bloxham to dub the term 'Auschwitz' the synecdoche of the **Holocaust**. This representative value is also reflected in the official memory of the genocide, for example Holocaust Memorial Day falls on the 27 January, the date of the camp's liberation. Further, the site has subsequently been turned into a museum, leading to much debate over the most appropriate ways to memorialise the horrific events that occurred at Auschwitz-Birkenau.

Unsurprisingly, then, Auschwitz has also become the focal point for some of the most prominent Holocaust deniers. This trend in revisionism began in earnest with the pro-Vichy essayist Maurice Bardeche's *Nuremburg ou la Terre promise*, which was published in 1947 and heavily critiqued the Nuremburg Trials. Subsequently, Paul Rassinier became another founding father of later trends in revisionism regarding the Holocaust. Often, this literature presents itself as a scientific attempt to get to the 'truth' of history, and so is dismissive of what it alleges are the emotive, pro-Jewish readings of events that had dominated the historical literature on the topic. Such sophistry was epitomised in 1973 when Thies Christophersen published a memoir called *Die Auschwitz-Lüge*, translated as *The Auschwitz Lie*. The book was soon banned in Germany, but subsequently, as the German-language version found outlets in other countries, this publication has become an inspiration for other revisionist writings. Christophersen has said of his writings on this subject: 'When I wrote my report, I was criticised on the grounds that, although I was in the camp and saw nothing of mass gassings, that fact did not necessarily mean that there were none [...] I have received thousands of letters and calls. Many of those who contacted me can confirm my statements, but are afraid to do so publicly. Some of those are SS men who were brutally mistreated and even tortured in Allied captivity.' He also argues that his book offered nothing that was in itself remarkable, and was merely 'written by someone who was in Auschwitz and who recorded his experiences and recollections'. Typically, he argued that, unlike much of the literature on the topic, his book was not a sensationalist report of Nazi atrocities. He even claimed that '[i]n the spirit of Martin Luther, I try to speak positively and influence things for the best. But I was accused of "popular incitement" [*Volksverhetzung*] for doing that.'

Over the years, many far-right ideologues have added to the Holocaust denial literature. The key themes here are attempts to find excuses for the existence of camps, and then to deny the worst aspects of their nature. Typical is David Irving, whose work has argued that Auschwitz was nothing more than a 'labour camp'. Similarly, in 1995 during a parliamentary debate, Jörg **Haider** talked of the 'punishment camps' of National Socialism. This line of reasoning implies that the victims of the Holocaust were in fact guilty of crimes, rather than innocent civilians. Haider later apologised for such rhetoric, demonstrating that the Far Right's legacy often remains intimately entangled with the events of World War II. Indeed, taking and retaking positions on the Holocaust issue allows far-right politicians to create and develop either more moderate or more radical political poses. Other far-right leaders have also taken controversial positions on the Holocaust. In Britain, for example, Nick **Griffin** has talked of the 'Holohoax', and has allegedly even criticised David Irving for admitting that several million Jews may have died at the hands of the Nazis.

Auschwitz, and the topic that it symbolises, then, is a key aspect of contemporary far-right politics. Far-right leaders continue to debate and discuss this issue in public, both in order to express their own beliefs and to present a particular public profile.

See also Anti-Semitism; The Holocaust *and Mein Kampf* by Adolf Hitler (Germany).

Further Reading
Evans, Richard J. 2002. *Telling Lies about Hitler: The Holocaust, History and the David Irving Trial.* London and New York: Verso.
Lipstadt, Deborah E. 1993. *Denying the Holocaust: The Growing Assault on Truth and Memory.* New York: Free Press.
Shermer, Michael. 2000. *Denying History: Who Says the Holocaust Never Happened and Why Do They Say It?* Los Angeles: University of California Press.

Austrian Freedom Party

The Austrian Freedom Party (*Freiheitliche Partei Österreichs*, FPÖ) was founded in 1956 as a liberal and nationalist movement. In its early days it was an unusual coalition of businessmen, anti-clericals and former Nazis, and helped to make and break various governing coalitions. The party's liberal faction, led by Norbert Steger, came to dominate in 1980, but the nationalist wing, under the leadership of Jörg **Haider**, reasserted itself in 1986 to take charge.

This led to a significant change in the party's electoral fortunes. Between 1956 and 1986 the party failed to score more than 10 percent in any national election, averaging between 4 and 7 percent. However, in 1986, it claimed a 9.7 percent share of the vote and thereafter broke through the 15 percent barrier, scoring 16.6 percent in 1990, and then 22.5 percent in 1994, 22 percent in 1995 and 26.9 percent in 1999. By 2000, the FPÖ, a sworn enemy of multiculturalism, had a place in government.

The emergence of the party in the corridors of power caused consternation and anger across the world. The EU imposed sanctions on Austria and many countries expressed their distaste at developments. The reason for the overwhelmingly hostile reaction was the ideology and programme of the FPÖ. On one level, it still believed in free enterprise and privatisation, but on another, it had metamorphosed into a party that was hard-line on **immigration** (wishing to restrict the Austrian citizenship law and halt the misuse of the asylum system) and the EU (insisting that EU policy should not impinge on Vienna, and that Austria's financial contribution to the EU should not be increased, as well as arguing against the accession of Turkey).

By 1990, the party had 40,000 members, most fairly young and well educated. The rise of the party provoked an anti-Haider movement and the appearance of various 'Austria Watch' websites. Here the argument was that Haider had neo-Nazi tendencies and that some of his comments implied that he had some sympathy, or even admiration, for the Hitler regime. Haider responded with the following statement: 'In the past, some remarks have been attributed to me in connection with Nazism which were certainly insensitive or open to misunderstanding. I am personally sorry for this, firstly because I believe I hurt the feelings of people who were themselves victims of Nazism or whose relatives were, and secondly because the statements were not in line with the personal values of tolerance and humanity which are the basis of my political work ... Where we in the Freedom Party have responsibility, no-one needs to pack their suitcases and no-one has to leave their home. Where we in the Freedom Party have responsibility, **freedom** and **democracy** are in good hands'.

Critics have made fun of the party's name, claiming that the FPÖ policy platform is diametrically opposed to the concept of 'freedom', especially its hostility to

5. Austrian far-right politician and Carinthia governor Jörg Haider, speaking at the Freedom Party (FPÖ) congress, 9 June 2002, Wiener Neustadt, Austria.

multiculturalism. But while he was at the helm of the party, Haider was undaunted. In 1995 he wrote: 'Our movement seeks to rally the friends of freedom to regenerate the old democracies and inspire the new. Our enemies are legion both in eastern **Europe** and the west ... The road will not be easy, but the rewards will be worth the struggle. That is the challenge for Austria. That is the vision for Europe. That is the freedom I mean'.

The FPÖ has been riven by internal disputes. There was always a fundamental tension between liberals and nationalists, but there have also been personality clashes and odd-looking tactical manoeuvres. In 2000, for example, Susanne Riess-Passer succeeded Haider as party leader; a ploy, it seemed, to take the pressure off the latter without changing the policy of the party. And in April 2005, after a series of arguments, Haider and a group of other members left the party to form a new organisation, the Alliance for the Future of Austria (BZÖ). The electoral effect of all this manoeuvring was not positive. In 2002, the FPÖ took only a 10 percent share of the vote and in 2006, 11 percent. There remained a significant overlap between BZÖ and FPÖ policy platforms and for a short period it was actually possible for individuals to belong to both movements.

Haider's exit and the internal bickering that prompted it should not take away from the significance of the Freedom Party as a model of far-rightism in action, and a case study in how far a populist-nationalist movement can progress. Quoting Paxton, it would seem that Haider's special ability was to aim 'winks of approval at Nazi veterans', while also breaking the 'immovable political monopoly [of the socialists and People's Party]'. But, according to Morrow, the problem for Austria was that, in its heyday, the FPÖ's commitment to liberal **democracy** was ambiguous at best.

See also Alliance for Austria's Future, Foundation by Haider (2005); Central Europe and the Far Right *and* Haider, Jörg (Austria).

Further Reading

http://www.bzoe.at (Alliance for the Future of Austria website).

http://www.fpoe.at (Freedom Party website).

Höbelt, L. 2003. *Defiant Populist: Jörg Haider and the Politics of Austria 1986–2000*. West Lafayette: Purdue University Press.

Morrow, D. 2000. 'Jörg Haider and the new FPÖ: beyond the democratic pale'. In *The Politics of the Extreme Right: From the Margins to the Mainstream*. Edited by Paul Hainsworth. London: Pinter.

B

The Berlin Wall (Germany)

The fall of the Berlin Wall in 1989, an event that symbolises the end of Communism in central and eastern Europe, had profound repercussions for European politics. In particular, it not only saw the end of the Far Right's ideological nemesis, it also resulted in a host of new countries transferring to democratic political systems. Invariably, this transition to **democracy** has created a number of new electorates. To greater and lesser extents, many of these new voters have shown interest in far-right politics.

Turning firstly to Germany, here we see that the Federal Republic of Germany (*Bundesrepublik Deutschland*, FRG) was experiencing a growth in far-right activity and political significance in the years preceding the fall of the Berlin Wall. The issue of re-unification was central to these groups; for example the key objective of the Republicans (*Die Republikaner*, REP) was the reformation of Germany 'as a whole'. However, the immediate effect of the fall of the Berlin Wall was to marginalise the Far Right, as its central goal of German re-unification had been met. Indeed, in the 1990 elections, the Far Right performed very badly. In the longer term, however, the effects of German reunification were arguably more beneficial to far-right concerns. For example, Germany experienced an increase in numbers of German re-settlers and asylum seekers. Meanwhile, the tensions created by this new wave of migrants from Eastern **Europe** was augmented by the sense of economic disparity between the former East and West Germany. Finally, a number of political scandals, alongside a more general impression that the re-unification of the country was handled badly, led to a growing mood of alienation from the political process among some German voters. This was particularly significant in the former East Germany, and the country's far-right parties were keen to target this new, disaffected electorate. Among the region's urban working classes, xenophobia and distrust in political systems is noticeably higher, and so far-right parties, especially the German People's Union (*Deutsche Volksunion*, DVU), have capitalised on these resentments.

The fall of the Berlin Wall also had a strange effect on the left-wing and communist parties that survived 1989. Essentially, these movements found themselves in a political vacuum, a kind of ideological limbo, and suddenly faced a tactical dilemma. Should the Far Left regurgitate the increasingly-dated Marxist ideology and become more and more irrelevant to the electorate? Or should the Far Left re-invent itself by adopting a new doctrine and creed? The second option was always going to be the more appealing, and so, for many ex-communist parties and activists, the solution to this problem was to accommodate and integrate nationalist and far-right ideas into their own discourse. For example, the leader of the far-right **Greater Romania Party** (*Partidul România Mare*, PRM), Corneliu Vadim **Tudor,** often praised Ceausescu's dictatorship before the fall of **Communism**, and has even been described as a 'court poet' of the regime.

We can turn to the break-up of Yugoslavia for the most succinct example of the old Far Left embracing the politics of the Far Right and ultra-nationalism. Here, political leaders like Franjo **Tuđman** in Croatia and Slobodan **Milošević** in Serbia moved their discourse dramatically to the right in an attempt to 'surf the waves' of political change in the Balkans. Both leaders were able to synthesise their pasts as leading members of the Communist Party of Yugoslavia (*Savez komunista Jugoslavije*) with their new roles as defenders of Croatian and Serbian interests. Their politics drew on the Tito-style authoritarian Communism, and reignited sympathies for this style of governance in the hearts of many of their fellow nationals with new and highly emotive readings of their nation's histories. Sometimes this nationalism has veered into Holocaust revisionism as a strategy to create a more positive national story. Furthermore, the national Communism that emerged from Tuđman and Milošević's politics ultimately led to many scenes that were reminiscent of World War II. Not only were memories of the Ustaše and Chetnik militants revived, but new programmatic campaigns of ethnic cleansing were committed in the wars of the 1990s. These shocked and shamed the rest of the world in equal measure as Yugoslavia dissolved into its constituent national parts over the course of the decade.

Another trend following the fall of the Berlin Wall was fear that the rise of the Far Right in former communist countries might result in a new, fascist-style regime. The success of Vladimir **Zhirinovsky**'s Russian Liberal Democratic Party (*Liberal'no-Demokraticheskaya Partiya Rossii*, LDPR) sparked such concern among some commentators in 1993, though these fears have since proved unfounded. The extreme nationalist sentiments unleashed by the end of Communism in Europe, then, were diverse. In Germany, the fall of the Berlin Wall took away a central aspect of the Far-Right's goals. Elsewhere, the Far Right emerged in countries that had not previously experienced democratic politics. Meanwhile, the descent into aggressive nationalism led to war atrocities in the former Yugoslavia.

See also Central Europe and the Far Right; Republican Party (Germany) *and* Schönhuber, Franz (Germany).

Further Reading

Ignazi, Piero. 2003. *Extreme Right Parties in Western Europe.* New York: Oxford University Press.
Kaldor, Mary and Vejvoda, Ivan, eds. 2002. *Democratization in Central and Eastern Europe.* London: Continuum.
Ramet, Sabrina, ed. 1999. *The Radical Right in Central and Eastern Europe since 1989.* University Park, PA: Pennsylvania State University Press.

Bernabeu Stadium (Spain)

In November 2004, Spanish soccer fans disgraced themselves by directing racist abuse at England's black players during a friendly international match held at Madrid's Bernabeu Stadium. Despite the fact that Spain lacks a far-right movement that is directly comparable to the **French National Front** (*Front National*, FN), for example, this does not mean that the country lacks a strong culture of far-right activity. In Spain's unique far-right dynamic, older supporters of the **Franco** regime are augmented by younger 'Ultras', namely politicised and deeply racist hooligans who meet at football matches. The international match between England and Spain, held at the Bernabeu Stadium in November 2004, broadcasted the behaviour of these far-right 'Ultras' on the international stage.

Portents were mounting before the game. For example, the manager of the Spanish side, Luis Aragonés, described Thierry Henry as 'that black shit', and the under-21 match the preceding evening was marked by racial abuse. During the game itself, these events were followed by Spanish supporters making monkey noises whenever black England players received the ball. The chanting came from both 'Ultras' and more well-healed members of the Spanish crowd, demonstrating how the racist views of the 'Ultras' have found wider popularity in recent times. Further, this type of chanting was part of a more general pattern of such behaviour, though it was this match that served to highlight the problem to the international football community. During the 2004–2005 season, Real Zaragoza incurred a fine of 600 euros when some of their fans racially abused Barcelona's Cameroonian forward, Samuel Eto'o. Meanwhile, Atlético Madrid, Deportivo La Coruña, Albacete and Getafe have also received significant fines for racist chanting at their grounds. Indeed, the problem is not limited to Spain, and links between far-right politics and football hooliganism is an international phenomenon.

This raises the question regarding the relationship between racist chanting at football grounds and the Far Right. On one level, of course, the connection is tenuous. The chanting is the work of a small minority of soccer fans without obvious organisational affiliations. The abuse is venomous, but also spontaneous, and by all accounts it does not appear to be part of a strategy laid down by a political party or movement. A more persuasive interpretation comes from Esteban Ibarra, president of the Movement Against Intolerance, a Madrid-based watchdog. He has likened the emergence of xenophobia and fear of difference to a subsoil of intolerance that is developing under the Spain's democratic political culture. Meanwhile, in the *Christian Science Monitor*, Lisa Abend agrees with such a perspective. Arguing that the evidence for a subsoil of intolerance is easy to discover, she describes how a far-right culture has emerged in Spanish football, one that elided fanaticism, racism, and fascist symbols. She also highlights that the key tropes of this racism are white pride combined with **anti-Semitism** and a strong propensity for **violence**. In this sense, the relationship between racist chanting at Spanish football grounds and the Far Right is a cultural rather than an institutional one.

See also Southern Europe and the Far Right.

Further Reading

Pingree, Geoff. 2006. 'The ugly game', Time, http://www.time.com/time/magazine/article/0,9171,9010 60403–1176955,00.html?cnn=yes (cited 31 December 2007).

Abend, Lisa. 2005. 'In Spain, signs that the far right is on the rise', Christian Science Monitor, http://www.csmonitor.com/2005/0411/p05s01-woeu.html (cited 31 December 2007).

Blocher, Christoph (b.1940) – Switzerland

Leader of the **Swiss People's Party** (*Schweizerische Volkspartei* SVP), Christoph Blocher came to national and international prominence in 2003 when his movement emerged as the largest party in the National Council in the Swiss election of 19 October, claiming a 27 percent share of the vote, and with Blocher himself topping the electoral lists in Zurich. The poll was a landmark: the SVP, once the smallest party in the Swiss governing coalition, had become the largest. Following the election he said: 'I thank you, for your trust in me personally, and for electing a government that is composed in accordance with the wishes of the people of Switzerland. I have no illusions: my election is the product of a variety of motives. But I will do everything in my power within this government to help jointly solve the problems our country faces, problems that I feel are more serious than they are generally assumed to be … I promise to do my utmost to justify your trust.' The election result enabled the SVP to claim two seats – rather than just the one – in the governing Swiss cabinet. The party leader took control of the Federal Department of Justice and Police.

Blocher's reputation is built on his wealth and notoriety. He made his money in the chemical industry through the EMS-Chemie corporation and he is thought to be a billionaire. He became leader of his party in Zurich in 1977 and has courted controversy ever since. He has been an active campaigner in recent referenda, campaigning against UN membership in 1986, abolition of the Swiss army (1989), Swiss involvement in the European Economic Area (1992), Swiss involvement in peacekeeping operations (1994), EU membership (2001), and UN membership and asylum abuse (2002). He has also entered the debate about his country's role during World War II, arguing in *Switzerland and the Second World War: A Clarification* that Switzerland should be proud of her record of neutrality during the conflict. Blocher's political powerbase has always been the German-speaking area around Zurich and he dominates the SVP's nationalist wing. Up until 2003, he led a mass lobby group: Action for an Independent and Neutral Switzerland (*Aktion für eine unabhängige und neutrale Schweiz*).

The anti-fascist magazine *Searchlight* has accused Blocher of fuelling a 'new populism'. The evidence is not hard to come by. He has campaigned against **immigration** and has been accused of racism (he has even used the word 'negro' in some of his public utterances). In 2006, he described two Albanian asylum-seekers as 'criminals', even though neither had been convicted of any offence. This kind of behaviour – and language – has led commentators to liken him to Jean-Marie **Le Pen**, leader of the FN in France. At the very least, the two men have similar political styles: both are known for their hard-hitting oratory and their willingness to engage with sensitive and taboo issues for political benefit. In an interview with Swissinfo he responded to such comparisons: 'These are nonsensical … I don't know those people personally; I've only read about them in the newspapers. Also, I'm not interested in their kind of politics. **Haider** is an opportunist and Le Pen a one-issue bruiser … A demagogue is a rabble-rouser. That's not me. I try to convince people; sometimes they agree with me and sometimes they don't. This is how **democracy** works. And I fight for my causes whether they are popular or not … I am a democrat by conviction.'

Weighing up the broader political significance of Blocher, it is important to point out that, almost single-handedly, he has undermined the consensus that seemed to dominate Swiss politics. It is not just that he has entered government and raised new issues, but he has helped to polarise debates in a very un-Swiss-like manner. He uses a new vocabulary and has pushed the boundaries of political discourse to the limit. It is tempting to see him as the latest in a line of European far-right leaders. He has the verbosity and larger-than-life appeal of a Le Pen or a **Schönhuber**, but also the modern political astuteness of a **Haider** or a **Fortuyn**. He is a crusading hero to some, a monster to others (the message on one YouTube page is 'Fuck Blocher'). Opponents fear that the Swiss national flag will end up in his toolbox and that his illiberal influence was at work in 2006 when Switzerland's laws on immigration were tightened. For these reasons, Blocher has been described by left-wing journalist Jean Martin Butner as 'the guy who just has the match and isn't there when the fire breaks out.'

See also Central Europe and the Far Right; Swiss People's Party *and Switzerland and the Second World War: A Clarification* by Christophe Blocher (Switzerland).

Further Reading
http://www.svp.ch (SVP website).
Blocher, Christoph. 1997. *Switzerland and the Second World War: A Clarification.* Schweizerische Volkspartei des Kantons Zürich.
Church, Clive H. 2003. *The Politics and Government of Switzerland.* Basingstoke: Palgrave Macmillan.
Fossedal, Gregory A. 2005. *Direct Democracy in Switzerland.* Transaction.
Farago, P., Kohli, M., Zarin-Nejadan, M. & Kriesi, H., eds. 2005. *Contemporary Switzerland: Revisiting the Special Case.* Houndmills: Palgrave Macmillan.

Blood and Honour Magazine (Great Britain)

In its own words, *Blood and Honour* 'is the longest running White Power music zine in the world and is now setting new boundaries for others to follow'. It was founded by skinhead activist, Ian Stuart Donaldson in the late 1980s. His editorial in issue no.1 read: 'This is *Blood and Honour*, a new independent Rock Against Communism paper. This paper will be run by people who really care about the Nationalist music scene, and not by people who are out to line their pockets, or further their own flagging political careers. This magazine will be your magazine and will be run as a service for you. We won't be pushing any one party's political message. We will mirror the views of all Nationalist music fans and we hope you'll be with us in the future. Racial Regards, Ian Stuart'. Today, the magazine is in full colour and contains news, information, interviews, reviews, articles and contact details relating to the British neo-Nazi scene. Donaldson was killed in a car crash in 1993, but his creation lives on. The individuals behind the publication have stated: 'Our magazine has come a long way since its birth. Our mailing list is at an all-time high and new subscribers are joining every week. This, however, is still not enough. To help realise Ian's dream, we need even more subscriptions and even more bulk sellers'. More broadly, *Blood and Honour* sees itself as a 'resistance network' promoting ideas of race and white supremacy across the world. The magazine styles itself as 'The Independent Voice Against Communism' and its imagery and reference points link it directly to Nazism. Front-page headlines over the decades include: 'THIS IS THE VOICE OF THE RIGHT', 'WHITE PRIDE' and 'PROTEST – SURVIVE'.

See also Communism.

Further Reading
Eatwell, Roger. 2000. 'The extreme right and British exceptionalism: the primacy of politics'. In *The Politics of the Extreme Right: From the Margins to the Mainstream.* Edited by Paul Hainsworth. London: Pinter.
Eatwell, Roger. 1994. 'Why has the extreme right failed in Britain?'. In *The Extreme Right in Europe and the USA.* Edited by Paul Hainsworth. London: Pinter.
Cable, Gerry. 1991. 'The far right in contemporary Britain'. In *Neo-Fascism in Europe.* Edited by Luciano Cheles, Ronnie Ferguson and Michalina Vaughan. London: Longman.
Eatwell, Roger. 1996. *Fascism: A History.* London: Vintage.

Bologna Bombing (1980)

The Bologna Bombing of 2 August 1980 left 85 people dead, most of whom were Italians, and many more were injured. Far-right terrorists had left a large bomb in a waiting room of the central Bologna train station. The blast devastated the building, causing the roof to collapse onto passengers in the waiting room, and damaged a train that was waiting at one of the station's platforms. In Italy, the event became known as the *Strage di Bologna* or the Bologna Massacre.

The impact of the *Strage di Bologna* was immediately felt across Italian society. For example, on 5 August 1980, a general strike was called to demonstrate solidarity with the victims and to express widespread outrage at the atrocity. There were some arrests in the aftermath of the event, and it was later discovered that the perpetrators included two members and one former member of the Military Intelligence and Security Service (*Servizio per le Informazioni e la Sicurezza Militare*, SISMI), the neo-fascist militants of the Armed Revolutionary Nuclei (*Nuclei Armati Rivoluzionari*, NAR) and the secretive right-wing Propaganda Due (P-2) Masonic Lodge. Either by coincidence or design, the bombing occurred on the same day that a Bologna court sent eight men, including renowned neo-fascist agitator Mario Tutti, to trial for an attack on a railway in 1974. Many legal proceedings have occurred since the bombing, though these have yet to reveal the full motives of the bombers. In November 1995, Italy's Supreme Court confirmed life sentences for two neo-fascist terrorists, Valerio Fioravanti and Francesca Mambro, who had been convicted of planting the bomb despite their claims of innocence.

The Bologna Bombing has been recorded as the worst terrorist atrocity in Italy's postwar history, and it has been commemorated every year since. Rationalising and understanding the motives for the attack is difficult, but the consensus is that it was a reactionary attempt to destabilise Italy while the country was trying hard to modernise and renew itself.

Recently, centre-left premier Romano Prodi claimed that it was 'one of too many black chapters in the history of our country'. Demonstrating how the *Strage di Bologna* remains a profoundly emotive issue among Italians, he continued by asserting that the bombing had opened up a deep wound that would take many years to heal. 'That day must never be forgotten' he stressed. 'We must work to ensure that truth and justice prevail and to show that the State will never give in to any attempt at destabilisation, hatred or division.'

See also Southern Europe and the Far Right *and* Violence.

Further Reading
Moss, David. 1993. *Italian Political Violence, 1969–1988: The Making and Unmaking of Meanings*. United Nations Research Institute for Social Development.
Willan, Philip. 1991. *Puppetmasters: The Political Use of Terrorism in Italy*. London: Constable.

Bradford, Burnley and Oldham (Great Britain)

Bradford, Burnley and Oldham, three towns in the north of England, hit the headlines in 2001 following riots involving Asian communities. Growing tension between the local Asian and white communities had been fuelled by a **British National Party**

(BNP) and **National Front** (NF) presence in the area ahead of the 7 June 2001 general election. Most prominently, the BNP had pledged to stand in two Oldham constituencies in the forthcoming general election, while the NF had threatened a march through the town centre, stirring up anti-Asian sentiments.

Oldham, an industrial suburb of Manchester, was the first area to witness the **violence**. These initial disturbances occurred mainly in the Glodwick area on 28 May, when rioting between local Asian youths led to the injury of 15 police officers and the arrest of 17 rioters. Following a fight between an Asian and a white **youth**, white youths began to assemble in the area. Later the same evening, an Asian-owned house was targeted by a violent gang of white youths, endangering the life of a pregnant woman. This led to retaliatory activities and rioting by the Asian community, including throwing petrol bombs at the *Live and Let Live* pub, again endangering lives. The Greater Manchester Police spoke of 'sheer carnage' when describing the riots.

Following these initial disturbances, rioting continued in Burnley. The town was home to a significant Asian community, but there was not a notable history of racial division in the area, and many locals interviewed by journalists tended to describe the community as well integrated. Again, BNP politicking in the general election was cited as a key factor in local Asian grievances, and the fact that the party did surprisingly well in the election on June 7 stoked further anger. Symbolising the rise of the Far Right, after the election, a BNP election banner with the slogan 'Save Your Country' remained hanging from a prominent factory site. At the end of June 2001, similar rioting broke out resulting in three nights of disturbances which culminated in the firebombing of a local pub in Burnley. When local Asians became angered over how police had dealt with an assault on a taxi driver, they began gathering on the streets. Eye-witnesses described how the Asians had clashed with a gang of white youths who had marched into the Stoneyholme area of Burnley, a predominantly Asian quarter.

The final flashpoint of the summer occurred a few days later in Bradford, a large multi-cultural city in West Yorkshire. Here, for the most part, various ethnic groups have cohabited peacefully over the decades, but occasionally trouble has flared up. The rioting followed a 7 July march by the Anti-Nazi League though the city. In an increasingly tense climate, the NF had been banned from organising a march through Bradford the previous month. During the Anti-Nazi League's (ANL) march, some of the protestors described how NF members were gathering in a city-centre pub. Soon, ANL and NF supporters confronted each other in the city centre, where an Asian man was stabbed. By the evening, these developments had triggered running battles between rioters and police, leading to the injury of around 200 people and 36 arrests. There was also much destruction within the local area, including severe damage to several pubs, a BMW dealership and Manningham Labour Club.

There were two major questions raised by these disturbances: Why did the riots happen? And what were their consequences? There were no easy answers to the first question. Clearly, Bradford, Burnley and Oldham had been multi-ethnic communities for generations. There was nothing *new* in large ethnic populations settling in British cities. But in 2001, other issues seemed to have come to the surface. Newspapers were quick to analyse the situation; for example, *The Guardian* described how a leaked Home Office report argued that the riots were a result of a lack of political leadership within local communities, combined with poorly planned regeneration projects and inequitable arrangements for social housing. Further, in all three locations there were many allegations of municipal authorities favouring the local Asian communities rather than the indigenous white population, with the result that the latter felt aggrieved. This sort of tension was easily exploited by far-right groups, such as the BNP and the NF. Other factors also seemed to be at play: rivalries between local drug gangs, police tactics, and even the unusually hot summer weather. Many reports have subsequently emerged on these riots, such as the *Cantle Report* produced by the Oldham Metropolitan Borough Council. This document argued for the need for clearer political leadership, and a greater willingness of the local community to transcend its segregated nature and develop a willingness to change 'from below'. For months following the riots, members of the cabinet attempted to comprehend how the Far Right was linked to the riots. Aside from official reports that demonstrated immediate official recognition of the Far Right's role in the violence, Home Office minister John Denham told parliament that Home Secretary David Blunkett was 'seeking out connections' between the unrest in the towns and criticised the exploitation of events by far-right groups.

Parties such as the BNP were certainly boosted by these riots, and felt the towns had an electorate that they could represent. They had targeted the towns because of the size of their ethnic populations. Indeed, demonstrating their success in these campaigns, during and after the riots, the BNP scored well in local and national elections. For instance, in the June 2001 general election the party won 6,552 votes or 16.4 percent in the Oldham West constituency, its strongest performance in the country. The following year, the BNP claimed three council seats in Burnley. However, in the long run, BNP electoral performances bottomed out, although the party would not admit this fact. In an official statement they said: 'The summer of 2001 is likely to be remembered as the turning point, when the British people began their long-overdue awakening to racial reality. Thus, an odyssey begins in which, instead of being reduced to a third-world country by traitor politicians and **immigration**, the British nation will once again assert its traditional values of honesty and fairness.'

See also British National Party; Griffin, Nick (Great Britain) *and* England, Race Riots in the North (2001).

Further Reading

BBC, '2001 summer violence: the reports', http://news.bbc.co.uk/1/hi/in_depth/uk/2001/summer_of_violence/default.stm (cited 31 December 2007).

Copsey, Nigel. 2004. *Contemporary British Fascism: The British National Party and the Quest for Legitimacy*. Basingstoke: Palgrave Macmillan.

Eatwell, Roger. 2004. 'The Extreme Right in Britain: the long road to "modernisation"'. In *Western Democracies and the New Extreme Right Challenge*. Edited by Roger Eatwell & Cas Mudde. London: Routledge.

British National Party

The British National Party (BNP) was founded in 1982 by John Tyndall. When it was formed it was viewed as the heir to the New National Front and the British Movement. Today, its leader is Nick **Griffin** and its organisational headquarters are in Waltham Cross, Hertfordshire. As if to emphasise its hard-line nationalism, its logo incorporates the letters 'B', 'N' and 'P' and imagery of the Union Jack.

The mission statement of the party reads: 'The British National Party exists to secure a future for the indigenous peoples of these islands in the North Atlantic which have been our homeland for millennia. We use the term indigenous to describe the people whose ancestors were the earliest settlers here after the last great Ice Age and which have been complemented by the historic migrations from mainland **Europe**. The migrations of the Celts, Anglo-Saxons, Danes, Norse and closely related kindred peoples have been, over the past few thousands of years, instrumental in defining the character of our **family** of nations'. This is the starting-point for BNP doctrine.

The movement hit the headlines in September 1993 when it won a local by-election victory in Tower Hamlets on the Isle of Dogs with 34 percent of the vote. It currently has over 50 local councillors. Although it scored only 0.7 percent in the 2005 general election, it actually received 192,850 votes – a massive increase on the 47,219 it polled in 2001. The number of parliamentary seats that the party has been able to contest is also a significant barometer of its profile and influence. In 1983, this figure was 53 and in 2005 it was 119.

In terms of doctrine, the party is defined by its stance on **immigration**: 'On current demographic trends, we, the native British people, will be an ethnic minority in our own country within sixty years'. It is also highly critical of Islam – the **religion** of many new and old British immigrants. In 2006, Griffin labelled it 'a wicked, vicious faith'. But the party emphasises that it is not one-dimensional. It is strong on **law and order**, hostile to the EU and wants to increase spending on defence. In the area of social policy it wants to pay mothers to stay at home and look after their children, and opposes the introduction of civil partnerships for homosexual couples. The mainstream parties in Britain have distanced themselves from the party and portray it as a racist and fascist organisation.

Party leader Nick **Griffin** has attempted to make the BNP more electable by talking about culture and religion, rather than colour, when he broaches the immigration issue, but he has not been helped by an array of court cases (some of which the BNP has actually won) and a belief that the party attempted to exploit the 2001 riots in northern England for political advantage.

In their analyses, academics have emphasised the political context in which the BNP has emerged. Writing in 1991, Gable focused on the issue of strategy. He referred to the thinking of veteran activist Colin Jordan, who said that part of the BNP's role was to 'rub shoulders with ultra-Tories'. And Gable said that, 'The BNP took in a number of former officers of the Federation of Conservative Students in 1986, and claims still to have members concealed in Conservative organisations'.

According to Eatwell – who has written extensively on the subject – the BNP should be interpreted as an extension of the National Front. But he also argues that the British Far Right is characterised by its fluidity and regular schisms; and it is possible that this could be a problem in the future.

Eatwell also portrays the BNP as a thoroughly modern political movement. It is very conscious of the media – developing its own, but also trying to combat negative stereotyping of its activities in the mainstream press. Moreover, the party also knows that its achievements will always provoke a backlash. Which is what happened in the Isle of Dogs; the seat that it so controversially won in 1993 was lost in 1994 following a hard-hitting anti-fascist campaign.

See also British National Party, Acquittal of Members (2006); England, Race Riots in the North (2001) *and* England, Race Riots in the North (2001).

Further Reading

www.bnp.org.uk (BNP website).

Eatwell, Roger. 2000. 'The extreme right and British exceptionalism: the primacy of politics'. In *The Politics of the Extreme Right: From the Margins to the Mainstream*. Edited by Paul Hainsworth. London: Pinter.

Eatwell, Roger. 1994. 'Why has the extreme right failed in Britain?'. In *The Extreme Right in Europe and the USA*. Edited by Paul Hainsworth. London: Pinter.

Cable, Gerry. 1991. 'The far right in contemporary Britain'. In *Neo-Fascism in Europe*. Edited by Luciano Cheles, Ronnie Ferguson and Michalina Vaughan. London: Longman.

Eatwell, Roger. 1996. *Fascism: A History*. London: Vintage.

Bragg, T., Griffin, N., Kerr, D. & Harrington, P. 2005. *Taking Liberties: A Third Way Special on the Attack on Civil Liberties in the UK*. Pamphlet.

Copsey, N., 2004. *Contemporary British Fascism: The British National Party and the Quest for Legitimacy*. Basingstoke: Palgrave Macmillan.

British National Party, Acquittal of Members (2006)

The 2006 acquittal of British National Party (BNP) duo, Mark Collett and Nick **Griffin**, on charges of racial hatred was a landmark event in the history of the party. Collett and Griffin were brought to trial following salacious comments made in 2004, which had been captured on camera by undercover BBC reporters. Subsequently, both were deemed not to have committed any offence at the 2006 trial.

Collett and Griffin had always denied that their comments had stirrred up racial hatred. On hidden camera, Collett described asylum seekers as 'a little bit like cockroaches', while Griffin had called Islam a 'wicked vicious faith'. Both Collett and Griffin viewed their acquittal as a vindication of their beliefs and their conviction in the wider political relevance of the BNP. At the end of the trial, Griffin described the verdicts as a 'tremendous victory for **freedom**'. He went on: 'This evening, millions of people in Britain will be holding their heads a little higher and walking a little taller. If the CPS [Crown Prosecution Service] feel they must continue to persecute us simply for telling the truth, then we will see them in court'. Seemingly suggesting a conspiracy by the BBC and the government, particular venom was reserved for the broadcasters: 'What has just happened shows Tony Blair and the government toadies at the BBC that they can take our taxes but they cannot take our hearts, they cannot take our tongues and they cannot take our freedom'. He also accused the BBC of being a 'politically correct organisation' arguing that the trial had been a waste of licence payers' money, and claimed that his organisation was a democratic party doing nothing more than articulating the truth. Responding to these assertions, the BBC stated that the decision to prosecute lay not with the corporation itself, but rather with the courts and prosecuting authorities. Further, the corporation stressed the widespread public concern regarding the nature of the BNP that immediately followed the broadcast. The fallout from the case also enveloped the then Chancellor of the Exchequer, Gordon Brown, who felt the need to comment on the issue. Brown stated that it was possible that laws regarding discrimination and incitement may have to be revised in light of the verdict, asserting: 'I think any preaching of religious or racial hatred will offend mainstream opinion in this country and I think we've got to do whatever we can to root it out from whatever quarter it comes. And if that means we've got to look at the laws again, I think we will have to do so'.

More generally, this case, alongside the political commentary that followed, has demonstrated the distinction between discrimination on the grounds of race and on the grounds of **religion**. The verdict demonstrates that it is easier for the Far Right to target Islam as a faith, rather than to directly highlight racial markers, such as skin colour. This fact could help explain why Islam has proved such a fertile ground for the Far Right in recent years. Further, the widespread use of hyperbolic language to describe asylum seekers within the British media also allows comments, such as those made by Collett, to be lost in a wider discourse arguing for tighter controls on **immigration**.

See also British National Party *and* Griffin, Nick (Great Britain).

Further Reading
BBC. 2006. 'BNP leader cleared of race hate', *BBC News,* http://news.bbc.co.uk/1/hi/england/ bradford/6135060.stm (cited 31 December 2007).
Copsey, Nigel. 2004. *Contemporary British Fascism: The British National Party and the Quest for Legitimacy.* Basingstoke: Palgrave Macmillan.

C

Campaign in Russia: The Waffen SS on the Eastern Front by Léon Degrelle (Belgium)

This memoir written by veteran Belgian fascist Léon **Degrelle** was published in 1985, nine years before his death in 1994. It tells of his experiences as a soldier, fighting for the Nazis, on the Eastern Front during the Second World War.

Degrelle's career straddled the inter-war and post-war years. He grew up as a hard-line integral Catholic but was ex-communicated by the Vatican for wearing a fascist uniform in church. He was entranced by Fascism and established his own party in Belgium, Rex. Gradually this movement was Nazified and by the outbreak of war, Degrelle was a passionate follower of Hitler.

In 1941, inspired by a passionate anti-communist ideology, Degrelle formed his own Walloon battalion which was ready to fight on the Eastern Front after the German invasion of the USSR. He started as a private and ended up as commander of what was known as the 28th SS Division 'Wallonia'. Hitler, it is said, thought very highly of him. Following the war, Degrelle went into hiding in Spain, but kept up his political activities. He published many books including *Open Letter to the Pope on His Visit to Auschwitz* (1979), *Epic: Story of the Waffen-SS* (1985), and *Hitler Century: Hitler – Born at Versailles* (1987). He also wrote *Campaign in Russia: The Waffen SS on the Eastern Front*, a detailed and, in places, almost poetic overview of the campaign.

In the book, Degrelle focuses on many key incidents including the Red Army's encirclement of Cherkassy-Korsun (1944) and his meeting with Hitler (the Führer suggested that he withdraw from the frontline, but Degrelle disobeyed, saying that his division needed his leadership skills). The volume paints a vivid picture of war, the savage conditions that fighters on both sides had to overcome, and the powerful ideological motivation that provoked individuals such as Degrelle into action.

Carinthia

See also Degrelle, Léon (Belgium).

Further Reading

Fields, E.R. 2005. *Léon Degrelle and the Rexist Party 1935–1940*. Spearhead.
de Bruyne, Eddy & Rikmenspoel, Marc. 2004. *For Rex and for Belgium: Léon Degrelle and Walloon Political and Military Collaboration 1940–45*. London: Helion and Company Ltd.
Conway, Martin. 1993. *Collaboration in Belgium: Léon Degrelle and the Rexist Movement, 1940–44*. New Haven, CT: Yale University Press.
Husbands, Christopher T. 1994. 'Belgium: Flemist legions on the march'. In *The Extreme Right in Europe and the USA*. Edited by Paul Hainsworth. London: Pinter.

Carinthia (Austria)

In recent years, Carinthia, the southern most state in Austria, has become the homeland of the **Austrian Freedom Party** (*Freiheitliche Partei Österreichs*, FPÖ), and especially its most high profile member, Jörg **Haider**. Now leader of the Alliance for the Future of Austria (*Bündnis Zukunft Österreich*, BZÖ), Haider's deployment of an emotional nationalism has won him many followers in his adopted Carinthia. Furthermore, this style of nationalist politics has often led to more direct references to interwar Fascism. Indeed, his rhetorical and semiotic strategy has seen him elide nods towards Nazism with a sense of traditional Austrian identity.

As Max Riedlsperger has observed, upon his election to party chairman in 1986, the Austrian magazine *Profil* typified the critical responses this generated. It depicted Haider wearing a traditional Carinthian outfit and standing in front of an image of another image of Haider; this time the then FPÖ politician was sporting a brown-shirt and a partially obscured Nazi armband. He has also earned many affectionate nicknames, such as *der Haider, Jörg* and, in an eerie echo of the Hitler **Youth** movement, HJ. In the public imagination, then, the ideological links between interwar politics and Haider's modern profile are often clear – both in the minds of his supporters and his critics. Moreover, Carinthia has become intimately associated with this rise of Haider and the far-right FPÖ.

Looking slightly deeper, we can locate some important themes in the relationship between the FPÖ stalwart and the state of Carinthia. First, Haider's links with the area are shrouded in controversy. In 1983, he inherited a large estate in Carinthia – Bärental, or the Valley of the Bears – that had previously been owned by his uncle. At the time he inherited this estate, it was valued at around $16m, and so this inheritance suddenly made Haider very wealthy. It also soon sparked controversy for Haider because it emerged that, until 1940, this estate had been owned by an Italian Jew. Further, Haider's uncle has been able to purchase the property at a knock-down rate in 1940 because, by this point in the war, Jews were fleeing Austria and were prepared to accept any meagre offer on their property. This revelation catapulted the young Haider into the headlines. The issue of Haider appearing to have profited directly from the actions of the Nazi regime made it easy for his opponents to argue that the FPÖ leader not only had deep-seated sympathies with the doctrine and policies of the Nazis, but even benefited personally from their reign of terror. Since this controversy, Carinthia has almost become Haider's personal fiefdom. He has served as its state governor for long periods, and it would probably be fair to say that it is the only region in which the FPÖ has a mass base and a track record of electoral success. In March 2004, for example, Haider polled 42.5 percent in state elections. He has also used the region as a kind of laboratory where he has experimented with various policies and agendas.

It is also important to note the distinctive political culture of Carinthia. The region is notorious for its conservative, nationalist and reactionary politics. The FPÖ, for example, is renowned for its hostility toward the Slovene minority in Carinthia, and in general there seems to be a meeting of minds between the province, its population and Haider's movement. This is reflected in Haider's new party, the BZÖ, which has to date received less support than the FPÖ, yet maintains a powerbase in Carinthia. Very rarely has one man's political fortunes been tied up so closely with one particular geographical region. As the BBC's correspondent in Austria put it, Carinthia is Haider's stronghold in the mountains. Not only was it in Carinthia that he made his notorious comments praising Nazi employment policies in the early 1990s, but also his re-election to state governor in 1999 had boosted his public profile so that 'despite or perhaps because of his attacks on immigrants and the EU, Carinthians have remained true to Mr Haider'.

See also Central Europe and the Far Right, *The Freedom I Mean* by Jörg Haider (Austria) *and* Haider, Jörg (Austria).

Further Reading
Ignazi, Piero. 2003. *Extreme Right Parties in Western Europe*. New York: Oxford University Press.
Riedlsperger, Max. 1992 '*Heil Haider!* The revitalization of the Austrian Freedom Party since 1986' in *Politics and Society in Germany, Austrian and Switzerland*. 4.3.

Carpentras (France)

With a history stretching back to the Roman era, the small town of Carpentras is located on a small tributary of the Ardèche River in the Provence-Alpes-Côte d'Azur region of France. It is also linked to a deeply-shocking episode in the history of the French Far Right. On 10 May 1990, thirty-four desecrated graves were discovered in a Jewish graveyard in the town. More disturbingly still, one body had even been exhumed and horribly mutilated by the vandals. Meanwhile, in Wissembourg, north-east Strasbourg, around twenty gravestones had also been damaged on the same night, leading politicians, including François Mitterrand and Jacques Chirac, to condemn the desecrations of these graves.

In the speculation that followed, suspicion quickly fell on Jean-Marie **Le Pen** and the **National Front** (*Front National*, FN), because of their thinly-veiled anti-Semitic discourse. Often, this commentary did not directly blame FN officials for carrying out the outrage, but rather media commentators stressed that the movement was responsible for encouraging a climate of xenophobia and racism. It was this growing, anti-Semitic culture that could well have encouraged the unknown perpetrators of the crime. Meanwhile, like other political leaders, Le Pen himself publicly condemned the actions.

In a subsequent, troubling development, a series of copycat crimes followed in other French towns and cities, leading to further soul-searching among the French regarding how to handle the situation. A wave of theories and counter-theories emerged to explain, or at least try to explain, the Carpentras episode and its aftermath. Also, marches against racism took place across France, the largest of which was held in Paris. This demonstration, estimated to be 80,000 strong, comprised all religions and political persuasions – with the exception of the FN – and was even joined by Mitterrand himself. Not since the liberation of Paris in 1945 had a French head of state protested in the streets. The fall-out could well have been fatal for the FN, but Le Pen's party has always possessed an ability to bounce back from disaster, and make good news out of bad news. Incredibly, the Carpentras events did no long-term damage to the party and its political fortunes. Meanwhile, in 1997, four neo-Nazi skinheads were convicted of the Carpentras crime.

See also Anti-Semitism; National Front (France) *and* Western Europe and the Far Right.

Further Reading
Davies, Peter. 1999. *The National Front in France: Ideology, Discourse and Power*. New York: Routledge.
Beyer, Lisa. 1990. 'France issues of color and of creed', *Time*, http://www.time.com/time/magazine/article/0,9171,970213,00.html (cited 31 December 2007).

Cold War

For far-right groupings of the 1950s, 1960s, 1970s and 1980s, the Cold War was a permanent backdrop. For those that came later, it became a key point of reference.

Technically speaking, the Cold War was an era of tension and occasional conflict between the US and USSR and the two countries' various proxy states. At root it was ideological: a period in which the capitalist Americans and communist Soviets displayed both suspicion and paranoia with regard to each other. There were junctures at which this relationship strained almost irrevocably, but other occasions when there was a thawing in relations. Most experts see the Cold War as lasting from the mid-1940s to the early 1990s.

For far-right movements active during the Cold War there was only one position to take: the American one. And so, they demonised **Communism** and depicted its agents as 'dangerous' and 'anti-national'. It was viewed as a 'foreign' and 'cosmopolitan' ideology that advanced utopian ideas such as equality. In the same vein, across **Europe**, the Far Right labelled communist political parties as 'undemocratic' and in tow to Moscow. **Le Pen** in France and **Schönhuber** in Germany were especially vehement in their anti-communist rhetoric, with the former arguing in 1984 that, 'communist hegemony endangers France and the whole of Western and Christian civilisation'.

In 1984, Nazi-hunter Simon Wiesenthal put forward his view. He argued that Russo-American hostility had unforeseen consequences, stating: 'Nazi criminals were the principal beneficiaries of the Cold War'. Wiesenthal said that many Nazi criminals found a hiding place for their views in far-right political movements; in effect, the Cold War enabled them to maintain their political personas and their political philosophies. The East German and Soviet regimes took advantage of this and tried to exaggerate the Nazi legacy in West Germany.

The fall of Communism in 1989 and 1990 was seen by the Far Right as a triumph. The enemy had been defeated – at last. Other targets now came into view including Third World **immigration** and Islamic terrorism.

In another sense, the Fall of the **Berlin Wall** and the end of the Cold War was a catalyst and heralded many new forms of far-right activity. Communism and its certainties had disappeared; and in its place, in some countries, emerged a strange communist-authoritarian-nationalist hybrid. This was exemplified best in Romania, **Russia** and the former Yugoslavia: in Romania, far-rightists of the 'radical continuity' type see themselves as heirs to national Communism and have actually exacerbated the xenophobic dimension to this ideology; in Russia the **National Bolshevist Party** has mixed neo-Nazi terror tactics with a nostalgic – and slightly warped – attachment to Bolshevism; and in their respective states, **Tuđman** and **Milošević** grafted fanatical nationalism onto traditional communist authoritarianism, but convinced few that they were anything other than old-fashioned demagogues with territorial ambitions.

See also Communism in Central and Eastern Europe, End of (1989) *and* The Ideology of the Far Right.

Further Reading

Ignazi, Piero. 2003. *Extreme Right Parties in Western Europe*. New York: Oxford University Press.
Kaldor, Mary and Vejvoda, Ivan, eds. 2002. *Democratization in Central and Eastern Europe*. London: Continuum.
Ramet, Sabrina, ed. 1999. *The Radical Right in Central and Eastern Europe since 1989*. University Park, PA: Pennsylvania State University Press.

Collaboration and Collaborationism

Collaboration occurred during the Second World War when indigenous governments and populations established a working relationship with the German or Italian occupiers. These relationships could take a number of forms, including economic, political or even personal and sexual. Turning to the term 'Collaborationism', this was a variation on the theme. Collaborationism came to denote the phenomenon of 'ideological' rather than 'governmental' or 'everyday' collaboration. As a concept, then, collaborationism is extremely important as it signifies 'voluntary' rather than 'involuntary' collaboration with the Nazis.

Many French Nazis, figures such as Robert Brasillach, Pierre Drieu la Rochelle and Jacques Doriot, were based in Paris during the Occupation, and were at the cutting edge of French collaborationism. Here, they expounded their pro-Hitler ideology, aped Nazi rituals, and openly declared their love for Germany. Collaborationists hoped that the Allies would be defeated. Thereafter, their support would be rewarded and they themselves would play a prominent role in Hitler's New **Europe**. On the whole, the French collaborationists were small in number and were viewed as irrelevant by both the Nazis and the Vichy regime.

The broader significance of collaboration and collaborationism lies in the fact that many countries did not come to terms with pro-Nazi wartime behaviour for decades after the war. This resulted in a succession of revelations, scandals and controversies, notably in France, Italy, Austria, Switzerland, the Balkans and the Baltic states. At the same time, some ex-collaborators and collaborationists established movements in the post-war years that attempted to fly the flag for the Far Right. A good example here is Maurice Bardéche, who founded the European Social Movement (*Mouvement Social Européen*, ESM) in France in 1951. This was an attempt to unite European nationalists and ultra-nationalists. Bardéche still had a National Socialist dream, even though he had been imprisoned in 1948 for trying to justify collaboration and the **Holocaust**. During the Second World War, he too had been pro-Vichy and anti-Resistance in his ideology. Following the war, other far-right movements also emerged and provided a home for pro-Nazis who still wanted to engage in political activity – for example, in Belgium both the **Flemish Bloc** (*Vlaams Blok*, VB) and Flemish Concentration (*Vlaamse Concentratie*) have acted in such a way.

In Austria, both Kurt **Waldheim** and Jörg **Haider** have been embroiled in controversy regarding positive links with the Nazi era. Further, in the nationalisms that have developed in Central and Eastern Europe following the end of the **Cold War**, memories and myths of collaboration have been used as a means to create a sense of discontinuity with the communist era. Indeed, in the worst instances of this trend, memories of the Ustaše and Chetnik atrocities committed under the Independent State of Croatia (*Nezavisna Država Hrvatska*, NDH) and the Nazi puppet Government of National Salvation (*Vlada Nacionalnog Spasa*) in Serbia were rekindled in the 1990s. For some, then, the tag of 'ex-collaborator' was a badge of honour in far-right circles. In time, as the world changed and moved on, for many within the Far Right the legacy of collaborationism has become something of a dirty secret.

See also Anti-Semitism; The Holocaust *and* The Ideology of the Far Right.

Further Reading
Davies, Peter. 2004. *Dangerous Liaisons: Collaboration and World War Two*. New York: Longman.
Gordon, Bertram M. 1980. *Collaborationism in France during the Second World War*. Ithaca, N.Y.: Cornell University Press.

Communism

Up until the collapse of the USSR, Communism was one of the great bugbears of the Far Right and unsurprisingly one of its primary objectives was to see world Communism come to an end. In the era of interwar Fascism, any permutation of Communism was seen as the antithesis of the ultra-nationalist cause. Everything that Fascists did not believe in could be found on Far Left: internationalism, belief in equality, and blind loyalty to the working class and class-based politics.

In the post-war period, this ideological inheritance has remained, and the Far Right continues to this day to oppose the ideology. Far-right discourse on this topic can turn into highly emotive, angry tirades. Often, anti-communist outbursts are used as the basis for more general attacks on the left, and tend to be loaded with sweeping generalisations, often invoking issues such as the Russian Revolution and Lenin and Stalin's totalitarianism in wide-ranging attacks. The far-right critique of the Far Left and Communism, then, has operated on several planes: ideological, historical and even philosophical.

Other factors are also worth noting in this regard. In the post-war period, it has often been the case that far-right parties have competed against parties of the Far Left for the protest vote. The tendency has been for these more extreme groupings to fight for third or fourth place in national elections, adding to the sense of rivalry between the two poles. Further, with the end of the USSR and the Communist Party of the Soviet Union in 1991, and following the tumultuous events of 1989, many sections of the Far Right believed that the left had lost this particular ideological battle, and so the Far Right could claim a victory against the old enemy in **Europe**. There were no significant Marxist/Leninist Communist parties to do battle with anymore but, of course, the philosophical battle between right and left continues. Therefore, some of the wider hopes and ideals of Communism have remained within far-left discourses. Nevertheless, for those on the Far Right, the enemy was no longer permutations of Communism, but a multicultural, globalising world.

In the political milieu of Central and Eastern Europe, the end of the USSR's communist domination of the region led to the emergence of myriad new far-right groupings. Some of the more significant of these include: Vladhimir Zhirinovsky's Russian Liberal Democratic Party (*Liberal'no-Demokraticheskaya Partiya Rossii*, LDPR), Corneliu Vadim **Tudor**'s **Greater Romania Party** (*Partidul România Mare*, PRM), the **Hungarian Justice and Life Party** (*Magyar Igazság és Élet Pártja*, MIÉP) and **League of Polish Families** (*Liga Polskich Rodzin*, LPR). These have acted as key ally figures for far-right groups in **Western Europe**. One example of this new trend was the brief emergence of the **Identity, Tradition and Sovereignty Group** in the European Parliament in 2007. Though short-lived, the emergence of this formal group demonstrates the new political clout of the Far Right in Eastern Europe after the fall of Communism. This political dynamic would have been unthinkable in the era of the **Cold War**.

See also Communism in Central and Eastern Europe, End of (1989) *and* The Ideology of the Far Right.

Further Reading

Ignazi, Piero. 2003. *Extreme Right Parties in Western Europe*. New York: Oxford University Press.
Kaldor, Mary and Vejvoda, Ivan, eds. 2002. *Democratization in Central and Eastern Europe*. London: Continuum.
Ramet, Sabrina, ed. 1999. *The Radical Right in Central and Eastern Europe since 1989*. University Park, PA: Pennsylvania State University Press.

Communism in Central and Eastern Europe, End of (1989)

The Fall of the **Berlin Wall** in 1989, and the consequent re-unification of Germany, changed the political landscape in **Europe**. Communist regimes were brought down throughout Eastern Europe. Within a matter of years, the USSR had disintegrated while new, non-communist states emerged across the region. In many of these countries, the vacuum left by parties and governments of the Far Left was, in part, filled by the ultra-nationalist Far Right.

It is worth citing some examples of this growth of the Far Right after the end of **Communism**. Romania has seen a growth of political parties that have played on the memory of the Iron Guard and Corneliu Codreanu, such as Corneliu Vadim **Tudor**'s **Greater Romania Party** (*Partidul România Mare*, PRM). Meanwhile, Hungary has seen the rise of the **Hungarian Justice and Life Party** (*Magyar Igazság és Élet Pártja*, MIÉP), and Poland has experienced coalition government by the **League of Polish Families** (*Liga Polskich Rodzin*, LPR). Further east, **Russia** has experienced the development of Vladimir **Zhirinovsky**'s Liberal Democratic Party (*Demokraticheskaya Partiya Rossii*, LDP), a virulently anti-Semitic organisation that reached its high-water mark in 1993.

Meanwhile, perhaps the most complex case has been the response of the German Far Right to the fall of the Berlin Wall and the reunification of Germany. In the western Federal Republic of Germany (*Bundesrepublik Deutschland*, FRG), this development realised the central goal of all post-war, far-right parties – the reunification of Germany. Meanwhile, in what was the German Democratic Republic (*Deutsche Demokratische Republik*, GDR), following reunification, a newfound sense of connection with Germany's ultra-nationalist past was one strategy through which people could achieve a sense of continuity with the past. Therefore, the Far Right was able to create new propaganda potential out of memories of Nazism. The **German People's Union** (*Deutsche Volksunion*, DVU) has been particularly successful at exploiting this new electorate.

Finally, it is worth commenting on the Yugoslav experience, which was undoubtedly the most bloody example of post-communist politics turning to the Far Right. The break-up of the country during the 1990s was both the product of, and prelude to, significant far-right political activity. As the end of one-party, communist states had an enormous impact on the prevailing political landscape, ethnic groups were encouraged and inspired by political leaders to reinvest their sense of national identity with new-found energy. In the context of Yugoslavia, this meant nationalist groups campaigning, sometimes violently, for independence from Belgrade. As the Yugoslav state disintegrated, various ultra-nationalist politicians and parties in various territories used the situation for their own personal and political gain. Croatian leader Franjo **Tuđman** and Serbian strongman Slobodan **Milošević** could both be categorised as ultra-nationalists and, by implication, men of the Far Right. Indeed, both leaders played on memories of the Second World War: Tuđman branded Milošević a latter-day Chetnik and Milošević portrayed Tuđman and his associates as heirs to the Ustaše. Tuđman and Milošević also stoked the fires of nationalism more generally: both looked back nostalgically to a 'golden age' in the history of their own states. As if to demonstrate their nationalist credentials to a worldwide audience, it has even been alleged that Tuđman and Milošević agreed to carve up Bosnia and Herzegovina in the interests of territorial aggrandisement.

The end of the old far-left ideological nemesis, then, created a new reality for the Far Right to exploit. New found support for the ideology has developed across Central and Eastern Europe from the 1990s onwards, providing political scientists with important new areas of far-right activity to research.

See also Communism *and* Cold War.

Further Reading

Ignazi, Piero. 2003. *Extreme Right Parties in Western Europe*. New York: Oxford University Press.
Kaldor, Mary and Vejvoda, Ivan, eds. 2002. *Democratization in Central and Eastern Europe*. London: Continuum.
Ramet, Sabrina, ed. 1999. *The Radical Right in Central and Eastern Europe since 1989*. University Park, PA: Pennsylvania State University Press.

Cosmopolitanism

Cosmopolitanism has come to be defined as the search for trans-national, universal values rather than local or national values. In the interwar period, the Nazi regime was diametrically opposed to the cosmopolitan ideal, as were other fascist groups. The post-war Far Right also tends to view such principles negatively, claiming they are 'weak', 'soft' and 'wishy-washy'. Further, it often regards cosmopolitan values as holding a clear ideological contrast with its brand of nationalism, and so the Far Right often ridicules such sympathies for prioritising the global over the national. The corollary is that anti-cosmopolitan parties come across as narrow, insular and bigoted as a result.

Modern far-right movements, such as the **National Front** (*Front National*, FN) in France have been at the forefront of this trend of vilifying the cosmopolitan ideal whenever they have encountered it. For a xenophobic and chauvinistic party committed to ultra-nationalism, such as the FN, cosmopolitan ideals like cultural diversity are anathema. Rather, the FN seeks to reconnect the nation with its national roots, an idea designed to counteract the growth of trans-national values. In France, cosmopolitan attitudes can be traced back to the revolutionary era and the *Declaration of the Rights of Man*. This document, one of the key outcomes of the French Revolution, laid out a new set of liberal guidelines for humanity to follow. The underlying message of the document was that all citizens were equal in their legal status, and so basic **freedom**s and liberties should be enshrined in law. The authors of the document also believed in universality: the principles laid out in the document were for the whole world, not just France. This meant Jews and immigrants – to name two distinguishable groups – were also included within the new concept of citizenship. This sense of inclusively on the basis of a legal code was one of the key reasons why interwar Fascists, such as Hitler, opposed so vehemently the ideals of the French Revolution. Indeed, many politicians on the Far Right have consciously styled their politics as a reaction against such a legalistic perspective, preferring an integralist or organic way of conceiving nationalism and the national community.

When we look at the FN during the 1980s and 1990s, we see that the party made great play of the fact that it believed that the Socialist Party, and the left-wing government that was led by François Mitterrand and Michel Rocard, was being hijacked by 'rights of man' fanatics. **Le Pen** and his party alleged that '*les droits de l'homme*' was becoming the 'new totalitarianism'. Indeed, they claimed that it was becoming impossible, almost *illegal*, to argue against such ideals. Arguably disproving their own claims, however, the FN continued its vocal critiques. To take the most controversial example, they believed that immigrants were being given *rights* when, actually, what should have been stressed were the *duties* and *responsibilities* involved in being a French citizen. In FN circles, this issue was seen as the major political battleground: nationals versus anti-nationals. In other words, for the FN, **immigration** was seen through a strict 'us verses them' lens. As a consequence, controversies surrounding **education** policies and nationality code reform were infused with a new potency in FN discourses. This allowed the party to raise divisive, anti-cosmopolitan questions, such as: Should French children learn about the history of foreign countries or should their studies focus on France alone? And, should so many immigrants be fast-tracked through France's naturalisation procedures? Thus, the anti-cosmopolitan argument stresses national difference rather than uniformity.

A similar battle was also waged in Sweden. Here, the far-right Sweden Democrats (*Sverigedemokraterna*, SD) have argued vehemently against cosmopolitan ideals. Typifying the new strand of nativism in far-right discourses that promotes multiple cultures just so long as they do not impact on the nation state in question, the party claims that cultural diversity is vital to the nature and survival of the human race.

However, it also claims that nations that have housed more than one cultural identity have been unable to protect these diverse elements in their pure form, leading to the eradication of original identities, and therefore an end to cultural diversity. Rather, it argues that cultural diversity needs to be protected through the paradigm of the nation-state, adding the caveat that this approach also needs to take into consideration relevant Human Rights issues. Such a position camouflages a more aggressive nativism in a language that ostensibly asserts the importance of cultural diversity.

In **Russia**, the war on cosmopolitanism was embraced by the ultra-nationalist party **Memory** (*Pamyat*). Through an anti-Semitic lens, Memory has argued that Zionists and Freemasons have created the concept of cosmopolitanism in order to combat their alleged enemies: national traditions and religious customs. The theme has been given a more contemporary twist by Vladimir **Zhirinovsky**, leader of the Russian Liberal Democratic Party (*Liberal'no-Demokraticheskaya Partiya Rossii*, LDPR). Zhirinovsky has talked about religious cosmopolitanism in a negative fashion, implying that his country has a dominant **religion**, eastern Orthodox Christianity, and that too many other religions are 'no good' for Russia. He has gone on to argue that the LDPR would attempt to control and limit all religious faiths and organisations other than Orthodox Christianity, including Catholic and Protestant versions of Christianity, all Eastern religions, as well as Islam.

See also Communism *and* The Ideology of the Far Right.

Further Reading

Davies, Peter. 1999. *The National Front in France: Ideology, Discourse and Power*. New York: Routledge.

Mudde, Cas. 2000. *The Ideology of the Extreme Right*. Manchester: Manchester University Press.

Ramet, Sabrina, ed. 1999. *The Radical Right in Central and Eastern Europe since 1989*.

University Park, PA: Pennsylvania State University Press.

Croatian Democratic Union

Formed in 1989, the Croatian Democratic Union (*Hrvatska Demokratska Zajednica*, HDZ) is an ultra-nationalist political party. It ruled Croatia between 1990 and 2000 and has also been in coalition government since 2003. Over the past two decades, it has been at the forefront of political conflict in Croatia, and also the former Yugoslavia more generally.

The HDZ is intimately connected with the political career of Franjo **Tuđman**. It was he who officially founded the movement in June 1989 and led it throughout the 1990s, up until his death in 1999. But the party was established in a period of political uncertainty. It had little money early on and legend has it that its first premises were nothing more than a shack.

In its early days, the party relied upon the Croatian expatriate community for financial support. This was significant in itself, but was also a key factor in helping to shape the doctrine and ideology of the HDZ. Almost immediately, the movement advertised itself as the party of Croatian patriots and nationalists and set itself up in opposition to the ruling Croatian Communist Party.

The date that is engrained in party history is 30 May 1990, when communist rule was replaced by HDZ rule. It is now a public holiday in Croatia – Statehood Day.

6. President of Croatia,
Franjo Tuđman, on
a visit to Budapest,
Hungary, March 1998.

Thereafter, the party oversaw Croatia becoming an independent state, in 1991, and being internationally recognised, in 1992. It also triumphed in parliamentary elections in 1992 and 1995.

In doctrinal terms, the HDZ styled itself as a party of the right, which believed in capitalism, privatisation, and also national reconciliation – a major issue during, and following, the various conflicts that Croatia was involved in as the state of Yugoslavia disintegrated, and both Croatia and Serbia sought to exert their influence in Bosnia.

Indeed, the rise of the HDZ is inseparable from the wars of the 1990s. Tuđman and his party put forward a powerful brand of ultra-nationalism which emphasised the cultural and historical specificity of Croats. They were vehement in their hatred and loathing of Serbia and Serbs, and this inspired many controversial military initiatives in the former Yugoslavia.

As HDZ leader, Tuđman personified this fanatical ultra-nationalism. One of his speeches, in 1995, contained the following passage: 'We knew what lessons to draw from our history in order to get to where we are now – **freedom** – which is truly the end of the Croatian crusade … The Croatian country is now stronger, not only stronger, but also fully consolidated following the liberation of Knin and central parts of Croatia. God willing, we shall liberate the remaining territory by peaceful means and without loss of life, with help from the international community. If this proves impossible, we shall use our force. Dear Croatian brothers and sisters … We must revive and build the whole of Croatia, so it can become a country of which every Croat can be proud'.

Tuđman's death in 1999 and a variety of policy setbacks meant that the HDZ lost support in the parliamentary and presidential elections of 2000. However, in the years that followed, the party underwent something of a transformation. Moderates gained the ascendancy over hardliners, and it reinvented itself as a movement of the centre-right, keen to fly the nationalist flag but also, at the same time, to divest itself of the less pleasant Tuđman-era memories.

New leader Ivo Sanader was the man to oversee the changes, and he reaped the electoral benefit. In the elections of 2003, the HDZ claimed 34 percent of the popular vote, 66 out of 151 seats, and Sanader became prime minister. He said: 'Croatian voters have shown that they trust the HDZ'.

Csurka, István

See also Horrors of War by Franjo Tuđman (Croatia); South-Eastern Europe and the Far Right *and* Tuđman, Dr Franjo (Croatia).

Further Reading
http://www.hdz.hr (HDZ website).
Tanner, Marcus. 1997. *Croatia: A Nation Forged in War*. New Haven, CT: Yale University Press.

Csurka, István (b.1934) – Hungary

István Csurka is currently the leader of the **Hungarian Justice and Life Party** (MIEP), a movement generally characterised as nationalist, xenophobic and anti-Semitic. Now in his 70s, Csurka is the personification of the Hungarian Far Right. He disseminates his populist, nationalist theories in his newspaper *Magyar Forum* and is famous for his clever political rhetoric and oratory.

Csurka has a background in the arts. His brother is the actor László Csurka and he himself has had a varied career in the Hungarian film industry, specialising in comedy and drama. As a writer, he was responsible for *Kertes házak utcája* (1962), *Miért rosszak a magyar filmek?* (1964), *A Férfi egészen más* (1966), *Hét tonna dollár* (1974), *A Kard* (1977), and *Amerikai cigaretta* (1978). And as an actor he starred in *Vízivárosi nyár* (1964), *Égi bárány* (1970) and *141 perc a befejezetlen mondatból* (1975). He was also involved in the 1980 film *Cserepek* as a consultant and in various theatrical works including *Móor es Páal*, *Döglött Aknák* and *Házmestersirató*.

Csurka formed the MIEP in 1993 when he and other ultra-nationalist activists left the Hungarian Democratic Forum (MDF), the ruling party at the time. At its peak – after the elections of 1998 – the MIEP boasted 14 seats (out of 386) in the Hungarian parliament and became the first movement of the Far Right to enter the legislature since the Second World War. In this period it was also allowed to form a parliamentary caucus. This brought the party representation on legislative committees, financial benefits and, in general, a higher parliamentary and media profile.

But, on the whole, Csurka and his party have performed poorly at the polls. In 1994 they did not pass the 5 percent threshold necessary to gain parliamentary representation; in the local elections of 1998, the party scored just over 5 percent of the vote and gained four mayorships (in Budapest it actually polled 9 percent of the vote and claimed six out of the sixty-six seats in the Budapest assembly); and in the European poll of 2004, it failed to cross the 5 percent barrier. Although two deputies left the MIEP during the post-1998 parliamentary session – leaving it with twelve representatives – and although the party has been beset by its fair share of internal disputes and squabbles, Csurka's authority has remained intact. His brand of extremism has won out and his party has even seen its influence rise with supporters being appointed to key posts in the state television company.

Research indicates that MIEP core supporters come from the top and bottom of society – from the aristocratic rich and the uneducated poor. Alina Mungiu-Pippidi has argued that the typical MIEP voter is both nationalist and authoritarian. This would seem to tie in with the main thrust of Csurka's ideology and his political style.

Over the years, Csurka has become notorious for his **anti-Semitism**. He portrays the Jews as a real threat to the Hungarian nation and routinely describes them as Communists. He is also close to revisionist writer David Irving, inviting him to Hungary and calling him a 'prominent British historian'. Csurka's language is coded. Any mention of 'Tel Aviv', 'global financial circles', 'cosmopolitans', 'globalisation', 'ethnic minorities' or 'non-Hungarian elements' automatically means the Jews. Likewise, he has put forward an array of conspiracy theories. According to one that was reported in 1997, because Israel could not cope with a mass influx of Jewish immigrants, Hungary would be invaded and designated as a 'safe haven' for homeless Jews.

The rest of Csurka's ideology is a rag-bag of nationalist concerns. He is anti-gypsy (he wants to expel all Roma from Hungary), anti-American (he opposed the invasion of Iraq), and proclaims that institutions such as NATO, the EU, the World Bank and the International Monetary Fund are working against the 'real Magyar interest'. The party's main slogan is: 'Neither right, nor left, Christian and Hungarian'. Csurka also believes that Hungary has legitimate territorial interests in the Balkans. Thus, at the end of the **Kosovo** conflict, he called on Serbia to cede Vojvodina to Hungary in true irredentist style.

In recent years, Csurka has forged links with **Le Pen** in France and has attended the FN annual congress in Strasbourg. He has likened his political battle in Hungary to Le Pen's in France and argues passionately for **Europe**-wide solidarity between nationalist movements to counter the liberal left. It is generally agreed that Csurka is a political maverick, a film star-turned-politician who is a lone voice on the Hungarian Far Right.

See also Hungarian Justice and Life Party *and* South-Eastern Europe and the Far Right.

Further Reading

http://www.miep.hu (MIEP website).
Körösényi, András. 2000. *Government and Politics in Hungary*. Budapest: Central European University Press.
Spirova, M. 2007. *Political Parties in Post-Communist Societies: Formation, Persistence, and Change.* New York: Palgrave.

D

Danish People's Party

The Danish People's Party (*Dansk Folkeparti*, DPP) was established in 1995 as successor to the Danish Progress Party. The party's leader is Pia Kjærsgaard, one of the most prominent, and controversial, female politicians in **Europe**. She has helped to create a centralised party structure – one which does not look kindly on dissension or internal criticism. Other prominent figures in the party include Søren Krarup and **immigration** spokesperson Jesper Langballe.

Since its formation, the party has steadily become more popular in electoral terms. In 1998, it claimed a 7.4 percent share of the national vote and thereafter broke through the 10 percent barrier. In 2001, it scored 12 percent, in 2005, 13.2 percent, and in 2007, 13.8 percent (thereby gaining 25 seats in the 179-member parliament and remaining the third largest political party in Denmark).

Danish People's Party

Since 2001, the DPP has positioned itself within the governing coalition. It does not have any ministers in the centre-right government, but given its hard-line stance on immigration, its opposition to multiculturalism and its unsympathetic attitude to Islam and Muslims during the cartoon controversy of 2006, it has insisted that, as a condition for its support, the government must act tough on issues related to nationality. And the executive has delivered, passing strict laws on immigration, tightening the asylum legislation and making it more difficult for Danish citizens to bring their foreign spouses into the country.

The party is hostile to the EU and its attacks on national sovereignty, and also believes in a small-state approach to taxation. As it says: 'The aim of the Danish People's Party is to assert Denmark's independence, to guarantee the **freedom** of the Danish people in their own country and to preserve and promote representative government and the monarchy. We are bound by our Danish cultural heritage and our responsibility towards each other as a people. For this reason, we wish to strength our country's internal and external security'. It also supports the national church and the monarchy.

The DPP has been branded racist and xenophobic because of its doctrine and ideology, and Kjærsgaard did little to dispel this image in a speech to the Danish parliament in October 2001. 'It has been mentioned that [the terrorist attacks of] September 11 were the beginning of a fight between civilisations. I don't agree about this, because a fight between civilisations would imply that there were two civilisations, and that is not the case. There is only one civilisation, and that is ours. Our opponents can't plead to belong to a civilisation, because a civilised world would never be able to carry out an attack which contains so much hatred, so much savagery, so much abomination. With this, I regard September 11 as an attack on civilisation itself. On the civilisation which decent people have built up during decades and centuries, and which is based on uprightness and freedom. The others want to implement ferocity, the primitive, the barbaric, the medieval'.

Most experts interpret the DPP as part of a wave of right-wing populism in **Scandinavia**. The Progress Party in Norway is not dissimilar in policies and political style and, independently, the two parties appear to have created an unusual blend of welfarism and anti-immigrant nationalism that has proved popular at the ballot box.

The DPP also has political daring. Only months after the cartoon controversy, the party unveiled a new advert for the 2007 elections. It read: 'Freedom of speech is Danish, censorship is not. We defend Danish values'. And Kjærsgaard justified it by saying that it was 'part of an election campaign centring on Danish values, which we want to push forward. Among them are gender equality and solidarity. The ad clearly falls under the issue of freedom of expression'.

According to one statement from the European Network Against Racism, Denmark has evolved almost overnight from a tolerant to a racist society, and one in which the DPP is happy to promulgate its slogan: 'Denmark for the Danes'. But Kjærsgaard is unrepentant and there is every sign that her party is here to stay.

See also Danish People's Party; Kjaersgaard, Pia (Denmark) *and* Scandinavia and the Far Right.

Further Reading

http://www.danskfolkeparti.dk (Danish People's Party website).
Arter, David. 1999. *Scandinavian Politics Today*. Manchester: Manchester University Press.
Andersen, J.G. 1994. 'Denmark: the Progress Party – populist neo-liberalism and welfare state chauvinism'. In *The Extreme Right in Europe and the USA*. Edited by Paul Hainsworth. London: Pinter.

Andersen, J.G. & Bjørklund, T. 2000. 'Radical right-wing populism in Scandinavia: from tax revolt to neo-liberalism and xenophobia'. In *The Politics of the Extreme Right: From the Margins to the Mainstream*. Edited by Paul Hainsworth. London: Pinter.

Danish People's Party, Growth of (2001–2005)

In November 2001, the far-right Danish People's Party (*Dansk Folkeparti*, DPP) claimed twenty-two parliamentary seats in national elections. The DPP became the third strongest party in Denmark, significantly building on the thirteen seats the party won in the 1998 election. The 2001 poll also marked the entry into government of a right-wing coalition, pledged to tightening **immigration**, led by Anders Fogh Rasmussen. Four years later, in February 2005, Rasmussen's coalition secured a second term in office, with the DPP netting two additional seats and increasing their share of the vote from 12 percent to 13.3 percent.

In the aftermath of the election, the leader of the DPP, Pia **Kjaersgaard**, stated: 'The last three and a half years have shown that we have the most influence doing things as we have done.' Indeed, between 2001 and 2005, the effect of the DPP's anti-immigration agenda had been felt. In 2003, 5,000 **family** reunification permits were granted, a notable 8,000 fewer than in 2001. Meanwhile, the number of successful asylum applications to Denmark also fell, from 31 percent in 2000 to 9 percent in 2003. To gain some sense of comparison, in the same period, the statistics regarding immigration for Sweden and Norway increased.

Unsurprisingly, Denmark's new found hard line on immigration has done nothing for intra-Scandinavian harmony. Indeed, the Swedish government in particular was quick to criticise the drift of Danish policy. Meanwhile, Kjaersgaard was certainly willing to vociferously argue her case. Of the Swedes she said: 'If they want to turn Stockholm, Gothenburg or Malmoe into a Scandinavian Beirut, with clan wars, honour killings and gang rapes, let them do it'.

See also Danish People's Party, Growth of (2001–2005); Kjaersgaard, Pia (Denmark) *and* Scandinavia and the Far Right.

Further Reading

Givens, Terri, E. 2005. *Voting Radical Right in Western Europe*. Cambridge: Cambridge University Press.
Ignazi, Piero. 2003. *Extreme Right Parties in Western Europe*. New York: Oxford University Press.

Degrelle, Léon (1906–1994) - Belgium

Degrelle was a charismatic Belgian fascist leader whose influence straddled both the pre-1945 and post-1945 eras. A hard-line integral Catholic, Degrelle was eventually ex-communicated by the Vatican for wearing a fascist uniform in church. He founded the Rex movement in 1936 and suffered a disastrous by-election defeat in April 1937; following this, Rex underwent a process of 'Nazification' and during the war he led the SS Walloon Brigade on the Eastern Front.

Born in 1906 in Bouillon, a small town in the Belgian Ardennes, his **family** was of French origin. After studying at a Jesuit college, Degrelle began a law degree at the University of Louvain, before leaving to become a journalist for the conservative Roman Catholic *Christus Rex*. During this time, he became interested in the integralist ideas of the French royalist thinker, Charles Maurras. In the early 1930s, he was a correspondent in Mexico during the Cristero War, which pitted Catholic (*Cristero*) and anti-clerical forces against each other. After returning to Belgium, he formed the *Éditions de Rex* and led a militant tendency inside the Catholic Party. In 1935, after causing increasing friction with the party's mainstream, his 'Rexist' group split to form the Parti Rexiste.

7. Léon Degrelle, on his return from the Russian Front. Belgium, April 1943.

Degrelle led the Parti Rexiste, which demanded radical political reform, the establishment of an authoritative corporative state of social justice and national unity. The party was essentially fascist and anti-communist. It drew its major support from Wallonia, and had a Flemish counterpart in the Vlaamsch Nationaal Verbond. The Rexists found a degree of political success in the 1936 elections, capturing 11.5 percent of the vote and twenty-one parliamentary seats. In the same year, Degrelle met with Mussolini and Hitler, who both agreed to provide financial support for the party. As a result, the Rexists added Nazi-style **anti-Semitism** to their political agenda; Degrelle also established links with other European fascist leaders, meeting with, among others, the Spaniard Jose Antonio Primo de Rivera and the Romanian Corneliu Zelea Codreanu. However, by the end of the 1930s, the popularity of the Rexists was in decline. In the 1939 elections the party won only four seats in the Belgium parliament.

Following the German invasion of Belgium, Degrelle was arrested as a collaborator and evacuated to France, only to be released by the Germans when their occupation began. He returned to Belgium and proclaimed that reconstructed Rexism was in union with the Nazis, despite a group of party members who were actively fighting against the Germans. Degrelle also began contributing to the Nazi propaganda newspaper *Le Pays Réel*. In 1941, following the German invasion of the Soviet Union, Degrelle formed a volunteer battalion of fellow Walloons to engage in what he saw as a pan-European crusade to crush **Communism**. He joined and began fighting as a private, before rising through the ranks to become commander of what finally came to be known as the 28th SS Division 'Wallonia'. He excelled in this role and was duly rewarded by Hitler.

At the end of the war, he took refuge in Spain where he arrived, with the help of the ODESSA network, on a plane provided by Hitler's former minister of armaments, Albert Speer. He was sheltered from extradition by **Franco** and in 1954 obtained Spanish citizenship, with false papers, as José León Ramírez Reina. In the post-war era, he was active in the neo-Nazi and Barcelona-based Círculo Español de Amigos de Europa (CEDADE), and continued to publish his own writings, which promoted neo-fascist ideology and also sought to question the **Holocaust**. He was brought to trial in Spain after publishing an *Open Letter* to Pope John Paul II on the concentration camp at Auschwitz and, after initially being cleared, he was found to have brought offence to the memory of the victims and was fined by the Supreme Court of Spain. He also wrote *Hitler: Born at Versailles*, the first in a planned series of works entitled *The Hitler Century*, which was published by the Institute for Historical Review in 1987.

Degrelle died in Malaga, Spain, on 1 April 1994 at the age of eighty-seven. As Eddy de Bruyne and Marc Rikmenspoel have shown, a plethora of small nationalist and fascist groups emerged in Belgium during the inter-war period. But the Rexists became the most prominent. **Degrelle** himself was unique: a man who had contact with Hitler and who also went on to become a mainstay of the post-war Far Right up to the 1990s.

See also Campaign in Russia: The Waffen SS on the Eastern Front by Léon Degrelle (Belgium); Flemish Bloc, Disbandment (2004) *and* Flemish Bloc/Flemish Interest.

Further Reading
Fields, E.R. 2005. *Léon Degrelle and the Rexist Party 1935–1940*. Spearhead.
de Bruyne, Eddy & Rikmenspoel, Marc. 2004. *For Rex and for Belgium: Léon Degrelle and Walloon Political and Military Collaboration 1940–45*. London: Helion and Company Ltd.
Conway, Martin. 1993. *Collaboration in Belgium: Léon Degrelle and the Rexist Movement, 1940–44*. New Haven, CT: Yale University Press.
Husbands, Christopher T. 1994. 'Belgium: Flemist legions on the march'. In *The Extreme Right in Europe and the USA*. Edited by Paul Hainsworth. London: Pinter.
Swyngedouw, Marc. 2000. 'Belgium: explaining the relationship between *Vlaams Blok* and the city of Antwerp'. In *The Politics of the Extreme Right: From the Margins to the Mainstream*. Edited by Paul Hainsworth. London: Pinter.

Democracy

Modern far-right movements generally have an ambivalent attitude towards democracy. On the whole, they uphold the concept in glowing terms, especially the more recent wave of neo-populist, far-right parties such as the **French National Front** (*Front National*, FN), the **British National Party** (BNP), and **Swiss People's Party** (*Schweizerische Volkspartei*, SVP). However, the lingering presence of neo-Nazism across the continent, typified by groups such as Combat 18 (C18) in Britain, demonstrates that not all far-right ideologues have converted to democratic methods.

According to many of their statements, members of the newer, populist, far-right parties are 'democrats' and they believe in 'democracy' and the 'democratic process'. Some even make reference to the idea in their official title – for example, the Liberal Democratic Party (*Liberal'no-Demokraticheskaya Partiya Rossii*, LDPR) in **Russia**.

Others speak passionately about the concept. For example, **Flemish Interest** (*Vlaams Belang*, VB) in Belgium says that it, 'believes that democracy and the rule of law are the best safeguards for personal **freedom**'. Meanwhile, the BNP has argued that its views are a vital component of the principle of a marketplace of ideas. However, because the contemporary political and cultural climate in Britain is governed by an allegedly oppressive political correctness, these views are stifled and remain unheard – surely destructive of a true democratic ideal, according to BNP thinking. Further, the party argues that Britain is the originator of modern democracy, claiming this tradition stretches back to the freedoms enjoyed in previous eras by the nation's Nordic, Anglo-Saxon and Celtic ancestors. Demonstrating the alleged state of decadence of modern Britain, then, according to the BNP, the modern British state is destructive of true democracy – a concept that the party maintains is the birthright of the British people. Indeed, this truth can only be revealed through an acceptance of the BNP's ideological reading of history and critique of contemporary politics.

Likewise, the **British National Front** (NF) argues that it is a genuine democratic party. It is critical of both houses of parliament in Britain, claiming the House of Commons should place greater power in selecting Committees, while the House of Lords should remove any lingering hereditary principles and be reformed into a more effective revising chamber. It also highlights its own internal working in this regard, arguing that unlike Britain's mainstream parties its policies are developed by its members at annual conferences, and these decisions are binding. Further, members of its upper echelons are all elected to their positions. Finally, the party is an advocate of proportional representation, stressing that this is a fairer means of representing the political will of the British people. However, the suspicion remains high regarding the validity of these types of arguments, positions on democracy that are recapitulated across **Europe** by other far-right movements. Reading between the lines, such assertions ultimately appear shallow, and should only really be viewed as the 'window dressing' for a more authoritarian style of politics.

Finally, it is worth noting how, in recent years, the Far Right has been able to claim many successes within Europe's democratic political culture; for example: the rise of the FN in France, from **Dreux** in 1983 to the 2002 presidential campaign; the growing political importance of the **Northern League** (*Lega Nord*, LN) and the **National Alliance** (*Alleanza Nazionale*, AN) in Italy, including Ganfranco **Fini** holding the Deputy Prime Minister post; the successes and notoriety of Jörg **Haider**'s **Austrian Freedom Party** (*Freiheitliche Partei Österreichs*, FPÖ); the **growth of the Danish People's Party** (*Dansk Folkeparti*, DPP), which has become a key player in the country's ruling coalition from 2001; the advance of the **Norwegian Progress Party** (*Framstegspartiet*, FrP), which has achieved a high level of success at national elections, making it a key voice in the country's political dynamic; **Flemish Interest** (*Vlaams Belang*, VB) has a large popular base in Flanders, allowing it to return members to the Belgian Chamber of Representatives, the Belgian Senate and the Flemish Parliament; Christoph **Blocher**'s **Swiss People's Party** (*Schweizerische Volkspartei*, SVP) has altered the political landscape in Switzerland in recent years; and in Russia, Zhirinovsky's LDPR scored very highly in the 1993 elections. Further, the Far Right can now claim many members of the European Parliament. For example, in 2007 this presence led to the brief existence of an official group in the EU parliament dedicated to far-right issues: the **Identity, Tradition and Sovereignty Group**.

See also The Development of the Far Right; The Ideology of the Far Right *and* The Origins of the Far Right.

Further Reading

Givens, Terri E. 2005. *Voting Radical Right in Western Europe*. Cambridge: Cambridge University Press.

Norris, Pippa. 2005. *Radical Right: Voters and Parties in the Electoral Market*. Cambridge: Cambridge University Press.

Denazification Laws (1946–1947)

The Denazification Laws of 1946–1947 were a profoundly important moment in the war against all forms of right-wing extremism and racialism in the aftermath of 1945. In essence, the laws made it difficult, at least in the short-term, for far-right movements to emerge again in **Europe**. Germany and Austria were the main countries affected by the legislation, but other countries were also involved. The laws were aimed at all sections of society, and included within their compass both individuals and groups. Of course, their primary objective was to eradicate every trace of Nazi influence. The directives were issued by the Allied Control Council and commenced in January 1946. Clearly, there were going to be logistical difficulties in implementing the laws, and it would probably be fair to say that they were put into practice unevenly across the various zones in Germany and elsewhere.

In short, the laws forbade post-1945 Nazis from expressing their beliefs in public, and prohibited them from creating movements that were capable of disseminating their ideas. In time, the physical symbols of Nazism would be removed, and so displaying the swastika and other Nazi imagery would become punishable by up to one year in prison. It was an ambitious, yet arguably vitally necessary, campaign. However, commentators have not been kind when assessing the successes of the laws. Brigitte Bailer-Galanda and Wolfgang Neugebauer claim that the programme to purge state institutions and the civil society of Nazi sympathies was beset by two problems. Firstly, they highlight that the sheer scale of the denazification was so vast that it was unlikely ever to succeed as planned. Secondly, they also stress that the Allies' administration of the programme was weighed down by many bureaucratic shortcomings. Most tellingly, they highlighted that failures could be easily spotted, simply because ex-Nazi party members had not been 'purged' of their views, and for the most part, their behaviour and prejudices remained intact. Furthermore, by 1949 they note that a new electorate came into existence: the 500,000 people registered as Nazis in 1945 who were disenfranchised immediately after the war. The size and sympathies of this new electorate was certainly a factor that post-war German parties could not disregard. The idea, then, that Nazi sympathies could be stopped immediately after the end of the war is largely a myth.

In a similar vein, Brandi M. McCary has argued that, following the war, the Allies put in place a systematic programme of re-**education** for the German people. This ambitions project soon ran into difficulties when they realised that it would be too impractical to exclude all ex-Nazis from the state apparatus and German society. Further, from the early 1950s onwards, aside from the most high-ranking Nazi officials, many ex-Nazis returned to their former roles, although most were loyal to the new government. Of course, some ex-Nazis remained firmly committed to their Nazi viewpoints and could not re-adjust to the new regime. Finally, it is worth noting that the Nuremburg Trials were another important aspect of the denazification of Germany – as Donald Bloxham has demonstrated. Not only did the trials have a direct goal of punishing key Nazis, they also were intended to help re-educate German society, revealing the true horrors of Nazism.

See also Central Europe and the Far Right *and Mein Kampf* by Adolf Hitler (Germany).

Further Reading

Bloxham, Donald. 2001. *Genocide on Trial: War Crimes Trials and the Formation of Holocaust History and Memory*. New York: Oxford University Press.
Thacker, Toby. 2006. *The End of the Third Reich: Defeat, Denazification and Nuremberg January 1944–November 1946*. Stroud: NPI Media Group.

Diorama Letterario Magazine (Italy)

Diorama Letterario is a Florence-based magazine of the right. It was edited by Marco Tarchi, a political scientist based at the University of Florence with an interest in concepts of revolution and ecology. Tarchi was an ex-member of the neo-fascist MSI and had also befriended the separatist **Northern League**. He also had close links with GRECE, a French new right organisation, and Alain de Benoist, the main ideologue of the French Nouvelle Droite. According to one writer, *Diorama Letterario* is 'one of the foremost organs behind the rethinking of neo-fascist ideology in the 1970s and 80s'.

See also Southern Europe and the Far Right.

Further Reading

Gallagher, Tom. 2000. 'Exit from the ghetto: the Italian far right in the 1990s'. In *The Politics of the Extreme Right: From the Margins to the Mainstream*. Edited by Paul Hainsworth. London: Pinter.
Sidoti, Francesco. 1992. 'The extreme right in Italy: ideological orphans and countermobilisation'. In *The Extreme Right in Europe and the USA*. Edited by Paul Hainsworth. London: Pinter.

Dreux (France)

Dreux, a small town on the edge of the Paris region, was led by a left-wing alliance in the 1970s and early 1980s. In terms of demography, the town was largely comprised of unskilled labourers living in public housing, but Dreux had also experienced rising levels of non-French migration in the 1970s. Indeed, by the early 1980s, **immigration** accounted for around 30 percent of the town's population. Into this climate stepped Jean-Pierre Stirbois, a close associate of Jean-Marie **Le Pen**. Stirbois quickly began to develop a **National Front** (*Front National*, FN) presence in the town, largely based on anti-immigration policies.

The success of this campaign bore fruit from 1982 onwards. In the cantonal elections in March of that year, the FN national average was a meagre 0.2 percent, whereas in Dreux West and Dreux East, the FN polled 12.58 and 9.58 respectively. In the local municipal elections the following year, the FN still polled a significant quantity of the vote, leading the Rally for the Republic (*Rassemblement pour la République*, RPR) and the Union for French **Democracy** (*Union pour la Démocratie Française*, UDF) to form a coalition with the FN. This coalition was narrowly defeated by the left-wing candidate. However, due to the electoral rules, this defeat was not by a significant enough margin for the left-wing candidate to claim victory. In the subsequent re-run of the election, Stirbois gained 16.7 percent of the vote in the first round, and so once again in the second round, the RPR and the UDF proposed an alliance with the FN. In this second round of the re-run municipal election, Stirbois actually won, thereby causing a major shift in French political thinking, both regarding the Far Right itself and regarding the more moderate right that had been tempted to form a coalition with the FN.

Meanwhile, this highly-significant election victory elevated the fortunes of the FN. Their new found power was met with massive media interest, allowing the movement to present its platform to a far-wider audience. Also, many among the more radically-inclined, conservative voters could now look to the FN and see a party that could claim genuine electoral credibility. A poll taken in early 1984 saw the FN opinion poll rating rise from 3.5 percent to 7 percent. The FN also received greater hostility from the radical left following the Dreux victories. As with hostile media coverage, these attacks probably had the opposite effect than the intended one. The very fact that the FN had been able to upset the radical left made it appear more appealing to potential supporters of Le Pen's brand of populist, ultra-nationalist anti-intellectualism.

See also Le Pen, Jean-Marie (France); National Front (France) *and* Western Europe and the Far Right.

Further Reading
Davies, Peter. 1999. *The National Front in France: Ideology, Discourse and Power*. New York: Routledge.
Kitschelt, Herbert. 1997. *The Radical Right in Western Europe: A Comparative Analysis*. Michigan: University of Michigan Press.

E

Economy

It is notoriously difficult to identify general patterns in the way that far-right movements have approached economic matters, and in recent decades, far-right movements have tended to be pragmatic in their attitude to the economy. Indeed, unlike the Far Left, which is often based on Marxist notions of revolution, the Far Right does not oppose capitalism in the same concise fashion. Rather, it tends to latch onto whatever economic policies appear to fit most succinctly its own agenda. Given the fact that most far-right parties have been permanently in opposition, often the economy has been a useful stick with which to beat the government of the day. Also, many far-right leaders have the luxury of knowing that it is unlikely that their ideas on the economy would ever be put to the test. This lack of an ideological predisposition to a particular economic perspective, alongside the strong impetus to oppose the government of the day, allows a great deal of malleability in far-right discussions on economics.

Economy

When we look at the origins of what could be described as the two most prominent far-right parties – the **Front National** (*Front National*, FN) in France and the **Freedom Party** (*Freiheitliche Partei Österreichs*, FPÖ) in Austria – we see that they both started life as parties inclined towards the free market and unfettered capitalism. In the 1990s, they evolved into movements that campaigned for greater regulation of markets and state intervention, especially where policies of controlling **immigration** and creating jobs were concerned. Meanwhile, in Italy, two-thirds of **National Alliance** (*Alleanza Nazionale*, AN) supporters favour the capitalist system, and in Sweden the Swedish Democrats (*Sverigedemokraterna*, SD) remain committed to the free-market approach. They argue that SD policies will help both entrepreneurs and small businesses, claiming that growth in this sector of the economy is central to the nation's future economic prosperity. By incentivising this growth through simpler taxation codes and lower rates of tax, alongside reduced bureaucracy, the SD argues that it can reduce unemployment and shore up the country's welfare state. The National Democratic Party (*Nationaldemokratische Partei Deutschlands*, NPD) in Germany has developed an alternative strategy. Its slogans have included, 'People's Economy – Yes! Globalisation – No!' Also, the party has even attacked employers and bosses and claimed that: 'The cartels of private interest have taken control of the state and betrayed the people'.

Another theme evident on the Far Right is economic nationalism. This doctrine says that all economic measures should be executed with the 'higher interests' of the nation in mind. In France, the FN have used this idea to justify preference-based polices that have favoured French nationals over immigrants. In Germany, the NPD has railed against the policy of recruiting information technology specialists from India. Likewise, the **British National Front** (NF) has also made statements based on this thinking. It argues that, should it attain power, the NF would take a radical approach to restoring prosperity to the nation. This sweeping programme would place at its core, the restriction of imports and the promotion of goods made in Britain. Destroying London's status as one of the key financial capitals of the world, speculation on the Stock Exchange would be eliminated, and hefty tariffs would be introduced to restrict imports. Through a policy of encouraging **workers** to take direct control of the workplace, reinvestment in British economy would also be encouraged. Finally, the party suggests that taxation could be drastically lowered through efficiency measures, and by reducing foreign expenditure. This belt-tightening includes cutting payments to the **European Union** and foreign aid, combined with an end to the 'race relations industry'. The British NF, then, blends a left-wing, syndicalist-style tenor of worker control over industry with far-right, ultra-nationalist ideology.

Unsurprisingly, then, some far-right statements on the economy have been ridiculed for their simplistic nature and utopianism. Parties like the FN in France alongside the **German People's Union** (*Deutsche Volksunion*, DVU) and the **Republican Party** (*Republikaner*, REP) in Germany have used the same tactic of eliding economic concerns with issues of race and immigration. In France, the following slogan typifies the FN attitude: 'Three million unemployed is three million immigrants too many'. Meanwhile, in Germany one reads: 'Send back 4 million immigrants and take 4 million off the dole'. Such slogans have reminded many commentators of the Nazi approach to economic nationalism in the 1930s. Meanwhile, if we turn to the 2001 programme of the Liberal Democratic Party (*Liberal'no-Demokraticheskaya Partiya Rossii*, LDPR) in **Russia**, we find that this document incorporates a hotchpotch of economic policies, which is worth quoting at some length: 'To enhance the functions of state control and management of economic processes [...] To restore Russia's economic sovereignty [...] To give an opportunity to everyone who wants to work and is capable of working to bring his talents into play and get worthy pay for good work [...] Land must belong to those who till it. Farm lands must be used only for efficient production of farm produce. The state should retain control over farm lands [...] To conduct state programme of employment, to retrain the workers released, to create jobs in small business and in the sphere of services [...] A clear-cut state programme of the production and sale of military hardware and weapons must be worked out [...] An all-round economic amnesty must be declared'. Here, **Zhirinovsky** embraces greater state control as a panacea for Russia's economic problems. However, arguably this contradicts the idea of liberalism enshrined in his party's name.

Finally, it is worth noting the role of successful businessmen in the recent successes of the Far Right. Though more centre-right in his political views, Silvio Berlusconi's stewardship of the Italian Far Right has undoubtedly allowed it to grow into a significant political force. Another example of a successful businessman turning to the Far Right can be found in Switzerland. Before leading the **Swiss People's Party** (*Schweizerische Volkspartei*, SVP) to electoral successes in recent years, Christoph **Blocher** made his fortune by turning around the Chemical firm Ems-Chemie. From the British NF's desire to abolish the Stock Exchange to Blocher's successful background in board room negotiations, then, the approaches to economic matter within the family of ideologies that are categorised as Far Right are highly diverse.

See also The Ideology of the Far Right and Workers.

Further Reading
Ignazi, Piero. 2003. *Extreme Right Parties in Western Europe*. New York: Oxford University Press.
Mudde, Cas. 2000. *The Ideology of the Extreme Right*. Manchester: Manchester University Press.

Education

Like all movements with political ambitions, the Far Right views education as a crucial battleground. The idea of changing school curricula so that they articulate a pro-far-right understanding of national identity and citizenship is a key theme within these discussions on education. As with many far-right ideals, it is difficult to make too many sweeping generalisations on the topic of education because each far-right interpretation of its national history holds numerous unique aspects and traditions. However, a far-right reinterpretation of national education policies often involves an attempt to radicalise, for ultra-nationalist ends, the educational standards of the nation in question. Also, the Far Right's interest in education policy correlates to their general interest in **youth**. Indeed, the Far Right would not be the first political faction to realise that individuals are at their most impressionable and malleable when they are young.

In France, Jean-Marie **Le Pen** has argued that all 'left-wing' text-books should be withdrawn, so that they can be replaced by more 'politically reliable' volumes. For him, French children should not be being 'brainwashed' with a '1789-centric' view of the world. Instead, the great national glories should be being passed down from generation to generation. In essence, then, education should be 'nationalised' in the sense that

French children should learn about the greatness of France, allowing them to connect with their national 'roots'.

Parties in other countries have articulated the need for a greater culture of pragmatism within educational standards. For example, the **Danish People's Party** (*Dansk Folkeparti*, DPP) has stated that it places at the core of its education ideals the development of what it calls 'useful knowledge', and that it has a high regard for all education, both teaching and research. Further, it considers technical training as a matter of equal importance as academic qualifications, because both are vital aspects of the skills base of the country. Moreover, like the FN and many other far-right positions on education, the DPP argues that all school pupils should be given a comprehensive understanding of Danish culture, history and values. This too is a seen as 'useful knowledge' by the DPP because an appreciation of Danishness lies at the core of a stable society.

8. Deputy Prime Minister and Minister of Education Roman Giertych speaking to journalists during a briefing about compulsory reading materials, 1 June 2007, Warsaw, Poland.

Meanwhile, in Britain, the **British National Party** (BNP) believes that the nation's educational standards have declined rapidly in recent years. Therefore, it takes a hard-line stance in order to improve standards and create a more unified society. The party has argued for a four point programme of reform for education. Firstly, it claims that it would retrain all teachers, in order to eliminate egalitarian views and anti-British dogmas that are supposedly at the core of the nation's educational problems. In its place, the party would instil in the outlook of all teachers the core BNP values of respect of British culture, excellence, and a belief in competition via this programme. Secondly, in a nod to more traditionally-minded Conservative Party voters, it proposes offering grammar schools to all communities that request one. Thirdly, in another throwback to a previous era, the BNP promises to re-introduce old-style 'O' and 'A' levels, ensuring they are conducted in a more rigorous manner than the current GCSE and 'A' Level exams. Fourthly, the party would ban all teaching aids and attempt to restore educational standards to the levels it argues existed in a previous era. World history and cultural studies would be replaced with an emphasis on the histories and cultures of the British nations, England, Wales, Scotland and Ireland. Further, the party would, as it puts it, 'prohibit all curricular pandering to the cultures of immigrants'.

Across **Europe**, then, the Far Right uses discussions on education as a vehicle for its own, wider ideals. A restored sense of nationalism lies at the core of this debate, and far-right policies tend to promote national histories and cultural identities. Further, it uses extant standards in education as a stick to beat the government of the day, implying that its own radical reforms are the only way to restore standards and return a sense of national greatness.

See also The Ideology of the Far Right.

Further Reading:

Hainsworth, Paul, ed. 2000. *The Politics of the Extreme Right: From the Margins to the Mainstream.* London: Pinter.

Ignazi, Piero. 2003. *Extreme Right Parties in Western Europe.* New York: Oxford University Press.

Kitschelt, Herbert. 1997. *The Radical Right in Western Europe: A Comparative Analysis.* Michigan: University of Michigan Press.

Empire Europe (Malta)

The Maltese party, Empire **Europe** (*Imperium Europa*) was founded in 1981. Led by Norman Lowell, it aims, rather grandly, to unite all European peoples under one flag. This is envisaged as a spiritual and racial awakening. The party is open about its white supremacist philosophy. Its slogan is 'The Lightning and the Sun - Action with Vision within a Racial context' and it goes on to state: 'Our aim is that Malta, this Sacred Island of Melita, this land of honey, will be the first liberated nation in the whole, White World – liberated from the enemy within and the enemy without'.

In 2004, Empire Europe scored 0.64 percent in European elections. Its vision for Europe is a product of historical and cultural analysis: 'The idea of Imperium Europa is gaining increasing attention at the highest cultural and political levels. An Imperium based on that of the Holy Roman Empire, with a central authority, embodying both the Political and the Spiritual. A centre, to which all the White World will refer and relate to. A hub, whereby all parts of the Empire would feel organically whole, while retaining the specific peculiarity of each region. Retaining initiative, diversity, interaction, castes, classes, character, personality, hierarchy: all converging to a superior idea. A common language will bind us all: Latin'. It seems that this new empire will be led by a new (pan-Aryan) aristocratic meritocracy – maybe 250,000 individuals across the continent. And Lowell clings to the belief that 2012 will be the date when his dreams turn into reality. He is regularly labelled a 'racist' and a 'neo-Nazi', but he has challenged all such accusations.

See also Southern Europe and the Far Right.

Further Reading

http://www.imperium-europa.org (Empire Europe website).

England, Race Riots in the North (2001)

Three towns in northern England were hit by race riots in the summer of 2001. **Oldham**, in Greater Manchester, was the first town to descend into **violence**. After a period of tension, things came to a head in late May when fifteen police officers were injured and seventeen local people were arrested after clashes between white and Asian youths. The district of Glodwick witnessed the worst of the rioting: buildings were set alight and the local police described the situation as 'sheer carnage'. The following month **Burnley**, in Lancashire, saw similar scenes, and the town hit the headlines. Again, white and Asian youths were involved in street skirmishes, with vehicles and local properties found themselves in the firing line. By July, the violence had spread to the Manningham area of **Bradford**, with more than 200 people injured and 36 people arrested. Here, the fault-line involved police and Asian youths.

The relationship between the Far Right and the Summer of Hate became an issue of great controversy and poignancy. It would be difficult to claim that the Far Right in Britain, especially organisations such as the **British National Party** (BNP), actually *caused* the riots. Editor of Spiked-Online.com, Brendan O'Neill, concurred with this perspective. In 2002, he argued that it is too simplistic to suggest that the BNP directly brought rioting to the streets of Oldham and elsewhere in the summer of 2000. Rather, he highlights that other important factors need to be taken into account as well. Primarily, he stresses that recent policies of anti-racism promoted by the New Labour administration had led to a widespread culture that tended to view social problems through a racial lens. This increasingly confrontational backdrop had heightened the sense of social unease within Oldham – which, he argued, had actually been subject to various tensions between ethic groups from the Second World War onwards. Indeed, the growth of an Asian workforce that was specifically tied to the city's cotton mill industry in the post-war period was another factor to be taken into account. A skilled Asian labour force was recruited from Pakistan, India and Bangladesh, and these **workers** tended to work the later, less desirable shifts. They were among the first to be laid off as the industry fell into decline in the 1970s. This economic downturn left the Asian migrants isolated, and open to exploitation by right-wing politicians who could blame the economic problems faced by white families on the presence of an increasingly undesirable immigrant workforce. With this historical backdrop, it is easier to see how the Far Right 'stirred things up,' and acted as *agents provocateurs*. For example, in a climate of growing racial tension and economic stagnation, the Far Right could be seen as a significant force. From the party's perspective, the riots were a god-send, and it was natural and predictable that they would work hard to capitalise on the situation by heightening a sense of crisis. Consequently, it is highly significant that, as soon as rioting began, car-loads of BNP activists arrived in the towns affected.

Indeed, if we view the BNP as the embodiment of organised intolerance expressing hatred of otherness, then it is difficult not to realise that the growing sense of instability between ethnic minorities and native English communities were of great benefit to the BNP. The sense of crisis that was stoked up by the party allowed it to appear more significant in the eyes of many, leading to greater media coverage for the organisation. Again, such attention shored up the legitimacy of the BNP, as media commentators discussed the organisation in terms of the Far Right playing a significant role in the activities, thereby publicising its hard-line stance on immigrant communities. Meanwhile, the aggressive nativism at the core of much of the party's literature could feed off the riots, citing them as a clear example of the growing tensions generated by multicultural societies. Consequently, it is clear that the Far Right benefited substantially from the summer's political fallout. Typically, *Socialism Today* argued that the riots and the atmosphere they engendered had opened the door to greater far-right influence.

Meanwhile, the disturbances made news across the world. For example, CNN reported that the series of riots in northern English towns was leading to growing concerns over the influence of the Far Right, and highlighted the growing activity of the BNP and the National Front (NF) in these areas ahead of the disturbances. These racial tensions, it continued, were typical of the growing influence of the Far Right across **Europe**. Indeed, the **French National Front** (*Front National*, NF), the **Austrian Freedom Party** (*Freiheitliche Partei Österreichs*, FPÖ), the **Flemish Bloc** (*Vlaams Bloc*, VB) and Pia **Kjaersgaard**'s **Danish People's Party** (*Dansk Folkeparti*, DPP) were cited as contemporary examples of this trend. A generalised concern over **immigration** and basic fears of rising crime levels, then, were seen as the oxygen that was fuelling this new trend in European far-right politics. Even the *Washington Post* joined the debate. In July 2001, it reported on British troubles with the headline 'Party Stokes Racial Ire In Britain'.

Anti-fascist groups certainly saw the riots as a key staging-post in the history of the British Far Right. In July 2001, *Searchlight* put the spotlight on Oldham. Its analysis highlighted the fact that the BNP achieved the highest general election vote in its history in June 2001, with Nick **Griffin** claiming 16 percent in Oldham West and Royton. Elsewhere, in Oldham East and Saddleworth, Mick Tracey won 11 percent of the vote, while in Ashton-under-Lyne Roger Wood took 4.5 percent. In total, *Searchlight*'s report claimed that the BNP won 12,000 votes, and argued that, spurred on by these results, the BNP felt that it was emerging from the political wilderness, capitalising on rising racial tensions through a professional and effective campaign strategy. Listing some of the significant electoral achievements made by the party, the article also highlighted that the BNP took an average of 3.9 percent of the vote and was able to save its deposit in five of the seats that it contested, putting it in a strong position to make further advances at local council elections to be held the following May. The article also warned that the local breakdown revealed further disturbing trends: 'A crude look at the ward breakdown is even more alarming. According to one councillor present at the count, the BNP gained over 50 percent of the vote in Fitton Hill, home of the Fitton Hill Crew and the Oldham Irregulars. In the more affluent Chadderton ward, it is estimated that the BNP polled between 20 and 30 percent'.

See also Bradford, Burnley and Oldham (Great Britain); British National Party *and* Griffin, Nick (Great Britain).

Further Reading
Searchlight, 'BNP profiting from hate', http://www.searchlightmagazine.com/index.php?link=template&story=101 (cited 31 December 2007).
Eatwell, Roger. 2004. 'The extreme right in Britain: the long road to "modernisation"'. In . *Western Democracies and the New Extreme Right Challenge*. Edited by Roger Eatwell, & Cas Mudde. London: Routledge.

Environment

Whatever some movements may say, it is probably fair to suggest that the relationship between the Far Right and ecology is a pragmatic one. For decades, parties on the extreme-right cared little for conservation and environmentalism. Rather, they generally had a negative view regarding these matters. The Far Right used to link environmentally aware policies to the 'eco-left', and ridiculed socialist, communist and ecological movements for their fashionable posturing on green issues. Over the course of the last two decades, the Far Right has changed tack and now engages seriously with ecological questions, embracing green ideas in its policy platforms and manifestos.

In the early 1990s, the Front National (*National Front*, FN) in France set the scene by defining 'the earth' and 'the environment' as issues that all nationalists had to be conscious of; this was because, in the final analysis, the earth and the environment *were* the nation. The FN's rhetoric harked back to French right-wing ideologues such as Maurice Barrès. Indeed, Barrès's writings invoked phrases such as 'the earth and the dead' when defining the essence of 'Frenchness'. The environmental spin-doctors used by the FN also broadened out the definition of ecology. Crime, social disorder and **immigration** were now linked to ecology, and so the environment was not just a debate over the preservation of flowers and trees, but rather could be shifted to include detailed, ideologically loaded discussions about community and society.

The **British National Party** (BNP) has echoed this line of thinking. They have called themselves 'hard green' rather than 'green' to distinguish the party from what it dubs the 'irrational left'. The BNP has claimed that the party respects the scientific evidence for climate change, and believes that people must take responsibility for the environment. Further, these solutions must be economically viable ones. Property owners have rights that need to be respected, but they must also appreciate they have duties too; if owners of land and industrial installations pollute the environment, then they must take responsibility for this. Demonstrating their nationalist perspective on this issue, the BNP also argues that protection of the British environment needs to be conducted within the framework of national sovereignty. Therefore, it rejects the notion that environmental issues can be tackled by international organisations. Also, perhaps in a coded message flagging up issues of migration, it argues that the urban habitats occupied by people are of concern to the party's 'environmental' perspective. Meanwhile, the **National Front** (NF) says it has a 'proud record' of environmental campaigning. One NF statement asserts that, even before the Green Party existed, the NF had called for greater investment in the rail network, tighter regulation on the use of chemicals in farming, and cleaner rivers. Its policies on the environment include ensuring all urban areas are made more attractive, increasing green areas in urban environments, and encouraging office **workers** to live in the inner cities. In rural areas, it argues that it would rejuvenate village life, and improve public transport to more remote areas. Finally, the party would promote the use of renewable energy sources.

It has actually become quite normal, then, for far-right parties to play up their ecological concern in the present climate of debate on this issue. Some do this in quite genuine fashion, without necessarily making the nationalist link. For example, the **Danish People's Party** (*Dansk Folkeparti*, DPP) has stated that the party will work to make sure that future generations reap the rewards of a sustainable environment. Further, it states that the DPP is willing to work with both national and international organisations so as to ensure the world's natural resources are used in a responsible, sustainable way. Meanwhile, the Sweden Democrats (*Sverigedemokraterna*, SD) has argued against animal testing, claiming that the saving of human life does not justify this suffering. Also, environmental damage must be eliminated: 'Human activities that permanently harm nature must end. Sverigedemokraterna is a political party with an ecological philosophy'.

Overall, this new concern for ecology may or may not be authentic, but it does say a lot about the Far Right as a political tendency. Indeed, often Far Right campaigning on this issue does appear, at least in part, to be genuine. Of course, the issue is also seen through the lens of far-right critiques of immigration and the need to create idealised myths of national homelands. Consequentially, environmental issues are also very useful rhetorical tools for far-right politics. Further, stressing environmentalist credentials may help the Far Right move on from the single-issue status of parties solely concerned with immigration.

See also The Ideology of the Far Right.

Further Reading
Kitschelt, Herbert. 1997. *The Radical Right in Western Europe: A Comparative Analysis.* Michigan: University of Michigan Press.
Olsen, Jonathan. 1999. *Nature and Nationalism: Right-Wing Ecology and the Politics of Identity in Contemporary Germany.* London: Macmillan.

Europe

All far-right parties are nationalist in their outlook, but they also construct this nationalism within a wider context of European history and culture. On the one hand, this common European identity gives far-right nationalisms wider compatibility with each other, a sense of common community through a collective, European history. On the other hand, it also raises the issue of numerous historical conflicts, especially over disputed territories, such as the emotive issue of Transylvania among Hungarian and Romanian ultra-nationalists, or the South Tyrol question. The idea of Europe, alongside its history and cultures, then, is central to far-right constructions of national identity.

In recent years, the Far Right has manifested a powerful hostility to the **European Union** as it is presently constituted. Indeed, a rejection of the idea of full-blown European integration is a common characteristic of the Far Right across the continent. Consequently, no far-right party is happy with the EU of the early **twenty-first century**, and they tend to present the institution as destructive of national sovereignty. **Flemish Interest** (*Vlaams Belang*, VB) in Belgium talk about the party's critical approach to the EU, claiming it is overly bureaucratic and has a tendency to interfere with national sovereignty. Likewise, the **Austrian Freedom Party** (*Freiheitliche Partei Österreichs*, FPÖ) believes that the EU's policy of free movement between member nations would conflict with its own stance on **immigration**. Contrastingly, the Far Right also regularly contests European elections, and there are currently many far-right MEPs. This has even led to the formation of a short-lived formal group in 2007, the Identity, Sovereignty and Tradition Group. Previously, in the 1980s the more stable formal group, the Group of the European Right, also brought together far-right parties across Europe. Unsurprisingly, such cooperation leads to the far-right parties taking all the benefits and perks from the supposedly corrupt EU that such a high status entails.

9. European deputies of the Identity, Tradition and Sovereignty group, Bulgarian Slavi Binev, Russian Desislav Chukolov, Bulgarian Dimitar Stoyanov and Frenchman Bruno Gollnish in Strasbourg, 12 November 2007.

At bottom, this hostility to the EU is linked directly to the exaggerated nationalism of far-right movements. After all, the Far Right asks: how can nations become united cultural entities with their own common-sense immigration policies when the EU encroaches on a wide range of national government activity? The **British National Party** (BNP) is particularly worried about this issue. It paints an almost apocalyptic picture of the future, claiming the EU is an attempt to create a monolithic super-state. This new state would impose foreign rule on the British people, who would be deprived of their ability to elect a sovereign British government. For the party, such an eventuality would be alien to many British traditions, such as personal **freedom** and **democracy**. Ultimately, this development would also lead to nothing less than the destruction of the British nation and its people. Meanwhile, claiming to hold a vision of a Europe of sovereign nation-states, the Sweden Democrats (*Sverigedemokraterna*, SD) have a similar attitude: 'Keep Sweden's independence! European cooperation is a good thing, but the establishment of a new European superstate is not'. It also claims to act as a party counteracting the movement towards closer European links. The SD, then, would like more cooperation between Scandinavian and Baltic states, particularly in security and defence policy, but it does not want Sweden to become swamped by a federal Europe.

For the **French National Front** (*Front National*, FN) the solution is a '*Europe des Patries*' – that is, a Europe of strong, independent countries that are conscious of their historic role. There is no need for artificial unity, according to the French Far Right, just a firm belief in the superiority of European civilisation, especially when compared to eastern and Islamic civilisations. The National Front (NF) in Britain has a similar approach. Like the SD and the FN, it envisions a future Europe where sovereign nation states conduct friendly relations with each other, and where the potential for states to interfere in each other's national affairs, such as via the EU, has been eliminated. Through cultural and sporting links especially, the NF believes that a new sense of European community could be developed, one respectful of national identity and cultural diversity. Like the BNP and others, then, the NF rejects the supposed moves towards a European super-state. Typically, the NF would take Britain out of the EU. In Belgium, the **Flemish Interest** (*Vlaams Belang*, VB) make a link between the issues of immigration and Europe. If immigrants cannot accept the values and ideals that it believes that Europe stands for, then they should leave. Conflating legal and cultural issues, for the VB, includes complying with the laws of the land as well as adapting to the moral and cultural values of Europe. The latter includes equality between men and **women**, freedom of speech, democracy, and the separation of church and state. The party also argues that 'For those aliens and immigrants who reject, ignore or contest the above, a policy of repatriation will be implemented, through appropriate legislation regulating political asylum, nationality, security and expulsion. Illegal and criminal aliens must be repatriated'.

See also European Union; The Ideology of the Far Right; The Identity, Tradition and Sovereignty Group, Rise And Fall (2007) *and* Treaty of Maastricht (1992).

Further Reading

Cheles, Luciano, Ferguson, Ronnie and Vaughan, Michalina, eds. 1995. *The Far Right in Western and Eastern Europe*. London and New York: Longman.

Ignazi, Piero. 2003. *Extreme Right Parties in Western Europe*. New York: Oxford University Press.

Kitschelt, Herbert. 1997. *The Radical Right in Western Europe: A Comparative Analysis*. Michigan: University of Michigan Press.

European Union, Treaty of Maastricht (1992)

Officially called the 'Treaty on European Union', the Maastricht Treaty was signed in February 1992 by the then twelve member states of the European Union. The essence of the treaty was the agreement to work towards a new level of European cooperation. The long-term goals included the creation of a common currency and a single European Central Bank; working towards a common foreign policy; increased cooperation over domestic affairs; and developing the concept of Union Citizenship as a way to symbolise far-greater political unity between European member states. The treaty was notoriously difficult to realise, and has been controversial among all stripes of the political spectrum ever since. What relevance did this treaty have to the Far Right?

This is a deeply problematic issue, but some core points are as follows. Given the traditional emphasis of the Far Right on nationalism, national integrity and **patriotism**, the ideas of closer European integration and the establishment of some form of European Union were always going to be anathema. But why was the idea of closer ties between European states so objectionable from such an ideological perspective? After all, the Far Right often alludes to ideas of a common European heritage in its numerous permutations of European nationalism. Despite this sense of European identity, and no matter how many caveats about respecting national traditions and cultures were written into the treaty, in the opinion of far-right parties it could only lead to a dilution of senses of national identity. This was because the treaty would invariably concentrate more power in the hands of seemingly anonymous Brussels Eurocrats, and weaken the enforcement of national borders and frontiers. In short, it would replace national sovereignty with an allegedly corrupt and inefficient European bureaucracy, turning sovereign nation-states into a federal set of states. For the Far Right, then, the Maastricht Treaty was the total antithesis of far-right nationalism and nationalist thinking, which emphasises strict notions of national identity.

If we turn to the thinking of one of the great theorisers of late nineteenth-century French nationalism, and the man identified by American academic Robert Soucy as the 'first French fascist', we see that Maurice Barrès played heavily on the conceptual metaphor of walls in his work. A hundred years on, it looked like the Maastricht Treaty was going to pull down the walls separating the European nations, replacing them with a single homogenous creation, one that the Far Right regarded as an inauthentic political structure. This sense of national identity coming under attack is a key trope of far-right discourses, and so the Maastricht issue has allowed the Far Right across the EU to argue that national sovereignty has migrated to the Brussels parliament. This sort of hyperbolic over-stating of the EU's actual powers has also allowed far-right politicians to claim, in an ostensibly common-sense fashion, that decision-making should remain within the nation.

If we look at France in 1992, the main opponents of Maastricht were either situated on the Far Right or the traditional right, and typically their argument centred on national sovereignty. The treaty was such a *cause célèbre* that a dedicated political party emerged to fight it, headed by the French aristocrat Philippe de Villers. If we move on 13 years and turn to the more recent arguments and votes surrounding the new EU Constitution, in many ways it looked as if the Maastricht debate was being replayed in France. Further, French political scientist Pascal Perrineau has argued that the **National Front** (*Front National*, FN) played a decisive part in the victory of the *'Non'* vote. Indeed, he argued that victory for the *'Non'* campaign was impossible without the support of the far-right electorate.

In Austria and Denmark too, it was the Far Right who spearheaded the attack on greater European integration. Regarding the new EU Constitutional Treaty, one **British National Party** (BNP) commentator from Cornwall laments the fact that Gordon Brown will send the son of a 'Belgian Marxist', i.e. David Miliband, to sign the treaty. Other pages from its website detail how the Treaty of Lisbon will remove key aspects of British sovereignty, and the party stresses that a pro-EU perspective is also pro-dictatorship.

See also Europe *and* The Identity, Tradition and Sovereignty Group, Rise and Fall (2007).

Further Reading
Baun, Michael J. 1996. *An Imperfect Union: The Maastricht Treaty and the New Politics of European Integration.* Boulder, CO, Oxford: Westview.
Hainsworth, Paul, ed. 2000. *The Politics of the Extreme Right: From the Margins to the Mainstream.* London: Pinter.

F

Family

In many ways modern far-right parties reveal their ultra-conservative political philosophies on the question of the family. Generations of right-wingers and Fascists before them have upheld the family as the primary unit in society, and have usually defined it in traditional terms, i.e. husband and wife plus children. This view has emerged from the teachings of Christianity – undoubtedly a key reference point for many on the Far Right – and from the more pragmatic desire of encouraging population growth as a way to stave off alleged national decline. The latter theme, then, is seen by the movement's ideologues as an important precondition for national renewal, an issue that is vital for all patriotic ultra-nationalists.

In France during the Second World War, the Vichy leader Marshal Pétain used to hand out special prizes to mothers with large families in order to encourage others to procreate for the nation. Half a century on, the **French National Front** (*Front National*, FN) were issuing special greetings cards decorated with white babies. Also, in official party literature, the names of FN politicians and authors are habitually accompanied by the words 'father of three' or something similar, in order to highlight the proactive procreation of FN party members. **Flemish Interest** (*Vlaams Belang*, VB) in Belgium have also talked about a 'birth dearth'. In other European countries, where the exigencies of reproduction are less engrained in the national psyche, far-right parties, like traditional conservative parties, have preached about the intrinsic goodness of the family unit. For example, the **Danish People's Party** (*Dansk Folkeparti*, DPP) has claimed that it places the family at the core of Danish society, and that securing the intimate bonds between parents and children are vital to the future of the country.

In Britain too, the **National Front** (NF) has lauded the idea of the family. It argues that all evidence points to the fact that a happy nuclear family represents the ideal **environment** for the healthy development of children. Typical of far-right discourse, is the attempt to evoke a sense of moral decline in the modern world, and the FN argues that modern society is detrimental to the formation of happy family environments. In part, it blames the government's taxation and welfare policies, especially the lowering of family allowances. As a solution, the FN argues that it would increase the financial support for families, and offer free school meals to all children. It also states that it would promote a change in media attitudes toward the family, which it stresses currently present the family unit as irrelevant in the modern world. There is slightly more urgency in the tone adopted by the Sweden Democrats (*Sverigedemokraterna*, SD). The party argues 'Sweden needs families! The family is the key component in a healthy society, and the children are our future'. The SD promotes the idea of state intervention, such as encouraging higher levels of child birth. It also argues that the government should maintain subsidies for kindergartens and offer additional benefits for parents who bring up their children without kindergarten care.

If the family is 'natural' and 'good', practices such as abortion and **homosexuality** are seen in equally one-dimensional terms as 'unnatural' and 'bad' by the Far Right. The FN, for example, has labelled abortion 'anti-national' in the sense that it has had a negative effect on the nation's birth-rate. Likewise, using fascist-style argumentation, the party has vilified homosexuals and homosexuality as 'perverted' and 'wrong'. Controversially and provocatively, just as late-nineteenth century nationalists identified syphilis as a metaphor for national decline, so **Le Pen** and the FN have used AIDS as an analogy. For the FN, SIDA (the French translation of AIDS) equates to '*Socialisme, Immigration, Affairisme, Delinquence*'. The FN's position finds an echo with the NF in Britain. It argues that the right of **women** to have an abortion would cease under an NF administration: 'The modern-day trend of having an abortion to fulfil one's career would be ended under a National Front government.' it opines. The party argues that the 1967 Abortion Act represents a crime against humanity and that, save for extreme cases, abortion should be forbidden. Conflating issues, the statement then goes on to argue that the NF views homosexual and lesbian relationships as aberrant, and it would introduce laws that would ensure homosexuality and its promotion was forbidden.

See also Homosexuality *and* The Ideology of the Far Right.

Further Reading

Glennerster, Howard and Midgley, James, eds. 1991. *The Radical Right and the Welfare State: an International Assessment*. London: Harvester Wheatsheaf.
Ignazi, Piero. 2003. *Extreme Right Parties in Western Europe*. New York: Oxford University Press.
Kitschelt, Herbert. 1997. *The Radical Right in Western Europe: A Comparative Analysis*. Michigan: University of Michigan Press.

Figaro Magazine (France)

In the late 1970s and early 1980s, the magazine published by *Le Figaro* newspaper came to be noted for its interest in new ideas and theses emanating from the *Nouvelle Droite* in France. Louis Pauwels established the magazine in 1978 and he also edited its cultural pages. Soon, Pauwels invited Patrice de Plunkett, Yves Christen, Jean-Claude Valla, Christian Durante, Grégory Pons, and Michel Marmin, to join him at the paper. They were all members of GRECE – a new far-right think tank that had been founded in 1968. The leader of GRECE, Alain de Benoist, was also involved in influencing the political direction taken by the notoriously high-brow magazine. GRECE's association with it lasted until 1981.

See also Western Europe and the Far Right.

Further Reading

Shields, J. 2007. *The Extreme Right in France: From Pétain to Le Pen*. London and New York: Routledge.
Davies, Peter. 2002. *The Extreme Right in France, 1789 to the Present: From De Maistre to Le Pen*. London and New York: Routledge.
Hainsworth, Paul. 1992. 'The extreme right in post-war France: the emergence and success of the Front National'. In *The Extreme Right in Europe and the USA*. Edited by Paul Hainsworth. London: Pinter.

Fini, Gianfranco (b.1952) – Italy

Born in Bologna in 1952, Gianfranco Fini is leader of the Alleanza Nazionale (AN), a grouping that incorporates former members of the neo-fascist **Italian Social Movement** (MSI). He studied psychology at university and went on to become a journalist before entering parliament in 1983 and being elected leader of the MSI in 1987. Fini is generally regarded as a suave and ultra-modern political operator, as a man who is trying to move beyond the memory of Mussolini and create some kind of post-Fascist political alternative in Italy. The fact that he supports the Lazio soccer team and has an attractive wife, Daniela (although they are now separated), has also helped his political and media appeal.

Fini became head of the party's **youth** movement in 1977. In his formative years he viewed Giorgio Almirante, the founding father of the MSI, as his chief mentor. Fini was secretary of the MSI from the late 1980s and a former candidate for Mayor of Rome. His election as party leader in 1987 was a landmark. He beat his opponent Pino Rauti by 727 votes to 608. Rauti was much older than Fini and belonged to a different political generation with different influences (such as Julius Evola and the Italian New Right). The result gave Fini a mandate to rebrand the MSI and mould it in his own image, even though he would always have to deal with opposing factions within the party.

Later, Fini helped to incorporate the bulk of the MSI into the AN, which won 109 seats in the 1994 parliamentary elections (although he himself chose to stay out of government). Throughout, his aim has been to 'sell' the AN as a modern, mainstream political party and to make it a natural party of government. In so doing, he has tried to distance himself and his movement from the legacy of Mussolini. In 1992 and 1994 he lauded *Il Duce* as 'the greatest statesman of the twentieth century' and declared that 'Fascism has a tradition of honesty, correctness and good government'. But later he commented: 'I was born in 1952, I am a post-Fascist and I hope that Italy stops talking about Fascism and anti-Fascism. I have said, and I repeat, that Fascism made a mistake with its 1938 race laws. This had horrible consequences.' He has also made friendly gestures towards the Jewish community in Italy and in 1999 visited Auschwitz in a conciliatory move.

Early on in his political career, Fini put the emphasis on protest and opposing the status quo. Tom Gallagher argues that he was also known for his irredentist nationalism – for claiming that Istria and Dalmatia were Italian, even though they were formally provinces of the new Croatia and the new Slovenia. He now champions a blend of free-market ideas, traditional Catholic values (which means he is opposed to abortion), and a hard-line attitude to **law and order**. He is also committed to constitutional change and wants Italy to become a presidential republic. Although he has targeted the **immigration** issue as vital to the AN, he has tried to disassociate himself from the more radical and vulgar elements on the Italian right. Fini intended the fusion with the AN to signify the end of the MSI, although a hardcore of MSI supporters has remained.

Fini has worked hard to make his party electable and respectable in the eyes of other players on the French political scene. It is in this context that his alliance with Silvio Berlusconi and his Forza Italia party should be viewed. The two men became allies during the 1990s and Fini was eventually appointed deputy prime minister in Berlusconi's government of June 2001, and then foreign minister in 2004. They have key characteristics in common: they are both right-wing modernisers who have tried to distance themselves them the memory of Fascism and **anti-Semitism**. But it hasn't been easy. During the general strike of April 2002 – Italy's first in a generation – placards read 'Berlusconi + Fini = Mussolini'.

There is now serious debate about where Fini stands on the political spectrum. In 2001, British Conservative MEP Charles Tannock stated: 'Mr Fini has worked hard to transform his party into a mainstream party ... [He] has been recognised as a democrat.' Fini's great achievement is that he has updated his party, enhanced its respectability and held key government positions. The move away from Fascism has not been without its problems and difficulties, but it is one that Fini and his colleagues have been forced to make.

See also Freedom Alliance, Victory in Italian Elections (1994); Italian Social Movement/National Alliance *and* Southern Europe and the Far Right.

Further Reading

www.alleanzanazionale.it (AN website).

Gallagher, Tom. 2000. 'Exit from the ghetto: the Italian far right in the 1990s'. In *The Politics of the Extreme Right: From the Margins to the Mainstream*. Edited by Paul Hainsworth. London: Pinter.

Sidoti, Francesco. 1992. 'The extreme right in Italy: ideological orphans and countermobilisation'. In *The Extreme Right in Europe and the USA*. Edited by Paul Hainsworth. London: Pinter.

Chiarini, Roberto. 1991. 'The "Movimento Sociale Italiano": a historical profile'. In *Neo-Fascism in Europe*. Edited by Luciano Cheles, Ronnie Ferguson and Michalina Vaughan. London: Longman.

Cheles, L. 1991. '"Nostalgia dell'avvenire": the new propaganda of the MSI between tradition and innovation'. In *Neo-Fascism in Europe*. Edited by Luciano Cheles, Ronnie Ferguson and Michalina Vaughan. London: Longman.

Eatwell, Roger. 1996. *Fascism: A History*. London: Vintage.

Amyot, Grant & Verzichelli, Luca, eds. 2007. *End of the Berlusconi Era?* Oxford; New York, N.Y.: Berghahn Books.

Bufacchi, Vittorio & Burgess, Simon. 2001. *Italy Since 1989: Events and Interpretations*. New York: St. Martin's Press.

Mack Smith, Denis. 1997. *Modern Italy: A Political History*. New Haven, CT: Yale University Press.

Flemish Bloc, Disbandment (2004)

On 15 November 2004, Frank Vanhecke, MEP and the then chairman of the Flemish Bloc (*Vlaams Blok*, VB), circulated a letter to party leaders announcing that the party had been dispended by its party council. This was due to the declaration by the Supreme Court of Belgium that VB was a racist party. This action was deemed necessary, the letter continued, as under the Belgian Anti-Racism Act, every party member was now potentially open to prosecution. It also stressed that the party's funding had been undermined by the court's decision. All political parties in Belgium are funded primarily through the state, with strict legislation preventing large-scale funding for parties by private individuals and a ban on any funding from corporations. Problematically, the charge of racism could lead to a parliamentary majority voting to withhold VB funds. Finally, the letter flagged up the fact that 1,000 ex-members of VB had met in **Antwerp** in order to form a new party from the ashes of the old one: **Flemish Interest** (*Vlaams Belang*, VB). As a sign of political continuity between the two parties, the letter included the new party manifesto for Flemish Interest.

Subsequently, Filip Dewinter has admitted that the new party is essentially the same organisation as the old one, although with a few cosmetic changes that enable it to negotiate Belgian laws. 'The style and the propaganda have changed', he told the *Observer* newspaper, 'but we are the same party underneath'. The sense of continuity between the old and the new VB means that, although the new VB is one of the most recent additions to the far-right family of parties, it is also very well established. Like the old party, the VB focuses on **immigration** issues and Flemish nationalism. Indeed,

Dewinter has even claimed that the reasoning for Flemish separatism is not economic but racial, and has been reported as claiming 'they [Walloons] are of Latin genes, we [Flemands] are from Nordic racial stock'. He also claimed that his party operated in a family of far-right parties. Jean-Marie **Le Pen**'s **National Front** (*Front National*, FN) was the grandfather of this family, while parties in Sweden and Switzerland also operated cognate national ideologies.

The move from the old party to the new one raises important questions regarding the most appropriate ways for moderate liberal democratic states to tackle the growth of far-right parties. Arguably, rather than unnecessarily banning parties that go on to reform themselves under new banners, but to all intents and purposes are the same movement, a more sophisticated approach might be to refrain from making such legal gestures against extremist parties – unless they are a direct and violent threat to the state's security – and rather prosecute individual party members for criminal offences if, and when, they occur.

See also Antwerp (Belgium) *and* Flemish Bloc/Flemish Interest.

Further Reading
Erik, Jan. 2005 'From Vlaams Blok to Vlaams Belang: the Belgian far-right renames Itself' in *West European Politics*. 28. 3.
The Observer, 'Far right strives to disguise its roots in bid for national power', http://www.guardian. co.uk/farright/story/0,,1890294,00.html (cited 31 December 2007).

Flemish Bloc/Flemish Interest

Flemish Bloc (*Vlaams Blok*, VB) was formed in 1978 to pursue the goal of an independent Flemish state. Its leader was Karel Dillen and the party incorporated a number of former pro-Nazi collaborators. It existed until 2004 when it was prohibited on account of its racist attitudes and behaviour. It then reconfigured itself as Flemish Interest (*Vlaams Belang*) and carried on its political battle, albeit under a different name. Just prior to its banning, it had scored 18 percent across Flanders in a general election – its best ever score. Previously it had only occasionally registered more than 10 percent in elections (2003, 11 percent and 12 percent, and 2004, 14 percent). Other Belgian parties had to deal with the success of the movement and eventually settled on a policy known as the *cordon sanitaire*, which meant the party was isolated and boycotted so far as agreements and alliances were concerned.

Flemish Bloc's main aim was an independent Flemish state, but it was also militant in its opposition to **immigration** and its belief in a tough policy on **law and order**. From the late 1970s onwards it thrived on the idea that it alone represented protest against, and opposition to, the status quo in Belgium. It even started to attract supporters who weren't particularly enthusiastic about the idea of Flemish independence, but rather just wanted to register their disgust with other political parties. Like many other parties, it had its fair share of internal quarrels and schisms – on issues such as immigration policy, separatism and religious affiliation – but it survived and flourished, even though some of its members flirted with **anti-Semitism** and Holocaust-denial theses. In 1996, Dillen, the party's main stalwart, handed over the presidency of the movement to Frank Vanhecke.

Flemish Bloc/Flemish Interest

The new, reinvented party, Flemish Interest, carried on where Vlaams Blok left off. It described itself as 'the political mouthpiece of the Flemish Movement as it has developed through time ... The Vlaams Belang is a party of Flemish patriots ... It is an instrument for the advancement of the national and cultural identity of Flanders ... Tradition, virtues and morality, as these have grown through time, must be respected and are constitutive elements of the society of the future. The Vlaams Belang strives for the secession of Flanders from the artificial Belgian state. Our aim is to dissolve Belgium and establish an independent Flemish state. This state will be sovereign over the Dutch-speaking territory of Belgium and will include Brussels, which is the capital of Flanders but will have a separate linguistic status ... Language is a constitutive element of a people's cultural identity. The Vlaams Belang defends the interests of the Dutch-speaking people wherever this is necessary, particularly along the linguistic border and in the international institutions'. The new movement scored 24 percent in regional elections in 2004 and opinion polls suggest that it is the second or third most popular party in Belgium today.

For specialists in Belgian politics, the phenomenon of Vlaams Blok/Vlaams Belang is a fascinating one. Not only is it a far-right movement with a separatist agenda; it is also unusual in being officially declared 'racist' and having to reinvent itself under a new name. As such, the party is moving into uncharted waters, but the first signs are that the legal ruling will possibly enhance its 'underdog' status, and even electoral popularity, with voters.

Both new and old parties have attracted significant support in **Antwerp**, where immigration-related tensions have been commonplace. Again, this is an interesting dimension to the movement. Swyngedouw has examined the sociological profile of the city and concludes that, 'The anti-immigrant slogans, populist anti-(party) political message, combined with a well-organised party apparatus supported by convinced party activists, in the specific political and historical context of the city of Antwerp at a time of difficult social and economic transition, are the threads from which the VB has woven its web of success in Antwerp'. Rarely is a far-right party so intimately associated with a major town or city.

The truth is that the VB has already had a significant impact on Belgian politics. As Husbands notes, governments have responded to the rise of the party by making more strenuous efforts to aid the integration of immigrants but, also, at the same time, by hardening policy on asylum seekers.

See also Antwerp (Belgium) *and* Flemish Bloc, Disbandment (2004).

Further Reading
Conway, Martin. 1993. *Collaboration in Belgium: Léon Degrelle and the Rexist Movement, 1940–44*. New Haven, CT: Yale University Press.
Husbands, Christopher T. 1994. 'Belgium: Flemist legions on the march'. In *The Extreme Right in Europe and the USA*. Edited by Paul Hainsworth. London: Pinter.
Swyngedouw, Marc. 2000. 'Belgium: explaining the relationship between *Vlaams Blok* and the city of Antwerp'. In *The Politics of the Extreme Right: From the Margins to the Mainstream*. Edited by Paul Hainsworth. London: Pinter.

Fortuyn, Pim (1948–2002) – The Netherlands

Wilhelmus Simon Petrus 'Pim' Fortuyn was born in 1948 and assassinated in 2002. Charismatic and openly gay, he became one of the Netherlands' most controversial politicians. He was bald, wore flashy Italian suits, had a butler, and lived with his two dogs, Kenneth and Carla, in a Rotterdam villa which came to be known as *Casa di Pietro*. He also had his own political party, List Pim Fortuyn (*Lijst Pim Fortuyn* [LPF]), and became notorious for his views on **immigration** and Islam.

Fortuyn studied sociology in Amsterdam and worked later as a lecturer at the Nyenrode Institute and associate professor at the University of Groningen. He was an expert on public transport and wage negotiation, and during the 1990s he moved to Erasmus University. He was known affectionately as Professor Pim. He had a catholic and socialist background and in 2001 he was elected to the Livable Netherlands' party list for the 2002 parliamentary elections. But in February 2002, he gave a controversial interview to a Dutch newspaper; he argued that Muslim immigration into the Netherlands should be stopped – and was immediately de-selected by his party. So he formed his own party to compete in elections: Lijst Pim Fortuyn. He achieved immediate success. In Rotterdam in March 2002, his movement claimed 36 percent of seats and dumped the left out of power.

10. Pim Fortuyn hit with cakes at an election rally, 15 March 2002, The Hague, Netherlands.

As a gay politician, Fortuyn was always going to attract attention, but his views on immigration and Islam made this inevitable. He told the Dutch newspaper *Volkskrant*: 'I don't hate Islam. I consider it a backward culture. I have travelled much in the world. And wherever Islam rules, it's just terrible'. And in an interview with the BBC he said: 'All those [immigrants] who are here can stay. I don't say send them home … I just say the Netherlands is a small country. We are already overcrowded, there's no more room and we must shut the borders. Muslims have a very bad attitude toward **homosexuality**; they're very intolerant. And **women**. For them, women are second-class citizens. What we are witnessing now is a clash of civilisations, not just between states but within them. This is a full country. I think 16 million Dutchmen are about enough.' His book, *Against the Islamicisation of Our Culture*, was published in 1997. Fortuyn was often likened to Jean-Marie **Le Pen** in France, but always rejected this comparison.

In 2002, nine days before national parliamentary elections, Fortuyn was assassinated in Hilversum only minutes after completing a radio interview. The attacker, Volkert van der Graaf, was an animal rights activist and he admitted in court to the crime: 'I confess to the shooting. He [Fortuyn] was an ever growing danger who would affect many people in society. I saw it as a danger. I hoped that I could solve it myself'. He was sentenced to eighteen years in prison. Fortuyn was buried on 20 July 2002, at Provesano di San Giorgio della Richinvelda in Italy. His legacy was a powerful one. His party won 26 out of 150 seats in the 2002 poll, although it faded thereafter, and by 2006 was devoid of a parliamentary presence.

In a sense, Fortuyn can be likened to other modern far-right leaders. He cut a smart, dashing figure like **Haider** and **Fini**, and his anti-Islamic discourse was reminiscent of Le Pen's. But, his intolerant attitude towards immigrants was not matched in other areas. He was gay, so would not have been able to understand traditional far-right attitudes toward homosexuality. He was also noted for his progressive attitude on issues such as prostitution (he wanted to legalise it), euthanasia (he approved of it) and drugs (he had campaigned in favour of marijuana being available over the counter).

It is impossible to understand Fortuyn without understanding the Netherlands. His sexuality and ultra-liberal attitudes on key issues reflected the modern, progressive nature of the Dutch state. He may have looked out of place when compared to some European far-right leaders; but when his political ideas were placed in the context of Dutch society and politics, he and his movement were entirely comprehensible. By contrast, his assassination was a most un-Dutch like event. This fact was reflected in the statement made by the prime minister of the Netherlands, Wim Kok, in the immediate aftermath of the killing: 'I am shocked. This is a deep tragedy for those close to him, for his loved ones and for our country and our **democracy**. This is not just an assassination attempt on Pim Fortuyn but also on Dutch democracy'.

See also Against the Islamisation of our Culture - Dutch Identity as Fundamental Value by Pim Fortuyn (The Netherlands); List Pim Fortuyn (The Netherlands) *and* Pim Fortuyn, Assassination of (2002).

Further Reading

Fortuyn, Pim. 1990. *Ordening Door Ontvlechting: Een Advies Over de Adviesstructuur in de Volksgezondheid*. Rijswijk/Den Haag, DOP: Ministerie van Welzijn.
Mudde, Cas. 2002. *The Ideology of the Extreme Right*. Manchester: Manchester University Press.
Sniderman, P.M. & Hagendoorn, L. 2007. *When Ways of Life Collide: Multiculturalism and Its Discontents in the Netherlands*. Princeton, NJ: Princeton University Press.
Mudde, Cas & Holsteyn, Joop Van. 2000. 'The Netherlands: explaining the limited success of the extreme right'. In *The Politics of the Extreme Right: From the Margins to the Mainstream*. Edited by Paul Hainsworth. London: Pinter.
Husbands, Christopher T. 1994. 'The Netherlands: irritants on the body politic'. In *The Extreme Right in Europe and the USA*. Edited by Paul Hainsworth. London: Pinter.

France, Student Riots and the French Far Right (1968)

A general strike by students and **workers** in France in May 1968 spiralled into one of the most infamous events of post-war in European history. Indeed, the various events of *mai 68* have been the subject of much myth making and hyperbolic discussion among commentators and academics alike. The idea of '1968' in the popular imagination is often symbolic of the watershed events not only in France, but around the world that, collectively, evoke the sense of elemental change that characterises the 1960s. These included the Tet Offensive and the My Lai Massacre in the Vietnam War; the assassination of Martin Luther King crystallising international opinion over the US civil rights movement; and the Prague Spring in Czechoslovakia holding the promise for human rights advances in the Warsaw Pact countries. Further, figures such as Che Guevara, Fidel Castro and Mao Zedong inspired left-wing radicals to revolt against bourgeois authority across the world. Meanwhile, another sign of changing times, alongside consternation within the Far Right thus created, was the outburst made by British Conservative Party politician Enoch Powell, who delivered his notorious Rivers of Blood speech in April 1968.

In France, the *mai 68* student protests and riots have come to symbolise a cultural transition from a conservative to a more liberal perspective on social issues. Although the protesting students did not succeed in their bid to overthrow the French regime, they did force Charles de Gaulle to call for fresh parliamentary elections in the summer. The demonstrations in France eventually petered out, but even in failure they seemed to symbolise the radicalism of the 1960s. In the popular imagination, then, *mai 68* is invariably associated with the left – for good reason because working people and radical thinkers alongside socialist and communist political groupings were at the forefront of events. However, the Far Right also played a role, albeit a minor one.

The most prominent far-right actions came in the shape of Occident, a small anti-communist group. Boasting slogans such as '*Écrasons les valets du Viêt-Cong!* [Stomp on the valets of the Viet Cong!]' and '*Mort aux Bolches! [Death to the Bolsheviks!]*', Occident was formed in 1964 by Pierre Sidos. Following its active participation in the tumultuous events in Paris, comprising mainly of street-fighting, the movement came to the attention of the Gaullist administration. In the aftermath of *mai 68*, the group was declared illegal by the authorities and it was formally dissolved by the end of 1968. However, from the ashes of Occident came New Order (*Ordre Nouveau*, ON). This group became highly dominant in French far-right circles during the 1970s, and comprised of many political positions that would later be taken over by the **National Front** (*Front National*, FN) including anti-Gaullism, national-revolution, Maurrassism and integralist nationalism. For the French Far Right, then, the rioting *mai 68* could also be regarded as a key reference point.

See also Western Europe and the Far Right.

Further Reading
Ignazi, Piero. 2003. *Extreme Right Parties in Western Europe*. New York: Oxford University Press.
Singer, Daniel. 1970. *Prelude to Revolution: France in May 1968*. London: Cape.

France, Success of the National Front (1982 to 2002)

The successes of the National Front (*Front National*, FN) in France between the early 1980s and the Presidential election of 2002 saw the larger-than-life personality of Jean-Marie **Le Pen** epitomise the growing impact of the Far Right in French politics. Indeed, between *L'Alternance* of 1981 and Le Pen's successes in 2002, we can see the dawn and climax of the Le Pen story.

France, Success of the National Front

To begin in the early 1980s, *L'Alternance* is the name given to the emergence of the left in power after decades in opposition. The victory by François Mitterrand's in the Presidential Elections of 1981 was not simply a milestone in the history of the French left, but also the trigger for the development of the Far Right in France. The theory goes that, up until 1981, with the conservative mainstream right dominating the political landscape and holding power almost perpetually, the Far Right lacked a party with which it could contrast itself. In a world dominated by Rally for the Republic (*Rassemblement pour la République*, RPR) and other Gaullists who stressed many traditional right-wing themes, the FN was unlikely to gain a significant political profile.

However, following François Mitterrand's Socialists victory in 1981, the French political landscape altered dramatically. Now, France's government had a vision and a policy agenda that was almost the exact opposite of the FN's. In the 1980s, there was a party in executive power that significantly contrasted with FN thinking, allowing the party's far-right position to stand out. Whereas Mitterrand lauded the Rights of Man as his guiding philosophy, and stressed the fact that France was a 'country of welcome' for immigrants and refugees from all over the world, Le Pen developed a doctrine of 'closed nationalism' and played on his belief in 'France for the French'. Now that the FN had an administration that it could reject out of hand, led by an executive that it could rail against passionately and vehemently, it found itself scoring electoral successes. By 1983, the FN had its first major by-election success in **Dreux**, and by 1984, its first significant parliamentary representation at the European Parliament in Brussels. More impressive results followed, including breaking the 15 percent barrier in the 1995 presidential elections.

If the changing political landscape that emerged after 1981 was the launch-pad for the FN, it could be argued that, after two decades of agitation and militant political activity, 2002 was lift-off. When we look again at these elections, we see that the Socialist Party (*Parti Socialiste*, PS) candidate, Lionel Jospin, did little to inspire the French population at large. With a weakened political left, the way was open for Le Pen to capitalise and present himself as the natural opposition to Jacques Chirac's Gaullist politics. Though Le Pen did not win the election, to the world's amazement, for the first time he reached the second round run-off for the presidency. This development caused shock and outrage in France and around the world, with the left, right and centre right uniting to defeat the Far Right in the second round of the election. One left-wing slogan typified the outrage of being presented with an allegedly corrupt conservative and a far-right extremist in the second round: 'vote for the crook, not the Fascist'.

In retrospect, 2002 will probably be seen as the highpoint of Le Pen's political career, for in 2007 he polled only 10 percent in the presidential elections that put Nicolas Sarkozy in the Elysée Palace. However, as he enters his political twilight years, the Le Pen story has a new chapter: the rising political star of his daughter. Marine Le Pen, MEP, is president of the **youth** organisation *Generations Le Pen*, and a leading member of the FN.

See also Le Pen, Jean-Marie (France); National Front (France) *and* Western Europe and the Far Right.

Further Reading

Davies, Peter. 1999. *The National Front in France: Ideology, Discourse and Power*. New York: Routledge.
Hainsworth, Paul. 2000. 'The *Front National*: from ascendancy to fragmentation on the French extreme right'. In *The Politics of the Extreme Right: From the Margins to the Mainstream*. Edited by Paul Hainsworth. London: Pinter.
Ignazi, Piero. 2003. *Extreme Right Parties in Western Europe*. New York: Oxford University Press.

Franco, Death of (1975)

On 20 November 1975, General Francisco Franco, the authoritarian Spanish leader, died after forty years in power. In the immediate aftermath of his death, many believed that there would be a level of continuity between Franco's Spain and the new regime. He was succeeded as head of state by his chosen successor, King Juan Carlos, and many of the *continuistas* believed the army and the new head of state would prevent a Spanish transition to **democracy**, at least in the short-term. In reality, neither the King nor the Army stood in the way of what has widely been regarded as a smooth transition from dictatorship to democratic governance. Indeed, confounding expectations, the King encouraged this transformation of Spain.

At the time, then, Franco's death and the move away from dictatorial style of government was a devastating blow to those on the Far Right of Spanish politics. Though groups attempted to present themselves as the new heirs to the *Falange* legacy in the immediate post-Franco era, these movements found little wide spread support. Fascist anthems, such as 'Face the Sun [*Cara al sol*]', were sung by this new generation of Falangists, and they even wore navy blue shirts sporting the Falangist logo. However, despite their anti-democratic philosophy, when they stood for the elections of 15 June 1977, they polled less that 1 percent of the vote.

In the years following the fall of Franco, the Far Right in Spain and across **Europe** have used the anniversary of his death as an excuse to parade their doctrines and beliefs. For example, in 2005, many newspapers carried the story of the commemoration of the 30th anniversary of Franco's death. These stories told of how, in Madrid's Plaza de Oriente, crowds gathered waving Spanish flags bearing Franco's Falange party insignia while shouting insults at Muslims and gays, and making fascist salutes. These crowds consisted of Italian, French and German far-right supporters, alongside Spanish Franco loyalists. The 1,000-strong throng that gathered at the plaza – a nostalgic meeting-point for Franco supporters – were addressed by Blas Piñar, who sketched out a picture of Spain falling into a state of decadence after the end of the Franco regime. Arguing the country was now corrupted by regional separatists who could tear the country apart, alongside rising crime rates, Piñar pinned the blame for this alleged decline in the nation's fortunes on the 1978 democratic constitution.

See also Franco, General Francisco (Spain) *and* Southern Europe and the Far Right.

Further Reading
Ellwood, Sheelagh. 1995. 'The Extreme Right in Spain: A Dying Species?' In *The Far Right in Western and Eastern Europe*. Edited by Luciano Cheles, Ronnie Ferguson and Michalina Vaughan. London: Longman.

Franco, General Francisco (1892–1975) – Spain

After a successful career in the Spanish army, General Francisco Paulino Hermenegildo Teódulo Franco Bahamonde led the Nationalist forces during the civil war, and following the triumph of the right, he governed Spain from 1939 until his death in 1975. While in power, he led a right-wing regime that was often characterised as Fascist; after his death he became an icon for those on the Spanish Far Right.

Franco, Death of

Franco was the son of a naval officer and studied at the Toledo Military Academy. He became a major in 1917, and in 1920 he was appointed second-in-command of the Spanish Foreign Legion. By 1926 he had become **Europe**'s youngest general. This came after several years of fighting in Morocco, where his tactical knowledge and all-round administrative capability impressed people. By 1928 he had been appointed head of the new military academy at Saragossa. Franco had good relations with the monarch Alfonso XIII and was also a supporter of the military dictatorship led by Miguel Primo de Rivera. However, there was no love lost between Franco and the Second Spanish Republic, established in 1931. Franco was known for his conservative views and in 1934 his right-wing credentials were highlighted when he helped to crush the Asturian miners' strike. This didn't endear him to the new republican regime, and so he was demoted and sent on unglamorous postings to Corunna and the Balearics. But, in 1935, the minister of war, José Maria Gil Robles, appointed Franco as his chief of staff.

11. General Francisco Franco leaves Capitania after being proclaimed head of the State and Generalissimo of the armies, 1 October 1936, Burgos, Spain.

Franco was becoming more and more politicised and he used his influence as chief of staff to promote monarchists and de-republicanise the army. In July 1936, he participated in a *coup d'état* against the legitimately elected Popular Front government. The *coup* failed but triggered the start of a bloody civil war. During this conflict, Franco emerged as leader of the right-wing Nationalists against the left-wing government.

After the Nationalists triumphed in the civil war, Franco dissolved Parliament and established a personal dictatorship, which lasted until his death in 1975 (and continued for three years thereafter until Spain was returned to **democracy**). It is tempting to talk about Franco in the same breath as Hitler and Mussolini, but Spain remained neutral during the Second World War. Franco actually turned down an invitation to join the Axis powers and only assisted Germany and Italy in a minor way during the conflict.

Franco is often depicted as a Fascist, but in essence, he was a traditional conservative who believed in values such as the **family**, hierarchy, **religion** and anti-Communism. A speech he made in 1942 illustrates this belief in tradition: 'Those are mistaken who dream of the establishment of democratic liberal systems in **Western Europe** ... Neither the highest cause of all, God, a cause never better served than under our regime, nor the interests of the country, never as well defended as in our days, nor the general welfare of our nation, embodied in our restored **economy**, reborn industries and flourishing fields, are safe from our enemies ... Divine assistance clearly has shown itself to us. With it, nothing and nobody shall vanquish us ... We know that with us is life, without us, death'.

That said, there were also unpleasant elements to his regime: disapproval of opposition, the creation of a police state and a cult of personality that had Franco – the *Caudillo* or *Generalísimo* – at its centre. The dictatorship also held Spain back. Under Franco's leadership, it remained under-developed economically and isolated in diplomatic terms. In essence, the key to Francoism was pragmatism. The General was able to do business with the fascist Falange and old fashioned Spanish monarchists, and also kept his independence in his dealings with Nazi Germany and Fascist Italy.

Although, in the post-war period, far-right activists in Spain have worshipped Franco and his memory – some of the time in exaggerated fashion –, the Far Right has never been a major force in Spanish politics. Franco is seen as the reason for this. While he was in power, he did little that was radical or new and actually kept the authentic voice of the Far Right (the Falange) at arm's length. He was by nature a conservative and traditionalist, and Fascism – radical, revolutionary Fascism – had little appeal for a man who was a born conservative. So he did little to encourage the growth of the Far Right, and after his death, far-right and neo-fascist movements in Spain found it difficult to put down roots. They idolised him – but his value-system was not theirs.

See also Franco, General Francisco (Spain) *and* Southern Europe and the Far Right.

Further Reading
Preston, Paul. 1995. *Franco: A Biography*. London: Fontana.
Payne, Stanley. 2008. *Franco and Hitler*. New Haven, CT: Yale University Press.
Ellwood, Sheelagh. 1991. 'The Extreme Right in Spain: A Dying Species?'. In Cheles, L., Ferguson, R., & Vaughan, M. 1991. *Neo-Fascism in Europe*. Edited by Luciano Cheles, Ronnie Ferguson and Michalina Vaughan. London: Longman.
Gilmour, John. 1994. 'The extreme right in Spain: Blas Piñar and the spirit of the nationalist uprising'. In *The Extreme Right in Europe and the USA*. Edited by Paul Hainsworth. London: Pinter.

Freedom

As with **democracy**, freedom is one of the key, abstract words that far-right movements have desperately tried to lay claim to. However, it is difficult for parties that forward policies such as the death penalty and reduce levels of **immigration** to make convincing cases for their deeply-held beliefs on freedom. The Far Right tends to argue for the freedom to pursue its ultra-nationalist agendas, and in the name of pursuing this freedom it seeks to introduce restrictions on all activities that, in their opinion, hinder such goals. An extreme example of the use of the language of freedom by the Far Right can be found in the **Austrian Freedom Party** (*Freiheitliche Partei Österreichs*, FPÖ). Founded in 1956, in its early incarnation the FPÖ was committed to the twin ideals of liberalism and nationalism. When it became less liberal and far more xenophobic, especially from the late 1980s onwards, its name alone became something of an ironic joke for those outside of a far-right ideological mentality. For the FPÖ, as with many other far-right parties, their notions of freedom are something of a Hobson's choice.

On the whole, then, parties of the Far Right have few qualms about using the word freedom in their manifestoes, even though they know that their kind of freedom is not unlimited and does have strict boundaries. The Far Right has sometimes trumpeted such ideas in quite grandiose fashion. For example, in its political programme, **Flemish Interest** (*Vlaams Belang*, VB) in Belgium talks about freedom as its number-one concern when it comes to values and morality. It claims that the VB is a movement dedicated to ensuring the freedom of the individual, protecting people from the powers of the state. It defends free speech, claiming it 'will respect, as a minimum, the rights and freedoms guaranteed by the European Convention for the Protection of Human Rights and Fundamental Freedoms of 4 November 1950, and the related protocols which apply in Belgium'. It also defends the right to free association and assembly, freedom of conscience, freedom of **education** and the right to life. Further, the VB argues that the right of ownership and free enterprise form the core of a successful **economy**. Finally, the VB maintains that its representatives will work towards ensuring the freedom to national self-determination for all nations. The last point is clearly born out of self-interest because independence for Flanders is the party's main objective. So too is the VB's concern with freedom of speech. Indeed, Flemish Interest came into existence because its predecessor, **Flemish Bloc** (*Vlaams Blok*, VB), was effectively prohibited by Belgian anti-racism laws. Such positions raise simple critical questions for the VB, such as: why not extend VB notions of freedom to immigrants, if the ideal of unlimited freedom is so central? And, why make the Islamic faith a belief system that is alien to Flemish identity? In a truly free society, should people not have the freedom to worship whichever **religion** they choose?

In Britain, both main far-right parties also articulate the rhetoric of freedom. The **British National Party** (BNP) stresses the idea of civil liberties in its programme. It argues that it works in the community to help people realise their civil liberties and combat discrimination by the state. The BNP stresses that indigenous (presumably white) British citizens in inner-cities are increasingly being discriminated against by people in positions of power: 'Increasingly our people are facing denial of service provision, failure to secure business contracts, as well as poor job prospects as both reverse discrimination excludes our people from the school room, workplace and boardroom. A key role of the British National Party is to provide legal advice and support to victims of repression and those denied of their fundamental civil rights'. Therefore, the key phrase seems to be 'our people'. For the BNP, freedom is a worthy cause to champion, but only for a select, racially-defined group within society. The **British National Front** (NF) is slightly vaguer in its recommendations, but the underlying tone is much the same. It argues that, throughout history, the British people have fought and died to preserve and extend their basic freedoms and liberties. The NF promotes the idea of introducing a British Bill of Rights that would outline these basic freedoms in a modern context. Specifically, it stresses that this Bill of Rights should touch on the following areas: 'Equal and free access to justice; Freedom of speech and publication and distribution of printed matter; Freedom of access to publicly owned assembly facilities; Freedom for orderly demonstrations in public; The right to vote and stand for election for public office without onerous financial or other qualifications; Freedom from arbitrary arrest'. Of course, the suspicion remains that this emphasis on freedom is mainly for external consumption and does not really square with the main thrust of BNP and NF policy.

A final theme worth noting is the assertion that immigrant communities are freer and more prosperous than their established national communities. Again, this position allows the Far Right to argue that it is working as a civil liberties movement, championing the rights of those nations who are having their rights restricted by foreign migrants. Freedom, then, is a key term in the discourse of the Far Right. Critiques of the ideology can easily pull apart the way freedom is actually defined on a case-by-case basis, and often, the term is used to mask a more authoritarian style of politics.

See also The Ideology of the Far Right *and* Law and Order.

Further Reading
Hainsworth, Paul, ed. 2000. *The Politics of the Extreme Right: From the Margins to the Mainstream.* London: Pinter.
Ignazi, Piero. 2003. *Extreme Right Parties in Western Europe.* New York: Oxford University Press.
Mudde, Cas. 2000. *The Ideology of the Extreme Right.* Manchester: Manchester University Press.

Freedom Alliance, Victory in Italian Elections (1994)

The March 1994 elections were a milestone in Italian political history, with Silvio Berlusconi's Pole of Freedoms (*Polo delle Libertà*) coalition sweeping into power with 58 percent of the vote. Controversy was supplied by Berlusconi, a flamboyant, well connected media tycoon, and also accompanied his choice of allies. Berlusconi and his conservative Forward Italy (*Forza Italia*, FI) party selected the **Northern League** (*Lega Nord*, LN) and the **National Alliance** (*Alleanza Nazionale*, NA) as electoral partners. This coalition was also known as the **Freedom** Alliance, and overall captured 156 seats out of a potential 315. Berlusconi became Prime Minister in May 1994, but was forced to resign by December of the same year after the LN pulled out of the alliance.

The significance of the 1994 elections lies in the fact that Berlusconi had openly allied himself with two movements of the Italian Far Right, the LN and the NA. Up until this point, the Far Right in **Europe** could almost be defined by its failure to reach high government office. Though the Far Right could win the odd local by-election, or land the occasional blow as an opposition force, real power at a national level was always something of a pipedream. But in Italy in 1994 this trend changed, and the Far Right, in the guise of two separate parties, became a key player in governmental circles, albeit for a short time. Following the victory, Gianfranco **Fini**, leader of the NA, said: 'It's time to put our cards on the table and sort out the differences that have emerged.' The victory of the right in 1994 also provoked the political left into responding. Most significantly, a huge movement of the working-classes emerged to oppose Berlusconi. Further, the coalition exposed the tensions within the LN regionalist agenda, and highlighted the fact that the NA at this point had not adopted its post-Fascist stance. This gave Berlusconi a negative international profile, especially as Fini notoriously commented at this time that he believed Benito Mussolini to be the greatest statesman of the 20th century' – a view that he has subsequently rejected.

See also Fini, Gianfranco (Italy); Italian Social Movement/National Alliance *and* Southern Europe and the Far Right.

Further Reading
Gallagher, Tom. 2000. 'Exit from the ghetto: the Italian far right in the 1990s'. In *The Politics of the Extreme Right: From the Margins to the Mainstream*. Edited by Paul Hainsworth. London: Pinter.
Ignazi, Piero. 2003. *Extreme Right Parties in Western Europe*. New York: Oxford University Press.

The Freedom I Mean by Jörg Haider (Austria)

Former **Austrian Freedom Party** leader Jörg **Haider** has written a collection of books about his political philosophy, including one called *Liberated Future beyond Left and Right* (*Befreite Zukunft, Jenseits von Links und Rechts*), but the one that stands out in terms of significance is *The Freedom I Mean*, also translated as *The Freedom I Want to Speak of*.

Haider led the Freedom Party between 1986 and 2000 and he wrote this volume in 1995. Critics have always maintained that the movement's name is a misnomer given its attitude to **immigration** and Austria's Nazi heritage, but in the book, Haider tries to square the circle: 'The concept of a "multicultural society" has become an ideology. Any policy of immigration must insist on assimilation and adaptation to the culture and norms of the indigenous population … Especially in **education** we have to defend Christian values. As more immigrants bring their children into **Western Europe**, the indigenous population is slowly being substituted by aliens. It's hard to understand why Catholic bishops and clerics march in the streets defending a multi-cultural utopia when the threat to Christianity is so obvious … From 1989–1992, 10,400 new jobs were created in eastern Austria and all of them were filled by cheap foreign labour. At the same time, employment of Austrians declined by 1,300 … For [our ruling politicians] it's more important to experiment with our **youth** as guinea pigs in abstract, multicultural programmes'.

The belittling of multiculturalism would not have pleased those on the left, but it actually persuaded Michael Krueger to join the party and serve as one of Haider's lieutenants. He signed up in 1993 and quickly became party spokesman for culture and the constitution, and then justice.

See also Alliance for Austria's Future, Foundation by Haider (2005); Austrian Freedom Party *and* Central Europe and the Far Right.

Further Reading
http://www.bzoe.at (Alliance for the Future of Austria website).
http://www.fpoe.at (Freedom Party website).
Höbelt, L. 2003. *Defiant Populist: Jörg Haider and the Politics of Austria 1986–2000*. West Lafayette: Purdue University Press.
Morrow, D. 2000. 'Jörg Haider and the new FPÖ: beyond the democratic pale'. In *The Politics of the Extreme Right: From the Margins to the Mainstream*. Edited by Paul Hainsworth. London: Pinter.

Freedom Newspaper (Great Britain)

The Voice of *Freedom* is the 16-page monthly newspaper of the BNP and styles itself as the 'only politically incorrect newspaper in the country!' Its banner slogan is 'For British Freedom, Security, Identity and **Democracy**'. It is edited by longstanding nationalist activist Martin Wingfield and carries news and information relating to BNP activities. The paper's editorials address major issues for the party and the nation. One that focused on a recent local election campaign read: 'Our election addresses were superb and the publicity that our media wing was able to generate was first class. But the greatest accolade that the BNP was able to claim was the high quality of our candidates, with almost all of those brave men and **women** standing for us at the polls proving to be fine ambassadors for the Party'.

Another on **immigration** began: 'The British people were never given the chance to vote on whether they wanted Britain to become a "multicultural" society. The **British National Party** is opposed to "multiculturalism" because it fragments society and generates conflict. The British National Party seeks to protect and preserve the ethnic and cultural integrity of the British people. Labour and Conservative Governments, for the past thirty years, have allowed large scale immigration into Britain from the Third World against the clear wishes of the British people'.

See also British National Party *and* Griffin, Nick (Great Britain).

Further Reading

www.bnp.org.uk (BNP website).

Eatwell, Roger. 2000. 'The extreme right and British exceptionalism: the primacy of politics'. In *The Politics of the Extreme Right: From the Margins to the Mainstream*. Edited by Paul Hainsworth. London: Pinter.

Eatwell, Roger. 1994. 'Why has the extreme right failed in Britain?' In *The Extreme Right in Europe and the USA*. Edited by Paul Hainsworth. London: Pinter.

Cable, Gerry. 1991. 'The far right in contemporary Britain'. In *Neo-Fascism in Europe*. Edited by Luciano Cheles, Ronnie Ferguson and Michalina Vaughan. London: Longman.

Eatwell, Roger. 1996. *Fascism: A History*. London: Vintage.

Bragg, T., Griffin, N., Kerr, D. & Harrington, P. 2005. *Taking Liberties: A Third Way Special on the Attack on Civil Liberties in the UK*. Pamphlet.

Copsey, N., 2004. *Contemporary British Fascism: The British National Party and the Quest for Legitimacy*. Basingstoke: Palgrave Macmillan.

Freedom Party, Coalition Government in Austria (2000)

International attention was cast on Austrian politics in 1999 when the Far Right made a significant incursion into the country's political dynamics. In 1999, the Austrian Freedom Party (*Freiheitliche Partei Österreichs*, FPÖ) scored 27 percent of the national vote. Indeed, the party finished in second place, ahead of the conservative Austrian People's Party (*Österreichische Volkspartei*, ÖVP), in the national parliamentary elections. The *Harvard International Review* reported on how international press reports had responded to **Haider**'s victory: typically, 'Heil Haider' was how one French paper greeted the news. The report also stressed how the ostentatious Haider used a xenophobic rhetoric during his campaign. Not only did the party run a poster campaign with a slogan claiming the FPÖ would protect Austria's children while sinister-looking Turkish men formed the poster's striking image, but also Haider reiterated his controversial views on the Second World War. These included describing Nazi concentration and death camps as punishment camps, thereby implying that the millions who died in the **Holocaust** were in fact criminals, and allegedly praising the Nazis' 'orderly employment policies'.

The 1999 poll result gave Haider's party significant political leverage. By 2000, the FPÖ was part of the ruling coalition, sharing power with Wolfgang Schüssel's ÖVP, albeit as the junior partner. Those on the political left were not surprised by this development. One socialist website discussed the issue, arguing that the 1999 result meant that Haider's rise to government power had become inevitable, polarising Austrian society. Indeed, the Haider issue had become the one subject that the whole country was talking about. Socialists also talked of the protests against Haider's politics, such as the hundreds of demonstrators who turned up to his final public rally in Vienna ahead of the election. The Haider controversy, then, was also able to draw out a mood of anti-racism, as well as the xenophobic prejudices of the electorate. Thus, it is clear the election success of the FPÖ in 1999 sent shockwaves through the Austrian body politic.

Unsurprisingly, after the election the FPÖ's ascendancy provoked a strong reaction. As if to emphasise this fact, one human rights organisation, Whatcom Human Rights Task Force (WHRTF), explained: 'The dramatic situation now unfolding by the hour in Austria has initiated our sister organisations to ask for our immediate assistance and public solidarity in the struggle for human rights in **Europe**.' Meanwhile, Graeme Atkinson of the European anti-racist and anti-fascist organisation *Searchlight* claimed that the development was an acid-test for human rights organisations, and called for an engagement with the rise of Haider by the international network created by *Searchlight*. Austrian human rights campaigners must be supported by the international human right movement, he continued, and, evoking the memory of past human rights abuses of the worst order, even reminded his readers of Primo Levi's famous novel *If Not Now When?*

At a diplomatic level, Israel recalled her ambassador from Vienna on account of Haider's well-known **anti-Semitism** and, rather hastily perhaps, some European countries decided to snub and boycott the pariah Austria at every opportunity, sending the country into the diplomatic equivalent of quarantine. The **European Union** voted to impose sanctions on Austria, while EU countries withdrew their ambassadors and even refused to indulge in common courtesies with representatives of the new government, such as shaking hands. However, the EU's position could not hold. Eventually, it was feared that the policy would become counter-productive, and so it was reversed in the summer of 2000. Haider continued to be a major player within the FPÖ until 2005 when he formed a new party, the Alliance for Austria's Future of (*Bündnis Zukunft Österreich*, BZÖ).

See also Alliance for Austria's Future, Foundation by Haider (2005), Austrian Freedom Party *and* Central Europe and the Far Right.

Further Reading
Morrow, Duncan. 2000. 'Jörg Haider and the new FPÖ: beyond the democratic pale?' In *The Politics of the Extreme Right: From the Margins to the Mainstream*. Edited by Paul Hainsworth. London: Pinter.
Ignazi, Piero. 2003. *Extreme Right Parties in Western Europe*. New York: Oxford University Press.

French Algeria

French Algeria (*Algérie Française*) was the issue around which many elements on the French Far Right coalesced as the independence of **Algeria** from France became a possibility, and then a reality, in the post-war years. It wasn't so much a party or even an organised movement – but rather a powerful and emotive cause that helped to unite a variety of individuals and groups.

In this period, the French Far Right comprised many elements: the army, French settlers in Algeria and various ultra-right parties and movements in Paris – some legal, others illegal. They all honoured the idea of an Algeria governed from Paris and hated the idea of their prized colonial possession acquiring independence and autonomy. In 1959 Colonel Bigeard outlined the general philosophy of the French army: 'We are not making war for ourselves, not making a colonialist war … We are fighting right here right now for them, for the evolution, to see the evolution of these people and this war is for them. We are defending their **freedom** as we are, in my opinion, defending the West's freedom. We are here ambassadors, crusaders'.

In 1958, 1960 and 1961, anti-Paris coups were launched in a vain attempt to prevent the Algerian nationalists from coming out on top. These were the work of right-wing generals supported by militant political activists. As de Gaulle – the man who eventually put paid to the dreams of *Algérie Française* – said in 1961: 'An insurrectional power has been established by military pronouncement. That power has an appearance. It has a reality: a quartet of retired generals and ambitious and fanatical officers. Now the nation is challenged, it has been humiliated, our position in Africa is compromised, and by whom? Alas, alas, alas, by the very men whose duty and whose honour it was, and whose reason for being it was, to serve and obey. In the name of France, I order that all the means, I repeat, all the means be taken to block the way to these men, until we reduce them. I forbid every French citizen, and most of all, every soldier to execute any of those orders … Men and **women** of France, think of the risk for the nation. Men and women of France, help me'.

De Gaulle was not alone in condemning the coup attempts. In mainland France, the plotters were viewed as extremists and fascists and it was no surprise that they failed in their efforts to thwart the civilian politicians in Paris and their plans for decolonisation. Algeria gained its autonomy in 1962 – but this was not the end of the matter.

The legacy of *Algérie Française* was immense. Politicians like Pierre Poujade in the 1950s and 1960s and Jean-Louis Tixier-Vignancour, extreme-right presidential candidate in 1965, aligned themselves with the issue. And today there is still a highly active caucus of *Algérie Française* veterans at the heart of the Front National. In fact, the doctrine and ideology of FN leader Jean-Marie **Le Pen** is conditioned to a large degree by his experience as a paratrooper in the **Algerian War**; for example, there would seem to be a link between his hard-line attitude on **immigration** and his bitterness at France's defeat and the full granting of independence to Algeria. Many in the FN still hark back to the conflict, and de Gaulle's 'surrender', at any opportunity; and at party rallies, it is unusual if nostalgic cries of 'Vive *Algérie Française!*' are not greeted with rapturous applause.

See also Algeria; Algerian War (1954–1962) *and* Western Europe and the Far Right.

Further Reading
Shields, J. 2007. *The Extreme Right in France: From Pétain to Le Pen*. London and New York: Routledge.
Arnold, E.J. 2000. *The Development of the Radical Right in France: From Boulanger to Le Pen*. Basingstoke: Macmillan.
Davies, Peter. 1999. *The National Front in France: Ideology, Discourse and Power*. New York: Routledge.
Davies, Peter. 2002. *The Extreme Right in France, 1789 to the Present: From De Maistre to Le Pen*. London and New York: Routledge.

French Algeria

Hainsworth, Paul. 2000. 'The Front National: from ascendancy to fragmentation on the French extreme right'. In *The Politics of the Extreme Right: From the Margins to the Mainstream*. Edited by Paul Hainsworth. London: Pinter.

Hainsworth, Paul. 1992. 'The extreme right in post-war France: the emergence and success of the Front National'. In *The Extreme Right in Europe and the USA*. Edited by Paul Hainsworth. London: Pinter.

Vaughan, M. 1991. 'The extreme right in France: "Lepenisme" or the politics of fear'. In *Neo-Fascism in Europe*. Edited by Luciano Cheles, Ronnie Ferguson and Michalina Vaughan. London: Longman.

G

Garda, Aivars – Latvia

Several far-right movements have emerged in Latvia in recent years, including the Latvian National Democratic Party, the Fatherland and Liberty Party, and the Party of (Ethnic) Latvians (LPF). Aivars Garda, the leader of the LPF, has become the most prominent personality on the Latvian Far Right in recent years.

First and foremost, Garda is a controversial political operator. He has also been involved in his share of controversy. He publishes extreme xenophobic literature via his publishing house, Vieda, and caused a furore when he decided to commemorate the activities of the pro-Nazi Latvian legionnaires of the Second World War.

But Garda's main concern is Latvia's population balance. His argument is that Latvia is an 'illegitimate state' because it has not eradicated the influence of the Russian 'occupiers'. Thus, his ultimate objective is to deport one million Russian speakers from Latvia in the interests of complete decolonisation from Moscow. He said: 'We are determined to expel these people from our Motherland, in a peaceful and legal manner, to **Russia** or any other country they may wish to go to. The **Latvian National Front** and the majority of the Latvian people support our ideals'. He also talked about the 'fair right of everyone to live in one's ethnic motherland without any interference on the part of outsiders'. Some of his followers have compared Russian people in Latvia to 'cockroaches'.

Garda has even talked in terms of practicalities. In a style eerily reminiscent of the Nazis and the **Holocaust**, he wrote in the LPF newspaper, *DDD*: 'Ethnic Latvians need at least 700,000 occupants to leave Latvia. This will require 20,000 railroad cars. If we look at the issue, we see that that is not a very large number of cars. As far as I know, there are four trains that depart to Russia every day. One train has at least 20 cars, and 700 occupants can leave in each of those trains. That means that in order to deport 700,000 occupants, we need 1,000 trains, and these can be sent to Russia over the course of 250 days.'

Given the nature and tone of his public pronouncements, it is no surprise that Garda has provoked opposition. In 2002, the Latvian Human Rights Committee (FIDH) produced a report on the protection of ethnic minorities in the country. It singled out the leader of the Party of Ethnic Latvians for special attention, albeit in imperfect English: 'In spring 2001, Aivars Garda, the director of a private publishing house announced a competition of essays on topics containing ideas of building ethnically clean Latvian state and encouraging repatriation of "colonists" i.e. Russians. The competition resulted in a publication of a book containing a spirit and remarks offending the honour primarily of persons of Russian ethnic origin ... An MP from the Social Democratic party signed the letter prepared by Aivars Garda and submitted to Guenter Verheugen, EU Commissioner for Enlargement, where integration of society in Latvia was called a "crime against humanity" ... A file for a criminal case was not opened in relation to Garda's activities, as the law enforcement authorities did not find that Garda acted with a purpose of inciting racial hatred.'

Over the years, the *DDD* newspaper has become the main vehicle for Garda's anti-Jewish, anti-Russian and anti-homosexual propaganda. In 2003, he found himself in the spotlight when Latvia's Special Minister for Integration, Nils Muiznieks, ordered an investigation into an article entitled 'Falsifiers of History' that appeared in the paper. The revisionist piece claimed that the Jews had purposefully spread the 'lie' of the Holocaust. In the same year, *DDD* also serialised 'The Protocols of the Elders of Zion' in an effort to spread its anti-Semitic prejudices. It has also described the Latvian government as a 'pederast-traitor' and 'Zionist-masonic' regime.

The LPF has had minimal electoral success, but it has gained important exposure in the media. Its leader has gained further publicity as an occasional lecturer at the 'Latvian Academy of Culture', while his female fans are now known as 'Garda girls'. In more general terms, Latvia and its Far Right fit a pattern. Many other countries that gained their independence after the fall of **Communism** have given birth to intolerant, xenophobic and racist parties. Garda also comes across as a typical far-right leader: outspoken and extreme, and also supported and encouraged by a party machine that craves controversy and media coverage more than anything else.

See also Latvian Marches (2005); Latvian National Front *and* Russia and the Far Right.

Further Reading
http://www.politika.lv (Latvian public policy site).
Smith, D.J., Purs, A., Pabriks, A. & Lane, T. 2002. *The Baltic States: Estonia, Latvia and Lithuania.* London and New York: Routledge.
Galbreath, David. 2005. *Nation-Building and Minority Politics in Post-Socialist States: Interests, Influence and Identities in Estonia and Latvia.* Stuttgart: Ibidem-Verlag.
Karklins, Rasma. 1994. *Ethnopolitics and Transition to Democracy: Collapse of the USSR and Latvia by Rasma Karklins.* Washington, DC: Woodrow Wilson Center Press.

German National Democratic Party

Founded in 1964, the German National Democratic Party (*National Demokratische Partei Deutschlands*, NPD) put forward a 'Third Way' policy agenda and became the most significant neo-Nazi party to emerge in Germany after the war. In electoral terms the party is a negligible force. In national polls it has never broken through the 5 percent barrier – and thus has never had any parliamentary representation. At local and regional level, though, it has done much better. It currently sends twelve representatives to the state parliament in Saxony, for example.

The German authorities have categorised the party as a 'threat to the constitutional order' on account of its ideology. It is nationalist, anti-immigrant and anti-EU, and has also hinted at territorial aggrandisement. The party is traditionalist in the sense that it believes in inequality and harks back to the glory days of the German Empire.

It also has a radical vision of Germany's constitutional future and wishes to replace the Federal Republic, which it views as illegitimate. Party leader Udo Voigt has stated: 'Politicians will do their utmost to serve the people, rather than to be served by them. Germany will honourably take her place among the world's nations as an equal partner and will no longer tolerate the blackmail methods used by her enemies because of the past. There will be a new economic as well as a new social order, which will ensure an honoured place for the German **family** and which will give financial support to young Germans in order to enable them to raise children, the most precious resource of [the country's] people. Foreigners will be welcomed as guests, but should live and work in their own countries'.

For tactical reasons, the NPD is wary of using violent means to achieve its goals, but it is clear that as an organisation, its instincts are both anti-democratic and racist. Over the decades, it has become notorious for its direct-action tactics and hostility to the Jews and Zionism. As the authorities put it in 2005: 'The party continues to pursue a "people's front" of nationals [consisting of] the NPD, DVU and forces not attached to any party, which is supposed to develop into a base for an encompassing "German people's movement". The aggressive agitation of the NPD unabashedly aims towards the abolishment of the parliamentary **democracy** and the democratic constitutional state ... Statements of the NPD document an essential affinity with National Socialism; its agitation is racist, anti-Semitic, revisionist and intends to disparage the democratic and lawful order of the constitution'.

For these reasons, there is a long-running debate about whether the NPD should be prohibited.

See also Central Europe and the Far Right; German People's Union *and* Republican Party (Germany).

Further Reading

http://www.npd.de (NPD website).

Kolinsky, E. 1994. 'A future for right extremism in Germany?'. In *The Extreme Right in Europe and the USA*. Edited by Paul Hainsworth. London: Pinter.

Backer, Susann. 2000. 'Right-wing extremism in unified Germany'. In *The Politics of the Extreme Right: From the Margins to the Mainstream*. Edited by Paul Hainsworth. London: Pinter.

Eatwell, Roger. 1996. *Fascism: A History*. London: Vintage.

Childs, David. 1991. 'The Far Right in Germany since 1945'. In *Neo-Fascism in Europe*. Edited by Luciano Cheles, Ronnie Ferguson and Michalina Vaughan. London: Longman.

Husbands, Christopher T. 1991. 'Militant neo-Nazism in the Federal Republic of Germany in the 1980s'. In *Neo-Fascism in Europe*. Edited by Luciano Cheles, Ronnie Ferguson and Michalina Vaughan. London: Longman.

Stöss, R. 1991. *Politics Against Democracy: Extreme Right in West Germany*. New York and Oxford: Berg.

German People's Union

The German People's Union (*Deutsche Volksunion*, DVU) has been one of the most influential far-right groups in post-war Germany. It was founded as an informal association in 1971 by Dr Gerhard Frey and evolved into an overtly electoral force in 1987 – DVU/Liste D. Throughout its history, it has never had enough electoral support to gain parliamentary representation (although it has won seats in state legislatures and claimed 13 percent of the vote in Saxony-Anhalt in 1998, thus becoming the first extreme-right party in Germany to enter a regional assembly).

The party's relations with other far-right movements have been mixed. Mutual hostility has characterised its relationship with the *Republikaner Party*, but with the NPD it entered a non-competition agreement for some state elections in 2004. The agreement continued into 2005 for the federal elections, with the NPD-DVU alliance winning 1.6 percent of the national vote. The wealthy Frey is the driving force behind the party. He publishes two national newspapers – *Deutsche National-Zeitung* and the *Deutsche Wochen-Zeitung/Deutscher Anzeiger*. *Deutsche National-Zeitung* is the DVU's in-house journal and, like Frey himself, has sought to campaign against asylum seekers and foreign **workers** without getting sucked into pro-Nazi rhetoric.

It is difficult to estimate membership figures, but according to official sources the highpoint of DVU recruitment was 1992 and 1993, when it had 26,000 registered members. In 1990, 1991 and 1994 it had 22,000, 24,000 and 20,000 members respectively, but between 1995 and 1997 the figure slipped to 15,000.

In terms of policy, the DVU is powerfully anti-European and anti-**immigration**, and there is a *völkisch* tone to much of their discourse on the **nation and nationalism**. In 1982, the controversial British revisionist historian, David Irving, spoke to DVU gatherings in ten German cities, implying that the party has some sympathy with his Holocaust-denial theses.

As with all parties of the Far Right in contemporary Germany, the DVU is monitored by the state authorities and was recently classified as 'right-wing extremist' and 'constitutionally hostile'. Today, the party mainly exists on the Internet.

See also Central Europe and the Far Right; German National Democratic Party *and* Republican Party (Germany).

Further Reading

http://www.dvu.de (DVU website).

Kolinsky, E. 1994. 'A future for right extremism in Germany?' In *The Extreme Right in Europe and the USA*. Edited by Paul Hainsworth. London: Pinter.

Backer, Susann. 2000. 'Right-wing extremism in unified Germany'. In *The Politics of the Extreme Right: From the Margins to the Mainstream*. Edited by Paul Hainsworth. London: Pinter.

Eatwell, Roger. 1996. *Fascism: A History*. London: Vintage.

Childs, David. 1991. 'The Far Right in Germany since 1945'. In *Neo-Fascism in Europe*. Edited by Luciano Cheles, Ronnie Ferguson and Michalina Vaughan. London: Longman.

Husbands, Christopher T. 1991. 'Militant neo-Nazism in the Federal Republic of Germany in the 1980s'. In *Neo-Fascism in Europe*. Edited by Luciano Cheles, Ronnie Ferguson and Michalina Vaughan. London: Longman.

Stöss, R. 1991. *Politics Against Democracy: Extreme Right in West Germany*. New York and Oxford: Berg.

German Voice Newspaper (Germany)

German Voice (*Deutsche Stimme*) is the monthly newspaper of the NPD in Germany. Its objective is to raise the profile of the German national movement. As such, it pedals a hard-line nationalist, anti-immigrant and anti-Semitic discourse that takes it to the edge of what is permissible in modern-day Germany. In its pages it has interviewed revisionist historian David Irving and in August 2002, it welcomed BNP leader Nick **Griffin** to one of its special festivals. In 1979 and 1980, Deutsche Stimme attacked a Hollywood television series, *Holocaust*, despite 65 percent of German people questioned in a poll saying that they were 'deeply moved' by it. The paper said it was simply 'Hollywood propaganda'. In May 2005, the NPD were forced to admit that Deutsche Stimme was printed in Jelenia Gora, south-west Poland, after police examined two Polish lorries and seized 21,000 copies of the paper in the eastern state of Saxony. Saxony's Interior Minister Thomas de Maiziere claimed that the find demonstrated the hypocrisy of the NPD. For the NPD, Holger Apfel revealed that he had been searching for a German publisher for three years. He stated: 'So the only solution for us was Poland.'

See also Central Europe and the Far Right.

Further Reading

http://www.npd.de (NPD website).

Kolinsky, E. 1994. 'A future for right extremism in Germany?' In *The Extreme Right in Europe and the USA*. Edited by Paul Hainsworth. London: Pinter.

Backer, Susann. 2000. 'Right-wing extremism in unified Germany'. In *The Politics of the Extreme Right: From the Margins to the Mainstream*. Edited by Paul Hainsworth. London: Pinter.

Eatwell, Roger. 1996. *Fascism: A History*. London: Vintage.

Childs, David. 1991. 'The Far Right in Germany since 1945'. In *Neo-Fascism in Europe*. Edited by Luciano Cheles, Ronnie Ferguson and Michalina Vaughan. London: Longman.

Husbands, Christopher T. 1991. 'Militant neo-Nazism in the Federal Republic of Germany in the 1980s'. In *Neo-Fascism in Europe*. Edited by Luciano Cheles, Ronnie Ferguson and Michalina Vaughan. London: Longman.

Stöss, R. 1991. *Politics Against Democracy: Extreme Right in West Germany*. New York and Oxford: Berg.

Giertych, Roman (b.1971) – Poland

Roman Giertych was born in Śrem, Poland. He is extremely tall (almost seven feet) and comes from a famous Polish political **family**. He is the son of veteran right-wing politician Maciej Giertych, and grandson of ardent Catholic-nationalist Jędrzej Giertych. It was no surprise, therefore, when he moved into politics at an early age and developed a right-wing, Catholic ideology. Today, Giertych Jnr – a minister in the Polish government – is one of the most controversial and outspoken politicians in **Europe**, regularly causing offence and outrage with his extremist views.

At university in Poznań, Giertych studied history and law to postgraduate level. In 1989, he re-founded the All-Polish **Youth** organisation and is still its honorary chairperson. He then became a member of the National-Democratic Party and the National Party, which eventually merged with a number of other organisations to form the **League of Polish Families** (*Liga Polskich Rodzin*, LPR) in 2001. Thereafter, he became a deputy chairman of the LPR's parliamentary grouping and was elected to the Polish parliament on the LPR list (both in 2001) and became chairman of the LPR Congress (2002) and president of the movement (2004). In 2006, he was appointed deputy prime minister and minister for **education**, but this decision caused a wave of protests in Poland with a big section of public opinion viewing Giertych as unfit for office.

An author of several books, Giertych says his aim is to 'sanitise' Poland's education system. In this crusade, he aligns himself closely with the Catholic Church. He has been accused of introducing 'wall-to-wall Catholicism' in Polish schools, with non-Catholics finding it hard to avoid periods of Catholic instruction and being told to follow a Catholic 'dress code'. That same year, he decided to boycott BBC interviews after the television station broadcast a documentary about 'paedophile priests'.

He has caused the greatest controversy with his views on **homosexuality** and abortion. With regard to the former, he stated in 2007: 'I found out recently that children ... will participate in a homosexual parade and that authorities of one of

European cities approved such propaganda ... Propaganda of homosexuality reaches younger and younger children. In some countries, children are not allowed to mention or read about mom and dad even in hospitals, as that might allegedly violate the rights of the minority. Let's shake ourselves free of this ill-advised political correctness ... We also cannot promote as normal same-sex partnerships when teaching youth, as those partnerships objectively constitute deviation from the natural law.' In the same speech he said: 'The missing truth about the tragedy of millions of Europeans killed every year by abortion is one of the mournful realities of our times ... A nation that kills its children is a nation without future. The continent that kills its children will be colonized by those who do not kill them ... Abortion should be immediately prohibited. Human life is the highest value on Earth'.

The speech – delivered at a meeting of EU education ministers in Heidelberg, Germany – caused shock and outrage. Around Europe, Giertych was depicted as a 'Nazi', 'fascist' and 'anti-gay demagogue', while at home he received torrents of criticism. The Polish Teachers Union said that his words could destroy 'the efforts of generations of Polish teachers who raised children in the spirit of tolerance, responsibility and openness towards different cultures, religions and beliefs'. Likewise, an online petition addressed to Giertych began, 'It is with anxiety that we notice that under your leadership the actions of the Ministry create the atmosphere which promotes in schools views which are based solely on pseudo-scientific theories, populist opinions and hurtful stereotypes. It is forbidden to present any different point of view.'

Giertych is also renowned for his hostility toward the EU. He criticises European treaties on a regular basis and has helped to reignite the age-old tension between Germany and Poland by questioning the rights of the German minority resident in Poland. (For its part, the EU took exception to an anti-Semitic pamphlet published by Giertych's father. Giertych Snr received an official reprimand from the president of the parliament).

For all these reasons, Giertych is a controversial figure in modern-day Europe. As a Pole, he is informed by traditional Catholicism, and so his unsympathetic attitude to homosexuality and abortion is at least logical. But in his public strictures, he has gone beyond the boundaries of decency and is now viewed as beyond the pale. The former Communist and Eastern Bloc states have given birth to an array of political mavericks since 1989, and Giertych is certainly one of them.

See also League of Polish Families.

Further Reading

http://www.lpr.pl (League of Polish Families website).
Giertych, M. 1963. *Thoughts for Thinking*. Publisher not known.
Blobaum, Robert. 2005. *Antisemitism and Its Opponents in Modern Poland*. Ithaca, NY: Cornell University Press.
Hancock, D.M., 2006. *Politics in Europe: An Introduction to the Politics of the United Kingdom, France, German, Italy, Sweden, Russia, Poland and the European Union*. Washington, DC: CQ Press.

Gothic Ripples Magazine (Great Britain)

British anti-Semite Arnold Leese founded *Gothic Ripples* in 1944. The magazine – often described as a 'hate sheet' – became a vehicle for violent and rabid anti-Semitic and anti-Communist diatribes. After the war, Leese's commentaries continued to rail against the supposed Jewish plot that sought to infiltrate and destroy British society. This threat was now all the greater considering Hitler's war against the Jews had been lost. Leese's racism also moved on to discuss the issue of African and Afro-Caribbean **immigration**. Typical of the deeply xenophobic tenor of this analysis was the 'Nigger Notes' column in the journal. Indeed, according to Leese's racist thinking, the face of leading Kenyan politician Jomo Kenyatta was, in fact, identical to a gorilla's.

After Leese's death in 1956, the publication passed into the hands of his protégé Colin Jordan, the founding father of the British Movement. Indeed, Jordan now seems to use the title in order to publish an irregular news sheet, disseminating Neo-Nazi and racist, far-right ideology. To give some examples of the tone of *Gothic Ripples* in recent years, the September 2001 issue offered a 'partial listing of the Hebrew millionaires financing the party of the puppet Blair'. It read:

The top six Labour Party donors for 2001:

1. Alan Sugar (Jew) £200,000

2. Lakshmi Mittal (Asian) £125,000

3. Christopher Ondaatje (Dutch/Indonesian) £102,500

4. Gulan Noon (Asian) £100,000

5. Ronald Cohen (Jew) £100,000

6. Sigmund Steinburg (Jew) £100,000

Not one Briton!

Another entry from the same period drew on a series of, ultimately manageable, national emergencies in Britain in order to paint a picture of a country falling into deep decline. Note especially the way the article conflates these issues, introducing a critique of immigration and a deeply racist tenor: 'Smoke and flames arise from farms far and wide as the foot-and-mouth disease bestrides our land […] The agricultural calamity has excited the urban zealots of liberalism – hothouse creatures of the concrete jungles who decry and agitate against anything and everything supportive of a national community of Aryans, such as immigration restriction or trade protection […] An open door to foreign food and foreign settlers are fundamental to the foreign mindedness of these deracinated frequenters of the bistros and wine bars of the big city who conceive the whole world as their habitat, and the global mobility of goods and bodies and ideas as the only way to peace and progress'.

Meanwhile, the paper has also spoken out on the **'War on Terrorism'**, again with a typically paranoid, hyperbolic reading of international affairs: 'George Bush, that puerile performer in the razzmatazz which characterises American presidential politics, was instantly supported in his pitiful display of blusterous bravado by Britain's posturing pygmy of a prime minister, Tony Blair, intent on proving all the promptitude of some Pavlovian poodle to the stimulus provided by his master'. The international folly of invading Afghanistan and Iraq would cost the British taxpayer hundreds of millions of pounds, he continued, which was 'just a small part of the colossal cost of foreign purposes entailed in the enforcement of the New World Order of Blair and Bush'. The anti-Semitic core of *Gothic Ripples* then came to the fore: 'The key to an understanding of all this weird procedure lies in the perception of the trouble spot of Israel as a foreign body in an Arab world, and the legitimate hostility in that world to an America and Britain who have allowed the foundation of that foreign body, upstart in its aspirations and tyrannical in its treatment of displaced Arabs, and upheld it despite its wrong doing, due to the power and pressure of their exceedingly powerful Jewish populations. Blair and Bush in their association thus with Israeli terrorism against the Palestinians are progenitors of Arab counter-terrorism'.

A final argument forwarded by the journal of late argues that 'Parliamentary **democracy** is a fraud: a confidence trick'. This could be proved by the alleged fact that the 'great majority of the British people never wanted the Coloured Invasion of their homeland'. The magazine contended that immigration had been forced on the public from above. Through heavy handed laws, the public had been compelled to accept what was described as 'alien occupation and control'. Further, 'this dishonest system [... presents] a deceiving façade of public consideration, deference and accountability, while effectively rigging the situation for the permanent dominance of its beneficiaries by shaping the public mind to its purposes by media indoctrination and by denying facilities to those other than its proprietorial parties and approved elements who are representative of a virtual dictatorship by the real ruling forces in the background'.

The magazine is typical of the minor publications produced on shoestring budgets that disseminate the thinking of the more extreme aspects of the Far Right. *Gothic Ripples* has been available recently by mail-order from an address in Harrogate, four issues for £3.

See also Anti-Semitism.

Further Reading
Eatwell, Roger. 2000. 'The extreme right and British exceptionalism: the primacy of politics'. In *The Politics of the Extreme Right: From the Margins to the Mainstream*. Edited by Paul Hainsworth. London: Pinter.
Eatwell, Roger. 1994. 'Why has the extreme right failed in Britain?' In *The Extreme Right in Europe and the USA*. Edited by Paul Hainsworth. London: Pinter.
Cable, Gerry. 1991. 'The far right in contemporary Britain'. In *Neo-Fascism in Europe*. Edited by Luciano Cheles, Ronnie Ferguson and Michalina Vaughan. London: Longman.
Eatwell, Roger. 1996. *Fascism: A History*. London: Vintage.

Greater Romania Party

As its name suggests, the Greater Romania Party (*Partidul România Mare*, PRM) is an ultra-nationalist movement and is usually pigeon-holed on the Far Right of the Romanian political spectrum. It was founded in 1991 by Corneliu Vadim **Tudor** and writer Eugen Barbu, and has acquired significant influence: it joined Nicolae Văcăroiu's cabinet between 1993 and 1995, and in 2000 its leader Tudor finished second in presidential elections. The party also hit the headlines in 2004 when it secured forty seats in parliament and twenty-one in the senate; a coalition with the ruling PSD was a possibility at this point, but the prime minister, Adrian Nastase, felt that such an alliance could prejudice his country's application to join the EU.

In terms of ideology, the party stands for a pure Romania devoid of troublesome minority groupings such as Hungarians, Jews, homosexuals and gypsies. It is also irredentist in the sense that the idea of a Greater Romania harks back to the inter-war period when all ethnic Romanians were united in a single state (the phrase was actually prohibited during the communist era). The party's flag actually incorporates a map of Greater Romania – as perceived by Tudor and colleagues – rather than Romania as it is today. As Tudor said in 1998: 'Yes, I am a nationalist. I'm a Romanian nationalist ... to be a nationalist means to love your fatherland'. But, in recent years, the party has tried to water down its programme (eg. by retracting much of its fiercely anti-Jewish discourse) in an attempt to make alliances in the European Parliament.

The party is obsessed by the Hungarian question. There is an age-old rivalry between Romania and Hungary, but the rhetoric of Tudor and the PRM has taken this to a new level. Speeches by party leaders have singled out Romania's ethnic Hungarians for harsh treatment. They are viewed as dangerous parasites, keen to destabilise the country at any opportunity. The PRM has taken things to the extreme and claims, on the basis of very little evidence, that Hungary is planning to annex the ethnically mixed region of Transylvania. But this tactic of playing on people's fears in exaggerated fashion has worked to an extent. Opinion polls suggest that the PRM is especially popular with the young and those who reside in Transylvania, where the Hungarian population is sizeable and, thus, where the party's inflamed rhetoric has the potential to resonate most.

It is not surprising that the activities of the PRM have had repercussions. The Democratic Union of Hungarians in Romania has become a significant political force with its aim to add strength to the liberal and left-wing forces that oppose the PRM. At the same time, mainstream politicians have begun to echo some of the party's main themes. The Social Democrats, for instance, have intimated that there might be problems for Romania's Hungarians if they accept full Hungarian citizenship.

In terms of election results, the movement has made great headway. In 1992, it scored 4 percent and in 1996, 5 percent, although this still meant it had twenty-seven seats in parliament. By 2000, though, it had become the second biggest party with 23 percent of the national vote and 126 seats. The party is also noted for its weekly journal *România Mare* and its daily paper *Tricolorul*.

The legacy of the Iron Guard, Codreanu's inter-war Fascist movement, can be seen in the rhetorical posturing of all Romania's modern-day nationalist parties, including the PRM, but Tudor has left his mark too. In 1998, he said that Romania needed to be governed 'from the barrel of a machine-gun', while more recently he commented: 'Romania is caught between anarchy and the Mafia. I will liquidate the Mafia so fast that they won't even have time to glance at their watches to let them know that Romania is ruled by an iron fist'.

See also Romania, Far Right Enters Coalition Government (1994); South-Eastern Europe and the Far Right *and* Tudor, Corneliu Vadim (Romania).

Further Reading

Shafir, M. 2000. 'Marginalization or mainstream? The extreme right in post-communist Romania'. In *The Politics of the Extreme Right: From the Margins to the Mainstream*. Edited by Paul Hainsworth. London: Pinter.

Greek Front

The Greek Front (*Hellenic Front*) was founded in 1994 and ceased to exist in 2004, when it merged with the Popular Orthodox Rally. It was led by lawyer Makis **Voridis** but had a minimal impact in elections. It scored only 0.12 percent in the European poll of 1999, 0.18 percent in the parliamentary elections of 2000, 1.4 percent in the municipal vote in 2002, and 0.09 percent in the parliamentary elections of 2004.

The party also boasted an organisation for young people – the Hellenic **Youth** Front, led by Ioannis Panayotakopoulos. This body was established in 1994 but only started to actively engage in politics in 1998. It said that its objective was to promote Greek **patriotism**, 'build a National Opposition Front, reverse the policy of national servitude and compliance to the orders of foreign interests and, at the same time, propose a modern way which, securing National Sovereignty, leads to **Freedom**, Creativity and Development'. Its newspaper and website was called Hellenic Lines and up to 1,000 people attended its annual youth festivals. The organisation had offices in ten towns and cities as well as the capital, Athens.

Ideologically, the Hellenic Front stood for patriotism and nationalism. It was hostile to outside foreign cultures (it was anti-Turkish and anti-Albanian) and also wished to abolish the Schengen and Maastricht treaties that furthered European integration. In terms of domestic policy, it campaigned for the death penalty.

The Front was particularly hard-line on illegal **immigration**. On this issue, the party had to deal with logistics and practicalities. As Voridis stated in 2002: 'The problem of illegal immigration in Greece is not a question of principles or ideology, but a policy issue, if we assume that there exists a structured national state. If there is a state, then there are borders too. It is known that there are three elements which define the existence of a state: the existence of definite territory, the existence of people living on this territory and the existence of power exercised within the boundaries of the territory for the benefit of the people. And if there exists a state, then the legal distinction between a native and an alien is absolutely legitimate and founded on our Constitution'. Voridis also complained about the anti-racists in the media and the corridors of power whose political correctness meant they rubbished any policy that aimed at reducing immigration levels.

See also Meligalas (Greece); South-Eastern Europe and the Far Right *and* Voridis, Makis (Greece).

Further Reading

http://www.e-grammes.gr/index_en.html (Hellenic Front website).
Dimitras, P.E. 1994. 'Greece: the virtual absence of an extreme right'. In *The Extreme Right in Europe and the USA*. Edited by Paul Hainsworth. London: Pinter.
Kapetanyannis, V. 1991. 'Neo-Fascism in modern Greece'. In *Neo-Fascism in Europe*. Edited by Luciano Cheles, Ronnie Ferguson and Michalina Vaughan. London: Longman.
Featherstone, K., ed. 2005. *Politics and Policy in Greece*. London: Routledge.
Close, D.H. 2002. *Greece Since 1945: A History*. London: Longman.

Griffin, Nick (b.1959) – Great Britain

Nick Griffin was born in London and attended public school in Suffolk before studying history and law at Downing College, Cambridge. He went into agricultural engineering and property before devoting himself to the **British National Party** (BNP), of which he is now chairman. Far-right politics run in the **family**: his mother, Jean, stood as a BNP candidate in the 2001 election and his father, Edgar, was expelled from the Conservative Party after assisting his wife in her role as membership secretary of the BNP. In recent years, Griffin has become the public face of the British Far Right, and in the process he has gained the reputation of being a confident and rather slick political operator.

After a short spell in the **youth** wing of the Conservative Party, Griffin joined the **National Front** (NF) at the age of 15. He became a hardworking political activist or, in the language of the NF itself, a 'political soldier'. He was a local secretary and also joined the party's governing body, the National Directorate, in 1980. He left the NF in 1989 and helped to establish the International Third Position (ITP), an organisation that opposed both capitalism and **Communism**. He switched to the BNP some time between 1993 and 1995, a move that was to transform him into a national political figure.

Griffin was elected leader of the BNP in 1999. Although some of his words and actions may suggest otherwise, his avowed aim has been to re-model the party, cut out its more extremist traits and, in general, make it more electable in local and national elections. In some ways he has been successful in his efforts. In the general election of June 2001, he scored 16 percent in Oldham West & Royton and actually pushed the Liberal Democrats into third place. In 2003, he scored 28 percent in a local council election in Chadderton, Oldham, and in 2005, he polled 9.16 percent in the general election in Keighley, West Yorkshire.

Controversy has surrounded Griffin's career in the BNP. In 1997, he revealed his hostility to the Jews, writing a booklet called *Who are the Mind Benders?* In 1998, he was prosecuted for inciting racial hatred in his role as editor of the anti-Semitic magazine, *The Rune*, and he has questioned the scale of the **Holocaust** on occasions. In 2004, he was arrested on suspicion of incitement to racial hatred and in 2005 he was charged with four offences of using words or behaviour likely to incite racial hatred. In 2006, he was acquitted of these crimes on two separate occasions.

It was during the 2006 court case that a particularly virulent Griffin speech, recorded by an undercover BBC reporter, was relayed. Arguing that the Qur'an condoned rape and paedophilia against non-believers, Griffin stated: 'These attacks are going to continue, because that is what the Qur'an says. The bastards that are in that gang, they are in prison so the public think it's all over. Well it's not. Because there's more of them. Their "good book" tells them that that's acceptable. If you doubt it, go and buy a copy and you will find verse after verse saying you can take any woman you want as long as they're not Muslim. These 18, 19 and 25-year-old Asian Muslims are seducing and raping white girls in this town right now. It's part of their plan for conquering countries. They will expand into the rest of the UK as the last whites try and find their way to the sea. Vote BNP so the British people really realise the evil of what these people have done to our country.'

Griffin lives with his wife and four children on a smallholding in mid-Wales. He has the final say on all matters to do with the party – from policy to finances. Commentators argue that Griffin is trying to modernise the BNP but emphasise that the traces of hard-line neo-Fascism remain. Others focus on Griffin's chameleon-like qualities – in particular, his ability to switch allegiances on and within the Far Right. In recent years, Griffin has been attacked for his links with ex-Ku Klux Klan activist David Duke and Libyan leader Muammar al-Qaddafi. But he has an ability to withstand criticism and take the attack to the opposition – which, in his view, is the ultra-liberal and political-correct British establishment. His electoral scores have been mixed, but he remains a key player on the British Far Right, articulate and forceful in the way that he makes the case for the BNP.

See also British National Party *and* British National Party, Acquittal of Members (2006).

Further Reading

www.bnp.org.uk (BNP website).

Eatwell, Roger. 2000. 'The extreme right and British exceptionalism: the primacy of politics'. In *The Politics of the Extreme Right: From the Margins to the Mainstream*. Edited by Paul Hainsworth. London: Pinter.

Eatwell, Roger. 1994. 'Why has the extreme right failed in Britain?' In *The Extreme Right in Europe and the USA*. Edited by Paul Hainsworth. London: Pinter.

Cable, Gerry. 1991. 'The far right in contemporary Britain'. In *Neo-Fascism in Europe*. Edited by Luciano Cheles, Ronnie Ferguson and Michalina Vaughan. London: Longman.

Durham, Martin. 1991. 'Women and the National Front'. In *Neo-Fascism in Europe*. Edited by Luciano Cheles, Ronnie Ferguson and Michalina Vaughan. London: Longman.

Eatwell, Roger. 1996. *Fascism: A History*. London: Vintage.

Bragg, T., Griffin, N., Kerr, D. & Harrington, P. 2005. *Taking Liberties: A Third Way Special on the Attack on Civil Liberties in the UK*. Pamphlet.

Copsey, N. 2004. *Contemporary British Fascism: The British National Party and the Quest for Legitimacy*. Basingstoke: Palgrave Macmillan.

H

Hagen, Carl (b.1944) – Norway

Carl I. Hagen was chairman of the **Norwegian Progress Party** (*Fremskrittspartiet*) between 1978 and 2006, having taken over following the death of previous leader Anders Lange. He is a veteran parliamentarian and under his stewardship the Progress Party gained in popular support, becoming the second largest party in the country between 1997 and 2001. In a country that prides itself on its liberal values, Hagen has gained a reputation as an outspoken and controversial political leader who has put race and **immigration** on the political agenda.

In 1968, Hagen gained a Higher National Diploma in Business Studies from the Institute of Marketing in London. Thereafter, he worked as an economics consultant and, between 1970 and 1974, a director of Tate & Lyle, Norway. Since 1974, he has been an active member of key standing committees, including those on government administration, finance, foreign affairs and the constitution, and scrutiny and constitutional affairs. He has also served on official Norwegian delegations to the Nordic Council and with responsibility for relations with the European Parliament. Between 1997 and 2001, he was also a member of the EEA Consultative Committee and deputy chairman of the Norwegian Delegation to the EFTA and EEA Parliamentary Committees. In parliament, he acted as deputy chairman (1976–1977) and chairman (1981–2005) of the Progress Party parliamentary group.

Hagen began his political career in the *Anders Langes* Party in 1973 and 1974, but by 1978 had become chairman of the Progress Party. He is also an experienced politician at local government level. Between 1979 and 1982 he was a member of the Oslo Executive Board and in three spells (1987–1991, 1995–1999 and 1999–2003) a member of Oslo City Parliament. Of most significance, however, is his contribution at a national level. In October 2001, he and his party agreed to support a coalition government comprised of Christian Democrats, Conservatives and Liberals, led by former prime minister Kjell Bondevik. This led to a media frenzy, with certain publications arguing that – although not in government – the Norwegian Far Right was closer to power than at any time since the days of Vidkun Quisling's pro-Nazi *Nasjonal Samling* (National Unity) party.

On an ideological level, Hagen – like his party – offers a strange blend of liberal and illiberal prescriptions for Norway's problems. He believes in *laissez-faire* economics, welfarism and an end to the big state. He also says that Norway is 'full up' and cannot accommodate any more immigrants, particularly when, in his opinion, many turn out to be criminals and terrorists. In 2004 Hagen commented: 'The Islamic fundamentalists, along the same lines as Hitler, made it clear a long time ago that their long-term plan is to "Islamify" the world. They're well underway ... We Christians are very concerned about children, "Let the children come to me," said Jesus. I can't see Mohammed saying the same. If he (Mohammed) did say such a thing, it must have been: "Let the small children come to me, so that I can exploit them in my effort to make the world Islamic."' This statement caused outrage in the media, among mainstream politicians and anti-racist organisations. Some Muslim groups threatened to sue Hagen for blasphemy.

Hagen has also demonstrated his solidarity with the State of Israel. He has argued that Israel is a 'symbolic issue' and 'must be defended'. Moreover, he has drawn a parallel between the fence that Israel erected to shut out the Palestinians and his party's belief in immigrant quotas. His view is that, 'We must remember our own values. We must show tolerance, we must accept, and we must forgive. But some times we also need to draw a few borders, and I believe those borders in Norway should say: Norway is founded in Christian values. We respect our ancestors. One of our values is that we must care for our children. But we should also show respect for our parents and grandparents, for the country they built, the country we have inherited, or at least borrowed for our lifetime. And we should say that when it comes to those Christian values our country is founded in, those must also apply to those who come to our country, even if they believe in another **religion**.'

Hagen is a curious figure. He established himself as a hardworking parliamentarian, but has also attracted criticism on account of his jocular media appearances – he recently took part in a celebrity game-show, *Den Store Klassefesten*, and also appeared on YouTube as the drummer in a rock band. Doctrinally, too, he is an odd blend of the libertarian and the authoritarian. He has been succeeded as Progress Party leader by Siv Jensen, but he remains an interesting and significant figure on the Norwegian Far Right.

See also Norway, Far-Right Gains (2001); Norwegian Progress Party *and* Scandinavia and the Far Right.

Further Reading

http://www.frp.no (Progress Party website).

Hagen, C.I. 1984. *Honesty is the Best Policy*. Publisher not known.

Andersen, J.G. & Bjørklund, T. 2000. 'Radical right-wing populism in Scandinavia: from tax revolt to neo-liberalism and xenophobia'. In *The Politics of the Extreme Right: From the Margins to the Mainstream*. Edited by Paul Hainsworth. London: Pinter.

Shaffer, W.R. 1998. *Politics, Parties, and Parliaments: Political Change in Norway*. Columbus, OH: Ohio State University Press.

Haider, Jörg (b.1950) – Austria

Jörg Haider was born to parents with direct links to the Nazi Party in Germany. His father, Robert, joined the NSDAP in 1929 and the 'Austrian Legion', a division of the Sturmabteilung, in 1934. He served on both Western and Eastern fronts during the Second World War and was discharged from the Wehrmacht with the rank of lieutenant. In 1945, he married Dorothea Rupp, who at the time worked as a leader in the Bund Deutscher Mädel (BDM) or League of German Girls – a branch of the Hitler **Youth**. This detail is significant given the reputation that Haider was to acquire during his political career – in short, a man who represented a modern Far Right and who also had praise for some of Hitler's policies.

Haider attended high school in Bad Ischl, where he first had contacts with organisations such as the Burschenschaft Albia, a right-wing, nationalist student group. He graduated in 1968 and moved on to study law in Vienna, where again he was affiliated to the Burschenschaften. After graduating from university in 1973, he was drafted into the Austrian army and took the option of extending his term beyond the statutory nine months, serving 'the voluntary one year'. In 1974 he started work at the University of Vienna in the department of constitutional law.

In 1970, Haider became the leader of the FPÖ youth movement, which he headed until 1974. He was made party affairs manager of the Carinthian FPÖ in 1976, and in 1979, aged 29, he became the youngest deputy in the Austrian parliament. After becoming leader of the Carinthian FPÖ in 1983, he started to emerge as a critic of the party leadership. His political breakthrough followed in 1986 when he defeated the Austrian vice-chancellor Norbert Steger in the vote for the leadership of the party. This ended the FPÖ's liberal coalition with the Social Democrat government, as Haider moved the party further to the right. In the same year, he attracted international attention by supporting the return of Walter Reder, an Austrian-born former major in the Nazi SS. Reder had been freed from a life sentence he was serving in Italy for his role in the mass killing of Italian civilians in 1944. Haider claimed that Reder was 'a soldier who had done his duty' and stated: 'If you are going to speak about war crimes, you should admit such crimes were committed by all sides'.

Haider became Governor of **Carinthia** in 1989. This first spell as regional chief ended in 1991 following remarks he made in response to criticism of his proposal to institute a Nazi-style policy during a debate on unemployment benefits. Haider claimed, 'it would not be like the Third Reich, because the Third Reich developed a proper employment policy, which your government in Vienna has not once produced'. He resigned during the subsequent furore, and the FPÖ-ÖVP coalition was replaced by an SPÖ-ÖVP alliance. However, the FPÖ came again. After receiving only 5 percent of the vote in the 1986 elections, the party claimed 22.6 percent in the 1994 poll. It also increased its representation in the 183-seat parliament from 13 seats in 1990 to 42. During this period, his leadership style became increasingly authoritarian, but he remained unchallenged due to the party's continued success.

Haider combined a nationalist, anti-**immigration** and anti-EU agenda with an anti-establishment populist stance which attracted many protest votes. However, his defence of Nazi policies and use of terminology reminiscent of the Nazis continued to cause problems in the early part of the decade. In October 1990, he announced a 'final solution to the farm question' and in 1995 the FPÖ was the only major Austrian political party absent from ceremonies marking the fiftieth anniversary of the liberation of the death camp at Mauthausen. Haider referred to Mauthausen as a 'punishment camp', implying that those interred there were criminals. In 1995, while addressing a gathering of war veterans, he said, 'A people that does not honour earlier generations is a people condemned to ruin. We shall prove that we are not to be wiped out ... We are morally superior to other people'. After amateur video footage of the speech was broadcast on television, Haider said that, 'the Waffen SS was part of the Wehrmacht and because of that it deserves every honour and recognition'.

However, with the increased success of the party, he also made attempts to detach his public image from the Far Right and improve his international standing. After a 1994 visit to the Holocaust Museum in Washington D.C., he declared: 'I think that even those individuals who don't know much about history will realise that we must do everything to enforce tolerance, everything to enforce human rights and everything to strengthen **democracy**'. He also visited the Simon Weisenthal Centre's Museum of Tolerance in Los Angeles in 1995, although this came at a time when the FPÖ was campaigning against a plan to make the famed Nazi-hunter Weisenthal an honorary Austrian citizen. Haider also appointed Peter Sichrovshky, a Jewish Viennese journalist, as his number-two candidate for the European elections in October 1996.

The party's continued rise in popularity throughout the 1990s culminated in the formation of a coalition government with the ÖVP in 2000, after the FPÖ had finished second in the elections, gaining 27 percent of the vote. The fourteen other members of the EU subsequently suspended dealings with the Austrian Government. Although EU sanctions lasted for only a few months, Haider resigned as leader of the FPÖ at the end of 2000. This was seen by many as simply an attempt to appease foreign criticism of the coalition, and he appeared to have effectively retained control of the FPÖ under the new leader, Susanne Reiss Passer.

After the high point of the 2000 election, the fortunes of the FPÖ declined rapidly and the elections in 2002 saw the party gain only 10.16 percent of the national vote. This followed internal rupture in the FPÖ at the September party convention. The so-called 'Knittlefeld Putsch' resulted in Reiss Passer losing the support of many party members, before resigning as federal vice-chancellor and party chairwoman. Haider was strongly linked to the events and subsequently demanded he be reinstalled as leader of the party. After being refused, he announced that he would leave federal politics permanently. Haider remained a popular figure in Carinthia and was elected governor again in 1999, when the FPÖ returned 42 percent of the vote. His position was reinforced in the 2004 elections, when a return of 42.5 percent of the vote saw him re-elected as governor and an FPÖ/ÖVP coalition government was formed.

After the decline of the FPÖ in national politics continued in the 2004 European elections, Haider moved to form a new political party. He joined with other leading members of the FPÖ, including his sister Ursula Haubner and the Austrian Vice Chancellor Hubert Gorbach, to form the Alliance for the Future of Austria (*Bündnis Zukunft Österreich* – BZÖ). The BZÖ retained links with the FPÖ, but despite this coalition, both remain on the fringes of domestic politics. Haider again caused international controversy in the aftermath of the 11 September attacks in 2001, through his sympathy for Saddam Hussain. He made a number of trips to meet the Iraqi leader, to reportedly discuss the 'Zionist and US conspiracy' against Iraq, and has also been linked to Abdul Monheim Jebara. Jebara is reportedly an Iraqi arms dealer who acts as a liaison between Saddam Hussein and sympathetic far-right groups in **Europe**.

Debate remains as to whether Haider is a genuine far-right politician or simply a populist opportunist. He is a slick and charismatic politician – famous for his smooth talking and fashionable suits. From this, one would assume that he is trying to disassociate himself from the more 'thuggish' elements on the Far Right. Yet, at the same time, he has repeatedly spoken in positive terms about aspects of the Nazi regime. In this respect, he is a contradiction, but he is also a product of Austrian political culture in the sense that many individuals and families will have had, and perhaps still have, connections with Nazism or neo-Nazism. Haider may have left the **Freedom Party** but he remains a prominent figure in Austrian politics.

See also Alliance for Austria's Future; Foundation by Haider (2005), Austrian Freedom Party *and* Carinthia (Austria).

Further Reading

http://www.bzoe.at (Alliance for the Future of Austria website).

http://www.fpoe.at (Freedom Party website).

Höbelt, L. 2003. *Defiant Populist: Jörg Haider and the Politics of Austria 1986–2000*. West Lafayette: Purdue University Press.

Morrow, D. 2000. 'Jörg Haider and the new FPÖ: beyond the democratic pale'. In *The Politics of the Extreme Right: From the Margins to the Mainstream*. Edited by Paul Hainsworth. London: Pinter.

The Holocaust (1939–1945)

The Nazis' policy of genocide as a 'Final Solution' to the 'Jewish Question' during the Second World War was so comprehensive that the term 'Holocaust' was introduced to convey its uniqueness. Translated from Greek and Latin, it roughly means 'burned offering', and is also sometimes called 'Shoah'. Approximately six million European Jews were killed as part of this organised programme of extermination. When gypsies, homosexuals, disabled people, religious minorities and prisoners of the regime are added to the death toll, the figure rises to about ten million people killed by the Nazis. Consequently, the Holocaust is widely regarded as the most horrific crime of the twentieth century, and of modern history more generally.

Since 1945, most far-right groups have had to deal with the legacy of the Holocaust in one way or another. This raises the following basic questions: Do you accept and acknowledge the Holocaust? Do you state at the outset that you do not wish to be linked in any way to this horrific phase in human history? Or do you locate your viewpoint somewhere else, for example by minimising and underplaying the scale of the Holocaust?

Typifying the final position, Jean-Marie **Le Pen**, the leader of the Front National (*Front National*, FN) in France, has 'crossed the line' of disassociating his politics from interwar Fascism and has made many provocative comments relating to the Holocaust. In one notorious example, on 13 September 1987, he said: 'I ask myself several questions. I'm not saying the gas chambers didn't exist. I haven't seen them myself. I haven't particularly studied the question. But I believe it's just a detail in the history of World War II.' Clearly, this statement should not be read at face value, and the attempt to argue that the nature of the concentration camps and death camps were mere details was a highly provocative gesture articulated by a politician who knew the impact value of these comments. Le Pen was later fined 1.2 million francs for this outburst. Other court actions have followed. For example, Le Pen also lost his immunity at the European Parliament in Strasbourg in 1997 so that he could be tried for comments he made in 1996, again arguing that the Holocaust was a minor 'detail of history': 'If you take a 1,000-page book on World War II, the concentration camps take up only two pages and the gas chambers 10 to 15 lines. This is what one calls a detail.' Finally, in June 1999, a German court found him guilty of 'minimising the Holocaust' and convicted and fined him accordingly.

Other far-right leaders have also been accused of historical revisionism. Jörg **Haider** in Austria has drawn on the memory of the Holocaust, and has attempted to rehabilitate many other Nazi policies. In 1994, however, he visited the Holocaust Museum in Washington DC and commented afterwards: 'I think that even those individuals who don't know much about history will realise that we must do everything to enforce tolerance, everything to enforce human rights and everything to strengthen **democracy**.' Nevertheless, his reputation still precedes him. In 2000, Haider was barred from Montreal's Holocaust Centre on an unannounced trip to Canada because of his notoriety. Haider and other far-right politicians, then, have used the Holocaust as a reference point, not only to parade their own radicalism, but also in attempts to present their views in a more moderate light. Other hard-line nationalists – ranging from Franjo **Tuđman** in Croatia to Nick **Griffin** in Britain – have also had to defend themselves against accusations of historical revisionism. Indeed, Griffin has even referred to the Holocaust as the 'Holohoax'.

One of the most significant Holocaust deniers of recent years has been David Irving – a publicist who often addresses far-right gatherings and who was convicted of **Holocaust denial** in Austria in 2006. Previously, Irving failed in an attempt to sue American academic Deborah Lipstadt for libel after she accused him of Holocaust denial. In a court case where Professor Richard Evens acted as an expert witness, Irving's scholarship on the Holocaust was revealed as deeply flawed. Other institutions promoting Holocaust denial within the Far Right include the US-based Institute for Historical Review. Recently, Iran held a conference dedicated to this topic, which was attended by many far-right Holocaust deniers, demonstrating the existence of a radical new politics between Islamist and far-right forms of **anti-Semitism**.

See also Anti-Semitism; Central Europe and the Far Right *and Mein Kampf* by Adolf Hitler, (Germany).

Further Reading
Evans, Richard J. 2002. *Telling Lies about Hitler: The Holocaust, History and the David Irving Trial*. London and New York: Verso.
Lipstadt, Deborah E. 1993. *Denying the Holocaust: The Growing Assault on Truth and Memory*. New York: Free Press.
Shermer, Michael. 2000. *Denying History: Who Says the Holocaust Never Happened and Why Do They Say It?* Los Angeles: University of California Press.

Homosexuality

In the canon of far-right doctrine, special vitriol is reserved for homosexuality. The **National Front** in Britain is representative: 'All the available evidence suggests that a happy **family** is the ideal **environment** in which children can grow and develop. Over the past twenty years there has been a marked decline in this type of arrangement ... The National Front does not regard homosexual or lesbian relationships as valid alternatives to normal heterosexual marriage. The NF would repeal the laws permitting homosexuality and its promotion'.

Across **Europe**, far-right movements have campaigned in favour of a pure and natural family unit. In this sense, they put forward text-book conservative attitudes: the family is the bedrock of society, it is traditional, and it is also the arrangement most conducive to demographic growth.

This last point is vital. In many European countries the Far Right is concerned about the issue of the birth-rate. And at times, this concern evolves into paranoia. In France *dénatalité* (population regression) has been a major issue for generations, with key figures on the Far Right (and also in the centre and on the left) advancing apocalyptic visions of a French nation in terminal decline. The FN has certainly taken up the gauntlet and has been ferocious in its opposition to contraception, abortion and, of course, homosexuality (which it refers to as *sodomie*).

In Britain the Far Right has been active on the issue. In August 2007, the National Front campaigned against the Gay Parade in Manchester. The party stated: 'Our message was seen by the homosexuals, lesbians, drag queens and assorted social misfits as they passed by in procession ... We were pleased that this year's parade seemed smaller than it was in 2006 ... Certainly the whole gay scene is being driven by Communists, mainly from within the mass media, as well as big business. Those promoting the homosexual agenda are the same people who push multi-racialism, alien culture, race-mixing and the need for more **immigration**. Leftists do this while at the same time they denigrate our **religion** and arts, as well as any form of British achievement'. Here, homosexuality is viewed not as normal and natural but as some kind of leftist plot.

The BNP has also joined the fray. In 2006, it protested against the Lesbian, Gay, Bisexual and Transgender/Transsexual history month being held in schools, calling the venture an 'atrocity' and railing against this 'unwholesome "alternative life-style" propaganda' and these 'unhealthy and unwanted social-engineering indoctrination exercises'. In response, Ben Summerskill, Chief Executive of Stonewall, said: 'Homopohobia is still widespread in too much of Britain and too many young lesbian, gay, bisexual and transgender people have attempted suicide by the time they are teenagers. **Education** is the only way to challenge this. Acceptance starts in schools ... The BNP's homophobia must be challenged nationally and locally'.

In France, the FN has opposed gay parades, and in Orange, Vitrolles, Marignane and Toulon – where it has held municipal power – the party worked hard to undermine festivals and events at which gay films were being shown. Other parties are more subtle in their discourse. In Norway the Progress Party says that it is 'totally opposed to discrimination on the basis of race, gender, religion and ethnic origin,' but interestingly does not mention sexuality.

The ultimate irony, of course, is that key far-right figures – individuals who have been at the forefront of anti-homosexual campaigns - are actually rumoured to be gay themselves.

See also Family; The Ideology of the Far Right *and* Women.

Further Reading

Glennerster, Howard and Midgley, James, eds. 1991. *The Radical Right and the Welfare State: an International Assessment*. London: Harvester Wheatsheaf.
Ignazi, Piero. 2003. *Extreme Right Parties in Western Europe*. New York: Oxford University Press.
Kitschelt, Herbert. 1997. *The Radical Right in Western Europe: A Comparative Analysis*. Michigan: University of Michigan Press.

Horrors of War by Franjo Tuđman (Croatia)

Horrors of War (*Bespuća Povijesne Zbiljnosti*) is the most notorious book written by former Croatian leader Franjo **Tuđman**. Published in Zagreb in 1989, the work gave Tuđman the necessary space in which to meditate on history, fate and political relationships in the Balkans. The title of the book also translates as *Wastelands of Historical Reality*.

The volume gained infamy during the Yugoslav wars of the 1990s because of Tuđman's claim that the Jasenovac concentration camp – run by the Croatian Ustaše during the Second World War – was slightly less murderous than mainstream historians had believed. The author quoted the figure of 60,000 for Serb, Jewish and gypsy deaths, while the consensus previously had been between 500,000 and 1,000,000. Half a century on, the scale of the killings became a major issue, with Serbs, Jews and the left claiming that Tuđman's revisionism had purposefully and maliciously underestimated the horror of the camp, with the Croats arguing against, and all of this feeding into the unsavoury conflicts and tensions of the period.

Tuđman's argument in the book has several strands: first, that the Ustaše-run Independent State of Croatia was pressurised by Hitler's Nazi regime; second, that Jasenovac was merely a 'work camp'; and third, that, anyway, **anti-Semitism** was not a major component of the wartime state's ideology. These lines of reasoning are blended with a number of lies and falsehoods, and an attempt to shift and share the blame. Four years after the book was published, in 1993, **Tuđman** became president of Croatia and it was translated into several languages.

Outrageous as the book's claims were, it is generally acknowledged to have increased Tuđman's standing with certain groups of Croat nationalists, in particular, many *émigrés* who were potential sponsors of his HDZ party. For most onlookers, however, it served to discredit Tuđman and his embryonic nation, and came close to infringing Holocaust-denial laws. Not surprisingly, the author was forced to publish an amended edition of the book.

Following the death of Tuđman in 1999, Croatia went on what can best be described as a public relations offensive. On 31 October 2001, President Stipe Mesic spoke to the Israeli parliament, claiming forgiveness and promising a new beginning in relations: 'I am speaking on behalf of democratic Croatia, which upholds the traditions of anti-Fascist and **freedom**-loving Croatia from the times of the Second World War. I am speaking on behalf of that Croatia which bows with respect and reverence to the memory of the millions of the victims of the Holocaust … I am using every opportunity to ask for forgiveness from all those who were harmed by the Croats at any time. Of course, from the Jews in the first place. As President of the Republic of Croatia, I profoundly and sincerely regret the crimes committed against the Jews during the Second World War on the territory of the Quisling entity called the Independent State of Croatia that was neither independent nor Croatian'. Tuđman and his book were obviously on everyone's minds as the president spoke. Later, in 2004, Croatian premier Ivo Sanader condemned his country's wartime record and paid tribute to the victims of Jasenovac.

See also Croatian Democratic Union; South-Eastern Europe and the Far Right *and* Tuđman, Dr Franjo (Croatia).

Further Reading
http://www.hdz.hr (HDZ website).
Tanner, Marcus. 1997. *Croatia: A Nation Forged in War*. New Haven, CT: Yale University Press.

Hungarian Justice and Life Party

The Hungarian Justice and Life Party (*Magyar Igazság és Élet Pártja*, MIÉP) was founded in 1993 and is currently led by István **Csurka**. Its share of the national vote has been 1.58 percent (1994), 5.47 percent (1998), 4.37 percent (2002) and 2.20 percent (2006).

MIÉP is an ultra-nationalist party. It believes in an imaginary Greater Hungary and speaks up for the Hungarian minority in Romania. Its **anti-Semitism** is well documented. Csurka is renowned for his inflammatory speeches that target the Jews and alarm the 20,000 Holocaust survivors who live in Hungary. He is also keen to emphasise the role of Jews in recent Hungarian history. In 2004, for example, at a rally organised to remember the uprising of 1956, Csurka made a point of reading out the names of communist leaders with obviously Jewish names; and in 2006 he claimed that a total of 178 Hungarian estate agencies were controlled by Jews.

In 2002, party vice-president Lóránt Hegedüs received an 18-month suspended prison sentence after demanding the segregation of Jews; and in their efforts to spread their doctrine and ideology, it has been claimed that the MIÉP is aided by the fact that the Hungarian media is notoriously open-minded and feels that it has to give air-time to the party.

12. The leader of the far right Hungarian Truth and Life Party (MIEP), István Csurka, addresses thousands of people gathered in Budapest's Heroes Square, 4 June 2000.

The movement has also called for the expulsion of all gypsies from Hungary. It describes its ideology as 'Neither right nor left, Christian and Hungarian'. Or as MIÉP spokesman Miklós Haraszti says: 'This party is anti-Western, anti-capitalist, anti-communist and anti-liberal, and believes that all these enemies are either Jewish or commanded by Jews'.

In 2005, the Hungarian Justice and Life Party formed an alliance with the Movement for a Better Hungary called The Third Way, and declared that its aim was to speak up for victims of crime and Hungarian minorities in other countries. It had previously neutralised Fidesz, the mainstream conservative party, by offering political support in exchange for what amounted to a non-hostility pact.

See also Curska, István (Hungary) *and* South-Eastern Europe and the Far Right.

Further Reading

http://www.miep.hu (MIEP website).

Körösényi, András. 2000. *Government and Politics in Hungary*. Budapest: Central European University Press.

Spirova, M. 2007. *Political Parties in Post-Communist Societies: Formation, Persistence, and Change*. New York: Palgrave.

I

I Was There by Franz Schönhuber (Germany)

I Was There (*Ich War Dabei*) is the controversial autobiography of German far-right politician Franz **Schönhuber**, published in 1981. In the book, the REP leader recounted his wartime career in the Waffen SS. Although he later proved that the memoir did not identify him with the Nazi regime, it was generally felt that he had minimised and underplayed the extent and gravity of Third Reich policy. Although the book turned out to be a bestseller, and gave Schönhuber a public profile that would help him make his mark as leader of the REP, it also resulted in him being sacked from his job as deputy chief editor of Bavarian television.

See also Central Europe and the Far Right; Schönhuber, Franz (Germany) *and* Republican Party (Germany).

Further Reading

http://www.rep.de (Republikaner Party website).

Kolinsky, E. 1994. 'A future for right extremism in Germany?' In *The Extreme Right in Europe and the USA*. Edited by Paul Hainsworth. London: Pinter.

Backer, Susann., 2000. 'Right-wing extremism in unified Germany'. In *The Politics of the Extreme Right: From the Margins to the Mainstream*. Edited by Paul Hainsworth. London: Pinter.

Eatwell, Roger. 1996. *Fascism: A History*. London: Vintage.

Childs, David. 1991. 'The Far Right in Germany since 1945'. In *Neo-Fascism in Europe*. Edited by Luciano Cheles, Ronnie Ferguson and Michalina Vaughan. London: Longman.

Husbands, Christopher T. 1991. 'Militant neo-Nazism in the Federal Republic of Germany in the 1980s'. In *Neo-Fascism in Europe*. Edited by Luciano Cheles, Ronnie Ferguson and Michalina Vaughan. London: Longman.

Stöss, R. 1991. *Politics Against Democracy: Extreme Right in West Germany*. New York and Oxford: Berg.

The Identity, Tradition and Sovereignty Group, Rise and Fall (2007)

On 9 January 2007, the Identity, Tradition, Sovereignty Group (ITS) published its formal charter and six days later, on 15 January, it made its parliamentary debut. Those on the Far Right who had been waiting for the opportunity to establish a formal group since July 2004 were aided by the entry of Romania and Bulgaria into the **European Union**. The arrival of five right-wing Romanian MEPs and one right-wing Bulgarian MEP then provided the necessary personnel because a formally constituted group needs to comprise at least nineteen MEPs from five different countries.

Critical comment was soon to follow. The Anti-Defamation League (ADL) called the development 'a disturbing show of unity among bigots.' National Director of the ADL Abraham H. Foxman argued that it was 'outrageous' that a group comprised of anti-Semites and racists could have achieved a level of support that qualified them for European Union funding. Despite the memory of the **Holocaust**, he claimed that the formation of the Identity, Tradition and Sovereignty Group represented a wider growth in cultures of intolerance, a politics where minorities and foreigners are targeted by far-right politicians. Foxman was adamant that the European Parliament was no place for the promotion of racism and **anti-Semitism**. Therefore, it was the duty of all politicians to condemn the activities and views of the group, and rather promote inclusion and opportunity rather than division and exclusion. Meanwhile, *Searchlight* magazine was bemused. Indeed, reporting of the emergence of the Identity, Tradition and Sovereignty Group, it highlighted the irony of this development: many far-right parties vociferously opposed Romanian and Bulgarian accession to the EU in 2007, but now the Far Right found ways to capitalise on the influx of far-right MEPs from these very same countries.

13. Italian European deputy Alessandra Mussolini leaves a meeting of the Identity, Tradition and Sovereignty group at the European Parliament, Strasbourg, 13 November 2007.

The leader of the new grouping was Bruno Gollnisch of the French Front National (*Front National*, FN). He sought to rekindle the memory of the previous far-right group in the European Parliament, which was led by Jean-Marie **Le Pen** in the 1980s and called the Group of the European Right. This had fallen apart in 1989 following the addition of the German Republicans (*Die Republikaner*, REP) to the group. The REP clashed with the **Italian Social Movement** (*Movimento Sociale Italiano*, MSI) over the South Tyrol question. A follow-on Technical Group of the European Right ran until 1994, headed by the FN, until fresh parliamentary elections led to the dissolution of this group due to a lack of potential members.

Immigration

In the end, the fate of the Identity, Tradition and Sovereignty Group was even less successful that these preceding groups. In November 2007, it split after members of the Greater Romanian Party (*Partidul România Mare*, PRM) resigned following comments by Alessandra Mussolini claiming that Romanians were 'habitual law-breakers'. PRM leader Corneliu Vadim **Tudor** responded by withdrawing his party from the group, claiming that they would conduct no further business with Mussolini. This walkout deprived the group of its requisite members, and so it has collapsed. This draws out the problems facing any attempt at far-right diplomacy on an international scale – the innate urge of the Far Right to make belligerent, nationalistic comments does not sit comfortably with international attempts at working together to achieve wider goals.

See also Europe *and* European Union, Treaty of Maastricht (1992).

Further Reading
Searchlight, 'Far-right bloc collapses', http://www.searchlightmagazine.com/index.php?link=template&story=215 (cited 31 December 2007).
Searchlight, 'Far right forms new group in European Parliament', http://www.searchlightmagazine.com/index.php?link=template&story=191 (cited 31 December 2007).

Immigration

If one issue has come to be linked almost permanently with the Far Right it is immigration. In previous eras, Jewish immigration and established local populations were seen as the primary targets for the ire of the Far Right, forming an easy scapegoat group. Indeed, in the late-nineteenth century and in the interwar period, **anti-Semitism** almost defined those on the extreme-right of the political spectrum. Epitomising this prejudice in intellectual circles were the writings of figures such as Edouard Drumont, Maurice Barrès and Charles Maurras in France, while Hitler has become symbolic of the elevation of anti-Semitism to executive office. However, in the post-war era, European society has undergone many cultural and social transformations and so the figures that are targeted by far-right scapegoating have moved on. Although there are still sizeable Jewish communities across the continent, in the post-war period it has been non-European migrants, especially Afro-Caribbean and Asian immigrants, who have become the primary focus of far-right scapegoating. Because of their skin colour, such migrants have been quickly identified as 'other' and so are easier to target and deploy as scapegoat figures in party literature and speeches. Arguably, immigration has become as central a concern to the current Far Right as anti-Semitism was to the Nazis.

In political terms, then, the issue of immigration, especially the consternation it can raise in the wider public imagination, has been a great boon for the Far Right. It is a topic that can be discussed in a simple black and white manner (sometimes literally), and can feed into a diverse set of wider issues such as asylum, liberal economics, housing and social welfare policies, as well as both levels of unemployment and levels of welfare support given to those seeking work. Typifying the link established between unemployment and immigration, in France one of the FN's most controversial slogans was 'Two Million Unemployed is Two Million Immigrants Too Many'.

Clearly, immigration is a highly emotive topic. From a far-right perspective, this has led many leaders to wax lyric about the purity of the national stock, stoking fears of internal threats to the nation from potential fifth columns of immigrants, alongside wild speculation concerning the future demographic make-up. Many far-right parties are also in denial regarding the historical trends of migration into the countries they champion. They each claim, falsely of course, that their country is somehow different, and uniquely has never been a country affected by immigration. Typifying this trope in far-right discourse, Jean-Marie **Le Pen** makes such claims of France. This is despite the fact that many colleagues in his party have surnames that suggest Italian or Portuguese ancestry.

In the **Danish People's Party** (*Dansk Folkeparti*, DPP), similar assertions have been made. It argues that Denmark has never been a country affected by inward migration, and so it should not develop a multicultural society in the future. The country's rule of law, it claims, must be developed along the lines of Danish culture, and needs to work as a system that protects Danish interests and values. It does agree that, in certain circumstances, foreigners can reside in Denmark, but only so long as they do not pose a security risk. Further, in limited situations, foreign nationals could be offered Danish citizenship, but only after they had conformed to a rigorous set of rules in accordance with the constitution. Similarly, the Sweden Democrats (*Sverigedemokraterna*, SD) have called for the end of a multicultural society. It argues that the trend towards a plural society jeopardises the homogenous composition of Sweden. Therefore, Swedish immigration laws need to be far tighter in order to protect Swedish culture from the modern trends of immigration from across the globe. 'The mass immigration of the past decades' it claims, 'has come to pose a serious threat to our national identity by creating huge areas populated by people who will never see themselves as Swedish nor as part of our culture or our history'.

By contrast, some far-right parties, like the National Front (NF) in Britain, still openly couch their hostility to immigration in terms of race and colour. It argues that, across the globe, there are a vibrant range of races and cultures which have developed over many hundreds of years. NF policies, allegedly, have the protection of this cultural diversity at heart. The party maintains that each culture is uniquely suited to an individual race, a relationship between race and culture that has accumulated over many generations. From this anthropological stance, the NF argues that it seeks nothing more than to promote the wish of the majority of the British people, which, it alleges, is for the country to remain a white nation. Therefore, it not only promotes the termination of all non-white immigration into Britain, but also endorses the phased repatriation of all coloured people living within British borders. Meanwhile, the **British National Party** (BNP) – perhaps kidding themselves that they are a future party of government – talk about practicalities involved in their immigration policies. They have offered five programmatic points on this issue. Firstly, the BNP claims that the rule of law must be maintained, so all illegal immigrants need to be deported immediately upon discovery. Secondly, it argues for far-tighter border controls as a way to maintain national sovereignty. Thirdly, it would abide by the obligations outlined by the 1951 United Nations Convention on Refugees. Fourthly, it would redraft laws and tighten up enforcement regarding immigration in order to guarantee that there were no lengthy appeal processes, and also to ensure that there were no *de facto* amnesties for current illegal immigrants. Finally, the party would enforce a lifetime ban on all people who broke the BNP's strict immigration laws, enforced by immediate deportation.

Immigration

In many European countries, immigration has also become tied up with issues of **religion**, especially Islam and the **'War on Terror'**. The fact that a good proportion of new immigrants into **Europe** come from North Africa and Asia has allowed far-right movements to spotlight Islam and its alleged iniquities as a faith. In recent years especially, Islam has been systematically vilified by the Far Right, whose politicians have portrayed the faith as a backward, evil and potentially dangerous ideology. The Danish cartoon debate in 2006 gave the Far Right even greater scope to criticise Islam. The BNP decided to distribute copies of the offending material, while the SD asked supporters to send in their own cartoons of the Prophet Mohammed – and promptly had their website shut down. The recent 'War on Terror', then, has played into the hands of far-right movements that are keen to demonise Muslim migrants and their religion because it has increasingly promoted the notion that world affairs should be viewed through the lens of a 'clash of civilisations'.

See also The Ideology of the Far Right *and* Islam and the Far Right.

Further Reading

Hainsworth, Paul, ed. 2000. *The Politics of the Extreme Right: From the Margins to the Mainstream.* London: Pinter.
Ignazi, Piero. 2003. *Extreme Right Parties in Western Europe.* New York: Oxford University Press.
Kitschelt, Herbert. 1997. *The Radical Right in Western Europe: A Comparative Analysis.* Michigan: University of Michigan Press.

Irving and Holocaust Denial (2006)

In February 2006, David Irving was imprisoned in Austria for the Holocaust denial. This conviction was both a legal milestone, and a further example of his work being discredited in a court of law. Indeed, the historical accuracy of Irving's work had already been undermined by a previous trial where he tried and failed to sue a historian of Jewish studies, Deborah Lipstadt, for libel after she had described Irving's work as Holocaust denial in her book *Denying the Holocaust*.

In the Austrian case, both the arrest and the trial of Irving were cloaked in drama. The story began when he was detained by police on a motorway in southern Austria on his way to give a lecture to a group of students. Subsequently, he was held in custody and then, when his court case began, he arrived in handcuffs but with a copy of his book, *Hitler's War*, under one arm. Irving also changed his line of augment whilst under examination. With reference to his earlier claim that Hitler *had not* killed millions of Jews, he told the court: 'I said that then, based on my knowledge at the time, but by 1991 when I came across the Eichmann papers, I wasn't saying that anymore and I wouldn't say that now. The Nazis did murder millions of Jews.' He also criticised the idea of being put on trial for simply giving his interpretation of the historical record: 'History is a constantly growing tree – the more you know, the more documents become available, the more you learn, and I have learned a lot since 1989 [...] Of course it's a question of **freedom** of speech.' He then added, 'I think within 12 months this law will have vanished from the Austrian statute book.'

Irving pleaded guilty to the charge, which was based on an interview and speech he gave in Austria in 1989. He was sentenced to three years in prison. After the verdict he commented: 'I made a mistake when I said there were no gas chambers at Auschwitz.'

But he said he was still shocked by the verdict, and declared his intention to contest the decision. Eventually, Irving served only 13 months of his three-year sentence, following a successful appeal. Meanwhile, other interested parties were keen to use the media coverage the trial generated to forward more critical perspectives regarding Irving's views. Karen Pollock of the Holocaust Educational Trust, for example, gave the following reaction: 'the Holocaust denial is **anti-Semitism** dressed up as intellectual debate. It should be regarded as such and treated as such.' Meanwhile, Lipstadt was reported as saying 'I am uncomfortable with imprisoning people for speech. Let him go and let him fade from everyone's radar screens.'

See also Anti-Semitism *and* The Holocaust.

Further Reading
Evans, Richard J. 2002. *Telling Lies about Hitler: The Holocaust, History and the David Irving Trial.* London and New York: Verso.
O'Neill, Brendan. 2006. 'Irving? Let the guy go home', BBC News, http://news.bbc.co.uk/1/hi/uk/4578534.stm (cited 31 December 2007).

Italian Social Movement/National Alliance

In 1994, the Italian Social Movement (*Movimento Sociale Italiano*, MSI) gave itself a political makeover and reconfigured itself as part of the National Alliance (*Alleanza Nazionale*, AN) coalition, claiming at the same time to have become post-Fascist. The aim was to try and distance itself from the legacy of Mussolini and inter-war Italian Fascism and become moderate and respectable – a tricky job given that the MSI had been formed by lesser officials of *Il Duce*'s regime. Gianfranco **Fini**, leader of the MSI between 1987 and 1989 and between 1990 and 1995, masterminded the tactical switch and became leader of the AN.

The MSI had been founded in 1946. At its peak in 1963, party membership was 240,063; in 1993, the year before its demise, membership was down to 202,715. The key personality in the early years of the party was Giorgio Almirante, who in 1970 oversaw the removal of overtly Fascist symbols from party literature and documentation. The party's official newspaper was *Il Secolo d'Italia*.

In terms of doctrine, the MSI espoused a third way between capitalism and **Communism**, and campaigned for a strong executive, as well as increased government intervention in social affairs. Particularly in its early days, it was vociferous in its hostility to **democracy** and traditional party politics, while also exhibiting a paranoid attitude towards Soviet-style Communism.

The birth of the AN in 1994 did not go without its hitches, with disenchanted members exiting the party and going on to form new political groupings, such as the Fiamma Tricolore, the Alternativa Sociale (Social Alternative) coalition, and the Nuovo Movimento Sociale Italiano – Destra Nazionale. But Fini was undaunted, declaring: 'In comparison with the MSI, the Alliance represents not only an evolution of the right, but a new identity, based on an unequivocal condemnation of all forms of totalitarianism, including that of the Fascist period'.

In due course, an MSI/AN manifesto was published. In philosophical language, it talked about a revolution happening before people's eyes: 'Until a few years ago in the era of the democracy of the parties, the Italians were convinced of exercising sovereignty by always voting "for someone" or sometimes "against something", but never "for something" ... Now a great chance for the introduction of a new model of political representation has been created by the failure of the partitocratic system, by the wiping out of the old parties brought about by the electorate, and by new personalities entering the political stage who are more representative and more reliable than their predecessors'. The message was clear: the birth of the MSI/AN heralded a new dawn in Italian politics, or so Fini and his colleagues hoped.

And almost immediately, the Alliance polled well. It scored 12 percent twice in 1994 (at parliamentary and European elections) and 16 percent in 1996. It claimed 12 percent of the vote again in 2001, 2004 and 2006 and remains a significant player in Italian party politics. Support for the party is particularly strong in central and southern Italy. In 1995, the AN allied itself to Silvio Berlusconi's Forza Italia (FI) and played a brief role in government. It did so again after 2001, with Fini becoming deputy prime minister – a major landmark for a party that was still pigeon-holed on the Far Right. Fini was also appointed foreign minister between 2004 and 2006.

In terms of ideology, the AN is nationalist, anti-communist and socially conservative because of its closeness to the Catholic Church. It would like to reduce illegal **immigration** and campaigns against the idea of a multicultural Italian society. It also wants to strengthen **law and order** – the aim is to double the number of police on the streets. On the **economy**, it believes in capitalism and privatisation and is keen to reduce Italy's tax burden. It has now done away with almost all the symbols and attitudes that harked back to the Mussolini era – hence its reputation for populism and pragmatism.

The AN has encountered its problems over the past decade. The movement is split into rival factions, there has been some opposition to Fini's leadership and relations with the other far-right party in Italy – the **Northern League** – have been tense at times. Nevertheless, it has achieved a lot in a short space of time and in 1998 it had a membership of just under half a million across 12,000 local branches.

The academic verdict is that Fini has a wonderful opportunity. Gallagher said that he had the 'scope to mould the AN and move it in the direction he wants it to go', while Eatwell argued that, 'Fini was more than ever convinced that the way forward was to turn the MSI into a "post-Fascist", moderate right-wing party, modelled loosely on the lines of French Gaullism'. It will be fascinating to see how the movement develops in the future.

See also Fini, Gianfranco (Italy); Italy, Coalition of Northern League and National Alliance (2001) *and* Southern Europe and the Far Right.

Further Reading
www.alleanzanazionale.it (AN website).
Gallagher, Tom. 2000. 'Exit from the ghetto: the Italian far right in the 1990s'. In *The Politics of the Extreme Right: From the Margins to the Mainstream*. Edited by Paul Hainsworth. London: Pinter.
Sidoti, Francesco. 1992. 'The extreme right in Italy: ideological orphans and countermobilisation'. In *The Extreme Right in Europe and the USA*. Edited by Paul Hainsworth. London: Pinter.
Chiarini, Roberto. 1991. 'The "Movimento Sociale Italiano": a historical profile'. In *Neo-Fascism in Europe*. Edited by Luciano Cheles, Ronnie Ferguson and Michalina Vaughan. London: Longman.
Cheles, L. 1991. '"Nostalgia dell'avvenire": the new propaganda of the MSI between tradition and innovation'. In *Neo-Fascism in Europe*. Edited by Luciano Cheles, Ronnie Ferguson and Michalina Vaughan. London: Longman.
Eatwell, Roger. 1996. *Fascism: A History*. London: Vintage.
Amyot, Grant & Verzichelli, Luca, eds. 2007. *End of the Berlusconi Era?* Oxford; New York, N.Y.: Berghahn Books.

Bufacchi, Vittorio & Burgess, Simon. 2001. *Italy Since 1989: Events and Interpretations*. New York: St. Martin's Press.

Mack Smith, Denis. 1997. *Modern Italy: A Political History*. New Haven, CT: Yale University Press.

Italy, Coalition Government of the Northern League and the National Alliance (2001)

Following the 2001 elections in Italy, Silvio Berlusconi promised Italians 'a new era' after the victory of his centre-right coalition, the House of Freedoms (*Casa delle Libertà*, CDL). Berlusconi claimed that the new government would respond to desires for politicians to talk less and act more. The new administration meant the entry of two far-right movements, the Northern League (*Lega Nord*, LN), and National Alliance (*Alleanza Nazionale*, AN), into coalition government – an echo of the 1994 *Polo delle Libertà*. The LN, who gained 4 percent of the vote, was awarded three cabinet posts by Berlusconi. Most significantly, the LN leader, Umberto Bossi, became Minister for Reforms and Devolution. Meanwhile, the NA, who gained 12 percent of the vote, was offered only one cabinet seat, Deputy Prime Minister. The rise of NA leader, Gianfranco **Fini**, to such high office was another key milestone in the history of the contemporary Far Right. The new coalition, which boosted two far-right parties in government, sent shockwaves around **Europe**.

The reaction of the left was curious. One campaigning workers' website, www. workers.org, struck a calm tone. Its report on the matter asserted that no-one was expecting that Berlusconi's new-found, far-right allies would lead to the style of state repression employed by the Fascist regime of the interwar years. Perceptively, the report argued that this was because, unlike Mussolini's National Fascist Party (*Partito Nazionale Fascista*, PNF), modern far-right political parties in Italy were devoid of a paramilitary dynamic. Rather, it argued that Italians should view the new coalition as akin to the Republican Party in the US. Furthermore, it warned that the new administration would be able to dominate private and government media. Meanwhile, one report on the left-wing website www.wsws.org was more cynical. This commentary was heavily critical of the moderate tenor struck by the NA, claiming this represented a successful assimilation of neo-Fascism into Italy's democratic system. It was keen to demonstrate the continuity between Mussolini's PNF, the **Italian Social Movement** (*Movimento Sociale Italiano*, MSI) and the NA. For example, it detailed how NA members had held celebratory demonstrations where they gave the traditional Fascist salute. Also, the website took particular issue with Francesco Storace, a prominent NA figure. This critique highlighted how Storace had become notorious for promoting the idea of reviewing all school books in the region of Latium, in order to purge them of what he alleged was communist bias. The article argued this communist bias mainly consisted of negative portrayal of interwar Fascism and Nazism.

Ahead of the 2006 elections, Berlusconi entered into negations with Allesandra Mussolini's Social Alternative (*Alternativa Sociale*, SA) coalition, and she agreed that the SA would support the CLD. However, in the subsequent polls, Berlusconi's CLD was defeated, and Mussolini's SA failed to secure any seats. Meanwhile, after the 2006 elections the LN made some noises in order to promote the idea of federalism, including Umberto Bossi claiming after the election that extreme separatists may resort to non-democratic means if a more moderate path towards **regionalism** could not be found. This veiled threat of separatist direct action sparked condemnation from CLD members. The NA, meanwhile, experienced a political fracture in 2007. July saw the proclamation of an offshoot party, The Right (*La Destra*), styled as a national conservative movement. The lasting impact of this split on the NA, and the Italian Far Right more generally, has yet to be fully understood.

See also Italian Social Movement/National Alliance; Northern League (Italy) and Southern Europe and the Far Right.

Further Reading

Gallagher, Tom. 2000. 'Exit from the ghetto: the Italian far right in the 1990s'. In *The Politics of the Extreme Right: From the Margins to the Mainstream*. Edited by Paul Hainsworth. London: Pinter.
Ignazi, Piero. 2003. *Extreme Right Parties in Western Europe*. New York: Oxford University Press.

Ivan Close Your Soul by Vladimir Zhirinovsky (Russia)

In July 2001, Vladimir **Zhirinovsky**, leader of the Russian LDP, published *Ivan Close Your Soul*, a book in which he meditates on his **family** background and related issues. Given his well documented outbursts of xenophobia and **anti-Semitism**, the media was particularly interested in the volume because of Zhirinovsky's comments about his Jewish father.

In the book, the author describes how his father swapped names – from Volf Isaakovich Eidelshtein to Volf Isaakovich Zhirinovsky. This prompts Zhirinovsky Jnr. to ask rhetorically: 'Why should I reject Russian blood, Russian culture, Russian land, and fall in love with the Jewish people only because of that single drop of blood that my father left in my mother's body?' This comment was interpreted as Zhirinovsky being slightly half-hearted in his new policy of honesty.

Even so, the publication of *Ivan Close Your Soul* is viewed as a milestone in Zhirinovsky's political career. He said: 'I don't say that Jews are bad, but simply there are not enough Russians around. Let's add a few more Russians, let's say, a few more Russian ministers. Jews are talented and clever. But there are very many of them at the top. There's much less anti-Semitism now. There cannot be any anti-Semitism in the party when my father was Jewish'. After 2001, he paid less attention to the Jewish threat and noticeably more to the Chechen conflict. Zhirinovsky's *Ivan Close Your Soul* was a follow-up to *My Struggle: The Explosive Views of Russia's Most Controversial Political Figure*.

See also Liberal Democratic Party of Russia; Russia and the Far Right *and* Zhirinovsky, Vladimir (Russia).

Further Reading

http://www.ldpr.ru (LDPR website).
Cox, M. & Shearman, P. 2000. 'After the fall: nationalist extremism in post-communist Russia'. In *The Politics of the Extreme Right: From the Margins to the Mainstream*. Edited by Paul Hainsworth. London: Pinter.
Zhirinovsky, Z. 1996. *My Struggle*. Barricade Books.
Morrison, J.W. 2004. *Vladimir Zhirinovsky: An Assessment of a Russian Ultra-nationalist*. Diane.
Solovyov, V. & Klepikova, E. 1995. *Zhirinovsky: Russian Fascism and the Making of a Dictator*. Da Capo Press.

K

Kjaersgaard, Pia (b.1947) – Denmark

Pia Kjærsgaard is the joint founder and current leader of the *Dansk Folkeparti* (Danish People's Party), which claims to be the third most influential political movement in Denmark today. Over the years, it has registered a number of impressive electoral scores, with Kjærsgaard at the forefront of the party's campaigns and successes. Jørgen Goul Andersen and Tor Bjorklund have argued that the key to Kjærsgaard's popularity has been her 'common sense' approach to politics. Nevertheless, she has been branded 'Denmark's **Le Pen**'. Her significance rests on the fact that she has risen to prominence in a country that once prided itself on its liberal values.

14. Pia Kjaersgaard's
60th birthday party,
Copenhagen, Denmark,
22 February 2007.

Kjærsgaard initially joined the Progress Party in 1978 and stood as a party candidate in the late 1970s and early 1980s. In 1984, she won a seat in parliament on the party ticket and worked as a deputy for more than a decade. By 1995, however, she had become disillusioned with the movement and split with its leader Mogens Glistrup. In the same year she helped to form the **Danish People's Party**. Since then she has made her name as a hard-hitting politician who goes where others fear to tread. She is in and out of court: in 2002 she was even fined DKK 3,000 for threatening a woman with a pepper spray, and a year later, in 2003, she was convicted on a charge of racism.

In ideological terms, Kjærsgaard has been particularly strong in her opposition to multiculturalism. She has called for the deportation of all imams who do not have Danish nationality and at the height of the Prophet Mohammed cartoon crisis in 2006 she wrote: 'The seeds of weeds have come to Denmark – Islamists and liars – who have fuelled the lethal fire through their tour of the Middle East. We will deal with them.' Not unnaturally perhaps, the saga – and the 9/11 attacks before it – helped to reignite the issue of **immigration** and multiculturalism in Denmark and in opinion polls Kjærsgaard and her party were to benefit.

Unlike some other far-right leaders, however, Kjærsgaard has not restricted herself to immigration and race. She has tried to outflank the Danish Social Democrats on 'left-wing' issues such as welfare and health, and is also passionate in her critique of the Iraq war and the EU. In a 1999 speech, she ridiculed the government: 'The Danish Minister of **Economy**, just a couple of weeks ago, described the EMU as "a fantastic success!" I ask you? If these quite frightening depreciations really represent a "fantastic success", how on earth would the Minister have controlled her comments if the Euro had increased in value? No – the fact of the matter is that the Euro is not a success at all. The first year has proved to be a thundering fiasco and the money weavers in Brussels and Frankfurt have feverishly been patching things up'.

A landmark was reached in 2001 when Kjaersgaard and her party scooped twenty-two seats in parliamentary elections. Her reaction to the result was short and sweet: 'We are in charge now,' she said. Following on from the elections, the People's Party was asked to take part in a centre-right government led by premier Anders Fogh Rasmussen. Over time, Rasmussen became a big fan of Kjærsgaard and at one birthday celebration famously said to her: 'There are a number of reasons for your success. With your background, you speak directly to common people and you have a nose for what's happening in the general population. You could say that you have continually taken advantage that not all parties have had the same receptiveness for shifting moods in the population'.

The emergence of Kjærsgaard and her party helps us to understand the changing nature of Denmark as a country. Before the 1990s, it was a distinctly white and monocultural society. But with an influx of immigrants from Islamic countries in the latter years of the twentieth century, all the old attitudes and assumptions seemed to die. Suddenly, the established political parties and the Danish establishment had to deal with the reality of a new ethnic mix. Critics have argued that this challenge was not met with sufficient vigour, and so a void opened up within Danish politics. Kjærsgaard and her party filled it – but instead of putting forward a discourse that validated the 'new society', they took the opposite line and actually campaigned against it. The signs are that Kjærsgaard will remain a key player in Danish politics.

See also Danish People's Party, Growth of (2001–2005); Danish People's Party *and* Scandinavia and the Far Right.

Further Reading

http://www.danskfolkeparti.dk (Danish People's Party website).

Arter, David. 1999. *Scandinavian Politics Today*. Manchester: Manchester University Press.

Andersen, J.G. 1994. 'Denmark: the Progress Party – populist neo-liberalism and welfare state chauvinism'. In *The Extreme Right in Europe and the USA*. Edited by Paul Hainsworth. London: Pinter.

Andersen, J.G. & Bjørklund, T. 2000. 'Radical right-wing populism in Scandinavia: from tax revolt to neo-liberalism and xenophobia'. In *The Politics of the Extreme Right: From the Margins to the Mainstream*. Edited by Paul Hainsworth. London: Pinter.

Klarström, Anders – Sweden

Anders Klarström was one of the most prominent figures on the Swedish Far Right. Between 1989 and 1995, he was the leader of the *Sverigedemokraterna* (Sweden Democrats), a movement generally regarded as Fascist and racist. He was also heavily involved in the Nazi rock scene. Klarström studied Music and Economics and – prior to the SD – was involved in *Nordiska Rikspartiet* (Nordic Reich Party), a Nazi movement that was founded in 1955. He was the first leader of the SD and came to personify its hard-line and uncompromising attitude to politics.

In terms of electoral scores, the SD has not been a significant player in Swedish politics. In 1994, for example, it received around 2,500 votes in Gothenburg, which equated to 0.6 percent of the vote and no seats on the local council. In other areas, they did gain some minor representation: in Eckerö, Stockholm, they gained 200 votes and one seat; in Höör they took a 5.4 percent share of the vote and won two seats; in Dals-Ed they also acquired two representatives; in Trollhättan they polled 2.1 percent; and in Lilla Edet 1.3 percent. In a sense, though, because of the nature of the party, elections and electoral performances have never been the be all and end all. Klarström and his party were better known than their poll results may suggest, and this is because of their style and rhetoric.

Klarström's political style was aggressive and hard-hitting. His background was in Nazi rock music and he was a member of Commit Suicide, a white power band that gained notoriety between 1983 and 1986. The band was based in Gothenburg, where they performed a variety of gigs, both indoor and outdoor. They also performed at SD political events. Originally, the SD was an authentic neo-Nazi movement, with many of its early leaders – including Klarström – having links to other hard-line groups. It did try to purge itself of its most extreme elements, but it was still popularly portrayed in the national media as a Nazi movement. Klarström certainly lived up to this reputation. In 1986, he was imprisoned for illegally possessing a firearm and making anti-Semitic threats to the entertainer Hagge Geigert.

Klarström has now converted to mainstream politics. Commentators are sceptical about this transformation and are prone to recall only his outrageous actions as leader of the SD. Swedish society is renowned for its liberalism and egalitarianism, but Klarström belonged to another universe. He was coarse and violent and stood for a brand of 'white power' politics that was totally anathema to the vast majority of Swedes.

See also New Democracy (Sweden) *and* Scandinavia and the Far Right.

Further Reading

http://www.sverigedemokraterna.net (Sweden Democrats website).

Arter, David. 1999. *Scandinavian Politics Today*. Manchester: Manchester University Press.

Andersen, J.G. & Bjørklund, T. 2000. 'Radical right-wing populism in Scandinavia: from tax revolt to neo-liberalism and xenophobia'. In *The Politics of the Extreme Right: From the Margins to the Mainstream*. Edited by Paul Hainsworth. London: Pinter.

Kosovo (Serbia)

In the late 1990s, the conflict in Kosovo focused international attention on the region. At the core of the issue was the attempt by Serbia to capitalise on the region's relative weakness in a bid to create a Greater Serbia from the dissolution of Yugoslavia. Kosovo itself is central to the politics and history of the region. Indeed, Kosovo has formed a key aspect of both Serbian and Albanian identity. The Battle of Kosovo of 1389 saw a Serbian nation defeated by the Ottoman army of the era, which then subjugated the whole Balkan region to centuries of domination. The Battle of Kosovo has subsequently been remembered by many far-right nationalists as an event that prevented Muslim forces from overrunning the whole of **Europe**. Further, in Serb nationalist literature, Kosovo has always formed a central part of the country's sense of identity.

During the post-war era, when Kosovo was a part of Tito's Yugoslavia, the region suffered relative poverty when compared to the rest of the country. Although Kosovo gained some political independence in the later years of Yugoslavia's history, this independence was removed in 1989 by Slobodan **Milošević** while Yugoslavia began to dissolve into its constituent nations. Further, during the communist era, Kosovo had seen a decline in its Serb population, dropping from around 30 percent of its population in 1946 to around 10 percent by the fall of the **Berlin Wall**. Drawing on a sense of history, on 28 June 1989, Yugoslav leader Slobodan Milošević made a now notorious speech about his ambitions for Kosovo to form part of the new-found sense of nationalism among Serbs: 'By the force of social circumstances this great 600th anniversary of the Battle of Kosovo is taking place in a year in which Serbia, after many years, after many decades, has regained its state, national and spiritual integrity [...] Serbia was at that time the bastion that defended the European culture, **religion**, and European society in general. [...] In this spirit we now endeavour to build a society, rich and democratic, and thus to contribute to the prosperity of this beautiful country, this unjustly suffering country, but also to contribute to the efforts of all the progressive people of our age that they make for a better and happier world. Let the memory of Kosovo heroism live forever! Long live Serbia! Long live Yugoslavia! Long live peace and brotherhood among peoples!' Such rhetoric, emphasising a sudden sense of national regeneration by intertwining history and myth in order to invoke a renewed sense of national destiny, was typical of Milošević's far-right nationalism.

During the wars in Croatia and Bosnia, Milošević sought to utilise the emotive political space that had been created by the exodus of Serbs in the Yugoslav era in order to boost Serb nationalism. Indeed, the Kosovo issue helped him to draw out powerful patriotic feelings among Serb nationals across the region. One example of this strategy was the policy of relocating Serbian refugees in Kosovo during the wars with Croatia and Bosnia, in order to augment the sense of deep-seated, demographic ties between Serbia and Kosovo. Meanwhile, other, high-profile Serbs also contributed to the debate. One of the most vocal of these was the radical-nationalist, Serbian opposition leader Vojislav Šešelj, who argued for the expulsion of Albanians from the Kosovo region, using force if necessary.

As the political situation in Kosovo deteriorated in the mid-1990s, the Kosovo Liberation Army (KLA) emerged to give Albanian Kosovans a military presence in the region. The organisation came of age in 1996, although its roots lay in growing frustration with the decision by leading Kosovan politicians, such as Ibraim Rugova, to take a moderate line in the face of Serb aggrandisement. As an alternate strategy to the more moderate tactic of creating an underground network of Albanian institutions, the emergence of the KLA led to a heightening of tensions in Kosovo. The growing frequency of KLA operations in 1998 resulted in the Serbian Army responding to these attacks with great ferocity. The Serbian military assault on Kosovo saw further acts of ethnic cleansing by the Serbian forces, perpetrated with the ultimate goal of creating a Serbian-dominated Kosovo.

By 1998, around 100,000 Albanians had fled Kosovo itself, while a further 200,000 were displaced within the region. Meanwhile, battles between the KLA and Serb forces continued. However, it was not until the Račak incident in January 1999 that international opinion crystallised into a formal condemnation of the Serb offensive. This widely reported act of mass murder saw the Organisation for Security and Co-operation in Europe document the deaths of forty-five unarmed civilians around the town of Račak in Kosovo. Following further inconclusive peace negotiations in the spring of 1999, NATO forces began a bombing campaign targeting Serbian military sites on 24 March. Eventually, this led to a Serbian withdrawal, and Kosovo was placed under transitional United Nations governance. Its long-term future remains unresolved in 2007. Meanwhile, Milošević was subsequently arrested and put on trial for war crimes. However, this trial ended inconclusively in 2006 following his death in custody.

See also Kosovo War, Responses (1999); Milošević, Slobodan (ex-Yugoslavia) *and* South-Eastern Europe and the Far Right.

Further Reading
Judah, Tim. 2002. *Kosovo: War and Revenge*. New Haven, CT: Yale University Press.
Markotich, Stan. 2000. 'Serbia: Extremism from the top and a blurring of right into left'. In *The Politics of the Extreme Right: From the Margins to the Mainstream*. Edited by Paul Hainsworth. London: Pinter.

Kosovo War, Responses (1999)

The Kosovo War of 1999 was one of the final chapters in the bloody break-up of the former Yugoslavia – though to argue that the instability in the region has been eliminated even by 2007 is to misinterpret subsequent events. The war between Serbia and NATO forces emerged from the deteriorating situation in **Kosovo** after Serbia launched attacks on the region, ostensibly only to counter the growing activity of the Kosovo Liberation Army (KLA).

Following the growing viciousness of the Serbian army's tactics in Kosovo, by early 1999 NATO began to take seriously the idea of military intervention in order to prevent localised instances of ethnic cleansing and further political and social deterioration in the Kosovo region. The world was divided over the question of military intervention by NATO. Unsurprisingly, then, the decision to go to war with Serbian president Slobodan **Milošević** in 1999, ultimately in order to protect Kosovo from further Serbian aggrandisement, was a controversial one. The reasoning for military intervention was based on the premise that an authoritarian political leader such as Milošević should not simply be allowed to run roughshod over a small, predominantly Muslim territory, Kosovo. Many queried whether this was a just conflict that would successfully protect a weak, minority group from state aggression, or whether it was another example of the West – and the US and UK in particular – developing ideas above its station, and clumsily stepping into an unwanted and potentially counter-productive military engagement.

For its part, the Far Right tended to come down on the anti-war side. Indeed, many within **Europe**'s Far Right saw the issue in terms of suppressing a belligerent Muslim threat. Perhaps simply because the NATO actions would aid the Muslims within Kosovo, the Far Right found such action highly objectionable. Furthermore, especially due to the high level of US involvement in the conflict, it excited the Far Right across the globe. For example, Texas-based ideologue Louis Beam, inventor of 'leaderless resistance', rejected the ideals presented by General Wesley Clark, and others, who stated that the objective of the conflict was specifically not to create an ethnically pure nation-state. For Clark, such a concept was a dangerous throwback to the utopianism of a previous century. Contrastingly, the idea of a multi-ethic state was, of course, anathema to the far-right ideologues such as Beam. Using the Battle of Kosovo Field of 1389 ideologically, Beam was typical of many far-right ideologues who argued that: '77,000 Christian knights and soldiers exact[ed] such a tremendous toll upon the Islamic soldiers that the advance into the heart of Europe was halted'. Further, history was repeating itself according to such far-right figures. So, as in 1389, it was necessary to see the conflict in terms of fighting the Muslim 'other' in Europe. Far-right voices around the world, then, tended to support Serbia's cause because they believed that Serbia had a right to expand its boundaries at the expense of the lives of Muslim Kosovans.

Moving forward to the end of 2007, the issue still excites the passions of the Far Right. For example, one **British National Party** (BNP) news report claimed that, should Kosovo declare full independence from Serbia, then Serbian nationalists would be justified in taking up arms. Arguing that these nationalist irregulars would be joined by the Serbian forces and a multitude of Russian volunteer fighters, the report refracts the Kosovo War through the lens of the **'War on Terror'**. According to its author, Lee Barnes, the KLA was in fact a part of al-Qaeda, and its primary aim was to create a 'jihadist base' in mainland Europe during the 1990s and beyond. Further, this development was backed by Britain and the 'US Corporatocracy', whose actions in the Kosovo War helped to arm Islamic terrorists determined to kill Christian Serbs. Indeed, according to Barns' analysis, the Serbian army during the Kosovo War was merely designed to protect Serbs from an ethnic cleansing campaign. Furthermore, the only ethnic cleansing to have occurred in the region was committed by the KLA, not the Serbian army. This conspiracy theory, arguing that the US and al-Qaeda were operating in harmony against the interests of European nationalists, demonstrates not merely the deeply paranoid style of analysis forwarded by the Far Right, but also how the Kosovo conflict can still excite the passions of far-right activists today.

See also Kosovo (Serbia); Milošević, Slobodan (ex-Yugoslavia) *and* South-Eastern Europe and the Far Right.

Further Reading

BNP, 'Kosovo flashpoint deadline looms', http://www.bnp.org.uk/?p=69 (cited 31 December 2007).
Intelligence Report, 'Kosovo and the Far Right', http://www.splcenter.org/intel/intelreport/article. jsp?aid=355 (cited 31 December 2007).
Pribićević, Ognjen. 1999. 'Changing fortunes of the Serbian far right'. In *The Radical Right in Central and Eastern Europe since 1989*. Edited by Sabrina Ramet. University Park, PA: Pennsylvania State University Press.

L

Latvian Marches (2005)

In March 2005, Riga, the capital of Latvia, was the scene of riots and arrests after a march by pro-Nazi, Latvian SS veterans was interrupted by pro-Russian, anti-Nazi activists. The incidents could not be understood without reference to Latvia's wartime experience, when Latvia's SS brigade fought the Soviet Army. The Latvian nationalists who held the event regard the brief era of Nazi occupation during the Second World War as a period of national independence before the country was subject to rule by the USSR. However, this neglects the historical detail that Latvia also spawned its own resistance movement during the war that fought against both Nazi and Soviet occupiers in the name of a sovereign Latvia. It was also significant that, in March 2005, the Latvian SS veterans were joined by a group of young Latvian nationalists. For many commentators, this highlights that a sense of continuity between memories of the Second World War and the present day is evident within the Latvian Far Right.

Turning to the 2005 march itself, the Latvian state authorities had given their blessing to the event. However, those on the anti-Fascist left viewed the march as highly provocative. They argued that, in sanctioning the march, Latvian president Vaira Vike-Freiberga was helping to rehabilitate Nazism. The government in Latvia was also criticised by the Russian Foreign Ministry, who claimed that the consent of Latvian authorities made the actions appear to them particularly cynical. Claiming that the timing was an affront to the memory of the Nuremburg Trials, where the SS was classified as a criminal organisation, **Russia** also claimed that Riga was attempting to revise the history of the Second World War, and added that 'only distorted logic' could, on the one hand, deploy police force against anti-Fascists, while, on the other hand, allow far-right protestors to march with impunity. Indeed, for the Russians, such 'distorted logic' was an affront to the very idea of **democracy**.

As a postscript, it should be noted that in March 2006 a similar march of veterans, singing nationalist songs took place. This march comprised 300 far-right activists, who were nicknamed 'ubernationalists' by the media. However, this time the Latvian authorities did not sanction the event. The 2006 march was attended by, among other groups, Klubs 415 and the **Latvian National Front**, led by Aivars **Garda**. According to some commentators, the controversy sparked by the marches brought to life a crucial dilemma for state authorities: should it uphold national security or **freedom** of speech?

See also Garda, Aivars (Latvia); Latvian National Front *and* Russia and the Far Right.

Further Reading
BBC News, 'Latvian SS march sparks clashes', http://news.bbc.co.uk/1/hi/world/europe/4353997.stm (cited 31 December 2007).
Eglitis, Daina Stukuls. 2002. *Imagining the Nation: History, Modernity and Revolution in Latvia.* University Park, PA: Pennsylvania State University Press.

Latvian National Front

This is the party of ultra-nationalist Aivars **Garda**. The party's newspaper is called *Deoccupation Decolonization Debolshevization* and is aimed at throwing off the yoke of Russian influence. It has become a vehicle for virulent **anti-Semitism**. It recently republished the *Protocol of the Elders of Zion*, the infamous anti-Semitic tract, and also allowed articles advancing Holocaust-denial theses to be published in its pages. It has also caused controversy by launching mischief-making essay competitions and gaining interviews with mainstream Latvian politicians. At one point, the paper was accused by a government minister of inciting racial hatred, but the authorities deemed that there was not enough evidence to begin a prosecution. On a practical note, the movement has engaged in public demonstrations calling for the 'decolonisation of Latvia'.

See also Garda, Aivars (Latvia); Latvian Marches (2005) *and* Russia and the Far Right.

Further Reading
http://www.politika.lv (Latvian public policy site).
Smith, D.J., Purs, A., Pabriks, A. & Lane, T. 2002. *The Baltic States: Estonia, Latvia and Lithuania.* London and New York: Routledge.
Galbreath, David. 2005. *Nation-Building and Minority Politics in Post-Socialist States: Interests, Influence and Identities in Estonia and Latvia.* Stuttgart: Ibidem-Verlag.
Karklins, Rasma. 1994. *Ethnopolitics and Transition to Democracy: Collapse of the USSR and Latvia by Rasma Karklins.* Washington, DC: Woodrow Wilson Center Press.

Law and Order

The Far Right often takes a tough approach to law and order issues. Some might say that this is somewhat paradoxical given the association between the ideology and the propensity for its organisations to break the law. This is another issue with which the Far Right can demonstrate its hard-line conservative principles, yet present itself as a more radical alternative to mainstream political parties, one that would deal with crime in an unsympathetic, ruthless manner.

Law and order, then, is where the Far Right reveals itself to be, fundamentally, of the *right*: not only is there a tough and uncompromising tone to its discourse, but the basic philosophical position – if the Far Right dealt in philosophical first principles – is that man is imperfect and flawed, and that the state has the right to intervene to punish criminals in order to protect the people. This point is neatly encapsulated by **Flemish Interest** (*Vlaams Belang*, VB) in Belgium, which argues that the state must ensure the **freedom** of citizens by upholding law and order. Therefore, for the VB, a tough stance on crime, including zero-tolerance strategies, is an urgently necessary measure. Further, it is imperative that this tough line is enforced by the judiciary and the prison service.

There is a legend that claims that, when the **French National Front** (*Front National*, FN) was thinking through its initial policy positions in the early 1970s, it commissioned an opinion poll to discover what French people cared most about. The story goes that, without delay, the top ten concerns became the top ten policy statements in the FN manifesto. Specifically, high on the list was law and order, and so law and order, or *sécurité*, has subsequently been a central pillar of FN doctrine. Here, key FN themes include campaigning for the death penalty and tougher punishments for non-French law-breakers.

This mix of populism and traditional right-wing thinking is evident across the continent. In 2001, the Liberal Democratic Party (*Liberal'no-Demokraticheskaya Partiya Rossii*, LDPR) in **Russia** spoke of toughening up the penalties for terrorist offences and murder and restoring capital punishment for the worst criminal acts. Meanwhile, the Sweden Democrats (*Sverigedemokraterna*, SD) say they are committed to the restoration of law and order – thereby implying it has already reached an unacceptable level. The SD argues that Swedish society currently is too soft on criminals. Rather, the SD is committed to helping the victims of crime instead of the state protecting criminals, as their material alleges. They argue for greater police powers to catch criminals, and for longer sentences that are seen more clearly by both criminals and wider society as a punishment. The implication seems to be that the left is weak on this issue, and that society needs a dose of tough, right-wing justice. The most recent **British National Front** (NF) manifesto strikes a similar tone. It claims that the preservation of the rule of law is vital for any society founded upon a legal structure. Therefore, there must be a clear correlation between crime and sentencing in the eyes of the public. The consequence of crime, then, must be a rapid conviction and harsh punishment. The NF argues for the introduction of birching for violent crimes, and would also introduce the death penalty for terrorist offences, murder and aggravated rape.

As with **immigration**, law and order policies of the Far Right demonstrate the strong authoritarian streak manifest in the ideology. Often, the world is seen in simplistic terms of good versus evil. Further, state institutions and liberal politicians, alongside the criminals themselves, are both presented on the same side of this stark binary – they are both part of the problem. The Far Right on the other hand presents itself as is doing nothing more than sticking up for the ordinary man-in-the-street who has the right to live his life free from the fear of crime. This populist appeal has a strong moral tenor, but fails to grasp the nuances and details in dealing with crime, and the complex social and psychological factors that cause it.

See also Freedom *and* The Ideology of the Far Right.

Further Reading
Hainsworth, Paul, ed. 2000. *The Politics of the Extreme Right: From the Margins to the Mainstream.* London: Pinter.
Ignazi, Piero. 2003. *Extreme Right Parties in Western Europe.* New York: Oxford University Press.
Mudde, Cas. 2000. *The Ideology of the Extreme Right.* Manchester: Manchester University Press.

League of Polish Families

The League of Polish Families (*Liga Polskich Rodzin*, LPR) was founded in 2001 and has its roots in the amalgamation of several smaller nationalist organisations, including the National-Democratic Party (*Stronnictwo Narodowo-Demokratyczne*) and the National Party (*Stronnictwo Narodowe*). The party has blossomed in the post-communist **environment** and is now a key player in Polish politics.

The LPR is led by Roman **Giertych** and claims to be the main successor to the inter-war party, the National Democrats. Its doctrine is based primarily on conservative nationalism. As the party states: 'We consider political activity merely as a means to serve Poland and the Polish Nation. We trust that our programme is in total agreement with Polish interest and its implementation is the best method of ensuring the maximum benefit for our Homeland ... Our participation in politics is based on the traditional morality of the Polish Nation with a fundamental role for Christianity, which is the backbone of our identity ... Our key pro-national political aim is to ensure the existence, continuity and the development of the Polish Nation'.

There are key dimensions to the party. In particular, it has attracted controversy on account of its anti-homosexual views, and in 2004 actually called for the suspension of the European Parliament, fearing that it was run by a gay conspiracy. Predictably, therefore, it is passionately pro-**family**: 'Families deserve particular attention from the government and, if necessary, social aid to ensure their comprehensive development. A family is the natural community of every human being. Human life should be protected by law from the moment of conception until the time of natural death. We demand a total ban on abortion, euthanasia, or cloning of a human being as these contradict the principles of morality and are in disagreement with social order in the state'.

In the national elections of 2001, the LPR won 38 out of the 460 seats with an 8 percent share of the vote. Three years later, in 2004, it improved its showing in European elections, claiming 15 out of the 54 Polish seats on 16 percent of the vote and joining the Independence and **Democracy** group. This made it the second largest Polish party at Strasbourg. Commentators say that in recent years, the party has benefited from the support of Catholic radio station Radio Maryja.

The party's **youth** organisation is called All-Polish Youth. It was originally formed in 1922 and re-established in 1989, thanks to the work of Giertych. Claiming to have 4,000 members, its main aim is to nurture its members 'in the spirit of national and Catholic values and inculcating them with a full sense of patriotic duties so that they try to be beneficial to their mother country when holding any post'.

See also Giertych, Roman (Poland).

Further Reading

http://www.lpr.pl (League of Polish Families website).

Giertych, M. 1963. *Thoughts for Thinking*. Publisher not known.

Blobaum, Robert. 2005. *Antisemitism and Its Opponents in Modern Poland*. Ithaca, NY: Cornell University Press.

Hancock, D.M. 2006. *Politics in Europe: An Introduction to the Politics of the United Kingdom, France, German, Italy, Sweden, Russia, Poland and the European Union*. Washington, DC: CQ Press.

Le Pen, Jean-Marie (b.1928) – France

Jean-Marie Le Pen founded the Front National in 1972 and has been its leader ever since. In the 1950s, he was a supporter of *Algérie Française* (the movement that aimed to prevent the decolonisation of Algeria) and the Poujadist *Union de Défense des Commerçants et Artisans* (UDCA). A colourful, charismatic and scandal-hit politician, Le Pen became as a key player in French politics in the mid-1980s. He has served as a Euro-MP and is probably one of the most successful far-right politicians to emerge in post-war **Europe**.

Le Pen was born in Brittany, the son of a fisherman, and was orphaned in 1942. In later writings and speeches, he has been known to play on these humble beginnings for political effect. He studied Political Science and Law at the University of Paris before joining the French Paratroop Regiment, and won recognition for his service in Indochina in 1953, Suez in 1956 and **Algeria** in 1957. His political career began in 1956 when he became the youngest member of the French National Assembly, elected as a Poujadist deputy for Paris. He became the General Secretary of the National Front of Combatants (FNC) in 1957, and in 1965, he was the campaign manager for the extreme-right presidential candidate Jean-Louis Tixier-Vignancour.

Le Pen formed the FN in 1972. Initially, it failed to break out of the political wilderness, winning only 0.7 percent of the vote in the 1974 presidential elections and only 0.3 percent of the vote in the legislative elections of 1981. The breakthrough came two years later, however, when the party won the city council and deputy mayorship in **Dreux**, near Paris. The party was in the ascendant during the rest of the 1980s, winning 11 percent of votes in the European elections of 1984 – when Le Pen won a seat in the European Parliament – and around 10 percent in the parliamentary elections of 1986 and 1988. In the presidential poll of 1988, Le Pen claimed 4.4 million votes or 14.4 percent of the total vote in the first ballot.

The controversial but charismatic leadership of Le Pen has been a key factor in the rise of the FN. It is generally agreed that he is one of the most effective media operators in modern France politics, and also one of the smartest and most savvy political strategists. But he has often crossed the line. In 1987, he described the Nazi gas chambers as a 'minor point of detail' in the history of the Second World War, and in 2005, he claimed that the occupation of France by Nazi Germany 'was not particularly inhumane'. He was also suspended from the European Parliament in 2000 after physically attacking the Socialist candidate for Mantes-la-Jolie, Annette Pleuvast-Bergeal, during the general election campaign of 1997.

In the 1990s, Le Pen consolidated his position in mainstream French political life. In 1992 and 1998, he was elected to the regional council of Provence-Alpes-Côte d'Azur and in 1999, he was re-elected to the European Parliament. His greatest success came in the 2002 French presidential election. He returned 16.86 percent of the vote in the first round, and became the first candidate from the Far Right to make it through to the second round of a presidential poll. The result caused a major international outcry and, even on the left, there were calls for Chirac to win through in the head-to-head ballot. One slogan used was, 'Vote for the crook, not the Fascist'. In the end, Chirac became president with 82 percent of the second-round vote.

Opposition to Le Pen also stemmed from those with whom he associated: in France, ex-Algeria veterans and former pro-Nazi collaborators; and in Europe, far-right leaders such as Franz Schönluber and Nick **Griffin**. It was inevitable that such a larger-than-life figure would end up creating opposition within his own party, and this is eventually what happened. In 1998, Bruno **Mégret** launched a failed bid to take over the leadership of the FN. He left the movement to found a rival right-wing party, claiming that the controversial image of Le Pen was preventing the party from gaining power. Mégret's defection was a setback for the FN, but the movement remains a key player in French politics, even though Le Pen himself could only manage a 10 percent share of the vote in the presidential elections of 2007.

For a number of reasons, Le Pen is a particularly important figure. His electoral results have ranged from the mediocre to the startling, and even though he fared little chance of making it to the Élysée Palace in 2002, the fact that he was in the second-round run-off at all was an enormous achievement. In a sense, though, the raw statistics tend to underplay Le Pen's influence in and on French politics. He has put issues on the national political agenda that other politicians have avoided – the best example being **immigration** – and he has forced the other parties to reposition themselves with regard to the FN.

He has also mixed tactics. He is part-old fashioned bully boy (the ex-paratrooper who fights with opposition politicians, is renowned for his fiery rhetoric, and casts doubt on the scale of the Holocaust) and part-twenty-first century politician (the smart-suited leader who boasts a clever PR machine and now sees ecologism and nationalism as sister ideologies). Le Pen is now an old man but it looks like his daughter, Marina, will keep the Le Pen flag flying when he is gone.

See also France; National Front (France); Success of the National Front (1982 to 2002) *and* Western Europe and the Far Right.

Further Reading
www.frontnational.com (FN website).
Shields, J. 2007. *The Extreme Right in France: From Pétain to Le Pen*. London and New York: Routledge.
Arnold, E.J. 2000. *The Development of the Radical Right in France: From Boulanger to Le Pen*. Basingstoke: Macmillan.
Davies, Peter. 1999. *The National Front in France: Ideology, Discourse and Power*. New York: Routledge.
Davies, Peter. 2002. *The Extreme Right in France, 1789 to the Present: From De Maistre to Le Pen*. London and New York: Routledge.
Hainsworth, Paul. 2000. 'The Front National: from ascendancy to fragmentation on the French extreme right'. In *The Politics of the Extreme Right: From the Margins to the Mainstream*. Edited by Paul Hainsworth. London: Pinter.
Hainsworth, Paul. 1992. 'The extreme right in post-war France: the emergence and success of the Front National'. In *The Extreme Right in Europe and the USA*. Edited by Paul Hainsworth. London: Pinter.
Eatwell, Roger. 1996. *Fascism: A History*. London: Vintage.
Vaughan, M. 1991. 'The extreme right in France: "Lepenisme" or the politics of fear'. In *Neo-Fascism in Europe*. Edited by Luciano Cheles, Ronnie Ferguson and Michalina Vaughan. London: Longman.

Lefebvre, Archbishop Marcel (1905–1991) – France

Archbishop Marcel Lefebvre gained notoriety in France because of his alleged far-right sympathies. In the 1980s, he seemed to become a *de facto* ally of Jean-Marie **Le Pen** and the FN in their campaign against North African and Islamic **immigration**.

Born in Tourcoing, Lefebvre attended the French Seminary in Rome and, after taking two years out of his studies for military service, was ordained in both Rome and Lille in 1929. He then completed his doctorate in theology in July 1930 before becoming a Holy Ghost Father in 1934 and, during the next decade, served as a missionary at various seminaries in Gabon. In 1945, a year after his father had died in the Nazi concentration camp at Sonnenburg, he returned to France to take up new duties as rector of the Holy Ghost Fathers seminary in Mortain. When the war was over, Lefebvre returned to Africa, was consecrated as a bishop in 1947, and became Archbishop of Dakar in 1955. In 1959, he was appointed to the Preparatory Commission for the Second Vatican Council and was transferred to the diocese of Tulle in France in 1962.

While sitting on the Second Vatican Council, Lefebvre became increasingly concerned about the nature of the discussions, which he saw as a threat to Catholic traditions. In particular, he feared that episcopal collegiality would undermine papal primacy. He also called for a specific condemnation of **Communism** by the Council and was particularly concerned with the debate about religious liberty.

As a result, in 1970 he founded the hard-line traditionalist Society of St. Pius X, which denounced and resisted the revisionist changes that had been brought about by the Second Vatican Council. The group was initially tolerated by Pope Paul VI, despite that fact that it was opening chapels in various dioceses around the world and Lefebvre was claiming that there was a crisis in Church leadership and life following the Second Vatican Council. However, in 1976 the SSPX was banned by the Vatican when, after being refused initial permission by the authorities, Lefebvre carried out ordinations and was suspended 'a divinis'. Unrepentant, and despite repeated attempts at reconciliation, the SSPX still continues its activities outside the jurisdiction of the Vatican. The Roman Catholic Church, however, does not class this as a schism, although in 1988 Lefebvre was ex-communicated after he consecrated four bishops.

Lefebvre and the SSPX have also been linked to various European right-wing groups. The Spanish translation of Lefebvre's book, *I Accuse the Council*, was launched at the headquarters of the New Forces Party – a Francoist fascist party – and Lefebvre was accompanied by Blas Pinar, the NFP's president, at the event. Lefebrve also publicly encouraged Catholics to vote for Jean-Marie **Le Pen** in French election campaigns and spoke of his desire for the election of 'a government that applies real Catholic principles, like **Franco** and **Salazar** did' in the Italian magazine *Secolo*, the organ of the MSI, Italy's main neo-fascist party.

In 1989, Lefebvre turned his attention to Muslim immigrants and warned a meeting of catholic traditionalists: 'It is your wives, your daughters, your children who will be kidnapped and brought to those secret places like in Casablanca'. Also in 1989 Richard Williamson, one of the four SSPX bishops who Lefebvre consecrated in the previous year, claimed during a speech in Sherbrooke, Quebec that: 'There was not one Jew killed in the gas chambers. It was all lies, lies, lies. The Jews created the **Holocaust** so we would prostrate ourselves on our knees before them and approve of their new state of Israel … Jews made up the Holocaust, Protestants get their orders from the devil, and the Vatican has sold its soul to liberalism.'

See also Religion *and* Western Europe and the Far Right.

Further Reading

Shields, J. 2007. *The Extreme Right in France: From Pétain to Le Pen*. London and New York: Routledge.

Arnold, E.J. 2000. *The Development of the Radical Right in France: From Boulanger to Le Pen*. Basingstoke: Macmillan.

Davies, Peter. 1999. *The National Front in France: Ideology, Discourse and Power*. New York: Routledge.

Hainsworth, Paul. 1992. 'The extreme right in post-war France: the emergence and success of the Front National'. In *The Extreme Right in Europe and the USA*. Edited by Paul Hainsworth. London: Pinter.

Vaughan, M. 1991. 'The extreme right in France: "Lepenisme" or the politics of fear'. In *Neo-Fascism in Europe*. Edited by Luciano Cheles, Ronnie Ferguson and Michalina Vaughan. London: Longman.

Liberal Democratic Party of Russia

The Liberal Democratic Party of Russia (*Liberal'no-Demokraticheskaya Partiya Rossii*, LDPR) was founded in 1990 and rose to prominence following the collapse of the USSR. It was the first opposition party to be sanctioned after the break-up of the country and quickly gained notoriety on account of its ultra-nationalist discourse and controversial leader, Vladimir **Zhirinovsky**. Though it attempts to network with other liberal-democratic parties across **Europe**, in the eyes of most commentators it is neither liberal nor democratic.

Even so, it has chalked up some impressive electoral performances – for example, 23 percent in the Duma elections of 1993, 12 percent in 2003 and 11 percent in 1995. In other polls, however, it has failed to make it into double figures, although Zhirinovsky finished a creditable third in the 1991 presidential elections.

Liberal Democratic Party of Russia

In many ways, the LDP is a reaction to the way that **Russia** has been governed since the end of **Communism**. It has railed against corruption, incompetence and national decline, and some commentators suggest that its 'clothes were stolen' by Vladimir Putin as he rose to power in the first years of the **twenty-first century**. The party has around 15,000 members, with almost half their supporters coming from the under-30 age group.

The party's anthem reveals much about its objectives and philosophy:

Through her deeds and by her word shall Russia revive herself,
With a new leader, who's worthy and honest,
With a strong party of whom her enemies are afraid,
For the good of the homeland and for free living.
There is a limit to how much we will put up with -
So now we choose the LDPR.
This is our way of restoring Russia,
With a party that is tough, smart and united.
For long enough have our people been on their knees,
And have had to bury their righteous sons.
Down with excess and with cruelty down -
On this the LDPR will help Russia.
This is our way of restoring Russia,
With a party that is tough, smart and united.
There is a limit to how much we will put up with, -
So now we choose the LDPR.
Now we choose the LDPR.

In terms of political style, the party is authoritarian and is known for its tough internal discipline. Ideologically, it stands for the reunification of the USSR under Russian control, a single language (Russian) and the annexation of Finland, Poland, Alaska and other territories to create a new Russian empire. It is hard-line on **law and order** and believes in the death penalty for murder and terrorist offences. It would also like to see itself as a modern, reforming party as it would like to reduce taxes, renovate the welfare system and abolish all religious sects in Russia. In this vein, the party said in 2002, that it wished to legalise prostitution to coincide with the 300th anniversary of the founding of St. Petersburg.

How should we interpret the Zhirinovsky phenomenon? Eatwell calls him a Fascist, while Paxton suggests that his star is on the wane after a series of gaffes and the revelation that, for all his high-profile **anti-Semitism**, his father was actually Jewish. Meanwhile, **Griffin** highlights the irredentist programme of the LDPR and argues that in its pomp it sounded 'alarm bells' for not just Russia but the West as well.

For their part, Russian specialists, Cox and Shearman argue that the LDPR is not Fascist in any traditional sense but, rather, a movement that has reformulated themes and emphases present in traditional Soviet ideology, albeit in a highly populist manner. Conspiracy theories assert that Zhironovsky is, actually, an establishment loyalist, but his political tactics and bizarre policy ideas suggest that, in truth, he is simply a political maverick.

See also Russia and the Far Right; Russia, Far Right Makes Electoral Gains (1993) *and* Zhirinovsky, Vladimir (Russia).

Further Reading

http://www.ldpr.ru (LDPR website).

Cox, M. & Shearman, P. 2000. 'After the fall: nationalist extremism in post-communist Russia'. In *The Politics of the Extreme Right: From the Margins to the Mainstream*. Edited by Paul Hainsworth. London: Pinter.

Zhirinovsky, Z. 1996. *My Struggle*. Barricade Books.

Morrison, J.W. 2004. *Vladimir Zhirinovsky: An Assessment of a Russian Ultra-nationalist*. Diane.

Solovyov, V. & Klepikova, E. 1995. *Zhirinovsky: Russian Fascism and the Making of a Dictator*. Da Capo Press.

List Pim Fortuyn (The Netherlands)

List Pim Fortuyn (*Lijst Pim Fortuyn*, LPF) is a relatively new political party in the Netherlands. For a few months – from February 2002 – the movement based itself around **Fortuyn** himself, but when he was assassinated in May 2002, it was forced to operate without its founder and first leader. Fortuyn established the party after leaving the *List Leefbaar Nederland* party.

Because of its doctrine and policies, List Pim Fortuyn was viewed in controversial terms. It wanted tougher government measures on **law and order**, less administration and bureaucracy throughout the Dutch state, more teachers, and shorter waiting lists for medical treatment.

But, instead, it became notorious for its attitude towards **immigration**. In general, the party wanted to penalise immigrants who did not make the necessary efforts to assimilate into Dutch culture. Fortuyn stated: 'All those who are here can stay. I don't say send them home like [Le Pen] does – I just say the Netherlands is a small country. We are already overcrowded, there's no more room and we must shut the borders. Muslims [also] have a very bad attitude to **homosexuality**, they're very intolerant. And **women**. For them women are second-class citizens. What we are witnessing now is a clash of civilisations, not just between states but within them'. The party became famous for its politically incorrect attitude to immigration – with Fortuyn himself totally unrepentant.

Fortuyn's new party participated in parliamentary elections in May 2002, even though they took place only days after his murder. And it did exceptionally well, scoring 17 percent and winning 26 seats in the 150-seat parliament. It became the second largest party in the country and entered the governing coalition, providing several cabinet members. This was a remarkable achievement given that it was such a new political movement and that its election candidates were so little known. There followed a period of scandals, internal squabbling and resignations, with the LPF losing a lot of credibility in the process.

In 2003, and with the party still operating under a cloud, the LPF collected only eight seats. This was better than some pre-election polls had forecast, but still a major disappointment after the heady heights of 2002. By this point the leadership of the party had switched to Mat Herben and Harry Wijnschenk. There was more internal feuding, with the eight LPF MPs exiting the movement and chaotic arguments taking place about the party name – the MPs eventually setting up a new party called the List Five Fortuyn (*Lijst Vijf Fortuyn*). During the 2006 elections, the new party did not receive enough votes to secure a seat in the Dutch parliament.

During its short-lived existence, the LPF had the backing of seven wealthy business people. Its MPs were a hotch-potch of academics, lawyers and medical professionals. One was a former ice hockey player and another was an ex-draughts world champion; and at least two had African origins – a key fact that Fortuyn was able to use in his defence when questioned about the racism of his party.

The shortlived Pim Fortuyn phenomenon has been interpreted in different ways. One view is that the LPF was a one-man show and, ultimately, with only second-rate spokesmen in reserve, could not survive the death of its charismatic founder and leader. Another view, put forward by Joop van Holsteyn and Galen A. Irwin, is that the party's appeal had little to do with traditional factors such as class, **religion** and economic status, but rather was exclusively political – it was simply the lure of a party that was willing to talk about immigration, asylum and other taboo issues.

Bizarrely, the LPF can be viewed as both liberal and illiberal. It was progressive on social matters – in particular, the issue of homosexuality – and received significant backing from immigrant groups who knew that it had nothing against foreigners who pulled their weight in Dutch society. But, on the other hand, it was hard-line in its critique of Islam.

The conventional wisdom is that the LPF was an anomaly in a country that prided itself on its tolerant attitudes, but in another sense it is surprising that any country in **Europe** could resist the rise of far-right politics for so long. Whether the LPF was populist or Fascist is a debate that will continue. The reality is that the party made a big impression in a short space of time, and its legacy has already been significant. In the post-Pim era the Dutch government has been talking tough on asylum and there are already plans in place to force all immigrants in the Netherlands to learn the Dutch language.

See also Against the Islamisation of our Culture - Dutch Identity as Fundamental Value by Pim Fortuyn (The Netherlands); Fortuyn, Pim (The Netherlands) *and* Pim Fortuyn, Assassination of (2002).

Further Reading

Fortuyn, Pim. 1990. *Ordening Door Ontvlechting: Een Advies Over de Adviesstructuur in de Volksgezondheid*. Rijswijk/Den Haag, DOP: Ministerie van Welzijn.
Mudde, Cas. 2002. *The Ideology of the Extreme Right*. Manchester: Manchester University Press.
Sniderman, P.M. & Hagendoorn, L. 2007. *When Ways of Life Collide: Multiculturalism and Its Discontents in the Netherlands*. Princeton, NJ: Princeton University Press.
Mudde, Cas & Holsteyn, Joop Van. 2000. 'The Netherlands: explaining the limited success of the extreme right'. In *The Politics of the Extreme Right: From the Margins to the Mainstream*. Edited by Paul Hainsworth. London: Pinter.
Husbands, Christopher T. 1994. 'The Netherlands: irritants on the body politic'. In *The Extreme Right in Europe and the USA*. Edited by Paul Hainsworth. London: Pinter.

M

Marignane, Orange, Toulon and Vitrolles (France)

In the mid-1990s, Marignane, Orange, Toulon and Vitrolles acquired notoriety and infamy when they were 'conquered' by the **National Front** (*Front National*, FN). In these four towns, the FN secured control of the town halls, giving the party a taste of power over local affairs. The party claimed victory in three of these towns – Marignane, Orange and Toulon – following the municipal elections of June 1995. Subsequently, Vitrolles fell to the FN in 1997. The four new mayors thus created were a major boon to the party's fortunes. In Marignane, the tall, urbane Daniel Simonpieri was regarded as the personification of 'light lepenism'. Meanwhile, in Orange, Jacques Bompard was regarded as a more charismatic and hard-line figure. In Toulon, Jean-Marie Le Chevallier, an intimate colleague of Jean-Marie **Le Pen**, took office. Finally, two years later in Vitrolles, Catherine Mégret, the wife of Bruno **Mégret**, became the final member of this set of FN mayors.

A single reason for these towns falling to the FN is somewhat difficult to formulate. Toulon is a large city with a major port, and so here there were many urban problems for Le Chevallier to exploit. Meanwhile, the party's success in Vitrolles, a suburb of Marseilles, could also be rationalised along similar lines. Again, this was a multi-ethnic suburb that possessed all the social problems that the FN associates with such areas, including crime, unemployment and *insecurité*. On the other hand, Orange was a most unlikely place to be associated with the rise of the FN at municipal level. A beautiful old Roman town, with a huge ampitheatre at its geographical centre, it did not suffer from any of the issues of urban decline – **immigration**, crime, unemployment and *insécurité* – that the FN usually thrives on. Rather, Orange remains a rather quaint tourist destination, attractive, historic and distinguished. Visitors come to experience the open-air *spectacles* and the highly cultural atmosphere. Literally and metaphorically, it is a very long way from the inner-city and the suburbs where the FN normally finds its constituency.

This begs the following question: why have the FN done so well electorally in such a town? Here, a combination of factors comes into play: the personality and charisma of Bompard, the effectiveness of the party's local organisation, and their skill in dealing with routine local issues. In fact, party spokesmen were keen to emphasise the fact that the Orange experience demonstrated very well the fact that the FN was an authentic political party and not the single-issue movement with an immigration obsession that many in the media would like to portray them as. There was also another theory among more critical commentators: that Orange was representative of a certain ideal of the French town, one that had not experienced significant levels of immigration and so retained a sense of 'pure' French identity. In such places, it was the fear of the unknown, ignorance, and the consternation regarding a future immigrant 'invasion' that motivated people to vote FN.

While in power, the new FN mayors never found themselves far away from controversy. They were the first representatives of the party to hold power in municipalities of such a size. Indeed, up until 1995, the party had had to content itself merely with the odd village mayor. Consequently, the new FN mayors were a walking news story. Every move they made and every word they uttered was jumped on by the local and national media. At the same time, they were determined to make their mark in policy terms. For the most part, they tried to steer clear of the predictable areas and, instead, focused on issues such as taxation and the **environment**, although observers delineated a pro-France undercurrent to many of the mayors' policy statements.

One of the key areas was the issue of culture. In the cultural policies enforced by the new mayors, one can see a clear attempt to promote the idea of French roots, alongside an anti-elitist attitude to cultural life. For example, Le Chevallier criticised the rap group *Nique Ta Mère* (Snub Your Mother or NTM) for their 'songs of hatred' and their 'insulting, scandalous and aggressive behaviour'. Such comments reveal more than a reactionary perspective. The campaign against NTM was presented as a cultural battlefield, with NF defending the concept of the nation and tradition while NTM symbolised the decadence of the modern world. For Le Chevallier, then, people needed to choose between 'either NTM or Le Pen'.

Meanwhile, another key issue was the spread of Islamic culture. In Orage, Bompard caused a stir after he asked locals to fill out a loaded questionnaire asking their opinions on whether the local authorities should allow the establishment of an Islamic school in the town. Controversially, the person filling in the form was asked to provide their full name, ostensibly as a bid to prevent people sending in more than one form. The move produced the desired results. Only those opposed to the creation of the school were prepared to put their names on the form, and so Bompart could claim legitimacy for his decision. In another minor conflict, Simonpieri asked schools not to make any special effort to provide non-pork meals for their pupils. The subtext of this pronouncement was to ruffle the feathers of Muslim and Jewish minorities, for whom such a decision would be a serious issue. However, Simonpieri dressed his argument for this shift in policy in the language of budgetary requirements.

Such events are the seemingly minor stuff of local politics. Nevertheless, political scientists should not dismiss such local issues out of hand, as they can significantly disrupt the flow of day-to-day life for those affected. Furthermore, the revelation of such antagonistic attitudes towards minorities, and the principled stands over other trivial issues in the name of the French nation, also offer us a glimpse of FN ideology in power, and therefore some appreciation of the reality of what an FN government in France might look like.

See also France; National Front (France); Success of the National Front (1982 to 2002) *and* Western Europe and the Far Right.

Further Reading

Davies, Peter. 1999. *The National Front in France: Ideology, Discourse and Power*. New York: Routledge.

Ignazi, Piero. 2003. *Extreme Right Parties in Western Europe*. New York: Oxford University Press.

New York Times, 'National Front wins control of a 4th city in Southern France', http://query.nytimes.com/gst/fullpage.html?res=9A06E7DB103CF933A25751C0A961958260 (cited 31 December 2007).

Mégret, Bruno (b.1949) – France

During the 1980s and 1990s, Bruno Mégret was credited with enhancing the electoral appeal of Jean-Marie **Le Pen**'s FN. He was a sharp-suited political operator and an intelligent electoral strategist. If Le Pen was the brawn, Mégret was the brains, so the popular cliché went. Not surprisingly perhaps, the two men eventually fell out, in the late 1990s.

Mégret is a senior civil servant by profession. He studied at the elite École Polytechnique and the École Nationale des Ponts et Chaussées before gaining a masters degree from the University of California at Berkeley. He is also a Cavalry captain in the reserve forces.

His first active involvement in politics came in 1979 when he joined the *Rassemblement pour la République* (Rally for the Republic, RPR), a conservative political party formed by Jaques Chirac. Shortly after, he became technical advisor to the minister of co-operation and joined the extreme right-wing *Club d'Horloge* think-tank. Mégret broke with the RPR in 1982, to establish the Committees of Republican Action (CAR), together with Jean-Claude Bardet, a former French Algerian colonist. He then joined the FN in 1985 and quickly became Le Pen's number-two, orchestrating the party's increasingly successful electoral campaigns. He masterminded Le Pen's election campaign in 1987, and devised the movement's controversial 'national preference' policy.

Described as a smooth, colourless and a consummate tactician, Mégret substituted his wife as FN candidate in the 1997 mayoral election in Vitrolles, when he was prevented from standing by a technicality. The campaign was successful, but controversy quickly followed when she received a suspended three-month prison sentence for racist remarks made in an interview published in the German daily newspaper *Berliner Zeitung*.

During the 1990s, Mégret became increasingly frustrated with Le Pen's extremist and controversial views, arguing that the leader's reputation prevented the FN from gaining mainstream recognition and access to executive political positions. After a failed attempt to gain control of the party, Mégret left to form the *Mouvement National Républicain* in 1998, declaring that the re-born Far Right would not lose itself in in-fighting, self-congratulation and empty gestures of protest. In response, Le Pen described his former deputy as a 'petty, undersized psychopath with Napoleonic delusions of grandeur'.

Although in keeping with Mégret's desire to enter the political mainstream the MNR considers itself to be a classical liberal nationalist party, many see it as of the Far Right. Its political agenda includes the promotion of *laissez-faire* economics and opposition to **immigration**, particularly Muslims. Mégret himself has described the party's ambition as to 'reclaim France's sovereignty and defend its identity, send immigrants home, establish state authority, repress crime and delinquency, promote traditional **family** values, and restore the pride of every French man and woman in the fact that they were born French'.

In the 2004 campaign for the regional elections, the MNR used the 'No to Islamisation' slogan and opposed the possible integration of Turkey in the **European Union**. Despite, or perhaps because of, its less confrontational image and leadership, the MNR remains lagging behind the FN as a representative of right-wing populism in France.

See also Le Pen, Jean-Marie (France); National Front (France) and Western Europe and the Far Right.

Further Reading

http://www.m-n-r.net (MNR website).

Shields, J. 2007. *The Extreme Right in France: From Pétain to Le Pen*. London and New York : Routledge.

Davies, Peter. 1999. *The National Front in France: Ideology, Discourse and Power*. New York: Routledge.

Davies, Peter. 2002. *The Extreme Right in France, 1789 to the Present: From De Maistre to Le Pen*. London and New York: Routledge.

Hainsworth, Paul. 2000. 'The Front National: from ascendancy to fragmentation on the French extreme right'. In *The Politics of the Extreme Right: From the Margins to the Mainstream*. Edited by Paul Hainsworth. London: Pinter.

Hainsworth, Paul. 1992. 'The extreme right in post-war France: the emergence and success of the Front National'. In *The Extreme Right in Europe and the USA*. Edited by Paul Hainsworth. London: Pinter.

Vaughan, M. 1991. 'The extreme right in France: "Lepenisme" or the politics of fear'. In *Neo-Fascism in Europe*. Edited by Luciano Cheles, Ronnie Ferguson and Michalina Vaughan. London: Longman.

Mein Kampf by Adolf Hitler (Germany)

'*Mein Kampf* is my bible,' said John Tyndall, founder of the BNP. Such a statement would also apply to the other neo-Nazis involved in political action in **Europe** post-1945. *Mein Kampf* ('My Struggle') was Hitler's most famous work – part-autobiography and part-ideological treatise with particular emphasis given to **anti-Semitism**. The two volumes that comprised *Mein Kampf* were published in 1925–1926. Since then some activists on the Far Right have used the book as both an inspiration and a source of reference. By way of illustration, it is worth pointing out that in 1996 for the first time since 1945, the book was reprinted in Hungary. Áron Mónus was the publisher – a man who previously had a conviction for his anti-Semitic distribe, *Conspiracy: The Nietzschean Empire*. Mónus's position was that *Mein Kampf* was an important element in the cultural heritage of Europe and should be available to Hungarians 'to set things straight'. In 2002, the President of France, Jacques Chirac, escaped an assassination. The would-be killer was 25-year-old Maxime Brunerie, a neo-Nazi activist with connections on the French extreme right. When police raided his home in the aftermath of the assassination attempt they found a wealth of pro-fascist literature including a copy of *Mein Kampf*. The book, obviously, still has currency among neo-Nazi activists in Europe.

See also Anti-Semitism *and* The Holocaust.

Further Reading
Eatwell, Roger. 1996. *Fascism: A History*. London: Vintage.
Childs, David. 1991. 'The Far Right in Germany since 1945'. In *Neo-Fascism in Europe*. Edited by Luciano Cheles, Ronnie Ferguson and Michalina Vaughan. London: Longman.
Husbands, Christopher T. 1991. 'Militant neo-Nazism in the Federal Republic of Germany in the 1980s'. In *Neo-Fascism in Europe*. Edited by Luciano Cheles, Ronnie Ferguson and Michalina Vaughan. London: Longman.

Meligalas (Greece)

In 2005, a small village in southern Greece hit the headlines when the Greek far-right movement Golden Dawn (*Chrysi Avyi*, CA) attempted to organise an international far-right jamboree on the historic site. The choice of Meligalas as the venue for this celebration of ultra-nationalism was highly symbolic. In 1944, during the Greek Civil War, communist fighters killed 1,400 **women** and children in the village, who were subsequently buried in a mass grave. CA organisers even boasted of how the event was deliberately timed to coincide with this massacre.

Initially, the police were reluctant to ban the event, while Dimitris Eleftheropoulos, spokesman for the group, claimed ahead of the jamboree that 'No-one can deny us our democratic right to assemble in public'. The now defunct website for Euro-fest 2005 boasted of how the far-right celebration would offer 'Three days of comradeship, with live shows, sport activities by the sea and the most important: Open Congress with speeches on defend [sic] of our European Identity'. CA promotional material boasted that the event would present a unique admixture of racial rock music and 'inspirational' talks from leading far-right figures. Indeed, regarding the latter, its line-up was scheduled to include Roberto Fiore from the Italian far-right party New

Force (*Forza Nuovo*, FN) and Udo Voigt from the **German National Democratic Party** (*Nationaldemokratische Partei Deutschlands*, NPD). There was even speculation that Jean-Marie **Le Pen** would make a guest appearance.

Unsurprisingly, in the lead-up to Euro-fest 2005, there was much condemnation from community leaders and concerned politicians. For example, the local mayor, Eleni Aliferi, spoke out on the tastelessness of the event, stating, 'For God's sake, our wounds from the civil war have yet to heal.' Meanwhile, the Jewish community was outraged. Spokesman Moses Constantides said, 'We've never seen any gathering of this scale being planned in Greece', while the Central Council of Jews in Greece released the following statement: 'We condemn the holding of this meeting and we ask the government to intervene in order to stop it from taking place in Greece'. The issue of Turkish membership of the **European Union** was especially topical. Indeed, 'Turkey, out of **Europe**' was one of the more prominent Euro-fest 2005 slogans, a message that did not go unnoticed in Ankara. The Turkish government was keen to maintain a calm relationship with Greece ahead of important talks regarding Turkish accession to the EU, and was rightly worried about the instability that could be produced if an anti-Turkish demonstration were to take place in Greece. However, Greek officials were also concerned that, by banning the jamboree, they could simply turn the far-right activists into martyr figures.

On Friday 16 September 2005, a spokesman for CA boasted to the BBC that around 500 supporters had already gathered from around Europe, and that the event was going ahead as planned. He also claimed that it would be held in a secret location, and would be accompanied by a march through Athens. The following day, the BBC reported that an estimated 150 CA supporters had gathered in Athens ahead of the now banned jamboree. They were addressed by Fiore, who spoke of the need to resist Turkish accession to the EU, after which the protestors gave the Nazi salute. The far-right demonstrators were then met by a gang of militant anarchists, and the event soon descended into chaos. Eventually, the anarchists became embroiled in clashes with the police, while the far-right protestors melted away.

After the event, the CA claimed that it had ceased its political operations, merging with the Patriotic Alliance (*Patriotiki Symmachia*) – another small, far-right organisation in Greece. However, in 2007, Nikolaos Michaloliakos announced that the movement was resuming its activities.

See also Greek Front; South-Eastern Europe and the Far Right *and* Voridis, Makis (Greece).

Further Reading
Kapetanyannis, Vassilis. 1995. 'Neo-Fascism in Modern Greece'. In *The Far Right in Western and Eastern Europe*. Edited by Luciano Cheles, Ronnie Ferguson and Michalina Vaughan. London: Longman.
BBC News, 'Street clashes in central Athens', http://news.bbc.co.uk/1/hi/world/europe/4256948.stm (cited 31 December 2007).
BBC News, 'Neo-Nazis gather for Greek fest', http://news.bbc.co.uk/1/hi/world/europe/4252494.stm (cited 31 December 2007).
New York Times, 'Far-right festival in Greece will proceed as planned, party says', http://query.nytimes.com/gst/fullpage.html?res=9B01E3D6173EF933A2575BC0A9639C8B63 (cited 31 December 2007).

Memory (Russia)

Memory (*Pamyat* or National Patriotic Front) was a shady nationalist and anti-Semitic movement that came to prominence in the late 1980s just as the Soviet Union was on the verge of collapse. In one form or another, it had actually been around since the 1970s, and in 1985 the group of political activists that came to form *Pamyat* split into rival factions.

The movement's leader was Dimitry Vasilijev. He is now in his 60s and has led the party since 1985. His background is in theatre, photography and the military. Significantly, given his movement's attachment to the history and heritage of **Russia**, he names a number of Russian historians as his heroes: people like A.Nechvolodov, I.E.Zabelin and S.F.Platonov.

On the same theme, Vasilijev has opposed the destruction of the old quarters of Moscow and other key Russian cities. And, as a result, in practical fashion, he and his party have restored key cloisters, churches and monuments: for example, the cloisters of St. Daniel, St. Dimitry, the Virgin of Tolgsk and the Cathedral of the Virgin of Kazan. On other issues, *Pamyat* members haven't been afraid to take their protests onto the streets and engage in direct-action tactics.

15. Sergei Vasiliev, Vladimir Orlov and Alexander Barshakov (L-R), nationalist Pamyat leaders, Russia.

On its official founding in 1987, *Pamyat* stated its belief in the 'renaissance' of Russia and laid down the traditional Russian values it would be led by: religious orthodoxy, national character and spirituality. Hence its old fashioned slogan: 'God! Tsar! Nation!' It sees the communist era as an illegal aberration: 'The aim of "Pamyat" is the restoration of the monarchy and rightful succession of autocratic power in Russia ... "Pamyat" does not recognise the legality of incumbent power because this power has succession to the illegal revolution of 1917 ... "Pamyat" takes overthrow of monarchy for an act of realisation of the zionistic and freemasonic conspiracy against Russia ... "Pamyat" appeals to all patriots to unite and be guided by the idea of restoration of the Autocratic Monarchy in Russia. You understand only too well – our strength in unity. Victory by Zionists in Russia is a pledge for victory in all countries!'

As can be discerned, a major theme in *Pamyat* discourse was **anti-Semitism**. The party talked about the Jews as 'the main source of the misfortunes of Russian people, disintegration of the **economy**, denationalisation of Russian culture, alcoholism and ecological crisis'. They saw Zionist plots everywhere and blamed the Jews for the Russian revolutions of 1905 and 1917. Accordingly, critics dubbed *Pamyat* ideology Fascist and Nazi.

Over the years, *Pamyat* made a point of cultivating relations with other far-right groupings across **Europe**. It congratulated **Haider**'s Freedom Party in Austria after its election successes and in 2000 it issued a statement in support of the German NDP, which was in danger of being prohibited by the authorities: 'The NDP's example shows the entire world that the national spirit and will of the German people are not broken … We Russian nationalists are following the struggle of our German comrades with deep concern … The basis for future peaceful and fruitful cooperation between Russia and Germany must be laid down by true patriots of both countries … Not only do we wish to announce our solidarity with the NDP and register our protest against its ban, but also we are offering our comrades-in-arms a strong and true hand of Russian friendship'.

In the early 1990s, *Pamyat* launched its own newspaper and radio station, but by the end of the decade it had virtually disappeared from view.

See also Protocols of the Elders of Zion Document (Russia) *and* Russia and the Far Right.

Further Reading

http://www.pamyat.ru/engl.html (Pamyat website).

Cox, M. & Shearman, P. 2000. 'After the fall: nationalist extremism in post-communist Russia'. In *The Politics of the Extreme Right: From the Margins to the Mainstream*. Edited by Paul Hainsworth. London: Pinter.

Milošević, Arrest of (2001)

On 1 April 2001, the Serbian president Slobodan Milošević was arrested following an armed stand-off at his Belgrade home. Police had surrounded his villa for 36 hours, and gun fire was heard by many witnesses. Finally, Milošević gave himself up and he was indicted on charges of 'misappropriation of state funds' and 'abuse of his official position'. By June 2001, he had also been handed over to the War Crimes Tribunal at The Hague to stand trial. At the time of his death in March 2006, he had been in the dock for four years. He was facing no less than 66 charges, including: genocide, war crimes and crimes against humanity. He pleaded not guilty to all of these accusations, and defended himself by saying that he did not order rapes and killings, and that whatever orders he had given were simply issued in the legitimate defence of the Serbian people.

During his time in power as president of Yugoslavia, Milošević was often referred to as the 'Butcher of the Balkans' on account of his systematic policy of ethnic cleansing aimed at Croatian, Bosnian and Albanian populations. For many commentators and analysts of Milošević's Serbia, it is clear that he gave the green light for numerous heinous crimes to be committed in the name of national aggrandisement. However, what is more difficult to ascertain is how easily Milošević can be pigeon-holed neatly on the Far Right of the political spectrum. In many ways he remained an old-style socialist who, after the fall of **Communism**, used the issue of national identity in an entirely pragmatic way in order to stay in power and dictate terms in the former Yugoslavia. Perhaps the same could also be said of his partners in the destruction of the region: Franjo **Tuđman**, Radovan Karadzic and Ratko Mladic. Notoriously, Misha Glenny has dubbed Miloševié's pursuit of power his 'basic instinct', an essential will to survive at all costs.

The Miloševié trial itself demonstrated many of the problems with prosecuting heads of state with war crimes charges. Defending himself, Miloševié used health problems and legal loopholes to draw out the court proceedings. Further, some commentators, such as Richard Dicker of Human Rights Watch (HRW), argued that Miloševié used the court case to produce a political defence of his war record, thereby solidifying his legacy in the eyes of Serbian nationalists in his final years. Further controversy occurred when, following his death, many of his supported alleged that Miloševié had been poisoned. However, an autopsy soon revealed that he in fact died of a heart attack. He was buried in Pozarevac, his home town, after calls for a state funeral were turned down.

See also Miloševié, Slobodan (ex-Yugoslavia); Serbian Radical Party *and* South-Eastern Europe and the Far Right.

Further Reading
Sell, Louis. 2002. *Slobodan Miloševié and the Destruction of Yugoslavia*. Durham, NC: Duke University Press.
BBC. 2006. 'Special report: death of Miloševié', http://news.bbc.co.uk/1/hi/in_depth/europe/2001/ yugoslavia_after_milosevic (cited 31 December 2007).

Miloševié, Slobodan (1941–2006) – Serbia

Slobodan Miloševié was president of Serbia between 1989 and 1997, and then of the Federal Republic of Yugoslavia from 1997 to 2000. He also headed Serbia's Socialist Party from its foundation in 1990. He belongs to a special **family** of leaders – those who began on the far left as old fashioned Communists and who, after the fall of the **Berlin Wall** in 1989, grafted ultra-nationalism onto their personal ideologies.

Miloševié was born in Pozarevac, Serbia. His father was an Orthodox priest and his mother a teacher and activist in the Communist Party (both ended up taking their own life). He gained a Law degree from the University of Belgrade in 1964 and went on to work as an economic advisor. He married Mirjana Markovic and had two children: Marko and Marija. His wife was seen as a major influence on his political life, if not the 'power behind the throne'. The rise of Miloševié through the ranks of the Communist Party was swift after he devoted himself to politics full-time in 1984. He was elected head of the Belgrade City Committee of the League of Communists in 1986, and became president of Serbia (within the ex-Yugoslavian state) in 1988. He was ousted as president of the rump Yugoslavia (Yugoslavia minus the states that had become independent) twelve years later in 2000.

The conversion of Miloševié from old-style Communist to new-style ultra-nationalist can be dated to a speech he made on 28 June 1989 to celebrate the six-hundredth anniversary of the Battle of **Kosovo**. The speech was full of aggressive nationalist posturing and finished with the words: 'Six centuries ago, Serbia heroically defended itself in the field of Kosovo, but it also defended **Europe**. Serbia was at that time the bastion that defended European culture, **religion** and European society in general ... In this spirit we now endeavour to build a society, rich and democratic and thus to contribute to the prosperity of this beautiful country, this unjustly suffering country, but also to contribute to the efforts of all the progressive people of our age that they make for a better and happier world. Let the memory of Kosovo heroism live forever! Long live Serbia! Long live Yugoslavia!'

Commentators doubt whether this was a total, complete, or even a genuine, metamorphosis, but the intention was there – to reinvent himself as a super-patriot. As a key player in the wars of the 1990s, he had a powerful belief in Serbian dominance and superiority; hence his attachment to the idea of a Greater Serbia comprising all those lands upon which, historically or mythically, the Serbs has a claim. This almost inevitably brought about conflicts with other states: inside Yugoslavia – Croatia and Bosnia, and outside – Albania over Kosovo. It was with good reason that Milošević was described as a 'strongman', a 'bully' and a 'late twentieth-century Hitler'.

16. Serbian Communist Party leader Slobodan Milošević addresses thousands of people headed for a Serbian nationalist rally, Belgrade, 19 November 1998.

Ironically, or perhaps predictably, he always had an uneasy relationship with the **Serbian Radical Party** and its leader Dr Vojislav Seselj. They were allies and rivals at the same time. Like Milošević, Seselj was a fanatical Serbian nationalist who dreamed of a Greater Serbia emerging and towering over other states in the Balkans. In 1992, Seselj's Radicals became the second force in Serbian politics after Milošević's Socialists, and for a short period the two parties worked together to eradicate the influence of moderate politicians such as Yugoslav prime minister Milan Panic (and, later, to campaign on Kosovo). But for the most part, their relationship was an antagonistic one with Seselj constantly portraying Milošević as a weak leader intent on surrender. In 1993 Seselj believed that Milošević was ready to make peace in Bosnia and two years later he condemned him for agreeing to the Dayton Accords that ended the wars in Bosnia. For his part, Milošević viewed Seselj as a nuisance and in the end had to resort to imprisoning him.

In 1999, Milošević was indicted by the War Crimes Tribunal in The Hague for his genocidal policies during the Yugoslavian wars of the 1990s, but was only arrested in 2001. His trial at The Hague started in 2002 but he died in 2006, before the trial could finish. His journey from old-style Yugoslavian Communism to modern Serb ultra-nationalism was an odd one, but one that was perfectly in keeping with his pragmatic style of politics. Stan Markotich argues that the highpoint of Milošević's expansionist nationalism was the period between 1987 and 1993, and that after this phase, he reverted to 'a socialist brand of intolerance' that was reminiscent of Tito. Arguably, therefore, Milošević's dalliance with the ideas of the Far Right were only temporary.

See also Milošević, Arrest of (2001); Serbian Radical Party *and* South-Eastern Europe and the Far Right.

Further Reading

www.slobodan-milosevic.org (personal website).

http://hague.bard.edu (War Crimes Tribunal).

Markotich, Stan. 2000. 'Serbia: extremism from the top and a blurring of right into left'. In *The Politics of the Extreme Right: From the Margins to the Mainstream*. Edited by Paul Hainsworth. London: Pinter.

LeBor, A. 2004. *Milosevic: A Biography*. London: Bloomsbury.

Thomas, R. 1999. *Serbia Under Milosevic: Politics in the 1990s*. London: Hurst & Company.

Murza, Mindaugas (b.1973) – Lithuania

Mindaugas Murza is a Lithuanian neo-Nazi who has led, and been involved with, a variety of far-right organisations in the last decade. He is a controversial figure who has gained notoriety because of his anti-Semitic views.

Murza is a former member of the Lithuanian voluntary defence force. His powerbase is Šiauliai, where he is a member of the local council. In fact, he and his party place great emphasis on political combat at municipal level – with the ultimate aim of winning 3 percent of the vote across Lithuania. Murza has been involved in the far-right newspaper Voice of the Nation (*Nacijos Balsas*) and claims his organisation has around 160 members (with many more reading the paper).

At the heart of Murza's ideology is **anti-Semitism**. He has equated 'globalism with Zionism', labelled the Jews 'the most cruel and crafty enemy of the European race and of all humanity', and promised to send 'world Jewry to the garbage dump of history'. As such, he has provoked a wave of reaction from local magistrates who have questioned whether Murza's hard-line rhetoric actually breaks the law and from Jewish groups who have lobbied in favour of enhanced Holocaust **education** to help minimise the threat from the Far Right in the future. On one occasion, Dr Efraim Zuroff, director of the Simon Wiesenthal Center, wrote to the president of Lithuania, stating: 'I have been a frequent visitor to Lithuania since it regained its independence and I have been closely involved in the efforts to illuminate Lithuania's Holocaust past … The fact that not a single Lithuanian Nazi war criminal has ever sat for one minute in jail in independent Lithuania clearly underscores the failure to date to deal effectively with this problem. Given the results of the recent municipal elections in which right-wing extremists such as Mindaugas Murza were elected to the city councils in Šiauliai and Alytus, the issue of confronting Lithuania's Holocaust past … assumes even greater significance and urgency.'

Murza has also hit the headlines. One Lithuanian newspaper, *Spinter*, asked 500 people across the five main cities of Lithuania to give their verdict on how other politicians and groups should interact with Murza. About a third of respondents said they agreed with local mayors' policy of 'not limiting the actions' of his party; almost 50 percent of people said that Murza and his men should be 'involved in public life' or 'negotiated with' where there was conflict between the authorities and the Far Right; and over a quarter of those questioned said they either approved or strongly approved of what Murza stood for.

In November 2006, a court in Siauliai found Murza guilty of incitement to spread ethnic and racial hatred because of his party's anti-Semitic beliefs. Many individuals and groups were in favour of a conviction and he was eventually fined $1,760 (5,000 litas). Other party members were also fined. Murza has also been convicted for possessing illegal weapons and in 2005 police seized his computer hard drive because of suspicions about his political activities.

Murza is an outspoken figure who flirts between legal and illegal political activity. He stands for an old fashioned neo-Nazism. He and his followers have shown their support for Lithuanian war criminals and paraded photographs of Hitler at special events. Murza has little electoral support.

See also Russia and the Far Right *and* United National Workers Party (Lithuania).

Further Reading
http://www.tau.ac.il/Anti-Semitism/asw2005/baltics.htm (Stephen Roth Institute).
Smith, David J., Purs, A., Pabriks, A. & Lane, T. 2002. *The Baltic States: Estonia, Latvia and Lithuania*. London and New York: Routledge.

N

Nation and Nationalism

In the lexicon of the Far Right, nation and nationalism are vitally important terms. For most far-right activists, a nation connotes a shared culture, language, ethnicity or history, forming the core factor of a person's identity, allowing him or her to connect to a historically and geographically conceived sense of community. For the Far Right, nationalism is seen as a 'closed' rather than 'open' form of identity. For example, it is regarded as more or less impossible for someone not born into a particular nationality to enter into one later in life. Indeed, like interwar Fascists, the Far Right tends to see the nation in organic rather than legal terms. Ultimately, a nation is something intuitively and deeply-felt; the essence of a nation is a living, breathing sense of folk community, and as such it is not an entity that can be articulated through legal frameworks of citizenship. Often, the Far Right manifests characteristics of what might be called ultra-nationalism, i.e. and extreme form of nationalism leading to the sort of political activity which typically places the supposed priorities of the nation above liberal-democratic legal statutes and structures.

As upholders of the nation's interests above all other concerns, far-right ultra-nationalism implies 'above all the glorification of the nation through political action'.

Nation and Nationalism

Nations, as envisaged by far-right movements, are pure entities that cannot and should not be breached by 'foreign' or 'outside' elements. So fundamental is the role of the nation and nationalism in far-right ideology that it has actually been likened to the role of class in left-wing and Marxist theory. The centrality of nationalism is most neatly demonstrated in the names that far-right movements choose for themselves. These include: the **National Front** (*Front National*, FN), the (British) **National Front** (NF), the **British National Party** (BNP), the **National Alliance** (*Alleanza Nazionale*, NA), **Flemish Interest** (*Vlaams Belang*, VB), the **Danish People's Party** (*Dansk Folkeparti*, DPP) and so forth. The centrality of nationalism can also be seen in slogans that the Far Right employs. For example, the FN use 'The French First', while the BNP and the NF have both used 'British Jobs for British **Workers**'.

Some movements go further and have actually spoken in terms of territorial aggrandisement, for example in **Russia**. Here, on behalf of the Russian Liberal Democratic Party (*Liberal'no-Demokraticheskaya Partiya Rossii*, LDPR), Vladimir **Zhirinovsky** has shocked many Russians by talking about reuniting Russia with its ex-Soviet satellites. He also says he dreams of the day when, as he puts it, 'Russian soldiers can wash their boots in the warm waters of the Indian Ocean'. Further, Zhirinovsky has advocated the annexation of Alaska, dumping Russian nuclear waste in Germany and launching a nuclear attack on Japan. This sort of thinking is not limited to mere rhetoric. Other far-right politicians who have held executive power have been responsible for some horrific crimes in the name of national aggrandisement. In the Balkans, ultra-nationalists such as Slobodan **Milošević** and Franjo **Tuđman** have been associated with the policy of ethnic cleansing, involving the systematic destruction of one ethnic group to make way for another.

For the most part, far-right parties have also interpreted nationalist policies in more pragmatic, day-to-day terms. For example, this has meant that they have put forward policies aimed at reducing **immigration** levels and giving nationals priority in the allocation of housing and welfare benefits. At other times, parties have made statements that have gone beyond **patriotism**, but have also been subtle enough to stave off accusations of xenophobia or racism. For example, in Denmark the DPP argue they assert the independence of Denmark, guaranteeing the **freedom** of the Danish people. They also stress that they back the monarchy and representative government, and want to empower the Danish people. Indeed, in their public rhetoric the DDP claim the party simply promotes the cultural heritage and communal responsibilities of the Danes, and believe that, because the DPP is 'bound by our Danish cultural heritage and our responsibility towards each other as a people', it must 'strengthen our country's internal and external security'.

In Britain, the BNP is stark in its nationalist message. It argues that the core goal of the party is national regeneration. They stress the need to uphold the nation's sovereignty, securing the British Isles as the 'homeland' for British people, ensuring that 'all economic and social structures, institutions and legislation must be built or developed around the fundamentals of ensuring the freedom and security of our people and maintaining our unique cultural and ethnic identity'. The party argues that this assertion of British patriotic and national interests will chime with the views of the 'ordinary British folk' who are dissatisfied with the current style of governance in Britain. The BNP, then, presents itself as a party capable of bringing about comprehensive change through what it often dubbed a common-sense approach to politics. The references to common-sense are typical of far-right nationalist diatribes. Jean-Marie **Le Pen** in France uses the phrase '*bon sens*' in the same way. This rhetoric suggests that far-right views are not ideological or theoretical but natural and obvious; it merely expresses what the man-in-the-street would also say about his country given the opportunity.

Another tactic of far-right nationalism and ultra-nationalism is to talk and reminisce about the 'good old days'. Often, such rhetoric implies that the nation in the present is in disarray, and so validates far-right calls for radical measures designed to achieve a national resurrection of some description. This is an older, but still highly effective, rhetorical strategy. In Russia, for example, the LDPR has talked about reconstituting the 'old Russia', which would imply amalgamation with Belarus, Ukraine and other ex-Soviet republics. The Sweden Democrats (*Sverigedemokraterna*, SD) also argue that the nation is in decline, and that, as the leading nationalist party, they have found ever-rising support since the party was founded in 1988. The SD stress that this is because Swedish citizens are increasingly becoming second-class citizens, and are systematically discriminated against in favour of the newer immigrant population. In 2003, it defined its own brand of nationalism. At its heart, the SD nationalism placed a sense of common identity and the promotion of cultural homogeny, both vital for a harmonic society and unified society. These values led directly to the need for a single nation expressed through a state. Therefore 'the principle of one state, one nation, is absolutely fundamental to the Sweden Democrats' political values'. The party argues that, according to the nationalist principle, both the boundaries of the nation's community of people and the borders of the state that houses this community should be the same, and that the nation-state should be ethnically pure.

From this discussion on far-right nationalism and ultra-nationalism, it is easy to see where accusations of xenophobia and racism against the Far Right originate. For the Far Right, nationhood is a central concept, and understanding how each party constructs its sense of nationality is vital to interpreting its unique political style and praxis.

See also The Ideology of the Far Right; Islam and the Far Right *and* Patriotism.

Further Reading
Griffin, Roger. 1993. *The Nature of Fascism*. London and New York: Routledge.
Hainsworth, Paul, ed. 2000. *The Politics of the Extreme Right: From the Margins to the Mainstream*. London: Pinter.
Hobsbawm, Eric. 1990. *Nations and Nationalism since 1780: Programme, Myth, Reality*. Cambridge: Cambridge University Press.

National Bolshevist Party

The National Bolshevist Party (*Национал-Большевистская партия*, NBP) operates in Estonia, Latvia, Moldova and Kyrgyzstan as well as **Russia**. It was formed in May 1993 by Eduard Limonov, who left the Liberal Democratic Party after falling out with the movement's maverick leader, Vladimir **Zhirinovsky**. The NBP claims to have more than 10,000 members.

Limonov – also known as Savenko – has had a colourful life. A writer and Soviet dissident, he spent time in the US and France as an *émigré*. He has been arrested and imprisoned for possessing arms in 2001 and again in 2003. He has also been charged with inciting terrorist activity, attempting to create a paramilitary body and calling for a coup, but he was acquitted on all of these charges. He supported Russia's Chechen war, has a vision of Russia as a powerful Eurasian power, and his political heroes include Stalin and Julius Evola. His most noted literary works are *It Is I, Eddie*, a memoir of life in the US, and *Memoir of a Russian Punk*, which focuses on life in his native Kharkov.

Apart from Limonov, the NBP's main spokesmen are Sergei Aksyonov and Alexander Dugin. Aksyonov helped to found the party's newspaper, *Limonka*, and was imprisoned with Limonov in 2003. Meanwhile, Dugin was a co-founder of the NBP and until he left the party in 1998, served as one of its main ideologues.

The NBP – which is home to many neo-Nazi skinheads – is renowned for its hostility to Jews, NATO, the EU and the Russian Orthodox Church. The MIPT Terrorism Knowledge Base states: 'The National Bolshevist Party seems to combine elements of Fascism, particularly nationalism, with socialism. In that sense, NBP fits into a wider collection of disaffected groups unhappy with the new Russia, as well as a worldwide anti-globalisation and anti-capitalist movement'.

The party's core aim is to protect the rights of Russian citizens and to oppose all signs of non-Russian influence. Their tactics have included armed resistance and bombing. MIPT continues: 'The NBP is not an organised, dangerous terrorist group. Though the group has many members across Russia, its primary activities are protests and the distribution of leaflets ... Some of the group's members have been connected to terrorist attacks, but these reflect the looseness of the organisation, not an organised, party-wide campaign of **violence**. The NBP has some terrorist members, but it is not a terrorist organisation. The NBP will remain active in Russia and in the major cities of the former Soviet Union for the foreseeable future. The group will continue to protest Putin's programme and attract those left behind in post-communist Russia. Some small-scale violence and hooliganism associated with the group is also likely to persist. However, their violent actions are not likely to proceed beyond isolated, minor incidents'. MIPT date the organisation's last terroristic attack to 2 April 1998.

Others have been fascinated by the name of the party. According to Dora Apel of Open **Democracy**, the National Bolshevik Party 'is in no way Bolshevik [but] echoes the name of the National Socialist Party founded by Adolf Hitler, which was in no way socialist'.

See also Russia and the Far Right.

Further Reading
Cox, M. & Shearman, P. 2000. 'After the fall: nationalist extremism in post-communist Russia'. In *The Politics of the Extreme Right: From the Margins to the Mainstream*. Edited by Paul Hainsworth. London: Pinter.

National Front (France)

The French National Front (*Front National*, FN) was founded in 1972 by Jean-Marie **Le Pen**, the man who has been its leader ever since. In its early days, the party was a negligible force – and in 1981 Le Pen couldn't even raise the requisite number of signatures to enable him to stand in the presidential elections of that year. But the party's breakthrough came in 1983 (at **Dreux** in a by-election) and in 1984 (at the European elections).

Thereafter, it became a major influence on French politics – not simply in terms of electoral scores but rather in the way that it was able to set the agenda and force other movements to confront difficult issues, primarily **immigration**. By 1995, Le Pen had passed the psychologically significant 15 percent barrier and in 2002 he confounded experts by making it through to the second round of the presidential elections. This achievement caused consternation and anger around the world, but within a few years the party had fallen into decline, and in the 2007 presidential poll, Le Pen finished fourth with only 10 percent of the national vote. Le Pen is now in his 70s and it is likely that he will hand over the leadership of his party to his daughter, Marine. Apart from the Le Pens, the key figures in the party are Bruno Gollnisch (general delegate), Carl Lang (general secretary) and Roger Holeindre (vice-president).

In many ways, the FN has been the prototype for other far-right movements around **Europe**. Its success came earlier than that of other parties and, in his leadership style and love of controversy, Le Pen seemed to set the tone for **Schönhuber**, **Haider**, **Fini**, **Fortuyn** and **Griffin** after him. The doctrine of the FN has been built around a powerful and defensive nationalism ('France for the French') which sees all non-French influences as threatening and thus undesirable.

In line with social change, the party's rhetoric has metamorphosed from being anti-Jew to anti-immigrant, with North African immigrants being viewed as harbingers of a crusading **religion** (Islam), un-French culture and customs, and disease. Also fundamental to FN doctrine has been a hard-line attitude to **law and order**, and hostility toward the over-bureaucratic EU. Interestingly, throughout the 1990s, the party's programme broadened to include ecologism.

The FN triumphed in four significant mayoral contests in the mid-1990s (Toulon, Marignane, Orange and Vitrolles), giving it 'real power' for the first time. In 1999, the movement split in two after the desertion of Le Pen's deputy Bruno **Mégret** to form the Front National-Mouvement National – renamed the MNR – but this secessionist organisation has fared poorly at the polls, peaking at only 3.28 percent in 1999.

Throughout, the FN has displayed a rare talent for hitting the headlines. Its leader has proved particularly good copy. Whether it is his love life, allegations of torture aimed at him during the **Algerian War**, fisticuffs on the streets of Paris, or his indiscreet tirades against immigrants and Jews, Le Pen has dominated the news agenda in recent times, so much so that the phrase, 'all publicity is good publicity', could have been devised with him in mind. The FN appears to have benefited accordingly.

Since the 1970s, the party has used a variety of high-profile political symbols. The *tricolor* is one, and it is used heavily in party literature and publicity. Joan of Arc is another. She is viewed as the incarnation of French **patriotism** and Le Pen has stated: 'My mission is similar to Joan's: expelling the invader'. Elsewhere, Le Pen has addressed her directly: 'Joan, your work at the time was political, patriotic and spiritual. You forcefully led the change in political power; you called the people to stand up to the foreign invader'. The fact that Joan carried out her work before France was recognisable as a sovereign state does not seem to worry Le Pen or the FN.

Academics have taken the FN's rise to prominence seriously and have tried to understand how the 'Le Pen phenomenon' emerged in the first place. The leader's personality has been crucial, as has the party's media strategy, but more fundamentally, political scientists have pointed to France's long history of far-right politics (which arguably begins in the 1880s with General Boulanger, a populist rabble-rouser who is often likened to Le Pen).

National Front (France)

The 'blame' has also placed on the head of François Mitterrand, French president in the 1980s, for introducing a system of proportional representation into elections which helped small parties, like the FN, find their feet. Other parties, too, have egged Le Pen on by mimicking his rhetoric or even, on occasions, aping his policies.

See also Le Pen, Jean-Marie (France); Mégret, Bruno (France) *and* Western Europe and the Far Right.

Further Reading
www.frontnational.com (FN website).
Shields, J. 2007. *The Extreme Right in France: From Pétain to Le Pen.* London and New York: Routledge.
Arnold, E.J. 2000. *The Development of the Radical Right in France: From Boulanger to Le Pen.* Basingstoke: Macmillan.
Davies, Peter. 1999. *The National Front in France: Ideology, Discourse and Power.* New York: Routledge.
Davies, Peter. 2002. *The Extreme Right in France, 1789 to the Present: From De Maistre to Le Pen.* London and New York: Routledge.
Hainsworth, Paul. 2000. 'The Front National: from ascendancy to fragmentation on the French extreme right'. In *The Politics of the Extreme Right: From the Margins to the Mainstream.* Edited by Paul Hainsworth. London: Pinter.
Hainsworth, Paul. 1992. 'The extreme right in post-war France: the emergence and success of the Front National'. In *The Extreme Right in Europe and the USA.* Edited by Paul Hainsworth. London: Pinter.
Eatwell, Roger. 1996. *Fascism: A History.* London: Vintage.
Vaughan, M. 1991. 'The extreme right in France: "Lepenisme" or the politics of fear'. In *Neo-Fascism in Europe.* Edited by Luciano Cheles, Ronnie Ferguson and Michalina Vaughan. London: Longman.

National Front (Great Britain)

The British National Front (NF) was formed in 1967 when three other movements – the Racial Preservation Society, **British National Party** and League of Empire Loyalists – merged. Its first chairman was A.K.Chesterton and it has been described variously as 'neo-Nazi', 'Strasserite' and 'Third Positionist'. Its heyday was in the 1970s when it tried to inch in on the traditional working-class and Conservative Party electorate, but it only scored 1.5 percent in the general election of 1979. Its white racist ideology has always targeted Asian and Afro-Caribbean immigrants primarily.

In the late 1960s, the NF was involved in violent clashes with left-wing and Jewish groups. In 1972, John Tyndall took over as leader and a new emphasis was placed on the battle against **immigration**. A year later, in 1973, the NF had one of its best by-election results when Martin Webster polled 5,000 (16 percent). The party fielded 90 candidates in the election of October 1974 and, away from the ballot box, specialised in confrontational marches and demonstrations. In 1977, a new party newspaper was launched, *National Front News*, but the movement admits that it went through a slump in the 1980s and early 1990s. It now claims to be in the midst of a resurgence. As it proclaims on its website: 'The National Front is back, and it is here to stay!'

In terms of doctrine and ideology, the NF has a set of core values. Its nationalism is based around the idea of a mono-racial society: 'We live in a nation that is historically of the white race and we will stabilise our population by introducing a complete halt to all further immigration into our country. Coupled with this we will begin a programme that will result in the repatriation of all non-White people living here to their countries of ethnic origin. The only alternative to this policy is racial conflict, much to the detriment of the indigenous White population and the non-Whites currently residing here. Multiracialism is an unnatural fantasy that will never work and will only result in catastrophe. Our repatriation policy is the only realistic alternative to this scenario and will be to the benefit of Black and White alike'.

Furthermore, the NF is tough on defence and **law and order**, and favours a policy of economic nationalism when it comes to the future of British industry. It is passionately pro-**family**: 'Financial measures would include the raising of family allowances and the universal provision of free school meals … The National Front does not regard homosexual or lesbian relationships as valid alternatives to normal heterosexual marriage'.

Gradually, the NF's role as the standard-bearer of the British Far Right was usurped by the BNP, formed in 1982. During the 1990s support for the NF declined as the popularity of the BNP increased. That said, there was little difference between the two parties in terms of policy and general outlook, though the perception was that the NF was more anti-black than the BNP, and the BNP said that it would stop homosexuals from holding high office. From time to time, some on the British Far Right have expressed the hope that the two movements might amalgamate.

See also British National Party.

Further Reading

http://www.natfront.com (National Front website).
Eatwell, Roger. 2000. 'The extreme right and British exceptionalism: the primacy of politics'. In *The Politics of the Extreme Right: From the Margins to the Mainstream*. Edited by Paul Hainsworth. London: Pinter.
Eatwell, Roger. 1994. 'Why has the extreme right failed in Britain?' In *The Extreme Right in Europe and the USA*. Edited by Paul Hainsworth. London: Pinter.
Cable, Gerry. 1991. 'The far right in contemporary Britain'. In *Neo-Fascism in Europe*. Edited by Luciano Cheles, Ronnie Ferguson and Michalina Vaughan. London: Longman.
Durham, Martin. 1991. 'Women and the National Front'. In *Neo-Fascism in Europe*. Edited by Luciano Cheles, Ronnie Ferguson and Michalina Vaughan. London: Longman.
Eatwell, Roger. 1996. *Fascism: A History*. London: Vintage.
Bragg, T., Griffin, N., Kerr, D. & Harrington, P. 2005. *Taking Liberties: A Third Way Special on the Attack on Civil Liberties in the UK*. Pamphlet.
Copsey, N. 2004. *Contemporary British Fascism: The British National Party and the Quest for Legitimacy*. Basingstoke: Palgrave Macmillan.

National Front (Spain)

The National Front (*Frente Nacional*, FN) was founded in 1986/1987 by Blas Piñar López as successor to the New Force (*Fuerza Nueva*), a Francoist movement that was dissolved in 1982. Its birth was actually assisted by **Le Pen**'s FN in France and the MSI in Italy – so keen were these two parties to have additional far-right strength in the European Parliament. The Spanish FN failed to win any seats in the 1987 or 1989 elections.

The movement has tried to update and tone down Falangist-Francoist ideology. Its four key principles – or 'living stones' – are faith, **patriotism**, **family** and justice, and it paints a bleak picture of modern-day Spain. In a 1988 speech, Piñar outlined the situation: 'I would like … to establish precisely what we see when we look at the

National Front (Spain)

Spain of today, the Spain in which we live, in which we survive. It is a Spain which is in tatters, unstable, desperate, timid, frightened … If we think of Spain as a nation and society, we mean a historical entity which has created itself in the course of centuries, which still remains today, however wounded and infirm, and which is moving into an uncertain future'.

This was stirring material, but quite early on, Piñar's new group started to haemorrhage members dissatisfied with the leadership of the movement. These individuals ended up joining other far-right movements, such as Spanish Councils (Juntas Españolas), Patriotic Union (*Unión Patriótica*) and the **Spanish Circle of Friends of Europe** (*Círculo Español de Amigos de Europa*, CEDADE). The party tried to revivify itself by creating a **youth** wing and making common cause with Spanish Councils – forming the Spanish National Front (Frente Nacional Español, FNE) – but it was never a significant political force, nor did it become one.

Many theories have been advanced in an effort to explain the failure of the FN. After the **Franco** experience there was widespread opposition to a restoration of authoritarian politics in Spain. We should also note the impact of flamboyant populist figures such as José María Ruiz Mateos and Jesus Gil y Gil, who had a skill for attracting support among discontented voters, the power of the neo-conservatives, and the strong competition emanating from the democratic-right party, Alianza Popular.

See also Franco, General Francisco (Spain) *and* Southern Europe and the Far Right.

Further Reading
Preston, Paul. 1995. *Franco: A Biography*. London: Fontana.
Payne, Stanley. 2008. *Franco and Hitler*. New Haven, CT: Yale University Press.
Ellwood, Sheelagh. 1991. 'The Extreme Right in Spain: A Dying Species?'. In *Neo-Fascism in Europe*. Edited by Luciano Cheles, Ronnie Ferguson and Michalina Vaughan. London: Longman.
Gilmour, John. 1994. 'The extreme right in Spain: Blas Piñar and the spirit of the nationalist uprising'. In *The Extreme Right in Europe and the USA*. Edited by Paul Hainsworth. London: Pinter.

National-Socialist Battlecry Newspaper (US - Germany)

In the one hundred-fifteenth and final edition of *NS Kampfruf* (National-Socialist Battlecry) Gerhard Lauck wrote the following: 'Over a period of more than twenty years of continuous political activism, I have experienced many success and many setbacks. It is easy to celebrate the victories'. And he went on: 'First: If the National Socialist idea can survive the military defeat in World War Two, the destruction of the Third Reich and the death of our beloved Leader Adolf Hitler, then it can certainly survive any other setback, too – even the loss of an important fighter, a leader or even an entire group of fighters. As long as even ONE National Socialist lives, THE FIGHT GOES ON! Second: As long as one White man and one White woman remain, the struggle for the survival of the White Race continues. Even though the White race is a minority on this planet, there are still hundreds of millions of White people. Third: Great, incredible world-historical changes are always possible. Nobody knows the future'. The article went on in a similar vein, idolizing Hitler and the Nazis, encouraging sacrifice, encouraging hope and condemning the Jews.

NS Kampfruf was published in the US, had an American base, and until its last issue was published in 1995, it was an openly national-socialist paper. It was a German-language publication, but observers claim that it was translated into ten languages including Hungarian, Dutch, French, Swedish, Spanish, Portuguese, Italian and English (the English version was known as *New Order*). The paper claimed to have between 10,000 and 20,000 readers in many different countries and was also available on CD. Lauck, one of the key individuals behind the publication, had a history of distributing pro-Nazi propaganda and paying the price in prison (his second jail sentence ran from 1995 to 1999).

See also Central Europe and the Far Right.

Further Reading

Eatwell, Roger. 1996. *Fascism: A History*. London: Vintage.

Childs, David. 1991. 'The Far Right in Germany since 1945'. In *Neo-Fascism in Europe*. Edited by Luciano Cheles, Ronnie Ferguson and Michalina Vaughan. London: Longman.

Husbands, Christopher T. 1991. 'Militant neo-Nazism in the Federal Republic of Germany in the 1980s'. In *Neo-Fascism in Europe*. Edited by Luciano Cheles, Ronnie Ferguson and Michalina Vaughan. London: Longman.

National Weekly Newspaper (France)

For more than two decades, National Weekly (*National Hebdo*) has campaigned on behalf of the **French** Far Right, and the FN in particular. It speaks for many party causes (opposition to North African **immigration** especially) but over the years it has loosened its formal ties to the movement in order to give it a little more leeway editorially. So, it is no longer the official journal of Jean-Marie **Le Pen** or the FN, but its concerns do overlap to a large extent. *National Hebdo* is tabloid in shape and style and has caused controversy with some of its hard-hitting and provocative front-cover images (one featured hundreds of French Muslims engaging in prayer outside a Paris landmark). On one level, it is a campaigning and crusading paper; on another it is simply a meeting-place for far-right activists and thus includes its fair share of news, views, notices and small ads. It has claimed a circulation of close to 20,000, with around half being sold on street-corner kiosks (a high figure for such an extreme and politicised journal). Because its direct association with the FN has lessened, the newspaper is now able to explore issues such as immigration and the **Holocaust** with greater **freedom**. That said, it is claimed that the FN is still one of the paper's major financial backers.

See also Le Pen, Jean-Marie (France); National Front (France) *and* Western Europe and the Far Right.

Further Reading

www.frontnational.com (FN website).

Shields, J. 2007. *The Extreme Right in France: From Pétain to Le Pen*. London and New York: Routledge.

Arnold, E.J. 2000. *The Development of the Radical Right in France: From Boulanger to Le Pen*. Basingstoke: Macmillan.

Davies, Peter. 1999. *The National Front in France: Ideology, Discourse and Power*. New York: Routledge.

Davies, Peter. 2002. *The Extreme Right in France, 1789 to the Present: From De Maistre to Le Pen*. London and New York: Routledge.

Hainsworth, Paul. 2000. 'The Front National: from ascendancy to fragmentation on the French extreme right'. In *The Politics of the Extreme Right: From the Margins to the Mainstream*. Edited by Paul Hainsworth. London: Pinter.

Hainsworth, Paul. 1992. 'The extreme right in post-war France: the emergence and success of the

Front National'. In *The Extreme Right in Europe and the USA*. Edited by Paul Hainsworth. London: Pinter.

Eatwell, Roger. 1996. *Fascism: A History*. London: Vintage.

Vaughan, M. 1991. 'The extreme right in France: "Lepenisme" or the politics of fear'. In *Neo-Fascism in Europe*. Edited by Luciano Cheles, Ronnie Ferguson and Michalina Vaughan. London: Longman.

Nationalist Action Party (Turkey)

The Nationalist Action Party (*Milliyetçi Hareket Partisi*, MHP) is an influential far-right nationalist movement in Turkey. It was originally established by Alparslan **Türkeş** in 1965 as the Republican Villagers Nation Party, but changed its name to the MHP in 1969. The party's ideology is based around 'The Nine Lights of Türkes': nationalism, idealism, morality, corporatism, science, populism, progressivism, technology and defence of the peasantry.

The party's nationalism is hard-line and based on a belief in national myths and common ancestry. The party has stated: 'Turks do not have any friend or ally other than other Turks. Turks! Turn to your roots. Our words are to those that have Turkish ancestry and are Turks ... Those that have torn down this nation [the Ottoman Empire] are Greek, Armenian and Jewish traitors, and Kurdish, Bosnian and Albanians ... How can you, as a Turk, tolerate these dirty minorities? Remove from within the Armenians and Kurds and all Turkish enemies'. In terms of doctrine, the party is also anti-communist, interventionist on economic matters and traditionalist in the way that it sees the role of **women** in society.

The MHP was banned in 1980 by the Turkish authorities as part of a wide-ranging attack on political parties. Some key individuals moved on to other groups, but the movement was re-established in 1983 as the Nationalist Task Party (*Milliyetçi Çalışma* Partisi) and reverted to its original name in 1992 – the Nationalist Action Party. Over the years the MHP has become a significant player in national elections. It polled only 1 percent in 1973 and 4 percent in 1977, but has also recorded a score of 23 percent, in 1999. The party's leader, Devlet Bahçeli, became deputy prime minister between 1999 and 2002.

Enemies of the MHP, whether leftists or Kurdish separatists, portray it as an extreme, racist and fascist organisation, but under current leader Devlet Bahceli, it has made a conscious effort to configure itself, simply, as a conservative and nationalist movement which emphasises the unitary nature of the Turkish state.

In fact, the party has moderated its discourse significantly over time. Cultural nationalism has taken the place of ethnic nationalism and the party has also made overtures to Turkey's practising Muslims in an effort to broaden its appeal. Moreover, the MHP has matured from a movement that had its own militias and hit squads to one that is now playing by the democratic rules. Some academics have questioned this 'makeover', but the reality is that the MHP is a force to be reckoned with and in 2002 the spectre of the quasi-fascist MHP gaining a foothold in power was contrasted, in a not very favourable light with some kind of Islamic movement taking power (seemingly the worst-case scenario for moderate Turkish voters).

In 2007, the MHP again performed well. It claimed 14.3 percent of the vote, which made it the third strongest political force in the country. Only Prime Minister Recep Tayyip Erdoğan's ruling party, the AHP, with 46.6 percent, and the Republican

People's Party, the CHP, with 21 percent recorded a higher share of the vote.

See also South-Eastern Europe and the Far Right *and* Türkeş, Alparslan (Turkey).

Further Reading
http://www.mhp.org.tr (MHP website).
Wilkinson, Paul. 1983. *The New Fascists*. London: Pan.

Netherlands-Europe Journal (Belgium)

Netherlands-Europe (*Dietsland-Europa*) was a Belgian far-right journal. It was published on a monthly basis by Were Di (*Verbond van Nederlandse Werkgemeenschappen*), a movement founded in 1962 by former Nazi collaborators including Karel Dillen, who went on to establish the VB. Were Di and its flagship publication put forward a pro-Flemish doctrine that aimed at undermining the Belgian state and promoting white supremacy. There is was a significant overlap between the VB and *Dietsland-Europa* in terms of personnel and ideas. The journal was particularly sympathetic to the **Holocaust denial** theses of Robert Faurisson and to the national-socialist heritage in **Europe**.

See also Degrelle, Léon (Belgium) *and* Flemish Bloc/Flemish Interest.

Further Reading
Sniderman, P.M. & Hagendoorn, L. 2007. *When Ways of Life Collide: Multiculturalism and Its Discontents in the Netherlands*. Princeton, NJ: Princeton University Press.
Mudde, Cas & Holsteyn, Joop Van. 2000. 'The Netherlands: explaining the limited success of the extreme right'. In *The Politics of the Extreme Right: From the Margins to the Mainstream*. Edited by Paul Hainsworth. London: Pinter.
Husbands, Christopher T. 1994. 'The Netherlands: irritants on the body politic'. In *The Extreme Right in Europe and the USA*. Edited by Paul Hainsworth. London: Pinter.

Neue Kronen Zeitung Newspaper (Austria)

Neue Kronen Zeitung is an Austrian daily newspaper that has been accused of aiding and abetting the rise of Jörg **Haider** and the FPÖ. Primarily it is other Austrian newspapers and left-wing intellectuals who have made the claim since the emergence of Haider in 1999. *Der Standard* argued that *Neue Kronen Zeitung* had anti-Semitic and racist sympathies and won a high-profile court case against the paper in August 2004. *Neue Kronen Zeitung*'s most famous journalist is Richard Nimmerichter, also known as Staberl. Critics maintain that Nimmerichter is too close to FPÖ ideas, particularly with regard to domestic policy, the Jews and the **Holocaust**. In 1992, for example, he wrote an article that seemed to minimise the significance of the Holocaust. On the other side of the fence is Elfriede Jelinek, a well known Austrian novelist and the newspaper's number-one critic. When she was awarded the Nobel Prize for Literature, the newspaper decided to ignore the story – as if fueling the war of words. At the height of the Waldheim Affair in the late 1980s, the high-circulation *Neue Kronen Zeitung* was also accused of far-right sympathies. The newspaper made it clear that it did not sympathise with the prevailing pro-resistance and anti-Nazi attitudes. The paper is also renowned for its anti-EU standpoint.

See also Austrian Freedom Party *and* Haider, Jörg (Austria).

Further Reading
http://www.bzoe.at (Alliance for the Future of Austria website).
http://www.fpoe.at (Freedom Party website).
Höbelt, L. 2003. *Defiant Populist: Jörg Haider and the Politics of Austria 1986–2000*. West Lafayette: Purdue University Press.
Morrow, D. 2000. 'Jörg Haider and the new FPÖ: beyond the democratic pale'. In *The Politics of the Extreme Right: From the Margins to the Mainstream*. Edited by Paul Hainsworth. London: Pinter.

New Democracy (Sweden)

New Democracy (*Ny Demokrati*, ND) was a relatively short-lived Swedish political party that was founded in 1991 by Ian Wachtmeister and Bert Karlsson. Capitalising on the growing sense of distrust with the traditional ruling elite that dominated Swedish politics at this time, ND emerged from nowhere and achieved parliamentary representation between 1991 and 1994. Indeed, in 1991, it easily passed the 4 percent threshold, gaining 6.7 percent of the national vote. Some commentators had predicted that the party would get an even higher share of the vote. However, this success was not consolidated by the party, and between 1991 and 1994 unprofessional behaviour, such as public quarrelling between leading ND members and the inability to develop an efficient party organisation, led to the party's lack of further electoral success. The ND scored only 1.2 percent in the 1994 elections, while in 1998 it achieved a mere 0.2 percent of the vote. Consequently, the party was wound up in 2000 following several years of infighting that stemmed from the defeat in the 1994 elections, alongside other differences.

The brief success of the party has to be understood in the context of Swedish politics of the late 1980s and early 1990s. At this time, a number of issues came together that created the short-lived political space for a radical populist party to win over a significant proportion of the electorate. These included: declining support for the Swedish Social Democratic Party (*Sveriges socialdemokratiska arbetareparti*) as it became increasingly indistinguishable from the more 'bourgeois' parties; a decreasing, and increasingly affluent, working class; rising taxes; and widespread public consternation at the decision to suddenly begin negotiations on joining the **European Union**. Finally, the **immigration** issue had become politicised by this point, following a dramatic increase in migrants during the 1980s. Several other xenophobic parties also emerged during this time, such as the Swedish Democrats (*Sverigedemokraterna*, SD). Meanwhile, the Swedish government itself developed new restrictions on immigration in order to curb the rise of radical, racist politics. This mixture of shifting political allegiances, the prospective loss of political neutrality through potential EU membership, and rising concerns over immigration, helped to create a more volatile electorate, one disenchanted with traditional parties and political institutions.

In terms of ideology, ND promoted a low tax and anti-state bureaucracy agenda, combined with a hard-line stance on immigration and foreign expenditure. Meanwhile, the anti-establishment tenor of the ND was also significant, allowing the party to be seen as a protest vote by an electorate that felt alienated from a seemingly corrupt political establishment. Turning to the party's leading personalities, Wachtmeister was an aristocrat and author of satirical novels, while Karlsson was a high-profile entrepreneur. The ND itself had emerged after a research institute headed by

Wachtmeister – which was close to the Swedish Employer's Federation (*Svenska Arbetsgivareföreningen*) – was converted into a political party following a meeting in 1990. Typical of the public behaviour of the party's two leaders was the way they became famous for addressing crowds while standing on beer cases during the 1991 election campaign. This gesture was taken as a sign of their populism and their desire to appear as 'different'.

Following the 1991 election success, it was not surprising that the ND were a controversial presence in Swedish national politics. They embarrassed the ruling coalition by supporting its policies on a number of occasions, and they provoked the occasional boycott by politicians who did not wish to be associated with an avowedly xenophobic movement. However, by 1994, the party was squeezed out of political significance by a discernible rightward turn among the conservative parties, alongside a loss of confidence in the ND among its voters. As with many far-right parties, the public spectacle of having its politics played out on the national stage helped to sow the seeds of the ND's destruction.

See also Klarström, Anders (Sweden) *and* Scandinavia and the Far Right.

Further Reading

http://www.sverigedemokraterna.net (Sweden Democrats website).
Arter, David. 1999. *Scandinavian Politics Today*. Manchester: Manchester University Press.
Andersen, J.G. & Bjørklund, T. 2000. 'Radical right-wing populism in Scandinavia: from tax revolt to neo-liberalism and xenophobia'. In *The Politics of the Extreme Right: From the Margins to the Mainstream*. Edited by Paul Hainsworth. London: Pinter.
Ignazi, Piero. 2003. *Extreme Right Parties in Western Europe*. New York: Oxford University Press.

Northern League (Italy)

Founded in 1991, the Northern League (*Lega Nord*, LN) is one of a small group of far-right Italian parties that pursue regionalist, and sometimes even separatist agendas. Not the easiest of organisations to pigeon-hole, the LN's policies manifest many far-right tendencies, including negative and aggressive attitudes towards asylum-seekers, immigrants, homosexuals, Communists and gypsies. This is combined with a typical deep distrust of the **European Union**. The LN's central idea promotes the concept of a separate, federal state for northern Italy, or **Padania**, as the party discourse describes the region. In the late 1990s, this goal was radicalised, and the party pushed for a separate Padanian nation-state, though it has subsequently dropped this aim. In this sense, the LN can be compared to **Flemish Interest** (*Vlaams Belang*, VB), as both pursue a far-right, regionalist agenda.

Emerging from the growing successes of regional movements within northern Italy during the 1970s and 1980s, the LN itself was created following the merger of several smaller political leagues. These included the Venetian League (*Liga Veneta*), which had achieved electoral successes from the early 1980s, and Lombardy League (*Lega Lombarda*), which was headed up by the future LN leader Umberto Bossi. In 1989, these various leagues contested the European parliamentary election as the Northern Alliance (*Alleanza Nord*, AN), and gained one seat. Spurred on by this success, the AN list of candidates gained nearly 6 percent of the national vote in the 1990 administrative elections. The Lombardy League was the dominant member of this group, and so Bossi's movement set the overarching tone for the campaign.

Unsurprisingly, this was strongly anti-southerner. Indeed, southern Italians were painted as corrupt, welfare-scrounging and work-shy, and so they allegedly contrasted negatively with the hard-working, morally upstanding northerners.

After its creation in 1991, the LN was boosted by the notorious 'Clean Hands' enquiry into party corruption. Indeed, the LN found widespread favour in the early 1990s because it represented a vote directed against a seemingly corrupt political establishment. From 1992, further Italian elections saw the LN consolidate its position on the national stage. In the general elections of 1992, overall the party gained 8.6 percent of the national vote, and achieved significant victories in Milan and Lombardy. In 1993, the LN won the mayorship of Milan, achieving 57.1 percent of the vote. Finally, in 1994, the party joined Silvio Berlusconi's Pole of Freedoms (*Polo delle Libertà*) coalition. However, it pulled out of this administration by the end of the year, causing the Pole of Freedoms to collapse.

After this flirtation with executive office, the late 1990s saw the LN take a more radical stance. Some of the more significant aspects of LN radicalisation at this time included: support for Milošević's Serbian aggrandisement in the break-up of Yugoslavia; increased hostility towards the powers of the EU; and the development of its own green shirted movement. Perhaps the most noteworthy step towards radicalisation in the later 1990s was for the party to pursue the policy of separatism for northern Italy. Consequently, despite not having the full support of his party, Bossi claimed independence for **Padania** in September 1996. Both the Catholic Church and the army condemned this stunt, and many media commentators responded with ridicule and astonishment. Unsurprisingly, then, this move towards a more extreme and unrealistic politics backfired, and the party soon noticed a downturn in its electoral fortunes.

The most prominent sign of dwindling interest in the LN was losing the mayorship of Milan in 1997, which was followed by a significant dip in LN support during the European parliamentary elections of 1998. This downturn prompted Bossi to reconfigure the party's policies, dropping the idea of Padanian independence. Indeed, by 2001, the LN had resumed cordial relationship with Berlusconi, joining his new House of Freedoms (*Casa delle Libertà*, CDL) coalition. The LN gained three ministers in this administration: Bossi himself headed up **regionalism** and devolution, Roberto Maroni picked up the labour and social affairs brief, and Roberto Castelli took over at the Ministry of Justice. This LN presence in high office lasted until 2006, when the CDL coalition was defeated in national elections.

The electorate responsible for putting the LN into power is interesting to analyse. Piero Ignazi and Tom Gallagher have offered some observations here. Ignazi's analysis notes that LN voters are often male and blue-collar. Despite this working-class appeal, the LN is actually proportionally less well represented in urban areas when compared to other far-right electorates. He also comments on the fact that the more rural LN voter often brings home a relatively high income. Despite this greater affluence, a sense of consistency with other far-right voters lies in a common authoritarian and xenophobic attitude, combined with a deep distrust of state institutions. Meanwhile, Tom Gallagher has noted that, during the 1990s, the LN's far-right politics allowed the party to steal some votes from the competitor far-right movement, the **Italian Social Movement** (*Movimento Sociale Italiano*, MSI), later the **National Alliance** (*Alleanza Nazionale*, AN). However, the LN's more extreme rhetoric also allowed the NA to appear as the more moderate party in comparison. Consequently, especially during the later 1990s, the radicalism of the LN helped to smooth the path for the emerging post-Fascist profile of the NA. Finally, Ignazi has noted the way that the LN's populist discourse has created its own demonised 'other' in the 1990s. Clustering themes such as anti-Rome, anti-southern Italy and anti-organised crime alongside anti-immigrant views, Bossi was able to reignite the north/south divide in a country notorious for its lack of a strong and stable sense of national identity. Combining a parochial localism with a critique of state politics, then, the LN has been able to tap into a profound sense of unease within modern Italy.

See also Fini, Gianfranco (Italy); Italian Social Movement/National Alliance *and* Southern Europe and the Far Right.

Further Reading

http://www.leganord.org (Northern League website).
Gallagher, Tom. 2000. 'Exit from the ghetto: the Italian far right in the 1990s'. In *The Politics of the Extreme Right: From the Margins to the Mainstream*. Edited by Paul Hainsworth. London: Pinter.
Ignazi, Piero. 2003. *Extreme Right Parties in Western Europe*. New York: Oxford University Press.
Amyot, Grant & Verzichelli, Luca, eds. 2007. *End of the Berlusconi Era?* Oxford ; New York, N.Y.: Berghahn Books.
Bufacchi, Vittorio & Burgess, Simon. 2001. *Italy Since 1989: Events and Interpretations*. New York: St. Martin's Press.
Mack Smith, Denis. 1997. *Modern Italy: A Political History*. New Haven, CT: Yale University Press.

Norway, Far-Right Gains (2001)

The growth of the Far Right in Norway in recent years was most dramatically felt in the national elections of 2001. This poll resulted in the following distribution of seats: Labour Party 43, Conservative Party 38, Progress Party 26, Christian People's Party 22, Socialist Left Party 23, Centre Party 10, Fisherman's Coastal Party 2, and the Red Electoral Alliance 1. After the election, the Conservatives Party and the Christian People's Party came together in a coalition government. The far-right Progress Party was not officially part of the coalition, but it did agree to support the legislative agenda of the new administration led by premier Kjell Bondevik. Interestingly, in one poll, 49 percent of Norwegian voters said they actually wanted the Progress Party to join the new government.

The election was an interesting landmark for the Progress Party. Although extremely respectable – especially when compared to the electoral results of other far-right parties in **Europe** – the vote was slightly down on some pre-election opinion-poll ratings for the movement. Indeed, at one point ahead of the vote their poll rating touched 30 percent. Even so, 15 percent of the vote and 26 seats catapulted the party into the mainstream *maelstrom* of Norwegian party politics. This rise to prominence became the issue of the moment, even though the Progress Party positioned itself outside the new ruling coalition. According to one left-wing website, wsws.org, a confused electorate saw the opportunity to register a protest vote in **Hagen**'s charismatic, man-of-the-people politics. This protest vote not only allowed the Progress Party to forward its policies opposing welfare and prompting strict controls on **immigration**, but more worryingly, the party had become a significant actor in the country's political milieu. Another article on the same website claimed that the Far Right in Norway was closer to power than at any time since the fall of Vidkun Quisling's National Unity (*Nasjonal Samling*) administrations – the Far Right, puppet government installed by the Nazis during the Second World War. The article also claimed that Hagen was a 'one-man band' backed by a largely ineffective local membership, and that his rise to prominence demonstrated a growing acceptance of the far-right perspective among the nation's political elites.

This said, the popularity of the Progress Party was not helped by other events. In one notorious example, in February 2001 a black teenager, Benjamin Hermansen, was murdered in Oslo. Subsequently, three neo-Nazis were imprisoned for the crime, an event that did nothing to help create a more moderate image for the Far Right in the Norwegian public imagination.

See also Hagen, Carl (Norway); Norwegian Progress Party *and* Scandinavia and the Far Right.

Further Reading

Ignazi, Piero. 2003. *Extreme Right Parties in Western Europe*. New York: Oxford University Press.
BBC, 'Norway far-right sets new course', http://news.bbc.co.uk/1/hi/world/europe/1603256.stm (cited 31 December 2007).

Norwegian Progress Party

The Norwegian Progress Party (*Fremskrittspartiet*) was established in 1973 by Anders Lange and was then known, rather laboriously, as Anders Lange's Party for a Reduction in Tax, Charges and Government Intervention. In the party's own words, it was 'founded as a protest movement against the nanny state and the interference in personal **freedom** associated with it'. Until 2006, the Progress Party was led by another key personality, Carl **Hagen**, and today the leader is a woman, Siv Jensen. It has made great strides since the early days. It won 5 percent of the vote and four seats in 1973, while in 2001 it claimed 15 percent of the popular vote and in 2005 it polled 22 percent (winning 38 seats and becoming the second largest party in the country in terms of parliamentary representation). Other landmark results were 1987 (12.3 percent), 1989 (13 percent), 1995 (12 percent), 1997 (15.3 percent), 1999 (13.5 percent), 2000 (14.6 percent) and 2003 (17.9 percent).

On one level, the party is liberal, and actually describes itself as 'libertarian': it is tied to free-market economics, privatisation, decentralisation, welfarism and the idea of a small state. It is progressive in many key areas. The party manifesto states: 'Welfare benefits must be directed increasingly towards those who need them ... It is both a private and a public responsibility to ensure a healthy **environment** and the adequate exploitation and use of Norway's natural resources ... *Fremskrittspartiet* will motivate the individual to work and activity by introducing a flatter fiscal system and by reducing the pressure of taxation. Funds that are required to meet necessary state responsibilities should, to an increasing extent, be raised from taxation on consumption, rather than taxation of the rewards of labour'.

On another level, it is very illiberal. It claims to be 'totally opposed to discrimination on the basis of race, gender, **religion** and ethnic origin' but, at the same time, it wishes to control **immigration** via quotas and opposes multiculturalism, saying that Norway should work hard to preserve its Christian identity in the face of increased Muslim immigration.

After 2001, the Progress Party supported the minority coalition government and, in a broader sense, has become a key player in Norwegian party politics. It has suffered its share of internal feuds, but has survived. It does not like being pigeon-holed on the Far Right, but its anti-immigrant discourse is strong. It has also helped to set the political agenda in Norway. Other parties may not approve of what the party stands for, but they have been forced to engage with the issues that it has raised. And the popularity of the Progress Party shows no sign of abating. In 2007, the *Norway Post* claimed that Jensen, the new party leader, had the support of 30.8 percent of the country's voters and it was thus the nation's largest political party.

17. Siv Jensen, 36, celebrates after she was elected leader of Norway's opposition far-right Progress Party in Gardermoen, 6 May 2006.

On the left, the Progress Party is viewed as a reactionary and xenophobic movement. Indeed, it has to be said that in recent years, the party has done little to dispel the perception that it is hostile to the idea of multiculturalism. In 2005, for example, it published a publicity brochure whose front-cover image featured a balaclava-wearing gunman alongside the caption, 'The perpetrator is of foreign origin … !' This was a fairly blunt and unsubtle attack on Norway's immigrant population, but party spokesman Per Sandberg was unapologetic: 'What we are focusing on is that we have had an immigration policy with a lack of integration and a lack of demands on immigrants. Many youngsters with an immigrant background end up in a route to crime … and we think it is important to focus on that. But if others want to put a lid on the problem and not debate it, we won't solve these problems'. At times the party's discourse has crossed the line between what is acceptable and what is not, and this is a case in point.

Research carried out by Jørgen Goul Andersen and Tor Bjørklund emphasises that the Progress Party has a very distinct electorate. Poll findings show that its voters were far more cynical than other voters, and also happy to endorse the view that immigrants are a 'threat to our national identity' and 'aid to foreign countries should be cut'. In fact, on the first question, the Progress Party was so far 'off the scale' that the Norwegian Conservatives were closer to the left on this issue than they were to their fellow right-wingers in Siv Jensen's movement.

See also Hagen, Carl (Norway); Norway, Far-Right Gains (2001) *and* Scandinavia and the Far Right.

Further Reading
http://www.frp.no (Progress Party website).
Hagen, C.I. 1984. *Honesty is the Best Policy*. Publisher not known.
Andersen, J.G. & Bjørklund, T. 2000. 'Radical right-wing populism in Scandinavia: from tax revolt to neo-liberalism and xenophobia'. In *The Politics of the Extreme Right: From the Margins to the Mainstream*. Edited by Paul Hainsworth. London: Pinter.
Shaffer, W.R. 1998. *Politics, Parties, and Parliaments: Political Change in Norway*. Columbus, OH: Ohio State University Press.

O

Oresund Bridge (Denmark)

The issue of **immigration** has become very prominent in Danish politics, with both the centre-right government and the far-right **Danish People's Party** (*Dansk Folkeparti*, DPP) exploiting trends in migration to forward aggressive political stances. Perhaps it is not surprising, then, that the Oresund Bridge – a feat of engineering comprising two lanes of trains and four lanes of motorway that stretches from Copenhagen in Denmark to Malmö in Sweden – is for many a negative symbol of the ease with which immigrants can enter Denmark. The centre-right government, led by Anders Fogh Rasmussen who came to power in 2001, has imposed some of the most hard-line, anti-immigration legislation in **Europe**. Moreover, the DPP's discourse on the subject is predicated on the assertion that the native Danish population will be overtaken by Muslim immigrants in the near future – for example, one DPP poster depicts a small, white Danish girl with the slogan 'When she retires, Muslims will be a majority in Denmark'.

Since its opening in 2000, the Oresund Bridge has played into the hands of the Danish Far Right, and in particular the DPP, led by Pia **Kjaersgaard**. She has raised the stakes of the immigration issue, arguing that if her party ever came to power it would look into the possibility of shutting the 10-mile road bridge. As the *New York Times* reported, Kjaersgaard has even claimed that Swedish immigration policies were transforming the country's cities, which she has dubbed 'Scandinavian Beiruts' that are riddled with 'gang warfare', 'honour crimes' and 'gang rapes.' By closing the bridge, she argues, Denmark could be protected from such an eventuality befalling the country. This discourse reflects the wider trend within the Scandinavian Far Right – especially in Denmark and Norway – to move away from a neo-liberal economic agenda, and to take ownership of the issue of immigration as a key tranche of its policy agenda. In turn, this has led to centre-right politicians offering a milder version of such concerns, in order to take the sting out of the Far Right.

In the Danish case, the result has been dramatic, and at times absurd. For example, the regulations surrounding Danish nationals marrying non-Danish spouses has led to much heartache. The *Sunday Times* offers one case study where a mixed nationality couple have been forced to relocate from Copenhagen to Malmö. One Danish, the other from New Zealand, they are unable to meet the stringent requirements for a mixed nationality marriage. These include a minimum age of twenty-four for both parties, and for the non-Danish national to be able to maintain the equivalent of £5,000 in savings for the duration of the application of the residency permit – a process that can take up to seven years to complete. As in many such cases, Danish nationals are forced to relocate to Malmö and commute via the Oresund Bridge to work in Copenhagen. The then immigration minister, Rikke Hvilshoj, claimed that the greatest beneficiaries of these strict new regulations were, in fact, young Muslim **women**. According to Hvilshoj, these regulations prevented forced marriages and helped young Muslim women to focus on their studies.

The emergence of a tough stance on the policies of immigration in Denmark is symbolised by the Oresund Bridge, but debate surrounding the significance of the structure taps into far deeper concerns within Danish political culture surrounding the threat of economic migration and asylum. These debates have allowed the Far Right to reposition itself as both a populist and a credible political force in Denmark.

See also Danish People's Party, Growth of (2001–2005); Danish People's Party *and* Scandinavia and the Far Right.

Further Reading

Sunday Times, 'Tough rules slash asylum in Denmark', http://www.timesonline.co.uk/tol/news/world/article379499.ece?print=yes&randnum=1197453238995 (cited 31 December 2007).
Givens, Terri, E. 2005. *Voting Radical Right in Western Europe*. Cambridge: Cambridge University Press.

P

Padania (Italy)

If one were to look for Padania on a map, one would find the task somewhat difficult. The proposal for Padania has emerged from recent ideas postulated by the **Northern League** (*Lega Nord*, LN) and roughly comprises the northern part of Italy, encompassing many of the industrial areas of the country. According to LN literature, Padania contains the major cities of northern Italy, and their surrounding regions, including Venice, Turin, Milan, Genoa, Trento, Trieste, Bologna, Florence and Perugia. Deriving the name Padania from the Po River Valley, the LN defines the region in cultural as well as geographical terms. Indeed, the role of regional dialects of the Italian language is central to the LN's cultural definition of Padania. In the 1990s, the LN has even proposed a national flag – a green Celtic cross on a white background – and a national anthem for Padania.

The LN itself was founded in the early 1980s, although it only rose to political prominence in the 1990s. Since its formation, its green-shirted activists have campaigned for a federal Italy, and at times even a separate Padanian state. The organisation, led by Umberto Bossi, is also hostile to **immigration**, multiculturalism and state interference in the **economy**. Consequently, some commentators, especially on the left, see the LN as neo-Fascist in political orientation. Since the fall of the **Berlin Wall**, the LN has claimed that the **end** of **Communism** has precipitated an economic crisis that requires the prosperous north of Italy to break away from the less economically developed south. Therefore, it argues that the LN 'is the party which gives political expression to the federalist movement and proposes implementation of the federalist idea as a solution to the cultural and economic crisis.'

The literature hosted on the LN website contains many of the core ideas of the movement. These documents include a national history of Padania, not only detailing its alleged roots in European culture but also emphasising how the creation of the Italian state in 1860 betrayed an older heritage of Padania. This national history also decries the degradation of the northern Italian dialects, which the LN claims comprise the Padanian language, and asserts the need for a modern Padanian consciousness and identity. Another key trope in this discourse is the assertion that, currently, the Italian state is impotent on the issue of organised crime – which the LN specifically associates with the allegedly corrupt nature of southern Italy. This factor, argues the LN literature, imparts a moral duty onto the movement: it is an organisation that seeks to end the decadence manifested by organised criminals murdering judges and police officers. This history of Padania concludes that the LN is fighting for **freedom**: 'Free from the oppression of Roman-style centralism. Free from the cancer of the Mafia. Free to manage its own problems. Free to remain part of **Europe**. Free to compete in international markets. Free to assist in the growth of peoples with less developed economies. Free to preserve and promote its own cultural identities.' This rhetoric of national and economic freedom is also styled to appeal to resentment over the redistribution of wealth from the more prosperous north to the less-well-off south of the country.

The Padanian cause was perhaps fought most vociferously in the 1990s. In the early part of the decade, the LN benefited from a growing sense of corruption in Italian politics, and by 1994 it had become a central player in the country's political milieu. Its policies of economic neo-liberalism combined with fiscal federalism for Italy chimed with an electorate that was worried about the economic imbalance between the north and the south, and who were also becoming increasingly distrustful of the state. However, by 1994, Silvio Berlusconi's Forward Italy (*Forza Italia*, FI) party had also entered this same political space, articulating a similar message, though in less virulent tones and with a greater national appeal. The LN's message of federalism for Italy was becoming more difficult to sell, and so, after the LN left Berlusconi's short-lived Pole of Freedoms (*Polo delle Libertà*) coalition, the party started to explore a more radical stance: independence for Padania. From 1995, it began debating the issue of separatism rather than federalism, initially covertly but later openly. In 1996, Umberto Bossi proclaimed the Republic of Padania – an English-language version of this declaration of independence is available on the LN's website. Reflecting this development, an unofficial Parliament of Padania was formed by the LN. Problematically for Bossi, he only had a minority of support within the LN for these increasingly radical steps. Nevertheless, in a country with a notoriously weak sense of national identity, Bossi hoped that the economic disparity between north and south would help the LN to strengthen the sense of solidarity among Italians living in Padania. However, the problems with this approach can be seen by the fact that, in 2001, the LN joined Berlusconi's new House of Freedoms (*Casa delle Libertà*) coalition. Subsequently, the movement downplayed its calls for independence, and it reverted to the federal ideal for Padania rather than the separatist path of the late 1990s.

See also Northern League (Italy); Regionalism *and* Southern Europe and the Far Right.

Further Reading
Ignazi, Piero. 2003. *Extreme Right Parties in Western Europe*. New York: Oxford University Press.
Northern League, http://www.seveso.org/English_version/home.htm (cited 31 December 2007).

Padina (Romania)

Located in Romania's Buzău County, the town of Padina has significant far-right connections. During the interwar period, it was the site of a legionary camp organised by Corneliu Codreanu's Legion of the Archangel Michael. More recently, it has regained notoriety after one strand of the Romanian Far Right sought to reconnect with this Iron Guard heritage. The miniscule organisation New Christian Romania (*Noua Românie Creştină*, NCR) – founded in November 1992 on Codreanu's birthday – has always promoted its theoretical, ideological links with the Iron Guard. NCR was created by a Bucharest based schoolteacher, Şerban Suru, and subsequently he has organised a series of events that have generated national media interest in the Romanian Far Right.

Echoing the organisational structure of the Iron Guard, in 1994, Suru began by launching the first 'nest' in Romania since the fall of **Communism**, which he dubbed the Horia Sima nest. This created fears amongst surviving Iron Guardists that their veterans' associations may become outlawed as a result of the controversy created by Suru's high-profile activities. Following on from this initial nest, there was a wave of new Iron Guard-style nests, located in Braşov, Sibiu, Constanţa and Chişinău. Meanwhile, Suru campaigned hard to promote the 'historical truth' about the Iron Guard in the mid-1990s. Aside from the formation of nests, other examples of this activity include the creation of a library in Bucharest dedicated to correcting the historical record regarding Codreanu's interwar political activities; and the formation of another organisation, the Christian Legion (*Legiunea Creştină*), again dedicated to promoting a pro-Iron Guard reading of the interwar years. The latter was later deemed unconstitutional by Romanian authorities, creating further media interest in the Iron Guard legacy in the country.

Building on these tensions, in the summer of 1995, Suru organised a legionary-style summer camp in Padina. The event itself comprised a heady mixture of prayer, work and indoctrination into Iron Guard thinking. Wearing green shirts, the uniform of the Iron Guard, Suru even sent participants to be interviewed by media reporters. Meanwhile, the Romanian Intelligence Service, SRI, deemed the camp a threat to state security. Further, these activities were not universally approved by veteran Legionaries and others seeking to build on the Iron Guard's legacy in post-communist Romania. For example, the September and November 1995 editions of *Gazeta de veste*, a pro-Iron Guard monthly publication, claimed that Suru's interpretation of the ideology was not an authentic one. The articles stressed that Suru failed to sufficiently internalise Iron Guard values, was simply 'showing off' and could even hinder the alleged progress that supporters of Sima had made since the collapse of Ceausescu's regime. Indeed, many of Sima's supporters gave their allegiances to the For the Fatherland Party (*Partidul 'Pentru Patrie'*, PPP) – itself another throwback to the interwar era. The following year, the Bucharest newspaper *Libertatea* reported a further camp organised by the resurgent Legionary movement, this time at Eforie-Sud, a resort on the Black Sea.

However, media attention aside, the real political significance of the assorted sub-groupings that attempted to rehabilitate the Iron Guard in post-communist Romania can be best measured in the election results of the 1990s. These movements failed to make significant electoral breakthroughs, and so could not capitalise on sensationalist media attention and create a significant popular desire to return to interwar Legionary politics.

See also Greater Romania Party; South-Eastern Europe and the Far Right *and* Tudor, Corneliu Vadim (Romania).

Further Reading

Shafir, Michael. 2000. 'Marginalisation or mainstream? The extreme right in post-communist Romania'. In *The Politics of the Extreme Right: From the Margins to the Mainstream*. Edited by Paul Hainsworth. London: Pinter.

Shafir, Michael, 'Radical politics in East-Central Europe Part IX: the Romanian Radical Return', *Radio Free Europe / Radio Liberty Reports*, http://www.rferl.org/reports/eepreport/2001/02/3-070201. asp (cited 31 December 2007).

Paris Riots (2005)

In October and November 2005, rioting spread across Paris and other major French cities. The events began in Clichy-sous-Bois on 27 October after two teenagers of foreign origin were accidentally killed following a police chase. By 8 November, and after twelve days of street **violence**, a state of emergency was declared by the government. In political terms, the events were a god-send to the **French** Far Right. They could forward their own agenda by playing on the non-French background of the two teenagers, alongside the breakdown of **law and order**, and the enveloping climate of *insécurité*.

At the time, Jean-Marie **Le Pen** claimed that: 'We are receiving thousands of new members, tens of thousands of e-mails. All of our offices are submerged, we don't know how to respond because we don't have the staff to reply to the wave of people who, 95 percent of them, salute and approve our positions.' In the aftermath of the riots, the **National Front** (*Front National*, FN) leader also argued that civil war was looming and that, if there had been a presidential election soon after the disturbances, his chances of being elected president would have increased tenfold. Less extreme right-wing politicians, especially the Union for a Popular Movement (*Union pour un Mouvement Populaire*, UMP) leader Nicolas Sarkozy, also capitalised on the riots by taking a hard-line position. Indeed, in what was seen as a direct appeal to the far-right electorate, Sarkozy argued for the expulsion of all non-French nationals involved in the disturbances. Rioters were for the most part Arab and Black youths, who were responding to a widespread sense of frustration with mainstream French society. From a position of seemingly total alienation, the rioters felt they had nothing to lose from rioting.

Across **Europe**, the Far Right was quick to capitalise on the rioting. This included raising fears that the disturbances could spread to other countries. Though there were isolated incidents in Belgium and Germany, the riots remained contained within French borders. In Italy, echoing the opinions of Le Pen, the **Northern League** (*Lega Nord*, LN) claimed the events were the result of years of socialist-style misrule of the country. Meanwhile, the National Democratic Party of Germany (*Nationaldemokratische Partei Deutschlands*, NPD) claimed that the riots represented an end to the argument for a multicultural European society, and reiterated its stance for the repatriation of migrants. Some commentators in the Netherlands, such as Geert Wilders, also called for tighter controls of the nation's borders in light of the rioting. Meanwhile, Pia **Kjaersgaard** claimed that the rioters were almost terrorists, again playing with the alarm generated by the spectre of Islamist terrorism. Even Russian far-right supporters used the events to promote their own nationalist ideals. The Paris

Riots, then, revealed the Far Right's underlying political message: **immigration** ultimately leads to social meltdown, so Europe needs to introduce more hard-line measures to curb the problem.

Reflecting this development, Thierry Balzacq of the think-tank Centre for European Policy Studies has argued that the post-9/11 political **environment** had made race relations politics more confrontational, especially as a result of new security concerns and legislation. He also claimed that the riots were helpful in polarising opinion; therefore, voters on the verge of aligning themselves with the Far Right may well do so following the riots. The Far Right, then, could easily suggest that today's rioters could become tomorrow's Islamist terrorists.

See also Le Pen, Jean-Marie (France); National Front (France) *and* Western Europe and the Far Right.

Further Reading

Murray, Graham. 2006. 'France: the riots and the Republic'. *Race and Class* 47.4.
New Zealand Herald, 'European far right seizes on French riots', http://www.nzherald.co.nz/section/2/story.cfm?c_id=2&ObjectID=10354708 (cited 31 December 2007).

Patriotism

Nationalism often connotes a coordinated political agenda and, more often than not, unscrupulous political means and ends. Patriotism, on the other hand, is often simply defined as a love for one's own country. Nevertheless, many parties of the Far Right thrive on this softer, patriotic sentiment as a way to garner wider support. However, this should not be seen as contradicting their more hard-line nationalist or even ultra-nationalist political ideologies.

The Far Right can also displease movements of the left by claiming that the right holds a monopoly on patriotic sentiment. Invariably, this is done by trying to exclusively link their movement to the national flag. For example, in France the **National Front** (*Front National*, FN) emblazons the tricolour over almost all of their publicity material, from leaflets and posters down to key rings and note paper. Further, the FN actually organises an annual festival called the Fête Bleu-Blanc-Rouge. Likewise, in Britain there was a time – especially in the 1970s and 1980s – when the Union Jack was more or less hijacked by the National Front (NF) and **British National Party** (BNP). Highlighting this problem, in the mid-1990s there was a minor controversy when Geri Halliwell, a member of the Spice Girls, decided to wear a Union Jack-themed dress at an awards ceremony – and was later forced to defend her choice of outfit. Many interpreted this as part of a wider cultural shift attempting to reclaim the British and English flags from their association with the British Far Right. *Guardian* columnist Gary Younge argued that this was an important debate to have. He summarised that the exploitation of the flag by far-right nationalists and their associated thugs was a means to invoke a particular style of national identity – one which was dominated by themes of pride in the empire, a colonial mentality to foreigners, and simplistic pride in King and country. The flag, then, became symbolic of this ideology, and became a useful tool to symbolically oppress immigrants, pacifists and internationalists. Countering these more belligerent associations, the newer patriotism that developed in Britain during the 1990s disassociated itself from the

Far Right. Indeed, its more refined exponents claimed that it was irresponsible to let the Far Right claim ownership of powerful cultural capital such as the British flag. A responsible patriotism then could reclaim this symbol from the extremists and in so doing relocate such emotive symbolism within a progressive sense of patriotic identity.

Across **Europe**, some parties that have been labelled far-right and ultra-nationalist have tried to articulate their political message in a soft, patriotic tone rather than in hard, nationalist terms. Typical of this line is Pia Kjærsgaard. The core of her party's politics has been a powerful sense of love for Denmark. She argues that the **Danish People's Party** (*Dansk Folkeparti*, DPP) is proud of Denmark, a feeling evoked though an appreciation of its history, its cultural heritage and its people. Such a strong love leads her to see the necessity of 'strong national defence' alongside 'secure and safe national borders'. Further, 'Only in a free Denmark can the country develop according to the will of the people'. Meanwhile, one policy statement from the Sweden Democrats (*Sverigedemokraterna*, SD) ends with the rallying cry, 'Patriots of the world, unite!' – an ironic and paradoxical form of words perhaps? The NF in Britain argues strongly that multi-racialism and large-scale **immigration** into Britain were errors, and that the British people had the right to be masters over their own future. It has also expressed its disappointment at seeing disunity among British 'white patriots'.

Patriotism tends to be a quality evoked through cultural production as much as through political tracts. Across Europe songs and stories are used by the Far Right to generate a wider sense of patriotic culture around the ideology. The Liberal Democratic Party (*Liberal'no-Demokraticheskaya Partiya Rossii*, LDPR) in **Russia** has used this tactic, but, purposefully perhaps, they do not mention **anti-Semitism** or Russia expanding westwards to re-take most of Eastern Europe (two key policy aims of the party), just some seemingly innocent patriotic sentiments. Further, the lyrics reveal key tropes of far-right cultural production. Not only do they imply a sense of national decline, but they present the far-right party, LDPR, as holding the only solution to this problem, all of which is couched in the tenor of a patriotic love of one's country. Patriotism, then, is a more complex quality within a far-right context. Many aspects of far-right patriotism can also be found in other forms of patriotism. Cultural products that appeal to the nation at large may also have a particular relevance to far-right ideologues. Further, teasing out the significance of a simplified, far-right notion of patriotism from more general patriotic sentiment raises complex research questions concerning the diverse range of patriotic cultures generated by the Far Right.

See also The Ideology of the Far Right *and* Nation and Nationalism.

Further Reading

Ignazi, Piero. 2003. *Extreme Right Parties in Western Europe*. New York: Oxford University Press. Kitschelt, Herbert. 1997. *The Radical Right in Western Europe: A Comparative Analysis*. Michigan: University of Michigan Press.

Pim Fortuyn, Assassination of (2002)

The assassination of maverick Dutch politician Pim Fortuyn in May 2002 made headlines throughout **Europe** and beyond. The murder was a genuine shock to the Dutch, astonishing politicians and the public in equal measure – indeed, many news reporters noted that the killing left the Netherlands confused, perplexed and mystified. In a normally peaceful political culture, this was the country's first political assassination in nearly 400 years. Fortuyn was shot by a lone gunman in the Dutch town of Hilversum, only minutes after taking part in a radio broadcast. Eleven months later, an animal rights activist, Volkert van der Graaf, was given an eighteen-year jail sentence for killing Fortuyn. Van der Graaf stated: 'I confess to the shooting. He was an ever growing danger who would affect many people in society. I saw it as a danger. I hoped that I could solve it myself.' Subsequently, van der Graaf's appeal against the sentence was rejected.

Fortuyn's politics combined a hard-line stance on **immigration** with a liberal perspective on social issues. Typical of the former was his notorious declaration that the Netherlands was 'full'. He was also an openly gay politician, and rejected the characterisation of his politics as extreme-right. Only three months prior to his death, Fortuyn had formed his own political party – Pim Fortuyn List (*Lijst Pim Fortuyn*, LPF) – which had emerged from the political wilderness and had begun to make significant waves in Dutch politics ahead of national elections. Even without Fortuyn's charismatic, maverick presence in the national elections that were held only a week following his murder, LPF took second place. This was undoubtedly a highly impressive performance given the circumstances surrounding the poll.

In the wake of this startling set of circumstance, many commentators argued that the party benefited from a widespread and entirely understandable sympathy vote. However, this level of support for LPF must also have signified that Fortuyn had been able to tap into deeper sympathies for a populist, anti-immigration style of politics among the Dutch population. By July 2002, the LPF had been invited to join the right-wing government led by Prime Minister Jan Peter Balkenende, a grouping that also included representatives of the liberal People's Party for **Freedom** and **Democracy** (*Volkspartij voor Vrijheid en Democratie*, VVD). However, in subsequent elections the party has diminished in significance. The death of Fortuyn, then, was ultimately also the death of LPF.

See also Against the Islamisation of our Culture - Dutch Identity as Fundamental Value by Pim Fortuyn (The Netherlands); Fortuyn, Pim (The Netherlands), *and* List Pim Fortuyn (The Netherlands).

Further Reading
Ignazi, Piero. 2003. *Extreme Right Parties in Western Europe*. New York: Oxford University Press.
Van Holsteyn, Joop and Irwin, Galen. 2003. 'Never a Dull Moment: Pim Fortuyn and the Dutch Parliamentary Election of 2002'. *West European Politics* 26.2.

Portuguese Popular Party

The Popular Party, led by ex-journalist Paulo Portas, claimed fourteen seats on 9 percent of the vote in the parliamentary elections of March 2002. As a result, it joined the centre-right Portuguese government and became the third most popular party in the country. Portas also became defence minister.

The party is noted for its anti-immigrant discourse and a range of practical policies it would like to introduce dealing with (what it sees as the problem of) **immigration** into Portugal; for example, setting up 'special integration programmes' for second-generation immigrants, making it compulsory for schoolchildren to sing the national anthem each day, strengthening the police presence in major towns and cities, and reducing the minimum age for prison sentencing.

It is anti-EU and anti-Spanish in its rhetoric, and socially conservative on issues such as abortion and same-sex partnership rights. It would like to raise the level of pensions, but reduce taxes. The party is linked to the newspaper *O Independente*, which has made a name for itself by publicising a number of corruption scandals, thus making Portas and his colleagues unpopular in the corridors of power.

See also Salazar, Dr António de Oliveira (Portugal) *and* Southern Europe and the Far Right.

Further Reading

Raby, D.L. 1991. *Fascism and Resistance in Portugal: Communists, Liberals and Military Dissidents in the Opposition to Salazar, 1941–74.* Manchester: Manchester University Press.

Derrick, M. 1972. *The Portugal of Salazar.* London: Campion.

Gallagher, Tom. 1994. 'Portugal: the marginalisation of the extreme right'. In *The Extreme Right in Europe and the USA.* Edited by Paul Hainsworth. London: Pinter.

Pinto, A.C. 1991. 'The radical right in contemporary Portugal'. In *Neo-Fascism in Europe.* Edited by Luciano Cheles, Ronnie Ferguson and Michalina Vaughan. London: Longman.

Protest and the Protest Vote

Challenged to explain the emergence and growing popularity of far-right parties around **Europe**, political scientists and media commentators habitually refer to the idea of protest. There are many examples of this choice of wording. In 2001, the BBC reported on the forthcoming elections in Italy: 'Aside from its core supporters, the Northern League is also expected to scoop up a significant protest vote'. The report stressed that the **Northern League** (*Lega Nord*, LN) was responding to a sense that the centre-left administration was not strong enough on issues such as prostitution, crime and illegal **immigration**. Similarly, in 2006, the BBC reported on the electoral successes of **Flemish Interest** (*Vlaams Belang*, VB) in Flanders. Highlighting its policy agenda, which included independence for Flanders and an anti-immigration stance, the BBC claimed that the VB was 'perhaps primarily a place for the protest vote, for people to register their dissatisfaction with the long-standing political status quo'. In a similar vein, political commentator Dominique Reynié has talked about the appeal of the **National Front** (*Front National*, FN): '**Le Pen**'s voters allure remains greater as a symbol of protest than as a proponent of sound policy'.

The way that the Far Right functions as a protest takes on a different form in different countries. In the Netherlands, it was often argued that Pim **Fortuyn**'s party **List Pim Fortuyn** (*Lijst Pim Fortuyn*, LPF) thrived on the widespread sense of disgruntlement with the centre-left government; in Britain, the **British National Party** (BNP) has been regarded in recent years as a protest vote against New Labour policies; in Romania, the **Greater Romania Party** (*Partidul România Mare*, PRM) has thrived on frustration with the Romanian Democratic Convention government that held power between 1996 and 2000; and in Finland, the True Finns (*Perussuomalaiset*) have made clear their opposition to the **European Union**, rising levels of immigration, the decline of public services, the status of the Swedish language in Finland, and even the phenomenon of golden handshakes. The protest vote, then, is a key aspect of the Far Right's popularity at the ballot box.

Why is the Far Right seen in such a light? First, it should be said that in European societies which are increasingly depoliticised and unpoliticised, a significant proportion of voters in most countries are attracted to the idea of using their vote in a negative way – that is, if they use their vote at all. Many voters want to make a statement, and can often feel that a negative one is an appropriate response. In some countries, the natural tendency was to vote for the Far Left in such instances. Particularly in the 1970s and 1980s, then, communist parties across Europe became the repository of the protest vote. France was a good example of this, and sweeping up the protest vote actually helped the French Communist Party (*Parti Communiste Français*, PCF) into government between 1981 and 1984. However, as the PCF became increasingly reformist rather than radical in the 1980s, it gradually lost it status as the protest vote *par excellence*. From this confusion, the FN was able to reap the benefit. It is also possible that negative stances attract voters. A disillusioned electorate could find it easier to put their faith in a party that was also disillusioned with the status quo. Such a statement holds true for far-right movements across Europe, and in France in particular. In its heyday in the late 1980s and 1990s, the FN railed against government corruption, a lax and decadent establishment, and the closed-shop nature of party politics, so much so that they christened the Socialist Party (*Parti Socialiste*, PS), French Communist Party (*Parti Communiste Français*, PCF), Union for French Democracy (*Union pour la Démocratie Française*, UDF) and Rally for the Republic, (*Rassemblement pour la République*, RPR) the 'Gang of Four'. The FN solution was a new 'Sixth Republic' to replace an allegedly unsalvageable Fifth Republic.

However, it would be dangerous to dismiss the Far Right only as a protest vote. To do so is to minimise its potential power when it gains office. Although it is important to recognise that the electoral success of the Far Right is often predicated on a protest vote, this analysis should not be used to conclude in a dismissive way that the Far Right is ultimately an insignificant political force.

See also The Ideology of the Far Right.

Further Reading

Givens, Terri E. 2005. *Voting Radical Right in Western Europe*. Cambridge: Cambridge University Press.

Norris, Pippa. 2005. *Radical Right: Voters and Parties in the Electoral Market*. Cambridge: Cambridge University Press.

Protocols of the Elders of Zion Document (Russia)

The Protocols of the Elders of Zion is a forged document, published in 1903, which far-right (and other) movements across **Europe** have used, bizarrely, as evidence of a Jewish and Masonic plot to take over the world. As such, it is seen as the starting-point for conspiracy theory literature on the Far Right.

The text was published originally in the Russian newspaper *Znamya*. Thereafter, the hoax was reprinted in a variety of forms in the early twentieth century, but, in essence, it takes the form of a speech which articulates the means of world domination – for example, taking over the control of the **economy** and the media. One theory is that it emanates from the minutes of the first meeting of the Zionist Congress in Switzerland in 1897.

Those opposed to the Russian Revolution referred to the Protocols, as did the Nazi Party and many groups of anti-Semites thereafter. Not unnaturally, it is far-right parties in Eastern Europe who have placed the greatest store on the forgery. These include *Pamyat* in Russia and the **Latvian National Front**.

See also Anti-Semitism *and* Memory (Russia).

Further Reading
Levy, R.S. 2005. *Antisemitism: A Historical Encyclopedia of Prejudice and Persecution*. Santa Barbara, CA: ABC-Clio (2 vols.).
Lacquer, Walter. 1996. *Fascism: Past, Present and Future*. New York: Oxford University Press.
Lee, Martin A. 1998. *The Beast Reawakens*. London: Warner Books.
Wistrich, Robert Solomon. 1991. *Anti-Semitism: The Longest Hatred*. London: Thames Methuen.

R

Redwatch Magazine (Great Britain)

Redwatch was a British far-right magazine which controversially tried to 'out' political opponents, and it has now evolved into a website with the same objective. While the magazine was first published in 1992, the website was launched in 2001. It takes its name from a Combat 18 newsletter of the 1990s. The first piece of text that surfers read when they log onto *Redwatch* is: 'This is a site designed and intended for people who are involved in the struggle against the spread of Marxist lies in the UK. This site should NOT be accessed by anyone who does not wish to be exposed to material that discusses the problems of sovietisation in the United Kingdom'. From this opening, it is a short step to disseminating anti-leftist propaganda and 'outing' anti-fascist campaigners by broadcasting personal information. There have been calls for the website to be taken down and claims that *Redwatch* has links to other far-right movements.

See also Communism.

Further Reading
Eatwell, Roger. 2000. 'The extreme right and British exceptionalism: the primacy of politics'. In *The Politics of the Extreme Right: From the Margins to the Mainstream*. Edited by Paul Hainsworth. London: Pinter.
Eatwell, Roger. 1994. 'Why has the extreme right failed in Britain?' In *The Extreme Right in Europe and the USA*. Edited by Paul Hainsworth. London: Pinter.
Cable, Gerry. 1991. 'The far right in contemporary Britain'. In *Neo-Fascism in Europe*. Edited by Luciano Cheles, Ronnie Ferguson and Michalina Vaughan. London: Longman.
Eatwell, Roger. 1996. *Fascism: A History*. London: Vintage.

Regionalism

Given the emphasis on the **nation and nationalism** in far-right discourse, it is perhaps surprising to discover that regionalism too is a key policy strand of the Far Right in some countries. Generalisations across the far-right spectrum are difficult on this issue because national circumstances are central to each party's own conception of regionalism and the role of regions in the nation's history. On the one hand, a powerful regionalism could be destructive of an overarching national identity, yet on the other, senses of local culture and tradition are key qualities in the cultures of the Far Right.

In France, Jean-Marie **Le Pen** says he is in favour of a healthy regionalism, one that does not disturb or threaten the nation and nationalism. Therefore, he is proud of being a Breton but would never countenance any step in the direction of Breton independence – hence his hostilities towards moves to autonomy for Corsica and New Caledonia. The context is very different in Belgium. Here, **Flemish Interest** (*Vlaams Belang*, VB) argues that it works tirelessly for the formation of Flanders as a separate state, which would take Brussels as its capital and would hold sovereignty over the Dutch-speaking areas of Belgium. Frank Vanhecke, President of the VB, has recently made the case for this separation, and it is worth looking at this argument in some detail. He has written that the response to a recent spoof television news report, claiming that Flanders had formally separated from Belgium, demonstrates that the goal of independence is a realistic one. He stressed that many within French-speaking Wallonia believed the report, backing the practicality of his cause. Vanhecke continued by asserting that Flemings no longer wanted to subsidise Wallonia, which he alleged had been the case for the 176 years of Belgium's history. Offering some statistics to back up such claims, he asserted that 20 percent of Flemings worked as civil servants compared to 40 percent of Walloons, and 8 percent of Flemings were unemployed as opposed to 20 percent of Walloons. Further, according to Vanhecke's figures 6.6 percent of the Gross Domestic Product of Flanders was transferred to Wallonia, where a culture of welfare state dependence was steadily developing. Socialist politicians and those who voted for them were ultimately to blame for all of this, and Vanhecke warned that the Walloons would lose their connection to Flanders if they continued to vote for left-wing governments. Further, this was the general view of Flanders, not just a position held by extreme nationalists. This point was backed up by a recent poll, which had shown that over 50 percent of the Flemish population favoured a split, and those who did not want a split tended to favour the idea of a confederation.

In Italy too, we can see a far-right grouping posing as the guarantor of a regional identity, the **Northern League** (*Lega Nord*, LN). It is also worth discussing the relationship between the LN and regionalism at some length. Perhaps the most extreme step here was the declaration of an independent state of **Padania** by the LN in the late 1990s. Indeed, the LN does not campaign for *one* regionalism, but rather *several*: the culture of Veneto, Lombardy and Piedmont. It even had contact with autonomist movements in the south. Its position, which oscillates between creating a separate federal region of Padania within the Italian nation-state and the formation of an independent nation-state of Padania, is difficult to pin down. All factors considered, the party can currently be classified as federalist in ideological terms, rather than simply regionalist, and it has actually stated that it would cease political activity if a truly federal state was ever realised. Of course, this political stance plays to the renowned issue of regionalism within Italian politics – in particular, the ever-present economic tensions between the urban north and the rural south. In 1997, Paolo Tripodi in the *Contemporary Review* commented on the declaration of independence for Padania made by the LN leader Umberto Bossi thus: 'The 15th of September 1996, marked one of the strangest days of Italy's recent history'. He also noted that Padania was given a new national flag and a new national assembly that would supposedly run in parallel with the Italian government. Tripodi also commented on the turnout for the event, which was less than Bossi's expectations, but nevertheless was sizable in number. At the time, many of the newspaper opinion leaders also saw the LN's initiative as a failure. In the *Corriere della Sera* Italian journalist Giulio Anselmi spoke of a 'Virtual Padania' as an 'illusory project'.

The regionalist position taken by the LN is unique in Italian politics. Over time too, the LN has tried to broaden out its political platform, building on the notion of regional separatism to advance a position of national populism in order to rid itself of the single-issue tag. This it has done successfully by putting forward traditional conservative positions on many issues. Regarding **immigration**, for example, it has not only talked tough but has also attracted much vitriol on account of its policy ideas, such as strict immigration quotas for each of Italy's twenty regions. This criticism is seen as good publicity for the LN. Paradoxically, though, the party's efforts to broaden its manifesto and become a serious player in Italian politics has backfired somewhat. In so doing, the regionalist dimension to its discourse has become drowned out. Further, LN regionalism has not been helped by the drift towards European integration, which has made the Padanian cause appear somewhat parochial as an ideology.

The Italian case demonstrates how difficult it is to discuss this issue through generalities – the political culture and history of each nation in question must be factored into any discussion of regionalism and the Far Right. In Romania and Hungary, the issue of Transylvania is crucial, while in Britain the **British National Party** (BNP) argues that it promotes the national identities and cultures not only of the English but also the Welsh, Scots and Irish. Regions and nations are highly complex issues that are taken very seriously by the Far Right. Serious study of the ideology, then, must also understand the ramifications of these emotive issues.

See also The Ideology of the Far Right; Nation and Nationalism *and* Northern League.

Further Reading

Hainsworth, Paul, ed. 2000. *The Politics of the Extreme Right: From the Margins to the Mainstream.* London: Pinter.

Ignazi, Piero. 2003. *Extreme Right Parties in Western Europe.* New York: Oxford University Press.

Kitschelt, Herbert. 1997. *The Radical Right in Western Europe: A Comparative Analysis.* Michigan: University of Michigan Press.

Religion

The relationship between religion and the Far Right has always been complex. In the interwar period, many fascist regimes benefited from the acquiescence of the Catholic Church. There was also a sense in which Catholic social teaching and the Church's strong dislike of **Communism** were actually compatible with the main thrust of fascist theory. In some cases, though, the Church made a point of distancing itself from fascist governments, or at least using its power and influence to draw out compromises from them. This trend was not limited to the Catholic Church. For example, the close links between Orthodox theology and the ideology of the Legion of the Archangel Michael in Romania reveals the way that far-right politics could be synthesised with the Christian faith; while the presence of Anglican clergy in Mosley's British Union of Fascists demonstrates the variegated appeal of Fascism to the actively religious in the interwar years. The relationship between ideology and religion was also complicated by the fact that members within the Nazi and Fascist regimes had grandiose dreams of creating some kind of new religion to replace traditional, established faiths. Typical here was Erich Ludendorff, who envisaged a new form of Germanic religion for the future salvation of the nation.

It is against this complex background intertwining faith and politics that far-right ideologues of the post-war years have had to negotiate the complex issue of their ideological heritage in the Christian faith. One of the key changes between the interwar years and post-war European society is that the influence of both the far-right and of religious leaders has waned. Hitler and Mussolini were actually in power during the interwar period, whereas today, for the most part, movements of the Far Right are in opposition. Therefore, their pronouncements on religion do not have the same impact. Nevertheless, within the thinking of the Far Right, religion is still a crucial factor, and it is often used as a marker of identity. Consequently, the simplification of world affairs into a Manichean battle between the Christian West and the Islamic East in recent years has been a vital fillip for far-right politicians, who have repeatedly drawn on this issue to inform and develop their political stances. The Far Right has also been able to exploit issues such as **immigration**, stressing the significant religious and cultural differences that exist between immigrant communities from North Africa and elsewhere and the native populations.

One example of religion being used as a marker of national identity comes from Jean-Marie **Le Pen**. His speeches on the changing architectural landscape of France articulate the theme of national decline epitomised through the trend of mosques and minarets replacing church towers on the skyline. He also uses such emotive images to paint an apocalyptical picture of an 'Islamic France' decades from now. This trend of using religion as a political tool can also be seen in Le Pen's Catholicism. Thus, Le Pen will talk about his Catholic beliefs as part of his personal value system. Indeed, Le Pen claims that he is Breton, French, European and Catholic. Christianity also informs his doctrine and ideology. For example, his opposition to abortion overlaps with the Church's position on this issue. Le Pen would say that his position is based on religious teachings; onlookers would argue that there are other factors at play, such as his fears of French population decline. Le Pen is also a traditionalist, and so he has always demonstrated his loyalty to the Latin Mass. This has always been celebrated very publicly at special FN events and festivals. Le Pen's use of the Latin Mass goes against the grain for many modern Catholics, but Le Pen and the FN in general remain unbowed to criticism from Catholic modernisers. Le Pen has even forged a controversial alliance with the maverick priest Mgr Marcel **Lefebvre**, who had also gone out on a limb to defend the FN's use of the Latin Mass.

Elsewhere in **Europe**, far-right leaders make political play over religious and national identities. Aside from the French case, it is not difficult to find examples of far-right politicians using religion as a marker of national identity. The **Danish People's Party** (*Dansk Folkeparti*, DPP) has used the controversial cartoons of Mohamed in election campaigns, sending out the message that Muslims are not a part of the DPP's vision for the country. Meanwhile, Fillip Dewinter actively tries to appeal to **Antwerp**'s Jewish community, an unusual electorate for the Far Right, in order to garner support for his opposition to Muslim immigration. Also, the **British National Party** (BNP) use the term 'Christian' almost as a synonym for 'white' and stress their deep concerns over the 'Islamification of Britain'. Meanwhile, **Christoph Blocher**'s **Swiss People's Party** (*Schweizerische Volkspartei*, SVP) has proposed that the building of minarets be banned in the country – a suggestion that has echoes across the continent.

The complexity of the relationship between the Far Right and religion is also demonstrated by Vladimir **Zhirinovsky** in **Russia**. His views are unique. In 1993, he claimed that he was closest to the Russian Orthodox Church and this theology informed his political views. Therefore, he promoted Russian nationalism by arguing for an end to religious **cosmopolitanism**, targeting oriental faiths, in particular Islam. Although critical of other Christian denominations, Zhirinovsky would not impose a ban on Catholics, Baptists, Lutherans, Pentecostals and so forth. Nevertheless, he was staunchly against these denominations taking over Eastern Orthodox Churches: 'Let Catholics build their own churches and works. I believe in full **freedom** for Christians of all denominations. The only thing I oppose is persecuting of Eastern Orthodox priests and temples'.

Religion, then, is a central issue for the Far Right. It is simplistic to assert that all far-right discussions on religion hold the subtext of national identity. Figures such as Le Pen and Zhirinovsky are undoubtedly genuine in their religious convictions – though whether this makes them good Christians is a matter for theologians to decide upon, not political scientists. This said, the heritage of Christianity as a part of national and European history is often an important factor for far-right politicians. Further, many of the moral principles articulated by the conservative Far Right are drawn from Christian teachings, though subsequently refracted through an ultra-nationalist lens. Finally, the use of Islam to denote an alien identity, thereby helping to define the national identity, has become a central issue when discussing the relationship between religion and the Far Right.

See also The Ideology of the Far Right *and* Islam and the Far Right.

Further Reading

Davies, Peter. 1999. *The National Front in France: Ideology, Discourse and Power*. New York: Routledge.
Feldman, Matthew and Turda, Marius, eds. 2007. '"Clerical Fascism" in Interwar Europe'. Special Issue of *Totalitarian Movements and Political Religions* 8.2.
Laqueur, Walter. 2003. *No End to War: Terrorism in the Twenty-First Century*. New York: Continuum.

Republican Party (Czech Republic)

For most of the 1990s, the nationalist Republican Party in the Czech Republic boasted representation in parliament, but in 1998 support for the movement nosedived and it wasn't able to scrape even a single deputy.

The party was founded by Miroslav **Sládek** in 1990 when Czechoslovakia still existed as a state. By 1992, it had secured a handful of representatives in the legislature, and in 1996 it claimed 18 seats. The movement came to be noted for its tough internal discipline and the omnipresence of Sládek – the personality who dominated the organisation from top to bottom in dictatorial fashion. It also produced a campaigning newspaper, *Politické Noviny Republika*.

The party believed in 'iron fist'-style **law and order** and was highly critical of the EU. But its doctrine centred around a powerful nationalism. It was hostile to **immigration** and all minority groupings. As party spokesman Jan Vik stated: 'We don't like seeing the so-called waves of migration from various East European countries, Asia, Africa and so on – because even with the best will [in the world] we've got enough problems of our own, for example with our gypsies. And we don't see why they should be reinforced from Romania, Ukraine and I don't know where else'.

The party has targeted Jews and gypsies, scapegoating these communities for perceived national decline. In 1995, Sládek was quoted as saying: 'The gypsies have a choice. Either they can live like us or they can leave, and it won't be our concern how, where, or for how much'. And elsewhere: 'It is not necessary … to pass special laws for them … Most gypsies are on disability insurance by the time they reach the age of 18 … We'll have a look at disability insurance. As soon as they don't have a source of money, they'll stop liking it here and they'll leave on their own'. In 1998, a gypsy organisation in the Czech Republic argued that the Republican Party was responsible for 'fuelling racism and xenophobia'. President Havel has consistently refused to meet with its representatives for this very reason.

The Republican Party was accused of having links with skinhead groups, and its rhetoric evolved in such a hard-line and anti-democratic direction that there were calls for it be prohibited. Party MP Josef Krejsa did not help matters when he declared: 'Our first task after winning [the election] will be to introduce a new constitution, a new legal order, and exemplary punishments … I have a machine gun at home. You'll see how people will be queuing up to join the party. Just wait until we win those elections! They'll come from all sides, mainly the political sides! At the firing range in Kobylisy I believe that [Prime Minister Václav] Klaus, [President Václav] Havel, and [Chamber of Deputies Chairman Milan] Uhde will be first in line. So that there's no chance that I would overlook them. Then we will separate the wheat from the chaff and after that it will be a piece of cake'.

After the 1998 election, the party almost disappeared from the political scene. It had little money and was also being chased by the police. The Patriotic Republican Party, or VRS, took its place on the Far Right of Czech politics. In 2000, Czech Radio reported that far-right groups were now converging around the VRS. Sládek tried to make a political comeback but was eventually banned from Czech politics due to the financial debts that the Republican Party had accrued.

See also Sládek, Miroslav (Czech Republic).

Further Reading

http://www.republikani.com (Republican Party website).
Mudde, C., ed. 2005. *Racist Extremism in Central and Eastern Europe*. London: Routledge.
Shepherd, R.H.E. 2000. *Czechoslovakia: The Velvet Revolution and Beyond*. Houndsmills: Macmillan.
Stein, E. 1997. *Czecho / Slovakia: Ethnic Conflict, Constitutional Fissure, Negotiated Breakup*. Michigan: University of Michigan Press.

Republican Party (Germany)

The Republican Party (*Die Republikaner*, REP) was founded in West Germany in 1983 by discontented ex-CSU members Franz **Schönhuber**, Franz Handlos and Ekkehard Voigt, with Schönhuber eventually emerging as the leader and embodiment of the movement.

Republican Party (Germany)

In many ways, the REP was styled from birth as a traditional conservative and nationalist party and – unlike other parties which came to be categorised as extreme right – it wished to be seen as being loyal to the constitution and the system of democratic politics that reigned in the old West Germany.

In the early years, the party's concerns were quite middle-of-the-road. It wanted to ensure that the process of reunification was completed successfully; it didn't want too much money spent on behalf of the soon-to-be former East Germany; and it was concerned that the CSU was monopolising political life in Bavaria.

However, in the second half of the 1980s, its vociferous nationalism and hostility to **immigration** led many to overlook its good intentions and place it firmly on the Far Right. It blamed immigrants for housing problems, crime and even pollution, and two of its most controversial policy ideas were a) placing German and non-German schoolchildren in separate classes, and b) wanting to ban all Islamic centres from engaging in political or cultural activities. The REP also suggested putting asylum-seekers in collection camps, 'to minimise the native population's existing and growing antipathy toward foreign residents'.

In the media, the REP is portrayed as anti-democratic, anti-European, anti-American, anti-Christian and anti-Semitic – the ultimate 'catch-all' protest party. In addition, it would be fair to say that in its public pronouncements it has tried to downplay the impact of the Nazi era on Germany. At other times, Schönhuber has tried to reassure German voters on a personal level: 'I have no Nazi past. Racism and Fascism led us into the most horrible catastrophe in our national history'.

The heyday of the REP was the late 1980s when Schönhuber came close to making it the German equivalent of the French FN. It boasted seats in the European Parliament and at regional level, but it failed to capitalise on its growing popularity and slid into obscurity during the 1990s.

The highpoint of this period was probably June 1989 when Schönhuber and five of his colleagues were elected to the European Parliament. In the same period, the party scored well in elections in Bavaria and Berlin. In retrospect, it is possible to argue that the late-1980s were particularly conducive to the growth of a nationalist party in West Germany. Issues surrounding reunification, relations with what was East Germany, and the growth of Turkish immigration all seemed to play into the hands of the REP.

Things, however, moved on, and with the collapse of the USSR and the completion of reunification, Schönhuber and his party had less favourable terrain on which to campaign. The party scored 2.1 percent in the all-Germany election of December 1990, and then only 1.9 percent in the elections of October 1994. A decade on, in the 2005 federal elections, the party took only 0.6 percent of the national vote.

Schönhuber was sacked as party chairman in 1994 for instigating talks with the DVU and he left the party in 1995. At this point in time, the REP claimed to have 23,000 members. Today, the German authorities continue to monitor the activities of the REP, a party they deem to be both 'right-wing extremist' and 'constitutionally hostile'.

It is clear that the REP has a claim to being one of the most significant expressions of far-right politics in post-war **Europe**. For in the late-1980s there was a feeling that Schönhuber's party in West Germany and **Le Pen**'s in France were at the vanguard of a new awakening on the nationalist right.

Academics became fascinated by the movement. **Griffin** saw it as crypto-fascist in political orientation e.g. it feigned loyalty to the democratic process while at the same time plotting against it. For his part, Eatwell noted the way in which the party evolved:

in terms of doctrine, from conservative nationalist to radical nationalist; and in terms of electorate, from a movement that mainly attracted older people to one that had a genuine appeal to younger voters. And of course, it would seem that these two changes are connected.

Backer and Childs have turned their attention to membership of the REP. Backer suggests that two groups were crucial. There were, first, the traditional right-wing extremists – those who had a history of political activism on the Far Right. And second, there were newer members, with less experience and more moderate views. The challenge for Schönhuber and the party leadership was to minimise the tension that existed between the two groups. Childs, meanwhile, records the fact that REP members were predominantly male, and also that many police officers joined the party. Here the authoritarian tone to party policy would seem to be the attraction.

Meanwhile, Kolinsky argues that Schönhuber's 'flair for the media' and 'ease of communication' were key factors in the REP's ascendancy. This is interesting because exactly the same has been said about Le Pen and the FN in France, and this would seem to strengthen the view which says that, as political movements, the REP and the FN were 'peas from the same pod'.

See also I Was There by Franz Schönhuber (Germany); Central Europe and the Far Right *and* Schönhuber, Franz (Germany).

Further Reading

http://www.rep.de (Republikaner Party website).
Kolinsky, E. 1994. 'A future for right extremism in Germany?' In *The Extreme Right in Europe and the USA*. Edited by Paul Hainsworth. London: Pinter.
Backer, Susann. 2000. 'Right-wing extremism in unified Germany'. In *The Politics of the Extreme Right: From the Margins to the Mainstream*. Edited by Paul Hainsworth. London: Pinter.
Eatwell, Roger. 1996. *Fascism: A History*. London: Vintage.
Childs, David. 1991. 'The Far Right in Germany since 1945'. In *Neo-Fascism in Europe*. Edited by Luciano Cheles, Ronnie Ferguson and Michalina Vaughan. London: Longman.
Husbands, Christopher T. 1991. 'Militant neo-Nazism in the Federal Republic of Germany in the 1980s'. In *Neo-Fascism in Europe*. Edited by Luciano Cheles, Ronnie Ferguson and Michalina Vaughan. London: Longman.
Stöss, R. 1991. *Politics Against Democracy: Extreme Right in West Germany*. New York and Oxford: Berg.

Romania, Far Right Enters Coalition Government (1994)

Following the end of Ceausescu's communist regime, Romania saw the growing influence of far-right politics. One of the most high-profile of these interventions by the Far Right came in 1994. Following the elections of 1992, the largest party in government – the Party of Social **Democracy** in Romania (*Partidul Democraţiei Sociale din România*, PDSR) – was forced into a coalition with, among others, Gheorghe Funar's Romanian National Unity Party (*Partidul Unităţii Naţionale a Românilor*, PUNR) and Corneliu Vadim **Tudor**'s **Greater Romania Party** (*Partidul România Mare*, PRM). PUNR has been characterised as a largely single-issue party concerned with promoting anti-Hungarian politics. Similarly, Tudor's PRM is also vociferously anti-Hungarian, as well as anti-Semitic, anti-Roma and homophobic. In 1994, PUNR caused the coalition problems when it demanded cabinet portfolios, and so, by the end of the year, Adrian Turicu became minister for communications, while Valeriu Tabara took the agriculture post.

18. Romanian President Traian Basescu, top, adjusts his microphone as ultra-nationalist leader Corneliu Vadim Tudor, right, shouts, attempting to interrupt the President's speech during a Parliament session, Bucharest, Romania, 18 December 2006.

At the time, it was feared that the Romanian government was becoming too dependent on the Far Right. For example, Human Rights Watch (HRW) lamented the fact that, following the failure of the PDSR to secure a working coalition with other parties, it had to rely on far right support to maintain its position in power. HRW contends that this led to the use of ethnic tensions as a means to achieve political goals. Its report also cited the ministerial portfolios held by Turiscu and Tabara as signifiers of a wider trend towards human rights abuses in Romania during this period. Subsequently, in 2000, Tudor ran in the country's presidential campaign, and reached the second round, though he was beaten by his rival Ion Iliescu. Meanwhile, in 2006 PUNR was absorbed by the Conservative Party (*Partidul Conservator*).

See also Greater Romania Party; South-Eastern Europe and the Far Right *and* Tudor, Corneliu Vadim (Romania).

Further Reading

Shafir, Michael. 2000. 'Marginalisation or Mainstream? The Extreme Right in Post-Communist Romania'. In *The Politics of the Extreme Right: From the Margins to the Mainstream*. Edited by Paul Hainsworth. London: Pinter.

Human Rights Watch. 2006. 'Romania', http://www.hrw.org/reports/1995/WR95/HELSINKI-12.htm#TopOfPage (cited 31 December 2007).

Russia, Far Right Makes Electoral Gains (1993)

The 1993 Russian elections threw up a major surprise in the form of Vladimir **Zhirinovsky** and his **Liberal Democratic Party of Russia** (*Liberal'no-Demokraticheskaya Partiya Rossii*, LDPR). Zhirinovsky's party won over 12 million votes, a 22.92 percent share, and thus claimed 59 of the 225 seats in the State Duma. The LDPR also claimed 5 out of the 225 seats reserved for single-member constituencies.

The party won more votes than all other parties, including Yegor Gaidar's Democratic Choice of Russia (DVR), Gennady Andreyevich Zyuganov's Communist Party of Russian Federation (*Kommunisticheskaya Partiya Rossiskoy Federatsii*, KPRF), Yekaterina Lakhova's **Women** of Russia (*Zhenshchiny Rossii*, ZhR) and Mikhail Lapshin's Agrarian Party of Russia (*Agrarnaya Partiya Rossii*, APR). The election also marked the zenith of Zhirinovsky's political career, for in 1991 he scored only 7.8 percent in the presidential elections, in 1995 only 11.2 percent in a parliamentary poll, 5.7 percent in the presidential vote, and 6 percent in further legislative elections. The 1993 result was also significant in other ways. In sixty-four out of eighty-seven regions, the LDPR emerged as the leading party, although it was unable to gain an absolute majority in any of them. It was also a fairly cross-sectional vote. The party scored 40 percent on average in towns with a population of less than 100,000, and 25 percent in some bigger towns and cities and agricultural areas. According to commentators after the 1993 poll, Zhirinovsky was no longer a 'lightweight politician'.

19. Vladimir Zhirinovsky, ultra-nationalist leader of the Liberal Democratic Party (LPDR) and candidate in Russia's March presidential elections protests outside the British embassy in Moscow, 23 January 2008.

Indeed, after the fall of **Communism**, the vote for Zhirinovsky catapulted radical Russian politics back into the headlines. The man himself acquired global fame, but this was as much for his eccentric and outlandish rhetoric as for the size of his electoral share. Demonstrating the wider international concern with this issue, *The Economist* argued that political extremism in Russia during the 1990s seemed a 'real threat', citing Zhirinovsky's 1993 breakthrough to back up this claim. Meanwhile, the BBC stated, 'Mr Zhirinovsky enjoys nothing more than shocking liberal opinion at home and abroad with outrageous threats and warnings'. With hindsight, it can be argued that the election result was something of a 'blip'. Commentators have become increasingly dismissive of Zhirinovsky's politicking. Many now regard the fierce ultra-nationalism that first became an international phenomenon in 1993 as nothing more significant than political theatrics. Zhirinovsky, then, is not currently regarded as a genuine threat to Russian and international politics.

See also Liberal Democratic Party of Russia; Russia and the Far Right *and* Zhirinovsky, Vladimir (Russia).

Further Reading
Cox, Michael & Shearman, Peter. 2000. 'After the Fall: National Extremism in Post-Communist Russia'. In *The Politics of the Extreme Right: From the Margins to the Mainstream*. Edited by Paul Hainsworth. London: Pinter.
Williams, Christopher and Hanson, Steven. 1999. 'National-Socialism, Left Patriotism, or Superimperialism? The "Radical Right" in Russia'. In *The Radical Right in Central and Eastern Europe since 1989*. Edited by Sabrina Ramet. University Park, PA: Pennsylvania State University Press.

Russian National Unity

Russian National Unity (RNU) was founded in 1990 by Aleksandr Barkashov and it has bases in Estonia, Latvia, Lithuania, Ukraine and **Russia**. Its main slogan is 'Russia for the Russians' and it is loyal to the idea of the 'Motherland' and the Russian Orthodox Church. Party leaders are hard-line in their opposition to minorities – including Jews and Freemasons – and believe in the reunification of Russia as well as 'cleansing' (what they view as) Russian territory of all non-Russian elements. At one point, the Russian authorities estimated that the party had around 100,000 members.

RNU has a strong military profile. Members wear black uniforms, use the raised-arm salute ('Hail Russia!'), boast a red swastika flag and are known as warriors. They have also formed the Russian Knights, a well trained paramilitary organisation, and glorified those who fought for the USSR during World War II. The party has been responsible for bombings, beatings, armed robberies and other crimes, with Jews and foreigners the main target. At the same time, though, Barkashov ran for the Russian presidency in 2000. Barkashov seems quite open about his party's attachment to both violent and democratic means.

The party's publications – *Russian Attack, New Order* and *For a Russian Order* – focus mainly on ideology and propaganda, but have had a limited circulation. Most policy statements have a conservative tone, and RNU spokesmen claim that the party has benefited politically from the endemic social problems in the post-Soviet states.

See also Russia and the Far Right.

Further Reading
Cox, M. & Shearman, P. 2000. 'After the fall: nationalist extremism in post-communist Russia'. In *The Politics of the Extreme Right: From the Margins to the Mainstream*. Edited by Paul Hainsworth. London: Pinter.

S

Salazar, Death of (1970)

In 1968, Portuguese dictator António de Oliveira Salazar was relieved of his duties as prime minister, and was succeeded by Marcello Caetano. Salazar had been the Portuguese dictator since 1932, emerging from a background as a university professor specialising in economics. Unlike many of the interwar dictators, Salazar's rule lacked a charismatic dimension, and his *Estado Novo* (New State) has been described by Roger Griffin, among other specialists, as a para-fascist, rather than a fascist, state. This was due to the way in which the *Estado Novo* was imposed from above and subsequently created a wider movement – the *União Nacional* – rather than the other way around, as in the case of Nazism and Italian Fascism. By 1968, Salazar was suffering from brain damage after a domestic accident. He died two years later in Lisbon, living the life of a recluse. His funeral was attended by thousands of his political supporters, and his coffin eventually came to rest in his home town, Santa Comba Dão. Salazar's death had a profound effect on the Portuguese Far Right.

The transition from the *Estado Novo* to a democratic political system began in earnest with a left-wing revolution in 1974. Many of Salazar's supporters were forced to flee and go into exile by this time. Indeed, far-right parties had actually been declared illegal in Portugal by the new left-wing politicians. When this situation was eventually relaxed, many Salazar loyalists preferred to join established conservative parties such as the Social Democratic Party (*Partido Social Democrata*, IPA) or the Democratic and Social Centre Party (*Centro Democrático e Social*, CDS) rather than establish their own far-right movements.

See also Salazar, Dr António de Oliveira (Portugal) *and* Southern Europe and the Far Right.

Further Reading
Griffin, Roger. 1993. *The Nature of Fascism*. London and New York: Routledge.
Pinto, António Costa. 1995. 'The Radical Right in Contemporary Portugal'. In *The Far Right in Western and Eastern Europe*. Edited by Luciano Cheles, Ronnie Ferguson and Michalina Vaughan. London: Longman.

Salazar, Dr António de Oliveira (1889–1970) – Portugal

Dr António de Oliveira Salazar was a Portuguese dictator between 1932 and 1968. His relationship to the Far Right is an ambiguous one. He is often depicted as a fascist and sometimes talked of in the same breath as **Franco** in Spain, Mussolini in Italy and Hitler in Germany. However, while it is not in doubt that Salazar occasionally gave off the impression that he was leading a fascist or far-right regime, the truth is that Salazar, like Franco, was nothing more than a traditional conservative.

Salazar had a humble background and at one time thought about going into the church (he eventually settled on a degree in Law). He became involved in politics in his late-20s and joined the Catholic Centre party, also gaining a seat in parliament. Salazar was close to government in the early 1920s and had a brief spell in the cabinet of José Mendes Cabeçadas in 1926. The major turning-point in his life came in 1928 when he was appointed minister of finance, and then four years later, in 1932, he became prime minister.

In 1933, Salazar introduced a new constitution, which gave him full executive power and, in effect, created a dictatorship. While in power, he was austere and lacking in charisma. It could be argued that he lacked a positive vision and was content to rely on the secret police, nullify opposition and remove republican sympathisers from key state jobs. In time, Salazar's Portugal came to revolve around the corporate *Estado Novo* (New State) and *União Nacional* (the 'artificial' movement set up to give the new regime an aura of legitimacy). His religious background was a key factor in the way that he configured his regime. He placed a heavy emphasis on conservative values such as hierarchy, economic stability and social harmony, and used the slogan 'God, Country and **Family**' to sum up his guiding philosophy.

He also took on extra roles: foreign minister between 1936 and 1947 and war minister during the period 1936 to 1944. He supported the Nationalists in the Spanish Civil War by sending aid, but purposefully did not become officially involved. Likewise, during World War II, he did not get close to Hitler or Mussolini, preferring to stay neutral and safeguard his relationship with Britain and Portugal's colonial empire. His strategy gained admirers outside his own country and in 1946, the American magazine *Time* put him on their front cover, dubbing him 'The Dean of the Dictators'. Salazar left power as a result of a medical condition in 1968 and died in 1970. Marcello Caetano succeeded him and ruled Portugal between 1968 and 1974. He tried to undo some of Salazar's authoritarianism, but he was thrown out of power by the democratic revolution of 1974.

20. Dr Oliveira Salazar, Premier of Portugal, addresses the National Assembly regarding India's demands that Portugal get out of her Indian enclaves, 3 December 1954, Lisbon, Portugal.

Historians tend to view Salazar's regime as para-fascist in nature. The task he set himself was to create the impression of Fascism – in effect, to stave off the appearance of *genuine* movements of the Far Right. He was quite effective in this, and when the dictatorship era came to a close in 1974 (after six years of his Caetano in power) movements of the Far Right were conspicuous by their absence (any that did exist were then banned by the new, post-dictatorship authorities).

In more general terms, Salazar is a strange figure. He led Portugal shrewdly, in a surefooted and safety-first manner, and yet he seemed to inspire little affection. This was particularly the case with the right-wing groups that emerged in the decades after exit from power. In his analysis, Tom Gallagher tries to square the circle: 'Outwardly, neo-fascists stood to gain from the extent to which two generations of Portuguese were indoctrinated in the schoolroom, from the pulpit, and through the media by conservative propaganda ... Salazar's longevity in power and his impact upon the Portuguese meant that, potentially, he was a powerful symbol available for co-option by neo-fascist bodies ... However, one has to look hard for signs of neo-fascist strength in democratic Portugal, and Salazar is a curiously understated figure in current ultra-right propaganda ... The reasons for neo-fascist weakness in Portugal ... and the often equivocal role of Salazar in neo-fascist ideology are not unconnected.'

So, he was a man who had some far-right traits, had connections with nationalist movements and fascist regimes, engaged in some ruthless operations against opposition forces, and created an appearance of Fascism in his own country, not least through an all-embracing corporative state. But at the same time, he was a careful and thoughtful political leader who, it is alleged, stymied the growth of the Far Right after his death as well as during his life.

See also Salazar, Death of *and* Southern Europe and the Far Right.

Further Reading

Raby, D.L. 1991. *Fascism and Resistance in Portugal: Communists, Liberals and Military Dissidents in the Opposition to Salazar, 1941–74*. Manchester: Manchester University Press.
Derrick, M. 1972. *The Portugal of Salazar*. London: Campion.
Gallagher, Tom. 1994. 'Portugal: the marginalisation of the extreme right'. In *The Extreme Right in Europe and the USA*. Edited by Paul Hainsworth. London: Pinter.
Pinto, A.C. 1991. 'The radical right in contemporary Portugal'. In *Neo-Fascism in Europe*. Edited by Luciano Cheles, Ronnie Ferguson and Michalina Vaughan. London: Longman.

SANU Memorandum (Serbia)

It is generally agreed that the SANU Memorandum of 1986 acted as a spur to those Serbian nationalists keen to dismantle the status quo in what became the ex-Yugoslavia. The statement, issued by the Serbian Academy of Arts and Sciences (SANU), has gone down in history as a landmark in the history of the Balkans, for it argued that Serbia had been exploited by the other Yugoslavian states. Some commentators argue that it was more than a mere 'spur'. Rather, the document represented a battle cry. There is no doubt that the emerging force of Serb nationalism – and Slobodan **Milošević** in particular – interpreted it as such. The president of SANU at the time the memorandum was published was Dobrica Cosic, a leading Serb intellectual and writer.

The document itself argued that Yugoslavia was falling into deep decline due to 'stagnating social development, economic difficulties, growing social tensions, and open inter-ethnic clashes'. This had led to declining standards in **law and order**, while the sense of crisis had come to engulf the entire political and economic spheres. Consequently, 'Idleness and irresponsibility at work, corruption and nepotism, a lack of confidence in and disregard for the law, bureaucratic obstinacy, growing mistrust among individuals, and increasingly arrogant individual and group egoism have become daily phenomena'.

The memorandum claimed that the central issue raised by the emergence of these problems was the position and power of Serbia in the Yugoslav system. Indeed, it specifically highlighted the growing influence of Serbian separatism and nationalism as a legitimate response to this issue. Regarding the new political reality created by the 1974 constitution, the document stressed the way this development had weakened Serbia, especially as a result of the formation of **Kosovo** and Vojvodina, which became increasingly independent entities as a result of the new constitution. Effectively, this development had divided Serbia into three equal parts, according to the memorandum. Claiming that any shortfall in formal status for Kosovo and Vojvodina was more than made up by an ability to 'interfere in the internal relations of Serbia proper through the republic's common assembly', the document highlighted the need for a stronger Serbian response to its relative loss of power. It advocated a thoroughgoing reform of the Yugoslav federal structure, alongside a move to a more social democratic style of governance for the country. Indeed, according to the memorandum's committee of authors, nothing less that the 'human resources of the entire country must be involved to the utmost extent' in order to meet this new challenge. Furthermore: 'The expulsion of the Serbian nation from Kosovo bears spectacular witness to its historic defeat. In the spring of 1981, a very special, but nevertheless open and total war, prepared by administrative, political and legal changes made at various periods, was declared against the Serbian people. Waged through the skilful application of various methods and tactics, with a division of functions, and with the active, not merely passive, and little concealed support of certain political centers within Yugoslavia (more pernicious than the support coming from outside), this open war, which has yet to be looked in the face and called by its proper name, has been continuing for almost five years'.

Indeed, it went on to argue that this 'physical, political, legal and cultural genocide perpetrated against the Serbian population of Kosovo and Metohija is the greatest defeat suffered by Serbia in the wars of liberation she waged between Orasac in 1804 and the uprising of 1941'. Elsewhere, the document placed enormous significance on the alleged genocide of Kosovan Serbs by Albanians. It is in this sense and others that Misha Glenny has argued that SANU 'prepared the ideological ground for Milošević' by focusing public opinion on the Kosovo issue'.

Christina Morus has emphasised the role of intellectuals and rhetoric in the SANU episode. She writes: 'The intellectual authority of prominent cultural intellectuals can affect a form of "cultural pedagogy" that can essentially re-educate an audience through constitutive discourses that can re-articulate that audience's identity, cultural framework and historical references, and in so doing can normalise mass **violence**. Serbian intellectuals and cultural elites played a prominent role in initialising the extreme nationalist mindset that increasingly polarized Yugoslavia throughout the 1980s'. By 2004 – after the conflict in the Balkans had ended – the memorandum was cited by lawyers at The Hague to argue that Serb nationalists had pre-planned their campaign of genocide in Bosnia, Croatia and Kosovo.

See also Milošević, Slobodan (ex-Yugoslavia) *and* Serbian Radical Party.

Further Reading

www.slobodan-milosevic.org (personal website).

http://hague.bard.edu (War Crimes Tribunal).

Markotich, Stan. 2000. 'Serbia: extremism from the top and a blurring of right into left'. In *The Politics of the Extreme Right: From the Margins to the Mainstream*. Edited by Paul Hainsworth. London: Pinter.

LeBor, A. 2004. *Milosevic: A Biography*. London: Bloomsbury.

Thomas, R. 1999. *Serbia Under Milosevic: Politics in the 1990s*. London: Hurst & Company.

Schönhuber, Franz (1923–2005) – Germany

Franz Schönhuber emerged in the 1980s as one of the main faces of the Far Right in **Europe**. His *Republikaner Party* (REP) had made its mark in German and European elections and he was viewed as the 'German **Le Pen**' – an ebullient and larger-than-life figure who was determined to disturb the status quo with his hard-hitting rhetoric and unique political style.

Schönhuber studied at the Gymnasium in Munich and became a member of the Hitler **Youth** and Hitler's Nazi Party. He also joined the Waffen SS and was awarded the Iron Cross for his work as an instructor and translator with the Charlemagne SS Division. Throughout his life he expressed admiration for the SS and its members; in his autobiography, he described them as 'decent, loyal and brave men'. At the end of the war, during the process of denazification, Schönhuber was actually described as a key participant by the Allies. After the SS he took up a journalistic career. He was editor-in-chief of the Munich-based newspaper *tz* and also wrote for the *Münchner Abendzeitung* and the *Deutsche Woche*. He then went on to work in television. Between 1975 and 1981, he was head of the Union of Bavarian Journalists.

21. Franz Schönhuber, Far Right Republican Party leader, at local council elections, Berlin, Germany, 1992.

Schönhuber founded the *Republikaner Party* in 1983 with two ex-members of the CSU: Franz Handlos and Ekkehard Voigt. At first it behaved like a traditional conservative party, pushing for German unity and posing as an alternative to the CSU. However, Schönhuber made a strategic decision to move the party to the right – the extreme right – and it immediately brought dividends. Other creditable electoral performances followed and in 1989, the party scored 7.1 percent in the European elections and gained six MEPs. Schönhuber played an active role at Strasbourg, joining up with Le Pen to form the Group of the European Right. He was a member of parliamentary committees dedicated to Political Affairs and Culture, Youth, **Education** and the Media and also served on delegations that focused on relations with Austria and the USSR and successor states.

In its day, the REP was the German equivalent of the French FN. Schönhuber and Le Pen were not just of the same generation with similar political styles and instincts. They also spoke the same kind of language. Schönhuber talked about a 'democratically purified **patriotism**' and stated: 'Multiracial society is a red flag to our party. We don't want it.' He did not approve of **Communism** or mass Turkish **immigration** into Germany and, like many other far-right leaders of his generation, he was hard-line on **law and order**. And, however much he denied it – 'I have no Nazi past. Racism and Fascism led us into the most horrible catastrophe in our national history' – he was constantly tainted by accusations that he was sympathetic to Hitler and the Nazi regime, an impression that his autobiography and some of his famous rhetorical flourishes did nothing to dispel.

Even though post-reunification problems in Germany were a godsend to the REP, the party descended into bickering and quarrelling. The major issue was relations with the NPD. Some members of the REP were fraternising with the NPD, but others, including Schönhuber, saw this as a betrayal because of the radical, socialist tone to NPD discourse. This schism seemed to establish Schönhuber as champion of the 'conservative', 'bourgeois' faction within the REP. Schönhuber was ousted as party chairman on two occasions – in 1990 and 1994 – and switched later to the DVU and NPD, eventually standing for both in national elections.

Schönhuber died in 2005. On the German Far Right he was mourned as a 'great nationalist fighter' but in electoral terms, he did not make a huge impression on the German body politic. In many ways, though, he was swimming against the tide. In post-war Germany – with anti-Nazism institutionalised throughout German society – it was always going to be difficult for a man of the Far Right to gain a significant political following. He was also 'unlucky'. Schönhuber wanted the reunification of Germany and he once stated: 'My service is to articulate relentlessly the uneasiness of the Germans. It is a very German feeling; the Germans tend toward neuroses. Germany must again be allowed to walk tall in the world'. However, the problems that followed reunification did little to help him or his party politically. Similarly, the end of the USSR was something he must have dreamed about but, strangely, it had an adverse effect on his political fortunes because suddenly he had nothing to position himself against.

See also I Was There by Franz Schönhuber (Germany); Central Europe and the Far Right *and* Republican Party (Germany).

Further Reading
http://www.rep.de (Republikaner Party website).
Kolinsky, E. 1994. 'A future for right extremism in Germany?' In *The Extreme Right in Europe and the USA*. Edited by Paul Hainsworth. London: Pinter.
Backer, Susann. 2000. 'Right-wing extremism in unified Germany'. In *The Politics of the Extreme Right: From the Margins to the Mainstream*. Edited by Paul Hainsworth. London: Pinter.
Eatwell, Roger. 1996. *Fascism: A History*. London: Vintage.
Childs, David. 1991. 'The Far Right in Germany since 1945'. In *Neo-Fascism in Europe*. Edited by Luciano Cheles, Ronnie Ferguson and Michalina Vaughan. London: Longman.
Husbands, Christopher T. 1991. 'Militant neo-Nazism in the Federal Republic of Germany in the 1980s'. In *Neo-Fascism in Europe*. Edited by Luciano Cheles, Ronnie Ferguson and Michalina Vaughan. London: Longman.
Stöss, R. 1991. *Politics Against Democracy: Extreme Right in West Germany*. New York and Oxford: Berg.

Serbian Radical Party

The Serbian Radical Party (SRS) was formed in 1991 after a merger between the People's Radical Party and the Serbian Chetnik Movement. The SRS has a twin strategy. On one level, it competes in elections and between 1998 and 2000 supported **Milošević**'s Socialist Party of Serbia in government, during which period its leader, Vojislav Šešelj, was appointed deputy prime minister. On another level, it engages in paramilitary activity; Šešelj has spent time in jail and is currently awaiting trial at the War Crimes Tribunal at The Hague. Tomislav Nikolić has led the party in Šešelj's absence and gained significant support in the 2004 presidential election.

In the 2003 parliamentary election, the movement claimed almost 28 percent of the popular vote and eighty-two seats. In 2007, it polled almost 29 percent and won eighty-one seats. Commenting on the 2007 result, the European media was aghast that a party led by such shady figures, and espousing such an extreme philosophy, could do so well in a democratic election. And this was after the US ambassador in Belgrade had urged voters to reject a party that had a 'retrograde vision' and that wanted 'to turn Serbia into an isolated island blinded by nationalism'.

The ultra-nationalism of the SRS means that it is loyal to the idea of a Greater Serbia – including **Kosovo** – and of honouring the ideal of Serbdom. In this sense it sees itself as heir to the Chetnik tradition. The corollary of this exaggerated nationalism is a hatred of other nationalities, particularly Croats. Šešelj once said: 'I hate the Croats so much that I would have liked to gouge their eyes out with a rusty spoon'. As such, the SRS applauded the approach of Milošević as Serbian leader, in life and now in death. For his part, Milošević looked upon the SRS as a useful ally on the nationalist right. Seselj once said: 'They say Milošević wanted Greater Serbia. I am the original ideologue of Greater Serbia and I will not let anyone take that away from me'.

The White Eagles are the movement's paramilitary arm. They played a key role in the 1990s when the state of Yugoslavia was disintegrating and Serbia was flexing its muscles in Bosnia and Croatia. At the height of the fighting, the White Eagles were equipped by the Serbian Ministry of Internal Affairs and were responsible for some of the worst bouts of ethnic cleansing, killing and torture in Bosnia-Herzegovina, most notably in Bratunac, Brcko, Prijedor, Visegrad, Zvornik and Bijeljina.

Today, the SRS puts great stress on trying to implement United Nations Resolution 1244, which would allow the Serbian police and army to protect Serbian citizens in the province of Kosovo, a province that is currently under UN administration, but which the Serbs lay claim to for cultural and historical reasons.

The party's organisational HQ is in Belgrade and its colours – like Serbia's – are red, white and blue. In December 2007, the Party of Serbian Unity, associated with Željko Ražnatović Arkan, merged into the SRS.

See also Milošević, Arrest of (2001) *and* Milošević, Slobodan (ex-Yugoslavia).

Further Reading

Markotich, Stan. 2000. 'Serbia: extremism from the top and a blurring of right into left'. In *The Politics of the Extreme Right: From the Margins to the Mainstream*. Edited by Paul Hainsworth. London: Pinter.

LeBor, A. 2004. *Milosevic: A Biography*. London: Bloomsbury.

Thomas, R. 1999. *Serbia Under Milosevic: Politics in the 1990s*. London: Hurst & Company.

Sládek, Miroslav (b.1950) – Czech Republic

Miroslav Sládek grew up in *Kostelec nad Orlicí* and studied information and library systems at the Charles University in Prague. Under **Communism**, it is said that he worked for the authorities and used his skills in informatics to help put censorship policies into practice. However, with the fall of Communism in 1989, Sládek was given a new lease of life and he founded the **Republican Party** in 1990. The name of the movement was something of a misnomer because its agenda was distinctly illiberal. Over the next decade his personality came to dominate the movement.

Between 1990 and 1995, Sládek edited the party's weekly newspaper, *Republika*, which became notorious for its xenophobic and racist content. He and others were tasked with articulating the party line and spreading propaganda; unsurprisingly, they were charged with inciting **violence** and hatred on more than one occasion. Sládek also put himself forward as a candidate at the presidential elections of 1992, 1993 and 1998. He received little support, but he was slowly putting himself and his party on the Czech political map. The party fared slightly better in national parliamentary elections. It gained some representation in the 1992 poll; by 1996 its strength had risen to eighteen seats in the Chamber of Deputies, which equated to 8 percent of the national vote. In parliament, Sládek's party acquired a pariah-like reputation because of its extreme politics, and as a result it turned to spoiling tactics. It was also shunned by the mainstream Czech media.

During the 1990s, Sládek himself took on various roles. In June 1992, he became a parliamentary deputy but this was a shortlived posting – by the end of 1992 the Federal Assembly of Czechoslovakia was no more (it split into Czech and Slovak republics) and the parliament body was dissolved. Between 1992 and 1998, Sládek also published his collected political speeches in five volumes. These were made available in hard-copy form and online. In their work on Czech extremism, Cakl and Wollmann argue that, as a politician and party leader, Sládek's style was authoritarian. Anyone with an opposing opinion was marginalised and branded a traitor; not surprisingly, many of his victims actually left the party, unable to operate under such a leadership.

Sládek seemed to court controversy as a matter of policy. In January 1997, he spoke during a demonstration that had been organised to protest against closer Czech-German diplomatic ties. Among other things, he stated: 'We can only be sorry for not having killed more Germans in the war.' This outrageous remark landed Sládek in prison on charges of inciting anti-German racial hatred and, perhaps more significantly, he was stripped of his parliamentary immunity. In 1998, he was found not guilty of any legal offence – it was said that he was merely expressing an opinion.

In terms of ideas, Sládek stood for a brand of populist nationalism: anti-immigrant, anti-gypsy, anti-EU and pro-death penalty. His rhetoric was so powerful and vindictive that, on occasions, it provoked a violent response, especially from the Roma community living in the Czech Republic. By 1999, his party was on the wane. The Czech media opined that Sládek had had his day and his style of politics was ill-suited to the new democratic framework in the Czech Republic. The view was that he was a liability and did not have the talent or the personality to win back voters who had deserted the Republican Party during the 1990s. But, in 2001, Sládek tried to reinvent himself. He founded a successor party, The Republicans of Miroslav Sládek (*Republikáni Miroslava Sládka*), but this sank without trace at the polls, even though Sládek himself was elected into the municipal government of Útěchov, a district of Brno. To add insult to injury, in 2006 he was fined because of the debts that the Republican Party had accrued during its lifetime.

In the context of the European Far Right, Sládek is significant for a number of reasons. The end of Communism let the 'genie out of the bottle' so far as xenophobia and racism was concerned. In post-1989 Czechoslovakia – and then in the Czech Republic – Sládek stood for a defensive brand of far-right populism that made scapegoats out of minority groups such as gypsies. Like other far-right politicians in **Central Europe** he also exhibited hatred for his near neighbours – in his case, Germany and the Germans. Sládek's politics were so shallow that it was no surprise when the Republican Party fell into disrepair and he was forced to create another movement to act as the vehicle for his xenophobic and racist discourse.

See also Republican Party (Czech Republic).

Further Reading

http://www.republikani.com (Republican Party website).
Mudde, C. (ed.). 2005. *Racist Extremism in Central and Eastern Europe*. London: Routledge.
Shepherd, R.H.E. 2000. *Czechoslovakia: The Velvet Revolution and Beyond*. Houndsmills: Macmillan.
Stein, E. 1997. *Czecho/Slovakia: Ethnic Conflict, Constitutional Fissure, Negotiated Breakup*. Michigan: University of Michigan Press

Slota, Ján (b.1953) – Slovakia

The Far Right in modern Slovakia is personified by Ján Slota. He became involved in politics after the Velvet Revolution of 1989 swept the Communist Party from power in the old Czechoslovakia. Since then, he has become a controversial player in Slovak politics, constantly berating the authorities while at the same time carving out a niche for himself as an effective municipal leader.

In 1990, Slota co-founded the **Slovak National Party** (SNS) and became its president. He was elected a member of the Federal Assembly and the National Council of the Slovak Republic. Between 1994 and 1999, he was also leader of the SNS. Yet his party has played a significant role in government. It was a partner in the Meciar-led coalition up until 1998 and it joined the government in 2006.

More than most politicians, Slota is intimately associated with one particular city, Žilina, where he was mayor between 1990 and 2006. Slota views Žilina as his personal fiefdom and his work as mayor has been much praised. In particular, he has been credited with transforming the city, creating a **twenty-first century** metropolis out of the ruins of a drab place that had borne the brunt of Czechoslovakia's communist rulers. In 2001, Slota stated: 'Last year we had a congressman from Pennsylvania who made it a point to come to Zilina. He had a great time. We have foreign visitors here all the time, and never have any problems. In Zilina, the Slovak expression "*Host do domu, Boh do domu*" (A guest in the home is like God in the home) holds true'.

Over the years, Slota has become infamous for his rants against foreigners, Jews, homosexuals and gypsies, among others. In 1998, he was quoted as saying that the best policy for Slovakia's gypsies was 'a long whip in a small yard'. He has also targeted his country's Hungarian minority. He has labelled them 'scoundrels' and, fearing that Slovakia's Hungarian Coalition Party might demand some kind of territorial autonomy, he has argued that Slovakia should not sacrifice a 'single centimetre' of its national territory. For his part, the Hungarian prime minister said that Slota's comments were 'not to be taken seriously'.

The corollary of this exclusionist discourse is a powerful belief in the nation and nationalist heroes. In this context, Slota has idolised Jozef Tiso, the head of Slovakia's wartime fascist regime, and described him as 'one of the greatest sons of the Slovak nation'. Slota's pro-Tiso rhetoric reached fever pitch in 1999, the year that marked the sixtieth anniversary of the founding of Slovakia's fascist state. On 13 March 1999, during a rally of skinheads and Fascists in central Bratislava, the cry was: 'Slovakia for the Slovaks' and 'Glory to Tiso'.

Slota has always been prone to controversial outbursts. He once called US secretary of state Madeleine Albright a 'Czech woman who calls herself an American and even the US secretary of state, and who wants to teach all Slovaks lessons about what sort of idiots we are'.

After a bout of internal feuding, Slota left the SNS in 2001 and established an alternative far-right party – the Real Slovak National Party. The two parties scored poorly in the 2002 elections but amalgamated in 2003, even though the arguments had not totally abated.

See also Slovak National Party.

Further Reading

http://www.sns.sk (SNS website).

Harris, E. 2002. *Nationalism and Democratisation: Politics of Slovakia and Slovenia*. Aldershot: Ashgate.

Henderson, K. 2002. *Slovakia: The Escape for Invisibility*. London: Routledge.

Trifunovska, S. 1999. *Minorities in Europe: Croatia, Estonia and Slovakia*. The Hague: Springer.

Slovak National Party

The Slovak National Party (SNS) was founded in December 1989 and sees itself as the successor to the movement of the same name that existed prior to 1939. Only twice has the party scored more than 10 percent in national elections (13.94 percent in 1990 and 11.6 percent in 2006). It currently has nineteen seats in the Slovak parliament and also had representation there between 1990 and 2002. As a proud nationalist party, it viewed the declaration of an independent Slovakia, on 1 January 1993, as a major landmark. It was led by Ján **Slota**, mayor of Žilina.

The party would like to think of itself as centre-right, but it is usually pigeon-holed on the Far Right due to its uncompromising and zealous nationalism, which singles out Czechs, Hungarians, gypsies and homosexuals as targets. Slota has stated: 'If the SNS is extremist, then Hungarians are radioactively extremist, they radiate more than Chernobyl. The best solution would be to entomb them with cement ... Hungarians are the cancer of the Slovak nation, without delay we need to remove them from the body of the nation ... I am sick when I see that the Hungarians set the pace in the Slovak Parliament. It is pathetic that the most stable party in the government is the Hungarian Coalition Party ... We are negativist only in saying that parasites have to be eliminated, and parasites are simply those who don't want to work, and the fact that among those people 95 percent are gypsies is just reality'.

This kind of rhetoric has caused much anger and resentment in the Hungarian and gypsy communities, as well as further afield. Critics argue that the SNS thrives on imaginary grievances and a 'them' and 'us' view of the world.

Between 1994 and 1998, the party shared in the government of Vladimír Mečiar In 2002, internal disagreements led to the formation of a Real Slovak National Party, which for a short time fought against the SNS. In 2006, the SNS joined the governing centre-left coalition, a move which caused huge controversy. The Party of European Socialists (PES) suspended the Slovak socialist party, Smer, for befriending the SNS – PES described the SNS as a 'political party which incites or attempts to stir up racial or ethnic prejudices and racial hatred' – and Hungarian interests also condemned the appointment of three SNS ministers with little sympathy for the Hungarian minority in Slovakia.

See also Slota, Ján (Slovakia).

Further Reading
http://www.sns.sk (SNS website).
Harris, E. 2002. *Nationalism and Democratisation: Politics of Slovakia and Slovenia*. Aldershot: Ashgate.
Henderson, K. 2002. *Slovakia: The Escape for Invisibility*. London: Routledge.
Trifunovska, S. 1999. *Minorities in Europe: Croatia, Estonia and Slovakia*. Springer.

Soini, Timo (b.1962) – Finland

Timo Juhani Soini is the leading figure on the Finnish Far Right. He is the leader of the **True Finns party** and someone who has gained prominence and national exposure in recent years. He argues that he and his party should not be pigeon-holed on the Far Right, but his policy programme does contain several key nationalist and ultra-nationalist pledges.

Soini graduated from the University of Helsinki in 1988 in social sciences. He is a city councillor in Espoo and, since 2003, a member of the Finnish parliament. He has a background in other organisations: for example, *Kehittyvän Suomen Nuorten Liitto* (**Youth** League of Developing Finland) and *Suomen Maaseudun Puolue* (Rural Party). He joined the True Finns when it was established in 1995, and became party leader in 1997 in succession to Raimo Vistbacka.

With Soini as leader, True Finns polled 1.7 percent in the 2003 general election – gaining three seats – and then he took a 3.4 percent share of the vote in the 2006 presidential poll. This result was a major success for the party, and it was during this election that Soini said: 'The True Finns will get exactly as many seats as they have the courage to take'. He has also served on a variety of parliamentary committees, including those devoted to legal affairs and international affairs, and is currently vice-chair of the True Finns' parliamentary grouping.

In terms of policies, Soini is in favour of Finland leaving the EU and encouraging immigrants to integrate more fully into Finnish society. He denies that he has links to other far-right parties – such as **Le Pen**'s FN in France – but does argue that Finland has the right to decide on its own **immigration** policy. He says he is opposed to uncontrollable levels of immigration, rather than immigrants *per se*. As he puts it: 'I am not against minorities. I am Catholic. I know what it's like to be a minority!' However, Soini's protestations have not been helped by comments attributed to one of his party colleagues, Tony Halme. Halme has been quoted as saying that 'people who have Somalians as neighbours either sleep very badly or not at all!'

On one occasion, Soini stated: 'I want nothing to do with hate. It's not about hate or racism or anything like that'. This may be so, but the anti-fascist magazine *Searchlight* has described his party as 'unashamedly Far Right'. The True Finns are most popular in the towns and cities of Finland, where immigration levels are highest, and thus produce a backlash at election time. It also does well in areas where there are significant numbers of Swedish-speakers. Again, he seems to benefit from fear and insecurity, this time among Finnish-speakers. This evidence suggests that Soini stands for a defensive form of nationalism, with his party determined to protect what it views as the true Finnish population from outsiders.

Soini is generally viewed as Finland's most colourful and controversial politician, partly because most Finnish politicians have a reputation for being slightly dull. He is a fine orator and, unusually, can also speak English. He converted to Catholicism while back-packing round **Europe** and supports the English football team, Millwall. Finland has no tradition of far-right politics to speak of, but Soini is now a key figure on the country's political scene.

See also Scandinavia and the Far Right *and* True Finns Party.

Further Reading

http://www.perussuomalaiset.fi/true_finns.html (True Finns website).
Andersen, J.G. & Bjørklund, T. 2000. 'Radical right-wing populism in Scandinavia: from tax revolt to neo-liberalism and xenophobia'. In *The Politics of the Extreme Right: From the Margins to the Mainstream*. Edited by Paul Hainsworth. London: Pinter.

Spanish Circle of Friends of Europe

Spanish Circle of Friends of **Europe** (*Círculo Español de Amigos de Europa*, CEDADE) was one of the first Europe-wide neo-Nazi organisations. It was founded in 1965 and was active until 1993 when it mutated into the National **Democracy** movement.

Although it was founded in West Germany, it was Spanish in inspiration and eventually came to be based in Barcelona. It has been described as a cultural association and study group, but this understates its role in publishing neo-Nazi material and disseminating it in a broader sense. It boasted a bookshop in Barcelona – Europa – which on occasion was raided by police who seized around 13,000 books and arrested CEDADE's leader, Pedro Varela. Ideologically, it stood for closer neo-Nazi cooperation across Europe, **anti-Semitism** and also dabbled in Holocaust denial. There were phases too when it looked towards Mussolini-style Fascism.

In 1979, it registered as a political party under the name European National Revolutionary Party (*Partido Europeo Nacional Revolucionario*) and claimed to have 2,500 members in Spain, including the son of Nazi Klaus Barbie. In 1989, it hosted an international centenary celebration of Hitler's birthday and until its demise – caused mainly by financial problems – it was led by Varela, a convicted neo-Nazi. The veteran Belgian activist Léon **Degrelle** was also a member.

See also Southern Europe and the Far Right.

Further Reading
Wilkinson, Paul. 1983. *The New Fascists*. London: Pan.
Eatwell, Roger. 1995. *Fascism*. New York: Oxford University Press.

Spearhead Magazine (Great Britain)

For most of the 1960s and 1970s, *Spearhead* magazine acted as the voice of the **British National Front**. It was launched in 1964 by John Tyndall and edited by him thereafter until his death in 2005. The publication was accused of promoting racist and fascist views – something that Tyndall denied.

It has now evolved into a webzine and a number of topics have been addressed in recent articles on the site, ranging from the quotidian to the extreme. One article praised the way that local authorities had decided to allow English people to define their ethnicity as English on official paperwork, rather than white British. The latter category rendered such people 'just one racial group among many others who now live in these wretched islands'. Of course, such sensitivity to national identity is a key marker of far-right ultra-nationalism. Launching into a diatribe against multiculturalism, the article argued that only Britain has pursued a multicultural agenda so vociferously. Not only were 'many tens of thousands of Anglo-Celts [...] leaving London each year', but immigrant communities were now beginning to develop their own separate areas, as in other countries such as the US. '**Immigration** on the present scale I consider to be morally and legally wrong,' the article continued, suggesting that such policies infringed on the human rights of British residents. Using such a line to invoke a sense of disenfranchisement from legal rights, it argued that local councils prioritised immigrant communities over native ones. Further, they did so undemocratically, without consulting local communities.

Aside from immigration, *Spearhead* has also tackled the '**War on Terrorism**'. For example, one article used the analogy of the Pied Piper of Hamelin to describe the relationship between Tony Blair and George W. Bush. Indeed, the magazine urged people to think about 'who truly has control over the US Government' when thinking about this subject. Aside from this conspiracy theory tenor, the article also articulated frustration with Blair and Bush through a racist lens: 'I am also confident that no one will disagree when I say that this "war on terror" ... has been against our national interests: a war into which we had no reason to go headlong and one that has given so much fuel to the hate against our nation in the Middle Eastern World (those who understand that our foreign policy is governed by our unconditional subservience to the United States and support of Israel) ... Whites are now the only group whose interests are not being promoted by state institutions, such as TV and the law'. This style of thinking on world affairs is typical of the analysis presented in *Spearhead* articles.

While Tyndall was alive, *Spearhead* also became a battleground among the British Far Right. After Tyndall left the NF to found the BNP, the magazine became the voice of the BNP. However, following Nick **Griffin**'s election as leader of the BNP, Tyndall started to use the magazine as a vehicle for destabilising the leadership of the party. In turn, Griffin banned the sale of the magazine at party meetings.

See also National Front (Great Britain).

Further Reading

Eatwell, Roger. 2000. 'The extreme right and British exceptionalism: the primacy of politics'. In *The Politics of the Extreme Right: From the Margins to the Mainstream*. Edited by Paul Hainsworth. London: Pinter.
Eatwell, Roger. 1994. 'Why has the extreme right failed in Britain?' In *The Extreme Right in Europe and the USA*. Edited by Paul Hainsworth. London: Pinter.
Cable, Gerry. 1991. 'The far right in contemporary Britain'. In *Neo-Fascism in Europe*. Edited by Luciano Cheles, Ronnie Ferguson and Michalina Vaughan. London: Longman.
Eatwell, Roger. 1996. *Fascism: A History*. London: Vintage.

Srebrenica (Bosnia and Herzegovina)

Of all the sites of mass murder during the break-up of Yugoslavia, Srebrenica stands apart. It claims the grizzly status of being the location of the largest mass murder since the end of World War II. In the communist era, especially under Tito, nationalism had largely been contained within Yugoslavia. However, as the country broke up into its constituent national parts in the 1990s, a powerful new trend of ultra-nationalism emerged. Consequently, the deadly combination of ultra-nationalist ideology and military force was unleashed with all its extremist potency. The Srebrenica Massacre itself was part of the Bosnian War that broke out when the proclamation of independence by Bosnian president, Aliza Izetbegović, was recognised by the international community on 6 and 7 April 1992. The atrocity was the culmination of a wider campaign of warfare, including ethic cleansing, which sought as its goal the creation of pure, national territory.

At the core of the Bosnian War, then, was the issue of national identity. The region comprised three distinct groups: Bosniacs (Muslim inhabitants of Bosnia), Croats and Serbs. After the Bosniac majority declared independence in 1992, Bosnia quickly became embroiled in the power struggle between an aggrandising Serbia and the other nationalities that comprised the cultural make-up of the region. Echoing the 'working towards the Führer' concept, this led to a dynamic whereby **Milošević** would encourage local Serbs in Bosnia to 'work towards a Greater Serbia', and where possible, he would aid these attempts through Serb-controlled troops. Often, analysts point to Slobodan Milošević's attempt to create a Greater Yugoslavia as the prime cause of the conflict. However, aside from this project, there were other national interests at play, and so political scientists should not regard the conflict through a simplifying good-versus-evil lens. For example, it would be wrong to ignore the fact that both Croats and Bosniacs also committed wartime atrocities in the Bosnian War. Nevertheless, Serbia's Milošević set the pace for the Bosnian War, and pro-Serbian forces committed the most extreme acts of ethnic cleansing. Further, the ideological thrust of the war for Bosnian Serbs is clear. Typifying this ideological lens, Richard Butler has observed that the execution of an estimated 8,000 Bosniac civilians at Srebrenica was militarily far less useful to the Bosnian Serb forces than if they had used them as a 'bargaining chip' when negotiating with the international community. Such tactics, however, were beyond the scope of the Bosnian Serb mentality, which saw the conflagration in ideological terms of creating territory devoid of Bosniacs.

Turning to the massacre itself, the region of Central Podrindre, which surrounded Srebrenica, was vital territory for the military campaign to create a Bosnian Serb controlled Republic of Srpska (*Republika Srpska*). Therefore, the Bosniac dominated town of Srebrenica became especially important to the Bosnian Serbs' campaign. In 1992, Srebrenica briefly fell under Serbian control. Some of its civilians were killed, while others were forced out of the town. Subsequently, Bosnian government forces recaptured Srebrenica, and in 1993 it was designated a 'Safe Area' by the United Nations. A UN Protection Force (UNPROFOR) entered the town on 16 April in order to enforce this move. Serbian forces, meanwhile, increasingly regarded the 'Safe Area' as a base for Bosnian government forces to attack them, one that was protected by the UN presence.

As the Bosnian War progressed, conditions within the 'Safe Area' around Srebrenica deteriorated. By 1995, its existence was regarded as a major problem for the Army of the Republic of Srpska (*Vojska Republike Srpske*, VRS), an organisation then under the direct command of Ratko Mladić. Further, according to the International Criminal Tribunal for the Former Yugoslavia (ICTY), the then president of the Republic of Srpska, Radovan Karadžić, gave the following order to the Bosnian Serb forces on the 8 March 1995: 'by well thought out combat operation, create an unbearable situation of total insecurity with no hope of further survival or life for the inhabitants of Srebrenica and Žepa.' By this time, locals were beginning to starve due to supply restrictions, and UNPROFOR troops were also becoming disillusioned with their campaign. Indeed, the tight restrictions on UNPROFOR activity not only depleted their morale but also arguably prevented them from at least hindering the massacre once it broke out in July 1995. Eventually, greatly out-numbered and severely restricted, they just watched on as the massacre unfolded.

After Serbian forces entered the 'Safe Area' in early July, the situation quickly descended into war crimes. By the 12 July, various pro-Serbian forces had full control of Srebrenica. Bosnian civilians were herded up by Bosnian Serb forces, and men were separated from **women** and children. The Bosnian Serbs even commandeered buses and compelled non-combatant, Bosnian Serb bus drivers to assist in the deportation of Srebrenica's women and children. In order to ensure their complicity in covering up the atrocity, these terrified bus drivers were also forced to kill Muslims. Having separated the men of fighting age from other civilians in the area, Bosnian Serb forces carried out a series of mass executions, leading to the deaths of around 8,000 people. According to the ICTY, these followed a simple formula: after a period of detention, the prisoners were taken by bus to another site, usually a remote location, for execution. These prisoners were unarmed, were often blindfolded and had their hands tied together. Sometimes their shoes were also removed, again to help disable them. After arrival at the execution site, they were formed into orderly lines and shot, any survivors were simply shot again. Earth-moving machinery was then used to bury the bodies; sometimes this began even before the execution operation had been completed. Aside from these premeditated acts of mass murder, locals, predominantly civilians, also made several attempts to flee and reach territory held by Bosnian government forces. Their attempts were also met with military force, and Bosnian Serb forces hunted down and shot many of these people too.

The Srebrenica Massacre was seen as a watershed moment in the Bosnian War, leading to a greater UN and NATO pressure on Belgrade to stop backing the actions of the Bosnian Serbs. Following the bombing of Serb positions in August 1995 and the threat of further NATO action, alongside continued economic sanctions on Serbia, the international community was able to persuade Milošević to back negotiations. Indeed, he was regarded as the one man capable of bringing peace to the region. This ultimately led to the signing of the Dayton Agreement in November 1995. As an internationally-recognised, sovereign country, Bosnia remained intact. However, internally it comprised a weak central state and two powerful regions: the Serb-dominated Republic of Srpska and the Muslim-Croat-dominated Federation of Bosnia-Herzegovina. Bosnian Serbs were granted many concessions by the Dayton Agreement, and the ethnic conflict of the war was simply formalised by the new Bosnia. Further, Srebrenica is located in what is now the Serb-dominated Republic of Srpska. Meanwhile, international arrest warrants issued by the ICTY, including for genocide during the Bosnian War, remain outstanding for both Mladić and Karadžić.

See also Milošević, Slobodan (ex-Yugoslavia) *and* Serbian Radical Party.

Further Reading
Judah, Tim. 2002. *Kosovo: War and Revenge*. New Haven, CT: Yale University Press.
Markotich, Stan. 2000. 'Serbia: extremism from the top and a blurring of right into left'. In *The Politics of the Extreme Right: From the Margins to the Mainstream*. Edited by Paul Hainsworth. London: Pinter.
Weitz, Eric D. 2005. *A Century of Genocide: Utopias of Race and Nation*. Princeton: Princeton University Press.

Stoyanov, Dimitar (b.1983) – Bulgaria

Dimitar Stoyanov is leader of the Attack (*Ataka*) Coalition in Bulgaria. He is a rising star on the Bulgarian Far Right and has benefited hugely from the political opportunities that have come his way after his country's accession to full EU membership. He is now an outspoken and controversial figure in the European Parliament.

The key to Stoyanov's involvement in politics is his **family**. His mother, Kapka Georgieva, is a journalist and his grandfather, Radoy Ralin, was a writer and dissident. His mother's partner is Volen Siderov, who helped to found the *Ataka* party, and his girlfriend, Denitsa Gadjeva, is a key member of *Ataka* and deputy chair of the movement's **youth** section.

When Stoyanov joined *Ataka* as a student – he studied Law at the University of Sofia – it was led by Siderov. At the age of 22, Stoyanov was elected as the youngest member of the Bulgarian parliament and soon after became an Observer to the European Parliament, serving from September 2005 to December 2006.

While working as an Observer, he became embroiled in controversy when, in a circular email, he objected to the nomination of Livia Jaroka (a Hungarian of Roma origin) for a parliamentary award. This was no coincidence, as the *Ataka* party were renowned for their anti-gypsy rhetoric.

Stoyanov has made many enemies at Strasbourg. One is Elly de Groen-Kouwenhoven, a Green MEP from the Netherlands. She has a special interest in south-east **Europe**, and Bulgaria in particular, and has labelled Stoyanov and his party dangerous and anti-democratic and campaigned for him to be expelled from the parliament. Her reaction to the Jaroka controversy was blunt: 'I got really shocked, when I read the text. That was not only a racialist but a sexist insult. This is a horrible misconduct. I am very sorry for both my colleague Livia Jaroka and for the Bulgarian delegation in the European Parliament. I know that the majority of the Bulgarian Observers in the European Parliament drew a line between themselves and this comment … This time Dimitar Stoyanov went too far'.

Stoyanov has also exhibited a strong hostility to what he calls the 'Jewish establishment' in Bulgaria. He was quoted in the *Daily Telegraph* as saying: 'There are a lot of powerful Jews, with a lot of money, who are paying the media to form the social awareness of the people. They are also playing with economic crises in countries like Bulgaria and getting rich. These are the concrete realities'. These comments were disowned by the only British member of the **Identity, Tradition and Sovereignty Group**, Ashley Mote.

Since 2007, Stoyanov has sat in the parliament as an *Ataka* representative, and as part of the larger Identity, Tradition and Sovereignty Group. He sits on parliamentary committees dedicated to Regional Development and Agriculture and Rural Development, and delegations that consider Relations with the Mashreq Countries and the Euro-Mediterranean Parliamentary Assembly.

Because he is so young for a politician, Stoyanov has been labelled the 'child prodigy' of the *Ataka* party. His hairstyle has attracted comment – he has a crew cut – and he also has a passionate interest in sport: he is currently a member of the management board of the Bulgarian Fencing Federation.

See also Attack Coalition (Bulgaria) *and* South-Eastern Europe and the Far Right.

Further Reading

http://www.ataka.bg (party website).

http://www.europarl.europa.eu (European Parliament).

Ganev, V.I. 2007. *Preying on the State: The Transformation of Bulgaria After 1989*. Ithaca, NY: Cornell University Press.

Giatzidis, E. 2002. *An Introduction to Postcommunist Bulgaria: Political, Economic and Social Transformation*. Manchester: Manchester University Press.

Crampton, R.J. 2005. *A Concise History of Bulgaria*. Cambridge Concise Histories.

Swiss People's Party

The Swiss People's Party (SVP) came to prominence in 2003 when it won 55 out of 200 seats in the Swiss lower house of parliament after securing almost 27 percent of the vote. It was asked to join the governing coalition and also gained two seats on the Swiss Federal Council. This was a milestone for a party that had veered towards the Far Right in the 1990s and early 2000s. It was also a significant moment in the history of Swiss politics for a decades-old tradition of consensus government had been broken. In 2007, the SVP maintained its position as the strongest party in the country, claiming 62 seats.

The SVP was formally established in 1971 after a merger between the Farmers, Artisans and Citizens' Party (BGB) and the Democratic Party (DP), so, in a sense, it can trace its history back to 1917 and the birth of the Farmers Party in Zurich. It is very much an anti or protest party. It is opposed to Swiss membership of the EU and UN and is hostile to growing (illegal) **immigration** levels and asylum applications. On the whole, the party is socially conservative, pro-**family** values and in favour of 'small government'.

In 2000, party leader Christoph **Blocher** outlined the 'Seven Secrets of the SVP', which essentially outlined the party's political position at that juncture. In confident fashion he looked to the future and gave his own movement some tips, including: 'Don't cultivate prestige, get on with the job!', 'Issues, not offices!', 'Understanding Switzerland as a special case', and finally, 'Thinking the unthinkable'. He also said that the party enjoyed confounding its critics: '"The SVP is doomed". This was the prophecy uttered a good 20 years ago by Helmut Hubacher, at that time chairman of the Swiss Socialist Party. "The SVP had," he said, "lost the support of so many voters that the party should be ejected from the Federal Council." But the truth is apparent: the red prophet was wrong – as are all red prophets!'

Three years later, in 2003, the SVP was the strongest force in Swiss politics, and seven years later, in 2007, the movement launched a major initiative against Islam and, in particular, the construction of minarets (though it should be stated that, at the time, Switzerland boasted only two – one in Zurich and one in Geneva). SVP member Ulrich Schlüer led the campaign, and he and his party were supported by the Federal Democratic Union of Switzerland. The first aim was to force the government into calling a referendum on the issue. Schlüer said that Swiss **democracy** meant, 'the fundamental right of every Swiss, not only to elect the parliament, but to decide in referendums on all questions of high interest. Direct democracy is, today in particular, threatened by international conventions, which Switzerland joined by government resolutions. As a consequence of such international agreements, more and more national related cases are no longer submitted to the population's vote, because they are determined through international agreements'.

22. An election poster of the Swiss Peoples Party (SVP) for federal elections in Basel, Switzerland, 6 October 2006.

Schlüer and his colleagues tried to emphasise that they were not targeting Muslims *per se*; rather, their contention was that the building of minarets went against notions of state secularism. The party has stated: 'Islam makes no distinction between Church and State, such that minarets become the expression of influence not only religious, but political, in nature. This conception is incompatible with Western secular tradition. Arguments that serve today to justify minaret construction will be used, in turn, to justify muezzins [those who call to prayer]. It's high time to let the Swiss people decide on the question of minarets in their nation'. SVP MP Oskar Freysinger continued: 'We don't want minarets. The minaret is a symbol of a political and aggressive Islam; it's a symbol of Islamic law. The minute you have minarets in **Europe**, it means Islam will have taken over'.

The future looks bright for the SVP, and Blocher has always been keen to emphasise the uniqueness of his movement. He talks about party members as being, 'united by a shared ideology and whose significance has in the meantime become apparent. Our members of parliament apply above-average commitment to the job in hand … Innumerable SVP members on all levels actively support the party through voluntary work – and even pay membership fees for the privilege! … The SVP as a movement has the strength to advance in the right direction and to curb any movement in the wrong political direction ... Our party has thus become THE driving force in Switzerland's political landscape. Over the past years the SVP has unswervingly developed powerful ideas, initiatives and motions. We present the solutions to the asylum problems, we know what should be done'.

See also Blocher, Christoph (Switzerland); Central Europe and the Far Right *and* Switzerland, Far Right Makes Electoral Gains (2003).

Further Reading

http://www.svp.ch (SVP website).

Blocher, Christoph. 1997. *Switzerland and the Second World War: A Clarification*. Schweizerische Volkspartei des Kantons Zürich.

Church, Clive H. 2003. *The Politics and Government of Switzerland*. Macmillan.

Fossedal, Gregory A. 2005. *Direct Democracy in Switzerland*. Transaction Publishers.

Farago, P., Kohli, M., & Zarin-Nejadan, M., & Kriesi, H., eds. 2005. *Contemporary Switzerland: Revisiting the Special Case*. Houndmills: Palgrave Macmillan.

Switzerland and the Second World War: A Clarification by Christophe Blocher (Switzerland)

In 1997, far-right Swiss politician Christophe **Blocher** gave a speech at a function organised by the Zurich branch of the SVP. It was delivered at the Hotel International, and in the oration he joined the debate about Switzerland's role in World War II, arguing that Switzerland should be proud of her record of neutrality during the conflict and not in any way embarrassed by it.

Blocher was ready to admit that some Swiss had let their country down during the conflict and kowtowed to the Nazis: 'There were weaklings, conformists and pussyfooters – there always have been, there are today, and there always will be. Isolated government measures, encouraged by high-handed officials out of touch with reality, are incomprehensible with hindsight and deserving of criticism. These include the identification stamp for Jews, regulations decreeing that Jews should bear the cost of Jewish refugees, the hermetically sealed border after 1942, the deportation of refugees, and the overly rigorous censorship by authorities. In some instances there was also evidence of an excessively compliant attitude towards a menacing Germany'.

But at the same time, as revisionist historians enquired into Switzerland's role during the conflict, and discussion ensued as to how the country behaved, Blocher argued that the facts were clear: 'Between 1933 and 1945, the Swiss people proved their resistance to Nazi thought and conviction. On the national level, almost 100 percent of the voters elected members of the democratic political parties which had remained Swiss! A single representative of the National Front was seated in Parliament for four years as of 1935. The Swiss were in no way Nazis'. He then went on to claim that no-one was mistreated by the Swiss state and that, 'a total of 800,000 men (20 percent of the population in a country of 4 million) safeguarded our national territory and strengthened armed neutrality. They were ready to give their lives for our country'.

In the context of the rise of the SVP, throughout the 1990s and into the 2000s, this was a significant statement to make. Many far-right leaders in **Europe** had been undone by their alleged Nazi sympathies – **Le Pen**, **Haider**, **Schönhuber** – and Blocher seemed to be saying that his country, never mind he and his party, was clean.

See also Blocher, Christoph (Switzerland); Central Europe and the Far Right a*nd* Swiss People's Party.

Further Reading
http://www.svp.ch (SVP website).
Blocher, Christoph. 1997. *Switzerland and the Second World War: A Clarification*. Schweizerische Volkspartei des Kantons Zürich.
Church, Clive H. 2003. *The Politics and Government of Switzerland*. Macmillan.
Fossedal, Gregory A. 2005. *Direct Democracy in Switzerland*. Transaction Publishers.
Farago, P., Kohli, M., & Zarin-Nejadan, M., & Kriesi, H., eds. 2005. *Contemporary Switzerland: Revisiting the Special Case*. Houndmills: Palgrave Macmillan.

Switzerland, Far Right Makes Electoral Gains (2003)

In October 2003, the far-right **Swiss People's Party** (*Schweizer Volkspartei*, SVP) emerged as the strongest force in parliament, claiming 28 percent of the national vote. It netted fifty-five seats, more than the Social Democratic Party of Switzerland (*Sozialdemokratische Partei der Schweiz*, SP), who won fifty-two seats, the Free Democratic Party of Switzerland (*Freisinnig-Demokratische Partei der Schweiz*, FDP) who won thirty-six, and the Christian Democratic People's Party of Switzerland (*Christlich Demokratische Volkspartei*, CVP), who won twenty-eight. By December 2003, the SVP, which had traditionally held one governmental seat, had garnered two out of seven cabinet posts – a major triumph.

The result came as no surprise to some commentators. For example, a month before the poll, the BBC correspondent in the country reported how the SVP's populist politics, characterised as 'ultra-conservative and fiercely patriotic', was making significant advances. Highlighting the way the SVP played on senses of alpine tradition and promoted Swiss independence, reports also highlighted a racist tenor to the party's **immigration** stance. Indeed, the BBC reported the ideas of one member based in Zurich, Will Eckler. 'We need foreigners to work in Switzerland and they are well paid,' claimed Eckler, 'but we don't need scroungers who cost money. The criminals should be kicked out or interned'. In the election campaign, the SVP campaigned on several key themes. It emphasised its hostility to immigrants and asylum seekers, it opposed membership to the **European Union**, courted controversy by using the word 'negro' in campaign posters, and even stated that the drugs industry was run by 'Albanians and black Africans'. The election result provoked varying reactions. For the SVP, Christoph **Blocher** commented: 'The fact that the Swiss have expressed such trust in the SVP means they want a change in policy.' On the other hand, centrist Barbara Polla was reported as saying 'I think there is a very large amount of work that needs to be done to reassure people, and to show that the presence of foreigners [...] is a positive factor, especially for the **economy**.'

Political analysts had a field day with the election result. Thomas Fleiner explained that Switzerland was experiencing an untypical period of political polarisation. This move away from the tradition of consensus politics raised profound questions regarding the future of Swiss politics: was it experiencing a temporary glitch, or did Blocher's rise signify long-term change? Similarly, Janwillem Acket argued that the rise of the SVP exposed the myth of Swiss political stability. Ackert also stressed that this was a mere prelude to further political instability and the country would see an end to the unique political status that Switzerland had enjoyed following the end of World War II. Even the US State Department noted that Switzerland 'has seen a gradual shift in the party landscape' in recent years.

The 2003 poll result did not come out of the blue. Internationally, Switzerland boasts a modern, progressive image, but there is also a darker element in its postwar political history. As far back as 1967, right-wing groups were campaigning to limit the number of foreign **workers** crossing the border into Switzerland. Further, in 2002 an independent study, the *Bergier Report*, found that the Swiss authorities knew more than they had previously disclosed regarding the fate of the Jews during World War II. Finally, twelve months after the 2003 election, voters in a national referendum decided not to liberalise the country's strict naturalisation laws, underscoring the centrality of the immigration issue in the country's political discourse. Meanwhile, in the 2007 election, the SVP increased its share of the vote to 29 percent. However, this still did not allow Blocher to form a majority government.

See also Blocher, Christoph (Switzerland); Central Europe and the Far Right *and* Swiss People's Party.

Further Reading

Plomb, Fabrice and Mileti, Francesca Poglia. 2007. 'Individual Expressions of Right-Wing Extremism – Understanding the Affinity to Radical Populism in Observing the Changes in the Work Field: The Case of Switzerland'. In *Changing Working Life and the Appeal of the Extreme Right*. Edited by Jörg Flecker. Aldershot: Ashgate.
BBC. 2003. 'Swiss right in political avalanche', *BBC News*, http://news.bbc.co.uk/1/hi/world/europe/3204412.stm (cited 31 December 2007).
Foulkes, Imogen. 2007. 'Swiss vote after ugly campaign', *BBC News*, http://news.bbc.co.uk/1/hi/world/europe/7050498.stm (cited 31 December 2007).

T

Taking Liberties: A Third Way Special on the Attack on Civil Liberties in the UK Essays (Great Britain)

This 2005 pamphlet was authored by a trio of British far-right activists: Tim Bragg, Nick **Griffin** and David Kerr, and edited by Patrick Harrington. It incorporated a series of essays aimed at defending civil liberties and was published by Harrington's Third Way movement.

The argument presented in the volume is that civil liberties are under threat in modern-day Britain. A range of examples are cited including cultural censorship and the gagging of BNP spokesmen. The proposed 'incitement to religious hatred' offence is also condemned. In his editorial, Harrington states: 'Let me nail my colours to the mast. I believe that speech (and other forms of expression) should be protected regardless of content or viewpoint. I am against any law that seeks to discriminate against any religious, racial or political group. I'm also against any law that favours one such interest group over another'.

The pamphlet presents the British Far Right as the guardian of civil liberties, and also the political current most threatened by a clampdown on them. But, at the same time, it is emphasised that civil liberties are generic and absolute and should not be denied to anyone.

The authors of the pamphlet came from a variety of backgrounds: Bragg is a musician and edits the nationalist journal *Steadfast*, Griffin is leader of the BNP and Kerr a member of Third Way. Harrington is a former Communist and National Front member and founder member of Third Way.

See also Griffin, Nick (Great Britain).

Further Reading

www.bnp.org.uk (BNP website).

Eatwell, Roger. 2000. 'The extreme right and British exceptionalism: the primacy of politics'. In *The Politics of the Extreme Right: From the Margins to the Mainstream*. Edited by Paul Hainsworth. London: Pinter.

Eatwell, Roger. 1994. 'Why has the extreme right failed in Britain?' In *The Extreme Right in Europe and the USA*. Edited by Paul Hainsworth. London: Pinter.

Cable, Gerry. 1991. 'The far right in contemporary Britain'. In *Neo-Fascism in Europe*. Edited by Luciano Cheles, Ronnie Ferguson and Michalina Vaughan. London: Longman.

Eatwell, Roger. 1996. *Fascism: A History*. London: Vintage.

Bragg, T., Griffin, N., Kerr, D. & Harrington, P. 2005. *Taking Liberties: A Third Way Special on the Attack on Civil Liberties in the UK*. Pamphlet.

Copsey, N., 2004. *Contemporary British Fascism: The British National Party and the Quest for Legitimacy*. Basingstoke: Palgrave Macmillan.

True Finns Party

The True Finns Party (*Perussuomalaiset*) was founded by Veikko Vennamo in 1995 as a successor to the Finnish Rural Party. Vennamo had made his name in the Agrarian League and the Rural Party before this. The Rural Party had actually taken part in government coalitions, but was generally dismissed as a protest party without charismatic leadership.

Today, the True Finns Party is proud of its doctrine: 'The ideals to which the True Finns subscribe require that all members of our society have the right to a life of human dignity. Every citizen is equally unique and valuable. No one has been born into this life in vain; we are all needed. Each and every one of us is entitled in our home country to housing, health care, work and security; these things are self-evident, but will they still be in the near future? The True Finns are willing to cooperate across party boundaries to enable the above-mentioned goals to be achieved. We are an independent, nationally minded party that presents an alternative, and serves as a counterweight to non-criticism of the EU. Standing on a foundation of Christian-social values, we have the courage to point out shortcomings and prompt a social discourse on them in plain Finnish'.

The party sees itself as an alternative voice in Finnish politics, particularly in its nationalism and anti-EU attitudes. As current party leader Timo **Soini** said recently: 'We need to escape from the heart of darkness in Brussels and stop licking the EU's boots'.

In a populist vein, the party says that it is in favour of equal regional development for Finland, a clean and first-rate Finnish food industry; increased pensions, child benefit allowances; enhanced **education** services and geriatric care; an equal distribution of welfare, common sense policy-making; sufficient resources for police, customs and border guard services; strong action against criminality and drugs; justice and security for everyone; referenda on important matters; inheritance tax reform; a belief in entrepreneurship and honest work; a credible national defence; and healthy families.

By contrast, it says that it 'works against': moves towards a federal EU, uncontrollable **immigration**; golden handshakes; reductions in services; the misuse of social benefits; the 'grey **economy**'; and the 'current forced status' of the Swedish language in Finland. But, it has to be said, it is easy for a small party, on the fringes of the political scene, to make grandiose statements such as these, with there being so little possibility of it ever coming to power.

The number of parliamentary seats held by the party has risen from one to five since 1999, and its share of the popular vote is up from 1 percent to 4.1 percent. Soini scored 3.4 percent in the 2006 presidential elections, finishing fifth out of eight candidates, and outscoring Ilkka Hakalehto (1 percent) in 2000. Interestingly, the party has performed less well in local and European elections, never breaking through the 1 percent barrier since 1996.

The party's five MPs are Raimo Vistbacka (chair of the parliamentary group), Timo Soini (vice-chair), Pentti Oinonen, Pirkko Ruohonen-Lerner and Pertti Virtanen.

See also Scandinavia and the Far Right *and* Soini, Timo (Finland).

Further Reading

http://www.perussuomalaiset.fi/true_finns.html (True Finns website).
Andersen, J.G. & Bjørklund, T. 2000. 'Radical right-wing populism in Scandinavia: from tax revolt to neo-liberalism and xenophobia'. In *The Politics of the Extreme Right: From the Margins to the Mainstream*. Edited by Paul Hainsworth. London: Pinter.

Tschokin, Georgy – Ukraine

Georgy Tschokin is leader of the far-right **Ukrainian Conservative Party** and rector of MAUP, the country's largest private university. He has many friends and contacts in the world of far-right politics and has become renowned for his hard-line anti-Semitic and anti-Zionist rhetoric.

MAUP – the Interregional Academy of Personnel Management – came under attack from the Anti-Defamation League (ADL) because of its highly politicised and anti-Semitic positions. In particular, Tschokin's establishment was censored for demanding that students subscribe to its two extremist newspapers, *Personnel* and *Personnel Plus*. It is not surprising, therefore, that MAUP has recently been nicknamed 'Ukraine's University of Hate'.

In the end, the ADL applauded the decision of the Ukrainian **Education** Ministry to close down seven of the university's regional campuses. In a letter to the Ukrainian education minister, the ADL stated: 'We applaud your courageous stand. A blow against MAUP and its xenophobic leadership is a move toward tolerance and **democracy** in Ukraine. We urge you to continue your bold efforts in order to ensure that MAUP is no longer able to spread its poisonous propaganda in the guise of education'. In some respects the university had a good name and hired some outstanding academics, but it sullied its reputation by employing individuals such as David Duke – the American white supremacist – who also gained his doctorate there.

Tschokin, Georgy

Tschokin is renowned for his anti-Semitic views and recently issued a statement of solidarity with Iranian President Ahmadinejad, who had threatened to delete Israel from the map of the world. Tschokin said: 'We'd like to remind you that the Living God Jesus Christ said to Jews two thousand years ago: "Your father is a devil!" … Israel, as known, means "Theologian", and Zionism in 1975 was acknowledged by the General Assembly of the UNO as the form of racism and race discrimination, that, in the opinion of the absolute majority of modern Europeans, is the biggest threat to modern civilisation. Israel is an artificially created state (classic totalitarian type) which appeared on the political Earth map only in 1948, thanks to the goodwill of the UNO.'

In March 2006, Tschokin and a number of MAUP colleagues caused controversy when they paid their respects to Andrei Yuschinsky, a young Christian boy whose death in 1911 has been ascribed – by them – to Jewish ritual murder. Tschokin would like the Orthodox Church to canonise Yuschinsky, regardless of the fact that Mendel Beilis, the Jew originally convicted of the murder, was also, later, acquitted.

See also Russia and the Far Right *and* Ukrainian Conservative Party.

Further Reading
http://www.adl.org (Anti-Defamation League).
Cox, M. & Shearman, P. 2000. 'After the fall: nationalist extremism in post-communist Russia'. In *The Politics of the Extreme Right: From the Margins to the Mainstream*. Edited by Paul Hainsworth. London: Pinter.

Tuđman, Dr Franjo (1922–1999) - Croatia

Dr Franjo Tuđman came to personify the hard-line ultra-nationalism that eventually gained Croatia its independence in 1990 and propelled it forcibly into the various Balkan wars of the 1990s. These conflicts were complex and complicated, but there is no doubt that, throughout, Tuđman's standpoint was the product of a powerful and extreme nationalism, which could easily be interpreted in far-right or neo-fascist terms.

What is interesting about Tuđman is his background and the distance he has travelled, in ideological terms, since his formative years. He was a military man by trade and, later, a historian. As a teenager, he fought on the Partisan side against the Nazi occupiers during World War II; and as an adult, he got sucked into the institutionalised communist system that was the hallmark of the Yugoslavian state.

But underneath, there was always a fanatical Croat nationalist trying to make his voice heard. He was expelled from the University of Zagreb in 1967 because of his ultra-nationalist outbursts; he also left the pan-Yugoslav League of Communists after objecting to the literary amalgamation of Croat and Serb languages. For his *travails*, he served two prison sentences – a significant badge of honour for the would-be saviour of the Croatian nation. In power, after 1990, Tuđman was quick to adopt the checkered red and white insignia of the Ustashe – the pro-Nazi Croat collaborators who murdered hundreds of thousands of Jews and Serbs. This was a highly provocative move that, at a stroke, aligned him with the nationalist and fascist tradition in Croatia's history.

After the Fall of the **Berlin Wall** in 1989 and the collapse of **Communism in Eastern Europe**, the state of Yugoslavia was living on borrowed time. Tuđman and his ultra-nationalist movement, the HDZ, were ready and waiting. He was elected president of the new Croatia in 1990, and his party claimed almost two-thirds of seats in the national parliament.

The following years were dominated by the conflict with Serbia and the war in Bosnia. For Tuđman, this was the perfect opportunity to display, in quite ostentatious fashion, his extreme brand of nationalism. For example, in 1995, on the liberation of Knin from Serbian control, he stated: 'Croatian **women** and men, dear Croatian **youth**, Croatian soldiers, dear citizens of Knin … Usually participants in historical events are not aware of the importance of the events which they take part in. What we have done today … is the laying of the foundations for an independent and sovereign Croatian state … Knin was not just the capital of Croatian king Zvonimir, Knin was the capital of the kingdom of Croatia at the time when we did not have our own rulers from our own blood until 1522 … And there can be no return to the past, to the times when they, the Serbs, were spreading cancer in the heart of Croatia'.

This passage reveals much about Tuđman's nationalism: it was rooted in a deep and extremely Croat-centred reading of history, became dominated by an 'us' and 'them' view of the Serbs, and was both rousing and highly jingoistic. In many ways his warmongering ideology was as unpleasant and dangerous as that of the much vilified Serb leader Slobodan **Milošević**. But, somehow, Tuđman was able to persuade Western governments that he was the 'good guy' in the Balkans and was determined to create a liberal **democracy** at home. He was also able to call on the support of many Croatian exiles in Australia, Canada and the US.

In truth, and on reflection, there was little to differentiate the bellicose brands of nationalism embodied by Tuđman and Milošević. This point is brought into sharper focus by the accusation (aimed at both men) that, besides being sworn ideological enemies in the Balkans, they were also engaging in *realpolitik* of the highest order by secretly engineering the future of the Balkans.

There was much mourning in Croatia when Tuđman died in 1999. He was acknowledged by all Croatians as the father of the new independent state – the man who had made it all possible. However, to neutral observers, it was clear that, as time went on, he became more and more illiberal and autocratic. There was a façade of liberalism and democracy, but, at bottom, it was as if he was trying to reconstitute the pro-Nazi Independent State of Croatia fifty years on. Tuđman was vindictively anti-Serb and anti-Semitic, and in his book, *Horrors of War*, he massively underestimated the amount of Serbian and Jewish casualties of the wartime Ustashe regime. For all these reasons, he can be categorised as a man of the ultra-nationalist Far Right.

See also Croatian Democratic Union *and Horrors of War* by Franjo Tuđman (Croatia).

Further Reading
http://www.hdz.hr (HDZ website).
Tanner, Marcus. 1997. *Croatia: A Nation Forged in War*. New Haven, CT: Yale University Press.

Tudor, Corneliu Vadim (b.1949) – Romania

Corneliu Vadim Tudor is leader of the **Greater Romania Party** (*Partidul România Mare*). In recent years, he has become the main personality on the Romanian Far Right, articulating an irredentist brand of nationalism which – as the name of his party implies – yearns for an expanded Romanian nation, to include Moldova and even parts of Hungary.

Known colloquially as 'Vadim', he has a degree in philosophy, some military training, and a background in political journalism. He has also experimented as a writer, authoring both poetry and plays. He toed the line during the communist era, and his political career only really started to develop after the fall of the **Berlin Wall** in 1989. He helped to found the nationalist journal *România Mare* (Greater Romania) in 1990, and in 1991 the political movement he leads today.

Thereafter, he has had varied fortunes. He has served as a Romanian senator since 1992 and threw in his lot with the left-wing coalition that governed the country between 1993 and 1996. In electoral terms, he has had his moments – scoring 28 percent in the 2000 presidential elections and 11 percent in 2004 – but he has never been able to rid himself of the reputation for being unpredictable and untrustworthy. That said, some of his electoral performances have impressed commentators – so much so that he has been nicknamed the 'Jean-Marie **Le Pen** of the Carpathians.'

Tudor's ideology is a rag-bag of populist concerns, mixing **anti-Semitism**, racism and pro-communist nostalgia. He is also anti-Hungarian, anti-gypsy and anti-homosexual. His ideas have evolved over time. He switched from national **Communism** to ultra-nationalism in 1996, and in recent years he has tried to moderate his language, most notably by retracting a controversial statement that inferred that the **Holocaust** had not taken place in Romania. He said: 'I know that I was wrong to have denied the Holocaust in Romania, which happened between 1941 and 1944 under Antonescu's regime'. So eager was he to repair relations with Israel and the Jewish community that he made a great play of his desire to hire Israeli Eyal Arad (Ariel Sharon's former campaign adviser) as his PR assistant. Many commentators were not convinced by his sudden change of heart.

See also Greater Romania Party; Romania, Far Right Enters Coalition Government (1994) *and* South-Eastern Europe and the Far Right.

Further Reading

Shafir, M. 2000. 'Marginalization or mainstream? The extreme right in post-communist Romania'. In *The Politics of the Extreme Right: From the Margins to the Mainstream*. Edited by Paul Hainsworth. London: Pinter.

Türkeş, Alparslan (1917–1997) – Turkey

Alparslan Türkeş was an ultra-nationalist leader who became a significant player in Turkish politics during the second half of the twentieth century. He was not simply a major personality on the Far Right; uniquely, he also straddled the worlds of military and civilian life. Many on the left would label him a Fascist and racist.

The name he was born with is the subject of mystery. Some claim his original name was Hüseyin Feyzullah, while others say he was born Ali Arslan. So, Alparslan Türkeş is, in reality, a *nom de guerre*, taken as his official name after 1934. To add to the confusion, he had a nickname among his followers – *Başbuğ* (*Führer*) – while his closest friends called him *Albay* (Colonel).

As a graduate of Kuleli, the military academy where Mustafa Kemal Ataturk also studied, Türkeş was always destined for a career in the army. But he also metamorphosed into a civilian politician. He joined the Republican Peasants Nation Party and in 1969 helped to found the MHP (National Action Party), which quickly became a vehicle for ultra-rightist activity. It stood for nine main principles: nationalism, idealism, moralism, societalism, scientism, independentism, ruralism, progressivism/populism, and industrialism/technologism. It also became notorious for its virulent anti-Kurdish and anti-Armenian rhetoric. Its **youth** movement came to be known as the Grey Wolves.

At the heart of Türkeş' personal ideology was a virulent pro-Turkish nationalism. He tapped into what was known as the 'Turanist' myth – which stated that the Turks were descended from a heroic race whose forefathers came from Central Asia. He was particularly harsh on the Kurds: he portrayed them as trouble-making separatists and then, in highly provocative fashion, went on to argue that they were, anyhow, descended from the Turks.

Over the course of his lifetime, he was involved in a number of key political events. He took part in the coup that brought down the government of Adnan Menderes in 1960, and in 1965 he published a pamphlet entitled *Dokuz Işık Doktrini*, which articulated the 'Nine Lights' doctrine of Turkish ultra-nationalists. In the 1970s, he was also implicated in a variety of political assassinations. He and a number of political associates were charged with instigating civil war in 1980, and after killing nearly 600 people after another coup attempt, the MHP was banned and Türkeş was given a prison sentence, although he was later released on medical grounds and pardoned.

Türkeş served as deputy prime minister in a number of right-wing cabinets. His political enemies included leftists, trade unionists and student leaders, all of whom were pointed in their criticisms of him: he was viewed as a racist and a Fascist, someone who believed in the superiority of Turks and Turkishness above everything else; he had little time for **democracy**; and it was also alleged that he accepted American support in the 1970s. He always existed on the fringes. Despite this – or probably because of this – he remains an icon for modern Turkish nationalists.

See also Nationalist Action Party (Turkey).

Further Reading
http://www.mhp.org.tr (MHP website).
Wilkinson, Paul. 1983. *The New Fascists*. London: Pan.

U

Ukrainian Conservative Party

Georgy **Tschokin**'s Ukrainian Conservative Party was formed in March 2005. But its name is something of a misnomer because it promulgates a vicious brand of ultra-nationalism and **anti-Semitism**.

Tschokin is not only leader of the movement, but also rector of MAUP, the country's largest private university. MAUP – the Interregional Academy of Personnel Management – has attracted widespread criticism because of its politicisation and anti-Semitic dogma. Likewise the Conservative Party has been allowed to compete in national polls by the Ukrainian Central Election Committee – much to the disgust of Jewish groups.

Ukrainian Conservative Party

The party does not attempt to disguise its anti-Semitism. Members of the party recently wrote to the Ukrainian president, Viktor Yushchenko, requesting that, 'Jews be prevented from teaching the Tanya in Jewish schools and synagogues, so as to stop the spread of this misanthropic religious system'. There is, in fact, a significant overlap in personnel and ideas between the party and MAUP.

See also Russia and the Far Right *and* Tschokin, Georgy (Ukraine).

Further Reading
http://www.adl.org (Anti-Defamation League).
Cox, M. & Shearman, P. 2000. 'After the fall: nationalist extremism in post-communist Russia'. In *The Politics of the Extreme Right: From the Margins to the Mainstream*. Edited by Paul Hainsworth. London: Pinter.

United National Workers Party (Lithuania)

The United National Workers Party was formed by Mindaugas **Murza** in Lithuania in April 2005. Its aim was to attract 3 percent of the national vote and to work hard at gaining a constituency at municipal level. In terms of ideology, it has railed against globalisation and Zionism. Murza has called the Jews, 'the most cruel and crafty enemy of the European race and of all humanity and the total inciter of war,' and gone on to say that, 'world Jewry will be thrown onto the dust heap of history'. Because of such rhetoric, the party leader has been accused of **anti-Semitism** and preaching hatred. Critics label the movement national-socialist and say that other parties and politicians should be wary of negotiating or liaising with it in any way.

See also Murza, Mindaugas (Lithuania).

Further Reading
http://www.tau.ac.il/Anti-Semitism/asw2005/baltics.htm (Stephen Roth Institute).
Smith, David J., Purs, A., Pabriks, A. & Lane, T. 2002. *The Baltic States: Estonia, Latvia and Lithuania*. London and New York: Routledge.

V

Violence

Whatever far-right parties might say about their respect for **democracy** and peaceful political strategies, in the wider public imagination many commentators remain convinced that there are strong links between the far-right and political violence. This sort of belligerent political culture is perhaps more typical of the neo-Nazi groups rather than the various populist, far-right parties that have enjoyed electoral success in recent years. Indeed, many within the Far Right before actively engaged with the democratic process have attempted to convey a more moderate, responsible profile in order to appear more electable. Therefore, the Far Right's relationship to violence contains a tension between an older association with interwar Fascism and

the memories of paramilitary politics, and newer far-right parties that are trying
to transcend such stereotyping. Nevertheless, some politicians who have chosen the
democratic road have also generated headlines for the wrong reasons. For decades,
Jean-Marie **Le Pen** in France has been dogged by accusations that he engaged in
torture tactics during the **Algerian War**. In a different context, he was also convicted
of assault in 1998 for throwing punches at a left-wing opponent during an election
campaign.

One of the worst acts of far-right violence in the post-war period was the **Bologna
Massacre**. Writing in 1981, Thomas Sheehan of the *New York Review of Books*
presented this attack as but one of a series of violent acts by neo-fascist terrorists.
Consequently, Sheehan also highlighted that on 26 September 1980, Gundolf Koehler
attempted to put a bomb at the entrance to Munich's famous Oktoberfest, and that a
bomb planted by a far-right activist exploded a week later in Paris. The latter explosion
occurred in front of a synagogue attended by Jews attending Sabbath services. This
sort of terrorist campaign was typical of how the Far Right of the period generated
public fears of terrorist attacks. It represented an emerging, coordinated campaign,
according to Sheehan. Indeed, with hindsight, he viewed these atrocities as the tip of
the iceberg. They were examples of the worst type of neo-fascist terrorism and violence.
But there were other groups too that believed in armed insurrection. Sheehan stressed
that the most extreme of these organisations consisted of 'assault groups like Honneur
de la Police, Delta, Pieper and Odessa, responsible for over one hundred terrorist
attacks in 1980 and at least three murders'. In short, the Far Right of this period
seemed to be increasing its aggressive tactics.

In the context of far-right violence, the term extreme, as in extreme-right, relates
to tactics and strategy as well as political ideas and ideology. Especially in Germany,
neo-Nazi violence was endemic in the 1980s. Christopher Husbands has offered the
following breakdown: there were 4,318 punishable offences with extreme right-wing
features between 1981 and 1983 and in 1985; 1,738 far-right extremists convicted of
punishable offences between 1977 and 1986; and 268 right-wing extremists involved
in various acts of planned or actual violence up to 1985. More troubling, in 2006 *Der
Spiegel* analysed a new set of official figures. These argued that in 2005 there were 985
racially motivated acts of violence, an increase of 23 percent over the previous year.
Further, there was a rise in the number which involved bodily harm. These figures also
estimated that the number of far-right supporters who considered themselves willing
to use violence has risen to 10,400. Finally, although cases of murder and arson were
down, the total number of far-right crimes was up a staggering 27 percent, a total of
15,361 cases. Many of these were related to the public display of swastikas and similar
imagery, an offence in Germany. The magazine was fearful that the statistics would
not paint a healthy picture of German society at a time when the country was getting
ready to host the football World Cup. Clearly, then, the issue of far-right violence has
not gone away among some sections of the Far Right.

In Britain too, there have been violent actions. The riots in **Oldham** and other
northern towns in the summer of 2001 were a significant development and were
egged on by the far right. But perhaps the most notorious examples of the Far Right's
continued propensity for violence was the nail-bombing campaign that David Copeland
inflicted on London in April 1999. Following two attacks in Brixton and Brick Lane
designed to hit Britain's black and Asian communities respectively, his final bomb
claimed the lives of three people. His target was the Admiral Duncan pub in Soho, which

served a predominantly gay clientele. Copeland had floated through a series of far-right organisations, such as the **British National Party** (BNP), and a tiny, Combat 18 (C18) offshoot, the National Socialist Movement (NSM). Typical of racially motivated violence, when asked by police why he carried out the attacks, he replied: 'Because I don't like them, I want them out of this country, I'm a national socialist, Nazi, whatever you want to call me, I believe in the master race'. Meanwhile, looking through the website of C18 and Redwatch.org, it is not difficult to get a sense of the genuine belligerence and para-militarism still abroad among sectors of the European Far Right.

However, in the early **twenty-first century**, with democracy well entrenched in most European countries, the actions of Copeland and others appears to be an anachronism even within the European Far Right. Indeed, for many parties there now seems little to be gained from straying from the increasingly-dominant, non-violent path that has characterised the successes of the Far Right in recent years. The ideology, then, had to choose between electoral politics and violence as a means to further its goals, and for the most part it has chosen to follow the path of electoral politics.

See also Bologna Bombing (1980) *and* The Ideology of the Far Right.

Further Reading

Ignazi, Piero. 2003. *Extreme Right Parties in Western Europe*. New York: Oxford University Press.
Laqueur, Walter. 2003. *No End to War: Terrorism in the Twenty-First Century*. New York: Continuum.
Sheehan, Thomas. 1981. 'Italy: Terror on the Right', *The New York Review of Books* 27..21 and 22, http://www.nybooks.com/articles/7178 (cited 31 December 2007).

Voridis, Makis (b.1964) – Greece

Makis Voridis has been the most prominent voice on the contemporary Greek Far Right. His party – the Hellenic Front – was never a major force in Greek politics and existed for only eleven years between 1994 and 2005. Nevertheless, Voridis articulated an ultra-nationalist discourse that was significant in terms of the themes it developed and the support it engendered from other European nationalist movements.

Voridis has a background in law and carried out his national military service in 1992 and 1993. He was particularly successful in the army, graduating as a class leader and serving as an artillery cadet reserve officer and second lieutenant. When he graduated from the military he went straight into politics. He founded the Hellenic Front in 1994 and became its first president. The Front described itself as a patriotic party and became politically active in 1998. It announced that its *raison d'être* was to 'build a National Opposition Front, reverse the policy of national servitude and compliance to the orders of foreign interests and, at the same time, propose a modern way which, securing National Sovereignty, leads to **Freedom**, Creativity and Development'.

In electoral terms, the Front had little success. Voridis failed in his bid to become mayor of Athens in 1998 and 2002. In 1998 the party scored 0.58 percent in local elections, in 1999, 0.12 percent in the European poll, and in the 2000 and 2004 general elections, 0.18 percent and 0.09 percent respectively. Only in 2002 at the local elections did the party pass the 1 percent barrier: across five districts it scored 1.4 percent (0.9 percent in Athens with Makis Voridis, 1.2 percent in Peiraeus courtesy of Christos Charitos, 1.2 percent in Thessalonica with Yannis Kouriannidis, 4.5 percent in

Karditsa thanks to Kostas Kardaras and 2.2 percent in Eastern Attica with Miltiades Kremmydas). Not surprisingly perhaps, the Front disappeared from view in 2005, merging into the Popular Orthodox Rally (LAOS) party. But Voridis is still active as a member of the LAOS political council and in 2006 was elected as a municipal councillor after winning 5 percent of the vote in East Attica.

Throughout, Voridis has become renowned for his xenophobia and his views on **immigration** and race. He is against Turkish membership of the EU and is hostile to the 'takeover' of Greece by illegal immigrants. In 2005 he wrote: 'The problem of illegal immigration in Greece is not a question of principles or ideology, but a policy issue, if we assume that there exists a structured national state. If there is a state, then there are borders too ... And if there exists a state, then the legal distinction between a native and an alien is absolutely legitimate and founded on our Constitution. Therefore any legal and legitimate policy exercised within the boundaries of the Greek State should aim at the service of the short, medium and long-term interests of the Greek people'. In recent years Voridis has fostered good relations with other far-right groups around **Europe** including the FN in France and the Greater Romanian Party.

See also Greek Front *and* Meligalas (Greece).

Further Reading

http://www.e-grammes.gr/index_en.html (Hellenic Front website).

Dimitras, P.E. 1994. 'Greece: the virtual absence of an extreme right'. In *The Extreme Right in Europe and the USA*. Edited by Paul Hainsworth. London: Pinter.

Kapetanyannis, V. 1991. 'Neo-Fascism in modern Greece'. In *Neo-Fascism in Europe*. Edited by Luciano Cheles, Ronnie Ferguson and Michalina Vaughan. London: Longman.

Featherstone, K. (ed.). 2005. *Politics and Policy in Greece*. London: Routledge.

Close, D.H. 2002. *Greece Since 1945: A History*. London: Longman.

W

Waldheim, Austrian President (1986–1992)

After serving as United Nations Secretary-General between 1972 and 1981, Austrian politician Kurt Waldheim turned his attention to domestic politics. On 4 May 1986, he stood for the presidency of Austria and outpolled his opponent Kurt Steyrer by 49.7 to 43.7 percent. In the run-off between the two leading candidates, staged on 8 June 1986, he claimed 54 percent of the vote.

The only problem for Waldheim was that, prior to the first election, it emerged that he had lied about his war record. It transpired that he had been an officer in the German Army during World War II, and also that his unit had committed atrocities in Yugoslavia. However, Waldheim himself denied any involvement in, or even knowledge of, such events. Further, in 1986 he sought to pre-empt even more controversy by appointing an international commission of historians to look into his wartime record. The commission took two years to report, and in the end it cleared him of committing any specific crime. On one level, this placated the Austrian population at large, but on another level the report, and the reaction to it, demonstrated that there was no widespread affection for Waldheim in Austria. As rumours persisted, his presidency from 1986 until 1992 was dogged by gossip and innuendo to the effect that he must have known more about the Yugoslavian events than he was admitting to. Except in partisan political and intellectual circles, there was no overwhelming demand for his resignation. On the other hand, everyone seemed to agree that a second term of office for Waldheim would probably not be desirable. It was no surprise, then, that Waldheim decided not to run for office again in 1992. If Waldheim's wartime record had come to light in the early 1970s, he would probably have been disqualified from serving as UN Secretary-General. However, despite the revelations, throughout his time at the UN and as Austrian president, Waldheim maintained friends in high places – Pope John Paul II perhaps being the most notable. The Pontiff was a personal friend and honoured Waldheim with the Knighthood of the Order of Pius 'for outstanding service as Secretary General of the United Nations'.

Waldheim came to personify a newfound deeper interest in Austria's wartime history. Indeed, with the benefit of hindsight, it is clear that the Waldheim affair and the subsequent saga of **Haider** and the rise of the **Austrian Freedom Party** (*Freiheitliche Partei Österreichs*, FPÖ) have much in common. Both have involved high-profile Austrian politicians revealing 'Nazi links' that have helped to open up debate on Austria's record in World War II. The country was often portrayed one-dimensionally as a victim of the Nazi regime, yet Waldheim's story opened up the opportunity to take a closer look and to question the historical record. In effect, the scandal forced Austria to do some serious soul-searching. Of course, this led to new stereotypes, with Austrians being equated to ex-Nazis or 'Nazi-lovers', or both, in the popular imagination. Austria has even suffered periods of international isolation as a result of Waldheim. For example, in April 1987, the US placed Waldheim on its watch list of undesirable aliens. Similarly, following Jörg **Haider**'s rise to power and international notoriety, the EU began a diplomatic boycott of Austria because of Haider's growing influence, and one can detect interesting similarities and continuities. The Waldheim affair, then, was significant not only because of the stature of Waldheim as a single, high-ranking politician, but also because it refracted a wider concern with the Austrian past.

See also Austrian Freedom Party; Central Europe and the Far Right *and* Waldheim, Kurt (Austria).

Further Reading

Saltman, Jack. 1988. *Kurt Waldheim: A Case to Answer?* London: Robson (in association with Channel Four Television Company).

International Commission of Historians. 1993. *The Waldheim Report.* Copenhagen: Museum Tusculanum Press, University of Copenhagen.

Waldheim, Kurt (b.1918) – Austria

Austrian statesman Kurt Waldheim gained notoriety in the 1980s when allegations were made about his Nazi past. He was tainted by the controversy and his career as a politician and diplomat was effectively ended. In broader terms, the 'Waldheim Affair' was interpreted as another example of Austria's Nazi past embarrassingly resurfacing; and with the rise of Jörg **Haider** – who admitted to admiration for some of Hitler's employment policies – the perception of Austria as a country with a strong far-right tradition gained even further ground.

Waldheim served as a German military officer during World War II. After the conflict, he returned to finish his studies in law at the University of Vienna, and in 1945 he began an illustrious career in the Austrian diplomatic service. Between 1948 and 1951, he was First Secretary of the Legation in Paris, worked in the Ministry for Foreign Affairs in Vienna from 1951 to 1956 and 1960 to 1964 and was Ambassador to Canada from 1956 to 1960. In 1964, he was appointed as the Permanent Representative of Austria to the United Nations and, after serving as the Federal Minister for Foreign Affairs in Austria from 1968 to 1970, became Secretary General of the UN in 1971. This appointment followed defeat in his first attempt to become the Austrian president in the same year. He was re-elected Secretary General of the UN in 1976, but was denied a third term in office when China blocked his candidacy in 1981.

Upon his return to Austrian politics in the 1980s, Waldheim became linked to the Far Right. He was successful in his second attempt to become president of Austria in 1981. However, this marked the beginning of what became known as the 'Waldheim Affair', as it came to light that he had failed to disclose a number of important details relating to his activities before and during the war.

Waldheim had been an officer in the SA-Reitercorps (Stormtroopers – Cavalrycorps), a paramilitary unit of the NSDAP before the war. He had also returned to service after recuperating from wounds, which he previously claimed had ended his time in the Wehrmacht, to serve as an intelligence officer in Germany's Army Group E. This unit committed mass murders in Kozara region of western Bosnia and Waldheim's name was found on the Wehrmacht's 'honour list' of those responsible for the atrocity. Later, in 1944, he was responsible for approving anti-Semitic propaganda leaflets, which were to be dropped behind Soviet lines, and included the message: 'Enough of the Jewish war, kill the Jews, come over.' Finally, it was revealed that he had in fact been wanted by the War Crimes Commission of the United Nations, the very organisation he would later head.

As a result of the revelations, Waldheim and his wife Elizabeth were shunned by the international community. He was placed on the United States watch list in 1987 and barred from entering the country. During his six-year term in office, he made virtually no state visits, other than to the Vatican City and some near-eastern states. The Austrian government appointed an international committee of historians to investigate the claims. They found that, while there was no evidence of his direct involvement in war crimes, he was 'excellently informed' of atrocities committed by German army units in Greece and Yugoslavia and made no attempt to stop them. A United States Justice Department report also found that, as a German military intelligence officer, Waldheim would have drafted orders on reprisals, made recommendations based on the interrogation of prisoners, and provided intelligence data to military units arresting civilians for deportation or final disposition. In 1988, accusations of his involvement in war crimes surfaced again when the Ministry of Defence claimed that he had taken part in the murder of British servicemen captured in Greece.

In February 1988, Waldheim spoke to a Vienna daily newspaper about his actions during the war and the findings of the Austrian Government report. He referred indirectly to his knowledge of the atrocities carried out by fellow German soldiers by stating: 'Yes, I admit I wanted to survive [by following orders] … I have the deepest respect for all those who resisted. But I ask understanding for all the hundreds of thousands who didn't do that, but nonetheless did not become personally guilty'.

See also Central Europe and the Far Right; Haider, Jörg (Austria) *and* Waldheim, Austrian President (1986–1992).

Further Reading
Waldheim, K. 1986. *In the Eye of the Storm: A Memoir*. London: Adler & Adler.
Morrow, D. 2000. 'Jörg Haider and the new FPÖ: beyond the democratic pale'. In *The Politics of the Extreme Right: From the Margins to the Mainstream*. Edited by Paul Hainsworth. London: Pinter.

'War on Terrorism'

The various wars against Muslim-dominated countries, such as the Gulf War of 1991 and the continuing conflicts in Afghanistan and Iraq, alongside the idea of the 'War on Terrorism', have given far-right parties in **Europe** the opportunity to put forward a range of views on world affairs. This has involved critical stances regarding the policies of the US and the UK, especially the personalities of George W. Bush and Tony Blair, as well as capitalising on a growing trend to see world affairs through the lens of a clash of civilisations. Indeed, given the high profile nature of this cluster of issues, it is not surprising that the Far Right has been able to build on this theme for its own politicking.

Regarding the First Gulf War, in 1991 Jean-Marie **Le Pen** controversially backed Iraq and Saddam Hussein in their attempt to take over Kuwait. Le Pen's argument was that Kuwait was not a natural country, but that an enlarged Iraq that also contained Kuwait would become such a natural entity. This pro-Saddam position was shared by Vladimir **Zhirinovsky** in **Russia**. A long-time friend of Saddam, Zhirinovsky talked about the democratic process in Iraq, and actually sent a military force called the 'Falcons of Zhirinovsky' to support the Iraqi president during the first Gulf War.

Following on from the 9/11 attacks on the World Trade Center and the Pentagon, we see that subsequent world events were not regarded in terms of material ideas, such as territorial aggrandisement, by western political leaders. Most significantly, the more recent prolonged conflicts in Afghanistan and Iraq, both fought by a US-led coalition of states against largely irregular Muslim forces, are seen as battles against al-Qaeda. The US-led coalition, then, believed that it is fighting a fundamentally new type of enemy: Islamic terrorism. The terrorist atrocities of 9/11 had a multitude of far-reaching consequences for the presidency of George W. Bush. For him, US national interests were best served by bringing regime change to Afghanistan and Iraq. The effects of this policy have shaped public perceptions of Islam not only in America, but around the world. In Europe, the 9/11 terrorist strikes have also had significant consequences for the continent's politics and culture. If we are to sum up the effect of this interrelated cluster of events on the Far Right in Europe, the primary consequence has been that 9/11 and the 'War on Terrorism' intensified the feelings and attitudes of Islamophobia among far-right movements and activists, and created a more receptive marketplace for such views.

Subsequent terrorist attacks by Islamists in Europe have been fuelling this growing fear of an Islamic 'other'. The most devastating of these terrorist attacks has been the Madrid bombing, which occurred on 11 March 2004. This attack killed 191 people, and led to the injury of many more. The Madrid bombing also generated new fears that the actions of Islamist terrorists could create an increased climate of fear and discrimination for Spain's Muslim population. In 2005, the Islamist attacks reached the streets of London with the 7/7 bombings. This strike killed a further fifty-two commuters. Subsequently, Glasgow International Airport was also subject to an Islamist attack, though this was more farcical than successful in the public imagination.

Meanwhile, across Europe, news reports highlight that police and intelligence services have uncovered further Islamist plots, sometimes leading to high-profile trials.

Unsurprisingly, as elsewhere, the Far Right in Britain was quick to exploit the 7/7 atrocity. One example of this came when the **British National Party** (BNP) used a notorious photo of a bombed London bus in one of its publicity leaflets. The accompanying message was: 'Maybe now it's time to start listening to the BNP'. The then Home Secretary, Charles Clarke, criticised the tactics, and said that the BNP 'have tried to cynically exploit the current tragic events in London to further their spread of hatred', while Bob Neill, the leader of the Conservatives in London, labelled it as 'disgraceful and sick [...] as contemptible an election tactic as I have ever seen in my life.' However, the BNP were unrepentant. The party's leader, Nick **Griffin**, claimed that, although an emotive, graphic image, the tactic was an attempt to summarise the failure of New Labour. Griffin claimed that it was the Labour administration that was ultimately to blame for the attacks, not the terrorists themselves. This was because the government had taken Britain into an illegal war in Iraq, resulting in the country becoming a target for terrorists. Further, the Labour government had neglected to police national borders effectively, thereby allowing an uncontrolled flow of potential extremists to enter the country, swamping police efforts to curb the problem of violent Islamism. Also, the government had failed to restrict Islamists preaching in Britain's mosques, according to Griffin. Elsewhere, party literature proclaimed that the BNP was the only political organisation genuinely opposed to the Islamification of British society, protecting its traditions and national identity. Revealing the organisation's ideological stance, which argues that Islam is alien to pure British culture, he went on to argue that the BNP was not opposed to Islam *per se*, but rather respected followers of Islam who practice the **religion**, though only 'in their own country'. It also stated that the BNP was opposed to American imperialism, Zionist lobbies and Britain's status as the puppet of the US in the 'War on Terror'.

A somewhat different tactic was deployed by Jean-Marie **Le Pen** on this issue. In the 2007 presidential campaign, he created a minor international stir by describing the 9/11 attacks as an 'incident'. In a bid to contrast 9/11 with the war in Iraq, he observed that more people were killed in Iraq every month than had been killed in the World Trade Center attacks, thereby implying 9/11 was less significant than many commentators have suggested. Le Pen went on to stress that an even greater number had died in the bombing of Dresden during World War II. Such controversial rhetoric echoed his previous attempts to minimise the **Holocaust** by describing it as a 'detail' of history. Similarly, ahead of the war in Iraq, the Anti-Defamation League (ADL) detailed how Jörg **Haider** backed Saddam Hussein in the face of growing international pressure on the regime, especially by the US and the UK governments. Such support allowed Haider to take a stance that was both anti-American and anti-Israeli – two points that would go down well with his supporters. As with Le Pen's comments, such a controversial position also allowed Haider to appear more significant on the international stage than his status of Governor of **Carinthia** actually merits.

The 'War on Terrorism', then, has seen a growth in the actual danger of Islamist terrorism. It has also seen the Far Right develop its own positions on the issue. It would be too simplistic to simply state that the Far Right rejects all Muslim politics; Le Pen and Haider demonstrate this is not the case. Rather, as with many other issues, the Far Right has been able to make political gains by suggesting that governments are incapable of dealing with the problem, and what is needed is a more hard-line stance, as provided by far-right parties. This has also seen parties such as the BNP draw on the issue to again assert that Islam is alien to a pure national identity in Europe.

See also Immigration and Islam and the Far Right.

Further Reading

Anti-Defamation League, 'Joerg Haider and Saddam Hussein: not-so-strange bedfellows', http://www.adl.org/extremism/haider-hussein.asp (cited 31 December 2007).
Laqueur, Walter. 2003. *No End to War: Terrorism in the Twenty-First Century.* New York: Continuum.
Eatwell, Roger & Mudde, Cas, eds. 2004. *Western Democracies and the New Extreme Right Challenge.* London: Routledge.

Women

Over the last century or so there has been a general assumption that fascism and far-right politics are a male preserve. Most leaders have been men, and the style of politics favoured by the Far Right has often been 'macho' and 'confrontational'. Indeed, much research has shown, sometimes by a ratio of 2:1, that it is men rather than women who are more likely to support far-right movements. Furthermore, traditionally the policies put forward by the Far Right have been anything but progressive, and so women have invariably been consigned to the roles of homemaker, housewife and mother. However, recent trends in far-right activities, especially within the neo-populist parties, have helped to confound these stereotypical views. The Far Right is targeting women as a potential source, not only of voters and members, but even leaders.

Many women do not now feel constrained by what society expects, or used to expect, of them. The same is true for women in contact with the Far Right. For example, *The Observer* has reported on one **British National Party** (BNP) activist, Wendy Edwards. She described how, sometimes, she would answer the phone when her BNP-supporting husband was not available to take questions regarding the party. She told the paper that it 'floors people' when they found out they were talking to a determined woman activist, adding that the tendency in the national movement was for women to let their husbands take the lead. Now things were changing, she argued, women were now working and 'fighting' alongside their husbands. Confounding and confirming far-right stereotypes in equal measure, the report also cited the words of Jackie Oakley of the White Nationalist Part (WNP): 'I headbutt, punch and kick just like a man. None of your poncey girly scratching for me; I'm up there with the men, and so are all the other women in the group'. Oakley is also head of the movement's women's section.

Several academics, such as Phyllis Rippeyoung, have tried to rationalise the appeal of the Far Right for women. She has argued that, to date, support for the Far Right in **Europe** has generally been a male phenomenon. Therefore, the reasons why women constitute a significant proportion of their membership has yet to be fully explained. From the minimal qualitative research that currently exists, the promotion of **family** values alongside fear of **violence** are cited as two key reasons for this membership. Male voters, she continues, tend to support far-right parties in terms of economic self-interest combined with a populist hatred of immigrants. However, a different perspective is taken by Amelia Hill, who argues that the traditional association between a hierarchy of races and a hierarchy of gender within far-right ideology has broken down in recent years. According to Hill, this has led to increased opportunities for women to take on more prominent roles within such parties. The Far Right has also embraced this development. Indeed, parties of the Far Right tend to believe that an increasingly female public profile will lead to greater mainstream appeal. Just as far-right politicians like Jörg **Haider** in Austria and Bruno **Mégret** in France started to wear designer suits, and populist movements went online with sophisticated, user friendly websites, modernisation can also be seen in far-right attitudes to gender. The explicit tactics of some parties, such as putting on family-friendly and women-friendly events, have been designed to make the Far Right appear more 'presentable' to the general public.

Further, since 1945, there have been few female far-right leaders, though again, this trend is changing. To give some examples: Siv Jensen is the current leader of the Progress Party in Norway; Susanne Riess-Passer succeeded Jörg Haider as Federal Chairperson of the **Austrian Freedom Party** (*Freiheitliche Partei Österreichs*, FPÖ) and held government office between 2000 and 2002; Pia Kjærsgaard was the co-founder of the **Danish People's Party** (*Dansk Folkeparti*, DPP) in 1995 and is now its leader; Alessandra Mussolini has gained fame and celebrity in far-right circles as the granddaughter of Benito Mussolini, and is currently an MEP; and Marine Le Pen, the daughter of Jean-Marie **Le Pen**, is likely to be the next leader of the FN in France. The advance of women in the neo-populist Far Right, then, has been a significant shift in far-right politics. However, the Far Right remains a force dominated by male activists and ideologues, and tends to be supported by male voters.

See also Family, Homosexuality *and* The Ideology of the Far Right.

Further Reading

Glennerster, Howard and Midgley, James, eds. 1991. *The Radical Right and the Welfare State: an International Assessment*. London: Harvester Wheatsheaf.
Hainsworth, Paul, ed. 2000. *The Politics of the Extreme Right: From the Margins to the Mainstream*. London: Pinter.
Ignazi, Piero. 2003. *Extreme Right Parties in Western Europe*. New York: Oxford University Press.

Workers

The relationship between the Far Right and workers is not a straightforward one. To summarise, we might say that it is about superficial promises that are rarely tested.

The bottom line is that in the **twenty-first century** far-right parties are contesting elections and thus, by necessity, have to make themselves look attractive, or as attractive as possible, to voters. Given that workers account for a significant proportion of national electorates, it is obvious that the Far Right has to make a play for these votes.

In some countries far-right parties have been successful in attracting the working-class vote. **Le Pen** in France has benefited dramatically from the decline of the French Communist Party and in 2002 he proved himself as attractive to working-class voters as the Socialist Party's presidential candidate, Lionel Jospin. In others, however, they have fared less well.

What is undeniable is that, in a fairly unsophisticated manner, far-right parties have developed policies with working-class voters in mind. Their subsidiary aim has been to drive a wedge between indigenous workers and immigrant workers. In **Scandinavia** parties of the Far Right have styled themselves as workers' champions and also developed a distinctive brand of welfarism. In Norway, the Progress Party, 'considers that work is a significant basis for well-being and prosperity ... *Fremskrittspartiet* considers it the state's responsibility to ensure a minimum standard of living. Welfare benefits must be directed increasingly towards those who need them. This can be done with increased use of means testing. If an increasing share of welfare benefits are linked to the role of employee, there will not be enough left for those who for various reasons do not participate in the labour market'.

Blunter is the 'National Preference' policy devised by the FN in France. Across a range of areas – including housing, employment and social security benefits – the party has stated that positive discrimination in favour of French nationals (and against foreign workers) is not only justifiable on philosophical grounds, but also necessary and desirable. Underlying such policy proposals is the belief that workers have been betrayed by left-wing parties and their false promises. The corollary of this is the feeling that the natural home of working-class voters is now on the Far Right.

The left is wise to this strategy. In **Europe**, socialist parties and trade unions have been at the forefront of anti-Nazi campaigns. They have pointed to the superficiality of the Far Right's platform but they have also rounded on parties of the centre-left. On the '**Youth** Against Racism in Europe' website, articles regularly appear which argue that ordinary working people have been forced into supporting far-right parties. One, focusing on the situation in Britain, stated that, 'the fundamental reasons for the growth of the far-right, racist and populist BNP are the betrayal of working-class people by Blair's New Labour government and the delay in the development of a new mass workers' party which could give a class-based political opposition to the onslaught of New Labour attacks on living standards, pay, conditions and our communities'. This shows that a new front has been opened in the war between left and right and European workers find themselves in the crossfire.

See also Communism *and* The Ideology of the Far Right.

Further Reading
Ignazi, Piero. 2003. *Extreme Right Parties in Western Europe*. New York: Oxford University Press.
Mudde, Cas. 2000. *The Ideology of the Extreme Right*. Manchester: Manchester University Press.

Y

Youth

One key bond linking inter-war Fascism with the post-war Far Right is their common attitude toward youth. Typical of the media-savvy, modern politician, in the interwar years, both Hitler and Mussolini engineered cringe-worthy moments when they were seen cradling young babies, and both put out propaganda posters that featured young, impressionable party members. The subtext always seemed to be that a brighter future awaited the nation's youth under Nazism and Fascism. Indeed, the idea that, for its supporters, the Far Right signifies youth and regeneration is one of the key factors that have distinguished the politics of the Far Right from more traditional conservatism.

Unsurprisingly, then, far-right movements after 1945 have placed no less emphasis on youth. For example, the **French National Front** (*Front National*, FN) established the youth wing 'Front National de la Jeunesse' in 1973. Its slogan is 'Youngsters with **Le Pen**', and the organisation currently has a membership of 10,000. Similarly, the **British National Party** (BNP) also has a youth wing, with a dedicated youth leader. Meanwhile, the Sweden Democrats (*Sverigedemokraterna*, SD) inaugurated their youth league in 1993, although it was later disbanded because it developed pro-Nazi tendencies. Elsewhere in **Scandinavia**, the Progress Party in Norway also has a youth movement. For far-right parties, then, the establishment of a youth wing has been part of a definite policy: to catch the attention of potential supporters when they are young, and to influence their way of thinking at an impressionable age. Critics might argue that this is an attempt at indoctrination and brainwashing. Nevertheless, far-left parties often make similar attempts to capture young minds, and even mainstream parties have youth organisations to help fill their ranks with future activists.

Another argument explaining why the ideology appeals to young people suggests that there is a natural affinity between the alleged rebelliousness of youth and the Far Right. Typical are the views of outreach worker Samuel Althof, who told the Swissinfo news service that neo-Nazi ideology and imagery had a major attraction for youngsters. He stressed that, although there may be other personal factors, through identification with aggressor figures, young people can feel empowered by neo-Nazi ideology. Althof contended that this allowed young people to transform themselves from losers into winners. In addition, he cited the shock value of embodying a social taboo, an important factor in the appeal of neo-Nazism. It acted both as a demonstration of strength and had the ability to create a sense of distance with their parents. So, in just the same way as teenagers may dye their hair or wear slashed jeans, in more extreme circumstances they might also join a far-right organisation. An alternative slant on the issue comes from **Russia**. One anti-fascist group claimed that the Russian National Union (*Russkiy Natsional'niy Soyuz*, RNU) thrived on social problems in the 1990s. It stressed that the RNU worked in the community with disadvantaged children – for example, by taking children off the streets and providing them with access to some sports facilities. Needless to say, this community work also incorporated a level of ideological indoctrination. Indeed, while undertaking these projects, the RNU actively recruited children. Unsuprisingly, then, most RNU recruits were typically young and male.

Another factor in the appeal of the Far Right to teenagers is music. As the anti-fascist group, D-A-S-H **Europe**, has argued, the Far Right has understood the importance of popular and everyday culture, and used these tools in its political praxis: 'Extreme-right *Kulturkampf* (i.e. culture war) directly targets infiltration of different music scenes and the youth styles associated with them. Whether it's […] singer-songwriters, dark wave, metal, techno or hip-hop, extreme-right groups can be found in any of these scenes'. The aim of this activity is simple enough. By dressing the ideology in more acceptable clothing, the Far Right can appeal to the youth market in a radical way, one that young people can also readily identify with. The implication is that music traditionally associated with the Far Right, such as Nazi chants and military marches, is no longer 'cool' (if it ever was!) and so new strategies have to be devised to attract potential young activists.

The youth vote, then, is something that the Far Right across Europe seeks to capture. It is an ideology that can appeal to the sense of radicalism associated with youth, and so the Far Right often tries to dress its ultra-nationalism in dynamic, youthful clothing. This is achieved especially through forms of music that manifest far-right ideological themes. The successes of these attempts to capture the minds of the young, of course, vary greatly from country to country.

See also Family *and* The Ideology of the Far Right.

Further Reading

Eatwell, Roger and Mudde, Cas eds. 2004. *Western Democracies and the New Extreme Right Challenge*. London: Routledge.

Ignazi, Piero. 2003. *Extreme Right Parties in Western Europe*. New York: Oxford University Press.

Laqueur, Walter. 2003. *No End to War: Terrorism in the Twenty-First Century*. New York: Continuum.

Z

Zhirinovsky, Vladimir (b.1946) – Russia

Born in Kazakhstan, Vladimir Volfovich Zhirinovsky is the son of a Jewish lawyer. He studied oriental languages and law at university and carried out his military service between 1970 and 1973. He then worked as director of legal services for Mir publishing, reviewer for the Soviet Committee for Defense of Peace and pro-rector (vice-president) at the Higher School of the Trade Union Movement. In post-communist **Russia** he found fame as the maverick and outspoken leader of the far-right Liberal Democratic Party (LDP).

He founded the LDP in 1988, presided at its first congress in 1990, and supported the hard-line anti-government coup in 1991. He also ran for the presidency in 1991 but only won 8 percent of the vote. Later, his electoral scores were 22.8 percent (1993 – parliamentary), 11.2 percent (1995 – parliamentary), 5.7 percent (1996 – presidential), 6 percent (1999 – parliamentary) and 2.7 percent (2000 – presidential). However, for a brief period, polls showed him to be the second most popular figure in Russia and in the early and mid-1990s, there was genuine alarm in the West about the future of the new Russia based on the electoral performances of Zhirinovsky. Predictably perhaps, his party's fortunes have declined since the emergence of Vladimir Putin and his nationalist policies in 2000.

Zhirinovsky has been called 'the single greatest eccentric in Russian politics'. His discourse and rhetoric is based on an exaggerated and irredentist nationalism. As he said in 1995, 'The Russian people have become the most humiliated nation on the planet. I will raise Russia from her knees'. A variety of policy propositions has flowed from this position. He has called for the restoration of Russia's borders as they were under the Soviet Union, or the Tsarist Empire, and says he dreams of a day, 'when Russian soldiers can wash their boots in the warm waters of the Indian Ocean'. He has questioned the existing frontiers of former Soviet republics and newly-independent East European states and has also threatened to seize Alaska from the United States, to launch a nuclear strike on Japan, to flood Germany with radioactive waste, and to occupy the Baltic states.

Moreover, Zhirinovsky is unpredictable when it comes to choosing his friends and foes. He befriended Iraqi dictator Saddam Hussein and members of the **Serbian Radical Party** and claimed that it was 'monstrous that **Europe**, which is fighting for human rights, refused Slobodan **Milošević** treatment when he was sick'. Not surprisingly, he has little time for the US and is renowned for his vicious personal attacks on the American secretary of state, Condoleezza Rice. On one occasion he said: 'The true reason for Ms Rice's attack against Russia is very simple. She is a very cruel, offended woman who lacks men's attention. Releasing such stupid remarks gives her the feeling of being fulfilled. This is the only way for her to attract men's attention'.

The rest of Zhirinovsky's policies are a blend of populist concerns. He openly advocates dictatorship and has spoken in favour of military police for Russia. He was a fervent supporter of the wars on Chechnya, has frequently struck a chord by campaigning for cheaper vodka, and even has a line on wildlife: 'We must force the government to stop the bird migration. We must shoot all birds ... and force migratory birds to stay where they are'.

It would be fair to say that Zhirinovsky is a colourful politician. On one level, he is the leader of an influential party and deputy speaker of the State Duma. He is a soldier by trade, and in 1995 was promoted to Lt Col, army reserve. But he has also sullied his reputation by brawling in parliament, fighting with a female deputy, Yevgenia Tishkovskaya, and throwing a drink in the face of a political rival, Boris Nemtsov, during a television debate.

In many ways, the rise of Zhirinovsky helps us to understand the nature of post-communist Russia. Once the shackles were removed (in the period 1989–1991) an amazing array of political animals came into view. Zhirinovsky's main success has been to channel a variety of ultra-traditional Russian concerns. The desire for empire, the belief in Slav solidarity, the policy on vodka – all these positions will have gone down well with the masses and will have added to his appeal and credibility. Although he and his movement scored almost 23 percent in the elections of 1993, power has remained a remote possibility. Zhirinovsky's popularity has declined and it looks now as if Russian voters view him in just the same light as Western governments – as a strange, oddball politician.

See also Liberal Democratic Party of Russia *and* Russia, Far Right Makes Electoral Gains (1993).

Further Reading

http://www.ldpr.ru (LDPR website).

Cox, M. & Shearman, P. 2000. 'After the fall: nationalist extremism in post-communist Russia'. In *The Politics of the Extreme Right: From the Margins to the Mainstream*. Edited by Paul Hainsworth. London: Pinter.

Zhirinovsky, Z. 1996. *My Struggle*. Barricade Books.

Morrison, J.W. 2004. *Vladimir Zhirinovsky: An Assessment of a Russian Ultra-nationalist*. Diane.

Solovyov, V. & Klepikova, E. 1995. *Zhirinovsky: Russian Fascism and the Making of a Dictator*. Da Capo Press.

Timeline

1945

Hitler kills himself.

Partisans murder Mussolini at Dongo.

1946

Founding of *Movimento Sociale Italiano*.

1947

Plebiscite confirms Franco's Spanish dictatorship as 'regency' regime.

1948

New Italian constitution outlaws attempts to reconstitute Fascist Party.

1950

Sozialistische Reichspartei founded in West Germany.

1952

West German courts ban *Sozialistische Reichspartei*.

1956

Founding of Freedom Party of Austria (FPÖ).

Poujadist movement wins 52 seats in French elections.

1958

Founding of Pro-Nazi Northern League.

Revolt of army and settlers in Algeria.

1960

Founding of British National Party.

'Barricades Week' in Algeria.

1961

'Generals' Putsch' against French Fourth Republic.

1962

Formation of World Union of National Socialists.

1964

Birth of the National Democratic Party of Germany.

Spearhead magazine launched by British National Front.

1965

Tixier-Vignancour wins 5 percent in French presidential elections.

Birth of Spanish Circle of Friends of Europe (CEDADE).

Alparslan Türkeş founds Nationalist Action Party in Turkey.

1967

Formation of British National Front.

'Colonels' coup' in Greece.

1968

Salazar leaves power in Portugal.

1969

Almirante becomes leader of the Italian MSI; Piazza Fontana bombing.

NPD wins 4.3 percent of vote in West German elections.

1970

Borghese launches coup attempt in Italy.

1971

A.K.Chesterton resigns from British National Front.

Birth of West German *Deutsche Volks Union*.

SVP founded in Switzerland.

1972

Birth of National Front in France.

Italian MSI scores 8.7 percent
in national elections.

1973

Danish Progress Party scores
16 percent in national elections.

Founding of Norwegian Progress
Party.

1974

Bologna bombing.

Collapse of Portuguese dictatorship.

1975

Death of Franco; King Juan Carlos I
becomes Head of State.

1977

Fini becomes head of MSI youth
movement in Italy.

1978

Founding of Flemish Bloc
in Belgium.

1979

Austrian FPÖ joins Liberal
International.

Blas Piñar Lopez elected to parliament
in Spain.

1980

MHP banned by Turkish authorities.

Second Bologna bombing.

1981

Founding of Maltese party Empire
Europe.

Franz Schönhuber publishes
autobiography *I Was There*.

1982

Birth of British National Party.

1983

French National Front makes electoral
breakthrough in Dreux by-election.

Republikaner party founded in West
Germany.

1984

French National Front passes 10
percent barrier in European elections.

1985

Pamyat splits into rival factions
in Russia.

Léon Degrelle publishes memoir
*Campaign in Russia: The Waffen SS
on the Eastern Front*.

1986

Kurt Waldheim elected Austrian
president; Haider takes over FPÖ.

French National Front wins 35 seats
in parliamentary elections.

Birth of the Spanish National Front.

Milošević issues SANU Memorandum
in Yugoslavia.

1987

Fini takes over as leader of Italian MSI.

West German DVU evolves into
electoral list.

1988

Le Pen wins 14.6 percent in French
presidential election.

British far-right activists make
controversial trip to Libya.

1989

French National Front win
parliamentary seat in Dreux
by election.

Republican Party in Germany win
7.1 percent of vote and 6 seats in Euro
elections.

Founding of Croatian Democratic
Union; Franjo Tuđman publishes
Horrors of War

Birth of Slovak National Party.

1990

Austrian Freedom Party pass
15 percent barrier in federal elections.

LDPR established in Russia.

Founding of Romania Cradle
movement.

Birth of Republican Party in Czech
Republic and SNS in Slovakia.

Russian National Unity founded
by Aleksandr Barkashov.

1991

Freedom Party win 23 percent
in Vienna local elections.

Fini restored as leader of Italian MSI.

Northern League founded in Italy.

Zhirinovsky finishes third in Russian
presidential elections.

Greater Romanian Party established
by Corneliu Vadim Tudor.

Birth of New Democracy in Sweden.

Founding of Serbian Radical Party.

Death of Archbishop Marcel Lefebvre.

1992

Birth of Party of Pure Rights and Party
of Rights Youth Group in Croatia.

Founding of Romanian Party of the
National Right.

1993

LDPR claim 23 percent in Duma
elections.

National Bolshevist Party formed
by Eduard Limonov in Russia.

Latvian Independence Party win
13 percent in national elections.

Party of National Right founded
in Romania.

BNP gain 34 percent in Isle of Dogs
election and first elected councillor.

Alessandra Mussolini stands in Naples
mayoral election.

Founding of Hungarian Justice and
Life Party.

1994

FPÖ win 22 percent in Austrian
parliamentary elections.

MSI leader Fini launches
National Alliance in Italy; NA
win 13.5 percent of vote in Italian
elections and gain five seats
in Berlusconi's cabinet.

Belgian and Danish ministers refuse
to shake hands with AN counterparts.

French National Front win
10.5 percent in European elections.

Hellenic Front founded in Greece.

Far right enters coalition government
in Romania.

Death of veteran Belgian fascist
Léon Degrelle.

1995

Haider makes controversial speech in
Austria praising SS veterans; he also
publishes *The Freedom I Mean*.

Birth of Danish People's Party.

Massacre at Srebrenica, Bosnia.

True Finns Party founded by Veikko
Vennamo.

Le Pen wins 15 percent in French
presidential election; his party wins
municipal power in Marignane, Orange
and Toulon.

Rutskoi forms *Derzhava* movement
in Russia

1996

Austrian FPÖ win 28 percent
in European elections.

AN win 15.7 percent in Italian
parliamentary poll.

Republican Party win 18 seats
in Czech Republic.

1997

Catherine Mégret wins power in
Vitrolles for French National Front.

Pim Fortuyn publishes *Against the
Islamisation of our Culture-Dutch
Identity as Fundamental Value.*

Norwegian Progress Party score
15 percent in national elections.

Christophe Blocher publishes
*Switzerland and the Second World
War: A Clarification.*

1998

People's Party score 7.4 percent
in Danish elections.

1999

Mégret splits from French Front
National and forms FN-MN.

Austrian Freedom Party win
23 percent and 5 seats in Euro
elections.

Death of Croatian leader Franjo
Tuđman.

2000

Freedom Party enter coalition
government in Austria.

Christoph Blocher outlines 'Seven
Secrets of SVP'.

Corneliu Vadim Tudor wins 28 percent
in Romanian presidential elections.

2001

Northern League and National Alliance
enter Berlusconi's governing party

in Italy; Fini becomes deputy prime
minister.

Progress Party support minority
coalition government in Norway.

League of Polish Families founded
in Poland.

Milošević arrested and charged with
genocide by War Crimes Tribunal.

People's Party positions itself within
governing coalition in Denmark.

Zhirinovsky publishes *Ivan Close
Your Soul.*

2002

Le Pen makes it through to second
round of French presidential elections.

Pim Fortuyn assassinated in the
Netherlands.

2003

Swiss People's Party win 55 out of 200
seats on 27 percent of vote.

HDZ secure 34 percent of vote and take
place in Croatian government.

Popular Party claim 9 percent of vote
in Portuguese elections.

2003

Norwegian Progress Party win
17.9 percent of national vote.

2004

Flemish Block reinvents itself
as Flemish Interest.

Greater Romania Party win 48 seats
in parliament and 21 in senate.

Hellenic Front disbanded.

League of Polish Families win 15 seats
on 16 percent of national vote.

2005

Attack coalition gains 21 out of 240
seats in Bulgarian election.

Birth of Georgy Tschokin's Ukrainian Conservative Party.

Haider and allies split from Austrian Freedom Party and form BZÖ.

United National Workers Party formed by Mindaugas Murza in Lithuania.

March by pro-Nazi Latvian SS veterans in Riga.

2006

Austrian Freedom Party win 11 percent of national vote in elections.

Danish 'cartoon controversy'.

BNP leaders acquitted of inciting racial hatred.

David Irving sent to prison for Holocaust denial.

Death of Slobodan Milošević.

2007

Le Pen finishes fourth in presidential poll with 10 percent of vote.

People's Party gain 25 seats in Danish parliament.

Rise and fall of Identity, Tradition and Sovereignty group at European Parliament.

SVP maintains position as strongest party in Switzerland with 62 seats.

SRS claim 29 percent of vote in Serbian elections.

2008

Far-right political leaders unveil plans for pan-European 'patriotic' party.

EUROPE

NORWAY

DENMARK

Oresu

IRELAND

Burnley   Bradford

Oldham

UK

NETHERLANDS   Hilversum

The
Hague

Antwerp

BELGIUM   GERMANY   Ber

Paris

Strasbourg

Dreux

FRANCE   SWITZERLAND

Orange   Carpentras   Bologna

Vitrolles

Marignane

Toulon

PORTUGAL   Bernabeu Stadium
Madrid   ITAL

SPAIN

List of Illustrations

1. Marches in Prague, 21 August 1999. Sean Gallup/Liaison. Getty Images.

2. Posters of Volen Siderov, Sofia, Bulgaria, 28 October 2006. Valentina Petrova/AFP. Getty Images.

3. Italian Foreign Minister Gianfranco Fini, Rome, Italy, 6 April 2006. Associated Press. PA Photos.

4. Jean-Marie Le Pen and Nick Griffin, Manchester, UK, 25 April 2004. Darren Staples/Reuters. Corbis UK Ltd.

5. Joerg Haider, 9 June 2002, Wiener Neustadt, Austria. Roland Schlager/Apa/Epa. Corbis UK Ltd.

6. President of Croatia Franjo Tudjman, Budapest, Hungary, March 1998. Sipa Press. Rex Features.

7. Léon Degrelle, Belgium, April 1943. LAPI/Roger Viollet. Getty Images.

8. Deputy Primer Minister and Minister of Education Roman Giertych, 1 June 2007, Warsaw, Poland. Tomasz Gzell/Pap. Corbis UK Ltd.

9. European deputies of the Identity, Tradition and Sovereignty group, Strasbourg, 12 November 2007. Dominique Faget/AFP. Getty Images.

10. Pim Fortuyn, 15 March 2002, The Hague, Netherlands. Ed Oudenaarden/Anp/Epa. Corbis UK Ltd.

11. General Francisco Franco, 1 October 1936, Burgos, Spain. Efe. Corbis UK Ltd.

12. Leader of the Hungarian Truth and Life Party (MIEP) Istvan Csurka, 4 June 2000. Associated Press. PA Photos.

13. Italian European deputy Alessandra Mussolini, Strasbourg, 13 November 2007. Dominique Faget/AFP. Getty Images.

14. Pia Kjaersgaard, Copenhagen, Denmark, 22 February 2007. Francis Dean. Rex Features.

15. Nationalist Pamyat leaders, Russia. Chris Niedenthal/Time Life Pictures. Getty Images.

16. Serbian Communist Party leader Slobodan Milošević, 19 November 1998, Belgrade, Serbia. Patrick Hertzog/AFP. Getty Images.

17. Siv Jensen, Norway, 6 May 2006. Morten Holm/AFP. Getty Images.

18. Romanian President Traian Basescu, Bucharest, 18 December 2006. Associated Press. PA Photos.

19. Vladimir Zhirinovsky, Moscow, 23 January 2008. Yuri Kochetkov/Epa. Corbis UK Ltd.

20. Dr Oliveira Salazar, Premier of Portugal, 3 December 1954, Lisbon. Bettmann. Corbis UK Ltd.

21. Franz Schönhuber, Berlin, Germany, 1992. Sipa Press. Rex Features.

22. An election poster of the Swiss Peoples Party (SVP), Basel, Switzerland, 6 October 2006. Ralph Orlowski. Getty Images.

General Bibliography

General Far Right

Abedi, Amir. 2004. *Anti-Political Establishment Parties*. London: Routledge.

Betz, Hans-Georg & Immerfall, Stefan, eds. 1998. *The New Politics of the Right: Neo-Populist Parties and Movements in Established Democracies*. New York: Palgrave Macmillan.

Betz, Hans-Georg. 1994. *Radical Right-Wing Populism in Western Europe*. New York: St. Martin's Press.

Blamires, Cyprian P. 2006. *World Fascism: A Historical Encyclopedia*. Santa Barbara, CA: ABC-Clio.

Carter, Elisabeth. 2005. *The Extreme Right in Western Europe: Success or Failure?* Manchester: Manchester University Press.

Casals, X., ed. 2005. *Political Survival on the Extreme Right: European Movements between the Inherited Past and the Need to Adapt to the Future*. Barcelona: Institut de Ciences Politiques i Sociales.

Cheles, L., Ferguson, R. & Vaughan, M., eds. 1991. *Neo-Fascism in Europe*. London: Longman.

Cheles, L., Ferguson, R. & Vaughan, M., eds. 1995. *The Far Right in Western and Eastern Europe*. London and New York: Longman.

Davies, Peter & Lynch, Derek. 2002. *The Routledge Companion to Fascism and the Far Right*. London: Routledge.

Eatwell, Roger. 1996. *Fascism: A History*. London: Vintage.

Eatwell, Roger & Mudde, Cas, eds. 2004. *Western Democracies and the New Extreme Right Challenge*. London: Routledge.

Eatwell, Roger & O'Sullivan, Noel, eds. 1992. *The Nature of the Right*. London: Pinter.

Givens, Terri E. 2005. *Voting Radical Right in Western Europe*. Cambridge: Cambridge University Press.

Griffin, Roger. 1994. *The Nature of Fascism*. London: Routledge.

Griffin, Roger, ed. 1995. *Fascism, Oxford Reader Series*. Oxford: Oxford University Press.

Hainsworth, Paul, ed. 1994. *The Extreme Right in Europe and the USA*. London: Pinter.

Hainsworth, Paul, ed. 2000. *The Politics of the Extreme Right: From the Margins to the Mainstream*. London: Pinter.

Hainsworth, Paul. 2008. *The Extreme Right in Western Europe*. London: Routledge.

Harris, Geoffrey. 1990. *The Dark Side of Europe: The Extreme Right Today*. Edinburgh: Edinburgh University Press.

Ignazi, Piero. 1992. 'The silent counter-revolution. Hypotheses on the emergence of extreme right-wing parties in Europe'. *European Journal of Political Research* 22: 3–34.

Ignazi, Piero. 2003. *Extreme Right Parties in Western Europe*. Oxford: Oxford University Press.

Kaldor, Mary & Vejvoda, Ivan, eds. 2002. *Democratization in Central and Eastern Europe*. London: Continuum.

Kitchen, Martin. 1982. *Fascism*. London: Macmillan.

Kitschelt, Herbert in collaboration with McGann, Anthony J. 1995. *The Radical Right in Western Europe: A Comparative Analysis*. Michigan: University of Michigan Press.

Laqueur, Walter, ed. 1982. *Fascism, A Reader's Guide*. Harmondsworth: Penguin.

Levy, Richard S. 2005. *Antisemitism: A Historical Encyclopedia of Prejudice and Persecution*. Santa Barbara, CA: ABC-Clio.

Mény, Yves & Surel, Yves, eds. 2002. *Democracies and the Populist Challenge*. London: Palgrave.

Merkl, Peter & Weinberg, Leonard, eds. 2003. *Right-Wing Extremism in the Twenty-First Century*. London: Frank Cass.

Mudde, Cas. 2000. *The Ideology of the Extreme Right*. Manchester: Manchester University Press.

Mudde, Cas. ed. 2005. *Racist Extremism in Central and Eastern Europe*. London: Routledge.

Mudde, Cas. 2007. *Populist Radical Right Parties in Europe*. Cambridge: Cambridge University Press.

Nolte, Ernst. 1965. *Three Faces of Fascism*. London: Weidenfeld and Nicolson.

Norris, Pippa. 2005. *Radical Right: Voters and Parties in the Electoral Market*. Cambridge: Cambridge University Press.

Payne, Stanley. 1995. *A History of Fascism 1914–1945*. London: UCL Press Limited.

Ramet, Sabrina, ed. 1999. *The Radical Right in Central and Eastern Europe since 1989*. University Park, PA: Pennsylvania State University Press.

Rees, Philip. 1990. *Biographical Dictionary of the Extreme Right*. New York: Simon & Schuster.

Schain, Martin, Zolberg, Aristide & Hossay, Patrick, eds. 2002. *Shadows over Europe: The Development and Impact of the Extreme Right in Western Europe*. New York: Palgrave Macmillan.

Szayna, Thomas S. 1997. 'The extreme-right political movements in post-Communist Central Europe'. In *The Revival of Right-Wing Extremism in the Nineties*. Edited by Peter H. Merkel and Leonard Weinberg. London: Frank Cass.

Tarchi, Marco. 2005. 'The far right Italian style'. In *Political Survival on the Extreme Right: European Movements between the Inherited Past and the Need to Adapt to the Future*. Edited by Xavier Casals. Barcelona: Institut de Ciences Politiques i Sociales.

von Beyme, Klaus. 1988. 'Right-Wing extremism in post-war Europe'. *West European Politics* 11.2: 1–18.

Wilkinson, Paul. 1983. *The New Fascists*. London: Pan.

Williams, Michel Hale. 2006. *The Impact of Radical Right-Wing Parties in Western Europe*. New York: Palgrave Macmillan.

Western Europe

Hainsworth, Paul. 2008. *The Extreme Right in Western Europe*. London: Routledge.

Minkenberg, Michael. February 2006. 'Repression and reaction: militant democracy and the radical right in Germany and France'. *Patterns of Prejudice* 40.1: 25–44.

Schain, Martin, Zolberg, Aristide & Hossay, Patrick, eds. 2002. *Shadows over Europe: The Development and Impact of the Extreme Right in Western Europe*. New York: Palgrave Macmillan.

France

Arnold, Edward J. 2000. *The Development of the Radical Right in France: From Boulanger to Le Pen*. New York: Macmillan.

Davies, Peter. 1999. *The National Front in France: Ideology, Discourse and Power*. New York: Routledge.

Davies, Peter. 2002. *The Extreme Right in France, 1789 to the Present: From De Maistre to Le Pen*. London: Routledge.

Shields, James. 2004. *The Extreme Right in France: From Pétain to Le Pen*. London: Routledge.

Belgium

Conway, Martin. 1993. *Collaboration in Belgium: Léon Degrelle and the Rexist Movement, 1940–1944*. New Haven, CT: Yale University Press.

de Bruyne, Eddy & Rikmenspoel, Marc. 2004. *For Rex and for Belgium: Léon Degrelle and Walloon Political and Military Collaboration 1940–45*. Solihull, UK: Helion and Company Ltd.

Fields, Edward R. 2005. *Léon Degrelle and the Rexist Party 1935–1940*. Spearhead.

Netherlands

Fortuyn, Pim. 1990. *Ordening Door Ontvlechting: Een Advies Over de Adviesstructuur in de Volksgezondheid*. Rijswijk/Den Haag, DOP: Ministerie van Welzijn, Volksgezondheid en Cultuur.

Husbands, Christopher T. 1992. 'The Netherlands: irritants on the body politic'. In *The Extreme Right in Europe and the USA*. Edited by Paul Hainsworth. London: Pinter.

Mudde, Cas & Holsteyn, Joop Van. 2000. 'The Netherlands: explaining the limited success of the extreme right'. In *The Politics of the Extreme Right: From the Margins to the Mainstream*. Edited by Paul Hainsworth. London: Pinter.

Sniderman, Paul. M. & Hagendoorn, Louk. 2007. *When Ways of Life Collide: Multiculturalism and Its Discontents in the Netherlands*. Princeton: Princeton University Press.

Great Britain

Bragg, Tim, Griffin, Nick, Kerr, David & Harrington, Patrick. 2005. *Taking Liberties: A Third Way Special on the Attack on Civil Liberties in the UK*. Pamphlet.

Cable, Gerry. 1991. 'The far right in contemporary Britain'. In *Neo-Fascism in Europe*. Edited by Luciano Cheles, Ronnie Ferguson & Michalina Vaughan. London: Longman.

Copsey, N. 2004. *Contemporary British Fascism: The British National Party and the Quest for Legitimacy*. Basingstoke: Palgrave Macmillan.

Eatwell, Roger. 2000. 'The extreme right and British exceptionalism: the primacy of politics'. In *The Politics of the Extreme Right: From the Margins to the Mainstream*. Edited by Paul Hainsworth. London: Pinter.

Eatwell, Roger. 1994. 'Why has the extreme right failed in Britain?' In *The Extreme Right in Europe and the USA*. Edited by Paul Hainsworth. London: Pinter.

Southern Europe

Italy

Amyot, Grant & Verzichelli, Luca, eds. 2007. *End of the Berlusconi Era?* New York: Berghahn Books.

Bufacchi, Vittorio & Burgess, Simon. 2001. *Italy Since 1989: Events and Interpretations.* New York: St. Martin's Press.

Cheles, Luciano. 1991. '"Nostalgia dell'avvenire": the new propaganda of the MSI between tradition and innovation'. In *Neo-Fascism in Europe.* Edited by Luciano Cheles, Ronnie Ferguson & Michalina Vaughan. London: Longman.

Chiarini, Roberto. 1991. 'The "Movimento Sociale Italiano": a historical profile'. In *Neo-Fascism in Europe.* Edited by Luciano Cheles, Ronnie Ferguson & Michalina Vaughan. London: Longman.

Gallagher, Tom. 2000. 'Exit from the ghetto: the Italian far right in the 1990s'. In *The Politics of the Extreme Right: From the Margins to the Mainstream.* Edited by Paul Hainsworth. London: Pinter.

Mack Smith, Denis. 1997. *Modern Italy: A Political History.* London: Yale University Press.

Sidoti, Francesco. 1994. 'The extreme right in Italy: ideological orphans and countermobilisation'. In *The Extreme Right in Europe and the USA.* Edited by Paul Hainsworth. London: Pinter.

Tarchi, Marco. 2005. 'The far right Italian style'. In *Political Survival on the Extreme Right: European Movements between the Inherited Past and the Need to Adapt to the Future.* Edited by Xavier Casals. Barcelona: Institut de Ciences Politiques i Sociales.

Spain

Ellwood, Sheelagh. 1991. 'The extreme right in Spain: a dying species?' In *Neo-Fascism in Europe.* Edited by Luciano Cheles, Ronnie Ferguson & Michalina Vaughan. London: Longman.

Gilmour, John. 1994. 'The extreme right in Spain: Blas Piñar and the spirit of the nationalist uprising'. In *The Extreme Right in Europe and the USA.* Edited by Paul Hainsworth. London: Pinter.

Payne, Stanley G. 2008. *Franco and Hitler.* New Haven, CT: Yale University Press.

Preston, Paul. 1995. *Franco: A Biography.* London: Fontana Press.

Portugal

Derrick, Michael. 1972. *The Portugal of Salazar.* London: Campion Books Ltd.

Gallagher, Tom. 1994. 'Portugal: the marginalisation of the extreme right' In *The Extreme Right in Europe and the USA.* Edited by Paul Hainsworth. London: Pinter.

Pinto, Antonio Costa. 1991. 'The radical right in contemporary Portugal'. In *Neo-Fascism in Europe.* Edited by Luciano Cheles, Ronnie Ferguson & Michalina Vaughan. London: Longman.

Raby, David L. 1991. *Fascism and Resistance in Portugal: Communists, Liberals and Military Dissidents in the Opposition to Salazar, 1941–1974.* Manchester: Manchester University Press.

Scandinavia

Andersen, Jørgen Goul & Bjørklund, Tor. 2002. 'Anti-immigration parties in Denmark and Norway: the progress parties and the Danish People's Party'. In *Shadows over Europe: The Development and Impact of the Extreme Right in Western Europe.* Edited by Martin Schain, Aristide Zolberg & Patrick Hossay. New York: Palgrave Macmillan.

Andersen, Jørgen Goul & Bjørklund, Tor. 2000. 'Radical right-wing populism in Scandinavia: from tax revolt to neo-liberalism and xenophobia'. In *The Politics of the Extreme Right. From the Margins to the Mainstream.* Edited by Paul Hainsworth. London: Pinter.

Andersen, Jørgen Goul. 2006. *Immigration and the Legitimacy of the Scandinavian Welfare State.* Aalborg University, Denmark, AMID Working Paper #53.

Kestilä, Elina. 2006. 'Is there a demand for radical right populism in the Finnish electorate?', *Scandinavian Political Studies* 29.3: 169–191.

Rydgren, Jens. 2006. *From Tax Populism to Ethnic Nationalism: Radical Right-Wing Populism in Sweden.* New York and Oxford: Berghahn Books.

Taggart, Paul. A. 1996. *The New Populism and the New Politics: New Protest Parties in Sweden in a Comparative Perspective.* London: Macmillan Press.

Central Europe

Germany

Backer, Susann. 2000. 'Right-wing extremism in unified Germany'. In *The Politics of the*

Extreme Right: From the Margins to the Mainstream. Edited by Paul Hainsworth. London: Pinter.

Childs, David. 1991. 'The far right in Germany since 1945'. In *Neo-Fascism in Europe.* Edited by Luciano Cheles, Ronnie Ferguson & Michalina Vaughan. London: Longman.

Husbands, Christopher T. 1991. 'Militant neo-Nazism in the Federal Republic of Germany in the 1980s'. In *Neo-Fascism in Europe.* Edited by Luciano Cheles, Ronnie Ferguson & Michalina Vaughan. London: Longman.

Kolinsky, Eva. 1994. 'A future for right extremism in Germany?' In *The Extreme Right in Europe and the USA.* Edited by Paul Hainsworth. London: Pinter.

Stöss, Richard. 1991. *Politics Against Democracy: Extreme Right in West Germany.* New York and Oxford: Berg.

Austria

Hobelt, Lothar. 2003. *Jorg Haider and the Politics of Austria 1986–2000.* West Lafayette: Purdue University Press.

Pick, Hella. 2000. *Guilty Victim - Austria from the Holocaust to Haider.* London: I.B.Tauris & Co Ltd.

Sully, Melanie A. 1998. *The Haider Phenomenon.* New York: Columbia University Press.

Wodak, R. & Pelinka, A. 2002. *The Haider Phenomenon in Austria.* London: Transaction Press.

Switzerland

Blocher, Christoph. 1997. *Switzerland and the Second World War: A Clarification.* Schweizerische Volkspartei des Kantons Zürich.

Church, Clive H. 2003. *The Politics and Government of Switzerland.* Basingstoke: Palgrave Macmillan.

Fossedal, Gregory A. 2005. *Direct Democracy in Switzerland.* New Brunswick, NJ: Transaction Press.

Farago, Peter, Kohli, Martin, Zarin-Nejadan, Milad & Kriesi Hanspeter, eds. 2005. *Contemporary Switzerland: Revisiting the Special Case.* Houndmills: Palgrave Macmillan.

Czech Republic and Slovakia

Harris, Erika. 2002. *Nationalism and Democratisation: Politics of Slovakia and Slovenia.* Aldershot, Hampshire, UK: Ashgate.

Henderson, Karen. 2002. *Slovakia: The Escape for Invisibility.* London: Routledge.

Shepherd, R.H.E. 2000. *Czechoslovakia: The Velvet Revolution and Beyond.* Houndsmills: Macmillan.

Stein, Erik. 1997. *Czecho / Slovakia: Ethnic Conflict, Constitutional Fissure, Negotiated Breakup.* Ann Arbor, Michigan: University of Michigan Press.

Trifunovska, Snezana, ed. 1999. *Minorities in Europe: Croatia, Estonia and Slovakia.* The Hague: TMC Asser Press.

Eastern Europe

Ishiyama, John T. & Breuning, Marijke. 1998. *Ethnopolitics in the New Europe.* Boulder, CO: Lynne Rienner.

Petrou, Michael. 24 February 2006. 'Neo-neo-Nazis: New fascist movements find fertile ground in the turmoil of Eastern Europe'. *Maclean's.*

Szayna, Thomas S. 1997. 'The extreme-right political movements in post-Communist Central Europe'. In *The Revival of Right-Wing Extremism in the Nineties.* Edited by Peter H. Merkel and Leonard Weinberg. London: Frank Cass.

Russia

Cox, M. & Shearman, P. 2000. 'After the fall: nationalist extremism in post-communist Russia' In *The Politics of the Extreme Right: From the Margins to the Mainstream.* Edited by Paul Hainsworth. London: Pinter.

Morrison, J.W. 2004. *Vladimir Zhirinovsky: An Assessment of a Russian Ultra-nationalist.* Darby, PA: Diane.

Shenfield, Stephen. 2000. *Russian Fascism: Traditions, Tendencies and Movements.* New York: M.E.Sharpe.

Solovyov, Vladimir & Klepikova, Elena. 1995. *Zhirinovsky: Russian Fascism and the Making of a Dictator.* New York: Da Capo Press.

Zhirinovsky, V. 1996. *My Struggle: The Explosive Views of Russia's Most Controversial Public Figure.* New York: Barricade Books.

Baltic States

Galbreath, David. 2005. *Nation-Building and Minority Politics in Post-Socialist States: Interests, Influence and Identities in Estonia and Latvia.* Stuttgart: Ibidem-Verlag.

Karklins, Rasma. 1994. *Ethnopolitics and Transition to Democracy: Collapse of the*

USSR and Latvia. Washington, D.C.: Woodrow Wilson Center Press.

Smith, David J., Purs, Aldis, Pabriks, Artis & Lane, Thomas. 2002. *The Baltic States: Estonia, Latvia and Lithuania.* London and New York: Routledge.

Poland

Blobaum, Robert. 2005. *Antisemitism and Its Opponents in Modern Poland.* Ithaca, N.Y.: Cornell University Press.

Giertych, Maciej. 1963. *Thoughts for Thinking. From student discussions at Oxford and Toronto.* London. Publisher not known.

Hancock, D.M. 2006. *Politics in Europe: An Introduction to the Politics of the United Kingdom, France, German, Italy, Sweden, Russia, Poland and the European Union.* Washington, D.C.: CQ Press.

Hungary

Hanebrink, Paul A. 2006. *In Defense of Christian Hungary: Religion, Nationalism, and Anti-Semitism, 1890–1944.* Ithaca, N.Y.: Cornell University Press.

Oltay, Edith. 26 March 1993. 'Hungary: Csurka launches "National Movement"', *RFE/RL Research Report* 2.13: 25–31.

Romania

Gallagher, Tom. 2005. *Modern Romania: The End of Communism, the Failure of Democratic Reform, and the Theft of a Nation.* New York: New York University Press.

Light, Duncan & Phinnemore, David. 2001. *Post-Communist Romania: Coming to Terms with Transition.* London: Palgrave MacMillan.

Shafir, Michael. 22 April 1994. 'Romania'. *RFE/RL Research Report* [Munich] 3.16.

Shafir, Michael. 2000. 'Marginalization or mainstream? The extreme right in post-communist Romania'. In *The Politics of the Extreme Right: From the Margins to the Mainstream.* Edited by Paul Hainsworth. London: Pinter.

South-Eastern Europe

Bugajski, Janusz. 2000. 'Nationalist majority parties: The anatomy of ethnic domination in Central and Eastern Europe'. In *The Politics of National Minority Participation in Post-Communist Europe: State-Building, Democracy, and Ethnic Mobilisation.* Edited

by Jonathan P. Stein. New York: EastWest Institute, 2000.

Glenny, Misha. 1996. 3rd revised edition. *The Fall of Yugoslavia: The Third Balkan War.* New York: Penguin.

Glenny, Misha. 2001. *The Balkans: Nationalism, War and the Great Powers 1804–1999.* New York: Penguin.

Roudometof, Victor. 2002. *Collective Memory, National Identity, and Ethnic Conflict: Greece, Bulgaria, and the Macedonian Question.* Westport, CT: Praeger.

Bulgaria

Crampton, R.J. 2005. *A Concise History of Bulgaria.* Cambridge: Cambridge University Press, Cambridge Concise Histories.

Ganev, Venelin I. 2007. *Preying on the State: The Transformation of Bulgaria After 1989.* Ithaca, N.Y.: Cornell University Press.

Giatzidis, Emil. 2002. *An Introduction to Postcommunist Bulgaria: Political, Economic and Social Transformation.* Manchester: Manchester University Press.Ivanov, Christo & Ilieva, Margarita. 2005. 'Bulgaria: Chapter 1'. In *Racist Extremism in Central and Eastern Europe.* Edited by Cas Mudde. London: Routledge.

Greece

Close, David H. 2002. *Greece Since 1945: A History.* London: Longman.

Dimitras, Panayote Elias. 1992. 'Greece: the virtual absence of an extreme right'. In *The Extreme Right in Europe and the USA.* Edited by Paul Hainsworth. London: Pinter.

Featherstone, K., ed. 2005. *Politics and Policy in Greece.* London: Routledge.

Kapetanyannis, Vassilis. 1991. 'Neo-fascism in modern Greece'. In *Neo-Fascism in Europe.* Edited by Luciano Cheles, Ronnie Ferguson & Michalina Vaughan. London: Longman.

Turkey

Lokman I. Meho. 2004. *The Kurdish Question in U.S. Foreign Policy: A Documentary Sourcebook.* Westport, CT: Greenwood Press.

Croatia

Bellamy, Alex J. 2003. *The Formation of Croatian National Identity: A Centuries-old Dream?* Manchester and New York: Manchester University Press.

Bulajic, Milan. 1992. *Tudjman's Jasenovac Myth: Ustasha Crimes of Genocide.* Belgrade:

Ministry of Information of the Republic of
Serbia.

Goldstein, Ivo. 1999. *Croatia: A History*.
London: C. Hurst & Co.

Jelavich, Charles. 1967. 'The Croatian problem'.
Austrian History Yearbook 3 (1967).

Tanner, Marcus. 1997. *Croatia: A Nation Forged
in War*. London: Yale Nota Bene.

Tudjman, Franjo. 1981. *Nationalism in
Contemporary Europe*. New York: Columbia
University Press.

Tudjman, Franjo. 1991. *Croatia at the
Crossroads*. Centre for Policy Studies.

Tudjman, Franjo. 1996. *The Horrors of War:
Historical Reality and Philosophy*. New York:
M. Evans & Co Inc.

Tudjman, Franjo. 1996. *Genocide & Yugoslavia:
Exposing the Myths*. Washington, D.C.:
Regnery Pub.

Serbia

Judah, Tim. 2000. *The Serbs: History, Myth and
the Destruction of Yugoslavia*. New Haven,
CT: Yale University Press.

Knezevic, Anto. 1992. *An Analysis of Serbian
Propaganda: The Misrepresentation of the
Writings of the Historian Franjo Tudjman
in Light of the Serbian-Croatian War*. Zagreb:
Domovina TT.

Pribićević, Ognjen. 1999. 'Changing Fortunes
of the Serbian Radical Right'. In *The Radical
Right in Central and Eastern Europe since
1989*. Edited by Sabrina Ramet. University
Park, PA: Pennsylvania University Press.

Macedonia

Jordan, Peter. 1999. 'Ethnische Gruppen in
Makedonien'. In *Makedonien: Geographie,
Ethnische Struktur*. Edited by Walter Lukan
and Peter Jordan. Vienna/Skopje: Peter Lang.

Liotta, Peter H. (Spring 2000). 'The "Future"
Republic of Macedonia: The Last Best Hope'.
European Security 9.1.

Muhic, Ferid. 1996. 'Macedonia – an Island
on the Balkan Mainland'. In *Yugoslavia and
After: a Study in Fragmentation, Despair and
Rebirth*. Edited by David A. Dyker & Ivan
Vejvoda. Harlow, United Kingdom: Longman.

Slovenia

Cox, John K. 2005. *Slovenia: Evolving Loyalties.
Postcommunist States and Nations*. New
York: Routledge.

Thompson, Mark. 1992. *A Paper House: The
Ending of Yugoslavia*. New York: Pantheon.

About the Editors and Contributors

Editors

Dr Peter Davies is Senior Lecturer in History and Media at the University of Huddersfield, UK. He has authored six books and co-authored two on a range of topics including fascism, the extreme right in France, the Front National, World War II, collaboration, the French Revolution, and small-group teaching and learning. He is also leader of a £50,000 Heritage Lottery Fund-sponsored project on the social history of cricket in Yorkshire.

Paul Jackson is currently a part-time lecturer in modern history at Oxford Brookes University, where he has recently completed his doctorate on British intellectuals and World War I. He has published articles on Bosnian radical nationalism and the Romanian Iron Guard, and is currently the co-Editor of the peer-reviewed academic journal *Totalitarian Movements and Political Religions*. He has taught Nazism and fascism at Oxford Brookes University, the University of Northampton and the University of Greenwich, and was the editorial assistant for *World Fascism: A Historical Encyclopedia*.

Contributors

Hans-Georg Betz is Associate Professor of Political Science at York University, Toronto, Canada

Tor Bjørklund is Associate Professor of Politics at the University of Oslo, Norway

Brendan Evans is Professor of Politics at the University of Huddersfield, UK

Matthew Goodwin is Research Associate at the Institute for Political and Economic Governance, University of Manchester, UK

Roger Griffin is Principal Lecturer in History at Oxford Brookes University, UK

Paul Hainsworth is Senior Lecturer in Politics at the University of Ulster, UK

Stan Markotich is an Independent Markets Analyst (Commodities) at Middlebury College, Vermont, USA

Peter Shearman is Senior Lecturer in Politics at the University of Melbourne, Australia

Rob Light is Research Assistant at the University of Huddersfield, UK

Index